Pittsburgh Series in Bibliography

H. L. MENCKEN

Courtesy of Enoch Pratt Free Library, Baltimore, Md.

H. L. Mencken

A DESCRIPTIVE BIBLIOGRAPHY

Richard J. Schrader

with the assistance of
George H. Thompson and
Jack R. Sanders

UNIVERSITY OF PITTSBURGH PRESS

Published by the University of Pittsburgh Press, Pittsburgh, Pa., 15261
Copyright © 1998, University of Pittsburgh Press
Manufactured in the United States of America
Printed on acid-free paper
10 9 8 7 6 5 4 3 2 1

Library of Congress Cataloging-in-Publication Data

Schrader, Richard J.
    H. L. Mencken : a descriptive bibliography / Richard J. Schrader ;
  with the assistance of George H. Thompson and Jack R. Sanders.
      p.   cm. — (Pittsburgh series in bibliography)
    Includes bibliographical references and index.
    ISBN 0-8229-4050-7 (alk. paper)
    1. Mencken, H. L. (Henry Louis), 1880–1956–Bibliography.
  I. Thompson, George H. (George Howard), 1930–   . II. Sanders, Jack R.
  III. Title.   IV. Series.
  Z8563.5.S37   1998
  [PS3525.E43]
  016.818'5209—dc21   97-40050
                                                        CIP

A CIP catalog record for this book is available from the British Library.

Eurospan, London

For Mary and Kathy,
Betty and Carol

M is for MENCKEN
   A Merry Mocker,
     A' Nawful Knocker,
      A Galvanizing Shocker.

But under all his jibes,
And diatribes,
At Morons, Babbits, and Democracy,
Lies the man's hatred of hypocrisy.

   —from *Maryland Miniatures 1634–1934*
   by *A Lover of Maryland*

Contents

Acknowledgments

FOR MORE THAN FOUR YEARS I have presided over an international collaboration. I am indebted most to my assistants named on the title page. George Thompson and Jack Sanders formed their magnificent collections out of a love for the writings of Mencken, who modestly called himself a "scout for scholars." His leadership took them on a scholarly adventure they could not have imagined when their interest in him began, and I was the ultimate beneficiary of their learning. George has the best private collection of Mencken material (and knows the significance of each item), while Jack brings an editor's eye to the problems of Mencken's texts.

During my visits to the Enoch Pratt Free Library, Vincent Fitzpatrick was a genial and expert guide to the resources of the Mencken Room, and he faithfully responded to the inevitable queries that I would send afterwards. I became indebted in many ways to others on the staff, particularly Neil R. Jordahl, John Sondheim, and Averil J. Kadis. While I was in town, Arthur J. Gutman, the dean of Mencken collectors, was always hospitable and helpful. Baltimore is everything that Mencken said it was.

At Boston College I had the help of my colleagues in the English Department, especially Christopher P. Wilson and Raymond G. Biggar. O'Neill librarians Jonas Barciauskas and Brendan Rapple assisted with electronic research; Shari Grove directed me to foreign bibliographies; and Marguerite McDonough and the long-suffering staff of Interlibrary Loan brought in scores of books. Thanks also to Stephen Vedder of the Photography Production Service, Takako Minami for Japanese translations, and Michael Connolly for his computer wizardry.

Several other scholars came to my aid: Robert H. Miller helped with the Reno Collection at the University of Louisville and did volunteer work at English libraries; Gordon B. Neavill provided advance word from his bibliography of Modern Library editions; Cynthia R. Bland found and analyzed some books at Cambridge University Library; G. Thomas Tanselle drew upon his immense bibliographical knowledge; Peter S. Prescott advised on Alfred A. Knopf; and S. L. Harrison sent photocopies of an obscure item. I had the benefit of correspondence with these preeminent students of Mencken and his circle: Marion E. Rodgers, Fred Hobson, and Terry Teachout.

Among the library workers whom I must thank are A. V. Clark, Photoduplication Coordinator, Princeton University Library; Steven E. Smith, Special Collections, Texas A&M University; Rita H. Warnock, Curator of Broadsides, John Hay Library, Brown University; Jane Siegel, Curator, Graphic Arts, Columbia University Libraries; Mark Dimunation, Curator of Rare Books, Cornell University Library; Gene DeGruson, Curator of Special Collections, Leonard H. Axe Library, Pittsburg State University; Dean H. Keller, Associate Dean of Libraries, Kent State University; Delinda Buie, Curator, Department of Rare Books and Special Collections, Ekstrom Library, University of Louisville; Alexandra Mason, Spencer Librarian, University of Kansas; Christina M. Deane, Public Services Assistant, Special Collections Department, Alderman Library, University of Virginia; Gwen Smith, Barbara Smith-LaBorde, John Kirkpatrick, and Richard W. Oram at the Harry Ransom Humanities Research Center, University of Texas, Austin; Stanley W. Brown, Curator of Rare Books, Baker Library, Dartmouth College; Judy Dixon at the Library of Congress; Martha McPhail, Special Collections Librarian, Love Library, San Diego State University; and my former student Kenneth Rodriguez, who corralled some elusive items at the Library of Congress. I am very grateful to the staffs of all the libraries I visited, including the one in my hometown (OCanS), which had a couple of printings not found elsewhere.

Among the booksellers who were generous with their time and loyal in alerting me to unlisted items are Thomas L. Edsall of the Nineteenth Century Shop; Peter B. Howard of Serendipity Books; Paul Bauer of Archer's Books; Harvey Sarner of Brunswick Books; Joe Hagood of Joe Hagood Books; Gary Oleson of Waiting for Godot; Vincent McCaffrey of Avenue Victor Hugo Bookshop; and Kenneth Hooker, The Wayward Bookman.

Some others I must not overlook: Betty Thompson, Brad Thompson, and Carol Sanders for their hospitality; Richard Newsome at the Office of Carter Burden; Mark Kavanagh at Routledge Kegan Paul in London; William Koshland at Alfred A. Knopf, Inc.; Brenan Murphey at the Perkins School for the Blind; Louise Forrestal at Time-Life Library; Antonia Fusco of the Book-of-the-Month Club; and the collectors listed in the introduction.

I am grateful to Cynthia Miller, Director of the University of Pittsburgh Press; Ann Walston, Design and Production Manager; Kathy McLaughlin, Managing Editor; and Jane Flanders, Senior Editor.

Letters and inscriptions are quoted by permission of the Beineke Library, Yale University (A 41, A 53.1.a, D 12, D 14); Dartmouth College Library

(B 188); the General Rare Book Collection, Department of Rare Books and Special Collections, Princeton University Library (A 46); the H. L. Mencken Papers, Manuscripts and Archives Division, The New York Public Library, Astor, Lenox and Tilden Foundations (A 19.2.a.i); the Houghton Library, Harvard University (shelf marks °AC9.M5223 927j [A 35.1.b] and Typ 970.35.5665 [A 45.1.a]); the Mugar Memorial Library, Boston University (B 131.1); and the Trustees of the Boston Public Library (A 53.1.a).

My research benefited from a NEH Summer Stipend and generous expense grants from Boston College.

Finally, profound thanks are owed to the editors of this series, Matthew J. Bruccoli, Joel Myerson, and William R. Cagle, who each gave the manuscript a careful reading. I am indebted further to Mr. Cagle for providing the Lilly Library locations and to Professor Bruccoli for thirty years of inspiration.

Introduction

THIS BIBLIOGRAPHY of the works of H. L. Mencken describes his publications from 1899 to 1996, with some exceptions. Betty Adler's enumerative bibliography, *H. L. M.: The Mencken Bibliography*, one of the best of its kind for an American author, remains the authoritative source for the countless articles and reviews Mencken wrote for newspapers and magazines. In fact, most of her book is given over to that crucial area of his career. Rather than duplicate it, I have simply added, in Section C, a few periodical items that she missed. Also excluded are works by Mencken making their second or later appearances in books (such as anthologies) or periodicals. My private list of such appearances, from 1904 to the present, now stands at more than 350 items.

I have not listed writings about Mencken unless they include works by him published for the first time. Adler's book and its supplements provide a secondary bibliography to 1981; they are augmented by Bulsterbaum and the quarterly issues of *Menckeniana*.

FORMAT

Section A lists chronologically the separate publications by Mencken—books, pamphlets, and broadsides that he authored, coauthored, compiled, or translated—also, collections edited by others when most of the works they contain are making their first book appearances.

The numbering system indicates the place of each edition, printing, and issue in the work's publishing history. Thus for *George Bernard Shaw: His Plays*, A 2.1.a indicates that this is the second book (A 2) published by Mencken, the first (and only) edition (1), and the first printing (a). Issues are designated by lower-case roman numerals. Hence, A 3.1.b.i marks the first issue of the second printing of the first (only) edition of Mencken's third separate publication, *The Philosophy of Friedrich Nietzsche*. States are differentiated within the entry.

The first entry for each title includes a facsimile of the title page of the first edition, first printing. The copyright page and any colophon or statement of limitation are transcribed. Page size, of the largest example noted of the innermost right-hand leaf of the first gathering, is followed by pagination and a collation of the gatherings. The collation formula for A 2 is $[1–8]^8 [9]^4$. Brackets indicate that all nine gatherings are unsigned. Superscripts indicate that the first eight gatherings have eight leaves each, and the ninth has four, making a total of sixty-eight. (In a normal gathering there must be the same number of leaves before and after the threads in the middle.) The formula for the second printing of *The Artist* (A 9) is $[1]^6 [2]^8 (1 + 2_1, 2_8+ 1) [3]^2$. In the second gathering there are eight integral leaves, but additional leaves are tipped in to the recto of the first leaf and the verso of the last leaf, making a total of ten. A cancel (the replacement of an excised leaf with another pasted to the stub) is indicated as with the first gathering of *The Antichrist* (A 23): $[1]^8 (\pm 1_2)$. This means that there are eight leaves in the gathering, but the second leaf is a cancel. Publishers' catalogues and the like, which are inserts, are described but not counted in the collation formula.

Contents describes the makeup of the volume. Full-length works may be assumed to be previously unpublished unless I have indicated otherwise. For some short pieces, # designates first appearance in print and * designates previous publication only in a periodical. Generally this applies when the text is made up of stories, poems, or recollections for the *Days* series. However, it was often impossible to use the symbols for Mencken's journalism and critical essays, which were usually revised (or transformed) for their book appearances and had their titles changed, making it extremely difficult to track down original appearances. In desperate cases, I give a general account in the notes, sometimes in Mencken's own words. To chart fully his cutting, pasting, and recycling would require another book. Beginning with item A 67, an essay that has been retitled or is a section of a larger piece is given with the original title of the complete essay in parentheses. To prevent confusion and to reduce the total number of entries, essays are indexed only by the original title.

Typography and paper first specifies the dimensions of a representative page of text: total height, including running head and page number at the bottom when present; in parentheses, the distance from the top of the first line of text to the foot of the last line or page number; width of the type page; number of lines. Next, running heads, if any, are described. Finally, the paper is classified, usually as wove or laid, and watermarks spelled out. All paper is white and ink is black unless otherwise indicated.

Binding information describes the casings of hardbound books and the wrappers of paperbacks; trim, gilding, and stain of edges; color of end papers; boxes of limited printings. Spines of bindings and dust jackets are printed horizontally unless otherwise specified. The cloth designations refer to those illustrated in Jacob Blanck, *The Bibliography of American Literature,* 9 vols. (New Haven: Yale University Press, 1955–1991), and further elaborated by G. Thomas Tanselle, "The Specification of Binding Cloth," *The Library* 21 (September 1966): 246–47.

Dust jackets are described in detail, with facsimiles provided when it was possible. (Some came "via" collectors, which means that the volumes they covered were not examined.) Unless the first English printing preceded the first American, its jacket is only transcribed. In my judgment, English jackets were not otherwise important enough to require facsimiles.

Publication records include date of publication, price, copyright number, and, when available, number of copies sold. The source of the price is indicated only when it is not obvious from prior data, such as the dust jacket. Frequently the price and/or official date of publication differ from that announced in the review copy or stated on the copyright pages of subsequent printings, but I have let such contradictions stand without comment. When both Library of Congress deposit copies were missing, the date when two copies were received is noted with the copyright number. If the two were received separately, and the earlier is missing, its date of reception is recorded in the same place. Also noted there is the official reception date when it differs from that stamped in the LC copies. This procedure was necessary because many deposit copies are missing, and it was rare to find both. The numbers sold by Alfred A. Knopf, Inc., were provided by William A. Koshland of the firm and are as of August 1988 (*Menckeniana* 107.12–13, 110.16). Copies sold by other publishers were calculated from Mencken's handwritten account book (1914–1928) and his collection of royalty statements (1916–1941) at the Pratt Library. The figures may not always be complete.

Printing specifies what is known of those responsible for the manufacture of the book.

Location shows where one may find the copies on which the description is based. Not all locations where copies were found are listed (especially when the books were rebound), and not all copies at any one location were necessarily examined. Deposit dates for the Library of Congress, the British Library, the Bodleian Library, and the Cambridge University Library are provided. (See abbreviations.)

Section A goes on to record all subsequent editions and printings of each work. Descriptions of second and later editions are generally reduced, but are fuller if the books represent substantial rewrites (like the four editions of *The American Language* [A 19] and the two of *Treatise on the Gods* [A 40]) or are first Knopf, English, Canadian, or (in one case) Tauchnitz editions. Reprintings are only briefly described. Items grouped under "later reprintings" are photo-offset unless otherwise indicated.

Section AA lists collections of Mencken's writings which for the most part have already appeared in books. The format is a reduced version of that used for Section A.

Section B is comprised of works edited and/or introduced by Mencken, or containing other material (including interviews and song lyrics) appearing in a book or pamphlet for the first time. In these works, most of the writing is not by Mencken. The title page of the first printing is transcribed; necessary publication information is provided from the copyright page or elsewhere; page size and a general description of the binding are entered; one or more locations are cited; and information on the previous publication of Mencken's contribution is given.

Section C lists first appearances of Mencken's writings in magazines and newspapers when they are lacking in Adler and its supplements.

Section D describes, in brief form, material printed by Mencken himself or privately with his approval: juvenilia, jokes, ephemera, and the like. Borderline items connected to his editing of *Smart Set* or *American Mercury* remain in Section A, as do errata slips privately printed for him.

Section E comprises keepsakes, offprints, pamphlet piracies, and promotional items. These works were restricted to a few copies, whether privately or commercially printed. None was for sale. Some borderline items remain in Section A when their contents were specially revised by Mencken. The works in Section E are first separate appearances, so they are fully described in the format of Section A.

Section F lists blurbs: Mencken's statements about other authors printed on dust jackets and wrappers, or in prelims. These are either original contributions or appear on or in a book for the first time, so the format is that of Section B. Subsequent appearances of these blurbs are not listed.

Section G lists items entered in other sources that either are ghosts or have not been located.

Section H describes translations in the format of Section B and lists Braille versions. Only separate appearances and collections are included. The information is primarily useful to collectors and to students of the reception, influence, and reputation of Mencken, particularly in the German connection.

TERMS

Edition. All copies of a book or pamphlet printed from the same setting of type and the plates made from it, including photo-offset reprintings. The rule of thumb is that when more than half of the type has been reset, it is a new edition.

Printing. All copies of a book or pamphlet, the sheets for which were printed at the same time—that is, during the same continuous process in which the standing type or plates were not removed from the press. By this definition, a change of paper or a reimposition generally requires a new printing.

Issue. Copies of a book or pamphlet whose sheets are from the same printing comprise separate issues when some include an alteration affecting the conditions of publication or sale. For example, a second issue results when the title leaf is excised from some copies of an American printing and a new title leaf, indicating an English publisher, is inserted; or when some copies of the first gathering are printed with a limitation notice and some without it. The term "binding issue" was used for three books. Knopf marketed twenty-five signed, large-paper copies, bound in buckram, of the first edition of *The American Language* (A 19); and an unknown number of signed, large-paper copies, bound in "Borzoi boards," of *Americana 1926* (A 32). The bindings, along with handwritten limitation numbers, are the only differences between the two issues of *Fante/Mencken* (A 79).

State. Copies of a book whose sheets are from the same printing comprise separate states when some include an alteration not affecting the condition of publication and sale. For example, a second state results when a leaf with an error is excised in some copies and replaced with a corrected leaf. Stop-press corrections result in sheets with variant texts; when bound, the different arrangements of corrected and uncorrected sheets comprise states.

Note on sequence. When the sequence of printings, issues, or states could not be determined, a reasonable order was created, and the first arguable printing, issue, or state is styled as *presumed*. The notes will explain how far down the sequence the doubt extends.

ABBREVIATIONS

Under *Location*, the symbols for libraries are those of the *National Union Catalog*, with the exception of four major American repositories and three

English libraries. They, along with private collections and dealers, are represented by the following abbreviations:

AJG	Collection of Arthur J. Gutman
BL	British Library, London
Bod	Bodleian Library, Oxford
Camb	Cambridge University Library
CB	Collection of Carter Burden
CW	Collection of Charles Wallen Jr.
D	Dealer catalogue(s) or bookstore ("Reported" means just that, not seen.)
EPL	Enoch Pratt Free Library, Baltimore
GHT	Collection of George H. Thompson
Harv	Harvard University libraries, Cambridge, Mass.
JRS	Collection of Jack R. Sanders
KK	Collection of Ken Knudson
LC	Library of Congress, Washington, D.C.
PB	Collection of Paul Bauer
RAW	Collection of Robert A. Wilson
RJS	Collection of Richard J. Schrader
SL	Collection of Steven Lauria
Yale	Beineke Library, Yale University, New Haven, Conn.

FREQUENTLY CITED WORKS

Adler	Betty Adler. *H. L. M.: The Mencken Bibliography*. Baltimore: Johns Hopkins University Press, 1961.
Andes	George M. Andes. *A Descriptive Bibliography of the Modern Library: 1917–1970*. Boston: Boston Book Annex, 1989.
Blanck	*Merle Johnson's American First Editions*, 4th ed. Rev. and enlarged by Jacob Blanck. New York: Bowker, 1942.
Bode, *Letters*	*The New Mencken Letters*. Edited by Carl Bode. New York: Dial, 1977. (A 73)
Books	Mencken's 1918 list. (D 21)
Bruccoli	Matthew J. Bruccoli. *F. Scott Fitzgerald: A Descriptive Bibliography*. Rev. ed. Pittsburgh: University of Pittsburgh Press, 1987.
Bulsterbaum	Allison Bulsterbaum. *H. L. Mencken: A Research Guide*. New York and London: Garland, 1988.

C1, C2	Betty Adler. *A Census of Ventures into Verse*. 1st and 2nd eds. Baltimore: Enoch Pratt Free Library, 1965, 1972.
ECB	*English Catalogue of Books*
Fanfare	Burton Rascoe, Vincent O'Sullivan, and F. C. Henderson [Mencken]. *H. L. Mencken*. New York: Knopf, 1920. (B 29)
Forgue	*Letters of H. L. Mencken*. Edited by Guy J. Forgue. New York: Knopf, 1961. (A 65)
Frey	Carroll Frey. *A Bibliography of the Writings of H. L. Mencken*. Philadelphia: Centaur Bookshop, 1924. (B 53)
Hobson	Fred Hobson. *Mencken: A Life*. New York: Random House, [1994].
Menckeniana	*Menckeniana: A Quarterly Review* 1 (spring 1962)– .
MLAE	H. L. Mencken. *My Life as Author and Editor*. Edited by Jonathan Yardley. New York: Knopf, 1993. (A 84)
NUC	*National Union Catalogue*
OCLC	Online Computer Library Center data base via First-Search / WorldCat.
PBSA	*Papers of the Bibliographical Society of America*
PW	*Publishers Weekly*
S1	Betty Adler. *The Mencken Bibliography: A Ten-Year Supplement 1962–1971*. Baltimore: Enoch Pratt Free Library, 1971.
S2	Vincent Fitzpatrick. *The Mencken Bibliography: A Second Ten-Year Supplement 1972–1981*. Baltimore: Enoch Pratt Free Library, 1986.
Thirty-five Years	H. L. Mencken. *Thirty-five Years of Newspaper Work: A Memoir*. Edited by Fred Hobson et al. Baltimore and London: Johns Hopkins University Press, [1994]. (A 85)
West	Herbert Faulkner West. *The Mind on the Wing: A Book for Readers and Collectors*. New York: Coward-McCann, [1947], chap. 6 (bibliography based on the Mandel collection at Dartmouth).

Updatings of this bibliography will be published from time to time by various means. Additions and corrections are earnestly solicited.

Boston College
Chestnut Hill, Mass.
September 1996

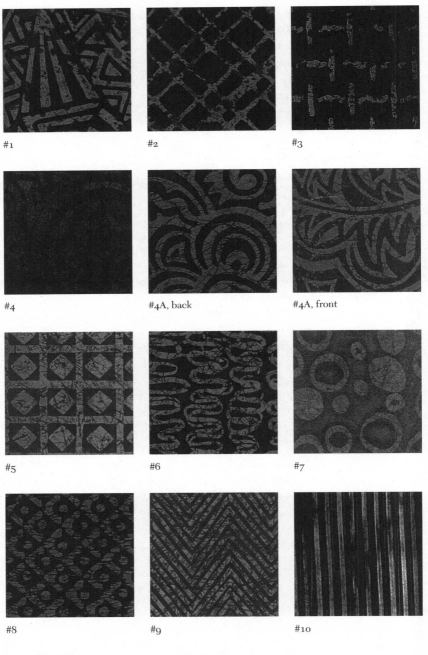

#1   #2   #3

#4   #4A, back   #4A, front

#5   #6   #7

#8   #9   #10

Borzoi boards designs

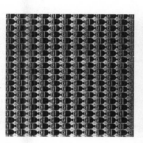

#11

#12

#13

#14

#15

#16

#17

#18

#19

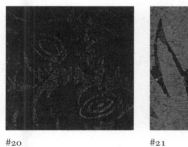

#20

#21

#22

Borzoi boards designs

The Borzoi Books logo

An example of the Borzoi device

The "winged A"

The "wallpaper" end papers

A. Separate Publications

Books, pamphlets, and broadsides authored, co-authored, compiled, or translated by Mencken. Also, collections made by others when most of the works they contain are making their first book appearances.

A 1 VENTURES INTO VERSE

A 1.1.a
Only edition, first printing (1903)

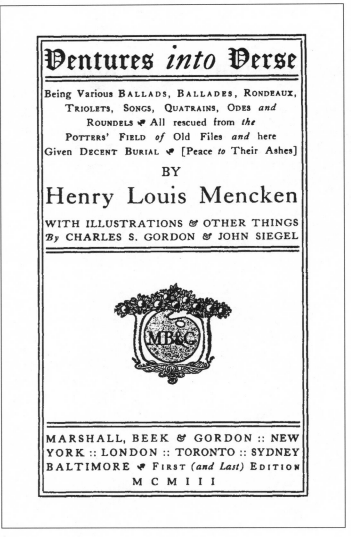

Title page: All rules green.

Copyright page: '[rule] | Copyright, 1903, by Henry L. Mencken'

Colophon: '[rule] | DONE [D occupies two lines] INTO TYPE AND PRINTED BY MARSHALL, BEEK & | GORDON IN THE CITY OF BALTIMORE AND ON THE | THIRD FLOOR OF THE TELEGRAM BUILDING, NORTH AND | BALTIMORE STREET CROSSING [ornament] ANNO DOMINI MCMIII'

7½″ × 4⅞″: [i–ii 1–4] 5–20 [21] 22–33 [34–35] 36–38 [39] 40–46 [47–50] = 52 pp. Extra wraparound binder's folio in binding B (wrappers).

[1]²⁶ = 26 leaves.

Contents: pp. i–ii: blank; p. 1: title; p. 2: copyright; p. 3: '*WARNING* | [green rule] | [ten-line acknowledgments]'; p. 4: '*PRELIMINARY REBUKE* | [motto and quatrain]'; pp. 5–46: text; p. 47: colophon; pp. 48–50: blank. In text: p. 34 blank. Divisional titles with green decorations on pp. 21, 35, 39. Black illustrations on pp. 7, 10, 13, 17, 20, 27, 31, 42, 46.

Text: "To R. K.,"° "The Song of the Olden Time,"° "The Spanish Main,"° "The Transport Gen'ral Ferguson,"° "A War Song,"° "Faith,"° "The Ballad of Ships in Harbor,"# "The Orf'cer Boy,"° "The Filipino Maiden,"° "The Violet,"# "The Tin-Clads,"° "September,"# "Arabesque,"# "A Ballade of Protest,"° "A Frivolous Rondeau,"° "The Rhymes of Mistress Dorothy,"# "A Few Lines,"° "A Rondeau of Two Hours,"° "An Ante-Christmas Rondeau,"° "Roundel,"° "In Vaudeville,"° "The Rondeau of Riches,"° "In Eating Soup,"° "Love and the Rose,"° "A Rondeau of Statesmanship,"° "Songs of the City,"° "A Madrigal,"° "A Ballad of Looking,"° "When the Pipe Goes Out,"° "A Paradox,"° "The Song of the Slapstick,"° "Il Penseroso,"# "Finis."#

Typography and paper: 5³⁄₁₆″ (4¾″) × 2¼″; 30 lines per page (width and lines vary with length and form of poems). Running heads: recto and verso, '[green double rule] | [gothic] Ventures [roman] *into* [gothic] Verse | [green rule]' (pp. 6–46). Green rule at bottom of pages with heads, sometimes with footnote between it and the page number. Laid paper.

Binding A: Plain boards with red V cloth spine. White paper label on front, printed in red (size of label varies): [all in a box] 'VENTURES INTO | VERSE | BY | [ornament] | HENRY LOUIS MENCKEN.' Stapled twice. White conjugate pastedowns, no free end papers. Trimmed, unstained. TxU copy: rear pastedown conjugate with free front end paper.

Binding B: Brown paper wrappers with same label on front. Coarse twine tied on outside through three holes.

Dust jacket: None recorded or found.

Publication: Published 6 June 1903 (C2.21). 60¢ boards, 50¢ wrappers (*PW*, 22 August 1903: 306). Copyright #A58559 (date of deposit of title page 30 April 1903).

Printing: See colophon.

Locations: GHT (2, bindings A and B), Harv (binding B, library stamp dated 2 December 1903), InU-Li (binding A), JRS (binding A), LC (9 June 1903, in boards, rebound), NjP (binding A), RJS (binding A), TxU (binding A).

Notes: 100 or slightly more copies were printed; those not distributed were destroyed in the Baltimore Fire of 1904. Forty-six are known to exist, sixteen in private hands. Earliest review in the first volume of Mencken's clippings (EPL): Baltimore *American,* 20 June 1903. For an annotated checklist of reviews, see Patrick S. Daly in *Menckeniana* 127.6–9.

   The prior appearances of the poems are listed in Adler's two censuses of the book (C1, C2). Her account of the known copies of *Ventures* was augmented and updated by Schrader in *PBSA* 83 (1989): 365–70. Since then, the Skirven copy has been donated to Goucher College, the copy Mencken presented to Peter Pry Shevlin was purchased by JRS in 1990, and the Schaefer copy was sold to William L. Clark of Chevy Chase, Md., 1991–92. In 1996 Clark purchased a copy in wrappers first sold from Goodspeed's cat. 580 (ca. 1975?); it was presented to Theodor Hemberger on 12 June 1908 and was formerly owned by Mrs. Charles Englehart. The owner of the Goodwin-Slater and Molstad copies was Carter Burden. According to Frey in his "Note Book" (see A 7 [Notes]), p. 14B, Ernest Boyd owned a copy; another was apparently sold by Marion Bloom (*In Defense of Marion* [B 230], p. 366).

   Adler 5, 40, 127–28, 133, 278, 339; Frey 15; Bulsterbaum 3, 25.

Review copy: As above (binding B), with slip (about 1⁵⁄₁₆″ × 2⅛″): [all in a box] 'FOR REVIEW | [rule] | [ornament] | KINDLY FORWARD CLIPPINGS | TO *MARSHALL, BEEK & GORDON* | Telegram BLG :: Baltimore'. *Location:* KyLoU (slip no longer in the copy; photocopy made before donation by Victor Reno).

A 1.1.b
Second printing: [Baltimore: Smith's Book Store, 1960].

Statement of limitation (p. 48): '250 | Copies Of This | Facsimile Edition Of | Ventures Into Verse | Have Been Printed For | Smith's Book Store | Baltimore 1, Maryland | This Is Copy No. | [number written in black]'. All printing in black. Brown wrappers, white paper label printed in red.

Locations: InU-Li, NjP (recased), RJS.

A 2 GEORGE BERNARD SHAW—HIS PLAYS

A 2.1.a
Only edition, first printing (1905)

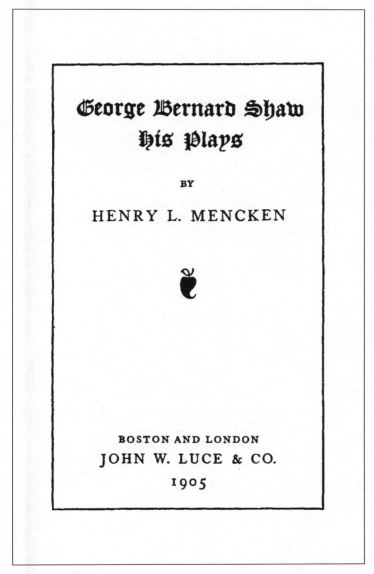

Title page: Title and ornament are orange.

Copyright page: 'Copyright, 1905, *by* | JOHN W. LUCE & COMPANY | *Boston, Mass., U. S. A.* | *The Plimpton Press Norwood Mass. U.S.A.*'

7⁹⁄₁₆″ × 5⅛″: [iii–vi] vii [viii–ix] x–xxix [xxx 1] 2–107 [108] = 136 pp.

[1–8]⁸ [9]⁴ = 68 leaves.

Contents: p. iii: title; p. iv: copyright; p. v: 'CONTENTS'; p. vi: blank; pp. vii–viii: 'PREFACE'; pp. ix–xxix: 'BY WAY OF INTRODUCTION'; p. xxx: blank; pp. 1–107: text, headed 'GEORGE BERNARD SHAW: | HIS PLAYS'; p. 108: blank. The text includes 'THE NOVELS AND OTHER WRITINGS' (pp. 82–89), 'BIOGRAPHICAL AND STATISTICAL' (pp. 90–101), 'SHAKESPEARE AND SHAW' (pp. 102–07).

Typography and paper: 5⁹⁄₁₆″ (5¼″) × 3½″; 28 lines per page. Running heads: recto, '*By Way of Introduction*' (pp. xi–xxix), chapter titles (pp. 3–107); verso, '*Preface*' (p. viii), '*By Way of Introduction*' (pp. x–xxviii), '*George Bernard Shaw: His Plays*' (pp. 2–106). Wove paper.

Binding: Deep blue V cloth. White paper label on front: [all within double-rule orange box] '*George Bernard Shaw* | *His Plays* | [floral ornament] | *By* Henry L. Mencken'. White paper label on spine: '[double orange rule] | *George* | *Bernard* | *Shaw* | *His Plays* | [double orange rule] | *By* | *Henry L.* | *Mencken* | [double orange rule]'. Fore and bottom edges roughly and unevenly trimmed, unstained. White end papers. The cover of one SL copy is 7¾″ tall; the others are 7⅝″.

Dust jacket: Reported but not seen.

Publication: Announced in *PW,* 16 December 1905: 1796. $1 (*PW* and *Books*). Copyright #A128044 (date of deposit of title page 6 October 1905).

Printing: See copyright page.

Locations: GHT, Harv, InU-Li, LC (12 December 1905), RJS (2), SL (2).

Notes: On some copies, to some eyes (including Frey and "Henderson" in Fanfare), the orange on the title page and labels is red. This was the first book published on Shaw. Adler 5; S1.3; S2.5; Frey 17; Bulsterbaum 4; Fanfare 21.

LATER REPRINTINGS WITHIN THE ONLY EDITION

A 2.1.b
New Rochelle, N.Y.: Edwin V. Glaser, 1969.

On copyright page: 'Reprint of 1905 Edition'.

Locations: EPL, GHT, Harv.

A 2.1.c
[Folcroft, Pa.:] Folcroft Library Editions, 1971.

Added title page. On copyright page: 'Limited to 150 copies'. Apparently the printing dated 1969 (OCLC) and 1970 (NUC 1968–72, 62.618).

Locations: EPL, GHT, MCR.

A 2.1.d
Folcroft, Pa.: Folcroft Library Editions, 1976.

Data from S2.5 and OCLC. Not seen.

A 2.1.e
Brooklyn, N. Y.: Haskell House, 1976.

On copyright page: 'Reprint of the 1969 ed. published by E. V. | Glaser'.

Location: GHT.

A 2.1.f
Norwood, Pa.: Norwood Editions, 1977.

Data from S2.5 and OCLC. Not seen.

A 2.1.g
[Darby, Pa.:] Arden Library, 1979.

Data from S2.5. Not located.

A 3.1.a
Only edition, presumed first printing (1908)

THE PHILOSOPHY OF FRIEDRICH NIETZSCHE

BY HENRY L. MENCKEN

> I shall be told, I suppose, that my philosophy is comfortless —
> because I speak the truth; and people prefer to believe that
> everything the Lord made is good. If you are one such, go to
> the priests, and leave philosophers in peace !
>
> *Arthur Schopenhauer.*

LUCE ET LABORE

BOSTON
LUCE AND COMPANY
MCMVIII

A 3.1.a

Copyright page: 'Copyright, 1908 | By Henry L. Mencken | *COLONIAL PRESS* | *Electrotyped and Printed by C. H. Simonds & Co.* | *Boston, U.S.A.*'

8⅛″ × 5½″: [A–B i–vi] vii–xiii [xiv 1–2] 3–59 [60–62] 63–251 [252–54] 255–325 [326–32] = 348 pp.

[1–21]⁸ [22]⁶ = 174 leaves. Seen with regular end papers, with first two leaves pasted down, and with first two and last two leaves pasted down. JRS copy: [1–21]⁸ [22]⁶ (± 22₅). The first and last leaves are pasted down; the penultimate leaf is a cancel (darker laid paper with vertical chain lines) serving as flyleaf.

Contents: pp. A–B, i–iv: blank; p. v: title, portrait of Nietzsche fronted by tissue paper tipped in; p. vi: copyright; pp. vii–xii: 'INTRODUCTION'; p. xiii: 'CONTENTS'; p. xiv: blank; pp. 1–321: text; pp. 322–25: 'BOOKS AND ARTICLES ABOUT NIETZSCHE'; pp. 326–32: blank. Blank pages in text: pp. 2,° 60, 62,° 252, 254° (° = after divisional title).

Typography and paper: 5⅞″ (5⁹⁄₁₆″) × 3½″; 31 lines per page. Running heads: recto, 'INTRODUCTION' (pp. ix–xi), chapter and section titles (pp. 5–325); verso, 'INTRODUCTION' (pp. viii–xii), 'FRIEDRICH NIETZSCHE' (pp. 4–324). Laid paper (chain lines horizontal, ⅞″ apart).

Binding: Maroon V cloth stamped in gilt. Front: '[rule] | FRIEDRICH NIETZSCHE | [rule] | [rule] | HENRY L. MENCKEN | [rule]'. Spine: '[rule] | THE | PHILOSOPHY | OF | NIETZSCHE | [rule] | MENCKEN | LUCE & | COMPANY'. Edges roughly and unevenly trimmed, unstained. White end papers, and see collation.

Dust jacket: Seen only on fifth printing.

Publication: Announced in *PW*, 21 December 1907: 1972 (number of pages estimated) and 8 February 1908: 806 (full description). $2 (*PW* and *Books*). Copyright #A196979 (date of deposit of title page 17 January 1908; two copies received 28 January 1908).

Printing: See copyright page.

Locations: EPL (2), GHT, Harv, JRS, RJS, Yale (2).

Notes: Copies with the six-leaf final gathering are presumably first printing; copies with the four-leaf are second, but one cannot tell for certain without the LC deposit copy. Thickness 1¹⁄₁₆″. Adler 5; S1.3; S2.5; Frey 18; Bulsterbaum 4.

A 3.1.b.i
Second printing, first issue

Same as A 3.1.a except:

8″ × 5⁷⁄₁₆″: [A–B i–vi] . . . [326–28] = 344 pp.

$[1-21]^8 [22]^4 = 172$ leaves.

Locations: GHT (2), RJS.

A 3.1.b.ii
Second printing, first English issue (1908)

Same as A 3.1.b.i except:

$7^{13}\!/_{16}'' \times 5\frac{1}{2}''$

Binding: Maroon V cloth stamped in gilt. Front: [all within blindstamped border] 'FRIEDRICH NIETZSCHE | HENRY L. MENCKEN'. Spine: '[rule] | THE | PHI-LOSOPHY | OF | NIETZSCHE | MENCKEN | T.FISHER *[sic]* UNWIN | [rule]'. Top edge trimmed and gilt, other edges rough and unevenly trimmed. White wove end papers.

Dust jacket: Not seen.

Publication: Published September 1908 (ECB 8.856). 7s.6d.

Locations: Bod (16 7 1910), Camb (AU 9 | 1910), GHT, RJS.

Notes: Adler 5; Frey 19.

A 3.1.b.iii
Second printing, second English issue

Same as A 3.1.b.ii except:

$7\frac{7}{8}'' \times 5\frac{1}{2}''$: [A–B i–vi] . . . 255–321 [322–24] = 340 pp.

$[1-21]^8 [22]^2 = 170$ leaves.

Contents: pp. A–B, i–iv: blank; . . . ; pp. 322–24: blank.

Binding: Some copies without free front end paper; a single white sheet used as pastedown, to which the first blank leaf (pp. [A–B]) is glued. White rear end papers.

Locations: BL (7 DE 09, rebound but not retrimmed), EPL, GHT, TxU.

Notes: 'BOOKS AND ARTICLES ABOUT NIETZSCHE' omitted (as prescribed by Frey and Adler) but not deleted from table of contents.

A 3.1.c
Third printing: Boston: Luce, MCMVIII.

Chain lines vertical, $1^3\!/_{16}''$ apart (not wove paper as Frey claims); thickness $1\frac{1}{4}''$. Retains 'BOOKS AND ARTICLES ABOUT NIETZSCHE'. Binding A: bound and trimmed as first printing. Binding B: $7\frac{7}{8}'' \times 5^5\!/_{16}''$; all edges trimmed; full title on spine; various numbers of initial blank leaves excised or pasted down. According to a

THE PHILOSOPHY OF FRIEDRICH NIETZSCHE

BY HENRY L. MENCKEN

I shall be told, I suppose, that my philosophy is comfortless —
because I speak the truth; and people prefer to believe that
everything the Lord made is good. If you are one such, go to
the priests, and leave philosophers in peace!

Arthur Schopenhauer.

LUCE ET LABORE

LONDON

T. FISHER UNWIN

MCMVIII

note in the TxU copy, signed "John W. Luce & Co. by Harrison Hale Schaff" and dated 18 December 1933, it is "one of the second edition of which only five hundred copies were printed. It is decidedly rarer than the first edition."

Locations: GHT (binding B), Harv (binding B), InU-Li (binding A), RJS (binding B), TxU (binding B), Yale (binding A).

A 3.1.d
Fourth printing: Boston: Luce, 1913.

On title page, beneath Schopenhauer quotation: '*Third Edition*'. On copyright page: '*COLONIAL PRESS* [final S broken] | . . . | . . . *U.S.A.*' New preface (dated November 1913); two chapters ('NIETZSCHE AS A TEACHER' and 'BOOKS AND ARTI-CLES ABOUT NIETZSCHE') omitted and two rewritten; 'HOW TO STUDY NIETZSCHE' and an index added. GHT copy signed and dated January 1914 by Mencken.

Locations: GHT, RJS.

A 3.1.e
Fifth printing: Boston: Luce, 1913.

Omits the Colonial Press information on copyright page, else same as fourth printing. InU-Li copy is inscribed to Louis Untermeyer and dated 1919. Cf. Frey 20; *Dreiser-Mencken Letters* (A 76), p. 385.

Locations: GHT (dj), InU-Li, RJS.

LATER REPRINTINGS WITHIN THE ONLY EDITION

A 3.1.f
Port Washington, N.Y.: Kennikat, [1967].

'*Third Edition*' on title page. On copyright page: 'Reissued in 1967'. Reproduction of 1913 Luce printings.

Location: GHT.

A 3.1.g
[Folcroft, Pa.:] Folcroft Library Editions, 1973.

Data from OCLC and NUC 1973–77, 84.163. Not seen.

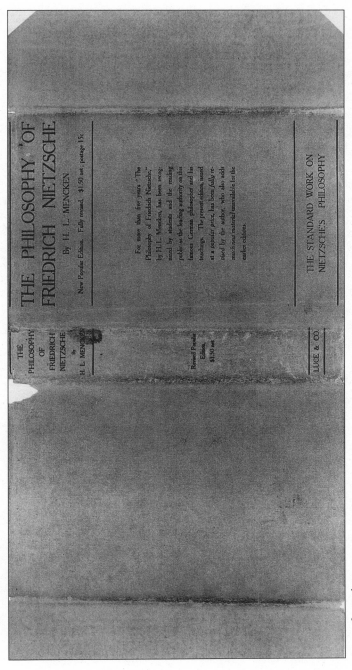

THE PHILOSOPHY OF
FRIEDRICH NIETZSCHE

By H. L. MENCKEN

New Popular Edition. Fully revised. $1.50 net; postage 15c

For more than five years "The
Philosophy of Friedrich Nietzsche,"
by H.L. Mencken, has been recog-
nized by students and the reading
public as the leading authority on this
famous German philosopher and his
teachings. The present edition, issued
at a popular price, has been fully revised by the author, who also adds
much new material unavailable for the
earlier edition.

THE PHILOSOPHY
OF
FRIEDRICH
NIETZSCHE
By
H. L. MENCKEN

New Popular
Edition.
$1.50 net

LUCE & CO

THE STANDARD WORK ON
NIETZSCHE'S PHILOSOPHY

A 3.1.e, dust jacket

A 3.1.h
[Folcroft, Pa.:] Folcroft Library Editions, 1976.

Added title page.

Location: Harv.

A 3.1.i
Norwood, Pa.: Norwood Editions, 1977.

Reproduction of 1908 Luce printings. Data from S2.5 and OCLC. Not seen.

A 3.1.j
Philadelphia: R. West, 1978.

Reproduction of 1908 Luce printings. Data from S2.5. Not located.

A 3.1.k
Torrance, Calif.: Noontide Press, MCMLXXXII.

Reproduction of 1908 Luce printings; paperback.

Location: GHT.

A 3.1.l
Torrance, Calif.: Noontide Press, MCMLXXXII *[sic]*.

On copyright page: 'Second Noontide | paperback printing | May, 1989'.

Location: GHT.

A 3.1.m
Friedrich Nietzsche. New Brunswick, N.J., and London: Transaction, [1993].

On copyright page: '© 1993'. Reproduction of 1913 Luce printings; introduction by Richard Flathman; paperback.

Locations: GHT, Harv, MChB.

A 4 A DOLL'S HOUSE

A 4.1.a.i
Only edition, only printing, first issue (1909)

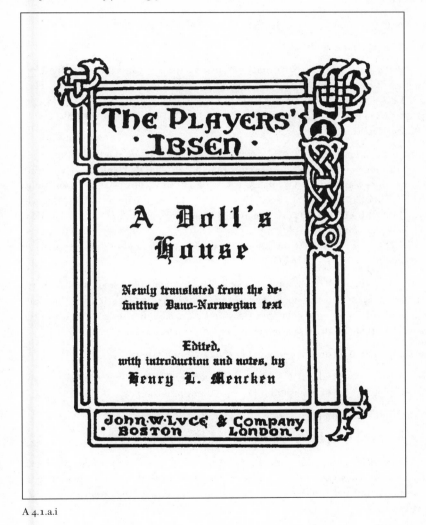

A 4.1.a.i

Title page: All text in red except 'Newly . . . text' and 'John . . . LONDON •'.

Copyright page: 'Copyright, 1909, | By HENRY L. MENCKEN | BOSTON, MASS., U.S.A. | Electrotyped and Printed at | THE COLONIAL PRESS: | C. H. Simonds & Co., Boston, U.S.A.'

$5^{15}/_{16}'' \times 4^{3}/_{8}''$: [i–iv] v–xxvii [xxviii] 1–150 [151–52] = 180 pp.

[1]² [2]⁴ [3–12]⁸ [13]⁴ = 90 leaves.

Contents: p. i: half title with two ornaments; p. ii: blank; p. iii: title; p. iv: copyright; pp. v–xxiv: 'INTRODUCTION'; pp. xxv–vi: 'TRANSLATOR'S NOTE'; p. xxvii: 'THE PEOPLE OF THE PLAY⁵' [note 5 is on p. 143]; p. xxviii: blank; pp. 1–136: text; pp. 137–48: 'NOTES'; pp. 149–50: 'BOOKS IN ENGLISH DEALING | WITH "A DOLL'S HOUSE"'; pp. 151–52: blank.

Typography and paper: $4^{1}/_{2}''$ $(4^{3}/_{16}'')$ × 3''; 26 lines per page (28 in introduction, 35 in notes). Running heads: recto, '[ornament] INTRODUCTION | [rule]' (pp. vii–xxiii), '[act number] [ornament] A DOLL'S HOUSE | [rule]' (pp. 3–135), '[ornament] NOTES | [rule]' (pp. 139–47); verso, 'INTRODUCTION [ornament] | [rule]' (pp. vi–xxiv), 'TRANSLATOR'S NOTE [ornament] | [rule]' (p. xxvi), 'A DOLL'S HOUSE [ornament] [act number] | [rule]' (pp. 2–136), 'NOTES [ornament] | [rule]' (pp. 138–48), 'BOOKS IN ENGLISH [ornament] | [rule]' (p. 150). Laid paper, watermarked 'Westminster | A.S.&B. | QUALITY'.

Binding: Red-orange V cloth, stamped in gilt. Front: crown above shield with halberd-bearing lion. Spine, reading up: '[interlace ornament] •A•DOLL'S•HOUSE• [interlace ornament]'. Trimmed, top edge gilt. Gray end papers, with interlaced boxes in the style of the title page and two ornaments like those on the spine.

Dust jacket: None recorded or found, but see *Little Eyolf* (A 5).

Publication: Announced in *PW*, 5 December 1908: 1718. 75¢ (*PW* and *Books*). Copyright #A234399 (date of deposit of title page 8 February 1909).

Printing: See copyright page.

Locations: GHT, Harv, LC (8 March 1909), RJS, Yale.

Notes: In collaboration with Holger A. Koppel, who "called off a rough but literal translation of each speech, and I compared it with two or three good German translations and we thus perfected the text" (Mencken, quoted in Adler). Adler 21; Frey 54; Bulsterbaum 65.

A 4.1.a.ii
Only edition, only printing, Canadian issue (1909)

Same as A 4.1.a.1 except:

A 4.1.a.ii

Title page: All text in red except 'Newly . . . text' and 'TORONTO . . . LIMITED'.

$5^{15/16}'' \times 4^{5/16}''$

[1]² (± 1₂) [2]⁴ [3–12]⁸ [13]⁴ = 90 leaves. The title/copyright leaf is a cancel.

Dust jacket: Not seen.

Location: GHT.

Notes: Not in Adler.

A 5 LITTLE EYOLF

A 5.1.a
Only edition, only printing (1909)

A 5

Title page: All text in red except 'Newly . . . text' and 'John . . . LONDON •'.

Copyright page: 'Copyright, 1909, | By HENRY L. MENCKEN | BOSTON, MASS., U.S.A. | Electrotyped and Printed at | THE COLONIAL PRESS: | C. H. Simonds & Co., Boston, U.S.A.'

$5^{15}/_{16}'' \times 4^{3}/_{8}''$: [i–iv] v–xxv [xxvi] 1–111 [112] 113–19 [120] 121–23 [124] 125 [126] = 152 pp.

$[1]^2 [2–10]^8 [11]^2 = 76$ leaves.

Contents: p. i: half title with two ornaments; p. ii: blank; p. iii: title; p. iv: copyright; pp. v–xxi: 'INTRODUCTION'; p. xxii: blank; pp. xxiii–iv: 'TRANSLATOR'S NOTE'; p. xxv: 'THE PEOPLE OF THE PLAY'; p. xxvi: blank; pp. 1–111: text; p. 112: blank; pp. 113–19: 'NOTES'; p. 120: blank; pp. 121–23: 'TRANSLATIONS AND PER- | FORMANCES'; p. 124: blank; p. 125: 'BOOKS IN ENGLISH DEALING | WITH "LITTLE EYOLF" '; p. 126: blank.

Typography and paper: $4^{1}/_{2}''$ $(4^{3}/_{16}'')$ $\times$ 3''; 26 lines per page (28 in introduction, 35 in notes). Running heads: recto, '[ornament] INTRODUCTION | [rule]' (pp. vii–xxi), '[act number] [ornament] LITTLE EYOLF | [rule]' (pp. 3–111), '[ornament] NOTES | [rule]' (pp. 115–19), '[ornament] TRANSLATIONS | [rule]' (p. 123); verso, 'INTRODUCTION [ornament] | [rule]' (pp. vi–xx), 'TRANSLATOR'S NOTE [ornament] | [rule]' (p. xxiv), 'LITTLE EYOLF [ornament] [act number] | [rule]' (pp. 2–110), 'NOTES [ornament] | [rule]' (pp. 114–18), 'TRANSLATIONS [ornament] | [rule]' (p. 122). Laid paper.

Binding: Red-orange V cloth, stamped in gilt. Front: crown above shield with halberd-bearing lion. Spine, reading up: '[interlace ornament] •LITTLE•EYOLF• [interlace ornament]'. Trimmed, top edge gilt. Gray end papers, with interlaced boxes in the style of the title page and two ornaments like those on the spine.

Dust jacket: The Yale copy has an unprinted glassine jacket, with clipped corners on the flaps.

Publication: Announced in *PW*, 5 December 1908: 1718. 75¢ (*PW* and *Books*). Copyright #A234400 (date of deposit of title page 8 February 1909).

Printing: See copyright page.

Locations: GHT, Harv, InU-Li, LC (8 March 1909), RJS, Yale (dj).

Notes: In collaboration with Holger A. Koppel; see A 4. Adler 21; Frey 54; Bulsterbaum 65.

A 6 THE GIST OF NIETZSCHE

A 6.1.a
Only edition, first printing (1910)

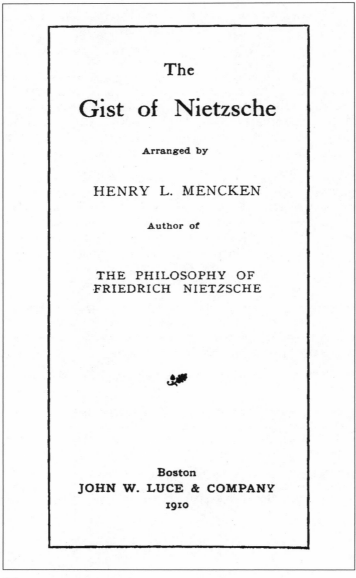

The

Gist of Nietzsche

Arranged by

HENRY L. MENCKEN

Author of

THE PHILOSOPHY OF
FRIEDRICH NIETZSCHE

Boston
JOHN W. LUCE & COMPANY
1910

A 6.1.a

Copyright page: 'Copyright 1910 | By L E Bassett'.

7½″ × 4½″: [i–x 1] 2–60 [61–62] = 72 pp.

[1–4]⁸ [5]⁴ = 36 leaves.

Contents: p. i: title; p. ii: copyright; p. iii: divisional half title; p. iv: blank; pp. v–vi: 'INTRODUCTION.'; pp. vii–viii: 'BIOGRAPHICAL NOTE.'; p. ix: half title; p. x: blank; pp. 1–60: text; p. 61: [within box] 'PRESS COMMENT | on | THE PHILOSO-PHY OF | NIETZSCHE.' | [four excerpts]; p. 62: [within box] 'THE PHILOSOPHY | of | FREIDRICH *[sic]* NIETZSCHE | by | Henry L. Mencken | [ad]'.

Typography and paper: 5½″ (5¹⁄₁₆″) × 3″; 30 lines per page. Running heads: recto, chapter titles (pp. 3–59); verso, 'NIETZSCHE | [rule]' (pp. 2–60). Wove paper.

Binding: Maroon V cloth. White paper label on front: [all within double-rule maroon box] '*The Gist of Nietzsche* | [maroon ornament: oil lamp] | HENRY L. MENCKEN'. White paper label on spine: '[double maroon rule] | THE | GIST | OF | NIETZ- | SCHE | [double maroon rule] | H. L. M. | [double maroon rule]'. Trimmed, unstained. White end papers.

Dust jacket: Unprinted glassine with evenly clipped corners on flaps.

Publication: Published 7 February 1910. 60¢ *(Books)*. Copyright #A259077 (two copies received 3 March 1910).

Printing: Printed by Commercial Financial Printing Co., Boston; bound by H. M. Plimpton and Co., Norwood, Mass.

Locations: EPL, dj via D and RAW, Harv, InU-Li, RJS (2), Yale (dj).

Notes: Arranged by Mencken and Harrison Hale Schaff. EPL copy in very dark maroon. Both cover labels vary in size. Adler 22; S1.6; S2.10; Frey 54; Bulsterbaum 65.

LATER REPRINTINGS WITHIN THE ONLY EDITION

A 6.1.b
Folcroft, Pa.: Folcroft Press, [1969].

"First published 1910; reprinted 1969." Data from NUC 1968–72, 70.4. Not seen. Perhaps these are the photo-offset copies seen without new imprints. Binding in same style as other Folcroft reprints: maroon (GHT) or green (MCR) buckram stamped in gilt on spine, reading down: 'THE GIST OF NIETZSCHE [ornament] MENCKEN'.

A 6.1.c

[Folcroft, Pa.:] Folcroft Library Editions, 1973.

Added title page. On copyright page: Library of Congress Cataloging-in-Publication Data.

Locations: EPL, GHT.

A 6.1.d

Belfast, Maine: Bern Porter, 1973.

Data from S2.10. Not located.

A 6.1.e

Norwood, Pa.: Norwood Editions, 1977.

Data from OCLC and NUC 1979, 11.211. Not seen.

A 6.1.f

[Norwood, Pa.]: Norwood Editions, 1978.

Added title page. Noted in blue buckram and green buckram.

Location: Harv (2, both), MCR (green).

A 7 MEN VERSUS THE MAN

A 7.1.a
Only edition, first printing (1910)

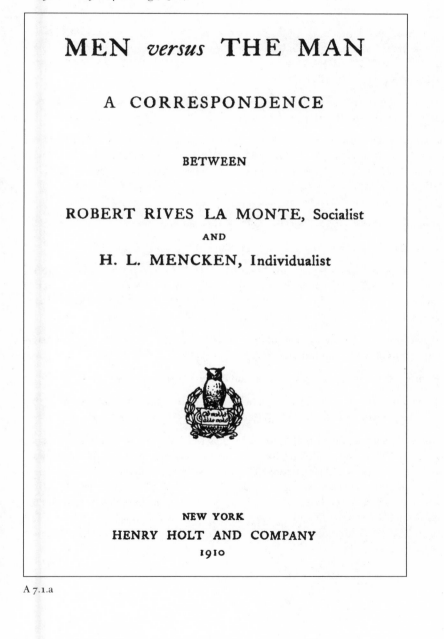

MEN *versus* THE MAN

A CORRESPONDENCE

BETWEEN

ROBERT RIVES LA MONTE, Socialist

AND

H. L. MENCKEN, Individualist

NEW YORK
HENRY HOLT AND COMPANY
1910

A 7.1.a

Copyright page: 'COPYRIGHT, 1910 | BY | HENRY HOLT AND COMPANY | [short rule] | *Published March, 1910*'

7⅜" × 4¹³⁄₁₆": [i–viii 1] 2–247 [248] 249–52 [253–64] = 272 pp.

[1–17]⁸ = 136 leaves.

Contents: pp. i–iv: blank; p. v: title; p. vi: copyright; p. vii: 'INTRODUCTION'; p. viii: blank; pp. 1–247: text; p. 248: blank; pp. 249–52: 'INDEX'; pp. 253–54: blank; pp. 255–64: ads: 'THE MIRAGE OF THE MANY . . . THE FRESH WATER AQUARIUM | AND ITS INHABITANTS'.

Typography and paper: 5¹¹⁄₁₆" (5⁷⁄₁₆") × 3⁵⁄₁₆"; 30 lines per page. Running heads: recto and verso, 'Men vs. the Man' (pp. 2–247); 'Index' (pp. 250–52). Wove paper.

Binding A: Vertically ribbed maroon T cloth stamped in gilt. Front: 'MEN VS. THE MAN | [short rule] | LA MONTE AND MENCKEN | [ornament with stylized owl]'. Spine: '[thick-thin rule] | MEN VS. | THE MAN | [short rule] | LA MONTE | AND | MENCKEN | [thin-thick rule] | [rule] | HENRY HOLT | AND COMPANY | [rule]'. Trimmed, unstained. White end papers.

Binding B: Maroon cross-filed ("rat-tail") cloth; same stamping.

Binding C: Red V cloth; same stamping but in black.

Dust jacket: Salmon paper. Front: 'MEN VS. THE MAN | [short rule] | LA MONTE AND MENCKEN | [ornament with stylized owl] | $1.35 NET | [six-line blurb]'. Spine: 'MEN VS. | THE MAN | [double rule] | LA MONTE | AND | MENCKEN | $1.35 net | [Holt device]'. Back: ads for three railroad books. Flaps: ads for six books.

Publication: Published 19 March 1910. $1.35. Copyright #A259618. Approximately 613 copies of the Holt printing sold.

Printing: Printed and bound by Quinn and Boden Co., Rahway, N.J.

Locations: GHT (binding B), Harv (2 in binding A), InU-Li (2, bindings A and C), LC (23 March 1910, binding A), MChB (binding A), RJS (2, bindings A and C [dj]).

Notes: Frey gives priority to the ribbed binding (A) and does not mention binding C, but in a "Bibliographical Note Book" he made from extra pages of the large-paper version of his book and annotated (EPL), he says: "Apparently three bindings. There is one in lighter red cloth, stamped in black. Mencken says, 'the small first edition was a complete flop. Several years later Holt bound up his remaining sheets, stamped the covers in black to save expense and remaindered them, at about 50 cts.'" Price of first printing $1.40 according to *Books*. Adler 22; S2.10; Frey 39; Bulsterbaum 4; *Menckeniana* 48.2.

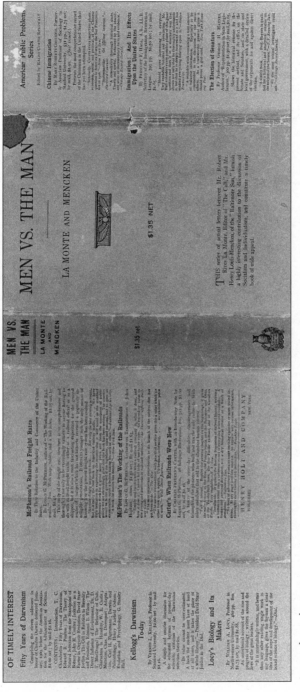

A 7.1.a, dust jacket

A 7.1.b
Second printing: New York: Arno Press and the *New York Times,* 1972.

Added title page. On copyright page: 'Reprint Edition 1972'. In series The Right Wing Individualist Tradition in America.

Locations: EPL, GHT.

A 8 WHAT YOU OUGHT TO KNOW ABOUT YOUR BABY

A 8.1.a
First edition, only printing (1910)

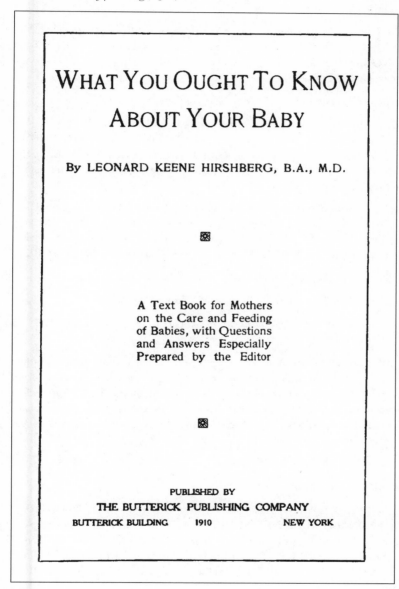

WHAT YOU OUGHT TO KNOW ABOUT YOUR BABY

By LEONARD KEENE HIRSHBERG, B.A., M.D.

A Text Book for Mothers
on the Care and Feeding
of Babies, with Questions
and Answers Especially
Prepared by the Editor

PUBLISHED BY
THE BUTTERICK PUBLISHING COMPANY
BUTTERICK BUILDING   1910   NEW YORK

A 8.1.a

Copyright page: 'COPYRIGHT, 1910, BY | THE BUTTERICK PUBLISHING COM-
PANY | NEW YORK'

$7^{15}/_{16}'' \times 5^{5}/_{16}''$: [i–x] 1–97 [98–102] = 112 pp.

$[1–7]^8$ = 56 leaves.

Contents: pp. i–ii: blank pastedown; pp. iii–iv: blank; p. v: title; p. vi: copyright; p. vii:
'TABLE OF CONTENTS'; p. viii: four-line dedication to George W. Wilder; p. ix: 'A
WORD TO MOTHERS | [15 lines]'; p. x: blank; pp. 1–97: text; pp. 98–100: blank; pp.
101–02: blank pastedown.

Typography and paper: $6^{1}/_{4}'' \times 3^{11}/_{16}''$; 40 lines per page. No heads. Wove paper.

Binding: Dark green V cloth. Front: [first four lines in double-rule box; raised dots
represent small triangles between words] 'WHAT•YOU•OUGHT | TO•KNOW•
ABOUT | YOUR•BABY | LEONARD KEENE HIRSHBERG, B.A., M.D. | THE
BUTTERICK PUBLISHING CO. | NEW YORK'. Spine blank. Trimmed, unstained.
No end papers.

Dust jacket: Grayish tan paper, printed only on front: '[in double-rule box, raised dots
between words representing triangles] WHAT • YOU • OUGHT | TO • KNOW •
ABOUT | YOUR • BABY | LEONARD KEENE HIRSHBERG, B.A., M.D. | [below
box] PRICE, 25 CENTS | THE BUTTERICK PUBLISHING CO. | NEW YORK'.

Publication: Published 29 April 1910. 25¢. Copyright #A261661.

Printing: Printed and bound by the Butterick Publishing Co., New York.

Locations: GHT (dj), Harv (2), InU-Li, KU-S (partial dj), LC (3 May 1910), RJS, TxU
(dj).

Notes: All ghost-written by Mencken except the questions and answers. According
to the editors of the third edition, "the book enjoyed reasonable popularity, went
through several printings, and continued to be issued by Butterick until 1923, when
the copyright was turned over to Leonard Hirshberg" (p. 15). No other printings have
been located. Parts previously published (*Delineator*, 72–74 [1908–1909]); Adler 22,
130; Bulsterbaum 25.

A 8.2.a
Second edition, only printing (1926)

Cover title: 'WHAT YOU | OUGHT TO KNOW [TO centered] | ABOUT THE BABY |
By | Dr. LEONARD KEENE HIRSHBERG | A. B., M. A., M. D. (Johns Hopkins
University) | Physician-in-Chief of the National Health Service | THE SCIENCE
OF REARING CHILDREN | Copyrighted, Published and Distributed | by the |
HEALTH SERVICE PUB. CO., Inc. | and the | NATIONAL HEALTH SERVICE |
17 West 60th Street, New York City

A 8.1.a, dust jacket

Copyright page: None.

7¹⁄₁₆″ × 4¾″ (?): [i–vi 1] 2–15 [16] 17–19 [20] 21–24 [25] 26 [27] 28–31 [32] 33 [34] 35–37 [38] 39–40 [41] 42–44 [45] 46 [47] 48–52 [53] 54–55 [56] 57–61 [62] 63–64 [65] 66–72 [73] 74–77 [78] 79–85 [86] 87–89 [90] 91 [92] 93–104 [105] 106 [107] 108–15 [116] 117–18 [119] 120–26 [127] 128 [129] 130–36 [137] 138 [139] 140–47 [148–54] = 160 pp.

[1–4]¹⁶ [5–6]⁸ = 80 leaves.

Contents: p. i: dedication; p. ii: blank; pp. iii–iv: 'FOREWORD | and | INTRODUC-TION'; p. v: 'PREFACE'; p. vi: biography of Hirshberg; pp. 1–147: text; pp. 148–49: order forms; pp. 150–52: ads for books; p. 153: list of foods; p. 154: order form.

Binding: Red wrappers (?) printed in black.

Location: DNLM (FEB-2 '26, rebound but gatherings intact).

Notes: Dated 1926 by NUC 247.342 and OCLC. The only copy located has been rebound.

A 8.3.a
Third edition, only printing (1990)

Title page: 'The H. L. Mencken | Baby Book | Comprising the Contents of H. L. Mencken's | What You Ought to Know | About Your Baby | with commentaries | [ornament: winged head above ring] | Howard Markel, M.D. [heavy dot] Frank A. Oski, M.D. | HANLEY & BELFUS, INC. | Philadelphia'

Copyright page: '[four-line publisher's address] | Copyright © 1990 by Hanley & Belfus, Inc. | [three lines reserving rights] | [seven-line Library of Congress Cataloging-in-Publication Data] | The H. L. Mencken Baby Book | ISBN 0–932883–22–2 | *Designed by Adrianne Onderdonk Dudden* | Printed in the United States of America | 9 8 7 6 5 4 3 2 1'

8⅜″ × 5⁷⁄₁₆″: [A–B i–vi] vii [viii] ix–xii 1–26 [26A–26H] 27–185 [186] 187–94 [195–202] = 224 pp. and page on postcard stock tipped in between last leaf and end paper.

[1–7]¹⁶ = 112 leaves.

Contents: pp. A–B: blank; p. i: half title; p. ii: blank; p. iii: title; p. iv: copyright; p. v: four-line dedication; p. vi: blank; p. vii: 'Contents'; p. viii: blank; pp. ix–x: 'Preface'; pp. xi–xii: 'Authors and Acknowledgments'; pp. 1–26: 'What You Ought to Know About | *What You Ought to Know | About Your Baby* | The Collaboration of H. L. Mencken, | Dr. Leonard K. Hirshberg, and Theodore Dreiser'; pp. 26A–26G: illustrations; p. 26H: 'Works of H. L. Mencken'; pp. 27–184: text; p. 185: 'Notes'; p. 186: blank; pp. 187–94: 'Index'; pp. 195–202: blank. The tipped-in page after p. 202 contains two business reply cards for ordering the book.

Binding: Mauve paper-covered boards; blue-green cloth spine stamped in gilt; dust jacket (price $18.95).

Locations: GHT (dj), RJS (dj).

A 9 THE ARTIST

A 9.1.a
First edition, presumed first printing (1912)

A 9.1.a

Copyright page: 'Copyright, *1909, by* | The Bohemian Publishing Company | *Copyright, 1912, by* | Henry L. Mencken | [gothic] The Four Seas Press | Sharon Mass *[sic]* U.S.A.'

6″ × 4½″: [1–10] 11–32 [33–38] = 38 pp.

[1]⁶ [2]⁸ (1 + 2₁) [3]⁴ = 19 leaves. The leaf with pp. 13–14 is tipped in to the following leaf.

Contents: pp. 1–2: blank; p. 3: half title; p. 4: blank; p. 5: title; p. 6: copyright; p. 7: 'DRAMATIS PERSONÆ'; p. 8: blank; p. 9: 'NOTE | [three lines]'; p. 10: blank; pp. 11–33: text; pp. 34–38: blank. Decorations at top and bottom of p. 7, top of p. 11, bottom of p. 33.

Typography and paper: 4⁹⁄₁₆″ (4⅛″) × 2⅝″; 19 lines per page (lines vary because of dialogue, stage directions, etc.). Running heads: recto and verso, '[between two ornaments] *The* Artist' (pp. 12–33). Wove paper.

Binding: Brown mottled paper-covered boards. Front: [within decorative box featuring lyre, piano, and infant, printed in brown, curved] 'The Artist'. Spine blank. Drab end papers. Trimmed, unstained.

Dust jacket: Unprinted glassine with corners of flaps unevenly clipped.

Publication: Announced in *PW,* 7 December 1912: n.p. 50¢. No record of copyright.

Printing: See copyright page.

Locations: EPL, GHT, dj via CB, Harv (3), RJS, Yale (2, dj).

Notes: The order of the first two printings is based on the review copy. Misimposed copy (Yale): [1]⁶ [2]⁸ (1 + 2₁) [3]⁴ (− 3₄); in the second gathering, the outer forme was perfected on itself instead of the inner, thereby producing two copies of each page in the outer forme (15, 18, 19, 22, 23, 26, 27, 30) instead of 15–30. Previously published (*Bohemian Magazine,* December 1909); Adler 6; S1.3; S2.5; Frey 20; Bulsterbaum 11; Matthew J. Bruccoli in *Menckeniana* 8.4–7.

Review copy: Same as above, with slip tipped in to free front end paper (2¾″ × 4″): 'THIS BOOK IS SENT FOR REVIEW IN YOUR PUBLICA- | TION . . . | THE PRICE OF THIS BOOK IS Net 50¢ [price handwritten over row of printed dots]'. *Location:* Yale.

A 9.1.b
First edition, second printing

Same as A 9.1.a except:

[1–10] 11–32 [33–36] = 36 pp.

[1]⁶ [2]⁸ (1 + 2₁, 2₈ + 1) [3]² = 18 leaves. The leaf with pp. 13–14 is apparently tipped in to that which follows it, and the one with pp. 31–32 to that preceding it.

Binding: Some copies with white end papers.

Locations: EPL, GHT (2), Harv, InU-Li, LC (28 April 1913).

A 9.1.c
Third printing: Boston: Luce, [1923].

Unchanged title page; copyright page changed to: ' . . . [roman] The Four Seas Press |
Boston, Mass., U.S.A.' 7″ × 4¾″; brown paper wrappers with design in darker brown,
glued on at spine and flaps; cream label on front printed in brown: [all within double-
rule box] '*The Artist* | A DRAMA WITHOUT WORDS | [ornament] | HENRY L.
MENCKEN'.

Locations: GHT, Harv (rebound), RJS.

LATER REPRINTINGS WITHIN THE FIRST EDITION

A 9.1.d
Folcroft, Pa.: Folcroft Press, [1969].

On copyright page: 'First Published 1912 | Reprinted 1969'. An EPL copy, without
title page, is bound in the Folcroft style.

Locations: EPL, GHT, MBU.

A 9.1.e
[Folcroft, Pa.:] Folcroft Library Editions, 1973.

Added title page. On copyright page: Library of Congress Cataloging-in-Publication
Data.

Location: EPL.

A 9.1.f
New York: Octagon, 1977.

Location: MBU.

A 9.1.g
[Norwood, Pa.:] Norwood Editions, 1978.

Added title page. Dated 1977 by OCLC and S2.5.

Location: PYoW.

A 9.1.h
Belfast, Maine: Bern Porter, 1979.

Data from S2.5. Not located.

A 9.1.i
[Darby, Pa.:] Arden Library, 1980.

On added title page: 'THIS IS LIMITED TO 150 COPIES | ARDEN LIBRARY 1980'.

Location: GHT.

A 9.2.a
Second edition, only printing (1917)

Cover title: 'THE ARTIST | A Satire in One Act | BY | H. L. MENCKEN. | [short rule] | [six lines of copyright notices and rights reservations] | CAUTION—The possession of this Acting Version of *The Artist* does | [eight lines requiring permission from HLM and noting it has been translated into French, German, and Danish] | NEW YORK 1917.'

Copyright page: See cover title.

$10^{13}/_{16}'' \times 8\frac{3}{8}''$: (only the rectos numbered) [1] 2–12 = 24 pp.

$[1]^{12}$ = 12 leaves.

Contents: p. 1: cover title and copyright; p. 2: 'FOR THE PRODUCER.'; pp. 3–12 text. All versos blank.

Binding: Self wrappers. All edges trimmed. Stapled twice.

Locations: EPL (3), InU-Li.

Notes: Published by Lane. Gray paper.

A 9.3.a
Third edition, only printing (1920)

Title page: 'THE ARTIST | A *Drama Without Words* | By | H. L. MENCKEN | [device] | SAMUEL FRENCH | *Incorporated 1898* | THOS. R. EDWARDS, *Managing Director* | 25 West 45th Street . New York City'

Copyright page: 'COPYRIGHT, 1916, 1920, BY ALFRED A. KNOPF, INC., | In volume, "A Book of Burlesques," | BY H. L. MENCKEN | ALL RIGHTS RESERVED | [17 lines on gaining permission]'

$7\frac{3}{8}'' \times 4^{15}/_{16}''$: [i–vi] 1–14 = 20 pp.

[1]^{10} = 10 leaves.

Contents: p. i: title; p. ii: copyright; p. iii: statement of permission received; p. iv: half title; p. v: 'CHARACTERS'; p. vi: blank; pp. 1–14: text.

Binding: Yellow-orange wrappers (7^{13}⁄$_{16}$″ × 5^{3}⁄$_{16}$″), printed in brown. Front reproduces title page with additional line: 'PRICE 50 CENTS'. Along "spine," reading down: 'THE ARTIST'. All edges trimmed. Stapled twice.

Locations: EPL (4), RJS.

Notes: 1,000 copies printed, 247 sold.

A 10 EUROPE AFTER 8:15

A 10.1.a
Only edition, only printing (1914)

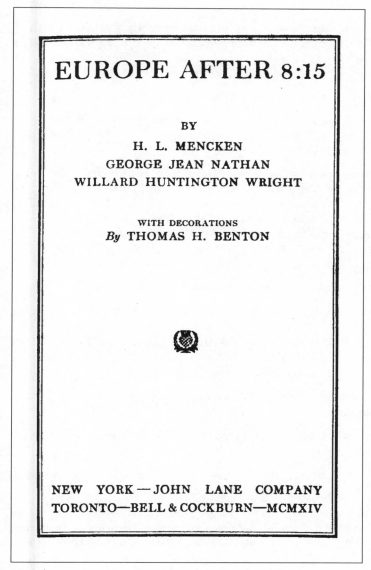

EUROPE AFTER 8:15

BY

H. L. MENCKEN
GEORGE JEAN NATHAN
WILLARD HUNTINGTON WRIGHT

WITH DECORATIONS
By THOMAS H. BENTON

NEW YORK — JOHN LANE COMPANY
TORONTO—BELL & COCKBURN—MCMXIV

A 10

Copyright page: 'Copyright, 1914 | By JOHN LANE COMPANY'

7⅜" × 4⅞" (binding A), 7⅜" × 4¾" (binding B): [1–6] 7–32 [33–34] 35–68 [69–70] 71–107 [108–10] 111–42 [143–44] 145–86 [187–88] 189–222 [223–24] = 224 pp.

[1–14]⁸ = 112 leaves.

Contents: p. 1: half title; p. 2: blank; p. 3: title; p. 4: copyright; p. 5: 'CONTENTS'; p. 6: blank; pp. 7–32: 'PREFACE IN | THE SOCRATIC MANNER'; pp. 33–222: text; pp. 223–24: blank. Blank pages of text following divisional half titles: pp. 34, 70, 110, 144, 188. Illustrations tipped in after pp. 2, 34, 54, 70, 110, 144, 188, 218.

Text: "Vienna," "Munich," "Berlin," "London," "Paris." See Notes.

Typography and paper: 5⅞₆" (5⅛") × 3⅗₆"; 23 lines per page. Running heads: recto, 'PREFACE' (pp. 9–31), chapter titles (pp. 37–221); verso, 'EUROPE AFTER 8:15' (pp. 8–222). Wove paper.

Binding A: Yellow-orange smooth V cloth. Design in very dark blue on front: '[rule] | [overstamped in gilt dots] EUROPE AFTER 8¹⁵ | [rule] | [woman seated at table underneath tree and Japanese lantern; beneath, flush right:] H. L. MENCKEN | GEORGE JEAN NATHAN | WILLARD HUNTINGTON WRIGHT | [double rule]'. Stamped in gilt on spine: 'EUROPE | AFTER | 8¹⁵ | [short rule] | MENCKEN | [short rule] | NATHAN | [short rule] | WRIGHT | JOHN LANE | COMPANY'. Trimmed, unstained. White end papers.

Binding B: Same except design in black on front.

Dust jacket: Black on dull yellow paper. Front repeats front cover. Spine repeats spine of cover, except: ' . . . WRIGHT | $1.25 net | JOHN LANE . . . '. Back: 'THE LATEST FICTION | [rule] | [ad for nine books: 'THE FORTUNATE YOUTH . . . YOUTH WILL BE SERVED'] | [rule] | JOHN LANE COMPANY, NEW YORK'. Front flap: blurb for the book. Rear flap: ad for the International Studio.

Publication: Published 29 May 1914. $1.25. Copyright #A376172. 610 copies sold (to 31 December 1916).

Printing: Printed by Vail-Ballou Co., Binghamton, N.Y.; bound by Grady Bookbinding Co., New York.

Locations: GHT (2, bindings A and B in dj), InU-Li (binding B), LC (3 June 1914, binding B?), RJS (2, bindings A and B [dj]).

Notes: Mencken wrote the preface, "Munich," and the first and last parts of "London." This was Benton's first book illustration. One or the other stamping on the front may represent the binding of the remainders reported by Mencken (Adler 23). Frey gives priority to the blue. Parts previously published (*Smart Set*, April 1913, June 1913); Adler 23, 131; Frey 40; Bulsterbaum 4.

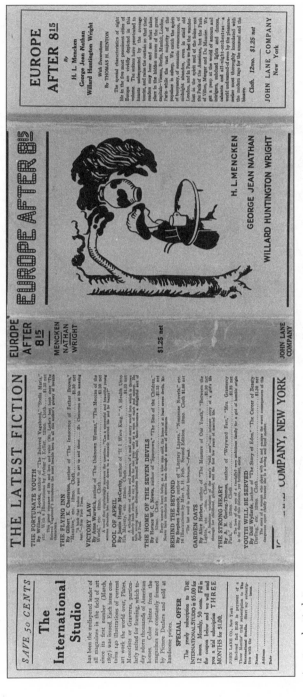

A 10.1.a, dust jacket

A 11 A NOTE TO AUTHORS
[1915?]

A 11, cover title

Head title: 'A NOTE | TO AUTHORS | [text follows]'

6⅛" × 3¼": 1–7 [8] = 8 pp.

[1]⁴ = 4 leaves.

Contents: pp. 1–7: text; p. 8: blank.

Typography and paper: 4¾" × 2⁵⁄₁₆"; 33 lines per page. No heads. Smooth wove paper.

Binding: Gray wrappers. Front: '[logo of *The Smart Set A Magazine of Cleverness* with a baby Pan figure connected by strings to winged hearts and a baby Cupid at bottom; in between:] Edited by | GEORGE JEAN NATHAN | and H. L. MENCKEN | A NOTE | TO AUTHORS'. All edges trimmed. Two staples.

Locations: EPL (2, both bound in books), TxU.

Notes: Text signed by both but written by Mencken. Dated 1915 by Adler, 1916 by Frey, "apparently . . . 1916" by Mencken in MLAE 197, and 1921 in typed index to one of the EPL volumes containing it. Adler 6; Frey 58.

A 12 THE EDITORS REGRET
(SMART SET REJECTION NOTICES) [1915?]

A 12.1
Single leaf

The
SMART SET

Edited by
George Jean Nathan
and
H. L. Mencken

25 WEST 45TH STREET, NEW YORK.

THE Editors regret that they are unable to use the enclosed at the moment. They read personally all manuscripts submitted and try to return all that are unavailable within five days. In case of acceptance payment is made at once, without regard to the date of publication.

Authors who are not already contributors to the magazine will perhaps find something of interest in the notices on the back of this card.

A 12.1, recto

3½″ × 5½″ (recto); 5½″ × 3½″ (verso)

Contents: Recto: '[*Smart Set* logo and address] | [initial T descends below the line] THE Editors regret that they are unable to use the enclosed at the | moment. They read personally all manuscripts submitted and try to | return all that are unavailable within five days. In case of acceptance | payment is made at once, without regard to the date of publication. | Authors who are not already contributors to the magazine will perhaps | find something of interest in the notices on the back of this card.' Verso has nine rules for submission.

Typography and paper: Recto: 2⁹⁄₁₆″ × 4³⁄₁₆″; 13 lines. Verso: 4¹⁄₁₆″ × 2½″; 23 lines. Wove paper.

Location: EPL.

Notes: Not in Adler.

A 12.2
Two-leaf

Title page: None.

6¼″ × 3⁵⁄₁₆″: [1–4] = 4 pp.

[1]² = 2 leaves.

Contents: p. 1 [same design as on cover of *A Note to Authors* (A 11)—Pan and Cupid with *Smart Set* logo—but instead of title]: 'The Editors regret that they | are unable to use the enclosed | at the moment. A glance at | the pages following will per- | haps suggest the submission of | other material. All manuscripts | received are examined by the | Editors personally, and an ef- | fort is made to return those | found unavailable within five | days. All accepted contribu- | tions are paid for at once, with- | out regard to the date of pub- | lication.'; p. 2: 'DON'T SEND US: | [twelve items]'; p. 3: 'WHAT WE WANT: | [eight items]'; p. 4: 'IMPORTANT | [ten items]'.

Typography and paper: 5″ × 2³⁄₁₆″; 32 lines per page (number of lines varies). Text on pp. 2–4 within 5⅜″ × 2⅝″ box. Wove paper.

Binding: None.

Location: EPL (2).

Notes: Dated 1915 by Adler, "1919, or thereabout" by Mencken in MLAE 197 ("a four-page expansion of our rejection slip"), but dated 1915 by him on an EPL copy. Adler 6.

The Editors regret that they are unable to use the enclosed at the moment. A glance at the pages following will perhaps suggest the submission of other material. All manuscripts received are examined by the Editors personally, and an effort is made to return those found unavailable within five days. All accepted contributions are paid for at once, without regard to the date of publication.

A 13 A LITTLE BOOK IN C MAJOR

A 13.1.a
Only edition, only printing (1916)

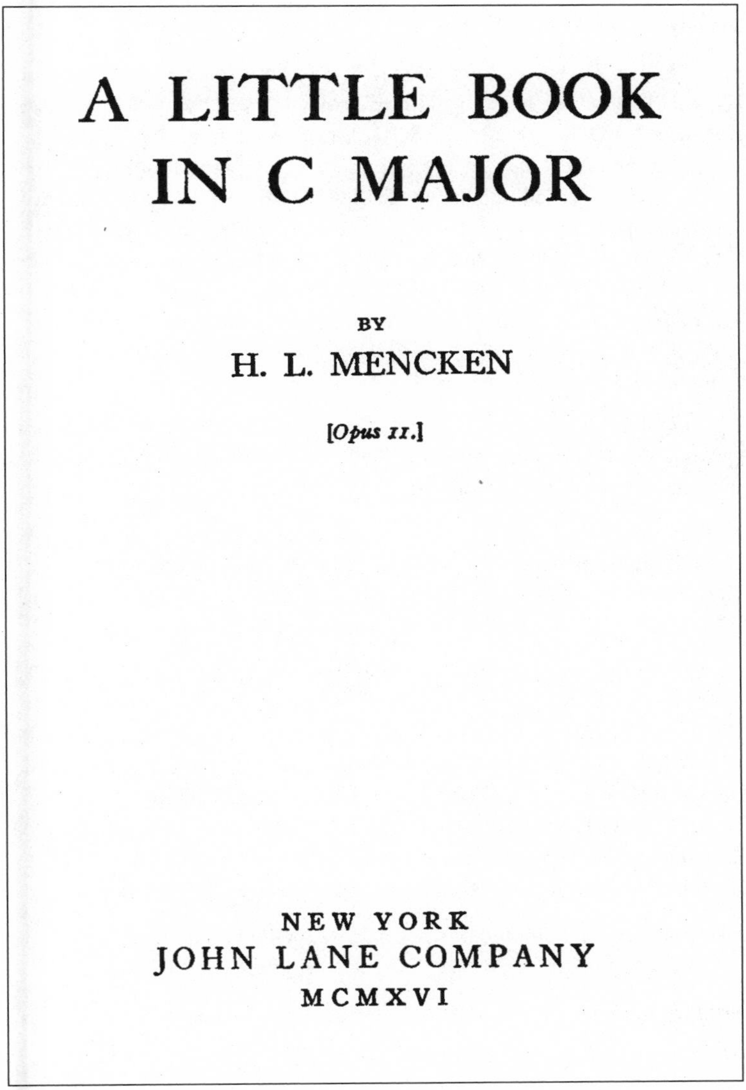

A LITTLE BOOK
IN C MAJOR

BY
H. L. MENCKEN

[*Opus 11.*]

NEW YORK
JOHN LANE COMPANY
MCMXVI

A 13

Copyright page: 'COPYRIGHT, 1916, | BY JOHN LANE COMPANY | Press of | J. J. Little & Ives Company | New York, U. S. A.'

7⅜″ × 4⅞″: [1–8] 9–16 [17–18] 19–26 [27–28] 29–35 [36–38] 39–46 [47–48] 49–56 [57–58] 59–69 [70–72] 73–79 [80] = 80 pp.

[1–5]⁸ = 40 leaves.

Contents: p. 1: half title between thin-thick and thick-thin rules; p. 2: [in box] 'BY THE SAME AUTHOR | [rule touching both sides of box] | A BOOK OF PREFACES | *Cloth $1.25 net* | A BOOK OF BURLESQUES | *Cloth $1.25 net*'; p. 3: title; p. 4: copyright; p. 5: three musical bars: first phrase of "Ich hatt' einen Kameraden"; p. 6: blank; pp. 7–79: text; p. 80: [all in a box] 'OTHER BOOKS BY H. L. MENCKEN | [thin-thick rule touching both sides of box] | [ads for 'A BOOK OF BURLESQUES' and '*IN PREPARATION* | [rule] | A BOOK OF PREFACES'] | [thick-thin rule touching both sides of box] | JOHN LANE COMPANY [on same line but smaller type, the first word over the next two:] PUBLISHERS NEW YORK'. Blank pages of text: pp. 8, 18, 28, 36, 38, 48, 58, 70, 72; all but pp. 36 and 70 follow pages with quotations that, with roman numerals, mark each division.

Typography and paper: 5″ (4⅝″) × 3″; 18 lines per page (lines vary with number of items on page). "Heads" are page numbers flanked right and left by parallel rules, except when pagination is at the bottom (pp. 9, 19, 29, 39, 49, 59, 73). Wove paper.

Binding: Maroon vertically ribbed T cloth, stamped in gilt. Front, within a musical bar with treble clef, each on a line: 'A LITTLE BOOK | IN | C MAJOR | H. L. MENCKEN'. Spine: 'A | LITTLE | BOOK | IN | C MAJOR | [small ornament] | MENCKEN | JOHN | LANE | CO.' Trimmed, unstained. White end papers.

Dust jacket: Maroon printing on white paper. Front: '[thick-thin rule] | A LITTLE BOOK | IN | [solid triangle] C MAJOR [solid triangle] | [rule] | By • H • L • MENCKEN | [rule] | [two paragraphs, each beginning with a paragraph symbol descending two lines:] A collection of about two-hundred | . . . | in the author's other works. | [rule] | JOHN LANE COMPANY, *Publishers,* NEW YORK | [thin-thick rule]'. Spine: 'A | LITTLE | BOOK | IN | C MAJOR | [short rule] | MENCKEN | 50 [on same line but smaller type, the first word over the rule over the second:] CTS. [rule] NET | John Lane | Company'. Back repeats p. 80 but reset. Flaps unprinted.

Publication: Published 22 September 1916. 50¢. Copyright #A437810. 885 copies sold.

Printing: Printed and bound by J. J. Little & Ives Co., New York.

Locations: GHT (dj), Harv (2), InU-Li, LC (25 September 1916), RJS.

Notes: "Nearly all the epigrams (226) in this little volume were first printed in the *Smart Set*" (Mencken, quoted in Adler 7). Adler 7, 158; S1.11; S2.6, 15; Frey 24; Bulsterbaum 71.

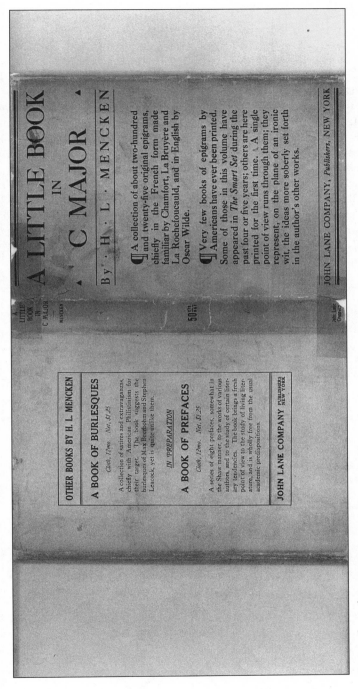

A LITTLE BOOK
IN
C MAJOR

By · H · L · MENCKEN

A collection of about two-hundred and twenty-five original epigrams, chiefly in the French form made familiar by Chamfort, La Bruyère and La Rochefoucauld, and in English by Oscar Wilde.

Very few books of epigrams by Americans have ever been printed. Some of those in this volume have appeared in *The Smart Set* during the past four or five years; others are here printed for the first time. A single point of view runs through them; they represent, on the plane of an ironic wit, the ideas more soberly set forth in the author's other works.

50 cts. net

JOHN LANE COMPANY, *Publishers*, NEW YORK

A LITTLE BOOK IN C MAJOR — MENCKEN

John Lane Company

OTHER BOOKS BY H. L. MENCKEN

A BOOK OF BURLESQUES

Cloth, 12mo. Net, $1.25

A collection of satires and extravaganzas, chiefly with American Philistinism for their target. The book suggests the burlesques of Max Beerbohm and Stephen Leacock, yet is quite unlike them.

IN PREPARATION

A BOOK OF PREFACES

Cloth, 12mo. Net, $1.25

A series of eight prefaces, somewhat in the Shaw manner, to the works of various authors, and to the study of certain literary tendencies. The book brings a fresh point of view to the study of living literature, and is wholly free from the usual academic predispositions.

JOHN LANE COMPANY PUBLISHERS NEW YORK

A 13.1.a, dust jacket

Note on opus numbers (JRS): Nos. 11–15 were assigned to A 13 (title page), A 14 (title page), A 16 (title page), A 17 (dust jacket of second edition), and A 18 (title page of second printing). Frey remarks: "The question has been asked, 'Why is this *fifth* book marked *Opus 11*?' The author himself has said that he is at a loss for an answer. So it must be that the publisher reckoned in the six well known books to which, previous to 1916, Mencken had contributed; according to the Henderson bibliographic check-list, there were six" (25). "Henderson" was Mencken himself in *H. L. Mencken* (B 29). Assuming that opus numbers apply only to books (not pamphlets) explicitly attributed to Mencken, with his name mentioned as either author, coauthor, or editor, the first ten opera in his reckoning were probably A 1–7, A 9, B 13, and A 10. "Henderson" lists the Ibsens (A 4–5) and *Blanchette* (B 13) among the "BOOKS EDITED BY H. L. MENCKEN" but does not mention books with anonymous contributions, such as *A Monograph of the New Baltimore Court House* (1899; B 1) or *What You Ought to Know About Your Baby* (1910; A 8).

A 14 A BOOK OF BURLESQUES

A 14.1.a
First edition, only printing (1916)

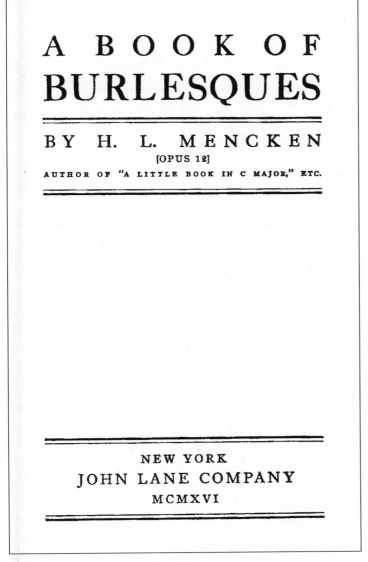

A BOOK OF
BURLESQUES

BY H. L. MENCKEN

[OPUS 12]

AUTHOR OF "A LITTLE BOOK IN C MAJOR," ETC.

NEW YORK
JOHN LANE COMPANY
MCMXVI

A 14.1.a

Copyright page: 'COPYRIGHT, 1916, | BY JOHN LANE COMPANY | Press of | J. J. Little & Ives Company | New York, U.S.A.'

7⅜″ × 4¹⁵⁄₁₆″: [1–10] 11–23 [24–26] 27–48 [49–50] 51–68 [69–70] 71–79 [80–82] 83–101 [102–04] 105–32 [133–34] 135–45 [146–48] 149–56 [157–58] 159–80 [181–82] 183–98 [199–200] 201–09 [210–12] 213–33 [234–36] 237–41 [242–44] 245–53 [254–56] = 256 pp., followed by tipped-in chart (7⅜″ × 27½″, verso blank)

[1–16]⁸ = 128 leaves and chart (folded seven times).

Contents: p. 1: half title between thick-thin and thin-thick rules; p. 2: [all in a box] 'BY THE SAME AUTHOR | [rule touching sides of box] | A LITTLE BOOK IN C MAJOR | *Cloth 50 cents net* | IN PREPARATION | A BOOK OF PREFACES | *Cloth $1.25 net* '; p. 3: title; p. 4: copyright; p. 5: between thick-thin and thin-thick rules, nine-line author's note signed 'H. L. M.'; p. 6: blank; p. 7: '[thick-thin rule] | CONTENTS | [thin-thick rule]'; p. 8: blank; pp. 9–256 and chart: text. Blank pages of text, all but those asterisked following divisional half titles: pp. 10, 24,° 26, 50, 70, 80,° 82, 102,° 104, 134, 146,° 148, 158, 182, 200, 210,° 212, 234,° 236, 242,° 244, 254,° 256.

Text: "Death: A Philosophical Discussion," "From the Programme of a Concert," "The Wedding: A Stage Direction," "The Visionary," "The Artist: A Drama Without Words," "Seeing the World," "From the Memoirs of the Devil," "Litanies for the Overlooked," "Asepsis: A Deduction in *Scherzo* Form," "Tales of the Moral and Pathological," "Epithalamium," "Portraits of Americans," "Panoramas of People" I–III, "The New Soule," "A Genealogical Chart of the Uplift." See Notes.

Typography and paper: 5⁹⁄₁₆″ (5¹⁄₁₆″) × 3⅛″; 28 lines per page (lines vary with the subject matter). Running heads: recto, chapter titles (pp. 13–253); verso, '[thick-thin rule] | [page number] *A Book of Burlesques* | [rule]' (pp. 12–252). Wove paper.

Binding A: Maroon T cloth stamped in gilt. Front: [letters appearing in maroon showing through gilt background in double box, boxed gilt foolscaps in the four corners] 'A BOOK OF | BURLESQUES | [short rule] | H. L. MENCKEN'. Spine: 'A BOOK | OF | BURLESQUES | [foolscap] | MENCKEN | JOHN LANE | COM-PANY'. 'COMPANY' is ¹³⁄₁₆″ wide, shorter than 'JOHN LANE'. Trimmed, unstained. White end papers.

Binding B: Same as binding A, but V cloth. 'COMPANY' is ¹⁵⁄₁₆″ wide, same width as 'JOHN LANE'.

Dust jacket: Maroon on white paper. Front: '[thick-thin rule] | • A BOOK OF • | BUR-LESQUES | [rule] | By H. L. MENCKEN | Author of "A Little Book in C Major," etc. | [rule] | [two paragraphs, each beginning with a paragraph symbol:] A collection of satires and extravaganzas, | . . . | possesses a deep insight into human nature. | [rule] | JOHN LANE COMPANY, Publishers, NEW YORK | [thin-thick rule]'. Spine: 'A BOOK | OF | BURLESQUES | [short rule] | MENCKEN | $1.25 | NET | JOHN

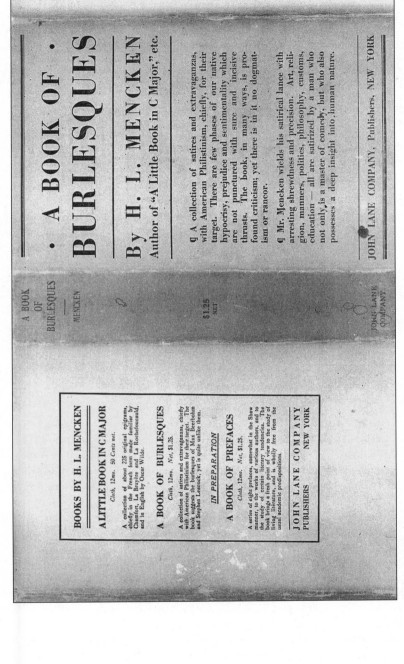

A 14.1.a, dust jacket

LANE | COMPANY'. Back: [all in a box] 'BOOKS BY H. L. MENCKEN | [double rule] | [ads for three books]'. Flaps unprinted.

Publication: Published 17 November 1916. $1.25. Copyright #A445738. 789 copies sold (to 30 June 1919).

Printing: Printed and bound by J. J. Little & Ives Co., New York.

Locations: EPL (2 in binding B), GHT (binding A, dj), InU-Li (binding B), JRS (2, bindings A and B), LC (22 November 1916, binding A), RJS (2, bindings A and B), Yale (2, bindings A and B).

Notes: In Frey's "Note Book" addenda (see Notes to *Men Versus the Man* [A 7]) he claims to own "a sort of rat-tail" binding as opposed to the "sort of ribbed cloth." See note on opus numbers at A 13. "These pieces cover three or four years, and are chiefly reprinted, though with many changes, from the *Smart Set,* the *Bohemian,* and the *Baltimore Evening Sun*" (author's note [p. [5]]). For "The Artist" see A 9. Adler 6, 142, 146; S1.4; S2.5; Frey 22; Bulsterbaum 71.

A 14.2.a
Second edition, first printing (1920)

Title page: '[rule] | A B O O K O F | BURLESQUES | [rule] | B y H. L. M E N C K E N | [rule] | [Borzoi device in oval] | [rule] | PUBLISHED AT THE BORZOI • NEW YORK • BY | A L F R E D • A • K N O P F | [rule]'

Copyright page: 'COPYRIGHT, 1916, 1920, BY | ALFRED A. KNOPF, INC. | PRINTED IN THE UNITED STATES OF AMERICA'

First state: 7¼" × 4¹⁵⁄₁₆": [1–10] 11–23 [24–26] 27–48 [49–50] 51–68 [69–70] 71–79 [80–82] 83–101 [102–04] 105–32 [133–34] 135–45 [146–48] 149–56 [157–58] 159–80 [181–82] 183–97 [198–200] 201–10 [211–12] 213–19 [220–22] 223–27 [228–30] 231–33 [234–40] = 240 pp. P. 198 blank. In both states the number is missing from the bottom of p. 237, unlike the first page of other sections. *Second state:* 7⁵⁄₁₆" × 4¹⁵⁄₁₆": . . . 183–98 [199–200] . . . = 240 pp. Pp. 197–98 replaced by a cancel.

First state: [1–15]⁸ = 120 leaves. *Second state:* [1–12]⁸ [13]⁸ (±13₃) [14–15]⁸ = 120 leaves.

Contents: First state: p. 1: half title; p. 2: [all within a box within a double-rule box] 'BY *H. L. MENCKEN* | [eleven titles:] VENTURES INTO VERSE | . . . | THE AMERI-CAN LANGUAGE | [*New edition ready 1921*] [brackets sic]'; p. 3: title; p. 4: copyright; p. 5: 'CONTENTS'; p. 6: blank; p. 7: ten-line author's note signed 'H. L. M.' and dated 1 February 1920; p. 8: blank; pp. 9–237: text; pp. 238–40: blank. Blank pages of text, all but those asterisked following divisional half titles: pp. 10, 24,° 26, 50, 70, 80,° 82, 102,° 104, 134, 146,° 148, 158, 182, 198, 200, 212, 220,° 222, 228,° 230, 234,° 236. *Second state:* same as first, except p. 198 is not blank.

Text: Omits "Epithalamium," "Portraits of Americans," "The New Soule," and "A Genealogical Chart of the Uplift," adds "The Jazz Webster," "The Old Subject," "Homeopathics" 1–5, and "Vers Libre."

Binding: Dark blue cloth. Front: Mencken arms blindstamped (see Notes). Spine, stamped in gilt: '[double rule] | A•BOOK•OF [double O linked] | BURLESQUES | [double rule] | H•L•MENCKEN | [double rule] | [double rule] | ALFRED•A• KNOPF | [double rule]'. Back: Borzoi Books logo blindstamped. Trimmed, top edge stained orange. White end papers.

Dust jacket: Blue-green on yellow paper. Front: '*New and Revised Edition* | [double rule] | A BOOK OF | BURLESQUES | [double rule] | By H. L. MENCKEN | [fourteen-line blurb:] THESE [T descending two and a half lines] satires and extravagances are | . . . | gone into common currency. | [double rule] | ALFRED A. KNOPF [intertwined AAK in box] PUBLISHER, N. Y. | [double rule]'. Spine: '[double rule] | A | BOOK | OF | BURLES- | QUES | [double rule] | H. L. | Mencken | [double rule] | [Borzoi Books logo] | [rule] | ALFRED A. | KNOPF | [rule]'. Back: 'BOOKS BY H. L. MENCKEN | [rule] | [six titles and Knopf imprint]'. Front flap: list of the first four Free Lance Books. Rear flap unprinted.

Locations: EPL (first state), GHT (2, first and second [dj] states), RJS (second state).

Notes: Reprinted from Lane's plates (*Dreiser-Mencken Letters* [A 76], p. 385) but with new author's note and new text from p. [199] on; ends on p. [240], no chart. In the third and fifth printings, this unstated first printing of the second edition is called '*Second Printing (revised), January, 1920*'. 9,500 copies of Knopf printings sold. The Mencken coat of arms: "Azure, a linden tree between two rehbock rampant, all proper; crest, a demi-rehbock on a helmet affrontée; wreath and mantling of the colors" (Frey 35). Adler 6.

A 14.2.b
Second edition, second printing: New York: Knopf, [1920].

On copyright page: '*New revised edition,* | *Published January, 1920* | *Second printing, April, 1920*'. It was actually published in August, according to Frey. In the third and fifth printings, this one is styled as '*Third Printing (again revised), August, 1920*'. A new author's note on p. [7] is dated 31 July 1920, and in it Mencken refers to this as the "third edition." Adler creates a ghost by claiming two different printings (April and August), saying that the latter has a different "Preface to the Third Edition." It seems that, beginning with his third printing, Knopf began counting the Lane printing as the first. Text adds "Panoramas of People" IV and "Homeopathics" 6–10.

Locations: EPL, MBU.

A 14.2.c.i
Second edition, third printing, American issue: New York: Knopf, [1921].

On copyright page: '*Fourth Printing (again revised), December, 1921*'. The preface is omitted. Adler claims wrongly that it has a new "Preface to the Fourth Edition." Text omits "Homeopathics" 5–10 and extends "Vers Libre." Freak copy: bound in the covers of Eugene O'Neill's *The Moon of the Caribees* (Boni) (GHT).

Location: GHT.

A 14.2.c.ii
Second edition, third printing, English issue (1923)

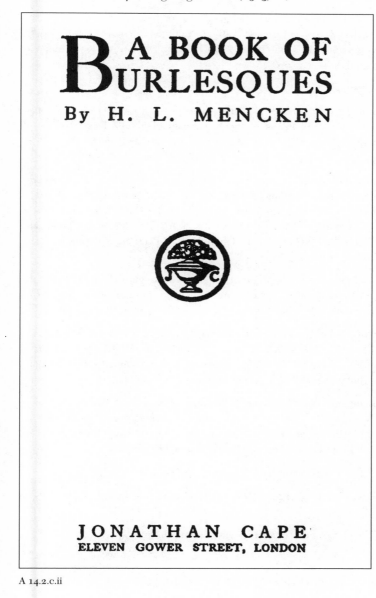

A BOOK OF BURLESQUES

By H. L. MENCKEN

JONATHAN CAPE
ELEVEN GOWER STREET, LONDON

Copyright page: 'First Published, 1923 | All Rights Reserved | Printed in the United States of America'

7½″ × 5″: [1–10] 11–23 [24–26] 27–48 [49–50] 51–68 [69–70] 71–79 [80–82] 83–101 [102–04] 105–32 [133–34] 135–45 [146–48] 149–56 [157–58] 159–80 [181–82] 183–98 [199–200] 201–10 [211–12] 213–19 [220–22] 223–29 [230–32] 233–34 [235–36] 237–39 [240] = 240 pp.

[1–15]^8 = 120 leaves.

Contents: p. 1: half title; p. 2: blank; p. 3: title; p. 4: copyright; p. 5: 'CONTENTS'; p. 6: blank; p. 7: half title; p. 8: blank; pp. 9–239: text; p. 240: blank. Blank pages of text, all but those asterisked following divisional half titles: pp. 10, 24,° 26, 50, 70, 80,° 82, 102,° 104, 134, 146,° 148, 158, 182, 200, 212, 220,° 222, 230,° 232, 236.

Text: "Death: A Philosophical Discussion," "From the Programme of a Concert," "The Wedding: A Stage Direction," "The Visionary," "The Artist: A Drama Without Words," "Seeing the World," "From the Memoirs of the Devil," "Litanies for the Overlooked," "Asepsis: A Deduction in *Scherzo* Form," "Tales of the Moral and Pathological," "The Jazz Webster," "The Old Subject," "Panoramas of People," "Homeopathics," "Vers Libre."

Typography and paper: 5⁹⁄₁₆″ (5¹⁄₁₆″) × 3⅛″; 28 lines per page (lines vary with the subject matter). Running heads: recto, chapter titles (pp. 13–239); verso, '[thick-thin rule] | [page number] *A Book of Burlesques* | [rule]' (pp. 12–238). Wove paper.

Binding: Yellow V cloth (very smooth) stamped in black. Front: 'A BOOK | OF BURLESQUES | H.L. MENCKEN'. Spine: 'A BOOK OF | BURLESQUES | H.L. MENCKEN | JONATHAN CAPE'. Top edge trimmed and stained yellow, fore and bottom edges rough trimmed. White end papers.

Dust jacket: Light gray paper. Front: [all within double-rule box] 'A BOOK OF | [blue] BURLESQUES | *by* | H. L. MENCKEN | Author of *Prejudice [sic]* | *In Defence of* | *Women, &c.* | [JC device in circle]'. Spine and back flap missing on example seen. Back unprinted. Front flap: 'A *Book of* | *Burlesques 7s. 6d. net* '.

Publication: Published May 1923 (ECB 11.1018). 7s.6d.

Locations: BL (31 MAY 23), Bod (JUN | 1923), Camb (JU 7 | 1923), GHT, RJS, dj (partial) via KK.

Notes: From the plates of the "fourth" (1921) Knopf printing. Adler 6.

A 14.2.d
Second edition, fourth printing: New York: Knopf, [1924].

On copyright page: '*Pocket Book Edition, Published April, 1924*'. From December 1921 printing.

Locations: EPL, GHT.

A 14.2.e
Second edition, fifth printing: New York: Knopf, [1924].

In original format of second edition. On copyright page: '*Fifth Printing, November, 1924*'. No preface.

Locations: EPL, GHT.

A 14.2.f
Second edition, sixth printing: New York: Knopf, [1925].

Borzoi Pocket Book. On copyright page: '*Second Printing, September, 1925*'.

Locations: EPL, GHT.

A 14.2.g
Second edition, seventh printing: New York: Knopf, [1928].

Borzoi Pocket Book. On copyright page: '*Third printing, February, 1928*'.

Locations: EPL, GHT.

LATER REPRINTINGS WITHIN THE SECOND EDITION

A 14.2.h
New York: Reprint House International, 1970.

Data from S1.4. Not located.

A 14.2.i
New York: Knopf; St. Clair Shores, Mich.: Scholarly Press, 1977.

Altered title page. On copyright page: '*Second printing, April, 1920* | [Library of Congress cataloging data]'.

Locations: EPL, NOneoU.

A 15 PISTOLS FOR TWO

A 15.1.a
Only edition, first printing (1917)

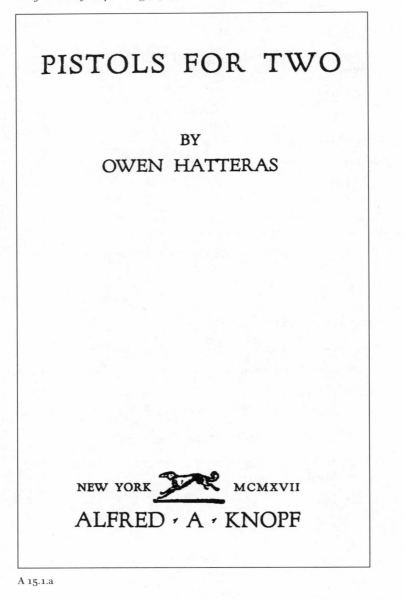

PISTOLS FOR TWO

BY
OWEN HATTERAS

NEW YORK   MCMXVII
ALFRED · A · KNOPF

A 15.1.a

Copyright page: 'Published, September, 1917 | PRINTED IN THE UNITED STATES OF AMERICA'

$7\frac{5}{16}'' \times 5\frac{1}{16}''$: [i–vi 1] 2–42 = 48 pp.

$[1–3]^8$ = 24 leaves.

Contents: p. i: half title with ten-pointed star ornament, 'AAK' intertwined in center; p. ii: blank; p. iii: title; p. iv: copyright; p. v: 'CONTENTS'; p. vi: blank; pp. 1–42: text.

Typography and paper: $5\frac{3}{4}''$ ($5\frac{1}{2}''$) $\times$ $3\frac{1}{2}''$; 36 lines per page. Running heads: recto and verso (page numbers at outer margins), 'PISTOLS FOR TWO | [rule]' (pp. 2–42). Wove paper.

Binding: Rose wrappers. Front: [within double-rule box] 'PISTOLS FOR TWO | BY | OWEN HATTERAS'. Back: intertwined 'AAK'. All edges trimmed. Sewed.

Locations: EPL, Harv (2), InU-Li, LC ('Gift | Author | OCT 1 1917'), RJS.

Notes: "HLM wrote the introductory and closing remarks, p. 1–5, 39–42, and the biographical sketch of Nathan, p. 5–21; Nathan wrote the sketch about HLM, p. 21–39. 'The plan of it was my idea . . . Nathan and I contributed $300 toward the cost of printing it. At the start, Knopf distributed it gratis, but the demand for it soon became so great that he began to sell it at, first *[sic]* for fifty cents and then for a dollar' " (Adler, quoting a Mencken note). 100 copies were sold. Glassine dust jacket reported (D). Adler 24; S2.10; Frey 41, 68; Bulsterbaum 11.

LATER REPRINTINGS WITHIN THE ONLY EDITION

A 15.1.b
Folcroft, Pa.: Folcroft Library Editions, 1977.

Data from NUC 1978, 10.888. Not seen. Copies noted (EPL, GHT) without new imprint, bound in the Folcroft style with title and author reading down on spine, $8\frac{3}{4}''$ $\times$ $5\frac{5}{8}''$.

A 15.1.c
[Norwood, Pa.:] Norwood Editions, 1978.

Added title page.

Location: GHT.

A 16 A BOOK OF PREFACES

A 16.1.a
Only edition, first printing (1917)

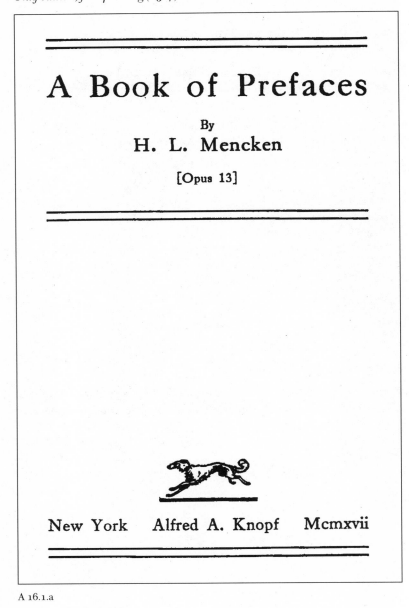

A 16.1.a

Copyright page: 'COPYRIGHT, 1917, BY | ALFRED A. KNOPF | *Published September, 1917* | PRINTED IN THE UNITED STATES OF AMERICA'

7⅝" (other pages 7¾") × 5¹⁄₁₆" (5⅜") (binding A), 7⅜" × 4¹⁵⁄₁₆" (binding B): [1–10] 11–64 [65–66] 67–148 [149–50] 151–94 [195–96] 197–283 [284–88] = 288 pp.

[1–18]⁸ = 144 leaves.

Contents: p. 1: half title within rules over ten-pointed device with 'AAK' in center; p. 2: '[in box within double-rule box] *BY H. L. MENCKEN* | [nine titles:] *Ventures into Verse (Out of | print)* | . . . | *A Little Book in C Major*'; p. 3: title; p. 4: copyright; p. 5: 'PREFACE'; p. 6: blank; p. 7: 'CONTENTS'; p. 8: blank; pp. 9–283: text; p. 284: blank; p. 285: within box an ad for Borzoi Books, with logo and address; p. 286: 'THE BORZOI RUSSIAN TRANSLATIONS | [eleven titles listed]'; p. 287: 'SPEAKING ABOUT RUSSIA- | [eight more titles]'; p. 288: blank. Blank pages of text, each following divisional half title: pp. 10, 66, 150, 196.

Text: "Joseph Conrad," "Theodore Dreiser," "James Huneker," "Puritanism as a Literary Force." See Notes.

Typography and paper: 5⅝" (5¼") × 3⁵⁄₁₆"; 27 lines per page. Running heads: recto, chapter titles (pp. 13–283); verso, '[between rules] [page number] *A BOOK OF PREFACES*' (pp. 12–282). Wove paper.

Binding A: Dark blue V cloth stamped in gilt. Front, dots representing solid inverted triangles: '[double rule] | A•BOOK•OF•PREFACES [double O linked] | [double rule] | [double rule the width of name] | H•L•MENCKEN | [double rule the width of name]'. Spine: '[double rule] | A•BOOK•OF [double O linked] | PREFACES | [double rule] | H•L•MENCKEN | [double rule] | [double rule] | ALFRED•A•KNOPF | [double rule]'. Back: blindstamped borzoi over intertwined 'AAK'. Untrimmed, unstained. White end papers.

Binding B: Same as binding A but trimmed, top edge stained orange.

Dust jacket: Ocher paper printed in blue. Front: '[double rule] | A BOOK OF PREFACES | [rule] | By H. L. MENCKEN | [double rule] | JOSEPH CONRAD | THEODORE DREISER | JAMES HUNEKER | [blurb in nineteen lines] | [double rule] | Alfred A. Knopf [interlocked 'AAK'] Publisher, N. Y. | [double rule]'. Spine: '[double rule] | A | BOOK OF | PREFACES | [rule] | H. L. | MENCKEN | [double rule] | $1.⁵⁰ net | A | BORZOI | BOOK | [Borzoi device over rule] | ALFRED A. | KNOPF | [double rule]'. Back: [all within frame with Borzoi device at top] 'Some Opinions of the Work | *of* | H. L. MENCKEN | [double rule] | [six blurbs]'. Front flap: 'About the Author | [rule] | [biography and bibliography]'. Rear flap: ad for Borzoi Books.

Publication: Published 8 October 1917. $1.50. Copyright #A476828 (first copy received 15 October 1917). 1,000 copies printed (MLAE 186). 6,300 copies of Knopf printings sold.

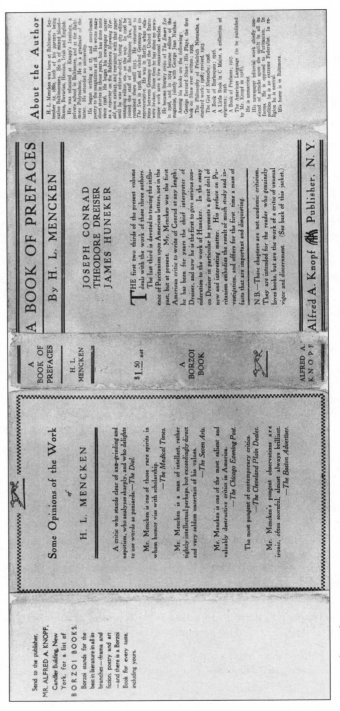

A 16.1.a, dust jacket

Printing: Printed and bound by the Plimpton Press, Norwood, Mass.

Locations: EPL (binding A), Harv (2 in binding B), InU-Li (binding B), JRS (binding B, dj), LC (30 October 1917, binding B), RJS (binding B), TxU (binding A).

Notes: "Of the first edition . . . , a few copies were issued with all edges uncut, and signed by the author" (Frey). On the front pastedown of the EPL copy Mencken has penciled in: '1ˢᵗ ed | large paper | uncut'; the pages are in fact cut at the top. No evidence in *PW* or elsewhere that this "issue" was offered for sale.

 "It had been gathering form and direction in my mind ever since I first began to feel my oats as a literary critic, and there were parts of it that dated back to my first writings about Joseph Conrad in the 1909–13 era, to my whooping up of Huneker at the same time, and to my ardent championing of Dreiser from 1911 onward. Not a little of the material that I had gathered for my 'American' articles in the *Smart Set,* from June of 1913 onward, went into it, and also a great deal of stuff from my contributions to the Baltimore *Evening Sun*—not always, to be sure, in the original form, but nevertheless in essence" (MLAE 170; cf. Adler 50–51).

 See note on opus numbers at A 13. Adler 7, 289; S1.8; S2.6; Frey 26; Bulsterbaum 13–14, 72.

A 16.1.b
Second printing: New York: Knopf, Mcmxviii.

'Second (Revised) Edition' on title page. Copyright page unchanged. Revised, with 'PREFACE TO THE SECOND EDITION' and index.

Locations: GHT, InU-Li.

A 16.1.c
Third printing: New York: Knopf, [1920].

On copyright page: '*Third edition, August, 1920*'. New preface, dated 12 September 1920.

Locations: GHT, Harv.

A 16.1.d.i
Fourth printing, American issue: New York: Knopf, [1922].

On copyright page: '*Third edition, August, 1920* | *Reprinted, January, 1922*'. New preface, dated 1 January 1922, in which he claims not to have made changes. Minor changes, according to Adler.

Locations: EPL, MCR.

A 16.1.d.ii
Fourth printing, English issue (1922)

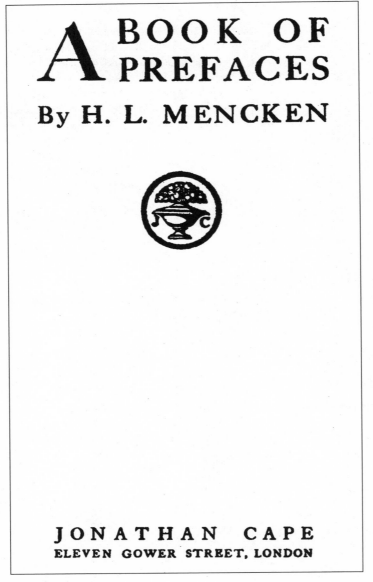

A BOOK OF PREFACES

By H. L. MENCKEN

JONATHAN CAPE
ELEVEN GOWER STREET, LONDON

Copyright page: 'First Published, 1922 | All Rights Reserved | Printed in the United States of America'

Presumed first state: 7½" × 5⅛": [1–10] 11–64 [65–66] 67–148 [149–50] 151–94 [195–96] 197–283 [284] 285–88 = 288 pp. *Second state:* 7½" × 5⅟₁₆": [3–10] . . . 285–88 = 286 pp.

Presumed first state: [1–18]⁸ = 144 leaves. *Second state:* [1]⁸ (-1₁, ±1₂) [2–18]⁸ = 143 leaves. The first leaf is excised; the second is a cancel.

Contents: p. 1: half title; p. 2: [in box within double-rule box] 'BY H. L. MENCKEN | [twelve titles]'; p. 3: title; p. 4: copyright; pp. 5–6: 'PREFACE TO THE FOURTH EDITION' [dated 1 January 1922]; p. 7: 'CONTENTS'; p. 8: blank; pp. 9–283: text; p. 284: blank; pp. 285–88: 'INDEX'. Blank pages of text, each following divisional half title: pp. 10, 66, 150, 196.

Text: "Joseph Conrad," "Theodore Dreiser," "James Huneker," "Puritanism as a Literary Force."

Typography and paper: 5⅝" (5¼") × 3⅟₁₆"; 27 lines per page. Running heads, all between rules with page numbers at outer margins: recto, chapter titles (pp. 13–283), 'INDEX' (p. 287); verso, 'PREFACE' (p. 6), 'A BOOK OF PREFACES' (pp. 12–282), 'INDEX' (pp. 286–88). Wove paper.

Binding: Yellow V cloth (very smooth) stamped in black. Front: 'A BOOK OF | PREFACES | BY H.L. MENCKEN'. Spine: 'A BOOK OF | PREFACES | H.L. MENCKEN | JONATHAN CAPE'. Top edge trimmed and stained yellow, fore and bottom edges unevenly trimmed. White end papers.

Dust jacket: Off-white paper. Front: 'A BOOK OF | PREFACES | H. L. MENCKEN | [JC device in circle] | [two blurbs in ten lines from the *English Review* and the *Saturday Review*] | Jonathan Cape, Eleven Gower Street, London'. Spine: '[double rule] | A BOOK OF | PREFACES | H. L. MENCKEN | [JC device in circle] | JONATHAN CAPE | [double rule]'. Front flap: 'By the same | Author | [ornament] | [three titles] | [ornament] | A Book of | Prefaces :: | [price clipped on example seen]'. Back flap unprinted.

Publication: Not in ECB; see dates of accession under *Locations*.

Locations: BL (28 MAR 22, rebound second state), Bod (APR. 1927, second state), Camb (AP 4 | 1922, second state), EPL (second state), GHT (second state, dj), InU-Li (second state), NhD (first state), RJS (second state).

Notes: The order of the states is based on the fact that English printings usually omit advertisements for Mencken's American books. Adler 7.

A 16.1.e
Fifth printing: New York: Knopf, [1924].

On copyright page: '*Fifth Printing, February, 1924*'. New preface, dated 15 March 1924.

Locations: EPL, GHT.

A 16.1.f
Sixth printing: Garden City, N.Y.: Garden City Pub. Co., [n.d.].

On copyright page: 'COPYRIGHT, 1917'. From fifth Knopf printing (1924 preface). A Star Book. "At about the same time [as Knopf brought out the Pocket Book printing (below)] the Garden City Publishing Company . . . bought the right to issue five thousand copies in its series of $1 reprints, and before the end of 1928 it had added five thousand more" (MLAE 186). Noted in purple stamping on green cloth and blue stamping on green cloth.

Locations: D, GHT.

A 16.1.g
Seventh printing: Garden City, N.Y.: Garden City Pub. Co., 1927.

Fifth printing indicated on copyright page (1924 preface). A Star Book. Gilt stamping on black cloth.

Locations: D, EPL, Harv, D.

A 16.1.h
Eighth printing: New York: Knopf, [1928].

On copyright page: '*Pocket Book Edition, January, 1928*'. Fifth Knopf printing reprinted as Borzoi Pocket Book. Bindings noted: gilt stamping on red cloth (extra leaf listing Pocket Books nos. 1–51) and silver on green (no extra leaf); the former dated 1927, the latter 1928, by Mencken in the EPL copies. The InU-Li copy of the latter is likewise dated 1928.

Locations: EPL (2), InU-Li.

A 16.1.i
Ninth printing: New York: Octagon, 1977.

Borzoi Pocket Book reprinted.

Location: EPL.

A 17 DAMN! A BOOK OF CALUMNY

A 17.1.a
First edition, first printing (1918)

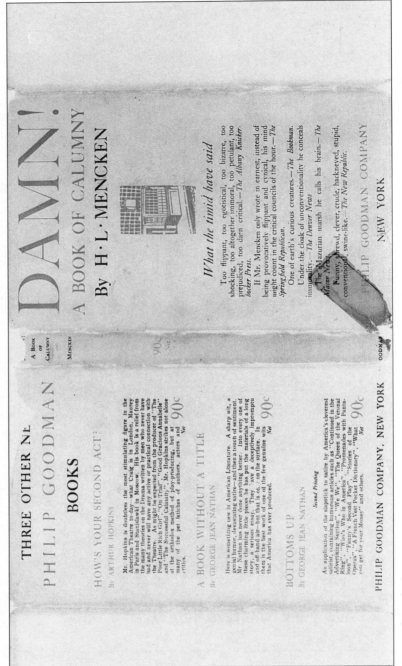

DAMN!
A BOOK OF CALUMNY
By H·L·MENCKEN

What the timid have said

Too flippant, too egotistical, too bizarre, too shocking, too altogether immoral, too petulant, too prejudiced, too darn critical.—*The Albany Knickerbocker Press.*

If Mr. Mencken only wrote in earnest, instead of being provocatively flippant and cynical, his mind might count in the critical councils of the hour.—*The Springfield Republican.*

One of earth's curious creatures.—*The Bookman.*

Under the cloak of unconventionality he conceals immunity.—*The Denver News*

The Mazurian marsh he calls his brain.—*The Macon News*

Funny, shrewd, clever, crude, hackneyed, stupid, conventional, swine-like.—*The New Republic.*

PHILIP GOODMAN COMPANY
NEW YORK

THREE OTHER NE PHILIP GOODMAN BOOKS

HOW'S YOUR SECOND ACT?
By ARTHUR HOPKINS

Mr. Hopkins is doubtless the most stimulating figure in the American Theatre to-day—what Craig is in London, Maurey in Paris and Stanislawki in Moscow. His book is a relief from the many theories on the Drama written by men who never have had and never will have any active or practical connection with the Theatre. As might be expected from the producer of "The Poor Little Rich Girl" "On Trial" "Good Gracious Annabelle" and "The Successful Calamity", Mr. Hopkins strikes not alone at the orthodox method of play-producing, but at many of the pet fetiches of authors, actors and critics.
Net 90c

A BOOK WITHOUT A TITLE
By GEORGE JEAN NATHAN

Here is something new in American Literature. A sharp wit, a genial humor, devastating satire—and then a touch of sentiment. Mr Nathan has never done anything better. Into every one of these charming little pieces he has put the materials of a long story ... a serious essay ... They have a deceptively impromptu and off-hand air—but that is ... on the surface. In them is the best work of one of the few genuine wits that America has ever produced.
Net 90c

BOTTOMS UP
By GEORGE JEAN NATHAN

Second Printing

An application of the slapstick to satire by America's cleverest satirist, containing humorous articles such as "Continued in the Advertising Section", "We We", "The Queen of the Verotial Ring", "Who's Who in America", "Promenades with Pantaloon", "Fanny's Second Play", "Stories of the Opera", "A French Vest Pocket Dictionary", "What you get for your Money" and others.
Net 90c

PHILIP GOODMAN COMPANY, NEW YORK

A 17.1.a, dust jacket

Title page: The storefront device is orange.

Copyright page: 'COPYRIGHT 1918 BY | PHILIP GOODMAN COMPANY'

7³⁄₁₆″ × 4¾″: [1–6] 7–103 [104] = 104 pp. Only part of the 6 on p. 68 is visible.

[1]⁴ [2–7]⁸ = 52 leaves.

Contents: p. 1: half title; p. 2: blank; p. 3: title; p. 4: copyright; pp. 5–6: 'CONTENTS'; pp. 7–103: text; p. 104: blank.

Typography and paper: 5⁵⁄₁₆″ × 3″; 32 lines per page. No heads. Wove paper.

Binding: Pea-green V cloth stamped in gilt. Front: 'DAMN! | A BOOK OF CAL-UMNY | By H•L•MENCKEN'. Spine: 'DAMN! | A BOOK | OF | CALUMNY | [short rule] | MENCKEN | GOODMAN'. Trimmed, unstained. White end papers.

Dust jacket: White paper. Front: [title, device, and Goodman line orange, the rest black] 'DAMN! | A BOOK OF CALUMNY | By H•L•MENCKEN | [device as on title page] | *What the timid have said* | [fifteen lines of attacks on Mencken] | PHILIP GOODMAN COMPANY | NEW YORK'. Spine: 'DAMN! | A BOOK | OF | CALUMNY | [short orange rule] | MENCKEN | [orange] 90c | [orange] *Net* | GOODMAN'. Back: 'THREE OTHER NEW | [orange] PHILIP GOODMAN | BOOKS | [blurbs for 'HOW'S YOUR SECOND ACT?', 'A BOOK WITHOUT A TITLE', and 'BOT-TOMS UP'; titles, authors, and prices in orange] | PHILIP GOODMAN COMPANY, NEW YORK'. Flaps unprinted.

Publication: Published 1 April 1918. 90¢. Copyright #A501208. 1821 copies of Good-man editions sold (includes Knopf issue).

Printing: Printed by Alliance Press, New York; bound by Robert Rutter & Co., New York.

Locations: GHT (dj), Harv, InU-Li, KU-S, RJS, TxU (partial dj), Yale.

Notes: Hand corrections (by the same hand) appear on pp. 63, l. 13 ("By" to "My"), and 96, l. 20 ("it is" to "is it"), in the RJS and GHT copies; the first correction alone is in the Yale copy. Fanfare (24) reports light blue cloth binding. Most of the forty-nine short pieces, here rewritten, appeared first in the *Smart Set* or New York *Evening Mail* (MLAE 227–28). Adler 8, 140 ("La Infamia"); S2.6; Frey 27; Bulsterbaum 72.

A 17.1.b

First edition, second printing: New York: Goodman, Nineteen Eighteen.

Indicated by '*Second Printing*' below the device on the title page. Errors on pp. 63 and 96 uncorrected. The surviving LC deposit copy is a second printing with most of the indication scraped off. Copies for sale have been noticed in the same condition.

Locations: GHT, LC (20 April 1918), MWalB.

A 17.1.c
First edition, third printing: New York: Goodman, Nineteen Eighteen.

Indicated by *'Third Printing'* below the device on the title page. Errors on pp. 63 and 96 uncorrected.

Location: JRS.

A 17.2.a.i
Second edition, only printing, first issue (1918)

Title page: 'D A M N ! | *A Book of Calumny* | BY H • L • MENCKEN | Philip Goodman • New York • 1918'

Copyright page: 'COPYRIGHT 1918 BY | PHILIP GOODMAN COMPANY | *Fourth Edition'*

$7^{7}/_{16}$" × $4^{7}/_{8}$" (binding A), $7^{7}/_{16}$" (larger pages, $7^{9}/_{16}$") × $4^{15}/_{16}$" (binding B): [i–iv] v–ix [x–xii] 13–139 [140–44] = 144 pp.

$[1–9]^{8}$ = 72 leaves.

Contents: p. i: half title; p. ii: 'BY THE SAME AUTHOR | [short rule] | IN DEFENSE OF WOMEN'; p. iii: title; p. iv: copyright; pp. v–ix: 'PREFACE' [dated July 1918]; p. x: blank; pp. xi–xii: 'CONTENTS'; pp. 13–139: text; p. 140: blank; p. 141: 'OTHER | PHILIP | GOODMAN | BOOKS'; pp. 142–44: blank.

Binding A: Light green cloth printed in black. Front: 'DAMN! | A BOOK OF CALUMNY | By H•L•MENCKEN'. Spine: 'DAMN! | A BOOK | OF | CALUMNY | [short rule] | MENCKEN | PHILIP | GOODMAN | COMPANY'. Bottom edge unevenly trimmed, unstained. White end papers.

Binding B: Same as binding A except rust cloth stamped in black.

Dust jacket: Not seen. Frey reports "Fourth (Revised) Edition" and "Opus 14" on the dust jacket.

Locations: GHT (2, bindings A and B), D (binding B), Harv (rebound), InU-Li (binding B), NWM (rebound), RPB (binding B).

Notes: Reset July 1918; price $1.25 (MLAE 228). Larger type, revised, preface added. Errors of first edition corrected on pp. 86 and 130. See note on opus number at A 13. Adler 8; Frey 28.

A 17.2.a.ii
Second issue

A Book of Calumny [First Printed as "Damn"]. New York: Knopf, [1918].

[9–12] 13–139 [140–44]. [1]⁴ [2–9]⁸. First gathering reset. "Later in 1918 Knopf took over such sheets as Goodman still had in stock, changed the title to *A Book of Calumny,* and reissued the book without the preface that I had written for Goodman's 'fourth' edition but with his (Goodman's) advertising page at the end. This Knopf edition, the price of which was raised to $1.35, was much sightlier than either Goodman printing, but it failed again and was soon scrapped" (MLAE 228). Copy noted with penultimate leaf, containing the Goodman ad, excised (D).

Location: RJS.

A 18.1.a
First edition, first printing (1918)

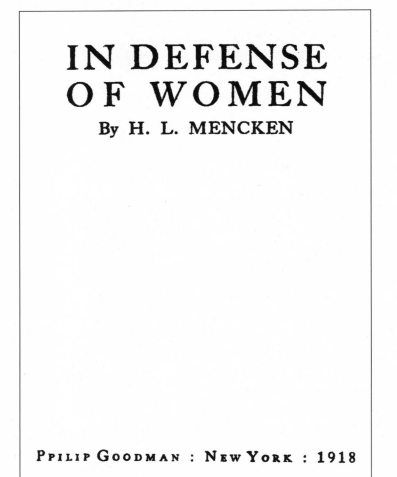

IN DEFENSE
OF WOMEN
By H. L. MENCKEN

PᴘɪʟɪP Gᴏᴏᴅᴍᴀɴ : Nᴇᴡ Yᴏʀᴋ : 1918

A 18.1.a

Copyright page: 'COPYRIGHT 1918 BY | PHILIP GOODMAN'

7½" × 4¹⁵⁄₁₆": [1–5] 6–218 [219–20] = 220 pp.

[1–13]⁸ [14]⁴ [15]² = 110 leaves.

Contents: p. 1: half title; p. 2: 'BY THE SAME AUTHOR | [short rule] | DAMN! A BOOK OF CALUMNY'; p. 3: title; p. 4: copyright; pp. 5–218: text; pp. 219–20: blank.

Typography and paper: 4¹³⁄₁₆" (4½") × 3"; 22 lines per page. Running heads: recto and verso, 'IN DEFENSE OF WOMEN' (pp. 6–218). Wove paper.

Binding A: Very dark blue T cloth, stamped in yellow. Front: [all within blindstamped border] 'IN | DEFENSE | OF | WOMEN | *By* | H•L•MENCKEN'. Spine: 'IN | DE-FENSE | OF | WOMEN | H. L. | MENCKEN | PHILIP | GOODMAN'. Back: square storefront device. Unevenly trimmed at bottom edge, unstained. White end papers.

Binding B: As above except light red V cloth printed in black, border printed and not blindstamped.

Dust jacket: White paper printed in black. Front: 'MENCKEN'S | L A T E S T ! | [square storefront device] | IN DEFENSE | OF WOMEN | *By* | H • L • MENCKEN | [seventeen-line blurb] | [short rule] | PHILIP GOODMAN.NEW YORK'. Spine: '[?] | $1³⁵ | GOODMAN'. Back: [all within box] [storefront device to left of next four lines] 'OTHER | PHILIP | GOODMAN | BOOKS | [four titles]'. Flaps unprinted. Top of spine missing on example seen.

Publication: Published 17 September 1918. $1.35. Copyright #A501934. Apparently 849 copies of Goodman printings sold. Another 975 copies earned no royalties in 1920; perhaps these were the sheets that went to Knopf.

Printing: Printed by Publicity Printing Co., New York; bound by Robert Rutter and Sons, New York.

Locations: Harv (2, bindings A and B), dj via AJG, InU-Li (binding A), LC (27 September 1918, binding A), RJS (binding A).

Notes: As with most of his books in this period, "substantial parts of it had been printed previously in the *Smart Set*" (Mencken, quoted in Adler 8). See B 81 for a Hungarian translation with a new (1928) preface. Adler 8, 141; S2.6; Frey 29; Bulsterbaum 4; .Fanfare 25.

A 18.1.b.i
Second printing, first issue (1918)

New York: Goodman, 1918.

Title page: 'IN | DEFENSE OF | WOMEN | BY H • L • MENCKEN | OPUS 15 | SECOND EDITION | PHILIP GOODMAN • NEW YORK • 1918'. [1–5] 6–218 [219–20].

[1]⁸ (± 1₂) [2–13]⁸ [14]⁴ [15]². The title/copyright leaf is a cancel. Same two bindings as in first printing. See note on opus numbers at A 13.

Locations: GHT (2, bindings A and B), RJS (binding A).

A 18.1.b.ii
Second printing, second issue (1919)

New York: Knopf, [1919].

[1–5] 6–218 [219–20]. [1]⁸ (-1₁,₂, +1₁₋₂) [2–13]⁸ [14]⁴ [15]². Two stubs precede p. [5], and two new conjugate leaves (pp. [1–4]) are tipped in between the first and the end paper. No date on new title page. On copyright page: 'COPYRIGHT, 1918, BY | ALFRED A. KNOPF, INC.' Dated 1918 by Adler, 1919 by Mencken (quoted in Adler 8), Fanfare (25), and Frey (29). "Early in June, 1919, I proposed that he [Goodman] turn over *In Defense of Women* to Knopf. . . . When they came to terms—just what those terms were I do not recall—Knopf bound Goodman's remaining sheets in the neat blue binding, with gilt stamping, that he had adopted for my books, and by the end of 1919 he had worked off the whole stock in hand and *In Defense of Women* went out of print" (MLAE 229–30). Binding A: dark blue cloth with title and author blindstamped on front in the style of Knopf's printings of *A Book of Prefaces* (1917; A 16) and *Damn* (1918; A 17). Bindings B–C: black cloth and dark blue cloth blindstamped on front with the Mencken arms in the style of *Prejudices: First Series* (1919; A 20) and later works. "Third Printing" on dust jacket (Fanfare).

Locations: GHT (2 in binding C), JRS (2, bindings A and B), RJS (binding A).

LATER REPRINTINGS WITHIN THE FIRST EDITION

A 18.1.c
New York: Octagon, 1977.

Locations: EPL, GHT, MBU.

A 18.1.d
New York: Octagon, 1980.

On copyright page of next item: '*Second Octagon printing 1980*'. Not seen.

A 18.1.e
New York: Octagon, 1985.

Location: MWiW.

A 18.2.a
Second edition, first printing (1922)

Title page: [all within double-rule borders on left, single on right, both the length of the page] 'THE FREE LANCE BOOKS. VI | EDITED WITH INTRODUCTIONS BY H. L. MENCKEN | [double rule from left side of page to right border, interrupting left vertical rules] | IN DEFENSE | OF WOMEN | By H. L. MENCKEN | [Borzoi device in oval] | [rule between borders] | NEW YORK ALFRED • A • KNOPF MCMXXII | [rule between borders]'

Copyright page: 'COPYRIGHT, 1918, BY | ALFRED A. KNOPF, INC. | COPYRIGHT, 1922, BY | ALFRED A. KNOPF, INC. | *Set up and printed by the Vail-Ballou Co., Binghamton, N. Y.* | *Paper (Warren's) furnished by Henry Lindenmeyr & Sons, New York, N. Y.* | *Bound by the Plimpton Press, Norwood, Mass.* | MANUFACTURED IN THE UNITED STATES OF AMERICA'

$7\frac{1}{4}'' \times 4^{15}\!/_{16}''$: [i–vi] vii–xviii [1–2] 3–22 [23–24] 25–62 [63–64] 65–122 [123–24] 125–78 [179–80] 181–210 = 228 pp.

$[1–13]^8 [14]^{10}$ = 114 leaves.

Contents: p. i: half title; p. ii: [all within a box inside a double-rule box] 'THE FREE LANCE BOOKS | [six titles in ad]'; p. iii: title; p. iv: copyright; p. v: 'CONTENTS'; p. vi: blank; pp. vii–xviii: 'INTRODUCTION'; pp. 1–210: text. Blank pages following divisional half titles: pp. 2, 24, 64, 124, 180.

Binding: Boards covered by pale yellow-green paper. Black cloth spine with pale yellow-green paper label. Front: [all within ornate borders] [within box] 'VI. In Defense of Women | By H. L. Mencken | [within another box] [intertwined AAK showing through square] | THE FREE-LANCE BOOKS [mark] EDITED BY H. L. MENCKEN [the hyphen slants up, and the mark resembles it but has another line coming down from the raised end]'. Spine: '[ornate border] | IN | DEFENSE | OF | WOMEN | [ornament] | H. L. MENCKEN | 1922 | [ornate border]'.

Dust jacket: Yellow paper printed in red. Front: [all words within double vertical rules] '[double horizontal rules] | IN | DEFENSE | OF | WOMEN | *By* H. L. Mencken | [rule] | [twelve-line blurb: 'This is a new edition . . . the sixth volume.'] | [double horizontal rule] | ALFRED A. KNOPF [Borzoi Books logo] PUBLISHER, N. Y.' Spine: 'FREE LANCE | BOOKS: VI | [continuation of horizontal rule] | IN | DEFENSE | OF | WOMEN | [short rule] | H. L. Mencken | [Borzoi Books logo] | [continuation of horizontal rule] | ALFRED A. | KNOPF'. Back: ad for Free Lance books. Front flap: short biography of Mencken. Rear flap: ad for Borzoi books.

Locations: GHT, RJS, Yale (dj).

Notes: Revised, with new introduction containing biographical information at the end. A 1921 Knopf brochure advertising the Free Lance Books describes the covers as

"Toyogami" (EPL). There is an example of the fourteen gatherings, untrimmed and unsewed, held together with string through two punched holes, in unprinted brown wrappers, and marked 'ADVANCE COPY' by a bookseller (CB). 21,800 copies of Knopf printings sold. Adler 8.

A 18.2.b
Second edition, second printing: New York: Knopf, MCMXXII.

On copyright page: '*Revised, Reset, and Republished, Jan., 1922* | *Second Printing, May, 1922*'.

Location: EPL.

A 18.2.c
Second edition, third printing: New York: Knopf, MCMXXII.

On copyright page: '*Third Printing, November, 1922*'.

Location: EPL.

A 18.2.d
Second edition, fourth printing: New York: Knopf, MCMXXIII.

On copyright page: '*Fourth Printing, August, 1923*'.

Locations: D, EPL, GHT.

A 18.2.e
Second edition, fifth printing: New York: Knopf, MCMXXIV.

On copyright page: '*Fifth Printing, March, 1924*'. Noted in green and yellow paper-covered boards.

Locations: EPL (green), RJS (yellow).

A 18.2.f
Second edition, sixth printing: New York: Knopf, MCMXXIV.

On copyright page: '*Sixth Printing, November, 1924*'.

Location: EPL.

A 18.2.g
Second edition, seventh printing: New York: Knopf, MCMXXV.

On copyright page: '*Seventh Printing, October, 1925*'.

Locations: D (2), EPL.

A 18.2.h
Second edition, eighth printing: New York: Knopf, MCMXXVI.

On copyright page: '*Eighth Printing, October, 1926*'.

Location: EPL.

A 18.2.i
Second edition, ninth printing: New York: Knopf, [1927].

On copyright page: 'NINTH PRINTING, MARCH, 1927'. Bound in the *Prejudices* (dark blue cloth) and not the Free Lance format; with this printing the biographical information is deleted from the introduction; a colophon is added on p. [211].

Locations: D, EPL, GHT.

A 18.2.j
Second edition, tenth printing: New York: Knopf, Mcmxxvii.

On copyright page: 'TENTH PRINTING, JUNE, 1927'. Noted in blue leatherette binding (in blue cardboard box) and maroon cloth, both with gold stamping, lavender end papers, top edge gilt. This is probably the "gift edition" mentioned on the dust jacket of *Selected Prejudices* (1927; AA 3).

Locations: EPL (2 in leatherette, box), GHT (2, both).

A 18.2.k
Second edition, eleventh printing: New York: Knopf, [1928].

On copyright page: 'ELEVENTH PRINTING, JUNE, 1928'. Bound in the *Prejudices* format.

Location: EPL.

A 18.2.l–m
Second edition, twelfth and thirteenth printings: Garden City, N.Y.: Garden City Pub. Co., [n.d.].

Dated 1931 and 1934 by NUC 375.491. Dated 1922 by Adler and OCLC, probably because of last year on copyright page. A Star Book. Noted on dust jackets: '31–7', '31–11', '34–5–6–7'.

Locations: EPL (dj), GHT (3 in dj), Harv, JRS (dj).

A 18.3.a
Third edition (first English edition), first printing (1923)

Copyright page: '*First published* 1923 | *All rights reserved* | *Printed in Great Britain by* Butler & Tanner, *Frome and London*'

In Defence of Women
by H. L. Mencken

Jonathan Cape
Eleven Gower Street, London

A 18.3.a

7½″ × 4¾″: [1–4] 5 [6] 7–17 [18–20] 21–39 [40–42] 43–79 [80–82] 83–137 [138–40] 141–91 [192–94] 195–223 [224] = 224 pp.

[A]⁸ B–I⁸ K–O⁸ = 112 leaves.

Contents: p. 1: half title; p. 2: blank; p. 3: title; p. 4: copyright; p. 5: 'CONTENTS'; p. 6: blank; pp. 7–17: 'INTRODUCTION'; p. 18: blank; pp. 19–223: text; p. 224: blank. Blank pages in text (° following divisional half title): pp. 20,° 40, 42,° 80, 82,° 138, 140,° 192, 194.°

Typography and paper: 5¼″ (5″) × 3⅛″; 29 lines per page. Running heads: recto, 'INTRODUCTION' (pp. 9–17), chapter titles (pp. 23–223); verso, 'INTRODUCTION' (pp. 8–16), 'IN DEFENCE OF WOMEN' (pp. 22–222). Wove paper.

Binding: Yellow V cloth stamped in black. Front: 'IN DEFENCE OF WOMEN | H.L. MENCKEN'. Spine: 'IN DEFENCE | OF WOMEN | H.L. MENCKEN | JONATHAN CAPE'. Back: Jonathan Cape device. Top and fore edges trimmed, bottom edge unevenly trimmed, top edge stained yellow. White end papers.

Dust jacket: Not seen.

Publication: Published March 1923 (ECB 11.1018). 6s.

Locations: BL (17 MAR 23, rebound), Bod (MAR | 1923), Camb (23 MR | 1923), EPL, GHT (2), InU-Li.

Notes: Additions were made to the introduction, which, with some minor changes, has the biographical information. Laid in the Bod copy is a two-leaf brochure advertising *Travels in Arabia Deserta,* by Charles M. Doughty (Cape). Adler 8.

A 18.3.b
Third edition, second printing: London: Cape, [1927].

On copyright page: 'FIRST ISSUED IN THE TRAVELLERS' LIBRARY 1927'. Inserted in this printing of September 1927 (ECB 12.1036) were catalogues of 53 and 114 titles, the latter announcing volumes to appear in the fall of 1928.

Locations: EPL, GHT (2), RJS (2).

A 18.3.c
Third edition, third printing: London: Cape, [1929].

Published in Travellers' Library series, October 1929. Data from 1935 printing. Not seen.

A 18.3.d
Third edition, fourth printing: London: Cape, [1933].

Published in Travellers' Library series, January 1933. Data from 1935 printing. Not seen.

A 18.3.e
Third edition, fifth printing: London: Cape, [1935].

Travellers' Library series. On copyright page: 'FOURTH IMPRESSION APRIL 1935'.

Location: CtFaU.

A 18.4.a.i
Fourth edition, first printing, first issue (1927)

Title page: 'IN DEFENCE | OF WOMEN | BY | H. L. MENCKEN | *COPYRIGHT EDITION* | LEIPZIG | BERNHARD TAUCHNITZ | 1927'

6" × 4⅜" (binding A), 6⁵⁄₁₆" × 4⁷⁄₁₆" (binding B): [1–7] 8–20 [21–23] 24–45 [46–49] 50–92 [93–95] 96–158 [159–61] 162–219 [220–23] 224–55 [256] = 256 pp. Copies in wrappers (binding B) have an inserted 32-page catalogue, stapled in the center, glued in following the last gathering.

[1]⁸ 2–16⁸ = 128 leaves and inserted 16-leaf catalogue.

Contents: p. 1: 'COLLECTION | OF | BRITISH AUTHORS *[sic]* | TAUCHNITZ EDITION | VOL. 4782 | IN DEFENCE OF WOMEN | BY | H. L. MENCKEN | IN ONE VOLUME'; p. 2: blank; p. 3: title; p. 4: blank; p. 5: 'CONTENTS'; p. 6: blank; pp. 7–20: 'INTRODUCTION'; pp. 21–255: text; p. 256: '[rule] | PRINTED BY BERNHARD TAUCHNITZ, LEIPZIG | [rule]'. Blank pages of text following divisional half titles: pp. 22, 48, 94, 160, 222; others: pp. 46, 220. The inserted catalogue is dated May 1927. Laid into the Harvard and GHT copies is a sheet printed on both sides advertising 'MODERN AMERICAN WORKS | IN THE TAUCHNITZ EDITION', none numbered higher than 4782.

Binding A: Deep red cloth (see Notes). Front: Tauchnitz logo blindstamped. Spine: [stamped in gilt, all within ornate black design] 'In | Defence | of | Women | by | Mencken | TAUCHNITZ | EDITION | [diamond]'. Trimmed, unstained. White end papers.

Binding B: White paper wrappers. Front: [all in double-rule box, outer rule thick] 'TAUCHNITZ EDITION | COLLECTION OF BRITISH AND AMERICAN AU-THORS | VOL. 4782 | [double rule] | IN DEFENCE OF WOMEN | BY | H. L. MENCKEN | IN ONE VOLUME | LEIPZIG: BERNHARD TAUCHNITZ | PARIS: LIBRARIE HENRI GAULON, 39, RUE MADAME | [double rule] | A complete catalogue of the Tauchnitz Edition, with a list of the latest | additions on page 1, is attached to this volume | [below box] *Not to be introduced into the British Empire*'. Spine: '[thick-thin rule] | [same] | TAUCHNITZ | EDITION | BRITISH | AND | AMERICAN | AUTHORS | [thick-thin rule] | VOL. 4782 | [thick-thin rule] | H. L. | MENCKEN | [thick-thin rule] | IN | DEFENCE | OF | WOMEN | [thick-thin rule] | PRICE | M 1.80 | [thick-thin rule] | [same]'. The front verso and rear covers provide a list of the 'Latest Volumes—May 1927' (nos. 4758–81). Uncut, unstained.

Dust jacket: Unprinted glassine over the wrappers in the Yale copy, with corners of flaps evenly trimmed; original issue according to the donor.

Locations: EPL (2, bindings A and B), GHT (binding B), Harv (binding B), Yale (binding B, dj).

Notes: Binding A was found only on an EPL copy signed and dated 1927 by Mencken; presumably it was the copy presented by the publisher. The cloth is the x9 variety in William B. Todd and Ann Bowden, *Tauchnitz International Editions in English 1841– 1955: A Bibliographical History* (New York: Bibliographical Society of America, 1988), p. 583; it is not recorded in the entry for Mencken's book. The first issue in wrappers is distinguished by the date May 1927 on the catalogue and on the back cover. Adler 9; Todd and Bowden 688.

A 18.4.a.ii–ix

Copies of the first printing have been noted with variant wrappers and catalogues; these are treated as issues by Todd and Bowden: June, July (2), August, September, October (GHT) 1927, July 1928, July 1929.

A 18.4.b.i–iv
Second printing

No date on the title page; published July 1929. Copies of this printing have been noted with variant wrappers and catalogues; these are treated as issues by Todd and Bowden: July 1929 (GHT), September 1932, February 1933.

A 18.5.a
Fifth edition, first printing (1963)

Title page: 'H. L. MENCKEN | [lavender] IN DEFENSE OF | [decorated letters] WOMEN | [TRP logo] TIME Reading Program Special Edition | TIME INCORPO-RATED • NEW YORK'

Copyright page: 'TIME INC. BOOK DIVISION | EDITOR *Norman P. Ross* | [eleven others listed in twelve lines] | COVER DESIGN *Marshall Arisman* | Reprinted by arrangement with Alfred A. | Knopf, Inc. © 1922 by Alfred A. Knopf, Inc. | Renewal copyright 1950 by H. L. Mencken. | Editors' Preface and cover design © 1963 | Time Incorporated. All rights reserved.'

Colophon: '[TRP logo] | [lavender] A NOTE ABOUT THE PRODUCTION OF THIS BOOK | The text of this special edition of *In Defense of Women* | was set in Linotype Granjon, the basic design of which | stems from 16th Century French sources. The type was set | by Haddon Craftsmen, Inc., Scranton, Pennsylvania, and |

printed by the Safran Printing Company, Detroit, Michigan. | The binding was done by J. W. Clement Co. of Buffalo, New | York. The cover was printed by Livermore and Knight Co., | a division of Printing Corporation of America, of Provi- | dence, Rhode Island. | Cover stock was supplied by the Plastic Coating Corp. of | Holyoke, Massachusetts. The paper is TIME Reading Text, | by The Mead Corporation of Dayton, Ohio.'

8″ × 5⅛″: [A–B i–vii] viii–xvi [xvii] xviii–xxiv [xxv–xxviii 1–3] 4–18 [19–21] 22–35 [36] 37–42 [43] 44–47 [48] 49 [50] 51 [52–55] 56–70 [71] 72–82 [83] 84–89 [90] 91–92 [93] 94–98 [99] 100–01 [102–05] 106–13 [114] 115–30 [131] 132–38 [139] 140–41 [142] 143–46 [147–49] 150–72 [173–78] = 208 pp.

Perfect bound.

Contents: pp. A–B: blank; p. i: half title; p. ii: blank; p. iii: title; p. iv: copyright; p. v: 'CONTENTS'; p. vi: blank; pp. vii–xvi: 'EDITORS' PREFACE'; pp. xvii–xxiv: 'AU-THOR'S INTRODUCTION'; pp. xxv–vi: blank; p. xxvii: half title; p. xxviii: blank; pp. 1–172: text; p. 173: blank; p. 174: colophon; pp. 175–78: blank. Blank pages of text (° following illustrated divisional titles): pp. 2,° 20,° 52, 54,° 102, 104,° 148.° List of contents, section and chapter titles, and initials in lavender. Initial letters decorated.

Binding: Multicolored, decorated covers in heavy stock paper with plastic coating. Inside of covers white.

Locations: GHT, RJS.

Notes: This printing with lavender is the one on file at Time-Life Library; no other records remain. No LC copy. Originally published as part of a set that also included *Brave New World, The Screwtape Letters,* and *The Bridge at San Luis Rey.* For Time Reading Program, not for public sale (S1.4).

A 18.5.b
Fifth edition, second printing: New York: Time, Inc., [n.d.].

All printing black. Added line on copyright page: 'Printed in the United States of America'. Colophon changed. 8″ × 5⅛″ (inside covers black), 8¹⁄₁₆″ × 5³⁄₁₆″ (green), 8″ × 5³⁄₁₆″ (blue). Initial letters not decorated.

Locations: GHT (3), NcWsU, NjP, RJS (3).

A 18.5.c
Fifth edition, third printing: Alexandria, Va.: Time-Life Books, [1982].

On copyright page: 'Reprinted 1982'. Time Reading Program Special Edition, issued in case with George G. Simpson, *Attending Marvels.* In paper wrappers as above (white inside) and in red fabricoid stamped in gilt.

Locations: GHT (2), RJS.

A 19 THE AMERICAN LANGUAGE

A 19.1.a.i
First edition, only printing, limited binding issue (1919)

THE
AMERICAN LANGUAGE

*A Preliminary Inquiry into the Develop-
ment of English in the United States*

BY
H. L. MENCKEN

NEW YORK
ALFRED · A · KNOPF
MCMXIX

A 19.1.a

Copyright page: 'COPYRIGHT, 1919, BY | ALFRED A. KNOPF, INC. | PRINTED IN THE UNITED STATES OF AMERICA'

Statement of limitation: 'OF THE FIRST EDITION OF | THIS BOOK FIFTEEN HUNDRED | COPIES HAVE BEEN PRINTED | AND THE TYPE DISTRIB- UTED | THIS IS NUMBER _____ [number handstamped in red] | [signature of Mencken]'

9⅝″ × 6⅛″: [i–iv] v–x 1–321 [322] 323–74 = 384 pp.

[1–24]⁸ = 192 leaves.

Contents: p. i: half title and ten-pointed device with intertwined 'AAK' in center; p. ii: limitation notice; p. iii: title; p. iv: copyright; pp. v–viii: 'PREFACE' (dated 1 January 1919); pp. ix–x: 'CONTENTS'; pp. 1–321: text; p. 322: blank; pp. 323–39: 'Bibliogra- phy'; pp. 340–67: 'List of Words and Phrases'; pp. 368–74: 'General Index'.

Typography and paper: 6½″ (6¼″) × 4″; 37 lines per page (lines vary with number of charts and footnotes). Running heads: recto, 'PREFACE' (p. vii), chapter titles (pp. 3–321), 'BIBLIOGRAPHY' (pp. 325–39), 'LIST OF WORDS AND PHRASES' (pp. 341–67), 'GENERAL INDEX' (pp. 369–73); verso: 'PREFACE' (pp. vi–viii), 'CON- TENTS' (p. x), 'THE AMERICAN LANGUAGE' (pp. 2–320), 'BIBLIOGRAPHY' (pp. 324–38), 'LIST OF WORDS AND PHRASES' (pp. 342–66), 'GENERAL IN- DEX' (pp. 370–74). Wove paper.

Binding: Very dark blue buckram, stamped in gilt on spine: '[double rule] | THE | AMERICAN | LANGUAGE | [double rule] | H•L•MENCKEN [dots represent inverted triangles] | [double rule] | [double rule] | ALFRED•A•KNOPF | [double rule]'. Untrimmed, unstained. White end papers.

Dust jacket: Red printing on pale blue-green paper. Front: 'THE | AMERICAN LANGUAGE | By H. L. MENCKEN | Author of "A Book of Prefaces," etc. | [twenty- one line blurb] | *This is a limited edition printed from type of which only* | 1500 *copies are for sale.* | Alfred A. Knopf [intertwined AAK device] Publisher, N. Y.' Spine: 'THE | AMERICAN | LANGUAGE | By | H. L. | MENCKEN | A | Limited | Edition | [typed on label pasted over regular price] 7.50 | [Borzoi device over rule of same width] | ALFRED A. | KNOPF'. Back: [all within ornate borders] 'SOME OPINIONS OF H. L. MENCKEN | [ten quotations and blurb for second (revised) edition of *A Book of Prefaces*]'. Front flap: 'ABOUT THE AUTHOR | . . . | In Defense of Women; 1918'. Back flap unprinted. In the example seen, the limitation number is crayoned on the front of the jacket, which overall is the size of the trade issue dust jacket, but the flaps have not been folded twice (i.e., it was not lifted off a [smaller] trade copy).

Publication: Published 14 March 1919. $7.50. Copyright #A512890. 66,000 copies of the four editions sold by Knopf, along with 8,500 sets of the fourth edition and the two supplements.

Printing: Printed by Vail-Ballou Co., Binghamton, N.Y.; bound by J. J. Little & Ives, New York.

Locations: EPL (no. 1), GHT (no. 15), JRS (no. 17, dj), NjP (no. 2).

Notes: According to Frey, Mencken signed twenty-five copies; apparently, the first twenty-five were this issue. No. 1 (EPL) was presented to the Knopfs. No. 2 (NjP) was donated by Mencken in 1942; presumably his personal copy, it is signed on the free front end paper and not beneath the statement of limitation. The dust jacket is the only evidence that it was offered for sale, but "7.50" was also penciled on the rear pastedown of an unjacketed copy seen in a bookstore. The book developed out of, and borrowed from, his many essays on the subject; see MLAE 294. Adler 9, 131, 281; S1.8, 11; Frey 31, 52; Bulsterbaum 5.

A 19.1.a.ii
First edition, only printing, trade issue

Same as A 19.1.a.i except:

Statement of limitation: Same but without Mencken's signature.

9¼″ × 6¼″

Binding: Fore and bottom edges rough and unevenly trimmed; top edge trimmed and stained dark blue.

Dust jacket: ' . . . Edition | $4.00 net | [Borzoi device over rule of same width] . . . '.

Publication: $4.00.

Locations: GHT (3 [2 in dj]), Harv, InU-Li, LC (1 April 1919, no limitation number), MBU, RJS (dj).

Notes: Nos. 26–1,500 were apparently so issued. A Harv copy, rebound, is without a limitation number, as is one reported by a dealer and the LC copy. The number in the InU-Li copy (921) is written in blue ink; the remaining examples have it handstamped in red (both higher and lower than 921).

A 19.2.a.i
Second edition, first printing, first issue (1921)

Title page: 'THE | AMERICAN LANGUAGE | [red] *An Inquiry into the Develop-ment* | [red] *of English in the United States* | BY | H. L. MENCKEN | Second Edition | Revised and Enlarged | [red Borzoi device in oval] | NEW YORK | ALFRED • A • KNOPF | MCMXXI'

Copyright page: 'COPYRIGHT, 1919, BY | ALFRED A. KNOPF, Inc. | [short rule] | COPYRIGHT, 1921, BY | ALFRED A. KNOPF, Inc. | [short rule] | *Revised Edition Published December,* 1921 | *Set up and printed by the J. J. Little & Ives Co., New York,*

THE
AMERICAN LANGUAGE

By H. L. MENCKEN
Author of "A Book of Prefaces," etc.

The first book to present with any intelligibility the origin, development and present state of the American dialect of English. All other existing works upon the subject deal exclusively with the vocabulary; this one aims to examine the more fundamental characters of the language—its idioms, its methods of word-change, its relation to other languages, its syntax, and its tendencies in grammar.

First, the salient differences between English and American are pointed out; secondly, they are analysed and an attempt is made to exhibit the laws and causes underlying them; and finally, there is a discussion of the forces operating, either to accentuate them or to counteract them. The book represents many years of labor, and offers much material not hitherto accessible. The widely dispersed and highly fragmentary literature of the subject has been studied and co-ordinated, and, in the presentation there are clarity and coherence.

The work is of value to American teachers of English, to students of English dialect, to those of American literature, and to all persons interested in the language spoken by 100,000,000 Americans. It is thorough, but it avoids pedantry. A comprehensive bibliography is appended.

This is a limited edition printed from type of which only 1500 copies are for sale.

Alfred A. Knopf Publisher, N. Y.

THE
AMERICAN
LANGUAGE

By
H. L.
MENCKEN

A
limited
edition

$4.00 net

ALFRED A.
KNOPF

ABOUT THE AUTHOR

H. L. Mencken was born at Baltimore, September 12, 1880. He is of mixed ancestry, chiefly German, Irish and English. His family has been settled in Maryland for nearly a century.

He was educated at Knopf's Institute, a private school in Baltimore, and at the Baltimore Polytechnic. He is a graduate of the latter, but turned from applied science to journalism almost at once. Beginning as a reporter on the old Baltimore *Morning Herald*, he closed seven years' service as editor-in-chief of that paper. Since then he has been attached to various other newspapers, chiefly as editor and writer. Among other assignments, he has acted as special correspondent ...

He has written for *Life* and *The Smart Set* ...

Among his books are the following:

George Bernard Shaw: His Plays, the first book on Shaw ever written.

The Philosophy of Friedrich Nietzsche, the standard work in English, now in its third edition.

Men vs. the Man, an argument against Socialism ...

A Little Book in C Major, a collection ...

In Defense of Women, 1918.

A 19.1.a.ii, dust jacket

N. Y. | *Paper (Warren's) furnished by Henry Lindenmey r [sic] Sons, New York, N. Y.* | *Bound by the H. Wolff Estate, New York, N. Y.* | [short rule] | MANUFACTURED IN THE UNITED STATES OF AMERICA.'

9¼″ × 6¹⁄₁₆″ (binding A), 9¼″ × 6⅛″ (binding B): [i–ii] iii–xvii [xviii 1] 2–112 3 *[sic]* 114–425 [426] 427–57 [458] 459–92 [493–98] = 516 pp.

[1]¹⁰ [2–32]⁸ = 258 leaves. Two additional nonconjugate binder's leaves, at the beginning of the first gathering and at the end of the last, take the place of end papers.

Contents: p. i: title; p. ii: copyright; pp. iii–vi: 'CONTENTS'; pp. vii–x: 'PREFACE TO THE FIRST EDITION'; pp. xi–xvii: 'PREFACE TO THE REVISED EDITION'; p. xviii: blank; pp. 1–387: text; pp. 388–425: 'APPENDIX'; p. 426: blank; pp. 427–57: 'BIBLIOGRAPHY'; p. 458: blank; pp. 459–82: 'LIST OF WORDS AND PHRASES'; pp. 483–92: 'INDEX'; pp. 493–98: blank.

Typography and paper: 7″ (6¹¹⁄₁₆″) × 4⁵⁄₁₆″; 37 lines per page. Running heads: recto, 'CONTENTS' (p. v), 'PREFACE TO THE FIRST EDITION' (p. ix), 'PREFACE TO THE REVISED EDITION' (pp. xiii–xvii), 'INTRODUCTORY' (pp. 3–43), section titles (pp. 47–387), 'APPENDIX' (pp. 389–425), 'BIBLIOGRAPHY' (pp. 429–57), 'LIST OF WORDS AND PHRASES' (pp. 461–81), 'INDEX' (pp. 485–91); verso, 'CONTENTS' (pp. iv–vi), 'THE AMERICAN LANGUAGE' (pp. viii–424), 'BIBLIOGRAPHY' (pp. 428–56), 'LIST OF WORDS AND PHRASES' (pp. 460–82), 'INDEX' (pp. 484–92). Wove paper.

Binding A: Blue buckram. Front: blindstamped Mencken arms. Spine, stamped in gilt: '[double rule] | THE | AMERICAN | LANGUAGE | [double rule] | H•L• MENCKEN [dots represent inverted triangles] | [double rule] | [double rule] | ALFRED•A•KNOPF | [double rule]'. Back: Borzoi Books logo blindstamped. Top edge trimmed and gilt, fore edge rough trimmed, bottom edge uncut. White pastedowns.

Binding B: Same as binding A but dark blue V cloth, top edge trimmed and stained blue.

Dust jacket: Dark blue printing on light blue paper. Front: '*New, completely revised edition* | THE | AMERICAN LANGUAGE | *By* H. L. MENCKEN | [twenty-one-line blurb] | ALFRED A. KNOPF [Borzoi Books logo] PUBLISHER, N. Y.' Spine: 'THE | AMERICAN | LANGUAGE | *By* | H. L. | MENCKEN | *New* | *completely* | *revised* | *edition* | [Borzoi Books logo] | ALFRED A. | KNOPF'. Back: 'Some Recent | European Opinions of | H. L. MENCKEN | [ornate rule, four blurbs and Knopf imprint]'. Front flap: biography and bibliography of Mencken; price $6.00. Rear flap: form to submit for placement on mailing list.

Locations: EPL (2 in binding A), GHT (2 in binding B, dj), InU-Li (2 in binding B, dj), RJS (binding B), Yale (2 in binding B).

Notes: Knopf to Mencken, 27 December 1921: "The single copy of THE AMERI-
CAN LANGUAGE I sent you was one of the five or six I had bound in buckram with a
gilt top. There were no uncut copies" (NN). One of the EPL copies was presented to
the Knopfs; Mencken marked the other 'uncut / buckram'. "A few copies, uncut, were
bound in dark blue buckram" (Frey 32). Adler 9; S1.7.

Salesman's dummy: A dealer reported a salesman's dummy that contains the title
page, copyright page, table of contents, and two prefaces.

A 19.2.a.ii
Second edition, first printing, English issue (1922)

Same as A 19.2.a.i except:

Copyright page: 'First published, 1922. | All rights reserved. | Printed in the United
States of America.'

$9^{5}/_{16}'' \times 6''$

[1]¹⁰ (±1₁) [2–32]⁸ = 258 leaves. The title/copyright leaf is a cancel. Two additional
nonconjugate binder's leaves, at the beginning of the first gathering and at the end of
the last, take the place of end papers.

Binding: Dark blue V cloth stamped in gilt on spine: 'THE | AMERICAN | LAN-
GUAGE | MENCKEN | JONATHAN CAPE'. Top and fore edges trimmed, bottom
edge uncut, unstained. White pastedowns.

Dust jacket: Not seen.

Publication: Published March 1922 (ECB 11.1018). 30s.

Locations: BL (28 FEB 22, rebound), Bod (May. 1922 [?]), Camb (MY 12 | 1922),
GHT, KU-S.

Notes: The rebound BL copy is trimmed ($9^{1}/_{4}'' \times 6''$), all edges speckled red. Adler 9.

A 19.2.b–c
Second edition, second and third printings.

Reprinted twice by Knopf, according to Frey. Not located.

A 19.3.a
Third edition, first printing (1923)

Title page: 'THE | AMERICAN LANGUAGE | *An Inquiry into the Development* | *of
English in the United States* | *by* | H. L. MENCKEN | THIRD EDITION | REVISED
AND ENLARGED | [Borzoi device in oval] | NEW YORK | ALFRED•A:KNOPF
[*sic*] | MCMXXIII'

THE
AMERICAN LANGUAGE

*An Inquiry into the Development
of English in the United States*

BY

H. L. MENCKEN

JONATHAN CAPE
ELEVEN GOWER STREET, LONDON

A 19.2.a.ii

Copyright page: 'COPYRIGHT, 1919, BY ALFRED A. KNOPF, INC. | COPY-
RIGHT, 1921, BY ALFRED A. KNOPF, INC. | COPYRIGHT, 1923, BY ALFRED
A. KNOPF, INC. | *Revised Edition Published December, 1921* | *Third Edition (Again
Revised), February, 1923* | *Set up and electrotyped by J. J. Little & Ives Co., New York.*
| *Printed by the Vail-Ballou Co., Binghamton, N.Y., on Warren's No. 66 paper [sic]* |
Bound by the H. Wolff Estate, New York. | MANUFACTURED IN THE UNITED
STATES OF AMERICA'

9⅜" × 6³⁄₁₆": [i–ii] iii–ix [x] 1–467 [468] 469–89 [490–94] = 504 pp.

[1–31]⁸ [32]⁴ = 252 leaves.

Contents: p. i: title; p. ii: copyright; pp. iii–vi: 'CONTENTS'; pp. vii–ix: 'PREFACE
TO THE THIRD EDITION'; p. x: blank; pp. 1–397: text; pp. 398–435: 'APPEN-
DIX'; pp. 436–67: 'BIBLIOGRAPHY'; p. 468: blank; pp. 469–84: 'LIST OF WORDS
AND PHRASES'; pp. 485–89: 'INDEX'; pp. 490–94: blank.

Typography and paper: 7" (6¹¹⁄₁₆") × 4⁵⁄₁₆"; 37 lines per page (lines vary with number of
lines in footnotes). Running heads: recto, 'CONTENTS' (p. v), 'PREFACE TO THE
THIRD EDITION' (p. ix), 'INTRODUCTORY' (pp. 3–45), section titles (pp. 49–
397), 'APPENDIX' (pp. 399–435), 'BIBLIOGRAPHY' (pp. 437–67), 'LIST OF
WORDS AND PHRASES' (pp. 471–83), 'INDEX' (pp. 487–89); verso, 'CON-
TENTS' (pp. iv–vi), 'PREFACE TO THE THIRD EDITION' (p. viii), 'THE AMER-
ICAN LANGUAGE' (pp. 2–434), 'BIBLIOGRAPHY' (pp. 438–66), 'LIST OF
WORDS AND PHRASES' (pp. 470–84), 'INDEX' (pp. 486–88). Wove paper.

Binding: Dark blue cloth. Front: Mencken arms blindstamped. Spine, stamped in gilt:
'[double rule] | THE | AMERICAN | LANGUAGE | [double rule] | H•L• MENCKEN
[dots represent inverted triangles] | [double rule] | [double rule] | ALFRED [flying A]
KNOPF | [double rule]'. Back: Borzoi Books logo blindstamped. Top edge trimmed
and stained orange, fore edge rough trimmed, bottom edge unevenly trimmed and
partly uncut. White end papers.

Dust jacket: Dark blue printing on yellow paper. Front: 'THE AMERICAN | LAN-
GUAGE | *An Inquiry into the Development* | *of English in the United States* | *by* | H. L.
| MENCKEN | [eight-line blurb] | *THIRD EDITION* | *(Revised)* | ALFRED A.
KNOPF [Borzoi Books logo] PUBLISHER, N. Y.' Spine: 'THE | AMERICAN |
LANGUAGE | *by* | H. L. | MENCKEN | *THIRD* | *EDITION* | *(Revised)* | [Borzoi
Books logo] | *Alfred A. Knopf.*' Back: '*Some Recent European Opinions* | *of* | H. L.
MENCKEN | [seven blurbs and Knopf imprint]'. Front flap: '*BOOKS BY* | H. L.
MENCKEN | [seventeen titles; price $6.00]'. Rear flap: table of contents for *Preju-
dices: Third Series.*

Locations: GHT (dj), Harv (2), InU-Li, RJS.

Notes: Adler 9.

A 19.3.b
Third edition, second printing: New York: Knopf, MCMXXVI.

On copyright page: 'REPRINTED NOVEMBER, 1926'.

Locations: EPL, GHT.

A 19.3.c
Third edition, third printing: New York: Knopf, MCMXXIX.

On copyright page: 'REPRINTED JANUARY, 1929'.

Location: D.

A 19.3.d
Third edition, fourth printing: New York: Knopf, MCMXXX.

On copyright page: 'REPRINTED AUGUST, 1930'.

Locations: EPL, GHT.

A 19.3.e
Third edition, fifth printing: New York: Knopf, MCMXXX.

On copyright page: 'REPRINTED OCTOBER, 1930'.

Location: EPL.

A 19.3.f
Third edition, sixth printing: New York: Knopf, MCMXXXI.

On copyright page: 'REPRINTED AUGUST, 1931'.

Location: EPL.

A 19.4.a.i
Fourth edition, first printing, first issue (1936)

Title page: 'FOURTH EDITION *corrected, enlarged, and rewritten* | [wide French rule] | T H E | *American Language* | AN INQUIRY | INTO THE DEVELOPMENT OF ENGLISH | IN THE UNITED STATES | BY | H. L. Mencken | [thick-thin rule] | 1936 | ALFRED A. KNOPF | NEW YORK | [Borzoi device]'

Copyright page: 'Copyright 1919, 1921, 1923, 1936 by Alfred A. Knopf, Inc. All rights | [four lines reserving rights] | PUBLISHED *March,* 1919 | REVISED EDITION *published December,* 1921 | THIRD EDITION *again revised published February,* 1923 | FOURTH EDITION *corrected, enlarged, and rewritten* | *published April,* 1936 | MANUFACTURED IN THE UNITED STATES OF AMERICA'

Colophon: 'A Note on the Type in which | this Book is Set | [ornament, twenty lines about Janson type, Borzoi device] | *Composed, printed, and bound by the Plimp-* | *ton Press, Norwood, Mass. Paper made by S. D.* | *Warren Co., Boston. Designed by* W. A. | Dwiggins.'

9⅚₆″ × 6³⁄₁₆″: [A–D i–iv] v–viii [ix] x–xi [xii 1–2] 3–697 [698] 699–769 [770] i–xxix [xxx–xxxii] = 818 pp. The last two pages are on a binder's leaf.

[1–51]⁸ = 408 leaves, followed by a binder's leaf tipped in to end paper.

Contents: pp. A–C: blank; p. D: thirteen Borzoi titles by Mencken; p. i: half title; p. ii: blank; p. iii: title; p. iv: copyright; pp. v–viii: 'PREFACE | TO THE FOURTH EDITION'; pp. ix–xi: 'Table of Contents'; p. xii: blank; p. 1: half title; p. 2: blank; pp. 3–615: text; pp. 616–97: 'APPENDIX | NON-ENGLISH DIALECTS IN AMERICAN'; p. 698: blank; pp. 699–769: 'LIST OF WORDS AND PHRASES'; p. 770: blank; pp. i–xxix: 'INDEX'; p. xxx: colophon; pp. xxxi–xxxii: blank.

Typography and paper: 7⅜″ (7⅛″) × 4⅛″; 40 lines per page (lines vary with amount of reduced type and number of footnotes, which are in double columns). Running heads: recto, *'Preface to the Fourth Edition'* (p. vii), *'Table of Contents'* (p. xi), section titles (pp. 5–615), *'Appendix'* (pp. 617–97), *'List of Words and Phrases'* (pp. 701–69), *'Index'* (pp. iii–xxix); verso, *'The American Language'* (pp. vi–viii, 4–696), *'Table of Contents'* (p. x), *'List of Words and Phrases'* (pp. 700–68), *'Index'* (pp. ii–xxviii). Wove paper.

Binding: Black cloth. Front: shield from Mencken arms blindstamped. Spine, stamped in gilt: '[bar] | [ornament with spread eagle] | [three rules, middle one thinner] | THE | AMERICAN | LANGUAGE | [double rule] | [script] H. L. Mencken | [double rule, bar, rule, bar, rule] | K N O P F | [double rule, bar, double rule] | [various ornaments]'. Back: Borzoi Books logo blindstamped. Top edge trimmed and stained black or deep blue, fore edge rough cut (some pages uncut), bottom edge unevenly trimmed. White end papers.

Dust jacket: Red and black printing on white paper. Front: [all between ornate red and black border at top, ornate black borders left and right] 'T H E | American | Language | [red] H. L. MENCKEN | Fourth Edition | *Corrected Enlarged and Rewritten* | [ten-line blurb inside ornate black borders top, right, and left, red bar at bottom]'. Spine: '[red ornament] | The | American | Language | H. L. | MENCKEN | [red ornament] | FOURTH EDITION | CORRECTED | ENLARGED | REWRITTEN | [Borzoi device] | ALFRED • A • KNOPF | [red ornament]'. Back: '[red] H. L. Mencken | [fifteen titles, leaflike ornament to left of first three] | [red Borzoi Books logo beside next two lines] ALFRED • A • KNOPF • PUBLISHER | NEW YORK'. Front flap: blurb, price $5.00. Rear flap: '[red] *What Critics Say:* | [eight blurbs]'.

Locations: EPL, GHT (dj), Harv, RJS (dj), Yale.

Notes: All copies noted, including the later printings and the English issues, misspell "Gettysburg" on p. vii, l. 14. Adler 9, 154, 156, 157, 158; S1.12; S2.6.

A 19.4.a.ii
Fourth edition, first printing, English issue (1936)

Same as A 19.4.a.i, except:

Title page: 'FOURTH EDITION *corrected, enlarged, and rewritten* | [wide French rule] | T H E | *American Language* | AN INQUIRY | INTO THE DEVELOPMENT OF ENGLISH | IN THE UNITED STATES | BY | H. L. Mencken | [thick-thin rule] | LONDON | KEGAN PAUL, TRENCH, TRUBNER & CO., LTD. | BROADWAY HOUSE: 68–74 CARTER LANE, E.C. | 1936'

Copyright page: 'PRINTED IN THE UNITED STATES OF AMERICA'

Colophon: None.

First state: $9'' \times 5\,^{15}/_{16}''$: [i–ii ix] x [iii–iv] v–viii xi [xii 1–2] 3–697 [698] 699–769 [770] i–xxix [xxx] = 812 pp. *Second state:* $9\,^3/_{16}'' \times 6\,^1/_8''$: [C–D i–iv] v–viii [ix] x–xi [xii 1–2] . . . [xxx] = 814 pp. *Third state:* $9\,^1/_4'' \times 6\,^1/_8''$: [A–D ix] x–xi [xii i–iv] v–viii [1–2] . . . [xxx] = 816 pp. *Fourth state:* $9\,^1/_4'' \times 6\,^1/_4''$: [A–D i–iv] v–viii [ix] x–xi [xii 1–2] . . . [xxx] = 816 pp.

First state: [1]^6 [2–51]^8 = 406 leaves. The first gathering is misimposed. *Second state:* [1]^6 (1$_6$ + 1) [2–51]^8 = 407 leaves. The leaf with pp. xi–xii is tipped in to p. x. *Third state:* Same as fourth state, except the four innermost leaves of the first gathering have been bound following the outer four. *Fourth state:* [1–51]^8 = 408 leaves.

Contents: pp. A–D: blank; . . . ; p. xxx: blank.

Binding: Black or very deep blue V cloth stamped in gilt on spine: 'THE | AMERI-CAN | LANGUAGE | H.L.MENCKEN | KEGAN PAUL'. Top edge trimmed and stained blue, fore edge rough trimmed, bottom edge unevenly trimmed. White end papers.

Dust jacket: Not seen.

Publication: Published July 1936 (ECB 14.1124). 21s.

Locations: BL (20 JUL 36, first state, rebound but gatherings intact), Bod (4 | FEB | 1937, fourth state), Camb (2 FE | 1937, second state), EPL (third state), GHT (fourth state), TxU (second state).

Notes: Adler 9.

A 19.4.b
Fourth edition, second printing: New York: Knopf, 1936.

On copyright page: '*reprinted May,* 1936'.

Locations: EPL, InU-Li.

A 19.4.c
Fourth edition, third printing: New York: Knopf, 1936.

On copyright page: '*reprinted August, 1936*'.

Location: EPL, MB.

A 19.4.d
Fourth edition, fourth printing: New York: Knopf, 1936.

On copyright page: '*reprinted October, 1936*'.

Location: EPL.

A 19.4.e
Fourth edition, fifth printing: New York: Knopf, 1937.

On copyright page: '*reprinted February, 1937*'. $9^{5}/_{16}'' \times 6^{1}/_{4}'' \times 1^{3}/_{4}''$; vertical chain lines $1''$ apart; top edge trimmed and stained, fore edge rough trimmed, bottom edge unevenly trimmed. The Book-of-the-Month Club dividend of April 1937 (free to new members) was apparently one of the 1937 printings. Presumably, the books were purchased from Knopf. Cf. Hobson 363.

Locations: EPL, MChB.

A 19.4.f
Fourth edition, sixth printing: New York: Knopf, 1937.

Same as A 19.4.e, but $9^{3}/_{8}'' \times 6^{1}/_{4}'' \times 1^{1}/_{4}''$; chain lines $3/_{4}''$ apart, unstained top, all edges trimmed.

Locations: EPL, GHT, MBU (2).

A 19.4.g
Fourth edition, seventh printing: New York: Knopf, 1938.

Same as A 19.4.f but 1938 on title page.

Locations: D, EPL, GHT.

A 19.4.h
Fourth edition, eighth printing: New York: Knopf, 1938.

On copyright page: '*reprinted November, 1938*'.

Locations: EPL, GHT, MCR.

A 19.4.i
Fourth edition, ninth printing: New York: Knopf, 1941.

On copyright page: '*reprinted September, 1941*'.

Location: EPL.

A 19.4.j
Fourth edition, tenth printing: New York: Knopf, 1943.

On copyright page: '*reprinted November, 1943*'.

Location: EPL.

A 19.4.k
Fourth edition, eleventh printing: New York: Knopf, 1945.

On copyright page: '*ninth printing, April, 1945*'; note on compliance with government regulations.

Locations: EPL, GHT, MBU.

A 19.4.l
Fourth edition, twelfth printing: New York: Knopf, 1946.

On copyright page: '*tenth printing, April, 1946*'

Locations: D, EPL, GHT, MB, MCR.

A 19.4.m.i
Fourth edition, thirteenth printing, American issue: New York: Knopf, 1947.

On copyright page: '*eleventh printing, June, 1947.*' Contains a 'NOTE' by Mencken (p. [2]), dated '*Baltimore, 1947*', in which he claims that "the surviving errors of both the author and the printer have been rectified," but "Gettysburg" is still misspelled on p. vii.

Locations: D, RJS.

A 19.4.m.ii
Fourth edition, thirteenth printing, English issue: London: Routledge and Kegan Paul, [1948].

Label (1⁵⁄₁₆″ × 4¼″) pasted on the title page below the thick-thin rule: 'LONDON | ROUTLEDGE AND KEGAN PAUL LTD. | BROADWAY HOUSE, 68–74 CAR-TER LANE, E.C. 4'. The two supplements were issued simultaneously (A 56.1.d.ii, A 59.1.a.ii).

Locations: BL (12 NOV 48), Bod (19 | NOV | 1948), Camb (19 NO | 1948).

A 19.4.n
Fourth edition, fourteenth printing: New York: Knopf, 1949.

Published October 1949 (D). Not seen.

A 19.4.o
Fourth edition, fifteenth printing: New York: Knopf, 1955.

On copyright page: '*thirteenth printing, May,* 1955'.

Location: OCanS.

A 19.4.p
Fourth edition, sixteenth printing: New York: Knopf, 1957.

On copyright page: '*fourteenth printing, August,* 1957'. Laid paper. Also published in a boxed set with the two supplements (A 56, A 59; June 1960 and May 1960 printings, respectively) and *A New Dictionary of Quotations* (A 53; September 1957 printing) ca. 1960 ("The American Language Reference Library"), each with dust jacket. Other noted printings of the four volumes in this set: August 1957, June 1960, May 1960, and September 1960; September 1960, October 1961, October 1961, and September 1960; August 1962, another August 1962 in dust jacket of first supplement, August 1962, and August 1962.

Locations: GHT (dj), MC.

A 19.4.q
Fourth edition, seventeenth printing: New York: Knopf, 1960.

On copyright page: '*fifteenth printing, September* 1960'. Laid paper.

Location: GHT.

A 19.4.r
Fourth edition, eighteenth printing: same title page as sixteenth printing, for Senjo (Tokyo).

Wove paper. In a three-volume set with the two supplements (A 56, A 59); on copyright page: August 1957, October 1956, and March 1956, respectively. Black cloth stamped in gilt, with 'KNOPF | SENJO' at the base of the spine of the cover. Senjo (of Tokyo) imprint and that of Knopf also on the front and spine of dust jacket, with table of contents in Japanese on the front flap, a Mencken chronology in Japanese on the back flap. A pale yellow-orange strip (white on the verso) wraps around the dust jacket, identifying the book in Japanese. Published 20 January 1962, and "500 (?)"

printed, according to a distributor's label pasted onto the free front end paper of the EPL copy (cf. S1.4).

Location: EPL (dj).

A 19.4.s
Fourth edition, nineteenth printing: same title page as seventeenth printing, for Book-of-the-Month Club.

Wove paper; blindstamped dot on back cover; 'W' on copyright page. The Book-of-the-Month Club dividend for May 1962 included the book in a set with the two supplements.

Location: GHT.

A 19.4.t
Fourth edition, twentieth printing: New York: Knopf, 1962.

On copyright page: '*sixteenth printing, August* 1962'. Laid paper.

Location: MChB.

A 19.4.u
Fourth edition, twenty-first printing: same title page as twentieth printing, for Book-of-the-Month Club.

Wove paper; blindstamped dot on back cover; 'W' on copyright page; '4322' on spine of dust jacket.

Location: GHT (dj).

A 19.4.v
Fourth edition, twenty-second printing: New York: Knopf, 1965.

On copyright page: '*seventeenth printing, November* 1965'. Laid paper.

Location: D.

A 19.4.w
Fourth edition, twenty-third printing: same title page as twenty-second printing, for Book-of-the-Month Club.

Wove paper; blindstamped dot on back cover; '4322' on spine of dust jacket.

Locations: Harv, RJS (dj).

A 19.4.x
Fourth edition, twenty-fourth printing: same title page as sixteenth printing, for Senjo (Tokyo).

Wove paper. In a three-volume set with the two supplements (A 56, A 59); on copyright page: August 1957, October 1956, and March 1956, respectively. Taupe cloth stamped in gilt. Printed and published in July 1968, according to slip (printed in Japanese) tipped in to recto of rear end paper.

Location: GHT.

A 19.4.y–aa
Fourth edition, twenty-fifth through twenty-seventh printings

Not seen.

A 19.4.bb
Fourth edition, twenty-eighth printing: New York: Knopf, 1977.

On copyright page: '*twenty-first printing, May 1977*'.

Location: D.

A 19.4.cc
Fourth edition, twenty-ninth printing: New York: Knopf, 1980.

On copyright page: '*twenty-second printing, January 1980*'. Wove paper.

Location: MBU.

A 19.4.dd
Fourth edition, thirtieth printing: same title page as twenty-ninth printing, for Book-of-the-Month Club.

Book-of-the-Month Club premium for September 1979, with the two supplements. Wove paper; blindstamped square on back cover.

Locations: D, GHT.

A 20 PREJUDICES: FIRST SERIES

A 20.1.a
Only edition, first printing (1919)

A 20.1.a

Copyright page: 'COPYRIGHT, 1919, BY | ALFRED A. KNOPF, INC. | PRINTED IN THE UNITED STATES OF AMERICA'

7¹¹⁄₁₆″ × 5⅛″ (binding A), 7¼″ × 4¹⁵⁄₁₆″ (binding B): [1–8] 9–254 [255–56] = 256 pp. [1–16]⁸ = 128 leaves.

Contents: p. 1: half title; p. 2: [all within a box inside a double-line box] 'BY H. L. MENCKEN | [twelve titles:] VENTURES INTO VERSE | *Out of print* | . . . | PREJUDICES: FIRST SERIES'; p. 3: title; p. 4: copyright; pp. 5–6: 'CONTENTS'; p. 7: half title; p. 8: blank; pp. 9–250: text; pp. 251–54: 'INDEX'; pp. 255–56: blank.

Text: "Criticism of Criticism of Criticism," "The Late Mr. Wells," "Arnold Bennett," "The Dean," "Professor Veblen," "The New Poetry Movement," "The Heir of Mark Twain," "Hermann Sudermann," "George Ade," "The Butte Bashkirtseff," "Six Members of the Institute," "The Genealogy of Etiquette," "The American Magazine," "The Ulster Polonius," "An Unheeded Law-Giver," "The Blushful Mystery," "George Jean Nathan," "Portrait of an Immortal Soul," "Jack London," "Among the Avatars," "Three American Immortals." See Notes.

Typography and paper: 5½″ (5¼″) × 3½″; 27 lines per page. Running heads: recto, essay titles (pp. 11–249), 'INDEX' (p. 253); verso, 'CONTENTS' (p. 6), 'PREJU-DICES: FIRST SERIES' (pp. 10–250), 'INDEX' (pp. 252–54). Wove paper.

Binding A: Dark blue V cloth. Front: Mencken arms blindstamped. Spine, stamped in gilt: '[double rule] | PREJUDICES | [rule] | FIRST SERIES | [double rule] | H•L• MENCKEN | [double rule] | [double rule] | ALFRED•A•KNOPF | [double rule]'. Edges rough and unevenly trimmed, unstained. White end papers.

Binding B: Same as binding A but trimmed, top edge stained orange.

Dust jacket: Green on yellow paper. Front: '[double rule] | P R E J U D I C E S | [thin rule] | F I R S T　 S E R I E S | [double rule] | By H. L. M E N C K E N | [initial letter descending to second line] A COLLECTION of brief and penetrating | [fourteen further lines of the blurb] | [double rule] | ALFRED A. KNOPF [intertwined AAK] PUBLISHER, N. Y. | [double rule]'. Spine: '[double rule] | Prejudices | [rule] | First Series | [double rule] | *H. L. MENCKEN* | [double rule] | $2.00 net | [Borzoi device over rule] | [rule] | ALFRED A. | KNOPF | [rule]'. Back: '*Books by H. L. Mencken* | [five titles and blurbs]'. Front flap: 'About the Author | [biography and bibliography]'. Back flap unprinted.

Publication: Published 20 September 1919. $2.00. Copyright #A536014. 16,500 copies of Knopf printings sold.

Printing: Printed and bound by the Plimpton Press, Norwood, Mass.

Locations: GHT (binding B, dj), Harv (2 in binding B), InU-Li (binding B), LC (2 October 1919, rebound), RJS (binding B), TxU (binding A), Yale (4 in binding B, dj).

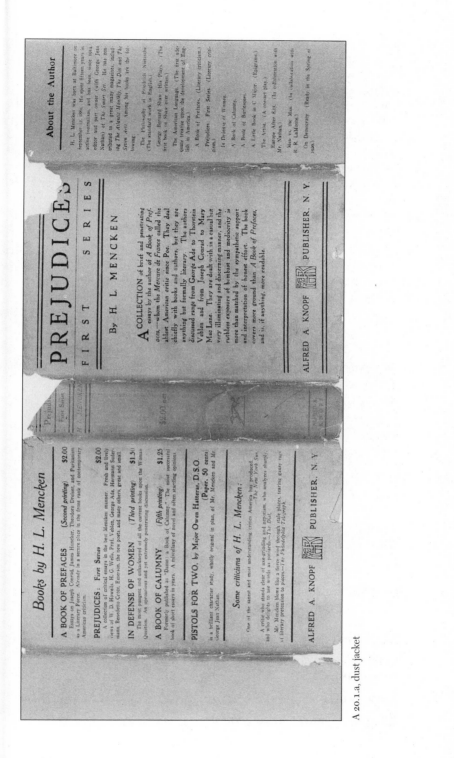

A 20.1.a, dust jacket

Notes: The copy in binding A is signed on the free front end paper. There were a few (Frey) or 50 (Blanck) uncut copies signed by Mencken. If 50, the large number points to an issue for sale, not presentation copies for the author; Mencken claimed: "from *A Book of Prefaces* onward Knopf has always given me twenty-five [free copies]" (MLAE 326). However, no other evidence suggests a separate issue for sale.

The book was "mainly made up of things that had been printed in the *Smart Set,* but I did some painstaking rewriting, and also added material from my articles in other magazines and in newspapers, and some stuff written especially for the book" (MLAE 300).

Frey says that the top edge is stained yellow in the second binding. Adler 10, 58, 158; S2.6, 14; Blanck 359; Bulsterbaum 14–16, 72; Fanfare 26; Frey 33.

Salesman's dummy: Title page lacks device, copyright page blank, 'CONTENTS' on pp. [7–8], text on pp. 9–20, the rest blank; 7⅜" × 5", trade binding. Different setting of type, and pp. 9–20 represent a different order from the trade edition: essays on "George Ade" and "The Butte Bashkirtseff." *Location:* EPL.

A 20.1.b
Second printing: New York: Knopf, [1920].

On copyright page: '*Second Printing January, 1920*'. Contains a "few slight changes" (Frey and Fanfare).

Locations: EPL, MBAt.

A 20.1.c
Third printing: New York: Knopf, [1920].

On copyright page: '*Third Printing April, 1920*'.

Location: EPL.

A 20.1.d.i
Fourth printing, American issue: New York: Knopf, [1921].

On copyright page: '*Fourth Printing March, 1921*'.

Locations: EPL, MBU.

A 20.1.d.ii
Fourth printing, English issue (1921)

Copyright page: '*First Published* 1921 | *All Rights Reserved* | *Printed in the United States of America*'

7½" × 5 1/16": [1–8] 9–254 [255–56] = 256 pp.

[1]^8 ($\pm 1_2$) [2–16]^8 = 128 leaves. The title/copyright leaf is a cancel.

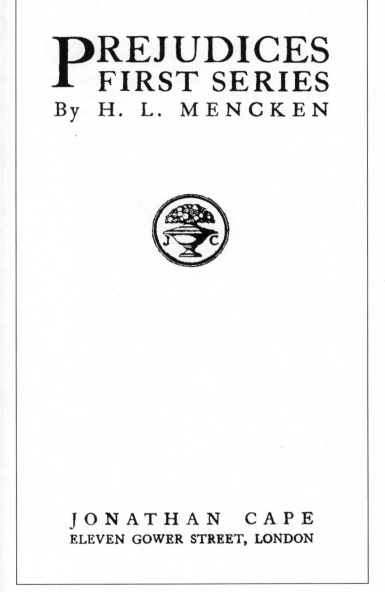

PREJUDICES
FIRST SERIES
By H. L. MENCKEN

JONATHAN CAPE
ELEVEN GOWER STREET, LONDON

A 20.1.d.ii

Contents: p. 1: half title; p. 2: blank; p. 3: title; p. 4: copyright; pp. 5–6: 'CONTENTS'; p. 7: half title; p. 8: blank; pp. 9–250: text: as in first printing; pp. 251–54: 'INDEX'; pp. 255–56: blank.

Typography and paper: Typography same as in first printing. Wove paper.

Binding: Very smooth yellow V cloth stamped in black. Front: 'PREJUDICES | FIRST SERIES | BY H. L. MENCKEN'. Spine: 'PREJUDICES | FIRST SERIES | H. L. MENCKEN | JONATHAN CAPE'. Top edge trimmed and stained yellow, fore and bottom edges rough and unevenly trimmed. White end papers.

Dust jacket: Ivory paper. Front: 'PREJUDICES | FIRST SERIES | BY H. L. MENCKEN | [blurb from G. B. Shaw in seven lines] | [JC device in circle] | *Published by* JONATHAN CAPE *London*'. Spine: '[bar over rule] | PREJUDICES | FIRST SERIES | H.L. MENCKEN | [JC device in circle] | JONATHAN CAPE | [rule over bar]'. Back: ad and blurb for *Mitch Miller,* by Edgar Lee Masters. Front flap: ad for *This Simian World,* by Clarence Day Jr. Back flap: invitation to be put on mailing list.

Publication: Published June 1921 (ECB 11.1018). 7s.6d.

Locations: BL (10 JUN 21), Bod (JUN. 1921), Camb (JU 17 | 1921), EPL, dj via KK, GHT, InU-Li, RJS, Yale.

Notes: The stamping on the covers is uniform with that of the second series printed by Cape, but not with that of the remaining four. Adler 10. The TxU copy is an English issue of some later American printing, with an integral title leaf. Its title and copyright pages have been reset; the first leaf of the first gathering is missing (its conjugate, pp. 15–16, may or may not have been tipped in); the printing on the covers is different, and a JC device appears on the back; and it has red and yellow-orange "wallpaper" end papers. The earliest known example of these end papers is in the fourth American printing of *Prejudices: Second Series* (February 1923; A 24.1.d).

A 20.1.e
Fifth printing: New York: Knopf, [1921].

On copyright page: '*Fifth Printing December, 1921*'.

Location: EPL.

A 20.1.f
Sixth printing: New York: Knopf, [1923].

Borzoi Pocket Book. On copyright page: '*Popular Edition, Published February, 1923*'.

Locations: EPL, GHT, MBU.

A 20.1.g
Seventh printing: New York: Knopf, [1923].

On copyright page: '*Sixth Printing, March, 1923*'.

Location: EPL.

A 20.1.h
Eighth printing: New York: Knopf, [1923].

Second Borzoi Pocket Book printing. On copyright page: '*Second Printing, November, 1923*'.

Locations: EPL, MChB.

A 20.1.i
Ninth printing: New York: Knopf, [1924].

On copyright page: '*Seventh Printing, August, 1924*'. Some copies noted in Borzoi boards design #18; EPL copy received by Mencken in 1924.

Location: EPL (2, regular and #18).

Note on sets in Borzoi boards: A boxed set of the first four series of *Prejudices* was advertised at $10 in the *American Mercury* (December 1924), xlii. According to Adler, "For the 1924 Christmas gift giving season, Knopf issued [the] first four volumes of *Prejudices* bound in Borzoi style" (10). A boxed set of the first five series was advertised, without price, in December 1926, lxxii. No *Mercury* ad could be found for a set of all six, and no copy of the lone Knopf trade printing of *Prejudices: Sixth Series* was located in Borzoi boards. The front dust jacket flap of *Selected Prejudices* (September 1927; AA 3) offers all six, boxed, for $15, but the front of the dust jacket for *Prejudices: Sixth Series* (October 1927; A 36) and the back of the dust jacket for *Treatise on the Gods* (1930; A 40) offer only the first five, at $12.50. None of the *Prejudices* in these sets was found in a jacket.

A 20.1.j
Tenth printing: New York: Knopf, [1924].

Third Borzoi Pocket Book printing. On copyright page: '*Third Printing, October, 1924*'.

Location: EPL.

A 20.1.k
Eleventh printing: New York: Knopf, [1924].

Title page partly in red-orange. On copyright page: '*Eighth Printing, November, 1924*'. Some copies noted in Borzoi boards design #18 (spine label in gold ink).

Location: D (regular), EPL (regular), GHT (2, regular and #18), JRS (#18).

A 20.1.l
Twelfth printing: New York: Knopf, [1926].

On copyright page: '*Ninth Printing, May, 1926*'. Some copies noted in Borzoi boards design #1.

Locations: D (#1), EPL (regular), GHT (#1), Harv (regular), NjP (#1), RJS (#1).

A 20.1.m
Thirteenth printing: New York: Knopf, [1926].

Fourth Borzoi Pocket Book printing. On copyright page: '*Fourth Printing, August, 1926*'.

Locations: EPL, Harv.

A 20.1.n
Fourteenth printing: New York: Knopf, 1929.

On copyright page: 'PUBLISHED SEPTEMBER, 1919 | REPRINTED TWELVE TIMES | NEW POCKET BOOK EDITION, APRIL, 1929'. Two bindings: green cloth with silver stamping; ecru buckram with black stamping. The plates were melted in 1933 (MLAE 301).

Locations: EPL (2, both), GHT (2, both), Harv (ecru).

LATER REPRINTINGS WITHIN THE ONLY EDITION

A 20.1.o
New York: Octagon, 1977.

Locations: EPL, Harv.

A 20.1.p
New York: Octagon, 1985.

Location: MChB.

A 20.1.q
New York: Octagon, 1987.

Location: MCR.

A 21 HELIOGABALUS

A 21.1.a
Only edition, presumed first printing (1920)

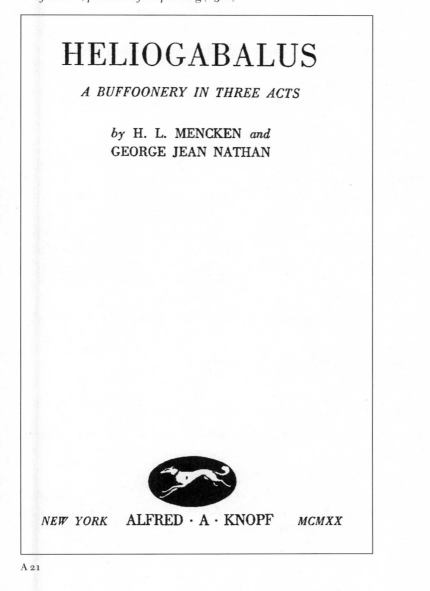

HELIOGABALUS

A BUFFOONERY IN THREE ACTS

by H. L. MENCKEN *and*
GEORGE JEAN NATHAN

NEW YORK ALFRED · A · KNOPF *MCMXX*

A 21

Copyright page: 'COPYRIGHT, 1920, BY | H. L. MENCKEN *and* | GEORGE JEAN NATHAN | All rights reserved, including that of translation into foreign | languages, including the Scandinavian. | [eighteen-line warning against unauthorized perfor- mance: 'In its present form this play is dedicated to the reading | . . . | Statutes, Title 60, Chap. 3.'] | PRINTED IN THE UNITED STATES OF AMERICA'

Statement of limitation: 'OF THIS BOOK SIXTY COPIES HAVE BEEN PRINTED | ON IMPERIAL JAPAN VELLUM AND AUTOGRAPHED | BY THE AUTHORS. FIFTY COPIES ONLY ARE FOR | SALE. THIS IS NUMBER _____ [number written in red; signatures below]'

$7^{13}/_{16}'' \times 5^{1}/_{4}''$: [1–4] 5 [6] 7 [8–10] 11–70 [71–72] 73–133 [134–36] 137–83 [184] = 184 pp.

[1–11]⁸ [12]⁴ = 92 leaves.

Contents: p. 1: half title; p. 2: limitation notice; p. 3: title; p. 4: copyright; p. 5: 'DRAMATIS PERSONÆ'; p. 6: blank; p. 7: scenes and times of the three acts; p. 8: blank; pp. 9–183: text; p. 184: blank. Blank pages of text following divisional half titles: pp. 10, 72, 136; also blank: p. 134.

Typography and paper: $5^{15}/_{16}''$ ($5^{5}/_{8}''$) $\times 3^{1}/_{2}''$; 27 lines per page (lines vary according to dialogue and stage directions). Running heads: recto (above rule), '[act number with bracket to right] HELIOGABALUS [page number]' (pp. 13–183); verso (above rule), '[page number] HELIOGABALUS' [act number with bracket to left]' (pp. 12–182). "Imperial Japan Vellum" (wove paper).

Binding: Mottled black paper-covered boards. White parchment spine stamped in gilt: 'HELIO- | GABALUS | [short rule] | MENCKEN | & | NATHAN | ALFRED [winged A] | KNOPF'. Fore and bottom edges unevenly trimmed, some fore edges uncut, top edge gilt. White end papers.

Dust jacket: None.

Publication: Published 25 January 1920. Price unknown. Copyright #A571938.

Printing: Printed by Vail-Ballou Co., Binghamton, N.Y.; bound by the Plimpton Press, Norwood, Mass.

Locations: GHT, Harv, RJS.

Notes: Written in 1919, the play was "at least nine-tenths mine" (quoted in Adler). Mencken's copy at EPL is no. 1, signed and dated 1919 on free front end paper; no. 9 was presented to Joseph Hergesheimer (CB). The order of the three printings is unknown. Adler 25; S1.6; Bulsterbaum 6; Frey 43.

A 21.1.b
Only edition, presumed second printing

Same as A 21.1.a except:

Statement of limitation: None.

8⅛″ × 5 1/16″: [i–ii 1–4] . . . [184–88] = 190 pp.

[1]⁶ (1₄ + 1) [2–12]⁸ = 95 leaves. The leaf with pp. 7–8 is tipped in to p. 6.

Contents: pp. i–ii, 1–2: blank; p. 3: title; . . . ; pp. 184–88: blank.

Typography and paper: Laid paper.

Binding: Tan paper printed in brown. Front: 'HELIOGABALUS | *by* H. L. MENCKEN *and* | GEORGE JEAN NATHAN'. Spine printed as above but in brown. Trimmed. No end papers.

Locations: EPL, GHT, InU-Li, LC (7 August 1920, original wrappers recased).

Notes: 150 (MLAE 291) or 200 copies (Frey 44, echoed by Adler 26) were given to the authors; none was for sale. Frey refers to this as an "acting edition," but Mencken never intended the play to be performed. The InU-Li copy is inscribed to Louis Untermeyer: "Dear Louis   An early extra-special edition for connoisseurs only, not for sale. Yours H. L. Mencken 1919". A copy was reportedly inscribed by Mencken "Prosit Neujahr, 1920!" (D).

A 21.1.c
Only edition, presumed third printing

Same as A 21.1.b except:

Statement of limitation: 'OF THIS BOOK TWO THOUSAND COPIES HAVE BEEN | PRINTED FROM TYPE AND THE TYPE DISTRIBUTED. | THIS IS NUMBER [following number handstamped in red]'

8 1/16″ × 5 3/16″: [i–iv 1–4] . . . [184–88] = 192 pp.

[1–12]⁸ = 96 leaves.

Contents: pp. i–iv: blank; p. 1: half title; p. 2: limitation notice; p. 3: title; . . . ; pp. 184–88: blank.

Binding: Black V cloth, stamped in gilt. Front: 'HELIOGABALUS | *by* H. L. MENCKEN *and* | GEORGE JEAN NATHAN'. Spine as above except: ' . . . MENCKEN | *AND* | NATHAN . . . '. Fore and bottom edges rough trimmed; top edge stained black. White end papers.

Dust jacket: Maroon printing on white paper. Front: 'HELIOGABALUS | *A Buffoonery* | *By* | H. L. MENCKEN | *and* | GEORGE JEAN NATHAN | [next three lines in a box] This edition is limited to 2,000 numbered copies, printed | from type. The type has been distributed and any reissue | in English is most unlikely. | ALFRED A. KNOPF [intertwined AAK in box] PUBLISHER, N. Y.' Spine: 'HELIO- | GABALUS

HELIOGABALUS
A Buffoonery

By

H. L. MENCKEN
and

GEORGE JEAN NATHAN

This edition is limited to 2,000 numbered copies, printed from type. The type has been distributed and any reissue in English is most unlikely.

ALFRED A. KNOPF   PUBLISHER, N. Y.

Other Books by the same Authors

BY MR. NATHAN:

Another Book on the Theatre.
Mr. George Jean Nathan Presents.
Bottoms Up. *(Out of print.)*
A Book Without a Title.
The Popular Theatre.
Comedians All.

BY MR. MENCKEN:

Ventures Into Verse. *(Out of print.)*
George Bernard Shaw: His Plays. *(Out of print.)*
The Philosophy of Friedrich Nietzsche.
Men vs. the Man. *(Out of print.)*
A Book of Burlesques.
A Little Book in C Major. *(Out of print.)*
In Defense of Women.
A Book of Prefaces.
A Book of Calumny. *(Out of print.)*
The American Language. *(New edition ready 1921.)*
Prejudices: First Series.

BY MESSRS. NATHAN AND MENCKEN:

Europe after 8:15. *(Out of print.)*
The American Credo.

Pistols for Two, by *Major Owen Hatteras, D.S.O.*
Contents: George Jean Nathan.
H. L. Mencken.

A 21.1.c, dust jacket

| A | BUFFOONERY | *By* | H.L. | Mencken | *and* | George Jean | Nathan | [Borzoi Books logo] | ALFRED A. | KNOPF'. Back: '*Other Books by the same Authors* | [rule] | [list of twenty books]'. Flaps unprinted.

Publication: Price unknown.

Locations: GHT, Harv, InU-Li, RJS (2, dj).

Notes: All copies sold before publication (MLAE 290).

Review copy: Marked "Press Copy" on statement of limitation (D).

A 22.1.a
First edition, first printing (1920)

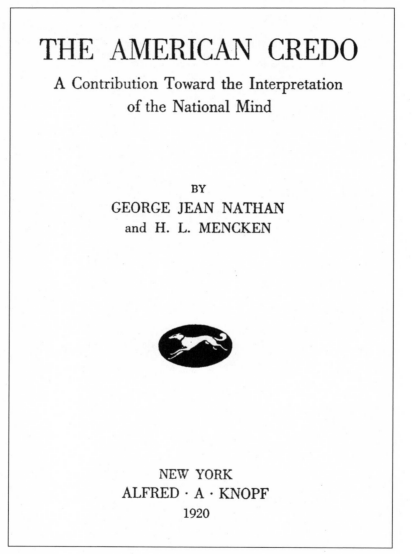

THE AMERICAN CREDO

A Contribution Toward the Interpretation
of the National Mind

BY
GEORGE JEAN NATHAN
and H. L. MENCKEN

NEW YORK
ALFRED · A · KNOPF
1920

A 22.1.a

Copyright page: 'COPYRIGHT, 1920, BY | ALFRED A. KNOPF, Inc. | PRINTED IN THE UNITED STATES OF AMERICA'

7½″ × 5⅛″: [1–6] 7–103 [104] 105 [106] 107–91 [192] = 192 pp.

[1–12]⁸ = 96 leaves.

Contents: pp. 1–2: blank; p. 3: half title; p. 4: '*BY H. L. MENCKEN AND GEORGE JEAN NATHAN* | [eleven joint and separate works]'; p. 5: title; p. 6: copyright; pp. 7–103: 'PREFACE'; p. 104: blank; p. 105: half title; p. 106: blank; pp. 107–91: text: 488 items; p. 192 blank.

Typography and paper: 5⁵⁄₁₆″ (5¹⁄₁₆″) × 3⁵⁄₁₆″; 25 lines per page. Running heads: recto and verso, 'THE AMERICAN CREDO | [bold rule]' (pp. 8–191). Wove paper.

Binding: Black V cloth, stamped in gilt. Front: 'THE AMERICAN CREDO | *By* GEORGE JEAN NATHAN | *and* H • L • MENCKEN'. Spine: 'THE | AMERICAN | CREDO | NATHAN | *and* | MENCKEN | ALFRED [winged A] | KNOPF'. Back: Borzoi Books logo blindstamped. Top edge trimmed and stained black, fore and bottom edges rough trimmed. White end papers.

Dust jacket: Yellow paper printed in red. Front: 'THE | AMERICAN | CREDO | [bold rule] | By GEORGE JEAN NATHAN | *and* H. L. MENCKEN | [in a box] A Contribution toward | the Interpretation of | the National Mind | [below box] ALFRED A. [period slightly raised] KNOPF [intertwined AAK in box] PUBLISHER, N. Y.' Spine: 'THE | AMERICAN | CREDO | NATHAN | *and* | MENCKEN | [Borzoi Books logo] | ALFRED A. | KNOPF'. Back: '*Other Books by the same Authors* | [rule] | [twenty titles]'. Flaps unprinted.

Publication: Published 6 February 1920. $2 (*PW,* 13 March 1920: 817). Copyright #A561981. 4,300 copies of the two Knopf editions sold.

Printing: Printed by Vail-Ballou Co., Binghamton, N.Y.; bound by the Plimpton Press, Norwood, Mass.

Locations: GHT, InU-Li, LC (24 February 1920), NjP, RJS, Yale (dj).

Notes: Mencken wrote the long preface and "at least half" the 488 articles (MLAE 323). Four-page ad for Nathan's books laid into SL copy. For their privately printed obscene addendum, see D 18. Adler 25; S2.10, 58 (West; cf. *Menckeniana* 45.16 [F. Scott Fitzgerald's contributions]; Bruccoli 259); Frey 45; Bulsterbaum 6.

A 22.1.b
First edition, second printing: New York: Octagon, 1977.

Locations: EPL, GHT.

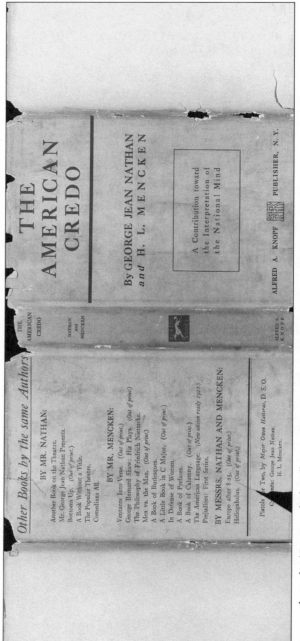

A 22.1.a, dust jacket (Courtesy of Yale Collection of American Literature, Beineke Rare Book and Manuscript Library, Yale University)

A 22.2.a
Second edition, only printing (1921)

Title page: 'THE AMERICAN CREDO | A Contribution Toward the Interpretation | of the National Mind | *Revised and Enlarged Edition* | BY | GEORGE JEAN NATHAN | and H. L. MENCKEN | [Borzoi device in oval] | NEW YORK | ALFRED • A • KNOPF | 1921'

Copyright page: 'COPYRIGHT, 1920, BY | ALFRED A. KNOPF, INC. | COPYRIGHT, 1921, BY | ALFRED A. KNOPF, INC. | PRINTED IN THE UNITED STATES OF AMERICA'

$7\%_{16}'' \times 5\frac{1}{8}''$. *First state:* [i–iv 1–2] 3–5 [6] 7–103 [104] 105 [106] 107–266 [267–68] = 272 pp. *Second state:* . . . [104–06]. . . . In the first state, the half title on p. 105 is paginated as in the first edition.

[1–17]^8 = 136 leaves.

Contents: p. i: half title; p. ii: '*BY H. L. MENCKEN AND GEORGE JEAN NATHAN* | [fifteen joint and separate works]'; p. iii: title; p. iv: copyright; p. 1: divisional half title: 'PREFACES'; p. 2: blank; pp. 3–5: 'PREFACE TO THE REVISED AND | ENLARGED EDITION'; p.6: blank; pp. 7–103: 'PREFACE TO THE FIRST EDITION'; p. 104: blank; p. 105: half title; p. 106: blank; pp. 107–266: text: 869 items; pp. 267–68: blank.

Binding: Black cloth, stamped in gilt; orange-yellow dust jacket reported (D).

Locations: Harv (second state), RJS (2, first and second states).

Notes: The preface underwent revision according to Frey; unchanged according to Adler. Entire gathering containing p. 105 reset? Adler 25; Frey 45. The original preface is partly quoted and the credos are recycled in George Jean Nathan, *The New American Credo: A Contribution Toward the Interpretation of the National Mind* (New York and London: Knopf, 1927). Adler 341; cf. MLAE 324.

A 23.1.a
Only edition, first printing (1920)

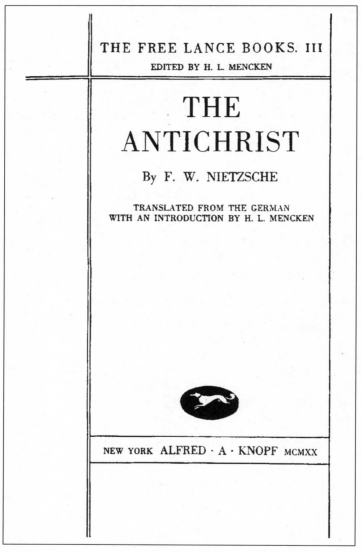

THE FREE LANCE BOOKS. III

EDITED BY H. L. MENCKEN

THE ANTICHRIST

By F. W. NIETZSCHE

TRANSLATED FROM THE GERMAN
WITH AN INTRODUCTION BY H. L. MENCKEN

NEW YORK ALFRED · A · KNOPF MCMXX

Copyright page: 'COPYRIGHT, 1920, BY | ALFRED A. KNOPF, INC. | PRINTED IN THE UNITED STATES OF AMERICA'

7³⁄₁₆″ × 5″: [1–6] 7–38 [39–40] 41–182 [183–84] = 184 pp.

[1]⁸ (± 1₂) [2–11]⁸ [12]⁴ = 92 leaves. The title/copyright leaf is a cancel.

Contents: p. 1: half title; p. 2 [in box within double-rule box]: '*THE FREE-LANCE BOOKS* [ad for first four volumes]'; p. 3: title; p. 4: copyright; p. 5: 'CONTENTS'; p. 6: blank; pp. 7–36: 'INTRODUCTION'; pp. 37–38: 'PREFACE'; p. 39: half title; p. 40: blank; pp. 41–182: text; pp. 183–84: blank.

Typography and paper: 5½″ (5¹⁄₁₆″) × 3⅛″; 25 lines per page. Running heads: recto and verso (all over bold rule), '*INTRODUCTION*' (pp. 8–36), '*PREFACE*' (p. 38), '*THE ANTICHRIST*' (pp. 42–182). Wove paper.

Binding A: Black V cloth spine; orange paper-covered boards. Front: [all within ornate border] [within box] 'III. The Antichrist | By F. W. Nietzsche | [within another box] [AAK logo] | THE FREE-LANCE BOOKS [mark] EDITED BY H. L. MENCKEN [the hyphen slants up, and the mark resembles it but has another line coming down from the raised end]'. Orange paper label on spine: '[ornamental border] | THE | ANTICHRIST | [ornament] | F. W. NIETZSCHE | 1920 | [ornamental border]'. Trimmed, unstained. White end papers.

Binding B: Same as binding A, but front unprinted and spine label dated 1921.

Dust jacket: Yellow paper printed in red. Front: [all words within double vertical rules] '[double rule passing under the verticals] | The | Antichrist | *By* F. W. NIETZSCHE | *Translated from the German by H. L. MENCKEN* | [rule] | [ten-line blurb: 'This [T descending two lines] is a new translation . . . ever written.'] | Introduction by H. L. MENCKEN | [double rule passing under the verticals] | ALFRED A. KNOPF [intertwined AAK in box] PUBLISHER, N. Y.' Spine: '[continuation of double rule] | THE | ANTI- | CHRIST | [rule] | *Nietzsche* | Introduction | by | H. L. | MENCKEN | [Borzoi Books logo] | [continuation of double rule] | ALFRED A. | KNOPF'. Back: ad for Free Lance Books. Flaps unprinted except for continuation of rules.

Publication: Published 18 February 1920. $1.75 (*PW,* 20 March 1920: 951). Copyright #A559898 (two copies received 3 March 1920). 7,300 copies of Knopf printings sold.

Printing: Printed and bound by the Plimpton Press, Norwood, Mass.

Locations: EPL (binding A), GHT (3, bindings A [2, dj] and B), RJS (binding A), Yale (binding A, dj).

Notes: A 1921 Knopf brochure advertising the Free Lance Books describes the covers as "Toyogami" (EPL). "The present translation of 'The Antichrist' is published by agreement with Dr. Oscar Levy, editor of the English edition of Nietzsche" (p. 35). Adler 26; Frey 55; Bulsterbaum 6.

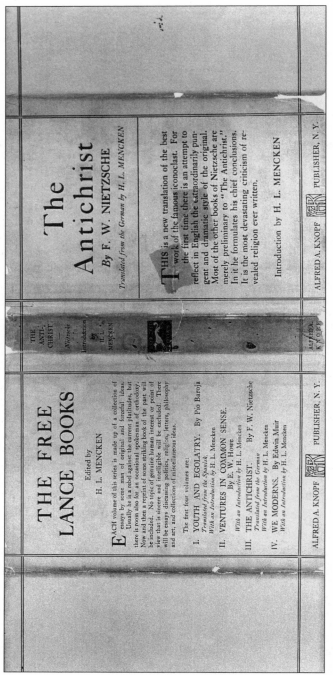

The Antichrist
By F. W. NIETZSCHE

Translated from the German by H. L. MENCKEN

THIS is a new translation of the best work of the famous iconoclast. For the first time there is an attempt to reflect in English the extraordinarily pungent and dramatic style of the original. Most of the other books of Nietzsche are merely preliminary to "The Antichrist." In it he formulates his chief conclusions. It is the most devastating criticism of revealed religion ever written.

Introduction by H. L. MENCKEN

ALFRED A. KNOPF ❦❦ PUBLISHER, N. Y.

Spine: THE ANTI-CHRIST · Nietzsche · Introduction by H. L. MENCKEN · ALFRED A. KNOPF

THE FREE LANCE BOOKS

Edited by
H. L. MENCKEN

EACH volume of this series is made up of a collection of essays by some man of original and forceful ideas. Usually he is a rebel against the current platitudes, but there is room also for an occasional spokesman of orthodoxy. Now and then a reprint of some striking book of the past will be included. No topic of genuine human interest or point of view that is sincere and intelligible will be excluded. There will be essays discussing politics, religion, letters, philosophy and art, and collections of miscellaneous ideas.

The first four volumes are:

I. YOUTH AND EGOLATRY. By Pío Baroja
   Translated from the Spanish.
   With an Introduction by H. L. Mencken

II. VENTURES IN COMMON SENSE.
   By E. W. Howe
   With an Introduction by H. L. Mencken

III. THE ANTICHRIST. By F. W. Nietzsche
   Translated from the German
   With an Introduction by H. L. Mencken

IV. WE MODERNS. By Edwin Muir
   With an Introduction by H. L. Mencken

ALFRED A. KNOPF ❦❦ PUBLISHER, N. Y.

A 23.1.a, dust jacket

A 23.1.b
Second printing: New York: Knopf, [1923].

On copyright page: '*Pocket Book Edition, Published September*, 1923'.

Locations: EPL, GHT.

A 23.1.c
Third printing: New York: Knopf, [1924].

Second printing as Borzoi Pocket Book. On copyright page: '*Second Printing, November, 1924*'.

Location: EPL.

A 23.1.d
Fourth printing: New York: Knopf, [1927].

Third printing as Borzoi Pocket Book. On copyright page: '*Third Printing, April, 1927*'. Noted in blue cloth stamped in gilt and green cloth stamped in silver.

Locations: D (blue), EPL (2, both), GHT (blue).

A 23.1.e
Fifth printing: New York: Knopf, 1931.

On copyright page: '*New edition September, 1931*'. Colophon added; bound in the *Prejudices* format.

Locations: EPL, Harv.

A 23.1.f
Sixth printing: New York: Knopf, 1941.

On copyright page: '*Published February, 1920*'; no further indication of printing history. Bound in the *Prejudices* format; styled a 'new edition' on the dust jacket.

Locations: JRS (dj), MCR.

LATER REPRINTINGS WITHIN THE ONLY EDITION

A 23.1.g
Torrance, Calif.: Noontide, 1980.

Published May 1980. Data from A23.1.h and OCLC. Not seen.

A 23.1.h
[Costa Mesa, Calif.:] Noontide, [1988].

On copyright page: 'Costa Mesa, California 92627 | Republished May, 1980 | November, 1988'.

Locations: GHT, MChB.

A 24 PREJUDICES: SECOND SERIES

A 24.1.a
Only edition, first printing (1920)

PREJUDICES
SECOND SERIES
By H. L. MENCKEN

PUBLISHED AT THE BORZOI · NEW YORK · BY
ALFRED · A · KNOPF

Copyright page: 'COPYRIGHT, 1920, BY | ALFRED A. KNOPF, INC. | PRINTED IN THE UNITED STATES OF AMERICA'

7$^{11}/_{16}$″ × 5$^1/_8$″ (binding A), 7$^3/_8$″ × 4$^{15}/_{16}$″ (binding B): [1–8] 9–248 [249–50] 251–54 [255–56] = 256 pp.

[1–16]^8 = 128 leaves.

Contents: p. 1: half title; p. 2 [all in a box within double-rule box]: '*By H. L. MENCKEN* | [fifteen titles:] PREJUDICES: FIRST SERIES | . . . | EUROPE AFTER 8:15 | [*With Mr. Nathan and W. H. Wright*]'; p. 3: title; p. 4: copyright; pp. 5–6: 'CONTENTS'; p. 7: half title; p. 8: blank; pp. 9–248: text; p. 249: divisional half title; p. 250: blank; pp. 251–54: 'INDEX'; pp. 255–56: blank.

Text: "The National Letters," "Roosevelt: An Autopsy," "The Sahara of the Bozart," "The Divine Afflatus," "Scientific Examination of a Popular Virtue," "Exeunt Omnes," "The Allied Arts," "The Cult of Hope," "The Dry Millennium," "Appendix on a Tender Theme." See Notes.

Typography and paper: 5$^{11}/_{16}$″ (5$^7/_{16}$″) × 3$^1/_2$″; 28 lines per page. Running heads: recto, essay titles (pp. 11–247), 'INDEX' (p. 253); verso, 'CONTENTS' (p. 6), '*PREJU-DICES: SECOND SERIES*' (pp. 10–248), 'INDEX' (pp. 252–54). Wove paper.

Binding A: Very dark blue V cloth. Front: Mencken arms blindstamped. Spine, stamped in gilt: '[double rule] | PREJUDICES | [rule] | SECOND SERIES | [double rule] | H•L•MENCKEN | [double rule] | [double rule] | ALFRED•A•KNOPF | [double rule]'. Edges roughly and evenly trimmed, unstained. White end papers.

Binding B: Same as binding A but trimmed, top edge stained orange.

Dust jacket: Red on green paper. Front: '[double rule] | P R E J U D I C E S | [thin rule] | S E C O N D   S E R I E S | [double rule] | B y   H. L. M E N C K E N | *Author of "A Book of Prefaces," etc.* | [fifteen-line blurb] | [double rule] | ALFRED A. KNOPF [intertwined AAK device] PUBLISHER, N. Y. | [double rule]'. Spine: '[double rule] | Prejudices | [rule] | Second Series | [double rule] | *H. L. MENCKEN* | [double rule] | [Borzoi Books logo] | [rule] | ALFRED A. | KNOPF | [rule]'. Back: four foreign blurbs. Front flap: biography and bibliography of Mencken; price $2.50. Rear flap: ad for first four Free Lance Books.

Publication: Published 27 October 1920. $2.50. Copyright #A604185. 7,600 copies of Knopf printings sold.

Printing: Printed and bound by the Plimpton Press, Norwood, Mass.

Locations: CSdS (binding A), Harv (2 in binding B), InU-Li (binding B), LC (17 November 1920, binding B), MBU (binding B), NhD (binding A), RJS (binding B), TxU (binding A), Yale (4 in binding B, dj).

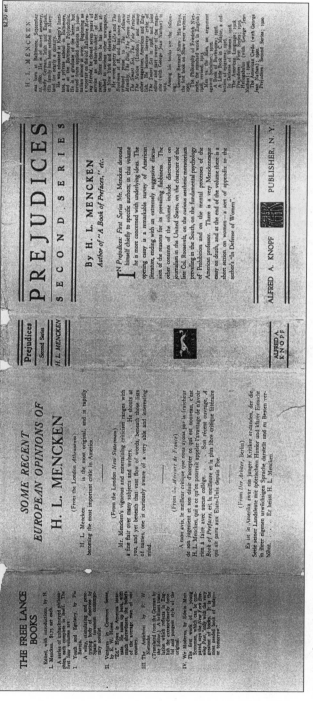

A 24.1.a, dust jacket

Notes: Copies in binding A signed on free front end paper. A few (Frey) or 25 (notation in the CSdS copy) uncut copies were signed by Mencken. No evidence suggests that this was a separate issue for sale.

The book "opened with a 93-page blast entitled 'The National Letters,' mainly made up of reworkings of my *Smart Set* reviews and my contributions to 'Repetition Generale,' but it also included some surplus material left out of the 1922 revision of *In Defense of Women,* under way in 1921, and some revisions of newspaper articles—for example, 'The Sahara of the Bozart,' from the New York *Evening Mail,* and 'The Divine Afflatus' from the same paper. 'Exeunt Omnes' came from the *Smart Set* for December, 1919, and 'Roosevelt: An Autopsy' was mainly lifted from my book article in the issue for March, 1920. 'The National Letters' was based upon an article called 'The National Literature' which I contributed to the *Yale Review* for June, 1920, but there was material in it from 'Observations Upon the National Letters' in the *Smart Set* for July of the same year, 'Notes and Queries' in the issue for September, and various other book articles" (MLAE 316).

Frey says that the top edge in the second binding is stained yellow. Adler 10, 157; S2.7, 20; Frey 35, 52; Bulsterbaum 13, 16–17, 73.

A 24.1.b.i
Second printing, American issue: New York: Knopf, [1921].

On copyright page: '*Second printing, June, 1921*'. The printing was "slightly revised" (Frey).

Location: Harv.

A 24.1.b.ii
Second printing, English issue (1921)

Copyright page: '*First published 1921* | *All rights reserved* | *Printed in the United States of America*'

7½" × 5 1/16": [1–8] 9–248 [249–50] 251–54 [255–56] = 256 pp.

[1–16]⁸ = 128 leaves.

Contents: p. 1: half title; p. 2: blank; p. 3: title; p. 4: copyright; pp. 5–6: 'CONTENTS'; p. 7: half title; p. 8: blank; pp. 9–248: text, as in first printing; p. 249: divisional half title; p. 250: blank; pp. 251–54: 'INDEX'; pp. 255–56: blank.

Typography and paper: Typography as in first printing. Wove paper.

Binding: Yellow V cloth stamped in black. Front: 'PREJUDICES | SECOND SE-RIES | BY H. L. MENCKEN'. Spine: 'PREJUDICES | SECOND SERIES | H.L. MENCKEN | JONATHAN CAPE'. Top edge trimmed and stained yellow, fore and bottom edges rough and unevenly cut. White end papers.

PREJUDICES
SECOND SERIES
By H. L. MENCKEN

JONATHAN CAPE
11 GOWER STREET · LONDON

Dust jacket: Off-white paper. Front: 'PREJUDICES | SECOND SERIES | By H. L. MENCKEN | [eight-line blurb on *Prejudices: First Series* from the *Morning Post*] | [JC device in circle] | *Published by* Jonathan Cape, *London*'. Spine: '[thick-thin rule] | PREJUDICES | SECOND SERIES | H. L. MENCKEN | [JC device in circle] | Jonathan Cape | [thin-thick rule]'. Back: ads for four Cape books. Front flap: blurb for *First Series*; price 7s.6d. Rear flap: publisher's note.

Publication: Published September 1921 (ECB 11.1018). 7s.6d.

Locations: BL (24 JAN 22), Bod (FEB. 1922), Camb (JA 27 | 1922), GHT (dj), InU-Li, NhD, RJS.

Notes: Adler 10.

A 24.1.c
Third printing: New York: Knopf, [1922].

On copyright page: '*Third Printing, February, 1922*'.

Location: EPL.

A 24.1.d
Fourth printing: New York: Knopf, [1923].

On copyright page: '*Fourth Printing, February, 1923*'. Title page partly in red-orange. The end papers are figured red and yellow ("wallpaper").

Locations: EPL, MChB.

A 24.1.e
Fifth printing: New York: Knopf, [1923].

On copyright page: '*Fifth Printing, December, 1923*'.

Location: EPL.

A 24.1.f
Sixth printing: New York: Knopf, [1924].

On copyright page: '*Sixth Printing, October, 1924*'. Some copies noted with Borzoi boards design #19. See note on sets in Borzoi boards at A 20.1.i.

Locations: D (regular), EPL (2, regular and #19 [received by Mencken in 1924]), MChB (regular).

A 24.1.g
Seventh printing: New York: Knopf, [1924].

On copyright page: '*Seventh Printing, December, 1924*'. Some copies noted with Borzoi boards designs ##1, 2, and 19.

Locations: D (#1), D (#2), EPL (regular), GHT (2, ##2, 19), Harv (regular), NjP (#2), RJS (2, ##2, 19).

LATER REPRINTINGS WITHIN THE ONLY EDITION

A 24.1.h
New York: Octagon, 1977.

Locations: EPL, Harv.

A 24.1.i
New York: Octagon, 1985.

Location: MChB.

A 24.1.j
New York: Octagon, 1987.

Location: MCR.

A 25 A PERSONAL WORD

1921

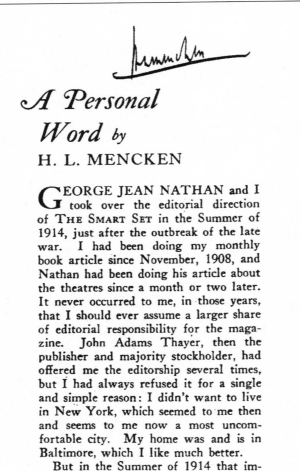

A Personal Word by
H. L. MENCKEN

GEORGE JEAN NATHAN and I took over the editorial direction of THE SMART SET in the Summer of 1914, just after the outbreak of the late war. I had been doing my monthly book article since November, 1908, and Nathan had been doing his article about the theatres since a month or two later. It never occurred to me, in those years, that I should ever assume a larger share of editorial responsibility for the magazine. John Adams Thayer, then the publisher and majority stockholder, had offered me the editorship several times, but I had always refused it for a single and simple reason: I didn't want to live in New York, which seemed to me then and seems to me now a most uncomfortable city. My home was and is in Baltimore, which I like much better.

But in the Summer of 1914 that impediment was suddenly removed. Thayer

A 25, p. [1]

Head title: 'A Personal | Word by | H. L. MENCKEN | [text follows]'

6″ × 3¼″: [1] 2–15 [16] = 16 pp.

[1]⁸ = 8 leaves.

Contents: pp. 1–16: text; p. 16: facsimile signature of Mencken.

Typography and paper: 4¹⁵⁄₁₆″ × 2⁵⁄₁₆″; 31 lines per page. No heads. Wove paper.

Binding: Self wrappers. All edges trimmed. Two staples.

Locations: EPL (2), GHT, Harv, LC.

Notes: The pamphlet "was got out early in 1921, after we had raised the news-stand price of the magazine [*Smart Set*] from twenty-five cents to thirty-five" (MLAE 197). Dated 1921 by Adler and by Mencken on an EPL copy, 1922 by Frey. Adler 10; Frey 60.

A 26 PREJUDICES: THIRD SERIES

A 26.1.a
Only edition, first printing (1922)

PREJUDICES
THIRD SERIES
By H. L. MENCKEN

PUBLISHED AT THE BORZOI · NEW YORK · BY
ALFRED · A · KNOPF

A 26.1.a

Title page: The rules, 'T H I R D   S E R I E S', and Borzoi device are dark red-orange.

Copyright page: 'COPYRIGHT, 1922, BY | ALFRED A. KNOPF, INC. | *Published, October, 1922* | *Set up, electrotyped, and printed by the Vail-Ballou Co., Binghamton, N.Y.* | *Paper furnished by W. F. Etherington & Co., New York, N.Y.* | *Bound by the Plimpton Press, Norwood, Mass.* | MANUFACTURED IN THE UNITED STATES OF AMERICA'

$7\frac{5}{16}'' \times 4\frac{15}{16}''$: [1–8] 9–328 = 328 pp.

$[1–20]^8 [21]^4$ = 164 leaves.

Contents: p. 1: half title; p. 2 [all within box inside double-rule box]: '*THE WORKS OF H. L. MENCKEN* | [sixteen titles]'; p. 3: title; p. 4: copyright; pp. 5–6: 'CONTENTS'; p. 7: half title; p. 8: blank; pp. 9–324: text; pp. 325–28: 'INDEX'. *First state:* without errata slip. *Second state:* errata slip ($6'' \times 3\frac{5}{16}''$, listing sixteen errors) following copyright page; tipped in to free front end paper in RJS copy.

Text: "On Being an American," "Huneker: A Memory," "Footnote on Criticism," "Das Kapital," "Ad Imaginem Dei Creavit Illum," "Star-Spangled Men," "The Poet and His Art," "Five Men at Random," "The Nature of Liberty," "The Novel," "The Forward-Looker," "Memorial Service," "Education," "Types of Men," "The Dismal Science," "Matters of State," "Reflections on the Drama," "Advice to Young Men," "Suite Americaine." See Notes.

Typography and paper: $5\frac{5}{8}''$ ($5\frac{7}{16}''$) $\times$ $3\frac{1}{2}''$; 28 lines per page. Running heads: recto, essay titles (pp. 11–323), '*INDEX*' (p. 327); verso, 'CONTENTS' (p. 6), '*PREJU-DICES: THIRD SERIES*' (pp. 10–324), '*INDEX*' (pp. 326–28). Both the title and the running head of chap. XIX are misspelled 'SUITE AMÉRICANE', though it is correct in the table of contents. Wove paper.

Binding: Very dark blue V cloth. Front: Mencken arms blindstamped. Spine, stamped in gilt: '[double rule] | PREJUDICES | [rule] | THIRD SERIES | [double rule] | H•L•MENCKEN | [double rule] | [double rule] | ALFRED•A•KNOPF | [double rule]'. Trimmed, top edge stained orange. White end papers.

Dust jacket: Dark red-orange on light blue paper. Front: '[double rule] | PREJU-DICES | [rule] | T H I R D   S E R I E S | [double rule] | B y   H. L. M E N C K E N | [initial letter descending to second line] IN this volume Mr. Mencken gives further | [ten lines of blurb] | are also a number of more "literary" chapters. | [double rule] | ALFRED A. KNOPF [Borzoi Books logo as light blue showing through dark red orange] PUBLISHER, N. Y. | [double rule]'. Spine: '[double rule] | Prejudices | [rule] | Third Series | [double rule] | H. L. MENCKEN | [double rule] | [Borzoi Books logo as light blue showing through dark red-orange] | [rule] | ALFRED A. | K N O P F | [rule]'. Back: ad for second edition of *The American Language*. Front flap: 'BOOKS BY THE SAME | AUTHOR | [seventeen titles] | $2.50 net'. Back flap: 'THE FREE LANCE | BOOKS | [six titles]'.

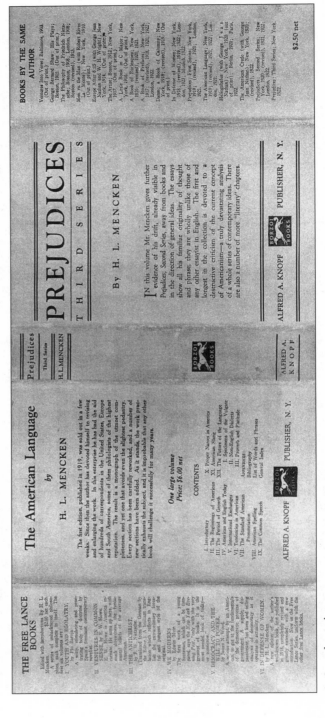

A 26.1.a, dust jacket

Publication: Published 6 October 1922. $2.50. Copyright #A686222 (two copies received 11 October 1922). 9,500 copies of Knopf printings sold.

Printing: See copyright page.

Locations: EPL (second state), Harv (3 in first state), InU-Li (second state), RJS (2, first [dj] and second states), Yale (second state).

Notes: There were a few uncut copies (Frey) or twenty-five copies not otherwise distinguished from the trade "edition" (Blanck) signed by Mencken. Harvard's Bamberger copy has written on its free front end paper (and nearly erased): "One of 25 copies signed by the Author"; the signature follows. Cf. B 67. The copy presented by Mencken to Alfred Knopf is the ordinary trade printing (EPL). Nothing in *PW* or the royalty statements at EPL indicates a limited issue. Privately printed errata sheets were later sent to friends and inserted in twenty-five copies signed for Blanche Knopf (MLAE 386).

As always in the series, the pieces generally derive from Mencken's essays and reviews in magazines and newspapers, sometimes in combination. "Footnote on Criticism," for example, is a revision of "The Motive of the Critic" (*New Republic,* 26 October 1921).

Frey says that the top edge is stained yellow. Adler 11, 140; S1.8, 9, 10, 11, 13; S2.7, 13; Frey 36; Bulsterbaum 17–19, 73; Blanck 359.

A 26.1.b
Second printing: New York: Knopf, [1922].

On copyright page: '*Second Printing, November, 1922*'. Contains the revisions on the errata slips.

Locations: EPL, Harv.

A 26.1.c.i
Third printing, American issue: New York: Knopf, [1923].

On copyright page: '*Third Printing, March, 1923*'.

Location: EPL.

A 26.1.c.ii
Third printing, English issue (1923)

Copyright page: '*First Published 1923 | All rights reserved | Printed in the United States of America*'

$7\frac{1}{2}'' \times 4^{13}\!/_{16}''$: [3–8] 9–328 = 326 pp.

$[1]^8 (-1_1, \pm 1_2) [2–20]^8 [21]^4$ = 163 leaves. The first leaf is excised; the title/copyright leaf is a cancel.

PREJUDICES
THIRD SERIES
By H. L. MENCKEN

JONATHAN CAPE
11 GOWER STREET · LONDON

A 26.1.c.ii

Contents: p. 3: title; p. 4: copyright; pp. 5–6: 'CONTENTS'; p. 7: half title; p. 8: blank; pp. 9–324: text, as in first printing; pp. 325–28: 'INDEX'.

Typography and paper: Typography same as in first printing. Wove paper.

Binding: Yellow V cloth stamped in black. Front: 'PREJUDICES | THIRD SERIES | H.L. MENCKEN'. Spine: 'PREJUDICES | THIRD SERIES | H.L. MENCKEN | JONATHAN CAPE'. Back: JC device. Trimmed, top edge stained yellow. White end papers.

Dust jacket: Off-white paper. Front: 'PREJUDICES | THIRD SERIES | H. L. Mencken | [JC device in circle] | *By the Same Author* | PREJUDICES, FIRST SERIES: PREJUDICES, SECOND SERIES | A BOOK OF BURLESQUES: IN DEFENCE OF WOMEN'. Spine: '[double rule] | PREJUDICES | THIRD SERIES | H. L. MENCKEN | [JC device in circle] | Jonathan Cape | [double rule]'. Back: ads for the four Mencken books. Front flap directs reader to back; price 7s.6d. Rear flap unprinted.

Publication: Published September 1923 (ECB 11.1018). 7s.6d.

Locations: BL (13 SEP 23), Bod (SEP | 1923), Camb (SP 25 | 1923), GHT (dj), InU-Li, KU-S, RJS.

Notes: The stamping on the covers is uniform with that of the remaining three series printed by Cape, but not with that of the first two. Adler 11.

A 26.1.d
Fourth printing: New York: Knopf, [1924].

On copyright page: '*Fourth Printing, February, 1924*'.

Location: EPL.

A 26.1.e
Fifth printing: New York: Knopf, [1924].

On copyright page: '*Fifth Printing, October, 1924*'. A stated fifth printing reportedly has been found in dust jacket stating fourth printing (D). Both noted copies are in Borzoi boards design #20. See note on sets with Borzoi boards at A 20.1.i.

Location: EPL (#20, received by Mencken in 1924), LC (#20).

A 26.1.f
Sixth printing: New York: Knopf, [1924].

On copyright page: '*Sixth Printing, December, 1924*'. All copies noted with Borzoi boards design ##2 or 21.

Locations: D (#2), GHT (2, ##2, 21), RJS (3, ##2, 21 [2]).

A 26.1.g
Seventh printing: New York: Knopf, [1926].

On copyright page: 'SEVENTH PRINTING, OCTOBER, 1926'. Copy noted in orange cloth stamped in blue.

Locations: EPL, GHT (orange), Harv.

LATER REPRINTINGS WITHIN THE ONLY EDITION

A 26.1.h
New York: Octagon, 1977.

Locations: EPL, MChB.

A 26.1.i
New York: Octagon, [1985?]

Identified by analogy with the second printing of other Octagon *Prejudices.* Not seen.

A 26.1.j
New York: Octagon, 1987.

On copyright page: '*Third Octagon printing 1987*'.

Location: MCR.

A 27 SUGGESTIONS TO OUR VISITORS

A 27.1
First edition (1922)

A 27.1, cover title

Copyright page: None.

5½″ × 3″: [1–4] = 4 pp.

[1]² = 2 leaves.

Contents: p. 1: cover title; pp. 2–4: text.

Typography and paper: 4¾″ × 2⁵⁄₁₆″; 31 lines on p. 2 (different number of lines on each page). No heads. Wove paper.

Binding: None.

Locations: EPL, GHT, RJS, Yale (2).

Notes: A leaflet, perhaps partly by George Jean Nathan, "ostensibly for the information of authors aspiring to contribute to the *Smart Set*" (MLAE 197). "I wrote nearly all of it" (quoted in Adler). Dated 1915? by Adler, 1923 by Frey, 1922 by Mencken on an EPL copy (he noted "by HLM" on another), "the 1921–1922 era" by Mencken in MLAE 197 and in his *Chrestomathy* (A 61), p. 608, where he claims authorship. Adler 6; Frey 60.

A 27.2
Second edition (1968)

Cover title: '[*Smart Set* logo in red] | GEORGE JEAN NATHAN [over] H. L. MENCKEN } *Editors* | SUGGESTIONS | [red rule] | TO OUR VISITORS | [red rule] | *Editorial Chambers:* | 25 *West 45ᵗʰ Street* | *New York*'

Copyright page: None.

Colophon: '*Printed by Grabhorn-Hoyem and presented to members of the Zam-* | *orano Club of Los Angeles and the Roxburghe Club of San Francisco* | *at their joint meeting on September 21–22,* 1968, | *Robert Grabhorn* | *Andrew Hoyem* | *Oscar Lewis*'

7½″ × 5½″: [1–8] = 8 pp.

[1]⁴ = 4 leaves.

Contents: pp. 1–2: introduction by Oscar Lewis; pp. 3–8: text; p. 8: colophon.

Binding: Grayish white paper wrappers. Front: cover title. All edges trimmed. Sewed.

Locations: EPL, InU-Li, RJS.

Notes: 150 copies (OCLC). S1.4.

A 28 THE UNDERSIGNED ANNOUNCE

1923

NEW YORK, October 10, 1923.
The undersigned announce that they are relinquishing the editorship of THE SMART SET with the issue for December, 1923, and that they have disposed of all their holdings in The Smart Set Company, Inc.

They have had this step in mind for several years; lately, on their completion of nine years' service as editors of the magazine, they decided upon it definitely. For six years before they assumed the editorship they were regular members of the staff. Thy have thus put in fifteen years of continuous service.

They are withdrawing from the work so long carried on together because they believe that, in so far as it is accomplishable at all, the purpose with which they began in 1908 has been accomplished. That purpose was to break down some of the difficulties which beset the American imaginative author, and particularly the beginning author, of that time—to provide an arena and drum up an audience for him, and to set him free from the pull of the cheap, popular magazine on the one side and of the conventional "quality" magazine, with its distressing dread of ideas, on the other—above all, to do battle for him critically, attacking vigorously all the influences which sought to intimidate and regiment him. This work is obviously no longer necessary. The young American novelist, dramatist or poet is quite free today, and the extent of his freedom is shown by the alarm and dudgeon of the pedants who still protest so vainly against it. That protest, in 1908, was yet potent and damaging; today it is only ridiculous.

The undersigned have enjoyed the combat and do not tire of it. They are not eager for a rest; they are eager for another round. But their desires and interests now lead them beyond belles lettres and so outside the proper field of THE SMART SET. They could not carry the magazine with them without changing its name, completely revolutionizing its contents, and otherwise breaking with its traditions—a business plainly full of practical difficulties. They have thought it wiser and more comfortable to withdraw from the editorship, dispose of their stock in the publishing company, and devote themselves to setting up an entirely new magazine. This they are now engaged upon in association with Mr. Alfred A. Knopf, the publisher. The new magazine will be THE AMERICAN MERCURY; its purpose will be to discuss realistically, not only American letters, but the whole field of American life. The first issue will be as of January, 1924.

George Jean Nathan

H. L. Mencken

Size: 9½″ × 5¹³⁄₁₆″ sheet printed on one side.

Contents: 'NEW YORK, October 10, 1923. | The undersigned announce that they are relinquishing the | editorship of THE SMART SET with the issue for December, | 1923, and that they have disposed of all their holdings in The | Smart Set Company, Inc. | . . . | [facsimile signatures of George Jean Nathan and Mencken at end]'

Typography and paper: 7⁹⁄₁₆″ (8¾″ with signatures) × 4⅝″; 43 lines of type. Wove paper, watermarked 'HAMMERMILL | BOND'.

Locations: EPL (4), Harv.

Notes: Mencken notes on one of the EPL copies: "by H.L.M." Adler 11; Frey 60.

A 29 PREJUDICES: FOURTH SERIES

A 29.1.a
Only edition, limited printing (1924)

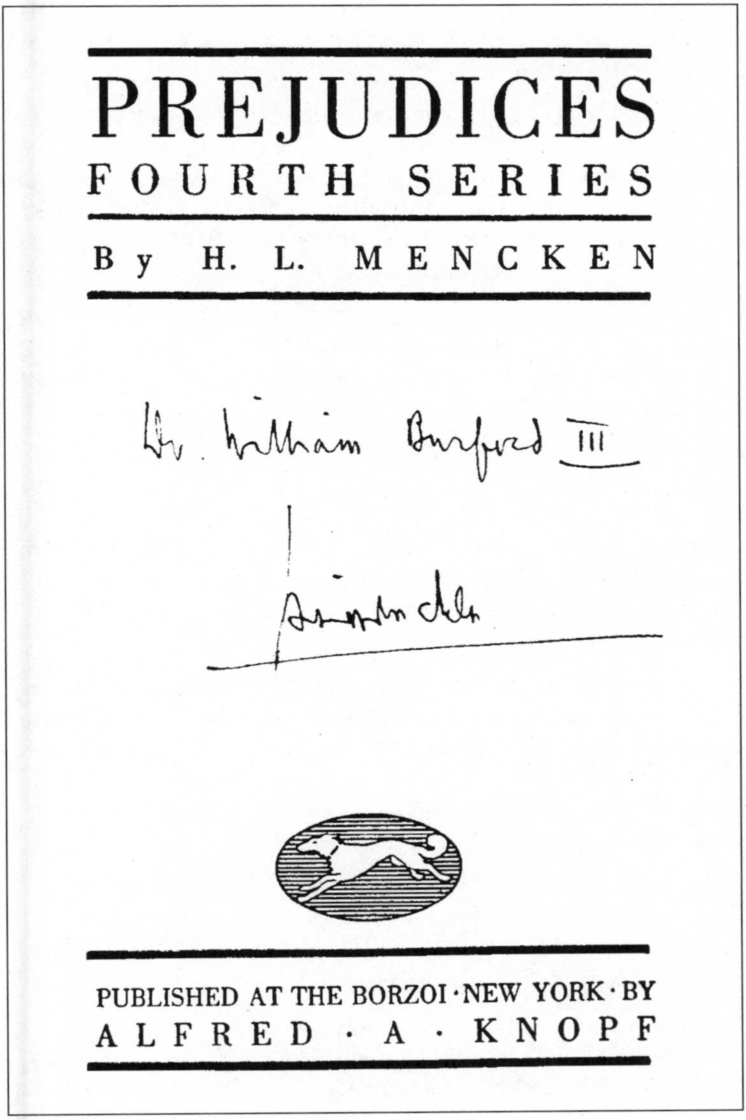

PREJUDICES

FOURTH SERIES

By H. L. MENCKEN

Dr. William Burford III

[signature]

PUBLISHED AT THE BORZOI · NEW YORK · BY
A L F R E D · A · K N O P F

A 29.1.a–b

Title page: All in black.

Copyright page: 'COPYRIGHT, 1924, BY ALFRED A. KNOPF, INC. | • PUB-LISHED, OCTOBER, 1924 • SET UP, AND | ELECTROTYPED BY THE VAIL-BALLOU PRESS, | INC., BINGHAMTON, N. Y. • PAPER FURNISHED | BY W. F. ETHERINGTON & CO., NEW YORK. | •PRINTED AND BOUND BY THE PLIMPTON PRESS, | NORWOOD, MASS.• | MANUFACTURED IN THE UNITED STATES OF AMERICA.'

Colophon: 'THE FIRST EDITION OF "PREJUDICES: | FOURTH SERIES" CONSISTS OF THIRTY-SIX | HUNDRED AND TEN COPIES AS FOLLOWS: | ONE HUNDRED AND TEN ON BORZOI WATER- | MARKED RAG PAPER, SIGNED BY THE AUTHOR | NUMBERED FROM 1 TO 110, ONE HUNDRED | OF WHICH ARE FOR SALE, AND THIRTY-FIVE | HUNDRED COPIES ON ENGLISH FEATHER- | WEIGHT WHITE PAPER.'

Statement of limitation: 'ONE HUNDRED TEN COPIES (OF WHICH ONE | HUNDRED ARE FOR SALE) HAVE BEEN | PRINTED ON BORZOI WATER-MARKED RAG | PAPER AND SIGNED BY THE AUTHOR | THIS IS NUMBER | [number handwritten] | [signature]'

9⅛" × 5⅞": [i–ii 1–8] 9–301 [302] 303–05 [306–10] = 312 pp.

[1–19]⁸ [20]⁴ = 156 leaves.

Contents: p. i: blank; p. ii: limitation; p. 1: half title; p. 2: [all in a box within double-rule box] '*THE WORKS OF H. L. MENCKEN* | [19 titles]'; p. 3: title; p. 4: copyright; pp. 5–7: 'CONTENTS'; p. 8: blank; pp. 9–301: text; p. 302: blank; pp. 303–05: 'INDEX'; p. 306: colophon; pp. 307–10: blank.

Text: "The American Tradition," "The Husbandman," "High and Ghostly Matters," "Justice Under Democracy," "Reflections on Human Monogamy," "The Politician," "From a Critic's Notebook," "Totentanz," "Meditations in the Methodist Desert," "Essay in Constructive Criticism," "On the Nature of Man," "Bugaboo," "On Govern-ment," "Toward a Realistic Aesthetic," "Contributions to the Study of Vulgar Psychol-ogy," "The American Novel," "People and Things." See Notes.

Typography and paper: 5¹¹⁄₁₆" (5⁷⁄₁₆") × 3½"; 28 lines per page. Running heads: recto, 'CONTENTS' (p. 5), essay titles (pp. 11–301), '*INDEX*' (p. 305); verso, 'CON-TENTS' (p. 4), '*PREJUDICES: FOURTH SERIES*' (pp. 10–300), '*INDEX*' (p. 304). Laid paper, watermarked with Borzoi Books logo.

Binding A: Orange and yellow on white paper-covered boards (design #14). Smooth blue V cloth spine with yellow paper label printed in blue: '[ornamental border] | PREJUDICES | FOURTH | SERIES | [ornament] | H. L. | MENCKEN | [ornamen-tal border]'. Edges rough and unevenly cut, unstained. White end papers. Spare label attached to rear pastedown. In cardboard box covered by blue paper, label on "spine" as on book, with limitation number written below bottom border.

Binding B: Same as binding A except green and yellow paper-covered boards.

Dust jacket: None reported or found.

Publication: Published 24 October 1924. Price unknown. Copyright #A807734 (two copies received 10 November 1924). 8,100 copies of Knopf printings sold.

Printing: See copyright page.

Locations: EPL (2, bindings A and B), GHT (binding A), Harv (binding A).

Notes: According to the copyright notice of the trade printing, the copies were numbered 'FROM 1 TO 100, AND A | TO J'. Lettered copies not seen. Signed errata slip (in RJS collection and laid into GHT copy); probably printed by Mencken and not Knopf. The slip ($5\frac{7}{16}'' \times 4\frac{3}{16}''$) lists errors on nineteen pages. An unsigned example is pasted on the first leaf of Mencken's copy (unnumbered) (EPL).

As in the previous volumes of the series, the pieces generally derive from Mencken's essays and reviews in magazines and newspapers, sometimes in combination. "The American Tradition," for example, in its first form was "The Nordic Blond Renaissance," appearing in the Baltimore *Evening Sun* (16 July 1923) and as a separate publication (E 13). Adler 11; S2.7, 14, 20; Frey 38; Bulsterbaum 19–20, 74; Blanck 359.

A 29.1.b
Only edition, first trade printing

Same as A 29.1.a except:

Title page: The rules, 'F O U R T H   S E R I E S', and Borzoi device are red.

Copyright page: 'COPYRIGHT, 1924, BY ALFRED A. KNOPF, | INC. • PUB-LISHED, OCTOBER, 1924 • SET UP, | AND ELECTROTYPED BY THE VAIL-BALLOU | PRESS, INC., BINGHAMTON, N. Y. • PAPER | FURNISHED BY W. F. ETHERINGTON & CO., | NEW YORK. • PRINTED AND BOUND BY THE | PLIMPTON PRESS, NORWOOD, MASS. • | THE FIRST EDITION OF "PREJU-DICES: FOURTH SERIES" | CONSISTS OF THIRTY-SIX HUNDRED AND TEN COPIES AS FOL- | LOWS: ONE HUNDRED AND TEN ON BORZOI ALL RAG PAPER | SIGNED BY THE AUTHOR NUMBERED FROM 1 TO 100, AND A | TO J; AND THIRTY-FIVE HUNDRED COPIES ON ENGLISH FEATHER- | WEIGHT PAPER. | MANUFACTURED IN THE UNITED STATES OF AMERICA'

Colophon and statement of limitation: None.

$7\frac{5}{16}'' \times 5''$: [i–ii 1–8] . . . [306] = 308 pp.

$[1]^2 [2–20]^8$ = 154 leaves.

A 29.1.b, dust jacket

Contents: p. i: half title; p. ii: '. . . *THE WORKS* . . .'; p. 1: title; p. 2: copyright; pp. 3–5: 'CONTENTS'; p. 6: blank; p. 7: half title; p. 8: blank; pp. 9–301: text; p. 302: blank; pp. 303–05: 'INDEX'; p. 306: blank.

Typography and paper: Wove paper.

Binding: Very dark blue V cloth. Front: the Mencken arms blindstamped. Spine, stamped in gilt: '[double rule] | PREJUDICES | [rule] | FOURTH SERIES | [double rule] | H•L•MENCKEN | [double rule] | [double rule] | ALFRED•A•KNOPF | [double rule]'. Trimmed, top edge stained orange. Red-orange and yellow "wallpaper" end papers, white on sides facing pages.

Dust jacket: Red-orange on ecru paper. Front: '[double rule] | PREJUDICES | [rule] | F O U R T H   S E R I E S | [double rule] | [nine-line blurb for the series] | PREJUDICES: FIRST SERIES, *7th Printing* | PREJUDICES: SECOND SERIES, *5th Printing* | PREJUDICES: THIRD SERIES, *4th Printing* | [double rule] | ALFRED A. KNOPF [Borzoi Books logo] PUBLISHER, N.Y.' Spine: '[double rule] | PREJU-DICES | [rule] | FOURTH SERIES | [double rule] | H. L. | MENCKEN | [double rule] | [Borzoi Books logo] | [rule] | ALFRED A. | KNOPF | [double rule]'. Back: 'THE FREE | LANCE BOOKS | Edited by H. L. MENCKEN | [double rule] | [eight-line blurb] | The first five volumes are: | [list of the *six* volumes and Knopf imprint]'. Front flap: list of 'BOOKS BY THE SAME | AUTHOR'; price $2.50. Back flap: a subscription form for *The American Mercury.*

Publication: $2.50.

Locations: GHT (dj), Harv (2), InU-Li, RJS (2, dj).

Notes: Errata slip reported in some copies (Adler, Blanck, D); none in the trade copies at EPL. Sheet advertising *American Mercury* (B 49) laid in GHT and RAW copies.

A 29.1.c
Second trade printing: New York: Knopf, [1924].

On copyright page: 'FIRST AND SECOND PRINTING BEFORE PUBLICA-TION'. Sheet advertising *American Mercury* laid in GHT copy. One copy noted with Borzoi boards design #4. See note on sets in Borzoi boards at A 20.1.i. An undeter-mined printing (bound without title/copyright leaf) was noted with design #13 (D, RJS).

Locations: EPL (regular), GHT (2, regular and #4), Harv (regular).

A 29.1.d
Third trade printing: New York: Knopf, [1924].

On copyright page: 'THIRD PRINTING, NOVEMBER, 1924'. Errors corrected in this printing. Some copies noted with Borzoi boards designs ##3 and 4A.

Locations: EPL (regular), GHT (#4A), MBU (regular), MChB (regular), NjP (#3).

A 29.1.e.i
Fourth trade printing, American issue: New York: Knopf, [1925].

On copyright page: 'FOURTH PRINTING, SEPTEMBER, 1925'. Some copies noted with Borzoi boards designs ##3 and 4A.

Locations: EPL (regular), GHT (#3), RJS (2 in #4A).

A 29.1.e.ii
Fourth trade printing, English issue (1925)

Copyright page: '*First Published 1925 | All rights reserved | Printed in U.S.A.*'

$7\frac{3}{8}'' \times 4\frac{3}{4}''$: [1–8] 9–301 [302] 303–05 [306] = 306 pp.

$[1]^8$ $(1 + 1_1)$ $[2–19]^8$ = 153 leaves. The title/copyright leaf is tipped in, recto to free front end paper, stub to p. 3.

Contents: p. 1: title; p. 2: copyright; pp. 3–5: 'CONTENTS'; p. 6: blank; p. 7: half title; p. 8: blank; pp. 9–301: text, same as in limited printing; p. 302: blank; pp. 303–05: 'INDEX'; p. 306: blank.

Typography and paper: Typography as in limited printing. Wove paper.

Binding: Yellow V cloth stamped in black. Front: 'PREJUDICES | FOURTH SE-RIES | H.L. MENCKEN'. Spine: 'PREJUDICES | FOURTH SERIES | H.L. MENCKEN | JONATHAN CAPE'. Back: JC device. Trimmed, top edge stained? Red and yellow "wallpaper" end papers, white on sides facing pages.

Dust jacket: Off-white paper. Front: 'PREJUDICES | FOURTH SERIES | H. L. Mencken | [JC device in circle] | *By the Same Author* | PREJUDICES, FIRST SERIES : PREJUDICES, SECOND SERIES | PREJUDICES, THIRD SERIES : A BOOK OF BURLESQUES | IN DEFENCE OF WOMEN'. Spine: '[double rule] | PREJUDICES | FOURTH SERIES | H. L. MENCKEN | [JC device in circle] | Jonathan Cape | [double rule]'. Back: ads for four of the five Mencken volumes. Front flap directs reader to back; price 7s.6d. Rear flap unprinted.

Publication: Published October 1925 (ECB 11.1018). 7s.6d.

Locations: BL (25 SEP 25), Camb (26 SP | 1925), EPL, GHT (dj), MeWC.

Notes: Cape moved from Gower Street to Bedford Square on 19 January 1925. Adler 11.

PREJUDICES
FOURTH SERIES
By H. L. MENCKEN

JONATHAN CAPE
30 BEDFORD SQUARE LONDON

A 29.1.e.ii

Review copy: Trade printing stamped in purple on title page: 'REVIEW COPY.' *Location:* Bod (SEP | 29 | 1925).

A 29.1.f
Fifth trade printing: New York: Knopf, [1927].

On copyright page: 'FIFTH PRINTING, JUNE, 1927'. Copy noted in orange cloth stamped in blue.

Locations: EPL, GHT (orange), InU-Li.

LATER REPRINTINGS WITHIN THE ONLY EDITION

A 29.1.g
New York: Octagon, 1977.

Locations: EPL, Harv.

A 29.1.h
New York: Octagon, 1985

Location: MChB.

A 29.1.i
New York: Octagon, [1987?]

Identified by analogy with the third printing of other Octagon *Prejudices*. Not seen.

A 30 AMERICANA 1925

A 30.1.a
First edition, only English printing (1925)

AMERICANA

1925

EDITED BY
H. L. MENCKEN
Editor of THE AMERICAN MERCURY

LONDON: MARTIN HOPKINSON & CO.
LTD., 14 HENRIETTA STREET, COVENT
GARDEN, W.C.2   1925

Copyright page: 'Copyright, 1925, *by Alfred A. Knopf Inc.* | PRINTED IN GREAT BRITAIN. | CHISWICK PRESS: CHARLES WHITTINGHAM AND GRIGGS (PRINTERS), LTD. | TOOKS COURT, CHANCERY LANE, LONDON.'

Colophon: [at the bottom of p. 309 is repeated from the copyright page:] 'CHISWICK . . . LONDON.'

8⁹⁄₁₆″ × 5½″: [i–iv] v–vii [viii] ix–x [xi–xii] 1–308 [309–12] = 324 pp.

[a]⁴ b² B–I⁸ K–U⁸ X⁴ = 162 leaves.

Contents: p. i: half title; p. ii: blank; p. iii: title; p. iv: copyright; pp. v–vii: 'PREFACE'; p. viii: blank; pp. ix–x: 'CONTENTS'; p. xi: half title; p. xii: blank; pp. 1–286: text; pp. 287–300: '[between rules] NOTES FOR FOREIGN STUDENTS'; pp. 301–09: '[between rules] GLOSSARY'; pp. 310–12: ads for twenty-one titles from 'DAI NIHON' to 'THE LORETTE SYSTEM OF PRUNING'.

Typography and paper: 6⅜″ (6″) × 3⅞″; 30 lines per page (lines vary with amount of reduced type). Running heads: recto, 'PREFACE' (p. vii), chapter titles (pp. 3–285), 'NOTES FOR FOREIGN STUDENTS | [rule]' (pp. 289–99), 'GLOSSARY | [rule]' (pp. 303–09); verso, 'PREFACE' (p. vi), 'CONTENTS' (p. x), 'AMERICANA 1925 | [rule]' (pp. 2–308). Wove paper.

Binding: Coarse blue V cloth stamped in gilt on spine: 'AMERICANA | 1925 | [short rule] | H.L.MENCKEN | HOPKINSON'. Trimmed, unstained. White end papers.

Dust jacket: Black and gray on off-white paper. Front: [all within double-rule box] '[man leaning against bar] | [next three lines in box as white showing through] AMERICANA | 1925 | *Edited by* H.L.Mencken | [in box beneath double-rule box] LONDON: MARTIN HOPKINSON & CO.Lᵀᴰ·'. Spine: '[rule] | Americana | 1925 | [ornament] | H. L. MENCKEN | HOPKINSON | [rule]'. Back: [all within box] '*A Self Portrait of the American People* | [rule] | [blurb for the book]'. Front flap: '*7s. 6d. net*'. Rear flap unprinted.

Publication: Published November 1925 (ECB 11.1018). 7s.6d.

Locations: BL (19 NOV 25), Bod (NOV | 21 | 1925), Camb (21 NO | 1925), EPL, GHT (dj), InU-Li, RJS (2, dj).

Notes: The text consists of contributions to the *American Mercury* edited by Mencken. This edition preceded the American, according to Mencken in MLAE 380, but note the dates of publication. Adler 28; Bulsterbaum 74.

A 30.2.a
Second (first American) edition, first printing (1925)

Copyright page: 'COPYRIGHT, 1925, BY ALFRED A. KNOPF, INC. | MANUFACTURED IN THE UNITED STATES OF AMERICA'

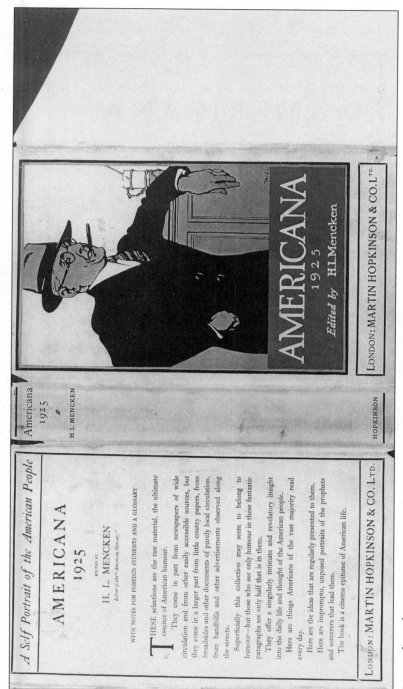

A Self Portrait of the American People

AMERICANA
1925

EDITED BY

H. L. MENCKEN
Editor of the "American Mercury"

WITH NOTES FOR FOREIGN STUDENTS AND A GLOSSARY

THESE selections are the raw material, the ultimate essence of American humour.

They come in part from newspapers of wide circulation and from other easily accessible sources, but they come in a larger part from little county papers, from broadsides and other documents of purely local circulation, from handbills and other advertisements observed along the streets.

Superficially this collection may seem to belong to humour—but those who see only humour in these fantastic paragraphs see only half that is in them.

They offer a singularly intimate and revelatory insight into the daily life and thought of the American people.

Here are things Americans of the vast majority read every day.

Here are the ideas that are regularly presented to them.

Here are impromptu, unposed portraits of the prophets and sorcerers that lead them.

The book is a cinema epitome of American life.

LONDON: MARTIN HOPKINSON & CO. LTD.

A 30.1.a, dust jacket

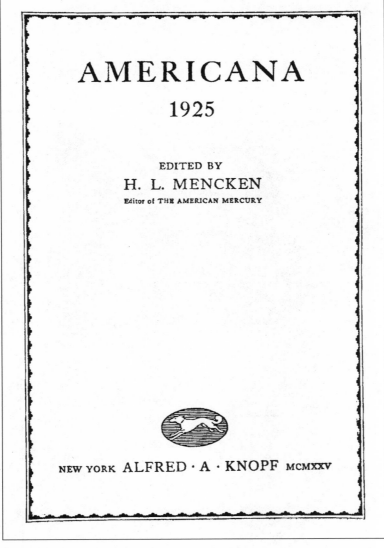

AMERICANA

1925

EDITED BY

H. L. MENCKEN

Editor of THE AMERICAN MERCURY

NEW YORK ALFRED · A · KNOPF MCMXXV

8⅜″ × 5½″ (binding A), 8³⁄₁₆″ × 5½″ (binding B): [i–iv] v–vii [viii] ix–x [xi–xii] 1–311 [312] = 324 pp.

[1–19]⁸ [20]¹⁰ = 162 leaves.

Contents: p. i: half title; p. ii: blank; p. iii: title; p. iv: copyright; pp. v–vii: 'PREFACE'; p. viii: blank; pp. ix–x: 'CONTENTS'; p. xi: half title; p. xii: blank; pp. 1–286: text; pp. 287–302: '[between rules] NOTES FOR FOREIGN STUDENTS'; pp. 303–11: '[between rules] GLOSSARY'; p. 312: blank.

Typography and paper: 6″ (5¹¹⁄₁₆″) × 3¹³⁄₁₆″; 30 lines per page (lines vary with number of items on page and amount of reduced type). Running heads: recto, 'PREFACE' (p. vii), chapter titles (pp. 3–285), 'NOTES FOR FOREIGN STUDENTS | [rule]' (pp. 289–301), 'GLOSSARY | [rule]' (pp. 305–11); verso, 'PREFACE' (p. vi), 'CONTENTS' (p. x), 'AMERICANA 1925 | [rule]' (pp. 2–310). Wove paper.

Binding A: Black V cloth stamped in gilt. Front: 'AMERICANA | 1925'. Spine: 'AMERICANA | 1925 | *Edited by* | H. L. | MENCKEN | ALFRED [winged A] KNOPF'. Back: Borzoi Books logo blindstamped. Edges untrimmed, unstained. White end papers.

Binding B: Same as binding A but top edge trimmed and stained blue, fore edge rough trimmed, bottom edge partly uncut.

Dust jacket, binding A: The GHT copy is in an unprinted brown jacket evenly bevelled on all four corners; its offset shadow was noted on the pastedowns and end papers of an unjacketed example.

Dust jacket, binding B: Green on gray paper. Front: '*THE PERFECT WEEK-END BOOK!* | [rule] | AMERICANA | 1925 | EDITED BY | H. L. MENCKEN | EDITOR OF *THE AMERICAN MERCURY* | [rule] | [nine-line blurb] | [rule] | ALFRED A. KNOPF [Borzoi Books logo] PUBLISHER, N. Y.' Spine: '[rule] | AMERICANA | 1925 | *Edited by* | H. L. | MENCKEN | [rule] | [Borzoi Books logo] | [rule] | *Alfred A. Knopf*'. Back: '[AM logo] THE [AM logo] | AMERICAN | MERCURY | [ad and subscription form]'. Front flap: list of '*Other books by* | H. L. MENCKEN'; price $2.50. Back flap: form to place one on the mailing list for *The Borzoi Broadside*.

Publication: Published 30 October 1925. $2.50. Copyright #A869972. 2,700 copies of Knopf printings sold.

Printing: Printed by Vail-Ballou Co., Binghamton, N.Y.; bound by H. Wolff Estate, New York.

Locations: GHT (2, bindings A and B in dj), Harv (2, bindings A and B), InU-Li (binding B, dj), LC (9 November 1925, rebound), RJS (3 in binding B, dj).

Notes: 50 signed copies, according to Blanck (360); the Harvard and GHT copies in binding A are signed on the free front end paper. On the question whether that is a

A 30.2.a, binding B, dust jacket

true issue or for author's presentation only, see Notes to A 20.1.a. Nothing else suggests that it was a separate issue for sale. Prospectus and subscription form for *The American Mercury* laid in (RAW, D).

A 30.2.b
Second edition, second printing: New York: Knopf, MCMXXV.

On copyright page: 'SECOND PRINTING, NOVEMBER, 1925'. Black cloth, gilt lettering (8⅛″ × 5¼″, top trimmed and stained blue, other edges rough trimmed) or green lettering (8″ × 5¼″, trimmed and unstained).

Location: GHT (2).

A 30.2.c
Second edition, third printing: New York: The American Mercury, MCMXXVI.

Copyright page same as A 30.2.b. Green covers with AM logo on front. Offered with subscription to the magazine for a total of $6 (April 1926: lv).

Locations: GHT, RJS.

A 31 TO THE FRIENDS OF THE AMERICAN MERCURY
1926

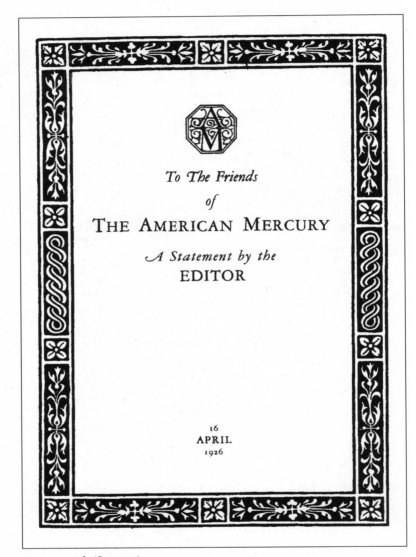

To The Friends

of

THE AMERICAN MERCURY

A Statement by the
EDITOR

16
APRIL
1926

A 31, cover title (first state)

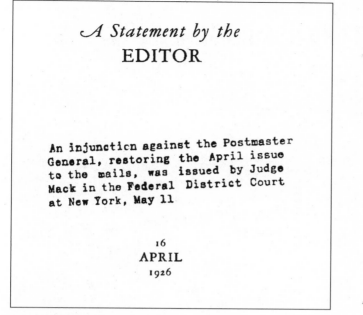

A Statement by the
EDITOR

An injunction against the Postmaster
General, restoring the April issue
to the mails, was issued by Judge
Mack in the Federal District Court
at New York, May 11

16
APRIL
1926

A 31, handstamping (second state)

Cover title: First state: Without handstamping. *Presumed second state:* [handstamped in blue between 'EDITOR' and '16'] 'An injunction against the Postmaster | General, restoring the April issue | to the mails, was issued by Judge | Mack in the Federal District Court | at New York, May 11'. *Presumed third state:* [handstamped in blue between 'EDITOR' and '16'] 'An injunction against the Postmaster | General, restoring the April issue to the | mails, was issued by Judge Mack in the | Federal District Court at New York | May 11.'

Copyright page: None.

8⁷⁄₁₆″ × 5½″: [1–8] = 8 pp.

[1]⁴ = 4 leaves.

Contents: p. 1: cover title; pp. 2–4: text; pp. 5–6: 'Appendix I' [Justice Parmenter's decision]; pp. 6–7: 'Appendix II' [district court opinion]; p. 8: blank.

Typography and paper: 6¹¹⁄₁₆″ × 4″; 44 lines per page. No heads. *Mercury* green wove paper.

Binding: Self wrappers. All edges trimmed. Two staples.

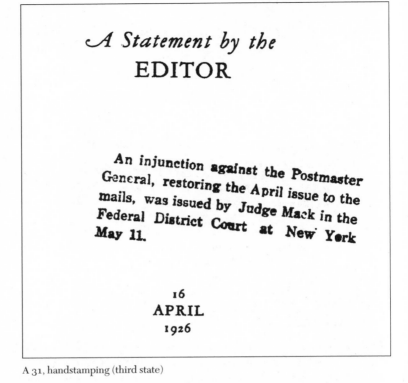

A 31, handstamping (third state)

Locations: EPL (4, first, second, and third [2] states), InU-Li (2, first and second states), LC (second state), NjP (second state), RJS (2, first and second states), SL (third state), Yale (3, first [2] and second states).

Notes: Concerns the "Hatrack" case, in which the April 1926 issue of the *American Mercury* was suppressed in Boston on the grounds of obscenity. The RJS copy in the first state was mailed to its recipient April 22. The true order of the presumed second and third states could not be determined. In the third, the handstamped addendum is also found at the end of the text on p. 4. The same handstamping is found on the pamphlet *Keeping the Puritans Pure,* by A. L. S. Wood, reprinted in the same format from the *American Mercury* of September 1925 (GHT). Adler 13.

A 32 AMERICANA 1926

A 32.1.a.i
Only edition, only printing, limited binding issue (1926)

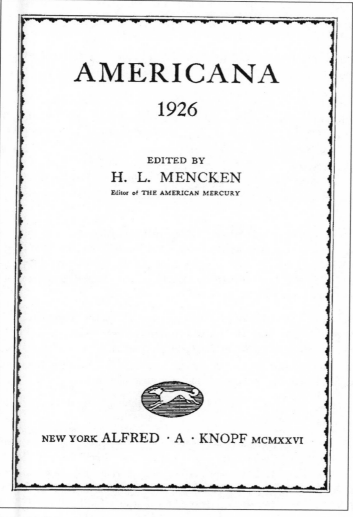

AMERICANA

1926

EDITED BY
H. L. MENCKEN
Editor of THE AMERICAN MERCURY

NEW YORK ALFRED · A · KNOPF MCMXXVI

A 32.1.a.i–ii

Copyright page: 'COPYRIGHT 1926 BY ALFRED A. KNOPF, INC. | MANUFAC-
TURED IN THE UNITED STATES OF AMERICA'

Colophon: 'A NOTE ON THE TYPE IN | WHICH THIS BOOK IS SET | [eleven
lines on the type based on Caslon] | [Borzoi device in oval] | SET UP, ELECTRO-
TYPED AND PRINTED BY THE | VAN REES PRESS, NEW YORK. • PAPER |
FURNISHED BY W. F. ETHERINGTON | & CO., NEW YORK. • BOUND BY |
THE H. WOLFF ESTATE, | NEW YORK'

8⁷⁄₁₆″ × 5½″: [i–iv] v–vii [viii] ix–xi [xii–xiv] 1–234 [235–36] 237–61 [262] 263–79
[280–82] = 296 pp.

[1–18]⁸ [19]⁴ = 148 leaves.

Contents: p. i: half title; p. ii [all in a box within a double-rule box]: '*THE WORKS OF
H. L. MENCKEN* | [twenty-four titles, including 'DAMNA: . . .']'; p. iii: title; p. iv:
copyright; pp. v–vii: 'PREFACE'; p. viii: blank; pp. ix–xi: 'CONTENTS'; p. xii: blank;
p. xiii: half title; p. xiv: blank; pp. 1–234: text; p. 235: [divisional title, between rules]
'APPENDIX FROM FOREIGN PARTS'; p. 236: blank; pp. 237–61: appendix; p.
262: blank; pp. 263–79: [between rules] 'NOTES'; p. 280: blank; p. 281: colophon; p.
282: blank.

Typography and paper: 6″ (5¹¹⁄₁₆″) × 3¹³⁄₁₆″; 28 lines per page (lines vary with number
of items on page and amount of reduced type). Running heads: recto, 'PREFACE' (p.
vii), 'CONTENTS' (p. xi), chapter titles (pp. 3–243), 'NOTES | [rule]' (pp. 265–79);
verso, 'PREFACE' (p. vi), 'CONTENTS' (p. x), 'AMERICANA 1926 | [rule]' (pp. 2–
278), 'NOTES | [rule]' (pp. 266–78). Wove paper.

Binding A: Borzoi boards #16 (blue and light green swirls flecked with blue), light
green V cloth spine. White paper label on spine printed in blue: '[two stars over three
stars] | [rule] | AMERICANA | 1926 | *Edited by* | H. L. MENCKEN | [rule] | [three stars
over two stars]'. Top edge uncut and unstained, fore and bottom edges rough cut.
White end papers. Duplicate label tipped in to inside back cover.

Binding B: Same except Borzoi boards #17 (vertical vinelike designs, blue-gray on
medium blue paper), orange V cloth spine.

Dust jacket: Black on green paper. Front: [all in double frame] '[man leaning on a bar]
| [in box] AMERICANA | 1926 | *Edited by* H.L.Mencken'. Spine: '[rule] | AMER-
ICANA | 1926 | *Edited by* | H. L. | MENCKEN | [rule] | [ornament with twenty-two
borzois] | [Borzoi Books logo] | *Alfred A. Knopf* | [rule]'. Back: humorous ad for *The
American Mercury* ('*Don't Forget Your Pastor!*'). Front flap: blurb; ad for the new
Notes on Democracy. Back flap: list of eleven books by Mencken. This is the same dust
jacket as on the trade issue, only larger to suit this format.

Publication: Published 1 October 1926. $5 (*PW*, 25 September 1926: index). Copy-
right #A950378. 1,400 copies sold.

A 32.1.a.i–ii, dust jacket

Printing: See colophon.

Locations: EPL (binding A), GHT (2, bindings A [dj] and B), Harv (binding A), RJS (binding A), Yale (binding B, dj).

Notes: All copies signed on free front end paper. The text consists of contributions to the *American Mercury* edited by Mencken. Adler 28; Bulsterbaum 75; Blanck 360.

A 32.1.a.ii
Only printing, trade issue

Same as above A 32.1.a.i except:

8⅛″ × 5½″ (binding A), 8″ × 5⁵⁄₁₆″ (binding B).

Binding A: Black V cloth stamped in gilt. Front: 'AMERICANA | 1926'. Spine: 'AMERICANA | 1926 | *Edited by* | H.L. | MENCKEN | ALFRED A. KNOPF'. Back: Borzoi Books logo blindstamped. Top edge trimmed and stained blue, fore and bottom edges rough and unevenly cut, some uncut. White end papers.

Binding B: Same as binding A except stamped in red. Spine: '. . . ALFRED•A• | KNOPF'. Logo on back is black showing through red.

Publication: $2.50 (*PW*, 25 September 1926: index).

Locations: GHT (2, bindings A and B in dj), InU-Li (binding A, dj), LC (8 October 1926, two copies, rebound and binding A), RJS (binding A, dj), Yale (binding A).

A 32.1.a.iii
Only printing, English copyright deposit issue

Same as A 32.1.a.ii except:

Title page: Handstamped twice in black: 'MARTIN HOPKINSON | & COMPANY LIMITED, | PUBLISHERS.'; below, in smaller font: '14, HENRIETTA STREET, COVENT GARDEN, LONDON, W.C. 2'.

Binding A.

Location: BL (6 OCT 26).

A 32.1.a.iv
Only printing, English trade issue (1926)

Copyright page: Same as in limited issue but reset.

7⅞″ × 5⅜″: [i–iv] v–vii [viii] ix–xi [xii–xiv] 1–234 [235–36] 237–61 [262] 263–79 [280] = 294 pp.

AMERICANA
1926

EDITED BY

H. L. MENCKEN
Editor of THE AMERICAN MERCURY

LONDON: MARTIN HOPKINSON &
CO. LTD., 14 HENRIETTA STREET,
COVENT GARDEN, W.C. 2   1926

[1]^8 ($-1_{1,2}$, $+1_{1-2}$) [2–18]^8 [19]^4 (-19_4) = 147 leaves. The first two leaves, which are conjugate, are a setting of pp. [i–iv] different from that of the other issues; they are pasted on the stubs of the two excised leaves. The last leaf of the final gathering is excised, and its stub is pasted to the free rear end paper.

Contents: p. i: half title; p. ii: blank; p. iii: title; p. iv: copyright; pp. v–vii: 'PREFACE'; p. viii: blank; pp. ix–xi: 'CONTENTS'; p. xii: blank; p. xiii: half title; p. xiv: blank; pp. 1–234: text; p. 235: [divisional title, between rules] 'APPENDIX FROM FOREIGN PARTS'; p. 236: blank; pp. 237–61: appendix; p. 262: blank; pp. 263–79: [between rules] 'NOTES'; p. 280: blank.

Typography and paper: Same as in limited issue.

Binding: Blue V cloth, stamped in gilt on spine: 'AMERICANA | 1926 | [short rule] | H.L.MENCKEN | HOPKINSON'. Trimmed, unstained. White end papers.

Dust jacket: Black and gray on off-white paper. Front: [all within box] 'AMERICANA | 1926 | With Study Notes, Glossary and an Appendix | "FROM FOREIGN PARTS" | Edited by | H. L. MENCKEN | [man leaning against bar in double-rule box] | MAR-TIN HOPKINSON & CO., LTD., LONDON | [below box] *For opinions of "1925" see back of jacket'*. Spine: '[rule] | AMERICANA | 1926 | Edited by | H. L. | MENCKEN | HOPKINSON | [rule]'. Back: '*SOME OPINIONS OF | AMERICANA 1925*'. Front flap: '*⅞ net*'. Back flap unprinted.

Publication: Published December 1926 (ECB 12.1036). 7s.6d.

Locations: Bod (MAR | 29 | 1927), Camb (29 MR | 1927), GHT (dj), RJS.

Notes: This issue preceded the American according to Mencken in MLAE 380, but the canceled leaves and American manufacture suggest otherwise. Adler 28.

A 33 NOTES ON DEMOCRACY

A 33.1.a
First edition, presumed first limited printing (1926)

NOTES ON DEMOCRACY

By H. L. MENCKEN

PUBLISHED AT THE BORZOI · NEW YORK · BY
ALFRED · A · KNOPF

A 33.1.a

Title page: The rules and the Borzoi device are red.

Copyright page: 'COPYRIGHT, 1926, BY ALFRED A. KNOPF, INC. | MANUFAC-TURED IN THE UNITED STATES OF AMERICA'

Colophon: 'A NOTE ON THE TYPE IN | WHICH THIS BOOK IS SET | [eleven lines on Bodoni type] | [Borzoi device in oval] | SET UP AND ELECTROTYPED BY THE | VAIL-BALLOU PRESS, INC., BING- | HAMTON, N.Y. • ESPARTO PAPER | MANUFACTURED IN SCOTLAND | AND FURNISHED BY W. F. | ETHER-INGTON & CO., NEW | YORK • PRINTED AND | BOUND BY THE PLIMP- | TON PRESS, NOR- | WOOD, MASS.'

Statement of limitation: 'THE FIRST EDITION OF NOTES ON DE- | MOCRACY CONSISTS OF TWO HUNDRED | AND THIRTY-FIVE COPIES, SIGNED BY | THE AUTHOR, AS FOLLOWS: THIRTY-FIVE | ON SHIDZUOKA JAPAN VEL-LUM (OF WHICH | FIVE ARE NOT FOR SALE) NUMBERED | FROM 1 TO 35, AND TWO HUNDRED COPIES | ON BORZOI RAG PAPER (OF WHICH EIGHT | ARE NOT FOR SALE) NUMBERED FROM | 36 TO 235 | THIS IS NUMBER | [number penned in, signature below]'

8⅞″ × 5¹³⁄₁₆″: [A–B i–iv] v [vi–viii 1–2] 3–68 [69–70] 71–144 [145–46] 147–92 [193–94] 195–212 [213–18] = 228 pp.

[1]¹⁰ [2–14]⁸ = 114 leaves.

Contents: p. A: blank; p. B: limitation notice; p. i: half title; p. ii: [all in a box within a double-rule box] '*THE WORKS OF H. L. MENCKEN* | [twenty-four titles listed]'; p. iii: title; p. iv: copyright; p. v: 'CONTENTS'; p. vi: blank; p. vii: half title; p. viii: blank; pp. 1–212: text; p. 213: colophon; pp. 214–18: blank. Blank pages in text following divisional half titles: pp. 2, 70, 146, 194.

Typography and paper: 5½″ (5¼″) × 3³⁄₁₆″; 26 lines per page. Running heads: recto, section titles (pp. 5–211); verso, '*NOTES ON DEMOCRACY* | [rule]' (pp. 4–212). "Shidzuoka Japan Vellum" (wove paper).

Binding: White vellum stamped in gilt. Front: four ornaments in corners of double-rule box, large ornament toward bottom of upper half. Spine: '[three stars] | [rule] | Notes on | Democracy | [star] | H. L. Mencken | [rule] | [three stars] | [ornament] | ALFRED A *[sic]* KNOPF'. Back: Borzoi Books logo. Top edge gilt, fore and bottom edges uncut. White end papers. In a cardboard box covered in the design of Borzoi boards #21 in purple. No label.

Dust jacket: None.

Publication: Published 20 October 1926. $25 (*PW*, 25 September 1926: index). Copyright #A950586. 6,100 copies of Knopf printings sold.

Printing: See colophon.

Locations: GHT, Harv.

Notes: Neither the order of the limited printings, nor the priority of limited and first trade, could be determined. Adler 12; S1.7, 26, 61; S2.7, 13, 14, 17; Bulsterbaum 6.

A 33.1.b
First edition, presumed second limited printing

Same as A 33.1.a except:

9⅛″ × 5⅞″

Typography and paper: Laid paper, watermarked with Borzoi Books logo.

Binding: Borzoi boards design #11 (purple on beige). Green V cloth spine with white paper label printed in black: '[three stars] | [rule] | Notes on | Democracy | [star] | H. L. Mencken | [rule] | [three stars]'. Uncut, unstained. White end papers. Extra label tipped in to rear pastedown. In cardboard box covered in gray paper. Label on "spine" as on cover but taller and, after last row of stars: '*number* | [limitation number penned in]'.

Publication: $10 (*PW*, 25 September 1926: index).

Locations: GHT, InU-Li, RJS.

A 33.1.c
First edition, first trade printing

Same as A 33.1.b except:

Statement of limitation: None.

7⁵⁄₁₆″ × 4¹⁵⁄₁₆″: [A–B i–iv] v [vi 1–2] . . . [213–16] = 224 pp.

[1]⁶ (1₃ + 1) [2–13]⁸ [14]⁸ (14₇ + 1) = 112 leaves. Pp. v–vi and 213–14 are tipped in.

Contents: pp. A–B: blank; . . . ; p. v: 'CONTENTS'; p. vi: blank; pp. 1–212: text; p. 213: colophon; pp. 214–16: blank. Blank pages in text as above.

Typography and paper: Wove paper.

Binding: Deep blue V cloth. Front: Mencken arms blindstamped. Spine, stamped in gilt: '[double rule] | NOTES ON | DEMOCRACY | [double rule] | H•L•MENCKEN [dots representing solid inverted triangles] | [double rule] | [double rule] | ALFRED• A•KNOPF | [double rule]'. Trimmed, top edge stained orange. Red and yellow "wallpaper" end papers, white on sides facing pages.

Dust jacket: Black on tan paper. Front: '[three rows of ornamental borzois] | N O T E S O N | DEMOCRACY | By H. L. MENCKEN | [five-line blurb] | [table of contents in five lines] | ALFRED • A • KNOPF | Publisher • New York | [three rows of ornamen-

NOTES ON DEMOCRACY

By H. L. MENCKEN

This terrific polemic embodies the final conclusions of the most uncompromising and devastating of all critics of American democracy. It issues naturally out of his past writings upon the subject, but it is by no means a reprint. Save for a few paragraphs, it is wholly new matter.

Contents

I. DEMOCRATIC MAN
II. THE DEMOCRATIC STATE
III. DEMOCRACY AND LIBERTY
IV. CODA

ALFRED · A · KNOPF
Publisher · New York

A 33.1.c, dust jacket

tal borzois and AK ligatures with Borzoi Books logo in center] | [row of ornamental borzois]'. Spine: '[two ornamental borzois and AK ligature] | NOTES ON | DEMOC-RACY | *by* | H. L. MENCKEN | [two ornamental borzois and AK ligature] | [group of ornamental borzois and AK ligatures] | [two ornamental borzois and AK ligature] | [Borzoi Books logo] | ALFRED [heavy dot] A [heavy dot] | K N O P F'. Back: list of '*Borzoi Books on Political Science*'. Front flap: list of '*OTHER BOOKS* | *by* | H. L. MENCKEN'. Back flap: ad and subscription form for *The American Mercury*.

Publication: $2.50 (*American Mercury*, August 1926: lxxv; *PW*, 23 October 1926: 1697).

Locations: GHT (dj), Harv, InU-Li (dj), LC (26 October 1926), RJS.

A 33.1.d
First edition, second trade printing: New York: Knopf, [1926].

On copyright page: 'PUBLISHED, OCTOBER, 1926 | SECOND PRINTING, NO-VEMBER, 1926'. Thinner (laid) paper.

Locations: EPL, GHT.

A 33.1.e
First edition, third trade printing: New York: Octagon, 1977.

Location: EPL.

A 33.2.a
Second edition (first English edition), only printing (1927)

Copyright page: 'FIRST PUBLISHED IN MCMXXVII | MADE & PRINTED IN GREAT BRITAIN | BY BUTLER & TANNER LTD | FROME AND | LONDON | [ornament]'

7½″ × 4¾″: [1–4] 5–6 [7–8] 9–76 [77–78] 79–154 [155–56] 157–203 [204–06] 207–24 = 224 pp.

[A]⁸ B–I⁸ K–O⁸ = 112 leaves.

Contents: p. 1: half title; p. 2: '*By the Same Author* | [three titles] | etc *[sic]*'; p. 3: title; p. 4: copyright; pp. 5–6: 'CONTENTS'; pp. 7–224: text. Blank pages in text following divisional half titles: pp. 8, 78, 156, 206; other: p. 204.

Typography and paper: 5⅜″ (5⅛″) × 3⁵⁄₁₆″; 24 lines per page. Running heads: recto, section titles (pp. 11–223); verso, 'CONTENTS' (p. 6), 'NOTES ON DEMOCRACY' (pp. 10–224). Wove paper.

Binding: Yellow V cloth stamped in black. Front: 'NOTES ON DEMOCRACY | H.L. MENCKEN'. Spine: 'NOTES ON | DEMOCRACY | H.L.MENCKEN | JONA-

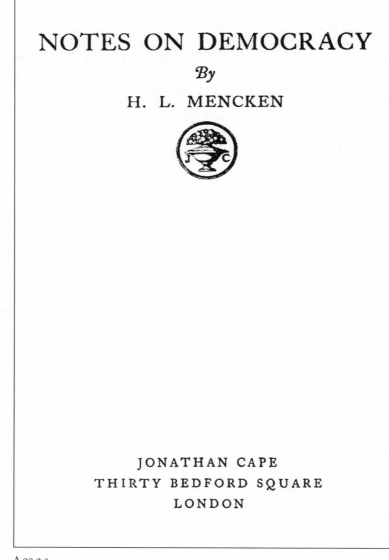

NOTES ON DEMOCRACY
By
H. L. MENCKEN

JONATHAN CAPE
THIRTY BEDFORD SQUARE
LONDON

A 33.2.a

THAN CAPE'. Top and fore edges trimmed, bottom edge unevenly trimmed, unstained. White end papers.

Dust jacket: Off-white paper. Front: [all within red ornamental frame] 'NOTES ON DEMOCRACY | by | H. L. MENCKEN | (Author of *Prejudices, In Defence of Woman* [*sic*], etc.) | [red JC device] | Jonathan Cape 30 Bedford Square'. Spine: '[red ornamental border] | *Notes | on | Democracy* | by | H. L. MENCKEN | [red JC device] | Jonathan Cape | [red ornamental border]'. Back: list of '*Some New Jonathan Cape Books*'. Front flap: blurb, price 6s. Back flap unprinted.

Publication: Published February 1927 (ECB 12.1036). 6s.

Locations: Bod (FEB | 7 | 1927), Camb (7 FE | 1927), GHT (dj), Harv (2), InU-Li, RJS.

Notes: Laid in the Bod copy is a two-leaf brochure on *The Travel Diary of a Philosopher,* by Count Hermann Keyserling, trans. J. Holroyd Reese (Cape), and a return postcard to request their house journal, *Now and Then*. Adler 12.

A 34 PREJUDICES: FIFTH SERIES

A 34.1.a
Only edition, limited printing (1926)

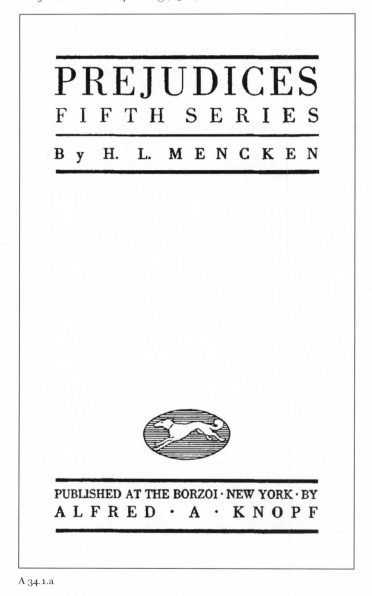

A 34.1.a

Title page: The rules, 'F I F T H   S E R I E S', and Borzoi device are red or red-orange.

Copyright page: 'COPYRIGHT, 1926, BY ALFRED A. KNOPF, INC. | MANUFACTURED IN THE UNITED STATES OF AMERICA'

Statement of limitation: 'OF THE FIRST EDITION OF PREJUDICES FIFTH | SERIES TWO HUNDRED COPIES HAVE BEEN | PRINTED AS FOLLOWS : EIGHT ON BORZOI RAG | PAPER SIGNED BY THE AUTHOR AND NUMBERED | FROM A TO H; ONE HUNDRED AND NINETY-TWO | COPIES ON BORZOI RAG PAPER SIGNED BY THE | AUTHOR AND NUMBERED FROM 1 TO 192. | THIS IS NUMBER | [letter or number penned in with period, signature below]'

$9\frac{1}{8}'' \times 5\frac{7}{8}''$: [A–B i–iv] v–vii [viii 7–8] 9–307 [308] = 312 pp. The 8 in 78 is raised, and the 0 in 80 is in a smaller font.

$[1]^{10}$ (1 + 1_1, 1_5 + 1) $[2–19]^8$ = 156 leaves. The first leaf is tipped in to the end paper. The leaf with pp. 7–8 is also tipped in.

Contents: p. A: blank; p. B: limitation notice; p. i: half title; p. ii: [all within box in double-rule box] '*THE WORKS OF H. L. MENCKEN* | [twenty-four titles]'; p. iii: title; p. iv: copyright; pp. v–vii: 'CONTENTS'; p. viii: blank; p. 7: half title; p. 8: blank; pp. 9–304: text; pp. 305–07: 'INDEX'; p. 308: blank.

Text: "Four Moral Causes," "Four Makers of Tales," "In Memoriam: W.J.B.," "The Hills of Zion," "Beethoven," "Rondo on an Ancient Theme," "Protestantism in the Republic," "From the Files of a Book Reviewer," "The Fringes of Lovely Letters," "Essay on Pedagogy," "On Living in Baltimore," "The Last New Englander," "The Nation," "Officers and Gentlemen," "Golden Age," "Edgar Saltus," "Miscellaneous Notes," "Catechism." See Notes.

Typography and paper: $5\frac{7}{16}''$ ($5\frac{1}{4}''$) $\times$ $3\frac{1}{2}''$ (some pages are $5\frac{5}{8}''$ [$5\frac{7}{16}''$] $\times$ $3\frac{1}{2}''$); 27 lines per page. Running heads: recto, chapter titles (pp. 11–303); 'INDEX' (p. 307); verso, '*PREJUDICES: FIFTH SERIES*' (pp. 10–302), 'INDEX' (p. 306). First chapter ('FOUR MORAL CAUSES') incorrectly headed '*BIRTH CONTROL*'. Laid paper, watermarked with Borzoi Books logo.

Binding: Borzoi boards design #12 (red and white marbled paper). Blue-gray V cloth spine with pink paper label: '[thick-thin rule] | PREJUDICES | [bracket pointed up] | *Fifth Series* | [bracket pointed down] | H. L. MENCKEN | [thick-thin rule]'. Untrimmed, unstained. White end papers. Spare label tipped in to rear pastedown. In cardboard box covered with beige paper. Label on "spine" as on cover but taller and, below bottom rule, '*Number* | [limitation number penned in]'.

Dust jacket: One GHT copy has a translucent dust jacket. Reported marble-paper example may be homemade (D).

Publication: Published 12 November 1926. $10 (*PW,* 25 September 1926: index). Copyright #A958080. 5,800 copies of Knopf printings sold.

Printing: See colophon of trade printing.

Locations: GHT (2, dj), Harv, InU-Li, RJS.

Notes: One GHT copy is lettered 'B.'. As in the previous volumes of the series, the pieces generally derive from Mencken's essays and reviews in magazines and newspapers, sometimes in combination. For example, "In Memoriam: W.J.B." began as "Bryan" (Baltimore *Evening Sun,* 27 July 1925) and then was greatly expanded for the *American Mercury* (October 1925). Adler 12, 98, 157, 158; S1.9; S2.7, 14, 19; Bulster-baum 20–22, 75.

A 34.1.b
Only edition, first trade printing

Same as A 34.1.a except:

Statement of limitation: None.

Colophon: 'A NOTE ON THE TYPE IN | WHICH THIS BOOK IS SET | [eleven lines on Bodoni type] | [Borzoi device in oval] | SET UP AND ELECTROTYPED BY THE | VAIL-BALLOU PRESS, INC., BING- | HAMPTON, N. Y. • ESPARTO PAPER | MANUFACTURED IN SCOTLAND | AND FURNISHED BY W. F. | ETHERINGTON & CO., NEW | YORK • PRINTED AND | BOUND BY THE PLIMP- | TON PRESS, NORWOOD, | MASS.'

$7^{7}/_{16}''$ × 5″: [i–iv] v–vii [viii 7–8] 9–307 [308–10] = 312 pp. Pp. 78 and 80 are as above.

[1–19]⁸ [20]⁴ = 156 leaves.

Contents: p. i: half title; . . . ; p. 308: blank; p. 309: colophon; p. 310: blank.

Typography and paper: Wove paper.

Binding A: Very dark blue V cloth. Front: Mencken arms blindstamped. Spine, stamped in gilt: '[double rule] | PREJUDICES | [rule] | FIFTH SERIES | [double rule] | H•L•MENCKEN [dots representing solid inverted triangles] | [double rule] | [double rule] | ALFRED•A•KNOPF | [double rule]'. Trimmed, top edge stained orange. Red and yellow "wallpaper" end papers, white on side facing pages.

Binding B: Borzoi boards design #2 (dark blue squares and rectangles on field speckled with red, blue, and orange). Yellowish tan V cloth spine with tan paper label printed in gold: '[ornamental rule] | PREJUDICES | [short ornamental rule] | FIFTH | SERIES | [short ornamental rule] | H. L. | MENCKEN | [ornamental rule]'. Top edge trimmed and stained black, fore and bottom edges rough and unevenly trimmed. White end papers. See note on sets in Borzoi boards at A 20.1.i.

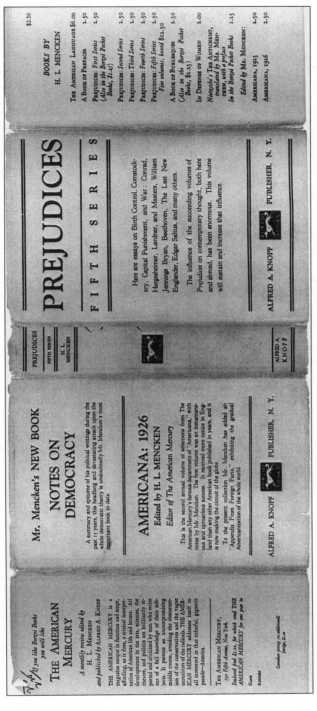

A 34.1.b, dust jacket

Binding C: Same as binding B except Borzoi boards design #13 (triangles and other shapes in gray and white with purple, red, blue, and orange flecks against a black background).

Dust jacket: Black on red paper (white on inside). Front: '[double rule] | PREJU-DICES | [rule] | F I F T H   S E R I E S | [double rule] | [two-paragraph, nine-line blurb] | [double rule] | ALFRED A. KNOPF [Borzoi Books logo, red showing through black] PUBLISHER, N. Y. | [double rule]'. Spine: '[double rule] | PREJUDICES | [rule] | FIFTH SERIES | [double rule] | H. L. | MENCKEN | [double rule] | [Borzoi Books logo, red showing through black] | [rule] | ALFRED A. | KNOPF | [double rule]'. Back: ads for *Notes on Democracy* and *Americana 1926*. Front flap: twelve titles by Mencken; price $2.50. Back flap: ad for *The American Mercury*.

Publication: $2.50.

Locations: D (binding B), D (binding C), GHT (2, bindings A [dj] and B), InU-Li (binding C), LC (20 November 1926, binding A), MBU (binding A), NjP (binding B), RJS (2, bindings A [dj] and B).

A 34.1.c.i
Second trade printing, American issue: New York: Knopf, [1926].

On copyright page: 'SECOND PRINTING, DECEMBER, 1926'. This printing not seen in Borzoi boards.

Location: MBU.

A 34.1.c.ii
Second trade printing, English issue (1927)

Copyright page: 'PRINTED IN THE UNITED STATES OF AMERICA'

$7\frac{1}{2}'' \times 4\frac{3}{4}''$: [i–iv] v–vii [viii 7–8] 9–307 [308–10] = 312 pp. The 8 in 78 is raised, and the 0 in 80 is in a smaller font.

$[1–19]^8 [20]^4$ = 156 leaves.

Contents: p. i: half title; p. ii: blank; p. iii: title; p. iv: copyright; pp. v–vii: 'CONTENTS'; p. viii: blank; p. 7: half title; p. 8: blank; pp. 9–304: text, same as in limited printing; pp. 305–07: 'INDEX'; pp. 308–10: blank.

Typography and paper: Typography same as in limited printing. Wove paper.

Binding: Yellow V cloth stamped in black. Front : 'PREJUDICES | FIFTH SERIES | H.L. MENCKEN'. Spine: 'PREJUDICES | FIFTH SERIES | H.L.MENCKEN | JONATHAN CAPE'. Back: JC device. Top edge trimmed and stained yellow, fore edge trimmed, bottom edge rough trimmed. White end papers.

PREJUDICES
FIFTH SERIES
By H. L. MENCKEN

JONATHAN CAPE
30 BEDFORD SQUARE · LONDON

A 34.1.c.ii

Dust jacket: Off-white paper. Front: 'PREJUDICES | FIFTH SERIES | H. L. Mencken | [JC device in circle] | *By the Same Author* | THE AMERICAN LAN-GUAGE: A BOOK OF PREFACES | IN DEFENCE OF WOMEN: NOTES ON DEMOCRACY'. Spine: '[double rule] | PREJUDICES | FIFTH SERIES | H. L. MENCKEN | [JC device in circle] | Jonathan Cape | [double rule]'. Back: ads for five Mencken books. Front flap directs reader to the back; price 7s. 6d. Rear flap un-printed.

Publication: Published March 1927 (ECB 12.1036). 7s.6d.

Locations: BL (24 FEB 27), Bod (MAR | 1 | 1927), Camb (1 MR | 1927), GHT (2, dj).

Notes: Dated 1927 by Adler (13).

LATER REPRINTINGS WITHIN THE ONLY EDITION

A 34.1.d
New York: Octagon, 1977.

Locations: EPL, Harv.

A 34.1.e
New York: Octagon, 1985.

Locations: MChB, MCR.

A 34.1.f
New York: Octagon, 1987.

Location: Harv.

A 35.1.a
Only edition, limited printing (1927)

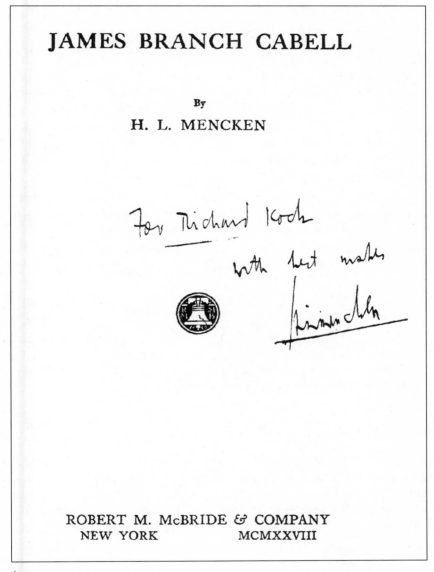

JAMES BRANCH CABELL

By

H. L. MENCKEN

ROBERT M. McBRIDE & COMPANY
NEW YORK   MCMXXVIII

A 35.1.a

Copyright page: 'COPYRIGHT, 1927, | BY ROBERT M. MCBRIDE & COMPANY | *Published, September, 1927* | PRINTED IN THE UNITED STATES OF AMERICA'

Statement of limitation: 'OF THE ONE HUNDRED AND TEN | COPIES OF THIS MONOGRAPH PRINTED | IN SEPTEMBER, NINETEEN HUNDRED | AND TWENTY-SEVEN, THIS COPY IS | NUMBER. . . . . [number penned in red]'

9½" × 6⅛": [1–6] 7–26 [27–28] 29–31 [32] = 32 pp.

[1–4]⁴ = 16 leaves.

Contents: p. 1: half title; p. 2: limitation notice; p. 3: title; p. 4: copyright; p. 5: half title; p. 6: blank; pp. 7–26: text; p. 27: divisional half title: 'BIBLIOGRAPHY'; p. 28: blank; pp. 29–31: 'THE BOOKS OF | JAMES BRANCH CABELL'; p. 32: blank.

Typography and paper: 6⅛" (5⅞") × 3½"; 31 lines per page. Running heads: recto, 'JAMES BRANCH CABELL' (pp. 9–29), 'BIBLIOGRAPHY' (p. 31); verso, 'JAMES BRANCH CABELL' (pp. 8–30). Laid paper, watermarked '[script] De Coverly Rag Laid'.

Binding: Greenish paper-covered boards front and back, ivory paper spine. White paper label on spine, reading down: 'JAMES BRANCH CABELL [ornament] *H. L. Mencken*'. Rough trimmed, unstained. White end papers.

Dust jacket: Unprinted glassine with evenly clipped corners on flaps.

Publication: Published 28 September 1927. Copyright #A1018051.

Printing: See below.

Locations: GHT, JRS (dj), RJS.

Notes: Glassine dust jacket also reported by dealer. Contrary to Adler, both printings appeared in 1927 (see below); the GHT copy was signed and dated by Mencken that year. This printing not for sale; fifty copies went to reviewers and thirty each to HLM and JBC (see below). Adler 13; S1.11; S2.11; Bulsterbaum 11.

A 35.1.b
Only edition, trade printing

Same as A 35.1.a except:

Copyright page: 'THE KALKI EDITION OF THE WORKS OF | *James Branch Cabell* | [short rule] | [seventeen titles] | [short rule] | COPYRIGHT, 1927, | BY ROBERT M. MCBRIDE & COMPANY | PRINTED IN THE UNITED STATES OF AMERICA'

Statement of limitation: None.

7⅜" × 4¹⁵⁄₁₆": [1–2] 3–32 = 32 pp., with portrait and illustration on outer leaves of glossy paper.

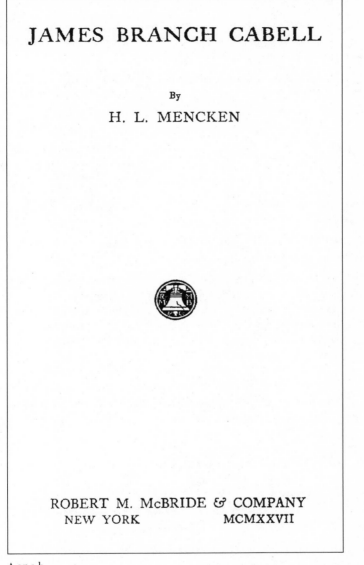

JAMES BRANCH CABELL

By

H. L. MENCKEN

ROBERT M. McBRIDE & COMPANY
NEW YORK   MCMXXVII

A 35.1.b

[1]^{16} = 16 leaves.

Contents: p. 1: title; p. 2: copyright; pp. 3–22: text; pp. 23–32: 'INDIVIDUAL COMMENT [reviews]'. A wraparound leaf on glossy paper contains a portrait on front verso and an illustration of a MS leaf on back recto.

Typography and paper: Running heads: recto, 'JAMES BRANCH CABELL' (pp. 5–21), 'INDIVIDUAL COMMENT' (pp. 25–31); verso, 'JAMES BRANCH CABELL' (pp. 4–32). Wove paper.

Binding: Slate blue or dark grayish green wrappers. Front: 'JAMES BRANCH CABELL | By | H. L. Mencken | [ornament with rearing horse]'. Trimmed, unstained. Two staples. Other reported wrappers are varying shades of green paper that varies in weight and smoothness; also, lightweight violet paper.

Printing: Printed by the Quinn and Boden Co., Rahway, N.J.; "not bound," according to copyright statement.

Locations: GHT, Harv, EPL, InU-Li, LC (30 December 1927, grayish green wrappers), RJS (2).

Notes: Form letter from the McBride Co. inserted in the Harv copy: "In accordance with your request we are sending you a copy of the paper bound edition of JAMES BRANCH CABELL by H. L. Mencken which we have prepared for free distribution. [¶] A limited cloth bound edition of one hundred and ten copies was also issued but it was not for sale, as it was intended only for Mr. Cabell, Mr. Mencken and a selected list of reviewers." A laid-in letter from Mencken to a Boston bookseller, dated 17 December [1927 on postmark], says, "The edition of the bound pamphlet seems to have been very small." Hence both were published in 1927. According to a note from Cabell in the EPL copy, McBride's told him that fifty of the deluxe printing went to reviewers, thirty each to him and to Mencken.

LATER REPRINTINGS WITHIN THE ONLY EDITION

A 35.1.c
James Branch Cabell   Three Essays by Carl Van Doren   H. L. Mencken   Hugh Walpole. Port Washington, N.Y.: Kennikat, 1967.

On copyright page: 'The three items issued for the first time together by | Kennikat Press in 1966 *[sic]*'. The essays are separately paginated.

Locations: EPL, GHT, Harv.

A 35.1.d
A 35.1.c was reprinted in 1971, according to S2.11. Not located.

A 36 PREJUDICES: SIXTH SERIES

A 36.1.a.i
Only edition, first trade printing, first issue (1927)

A 36.1.a.i

Title page: The rules, 'S I X T H   S E R I E S', and Borzoi device are red.

Copyright page: 'COPYRIGHT 1927 BY ALFRED A. KNOPF, INC. | PUBLISHED OCTOBER, 1927 | MANUFACTURED IN THE UNITED STATES OF AMERICA'

Colophon: 'A NOTE ON THE TYPE IN | WHICH THIS BOOK IS SET | [ten lines on Bodoni type] | [Borzoi device in oval] | SET UP AND ELECTROTYPED BY THE | VAIL-BALLOU PRESS, INC., BING- | HAMTON, N. Y. • PRINTED AND | BOUND BY THE PLIMPTON PRESS, | NORWOOD, MASS. • ESPARTO | PAPER MANUFACTURED IN | SCOTLAND AND FURNISHED | BY W. F. ETHERINGTON | & CO., NEW YORK'

$7^{5}/_{16}'' \times 4^{15}/_{16}''$: [i–iv] v–vi [7–8] 9–311 [312] 313–17 [318–20] = 320 pp.

$[1–20]^{8}$ = 160 leaves.

Contents: p. i: half title; p. ii: [all in a box within a red double-rule box] '*THE WORKS OF H. L. MENCKEN* | [fifteen titles]'; p. iii: title; p. iv: copyright; pp. v–vi: 'CONTENTS'; p. 7: half title; p. 8: blank; pp. 9–311: text; p. 312: blank; pp. 313–17: 'INDEX'; p. 318: colophon; pp. 319–20: blank. Errata slip ($2^{1}/_{2}'' \times 4^{7}/_{8}''$) with omissions from the table of contents (II.1–5) tipped in to p. 7 on four copies examined. Found on p. v of one copy and on p. iii of another (rebound); reportedly laid in (D).

Text: "Journalism in America," "From the Memoirs of a Subject of the United States," "The Human Mind," "Clarion Call to Poets," "Souvenirs of a Book Reviewer," "Five Little Excursions," "Hymn to the Truth," "The Pedagogy of Sex," "Metropolis," "Dives into Quackery," "Life Under Bureaucracy," "In the Rolling Mills," "Ambrose Bierce," "The Executive Secretary," "Invitation to the Dance," "Aubade," "Appendix from Moronia." See Notes.

Typography and paper: $5^{11}/_{16}''$ ($5^{7}/_{16}''$) $\times 3^{1}/_{2}''$; 28 lines per page. Running heads: recto, essay titles (pp. 11–311), 'INDEX' (pp. 315–17); verso, 'CONTENTS' (p. vi), 'PREJUDICES: SIXTH SERIES' (pp. 10–310), 'INDEX' (pp. 314–16). Wove paper.

Binding: Dark blue V cloth. Front: Mencken arms blindstamped. Spine, stamped in gilt: '[double rule] | PREJUDICES | [rule] | SIXTH SERIES | [double rule] | H•L• MENCKEN [dots represent solid inverted triangles] | [double rule] | [double rule] | ALFRED•A•KNOPF | [double rule]'. Trimmed, top edge stained orange. Red and yellow "wallpaper" end papers, white on sides facing pages.

Dust jacket: Blue on orange paper. Front: '[double rule] | PREJUDICES | [rule] | S I X T H   S E R I E S | [double rule] | In general plan this volume is like its compan- | [nine more lines of blurb] | [five lines stating the number of printings of the first five series] | The first five volumes of Prejudices, specially bound in Borzoi Batik and boxed, | are to be had at $12.50 a set. | [double rule] | ALFRED A. KNOPF [Borzoi Books logo as orange showing through blue] PUBLISHER, N. Y. | [double rule]'. Spine: '[double rule] | PREJUDICES | [rule] | SIXTH SERIES | [double rule] | H. L. |

A 36.1.a.i, dust jacket

MENCKEN | [double rule] | [Borzoi Books logo as orange showing through blue] | [double rule] | ALFRED A. | KNOPF | [double rule]'. Back: ads for six books edited or introduced by Mencken. Front flap: twenty books by Mencken; price $2.50. Rear flap: ad for *The American Mercury.*

Publication: Published 21 October 1927. $2.50. Copyright #A1007848. 4,100 copies of Knopf printings sold.

Printing: See colophon.

Locations: GHT, InU-Li (dj), LC (24 October 1927, with errata slip), RJS (2, dj).

Notes: As in the previous volumes of the series, the pieces generally derive from Mencken's essays and reviews in magazines and newspapers, sometimes in combination. "Aubade" appeared first as "Editorial" in *American Mercury,* August 1927, and later, with the same title, in *From the American Mercury 1927* (New York: Knopf, [January] 1928; limited to 600 copies), pp. [145]–55. See note on sets in Borzoi boards at A 20.1.i. Adler 13, 30, 154, 157; S1.15; S2.7, 14, 21; Bulsterbaum 22–24, 75.

Review copy: Same as above, except bound in orange wrappers printed in blue (the dust jacket); 7⁹⁄₁₆″ × 5⅛″; unstained, fore and bottom edges unevenly trimmed. No errata slip, errors uncorrected. *Location:* GHT.

A 36.1.a.ii
Only edition, first trade printing, English issue (1928)

Same as A 36.1.a.i except:

Title page: The rules, 'S I X T H   S E R I E S', and JC device are red.

Copyright page: 'PRINTED IN THE UNITED STATES OF AMERICA'

7⅜″ × 4¹⁵⁄₁₆″

Contents: p. i: half title; p. ii: blank; p. iii: title; p. iv: copyright; pp. v–vi: 'CONTENTS'; p. 7: half title; p. 8: blank; pp. 9–311: text, same as in first issue; p. 312: blank; pp. 313–17: 'INDEX'; pp. 318–20: blank. No errata slip, table of contents uncorrected.

Binding: Smooth yellow V cloth stamped in black. Front: 'PREJUDICES | SIXTH SERIES | H.L. MENCKEN'. Spine: 'PREJUDICES | SIXTH SERIES | H.L. MENCKEN | JONATHAN CAPE'. Back: JC device. Trimmed, top edge stained yellow. White end papers.

Dust jacket: White paper. Front: 'PREJUDICES | SIXTH SERIES | H. L. Mencken | [JC device] | *By the Same Author* | IN DEFENCE OF WOMEN : A BOOK OF PREFACES | SELECTED PREJUDICES : NOTES ON DEMOCRACY'. Spine: '[double rule] | PREJUDICES | SIXTH SERIES | H. L. MENCKEN | [JC device in circle] | Jonathan Cape | [double rule]'. Back: ad for three Cape books. Front flap: blurb from *English Review;* price 7s.6d. Rear flap unprinted.

PREJUDICES
SIXTH SERIES

By H. L. MENCKEN

JONATHAN CAPE
30 BEDFORD SQUARE · LONDON

A 36.1.a.ii

Publication: Published January 1928 (ECB 12.1036); 1928 (Adler). 7s.6d.

Locations: BL (18 JAN 28), Bod (JAN | 19 | 1928), Camb (19 JA | 1928), GHT (dj), JRS (dj), KU-S, RJS.

Notes: Adler 13.

A 36.1.b
Only edition, presumed first limited printing

Same as first American trade printing except:

Colophon: 'A NOTE ON THE TYPE IN | WHICH THIS BOOK IS SET | [ten lines on Bodoni type] | [Borzoi device in oval] | SET UP AND ELECTROTYPED BY | THE VAIL-BALLOU PRESS, INC., | BINGHAMTON, N. Y. • PRINTED | AND BOUND BY THE PLIMPTON | PRESS, NORWOOD, | MASS.'

Statement of limitation: 'OF THE FIRST EDITION OF PREJUDICES SIXTH | SERIES ONE HUNDRED NINETY COPIES HAVE | BEEN PRINTED AS FOL-LOWS: FIFTY COPIES | ON JAPAN VELLUM, BOUND IN VELLUM AND | SIGNED BY THE AUTHOR, NUMBERED FROM | 1 TO 50; ONE HUNDRED FORTY COPIES ON | BORZOI ALL RAG PAPER, SPECIALLY BOUND | AND SIGNED BY THE AUTHOR, NUMBERED | FROM 1 TO 140. | THIS IS NUM-BER | [number penned in, followed by signature]'

9" × 5⅞": [A–B i–iv] . . . [318] = 320 pp.

[1]⁸ (± 1₄) [2–20]⁸ = 160 leaves. The inserted leaf (pp. v–vi) is a corrected table of contents.

Contents: p. A: blank; p. B: statement of limitation; . . . ; p. 318: colophon. No errata slip.

Typography and paper: "Japan Vellum" (wove paper).

Binding: Vellum stamped in gilt. Front: four ornaments in corners of double-rule box, large ornament toward bottom of upper half. Spine: '[double rule] | PREJUDICES | [rule] | SIXTH SERIES | [double rule] | H• L• MENCKEN [dots represent solid inverted triangles] | [double rule] | [ornament] | [double rule] | ALFRED • A • KNOPF | [double rule]'. Back: Borzoi Books logo. Top edge gilt, fore and bottom edges unevenly trimmed. White end papers. In cardboard box covered in light orange paper, label of same color on "spine": 'PREJUDICES | [wavy line] | *SIXTH* | *SERIES* | [wavy line] | H. L. MENCKEN'. Limitation number written at base of "spine."

Dust jacket: None reported or seen.

Publication: $25 (*PW*, 24 September 1927: index).

Locations: GHT, Harv.

Notes: The order of the two limited printings could not be determined, but they are presumed to have followed the first trade printing because of the cancel that corrects the errors.

A 36.1.c
Only edition, presumed second limited printing

Same as A 36.1.b except:

Statement of limitation: First state: unnumbered and unsigned. *Second state:* numbered and signed as in first limited printing.

$9\frac{1}{16}'' \times 5\frac{7}{8}''$

First state: pp. v–vi integral and uncorrected. *Second state:* pp. v–vi a cancel as in first limited printing.

Typography and paper: Laid paper, watermarked with Borzoi Books logo.

Binding: Borzoi boards #15 (yellow, light blue, and brown on black with white spider-webbing). Oatmeal V cloth spine with yellow paper label: 'PREJUDICES | [wavy line] | *SIXTH* | *SERIES* | [wavy line] | H. L. MENCKEN'. Uncut, unstained. Extra label tipped in to inside rear cover. White end papers. *First state:* unboxed. *Second state:* in box, as in first limited printing.

Dust jacket: Unprinted glassine.

Publication: $10 (*PW,* 24 September 1927: index).

Locations: EPL (second state), GHT (2, first and second states), RJS (second state, dj).

LATER REPRINTINGS WITHIN THE ONLY EDITION

A 36.1.d
New York: Octagon, 1977.

Locations: EPL, Harv, MChB.

A 36.1.e
New York: Octagon, [1985?].

Identified by analogy with the second printing of other Octagon *Prejudices.* Not seen.

A 36.1.f
New York: Octagon, 1987.

On copyright page: '*Third Octagon printing 1987*'.

Location: MCR.

A 37 MENCKENIANA: A SCHIMPFLEXIKON

A 37.1.a
Only edition, presumed first limited printing (1928)

A 37.1.a–c

Title page: The Borzoi device is orange (the sprigs black).

Copyright page: [all in a box] 'COPYRIGHT 1928 | BY ALFRED • A • KNOPF • INC • [last dot slightly below center] | [heavy dot slightly open toward bottom] | EXPURGATED EDITION | MANUFACTURED | IN THE UNITED STATES OF | AMERICA'

Colophon: 'A NOTE | ON THE TYPE | IN WHICH THIS BOOK IS SET | [short rule] | [eleven lines on Bodoni type] | [Borzoi device in oval] | SET UP, ELEC-TROTYPED | PRINTED AND BOUND BY THE PLIMPTON PRESS | NOR-WOOD • MASSACHUSETTS | PAPER FURNISHED | BY THE JAPAN PAPER COMPANY | NEW YORK.'

Statement of limitation: 'OF THE FIRST EDITION OF | "MENCKENIANA" | EIGHTY COPIES (OF WHICH SEVENTY-FIVE | ARE FOR SALE) HAVE BEEN PRINTED ON | INOMACHI JAPAN VELLUM, | NUMBERED FROM 1 TO 80 | EACH COPY IS SIGNED BY H. L. MENCKEN | THIS IS NUMBER | [number penned in, signature below]'

$8\frac{3}{4}'' \times 5\frac{5}{8}''$: [i–xiv 1] 2–132 (first page of each section unnumbered: 1, 11, 16, 20, 22, 28, 36, 40, 48, 55, 59, 61, 65, 72, 76, 81, 82, 85, 95, 109, 115, 119, 121) [133–38] = 152 pp.

$[1-9]^8 [10]^4$ = 76 leaves.

Contents: pp. i–iii: blank; p. iv: limitation notice; p. v: half title; p. vi: blank; p. vii: title; p. viii: copyright; pp. ix–x: [gothic] 'Note' [signed *'THE PUBLISHER'*]; pp. xi–xii: [gothic] 'Contents'; p. xiii: half title; p. xiv: blank; pp. 1–132: text; p. 133: colophon; pp. 134–38: blank.

Typography and paper: $5\frac{5}{16}''$ ($4\frac{15}{16}''$) $\times$ $3\frac{1}{8}''$; 18 lines per page (lines vary with number of entries on the page). Running heads: recto, '[gothic] A Schimpflexikon | [rule]' (pp. 3–131); verso, '[gothic] Menckeniana | [rule]' (pp. 2–132). "Inomachi Japan Vellum" (wove paper).

Binding: Bright orange-red vellum stamped in gilt. Front: [all in a box] '[appearing as orange-red showing through gilt background] MENCKENIANA | [sprigs flanking quarter moon in large dot] | A | Schimpflexikon [last two in gothic]'. Spine: '[appearing as orange-red showing through gilt background] [rule] | [reading down] MENCKE-NIANA [beneath previous word, reading down in gothic] A Schimpflexikon | [rule]'. Back: Borzoi Books logo. Uncut, unstained. Black end papers, white on sides facing pages. In orange paper-covered box with black paper label stamped in gilt on front, in design of front cover. The limitation number is written on top of "spine."

Dust jacket: None reported or seen.

Publication: Published 20 January 1928. $25 (*PW,* 7 January 1928: index). Copyright #A1061459. 2,000 copies of Knopf printings sold.

Printing: See colophon.

Locations: GHT, Harv, InU-Li.

Notes: Anti-Mencken invective collected by Sara Powell Haardt and edited by Mencken. Neither the order of the limited printings, nor the priority of limited and first trade, could be determined. Adler 29; S2.10; Bulsterbaum 76.

A 37.1.b
Only edition, presumed second limited printing

Same as A 37.1.a except:

Colophon: '. . . PAPER FURNISHED | BY THE WORTHY PAPER ASSOCIATION COMPANY | MITTENEAGUE, MASSACHUSETTS'

Statement of limitation: 'OF THE FIRST EDITION OF | "MENCKENIANA" | TWO HUNDRED AND THIRTY COPIES HAVE | BEEN PRINTED ON | BORZOI RAG PAPER | NUMBERED FROM 1 TO 230. EACH COPY IS | SIGNED BY H. L. MENCKEN | THIS IS NUMBER | [number penned in, signature below]'

$9\frac{1}{8}'' \times 5\frac{7}{8}''$

Typography and paper: Laid paper, watermarked with Borzoi Books logo.

Binding: Orange paper-covered boards, yellow V cloth spine. Black paper label on front, stamped in gilt leaving a black border, appearing as black showing through gilt, in a box: 'MENCKENIANA . . .'. Black paper label on spine, as on front without box: '[rule] | [reading down] MENCKENIANA [beneath previous word, reading down in gothic] A Schimpflexikon | [rule]'. Uncut, unstained. Black end papers, white on sides facing pages. In black paper-covered box with black and orange paper label on front (design of label on front cover).

Dust jacket: Glassine dust jacket reported (D).

Publication: $10 (*PW,* 7 January 1928: index).

Locations: Harv, InU-Li, RJS.

A 37.1.c
Only edition, first trade printing

Same as A 37.1.b except:

Colophon: 'A NOTE | ON THE TYPE | IN WHICH THIS BOOK IS SET | [short rule] | [eleven lines on Bodoni type] | [Borzoi device in oval] | SET UP, ELECTROTYPED, PRINTED | AND BOUND BY | THE PLIMPTON PRESS | NORWOOD • MASS. | PAPER FURNISHED BY W. F. | ETHERINGTON & CO. | NEW YORK'

$2.00

Few Americans of the present age have been denounced more copiously and more violently than H. L. Mencken. His attacks upon Babbitts, professors, patriots, and politicians have met with an excessively hearty response. This *Schimpflexicon* (i. e., Dictionary of Abuse) is a selection from these denunciations. One section is made up of waspish replies from authors to whom Mr. Mencken has paid his respects—among them, Arnold Bennett, Christopher Morley, Dr. Frank Crane and William Allen White. Two of the mildest citations in the volume are its first, "I will content myself with 'the bald statement that he is a weasel'" and its last, "A Baltimore Babbitt."

By H. L. Mencken

A BOOK OF PREFACES (1917)

IN DEFENSE OF WOMEN (1909)

THE AMERICAN LANGUAGE (1919)

PREJUDICES: FIRST SERIES (1919)

A BOOK OF BURLESQUES (1920)

PREJUDICES: SECOND SERIES (1920)

PREJUDICES: THIRD SERIES (1922)

PREJUDICES: FOURTH SERIES (1924)

PREJUDICES: FIFTH SERIES (1926)

NOTES ON DEMOCRACY (1926)

PREJUDICES: SIXTH SERIES (1927)

SELECTED PREJUDICES (1927)

Edited by H. L. Mencken

AMERICANA (1925)

AMERICANA (1926)

A 37.1.c, dust jacket

Statement of limitation: None.

7½″ × 4⅝″: [i–xii 1] . . . [133–36] = 148 pp.

[1]¹⁰ [2–9]⁸ = 74 leaves.

Contents: pp. i–ii: blank; p. iii: half title; p. iv: blank; p. v: title; p. vi: copyright; pp. vii–viii: [gothic] 'Note' [signed *'THE PUBLISHER'*]; pp. ix–x: [gothic] 'Contents'; p. xi: half title; p. xii: blank; pp. 1–132: text; p. 133: colophon; pp. 134–36: blank.

Typography and paper: Wove paper.

Binding: Orange V cloth stamped in gilt. Front, within box, appearing in orange showing through gilt background: 'MENCKENIANA | [sprigs flanking quarter moon in large dot] | A | Schimpflexikon [last two in gothic]'. Spine, appearing in orange showing through gilt background: '[double rule] | [sprig] | [double rule] | [reading down] MENCKENIANA [beneath previous word, reading down in gothic] A Schimpflexicon | [double rule] | [sprigs and moon as on front only vertical and moon reversed] | [double rule] | ALFRED | •A• | KNOPF | [double rule]'. Back: Borzoi Books logo blindstamped. Fore and bottom edges rough and unevenly trimmed, top edge gilt. End papers light blue with light orange mottling.

Dust jacket: Acetate, transparent except for flaps, which are printed in black and orange. Front flap: blurb; price $2. Back flap: fourteen titles by Mencken.

Publication: $2.00.

Locations: GHT (dj), InU-Li (dj), LC (30 January 1928, rebound), RJS, Yale (dj).

Review copy: Reported with tipped-in review slip (D).

A 37.1.d
Second trade printing: New York: Knopf, MCMXXVIII.

On copyright page: '*Second Printing January, 1928*'.

Locations: D, EPL.

A 37.1.e
Third trade printing: New York: Octagon, 1977.

Locations: EPL, GHT, Harv, MBU.

A 38 H. L. MENCKEN, TREATISE ON THE GODS
1929

H L MENCKEN

TREATISE

ON

THE GODS

1929 ALFRED A KNOPF NEW YORK

A 38

Title page: Vertical and zigzag lines are green.

Copyright page: 'COPYRIGHT 1929 BY ALFRED A. KNOPF INC. | MANUFAC-TURED IN THE UNITED STATES OF AMERICA'

$7\frac{5}{8}'' \times 5\frac{1}{16}''$: [i–iv] 1–12 = 16 pages.

$[1]^8$ = 8 leaves.

Contents: p. i: blank; p. ii: blurb; p. iii: title; p. iv: copyright; pp. 1–12: text.

Typography and paper: $5\frac{1}{2}''$ ($5\frac{1}{4}''$) $\times$ $3\frac{1}{2}''$; 24 lines per page. Running heads: recto, 'The Nature of Religion' (pp. 3–11); verso, 'Treatise on the Gods' (pp. 2–12). Wove paper.

Binding: Self wrappers. All edges trimmed. ? staples.

Location: EPL.

Notes: EPL copy bound in a book. The text is an earlier version of what was published in March 1930 (A 40) as pp. 1–11, l. 20. The blurb gives as probable date of publication 25 October 1929. Not in Adler.

A 39 MR. MENCKEN TO THE BOOK PUBLISHERS
1929

Mr.
MENCKEN
TO THE
BOOK PUBLISHERS

——

NEW YORK
The American Mercury
1929

A 39, cover title

Head title: 'Mr. Mencken to the Book Publishers | [thick-thin rule] | [text follows]'

Colophon: 'Two hundred and fifty copies of this booklet have been | printed from Garamond type by | THE AMERICAN MERCURY | November 25, 1929.'

6½" × 4¾": 1–4 = 4 pp.

[1]² = 2 leaves.

Contents: pp. 1–4: text; p. 4: colophon.

Typography and paper: 5⅛" (4⁵⁄₁₆") × 3"; 20 lines per page. Running heads: recto and verso, 'Mr. Mencken to the Book Publishers | [thin-thick rule]' (pp. 1–4). Laid paper.

Binding: Light green wrappers (7" × 5"). Cover title: 'Mr. | M E N C K E N | TO THE | BOOK PUBLISHERS | [thick-thin rule] | NEW YORK | *The American Mercury* | 1929'. Front verso: '*P R E F A T O R Y   N O T E*'. Folded sheet glued into EPL copy, laid in to TxU and NhD copies.

Locations: EPL, NhD, TxU.

Notes: The prefatory note indicates (perhaps jokingly) that this originated as a speech recorded on a single gramophone record. Adler 14.

A 40 TREATISE ON THE GODS

A 40.1.a
First edition, limited printing (1930)

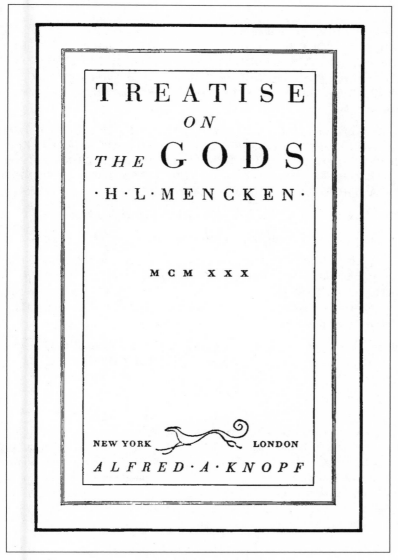

A 40.1.a–b

Title page: The triple-rule box and Borzoi device are red.

Copyright page: 'COPYRIGHT 1930 BY ALFRED A. KNOPF, INC. | ALL RIGHTS RESERVED INCLUDING THE RIGHT TO REPRODUCE | THIS BOOK OR PARTS THEREOF IN ANY FORM | MANUFACTURED IN THE UNITED STATES OF AMERICA'

Colophon: [the whole text in diamond shape] 'A | NOTE | ON THE | TYPE IN | WHICH THIS | BOOK IS SET | [rule] | [fifteen lines on Bodoni type] | [rule] | SET UP, ELECTROTYPED, PRINTED | AND BOUND BY THE PLIMPTON | PRESS, NORWOOD, MASS• | PAPER MADE BY THE | WORTHY PAPER CO., | MITTINEAGUE, | MASSACHUSETTS | [Borzoi device in oval] | [three rules] | [ornament]'

Statement of limitation: 'OF THE FIRST EDITION OF | *TREATISE ON THE GODS* | THREE HUNDRED SEVENTY-FIVE COPIES | (OF WHICH THREE HUNDRED SIXTY-FIVE | ARE FOR SALE) | HAVE BEEN PRINTED ON | *BORZOI RAG PAPER* | NUMBERED FROM 1 TO 375 | EACH COPY IS SIGNED BY THE AUTHOR | THIS IS NUMBER | [number penned in red, signature below]'

$9\frac{1}{8}'' \times 5\frac{7}{8}''$: [A–D i–iv] v–ix [x–xiv] 1–363 [364] i–xii [xiii–xvi] = 398 pp.

$[1]^8 (1_1 + 1) [2–24]^8 [25]^6$ = 199 leaves. The leaf containing pp. C–D is tipped in.

Contents: pp. A–C: blank; p. D: limitation notice; p. i: half title; p. ii: [all in a triple-rule red box within a box] '•H•L•MENCKEN• | [seventeen titles]'; p. iii: title; p. iv: copyright; pp. v–ix: 'PREFACE'; p. x: blank; p. xi: 'CONTENTS'; p. xii: blank; p. xiii: half title; p. xiv: blank; pp. 1–353: text; pp. 354–64: 'BIBLIOGRAPHICAL NOTE'; pp. i–xii: 'INDEX'; p. xiii: colophon; pp. xiv–xvi: blank.

Typography and paper: $6\frac{1}{8}''$ ($5\frac{7}{8}''$) $\times 3\frac{1}{2}''$; 29 lines per page. Running heads: recto, 'PREFACE' (p. vii–ix), chapter titles (pp. 3–353), 'BIBLIOGRAPHICAL NOTE' (pp. 355–63), 'INDEX' (pp. iii–xi); verso, 'PREFACE' (p. vi–viii), 'TREATISE ON THE GODS' (pp. 2–364), 'INDEX' (pp. ii–xii). Laid paper, watermarked with Borzoi Books logo.

Binding: Deep blue vellum-covered boards. Front, stylized blindstamped: 'HLM'. Spine, stamped in gilt: '[crownlike ornament] | TREATISE | *ON* | THE [HE ligature] GODS | [rule] | H. L. MENCKEN | [floral ornament with borders at top and bottom] | [script] Alfred A *[sic]* Knopf'. Back: Borzoi Books logo blindstamped. Top edge rough trimmed, gilt, fore edge rough trimmed, bottom unevenly cut. White end papers. In deep blue or black paper-covered box stamped in gilt on "spine" to match spine of book, limitation number penned in red at bottom.

Dust jacket: White paper folding over the three edges of the front and back covers. Spine: 'TREATISE | *ON* | THE [HE ligature] GODS | [rule] | H. L. MENCKEN'.

TREATISE
ON
THE GODS
H. L. MENCKEN

A 40.1.a, dust jacket

Publication: Published 14 March 1930. $15 (promotional form letter [JRS]; *American Mercury,* April 1930: xlviii). Copyright #A21163. 20,000 copies of the three Knopf editions sold.

Printing: See colophon.

Locations: GHT (dj), Harv, RJS (dj).

Notes: The leaves with the limitation notice were signed by Mencken in England (*Thirty-five Years* 196). One copy is noted in rust cloth without labels or lettering, signed but not numbered or boxed (GHT). Adler 15, 275; S1.4; S2.11, 14; Bulster-baum 6; Mary Miller Vass and James L. W. West III in *Menckeniana* 88.9–16 (on the book's composition and revision, noting there are thirty-five plate changes between first and tenth printings [13]).

A 40.1.b
First edition, first trade printing

Same as A 40.1.a except:

Colophon: '. . . | PAPER MADE BY CURTIS | & BROTHER, NEWARK, | DELA-WARE | . . .'

Statement of limitation: None.

8¹⁄₁₆" × 5½": [A–B i–iv] . . . = 396 pp.

[1–24]⁸ [25]⁶ = 198 leaves.

Contents: pp. A–B blank; p. i: half title;. . . .

Binding: Smooth blue V cloth. Front, spine, and back as above. Top edge trimmed, stained yellow, fore edge rough trimmed, bottom edge unevenly trimmed. White end papers.

Dust jacket: White paper with full-length red ornamental borders at top and bottom. Front: '• *H• L • M E N C K E N* • [dots in red] | T R E A T I S E | O N | *T H E G O D S* | *Nothing in this book has been printed before,* | *either in* T H E *A M E R I C A N* M *E R C U R Y or elsewhere.* | *It is the first book by Mr. Mencken since 1927.* | THE CONTENTS | [the chapter titles in five lines] | ALFRED•A•KNOPF [Borzoi Books logo as white showing through red] PUBLISHER•N•Y•'. Spine: '*H• L•* [dots in red] | • *M E N C K E N* • [dots in red] | T R E A T I S E | O N | *T H E* G O D S | ALFRED•A•KNOPF'. Back: '•*H•L•MENCKEN•* [dots in red] | [list of thirteen books, Knopf imprint]'. Front flap: blurb; price $3.00. Rear flap: list of five 'BORZOI BOOKS | *On Religion*'.

Publication: $3.00.

Locations: BL (31 MAR 1930), Bod (MAY | 24 | 1930), Camb (22 MY | 1930), Harv, InU-Li (dj), LC (17 March 1930, two copies), MBU, RJS (dj).

A 40.1.b, dust jacket

Notes: The MBU copy was presented to Charles Angoff and dated 24 February 1930 by Mencken.

A 40.1.c.i
First edition, second trade printing, American issue: New York: Knopf, 1930.

On copyright page: 'Published March 1930 | First and Second Printings Before Publication'.

Location: EPL.

A 40.1.c.ii
Second trade printing, English issue (1930)

Title page: The triple-rule box and Borzoi device are red.

Copyright page: 'FIRST PUBLISHED, 1930, BY ALFRED A. KNOPF, LTD. | ALL RIGHTS RESERVED INCLUDING THE RIGHT TO REPRODUCE | THIS BOOK OR PARTS THEREOF IN ANY FORM | PRINTED IN THE UNITED STATES OF AMERICA'

$8'' \times 5\frac{3}{8}''$: [A–B i–iv] v–ix [x–xiv] 1–363 [364] i–xii [xiii–xvi] = 396 pp.

$[1-24]^8 [25]^6$ = 198 leaves.

Contents: pp. A–B: blank; p. i: half title; p. ii: blank; p. iii: title; p. iv: copyright; pp. v–ix: 'PREFACE'; p. x: blank; p. xi: 'CONTENTS'; p. xii: blank; p. xiii: half title; p. xiv: blank; pp. 1–353: text; pp. 354–64: 'BIBLIOGRAPHICAL NOTE'; pp. i–xii: 'INDEX'; pp. xiii–xvi: blank.

Typography and paper: Typography same as in limited printing. The laid paper, watermarked with the Borzoi Books logo, is the same as that of the first and second American trade printings.

Binding: Maroon V cloth. Spine: '[black ornamental border] | [gilt] TREATISE | ON | THE GODS | [black ornamental border] | [gold] MENCKEN | [black ornamental border] | [black ornamental border] | [gold] KNOPF | [black ornamental border]'. Back: Borzoi Books logo as maroon showing through black.

Dust jacket: White paper with full-length red ornamental borders at top and bottom. Front: '• *H• L • M E N C K E N* • [dots in red] | T R E A T I S E | O N | *T H E* G O D S | *Nothing in this book has been printed before,* | *either in* THE AMERICAN MERCURY *or elsewhere.* | *It is the first book by Mr. Mencken since 1927.* | THE CONTENTS | [the chapter titles in five lines] | ALFRED•A•KNOPF [Borzoi Books logo as white showing through red] L O N D O N'. Spine: '*H• L•* [dots in red] | • *M E N C K E N* • [dots in red] | T R E A T I S E | O N | *T H E* G O D S | ALFRED•A•KNOPF'. Back: '• H • L• MENCKEN • | [list of eleven books] | [Knopf imprint]'. Front flap: blurb; price clipped in example seen. Rear flap: unprinted except for continuation of border.

TREATISE
ON
THE GODS
·H·L·MENCKEN·

M C M . X X X

LONDON   NEW YORK
A L F R E D · A · K N O P F

A 40.1.c.ii

Publication: Published May 1930 (ECB 12.1037); April 1930 (Mencken quoted in Adler). 10s.6d.

Locations: EPL, GHT (dj), InU-Li, RJS.

Notes: Mencken wrote on the free front end paper of the EPL copy: "Note exchange of 'New York' and 'London' in date on title page." BL, Bod, and Camb acquired the first trade printing. Adler 15.

A 40.1.d
First edition, third trade printing: New York: Knopf, MCMXXX.

On copyright page: 'Third Printing March 1930'.

Location: EPL.

A 40.1.e
First edition, fourth trade printing: New York: Knopf, MCMXXX.

On copyright page: 'Fourth Printing March 1930'.

Location: EPL.

A 40.1.f
First edition, fifth trade printing: New York: Knopf, MCMXXX.

On copyright page: 'Fifth Printing April 1930'.

Locations: EPL, Harv, MChB.

A 40.1.g
First edition, sixth trade printing: New York: Knopf, MCMXXX.

On copyright page: 'Sixth Printing June 1930'.

Location: D, EPL.

A 40.1.h
First edition, seventh trade printing: New York: Knopf, MCMXXX.

On copyright page: 'Seventh Printing October 1930'.

Location: EPL, MBU, MC.

A 40.1.i
First edition, eighth trade printing: New York: Blue Ribbon Books, [1932].

On copyright page: 'Eighth Printing March 1932'. The lines of type indicating the eighth, ninth, and tenth printings are not uniform with those of the first seven.

Locations: EPL, GHT, Harv, MBU.

A 40.1.j
First edition, ninth trade printing: New York: Blue Ribbon Books, [1932].

On copyright page: 'Ninth Printing May 1932'.

Location: D.

A 40.1.k
First edition, tenth trade printing: New York: Blue Ribbon Books, [1933].

On copyright page: 'Tenth Printing February 1933'.

Locations: D, EPL.

A 40.2.a
Second edition, first printing (1946)

Title page: 'Treatise on | T H E   G O D S | *H. L. Mencken* | [ornament] Second edition: corrected and rewritten | [Borzoi device in circle] | *New York* : 1946 | ALFRED A. KNOPF'

Copyright page: 'PUBLISHED MARCH 1930. REPRINTED NINE TIMES | SECOND EDITION: CORRECTED AND REWRITTEN | *Copyright* 1930, 1946 *by Alfred A. Knopf, Inc. All rights reserved. No* | [three lines reserving rights] | *Manufactured in the United States of America* | *Published simultaneously in Canada by The Ryerson Press* | *This is a Borzoi Book, published by Alfred A. Knopf, Inc.*'

Colophon: 'A NOTE ON THE TYPE | [ten lines on Granjon type] | *The book was composed, printed, and bound by* THE PLIMP- | TON PRESS, *Norwood, Massachusetts. The typography and* | *binding are by* W. A. DWIGGINS. | [ornament with linked WAD]'

8⅜" × 5⅝": [A–B i–iv] v–vii [viii] ix [x 1–2] 3–302 i–xvii [xviii–xxii] = 336 pp.

[1–21]⁸ = 168 leaves.

Contents: p. A: blank; p. B: 'ALSO BY MR. MENCKEN | [seven Borzoi Books]'; p. i: half title; p. ii: blank; p. iii: title; p. iv: copyright; pp. v–viii: 'Preface to the Revised Edition'; p. ix: 'Contents'; p. x: blank; p. 1: half title; p. 2: blank; pp. 3–293: text; pp. 294–302: 'Bibliographical Note'; pp. i–xvii: 'Index'; p. xviii: blank; p. xix: colophon; pp. xx–xxii: blank.

Binding: Black cloth. Front: Mencken arms blindstamped. Spine, stamped in gilt: '[ornament: thick rule | rule | row of dots | rule | row of heavy dots | rule | row of dots | rule | thick rule] | TREATISE | ON | THE [HE ligature] GODS | [same ornament as at top] | H•L•Mencken | [three ornaments as at top] | KNOPF | [ornament as at top]'.

Back: Borzoi logo blindstamped. Top edge trimmed and stained black, fore and bottom edges unevenly trimmed. Light brown end papers.

Dust jacket: White paper. Front: [appearing as white showing through black, all in a box with multiple orange borders top, left, and right] 'TREATISE | *ON THE* | GODS | BY | H. L. MENCKEN | [seven-line blurb] | [black on white, in an orange box with white ornamental borders on the sides showing though orange] T H E   C O N T E N T S | [the chapter titles in three lines]'. Spine: '[two orange bars] | *Treatise* | ON THE | Gods | [two orange bars] | NEW EDITION | REVISED AND | REWRITTEN BY | *H. L.* | *Mencken* | [two orange bars] | [orange bar] | BORZOI | [Borzoi device within orange rules] | BOOKS | [thick orange rule] | KNOPF | [orange bar]'. Back: photo, biography, and bibliography of Mencken. Front flap: four excerpts from reviews; price clipped in GHT, JRS, and RJS copies and replaced with handstamped '$3.50 | net.' Rear flap: blurb for *The American Language* and *Supplement One*.

Locations: Harv, RJS (dj).

Notes: Month of printing (October 1946) stated on copyright page of subsequent printings. The English printing of the second edition claimed by Adler (15) is a ghost. No copies with a Canadian imprint were found.

A 40.2.b
Second edition, second printing: New York: Knopf, 1948.

On copyright page: 'REPRINTED DECEMBER 1948'.

Locations: D, D.

A 40.2.c
Second edition, third printing: New York: Knopf, 1956.

On copyright page: 'REPRINTED MARCH 1956'. The dust jacket of this printing is in the style of that of *Minority Report* with squares on the front.

Location: GHT (dj).

A 40.2.d
Second edition, fourth printing: New York: Knopf, 1959.

On copyright page: 'REPRINTED JUNE 1959'.

Locations: D, GHT.

A 40.2.e
Second edition, fifth printing: New York: Knopf, 1965.

On copyright page: 'FIFTH PRINTING, MAY, 1965'.

Location: GHT.

A 40.3.a
Third edition, only printing (1963)

Title page: 'TREATISE | ON | THE | GODS | [star] | *H•L•MENCKEN* | [star] | [device: sun with face] | VINTAGE BOOKS | *A Division of Random House* | NEW YORK'

Copyright page: 'FIRST VINTAGE EDITION, *February, 1963* | VINTAGE BOOKS | *are published by* ALFRED A. KNOPF, INC. | *and* RANDOM HOUSE, INC. | Copyright 1930 by Alfred A. Knopf, Inc. Renewed 1958. | All rights reserved under International and Pan-American Copy- | right Conventions. Published in New York by Random House, | Inc., and in Toronto, Canada, by Random House of Canada, | Limited. | Reprinted by arrangement with Alfred A. Knopf, Inc. | MANUFACTURED IN THE UNITED STATES OF AMERICA'

Colophon: '[fourteen-line biography] | [device: sun with face] | [six lines on Electra type, designed by W. A. Dwiggins] | a feeling of fluidity, power, and speed. Composed, printed, | and bound by H. WOLFF BOOK MANUFACTURING CO. Cover | design by George Salter.'

7³⁄₁₆″ × 4⅜″: [i–vii] viii–x [1–3] 4–46 [47] 48–99 [100] 101–59 [160] 161–224 [225] 226–68 [269] 270–77 [278–79] 280–87 [288–94] = 304 pp.

[1–7]¹⁶ [8]⁸ [9–10]¹⁶ = 152 leaves in binding A; gatherings in binding B appear to be glued, not sewed, if not perfect bound.

Contents: p. i: half title; p. ii: 'OTHER WORKS BY *H. L. Mencken* ALSO AVAILABLE | IN THE VINTAGE SERIES ARE: | [three titles]'; p. iii: title; p. iv: copyright; p. v: '*Contents*'; p. vi: blank; pp. vii–x: '*Preface to the Revised Edition*'; p. 1: half title; p. 2: blank; pp. 3–268: text; pp. 269–77: '*Bibliographical Note*'; p. 278: blank; pp. 279–87: '*Index*'; p. 288: blank; p. 289: colophon; pp. 290–94: catalogue.

Binding A: Green buckram stamped in gilt.

Binding B: Thick white paper wrappers printed in brown, black, and blue (series no. V–232; price $1.95).

Locations: GHT (2, bindings A and B), RJS (binding B).

Notes: Text of second edition. No copies with a Canadian imprint were found.

A 41 THE 10,000 BEST AMERICAN BOOKS IN PRINT

1930

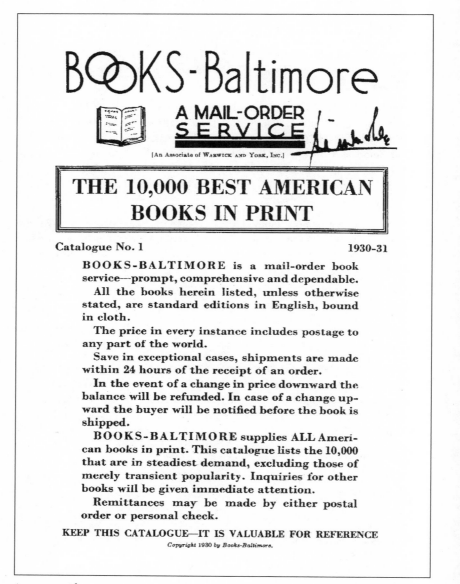

BOOKS-Baltimore

A MAIL-ORDER SERVICE

[An Associate of WARWICK AND YORK, INC.]

THE 10,000 BEST AMERICAN BOOKS IN PRINT

Catalogue No. 1   1930-31

BOOKS-BALTIMORE is a mail-order book service—prompt, comprehensive and dependable.

All the books herein listed, unless otherwise stated, are standard editions in English, bound in cloth.

The price in every instance includes postage to any part of the world.

Save in exceptional cases, shipments are made within 24 hours of the receipt of an order.

In the event of a change in price downward the balance will be refunded. In case of a change upward the buyer will be notified before the book is shipped.

BOOKS-BALTIMORE supplies ALL American books in print. This catalogue lists the 10,000 that are in steadiest demand, excluding those of merely transient popularity. Inquiries for other books will be given immediate attention.

Remittances may be made by either postal order or personal check.

KEEP THIS CATALOGUE—IT IS VALUABLE FOR REFERENCE

A 41, cover title

Copyright page: See cover title.

9″ × 5⅞″: 1–91 [92–96] = 96 pp.

[1]⁴⁸ = 48 leaves.

Contents: pp. 1–90: text, mostly in fine print in three columns; p. 91: order instructions; p. 92: blank; pp. 93–96: order forms.

Typography and paper: 7⅝″ (7¼″) × 4¹³⁄₁₆″; 71 lines per column (number of lines varies). Running heads: recto and verso, '1930–31 [book] BOOKS-Baltimore [O's linked] A MAIL-ORDER [over] SERVICE [over rule over bar] Catalogue No. 1 [all in one line over rule]' (pp. 2–90). Smooth wove paper.

Binding: Light green paper wrappers printed in green. Front: cover title. Back: blurbs. Inside front and back: index. All edges trimmed. Two staples.

Locations: EPL (3), Yale.

Notes: A note from August Mencken tipped in to an EPL copy ascribes "probably all of it" to Mencken, in association with H. E. Buchholz of Warwick and York. Mencken wrote in another copy, "I compiled this," and in the Yale copy, "I made up this list." In a note quoted in Adler he describes it as a joint venture with Buchholz. Adler 30.

A 42 A LITERARY HISTORY OF THE AMERICAN PEOPLE,
BY CHARLES ANGOFF
[1930?]

I wrote this

Publication date: March 13, 1931

A LITERARY HISTORY
OF THE
AMERICAN PEOPLE

BY CHARLES ANGOFF

VOLUME ONE

*From 1607 to the Beginning
of the Revolutionary Period*

•

VOLUME TWO

From 1750 to 1815

If you are a teacher and desire an examination set
with a view to adoption for class or reference purposes,
we shall be glad to bill the books to you less our educational discount. If an adoption follows, the charge
against you will be cancelled.

$5.00 *each volume*

Size: 6¼″ x 9¾″; set on the linotype in Caslon Long Descenders
and printed on a natural eggshell wove paper. The binding is of
black silk-patterned cloth stamped in gold and blind.

ALFRED·A·KNOPF BORZOI BOOKS **PUBLISHER·N·Y**

A 42, cover title

Copyright page: None.

8½″ × 5½″: [1–4] = 4 pp.

[1]² = 2 leaves.

Contents: p. 1: cover title; pp. 2–4: text.

Typography and paper: 6⅜″ × 4³⁄₁₆″; 30 lines per page (number of lines varies). No heads. All pages have bold French rules at top and bottom. Laid paper.

Binding: None.

Location: EPL.

Notes: Dated 1930 by Adler. An advertising brochure for the first two volumes (published 1931), the remaining two projected. The EPL copy is inscribed "I wrote this" by Mencken. Adler 14.

A 43 MAKING A PRESIDENT

A 43.1.a
Only edition, first printing (1932)

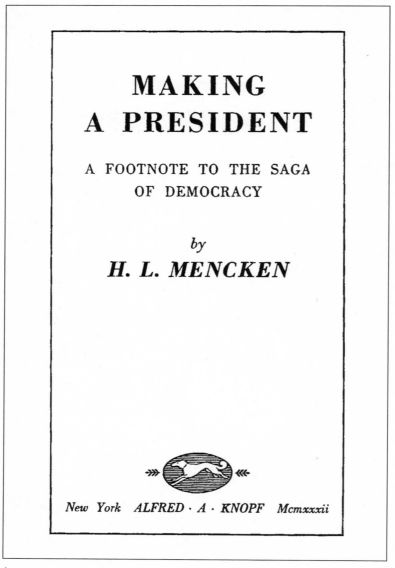

MAKING
A PRESIDENT

A FOOTNOTE TO THE SAGA
OF DEMOCRACY

by

H. L. MENCKEN

New York   ALFRED · A · KNOPF   Mcmxxxii

Copyright page: 'COPYRIGHT 1932 BY | ALFRED A. KNOPF, INC. | All rights reserved–no part of this book may be | [five lines of warning] | FIRST EDITION | MANUFACTURED IN THE UNITED STATES | OF AMERICA'

Colophon: 'A NOTE | ON THE TYPE | IN WHICH THIS BOOK IS SET | [short rule] | [eleven lines on Bodoni type] | [Borzoi device in oval] | SET UP, PRINTED, AND BOUND BY | HARRIS WOLFF ESTATE | NEW YORK | PAPER MADE BY | S. D. WARREN CO. | BOSTON, MASS.'

7¼″ × 4¼″: [A–F i–ii] iii–xiii [xiv] xv [xvi 1–2] 3–33 [34] 35–48 [49] 50–64 [65] 66–69 [70] 71–77 [78] 79–83 [84] 85–126 [127] 128–31 [132] 133–46 [147] 148–67 [168] 169–76 [177] 178–85 [186–90] = 212 pp.

[1]¹⁰ [2–13]⁸ = 106 leaves.

Contents: pp. A–C: blank; p. D: '*Mr. Mencken has also written* | [thirteen titles]'; p. E: half title; p. F: blank; p. i: title; p. ii: copyright; pp. iii–xiv: 'PREFACE'; pp. xv–xvi: 'CONTENTS'; p. 1: half title; p. 2: blank; pp. 3–186: text; p. 187: blank; p. 188: colophon; pp. 189–90: blank.

Typography and paper: 5⅞″ (5¹¹⁄₁₆″) × 3³⁄₁₆″; 25 lines per page. Running heads: recto, 'PREFACE' (pp. v–xiii), chapter titles (pp. 5–185); verso, 'PREFACE' (pp. iv–xiv), 'CONTENTS' (p. xvi), 'MAKING A PRESIDENT' (pp. 4–186). Wove paper.

Binding: Black S cloth. Front: [stamped in blue, within a box, appearing as black showing through blue background] 'MAKING | A PRESIDENT | [sprigs flanking quarter moon] | H • L *[sic]* | MENCKEN'. Spine: [as black showing through blue background] '[double rule] | [sprigs and moon as on front, only vertical] | [double rule] | [reading down] MAKING [over] A PRESIDENT | [double rule] | [reading down] H•L•MENCKEN | [double rule] | ALFRED•A *[sic]* | KNOPF | [double rule]'. Back: Borzoi Books logo blindstamped. Top edge trimmed, stained blue, fore and bottom edges rough trimmed. White end papers.

Dust jacket: White paper printed in brown. Front: '[photo of Mencken at typewriter] | [the rest as white showing through brown background] MAKING | A PRESIDENT | *H.L.MENCKEN*'. Spine: [as white showing through brown background, reading down] 'MAKING A PRESIDENT [diamond] *H.L.MENCKEN*'. Back: blurb for *Treatise on the Gods.* Front flap: blurb; price $1.50. Rear flap: ad for *The American Mercury.*

Publication: Published 1 September 1932. $1.50. Copyright #A54661 (two copies received 6 September 1932).

Printing: See colophon.

Locations: GHT (dj), InU-Li (dj), RJS, Yale (dj).

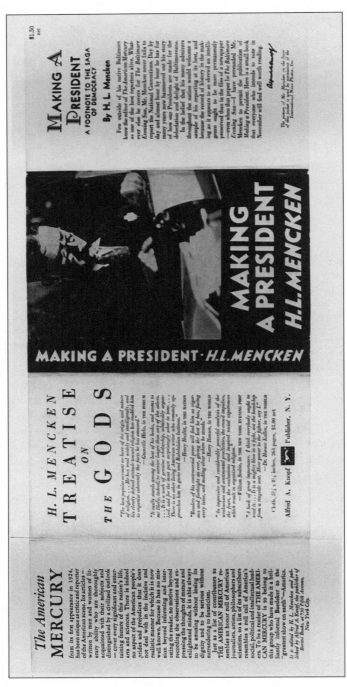

A 43.1.a, dust jacket

Notes: The book is made up "mainly of my reports of the two national conventions of 1932 for the Baltimore *Evening Sun* . . ." (p. iii). Adler 15, 87–88; Bulsterbaum 58, 76.

Review copy: As above, with light blue slip (2¼″ × 4″) laid in: 'This book will be published | [handstamped] SEP 1 1932 | [rule] | Please do not release reviews | until the above date. | *Alfred A. Knopf'*. *Location:* RJS.

Salesman's dummy: Title page and binding as above, 7¼″ × 4⅜″, no copyright page, has pp. iii–xvi, 3–10, the rest blank. *Location:* EPL.

A 43.1.b
Second printing: New York: Knopf, Mcmxxxii.
On copyright page: 'Published September 1, 1932 | Second Printing September, 1932'.

Location: GHT.

A 44 TREATISE ON RIGHT AND WRONG

A 44.1.a
First edition, first printing (1934)

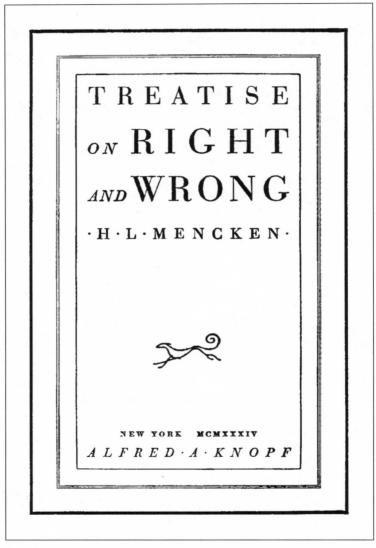

Title page: The triple-rule box and Borzoi device are red.

Copyright page: 'Copyright 1934 by Alfred A. Knopf, Inc. | [four lines reserving rights] | FIRST EDITION | *Manufactured in the United States of America*'

Colophon: 'A NOTE ON THE TYPE IN | WHICH THIS BOOK IS SET | [twenty-seven lines on Bodoni type] | [Borzoi device] | THIS BOOK WAS COMPOSED, PRINTED, AND BOUND BY | THE PLIMPTON PRESS, NORWOOD, MASS. THE PAPER | WAS MADE BY S. D. WARREN CO., BOSTON'

$8\frac{1}{16}'' \times 5\frac{1}{2}''$: [A–B i–iv] v–viii [ix–xii] 1–331 [332] i–xix [xx–xxii] = 368 pp.

$[1–23]^8$ = 184 leaves.

Contents: p. A: blank; p. B: '*Mr. Mencken has also written* | [thirteen titles]'; p. i: half title; p. ii: blank; p. iii: title; p. iv: copyright; pp. v–viii: 'PREFACE'; p. ix: 'CONTENTS'; p. x: blank; p. xi: half title; p. xii: blank; pp. 1–331: text; p. 332: blank; pp. i–xix: 'INDEX'; p. xx: colophon; pp. xxi–xxii: blank.

Typography and paper: $6\frac{1}{16}''$ ($5\frac{13}{16}''$) $\times 3\frac{1}{2}''$; 29 lines per page. Running heads: recto, 'PREFACE' (p. vii), chapter titles (pp. 3–319), 'BIBLIOGRAPHICAL NOTE' (pp. 321–31), 'INDEX' (pp. iii–xix); verso, 'PREFACE' (pp. vi–viii), 'TREATISE ON RIGHT AND WRONG' (pp. 2–330), 'INDEX' (pp. ii–xviii). Laid paper, watermarked 'WARREN'S | OLDE STYLE'.

Binding: Blue V cloth. Front: blindstamped 'HLM' as on first trade binding of *Treatise on the Gods* (A 40). Spine, stamped in gilt, as on *Gods* except: '. . . | TREATISE | ON | RIGHT | & WRONG | . . .'. Back: Borzoi Books logo blindstamped. Top edge trimmed, stained yellow, fore and bottom edges unevenly trimmed. White end papers.

Dust jacket: Blue on gray paper, in the style of the dust jacket of *Treatise on the Gods*, with full-length purple ornamental borders at top and bottom. Front: '*H • L • MENCKEN'S* [purple dots] | *FIRST BOOK SINCE 1930* | [short rule] | TREATISE ON | RIGHT *AND* | WRONG | *Nothing in this book has been printed before,* | *either in* THE AMERICAN MERCURY *or elsewhere.* | THE CONTENTS | [chapter titles in five lines] | ALFRED•A•KNOPF [Borzoi Books logo as gray showing through purple] PUBLISHER•N•Y•'. Spine: '•*H•L•* [dots purple] | •*MENCKEN•* [dots purple] | TREATISE | ON | RIGHT | *AND* | WRONG | [Borzoi Books logo as gray showing through purple] | ALFRED•A•KNOPF'. Back: '• *H • L • MENCKEN* • [dots purple] | [fourteen titles and Knopf imprint]'. Front flap: blurb; price $3.00. Rear flap: three titles by Oswald Spengler.

Publication: Published 5 April 1934. $3.00. Copyright #A71218. 4,700 copies of the Knopf printing sold.

Printing: See colophon.

Locations: GHT (2 in dj), Harv, InU-Li (dj), LC (11 April 1934), MCR, RJS (dj).

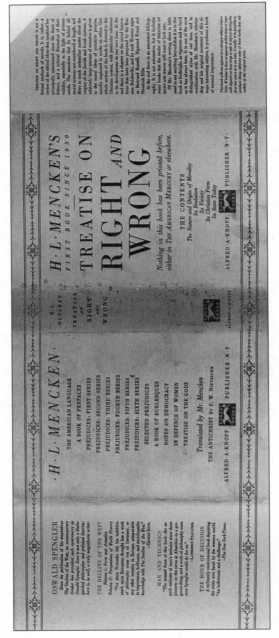

A 44.1.a, dust jacket

Notes: The RJS and InU-Li copies and one of two GHT examples have a pink sticker on front of dust jacket, a star in each corner: '*Recommended by* | *The [sic]* BOOK-OF-THE- | MONTH CLUB'. The sticker also seen on a dealer's copy. The BOMC recommendation was April 1934. Laid in the RJS copy is an ad for Thomas Mann's *Joseph and His Brothers* (publication date 6 June). The work took much longer to complete than Mencken planned. "I had hoped to get the book into Knopf's hands by the end of the year [1931], but it now seems likely that it will hold me until the Spring" (*Diary* [A 80], p. 37). This accounts for the date of the salesman's dummy. Adler 15; S2.8, 14; Bulsterbaum 7.

Salesman's dummy: Title page ('MCMXXXII'), copyright page ('1932'), table of contents, and first ten pages of text in a different setting of type from that of the trade printing; the rest blank. Trade binding and page size, but in a different dust jacket. Pasted on inside front cover is a publisher's announcement claiming that the book will be published in April at $3. *Location:* ViU.

LATER REPRINTINGS WITHIN THE FIRST EDITION

A 44.1.b
New York: Octagon, 1977.

Location: EPL.

A 44.1.c
New York: Octagon, 1980.

Data from OCLC. Not seen.

A 44.1.d
New York: Octagon, 1985.

"Third Octagon Printing 1985." Data from OCLC. Not seen.

A 44.2.a
Second edition (first English printing) (1934)

Copyright page: 'Printed in Great Britain by Butler & Tanner Ltd., Frome and London'

$7^{15}/_{16}'' \times 5^{1}/_{4}''$: [i–iv] v–vii [viii] ix [x] 1–277 [278] = 288 pp.

[A]^8 ($\pm$ A$_2$) B–I^8 K–S^8 = 144 leaves. The title/copyright leaf is a cancel.

Contents: p. i: half title; p. ii: blank; p. iii: title; p. iv: copyright; pp. v–vii: 'PREFACE'; p. viii: blank; p. ix: 'CONTENTS'; p. x: blank; pp. 1–256: text; pp. 257–64: 'BIBLIO-GRAPHICAL NOTE'; pp. 265–77: 'INDEX'; p. 278: blank.

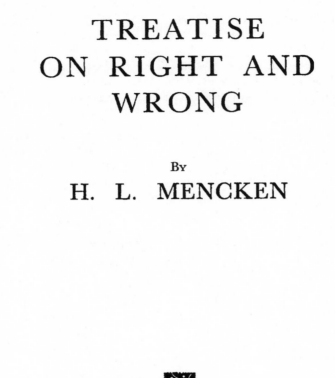

TREATISE
ON RIGHT AND
WRONG

By

H. L. MENCKEN

LONDON
KEGAN PAUL, TRENCH, TRUBNER & CO. LTD.
BROADWAY HOUSE: 68-74 CARTER LANE, E.C.
1934

A 44.2.a

Typography and paper: 6⅛″ (5⅞″) × 3¹¹⁄₁₆″; 34 lines per page. Running heads: recto, 'PREFACE' (p. vii), chapter titles (pp. 3–255), 'BIBLIOGRAPHICAL NOTE' (pp. 259–63), 'INDEX' (pp. 267–77); verso, 'PREFACE' (p. vi), 'TREATISE ON RIGHT AND WRONG' (pp. 2–256), 'BIBLIOGRAPHICAL NOTE' (pp. 258–64), 'INDEX' (pp. 266–76). Wove paper.

Binding: Red V cloth stamped in gilt on spine: 'TREATISE | ON | RIGHT | AND WRONG | H. L. MENCKEN | KEGAN PAUL'. Trimmed, unstained. White end papers.

Dust jacket: Off-white paper. Front: [all within ornate red border] 'TREATISE ON | RIGHT AND | WRONG | *By* | H. L. MENCKEN | *Author of "In Defence of Women,"* etc. | *The Nature and Origin of Morality* | *Its Evolution   Its Variety* | *Its Christian Form* | *Its State To-Day*'. Spine: '[ornate border] | H. L. | MENCKEN | [red] TREA-TISE | ON | [red] RIGHT | AND | [red] WRONG | *A* | *history of* | *the origin, growth* | *and present state* | *of morals* | [KP device] | KEGAN PAUL | [ornate border]'. Back: 'NEW BOOKS | FROM | ROUTLEDGE AND KEGAN PAUL | [eleven titles, including this book at 10s.6d]'. Front flap: blurb, possibly price (examined copy clipped). Back flap: list of 'THE | NEW WORLD | SERIES'.

Publication: Published September 1934 (ECB 13.1165); Autumn 1934 (*Routledge Kegan Paul Autumn Books 1934*, p. 25). 10s.6d.

Locations: BL (12 SEP 34), Bod (DEC | 6 | 1934), Camb (1 DE | 1934), EPL, GHT (dj), RJS.

Notes: A reprint in the New World Series and a Canadian issue, both claimed by Adler (15), are ghosts.

A 45 EREZ ISRAEL

A 45.1.a
Only edition, only printing (1935)

A 45, first state

Title page: Presumed first state: in Hebrew. *Presumed second state:* in English.

Copyright page: 'Copyright, 1934, and reprinted by courtesy of | The Evening Sun, Baltimore'

Colophon: 'This is one of twenty five [sic] copies, for presentation only, | printed by B. P. Safran at The New School.'

8⅜" × 5¼": [i–iv 1–2] 3–15 [16–20] = 24 pp.

[1–3]⁴ = 12 leaves.

Contents: pp. i–ii: pastedown; pp. iii–iv: blank; p. 1: title; p. 2: copyright; pp. 3–15: text; p. 16: colophon; pp. 17–18: blank; pp. 19–20: pastedown.

Typography and paper: 6⅜" (6¹⁄₁₆") × 3½"; 25 lines per page. Running heads: recto and verso, '*Erez Israel*' (pp. 4–15). Laid paper. See Notes.

Binding: Light green V cloth. White paper label on front: [within ornate border] 'EREZ ISRAEL | BY H • L • MENCKEN'. White paper label on spine, reading up: 'EREZ ISRAEL • MENCKEN'. Uncut, unstained. The first and last leaves are the pastedowns, no free end papers.

Dust jacket: None reported or seen.

Locations: BL (15 MAR 76, second state), EPL (3, first and second [2] states), Harv (first state), NhD (second state), NjP (second state).

Notes: Letter from Safran to Philip Hofer (13 May 1943) laid in the Harv copy: ". . . Mr. Mencken revised it especially from two articles he had written for the Baltimore Sun. [¶] I printed it on the hand-press of the New School for Social Research in New York while studying under Joseph Blumenthal. It is hand-set in 14 pt. Lutetia, and done on hand-made paper. [¶] This is one of three copies made with the Hebrew title page." The order of the two states could not be determined. An inscription in the BL copy is dated October 1935. Previously published (Baltimore *Evening Sun,* 2 and 9 April 1934); Adler 16, 79; Bulsterbaum 12, 58.

EREZ ISRAEL

BY H·L·MENCKEN

PRIVATELY PRINTED · NEW YORK

1935

A 45, second state

A 46 HERE IS ONE CHAPTER
1936

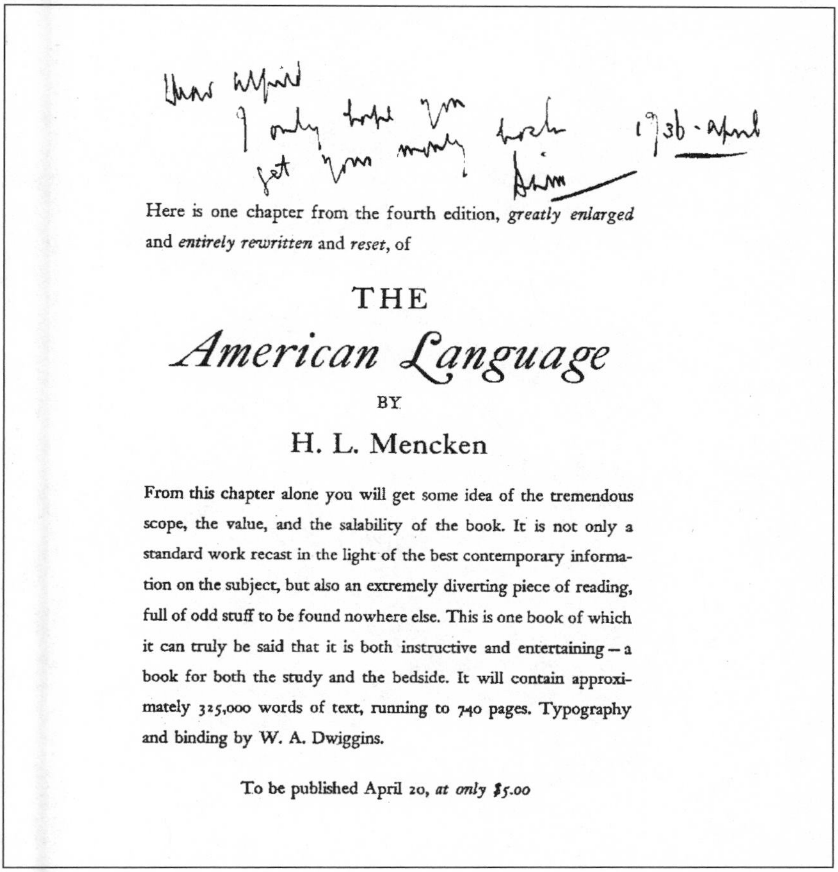

[handwritten inscription]

Here is one chapter from the fourth edition, *greatly enlarged*
and *entirely rewritten* and *reset*, of

THE
American Language
BY
H. L. Mencken

From this chapter alone you will get some idea of the tremendous
scope, the value, and the salability of the book. It is not only a
standard work recast in the light of the best contemporary information on the subject, but also an extremely diverting piece of reading,
full of odd stuff to be found nowhere else. This is one book of which
it can truly be said that it is both instructive and entertaining — a
book for both the study and the bedside. It will contain approxi-
mately 325,000 words of text, running to 740 pages. Typography
and binding by W. A. Dwiggins.

To be published April 20, *at only $5.00*

A 46, cover title

Copyright page: None.

9¼″ × 6⅛″: [iii–iv] v–viii [ix] 474–554 = 88 pp.

[1]⁴⁴ = 44 leaves.

Contents: p. iii: cover title and blurb; p. iv: blank; pp. v–viii: 'PREFACE | TO THE FOURTH EDITION'; p. ix: blank; pp. 474–554: 'X | PROPER NAMES IN AMERICA'.

Typography and paper: 7⅜″ (7⅛″) × 4⅛″; 44 lines per page, including 15 lines of notes in two columns (number of lines varies with amount of reduced type and number of notes). Running heads: recto, '*Preface to the Fourth Edition*' (p. vii), '*Proper Names in America*' (pp. 475–553); verso, '*The American Language*' (pp. vi–554). Wove paper.

Binding: Self wrappers. All edges trimmed. Three staples.

Locations: EPL, NjP.

Notes: Another NjP copy was trimmed and rebound by Elmer Adler. A letter to him from Alfred A. Knopf (3 April 1936) is pasted to the free front end paper: "Here's a Mencken curiosity or what will be one some day." Not in Adler.

A 47 THE SUNPAPERS OF BALTIMORE

A 47.1.a.i
Only edition, only printing, presumed first issue (1937)

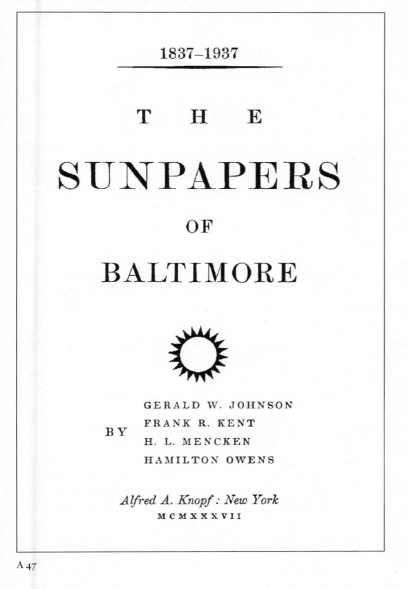

Copyright page: 'FIRST EDITION | *Copyright 1937 by Alfred A. Knopf, Inc.* | [four lines reserving rights] | *Manufactured in the United States of America*'

Colophon: 'A NOTE ON THE TYPE IN | WHICH THIS BOOK IS SET | [thirteen lines on Scotch type] | [Borzoi device in oval] | THIS BOOK HAS BEEN DE-SIGNED BY | W. A. DWIGGINS AND MANUFAC- | TURED BY THE PLIMP-TON | PRESS, NORWOOD, MASS. | PAPER MADE BY S. D. | WARREN CO., | BOSTON'

9¼″ × 6¼″: [A–B i–vi] vii–ix [x] xi–xii [1–2] 3–430 i–xvi [xvii–xx] i–xvi = 480 pp.

[1–30]⁸ = 240 leaves.

Contents: pp. A–B: blank; p. i: half title; p. ii: blank; p. iii: title; p. iv: copyright; p. v: 'TO THE MEMORY OF | ALL OLD SUN MEN | [sun ornament]'; p. vi: blank; pp. vii–viii: 'PREFACE'; p. ix: 'TABLE OF CONTENTS'; p. x: blank; pp. xi–xii: 'LIST OF ILLUSTRATIONS'; p. 1: half title; p. 2: blank; pp. 3–430: text; pp. i–xvi: 'IN-DEX'; p. xvii: blank; p. xviii: colophon; pp. xix–xx: blank; pp. i–xvi: 'A LIST OF | Officers, Editors, Correspondents, Carriers, and Employés | of the *Sunpapers* on January 1, 1937'. Illustrations inserted after pp. ii, 22, 84, 146, 168, 210, 222, 260, 288, 342, 370.

Typography and paper: 7⅛″ (6⅞″) × 4⅛″; 33 lines per page. Running heads: recto, chapter titles (pp. 5–429), 'INDEX' (pp. iii–xv), 'LIST OF SUNPAPER EMPLOY-ÉS' (pp. iii–xv); verso, 'PREFACE' (p. viii), 'LIST OF ILLUSTRATIONS' (p. xii), 'THE SUNPAPERS OF BALTIMORE' (pp. 4–430), 'INDEX' (pp. ii–xvi), 'LIST OF SUNPAPER EMPLOYÉS' (pp. ii–xvi). Laid paper.

Binding: Maroon V cloth, stamped in gilt. Front: original *Sun* vignette with motto 'LIGHT FOR ALL'. Spine: '[rising sun over rule] | [row of adjacent half dots] | T H E | SUNPAPERS | O F | BALTIMORE | B Y | *Gerald W. Johnson* | *Frank R. Kent* | *H. L. Mencken* | *Hamilton Owens* | K N O P F'. Back: Borzoi Books logo blindstamped. Top edge trimmed, stained maroon, fore and bottom edges rough trimmed. White end papers.

Dust jacket: Black, red, and gold on white paper. Front: '[script] THE | [roman] SUN= [hyphens slanting up] | PAPERS OF | BALTIMORE | [within sunburst partially covered by the above and next] 1837–1937 | [in scroll] LIGHT FOR ALL | GERALD W. JOHNSON | FRANK R. KENT | H. L. MENCKEN | HAMILTON OWENS | [gold bar on white field] | ALFRED•A•KNOPF [Borzoi Books logo] PUBLISHER •N•Y•'. Spine: '[script] The [roman] SUN = [hyphens slanting up] | PAPERS | OF | BALTIMORE | 1837–1937 | GERALD W. JOHNSON | FRANK R. KENT | H. L. MENCKEN | HAMILTON OWENS | [Borzoi Books logo] | [continuation of gold bar on white field] | ALFRED•A• | KNOPF'. Back: '*THE AUTHORS OF* | THE SUN-PAPERS OF BALTIMORE | [biographies]'. Front flap: blurb; price $3.75. Back flap: ad for a Borzoi Books catalogue.

A 47.1.a, dust jacket

Publication: Published 3 May 1937. $3.75. Copyright #A106079. 1600 copies sold.

Printing: See colophon.

Locations: GHT (dj), RJS (dj).

Notes: Mencken wrote chapters XI–XVIII, had a hand in other parts, and served as general editor (p. vii). The true order of the two issues could not be determined. A letter from "Ladd" of Plimpton Press (4 February 1937) says that there were to be 1,000 copies with the employees' names on the orders of Sidney Jacobs of Knopf (Dwiggins Collection at MB); 1,000 is also the figure in a November 1936 memo from Mencken to Knopf in the Mencken chapter of Knopf's unpublished autobiography, p. 69 (TxU: Knopf Box 13a/Mencken). Card ($4'' \times 4^{15}/_{16}''$) attached to front pastedown of GHT copy: 'COMPLIMENTS OF | THE SUNPAPERS | OF | BALTIMORE'. This copy is signed by several employees and dated 24 April 1937. Some covers noted are in reddish orange and light orange; light brown reported (D). Adler 32; Bulsterbaum 7.

Salesman's dummy: Mentioned in letters from Sidney Jacobs of Knopf (21 December 1936; 1 February 1937) (Dwiggins Collection at MB).

A 47.1.a.ii
Only edition, only printing, presumed second issue

Same as A 47.1.a.i except:

. . . [xvii–xx] = 464 pp.

[1–29]^8 = 232 leaves.

Contents: Same as first issue but without the sixteen-page list of employees at the end.

Locations: Harv, LC (10 May 1937, rebound), RJS (2, dj).

AN AMERICAN EDITOR SPEAKS

Four Editorials on "Fake" Neutrality by H. L. MENCKEN

From "THE SUN," Baltimore, Maryland

Why Not Be Honest?

Since the Hon. Mr. Roosevelt, in the great moral campaign of 1932, made his solemn vow to reduce governmental expenditures, get rid of useless jobholders and balance the budget, his customers have had a lot of hard exercise in reconciling his promises and his performances, and some of them have attained to a degree of virtuosity without parallel since Apostolic times. They will need every kilowatt of that virtuosity during the next several months. For at the moment of this writing he is testing them with an imposture so vast, so bold and so shameless that one can imagine sane men falling for it only by an effort comparable to that involved in believing that the late Gen. Robert E. Lee was of African birth and blood, and that Jonah, after clawing his way out of the whale's esophagus, turned round and swallowed the whale. I allude, of course, to his preposterous rumble-bumble about American neutrality in the current war.

Why the Hon. Mr. Roosevelt should indulge himself in this transparent hocus-pocus I do not know, and it would probably be vain to inquire. It may be that false pretenses run inevitably with the practice of statecraft; it may be only that quacks, in the long run, always swallow their own buncombe. But whatever the cause, the fact is surely plain enough. The hon. gentleman is actually no more neutral in this war than the British Ambassador. According to Dr. Raymond Moley, writing in the *Saturday Evening Post*, he has been strongly partisan in private since 1935, and certainly he has been partisan in public since 1937. On October 5 of that year he made a speech in Chicago that was as palpably a brief for the English case as anything ever uttered by the Right Hon. Neville Chamberlain, or even by the Right Hon. Winston Churchill, and at this very moment he is rooting for that case by every device at hand, and making obvious plans to give it more material aid at the first chance.

I pass over the curious and instructive example of the detention of the *Bremen*—a perfectly legal act, to be sure, but carried out with such studied unfairness that its intent was plain to everyone—and turn to an episode even more singular. Its central figure was the hon. gentleman's estimable and gifted consort—and if I am rebuked for mentioning her in connection with a political matter, I can only answer that she has already mentioned herself. Moreover, it has been suggested seriously by persons close to the throne, and without challenge, that she may herself run for the Presidency next year, and only the other day Comrade Arthur Krock, of the New York *Times*, was warning its readers that anything she says or writes must be accepted today as "required political reading."

My reference is to her article of September 2, last Saturday. In that article she spoke of herself categorically as the "representative" of her husband, and devoted about a third of it to a description of her participation in an official ceremonial. The other two-thirds she gave over to a bitter denunciation of the Hon. Adolf Hitler, naming him by name, and arguing eloquently [a] that Danzig was actually a Polish city, [b] that Hitler himself was an ignoramus and a man of no integrity, and [c] that his bombing of Polish towns was "war on women and children." All this she prefaced with the statement that her information about the war that had just broken out came from her husband, who had called her up at 5 o'clock in the morning to let her in on Hitler's wickedness.

Let no one, however prejudiced, mistake the clear issue here. It is not whether the hon. gentleman and his lady are right or wrong about Hitler, or whether they have or have not a right

1

Head title: 'AN AMERICAN EDITOR SPEAKS | Four Editorials on "Fake" Neutrality by H. L. MENCKEN | From "THE SUN," Baltimore, Maryland | [rule] | [text follows]'

Colophon: 'Single copies by mail 5 cents in stamps. 10 for 25 cents; 100 for $2.00, cash with order. | All shipments sent prepaid. Order from | THE CONCORD PRESS, BOX 428, MOUNT VERNON, WASH. (State)'

9¹⁄₁₆″ × 6¾″: 1–7 [8] = 8 pp.

[1]⁴ = 4 leaves.

Contents: pp. 1–8: text in two columns; p. 8: colophon.

Text: "Why Not Be Honest?,"° "Heavyweight Bout,"° "Notes on a Moral War," "Idealism Marches On."°

Typography and paper: 8″ × 5¾″; 51 lines in right column (number of lines varies). No heads. Newsprint.

Binding: Self wrappers. All edges trimmed. Two staples.

Location: Yale.

Notes: Dated 1940 by Adler. Previously published (Baltimore *Sun,* 10 and 24 September, 8 and 15 October 1939; "Notes on a Moral War" also in B 144); Adler 16, 105.

A 49 HAPPY DAYS

A 49.1.a
First edition, first printing (1940)

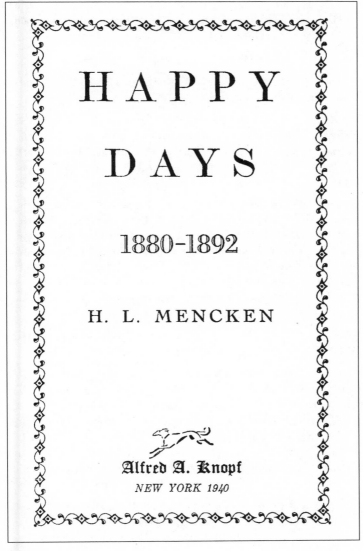

HAPPY

DAYS

1880–1892

H. L. MENCKEN

Alfred A. Knopf
NEW YORK 1940

A 49.1.a

Copyright page: 'Copyright 1939, 1940 by Alfred A. Knopf, Inc. | [four lines reserving rights] | FIRST EDITION | Manufactured in the United States of America | Published simultaneously in Canada by | The Ryerson Press | [three-line acknowledgement to the *New Yorker*]'

Colophon: 'THE TYPE | [fifteen lines on Scotch Modern type] | The book was designed by W. A. Dwiggins and | manufactured by The Plimpton Press, Norwood, | Massachusetts. The paper was made by S. D. | Warren Company, Boston.'

8⅝" × 5¾": [A–D i–iv] v–ix [x] xi [xii 1–2] 3–313 [314–20] = 336 pp.

[1–21]⁸ = 168 leaves. A nonconjugate leaf is inserted after p. [ii], with a childhood photograph of Mencken on the verso dated 'OCTOBER 8 1888'.

Contents: pp. A–C: blank; p. D: '*Mr. Mencken has also written* | [fourteen Borzoi titles]'; p. i: half title; p. ii: blank; p. iii: title; p. iv: copyright; pp. v–ix: [gothic] 'Preface' (signed 'BALTIMORE, 1939. H. L. M.'); p. x: blank; p. xi: 'TABLE OF | CONTENTS'; p. xii: blank; p. 1: half title; p. 2: blank; pp. 3–313: text; p. 314: blank; p. 315: colophon; pp. 316–20: blank.

Text: "Introduction to the Universe,"# "The Caves of Learning,"° "Recollections of Academic Orgies,"° "The Baltimore of the Eighties,"# "Rural Delights,"# "The Head of the House,"# "Memorials of Gormandizing,"° "The Training of a Gangster,"# "Cops and Their Ways,"# "Larval Stage of a Bookworm,"° "First Steps in Divinity,"° "The Ruin of an Artist,"° "In the Footsteps of Gutenberg,"° "From the Records of an Athlete,"# "The Capital of the Republic,"# "Recreations of a Reactionary,"° "Brief Gust of Glory,"° "The Career of a Philosopher,"° "Innocence in a Wicked World,"° "Strange Scenes and Far Places."#

Typography and paper: 6⁷⁄₁₆" (6¹⁄₁₆") × 3¼"; 30 lines per page. Running heads: recto and verso, 'PREFACE' (pp. vi–ix), chapter titles (pp. 4–313). Wove paper.

Binding: Oatmeal coarse grain linen cloth. Front, stamped in red, as on first trade binding of *Treatise on the Gods* (A 40): 'HLM'. Spine: '[stamped in blue, a row of adjacent triangles over a rectangular decoration] | [in red] HAPPY | DAYS | 1880•1892 | [in blue, a rectangular decoration, like the first but upside down, over a row of upside-down adjacent triangles] | [in red script] *H. L.* | *Mencken* | [in red roman] ALFRED A [*sic*] | KNOPF'. Back: Borzoi device stamped in blue. Top edge trimmed, stained purple, fore edge rough and unevenly trimmed, bottom unevenly trimmed, last gathering uncut. White end papers.

Dust jacket: Blue, red, and green on white paper. Front: 'H. L. Mencken | [in scroll over circular ornament] HAPPY | 1880•1892 | DAYS | [below scroll, ornate border top and right, tilted left] This [T tall] book offers the record, | not only of the man whose name is signed to | it, but also of a whole era, now fast fading | into the shadows of forgotten history.[arrow]'. Spine has same design as on that of cover but with different colors and, following script '*Mencken*': '[Borzoi Books logo] | ALFRED•A•KNOPF'.

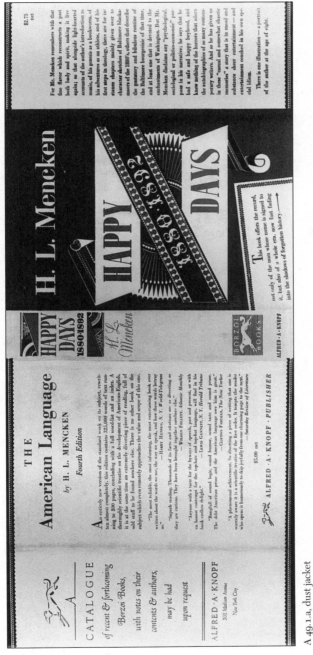

A 49.1.a, dust jacket

Back: blurb for fourth edition of *The American Language*. Front flap continues text of front; price $2.75. Back flap: ad for catalogue.

Publication: Published 22 January 1940. $2.75. Copyright #A137434. 17,200 copies of Knopf printings sold.

Printing: See colophon.

Locations: GHT, Harv, InU-Li (dj), RJS (dj).

Notes: Thickness 1⅟₁₆″. "Some of these chapters have appeared, either wholly or in part, in the *New Yorker*" (p. [iv]). No copies with a Canadian imprint were found. Adler 16, 18, 153–57; S1.7; S2.13, 21; Bulsterbaum 7, 9.

Review copy: Same as above except bound in the dust jacket as wrappers, attached at spine, flaps folding over "pastedowns"; 8½″ × 5⅝″; trimmed, unstained, stamped 'SAMPLE COPY' on top edge; light blue review slip (2¾″ × 2″) laid in: 'This book will be published: | DATE: [red handstamp] JAN 22 1940 | PRICE: [red handstamp] $2.75'. Unstamped copy noted. *Location:* GHT (2).

A 49.1.b
First edition, second printing: New York: Knopf, 1940.

On copyright page: 'PUBLISHED JANUARY 22, 1940 | FIRST AND SECOND PRINTINGS | BEFORE PUBLICATION'. The preface in this and subsequent print-ings is signed 'ROARING GAP, N. C., 1939. H. L. M.'

Locations: Harv, LC (26 January 1940), MChB.

A 49.1.c
First edition, third printing: New York: Knopf, 1940.

On copyright page: 'THIRD PRINTING, FEBRUARY 1940'. Published in box with *Newspaper Days* for Christmas 1941, according to Blanche Knopf correspondence with Mencken (HLM, 31 December 1941; BK, 2 January 1942; HLM, 13 January 1942 [EPL]).

Locations: EPL, MBU.

A 49.1.d
First edition, fourth printing (first English printing) (1940)

Copyright page: 'First Published in England 1940 | [three-line credit to *New Yorker*] | Printed in Great Britain by Butler & Tanner Ltd., Frome and London'

Colophon: None.

8⁹⁄₁₆″ × 5⁷⁄₁₆″: [i–iv] v–ix [x] xi [xii 1–2] 3–313 [314–16] = 328 pp.

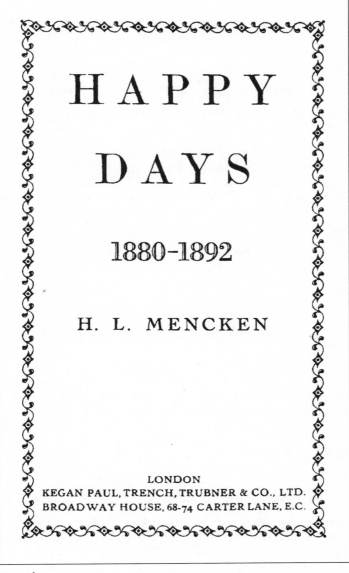

HAPPY

DAYS

1880-1892

H. L. MENCKEN

LONDON
KEGAN PAUL, TRENCH, TRUBNER & CO., LTD.
BROADWAY HOUSE, 68-74 CARTER LANE, E.C.

A 49.1.d

[A]⁸ B–I⁸ K–U⁸ X⁴ = 164 leaves.

Contents: p. i: half title; p. ii: '*Mr. Mencken has also written* | [fourteen titles]'; p. iii: title; p. iv: copyright; pp. v–ix: 'Preface'; p. x: blank; p. xi: 'TABLE OF | CONTENTS'; p. xii: blank; p. 1: half title; p. 2: blank; pp. 3–313: text, same as in first printing; pp. 314–16: blank. Portrait of Mencken on glossy paper tipped in to p. ii.

Typography and paper: Typography same as in first printing. Wove paper.

Binding: Red cloth stamped in gilt on spine: 'HAPPY | DAYS | 1880–1892 | [diamond] | H.L.MENCKEN | KEGAN PAUL'. Trimmed, unstained. White end papers.

Dust jacket: White paper. Front: '[red] HAPPY | [slanting up] 1880–1892 | [red] DAYS | An account of his | first twelve years | *by* | [red] H. L. MENCKEN | *author of "The American Language"*'. Spine: '[bar] | HAPPY | DAYS | [red] 1880–1892 | *by* | H. L. *Mencken* | KEGAN PAUL | [bar]'. Back: list of 'NEW AND RECENT BOOKS'. Front flap: blurb; in example seen, price of 15s covered by sticker (black on brown and white, on design of lion over open book): '16/6 | NET'.

Publication: Published October 1940 (ECB 14.1124). 15s (ECB, but see dust jacket above).

Locations: BL (21 OCT 40), Bod (FEB | 24 | 1941), Camb (12 FE | 1941), GHT (dj), NhD.

Notes: Adler 17.

A 49.1.e
First edition, fifth printing: New York: Knopf, 1945.

On copyright page: 'FOURTH PRINTING, MARCH 1945'. Contains notice 'To THE *Purchaser*' regarding wartime paper restrictions (p. [C]), thinner paper (8⅜" × 5½" ×⅝"), smooth binding.

Locations: EPL, GHT, JRS, MCR.

A 49.1.f
First edition, sixth printing: New York: Knopf, 1947.

Added title page: '[ornate border] | [all within rules top and bottom, row of diamonds left and right] THE DAYS OF | H. L. MENCKEN | *Happy Days* | *Newspaper Days* | *Heathen Days* | [Borzoi device in triple circle] | [the remainder outside box] ALFRED A. KNOPF *NEW YORK* 1947 | [rule] | [same ornate border but upside-down]'. On copyright page: 'FIRST PRINTING'. An '*Author's Note*' added on pp. v–vi (dated Baltimore, 1947). Individual title pages have dates changed to 1947; separate pagination; colophon (p. [300]) as in *Newspaper Days* (A 51) and *Heathen Days* (A 54), followed by ornament with linked 'WAD'. 8⅜" × 5½". Blue cloth blindstamped on front, stamped in gilt on spine. 3,800 copies of Knopf printing sold. The 1963 (OCLC) and 1968 (NUC 1973–77, 75.342) printings of this book are ghosts.

Locations: GHT, Harv (rebound), MBU, RJS.

A 49.1.g
First edition, seventh printing: New York: Knopf, 1955.

On copyright page: 'FIFTH PRINTING, JANUARY 1955'.

Location: EPL.

A 49.1.h
First edition, eighth printing: New York: Knopf, 1963.

On copyright page: 'SIXTH PRINTING, AUGUST 1963'.

Locations: D, MBU.

A 49.1.i
First edition, ninth printing: New York: Knopf, 1968.

On copyright page: 'SEVENTH PRINTING, 1968'.

Locations: D, EPL.

A 49.1.j
First edition, tenth printing: New York: Knopf, 1973.

Data from title page of next entry. Not seen.

LATER REPRINTINGS WITHIN THE FIRST EDITION

A 49.1.k
New York: AMS, [n.d.].

Added title page (New York: Knopf, 1973, retained on original). On copyright page: '. . . from the edition | of 1973'. Dated 1986 by OCLC.

Location: GHT.

A 49.1.l
New York: Dorset, [1989].

Second printing of *The Days of H. L. Mencken* (sixth printing, above). On copyright page: '1989 Dorset Press'. Portrait omitted.

Locations: D, GHT.

A 49.1.m
Baltimore and London: Johns Hopkins University Press, [1996].

On copyright page: 'Maryland Paperback Bookshelf edition, 1996 | 05 04 03 02 01 00 99 98 97 96   5 4 3 2 1'. 8⁷⁄₁₆″ × 5⅜″. White wrappers printed in black, gray, and blue.

Location: GHT.

A 49.2.a
Second edition, only printing (n.d.)

Title page: [all within double-rule box] '[to left of a vertical rule] PUBLISHED BY ARRANGEMENT WITH | ALFRED A. KNOPF, INC., NEW YORK | [six lines reserving rights] | COPYRIGHT 1936, 1937, 1939, 1940 | BY ALFRED A. KNOPF, INC. || [to right of rule] HAPPY | DAYS | 1880–1892 | *By* H. L. MENCKEN | *Armed Services Editions, Inc.* | A NON-PROFIT ORGANIZATION SPONSORED BY THE | COUNCIL ON BOOKS IN WARTIME. NEW YORK'

Copyright page: 'MANUFACTURED IN THE UNITED STATES OF AMERICA'

3⅞″ × 5⅜″: [1–2] 3–7 [8–11] 12–287 [288] = 288 pp.

Perfect bound.

Contents: p. 1: title; p. 2: copyright; pp. 3–7: [within double rule at top, rule at bottom] '*PREFACE*'; pp. 8–9: [within same] '*CONTENTS*'; p. 10: blank; pp. 11–287: text, same as in first edition, first printing; p. 288: blank.

Binding: Perfect bound with staple front to back. Red, white, blue, black, and yellow paper wrappers (series no. F-159).

Locations: InU-Li, RJS (2).

Notes: "Moszkowski" spelled correctly (p. 182); z missing in trade edition (p. 194). Not in Adler.

A 50 GENERALLY POLITICAL
1940

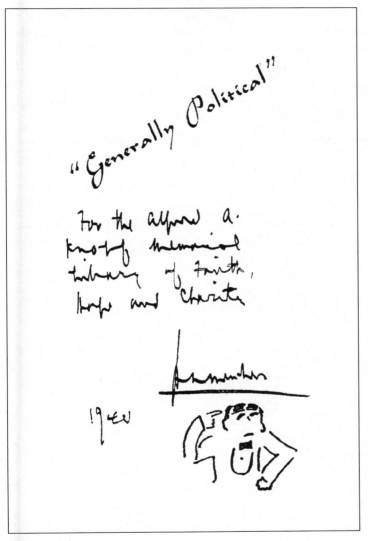

A 50, cover title

Cover title: '[slanting up, in red] "Generally Political" | [red caricature, perhaps of Mencken]'

Copyright page: None.

Colophon: '[red rule] | "Generally Political" was written for the | INSTITUTE OF ARTS AND SCIENCES | at Columbia University by | H. L. MENCKEN | [red rule] | *Price 15c at the Bookstall and at the Bookstore*'.

6$\frac{3}{16}$" × 3$\frac{7}{16}$": [1] 2–15 [16] = 16 pp.

[1]^8 = 8 leaves.

Contents: p. 1: cover title; pp. 2–16: text; p. 16: colophon.

Typography and paper: 5" × 2½"; 30 lines per page. No heads. Paginated in red. Wove paper.

Binding: Self wrappers. All edges trimmed. Two staples.

Location: EPL (4).

Notes: From a lecture delivered at Columbia on 4 January 1940 (*A Mencken Chres-tomathy* [A 61], p. 148). Two EPL copies are signed and dated 1940 by Mencken. Dated [1944] by NUC 375.489. Adler 16.

A 51.1.a
Only edition, first printing (1941)

NEWSPAPER

DAYS

1899-1906

H. L. MENCKEN

ALFRED A KNOPF
NEW YORK, 1941

A 51.1.a

Copyright page: 'Copyright 1940, 1941, by Alfred A. Knopf, Inc. All | [four lines reserving rights] | *or newspaper. Manufactured in the United States of* | America. *Published simultaneously in Canada by The* | *Ryerson Press.* | FIRST EDITION'

Colophon: 'THE TYPE | [fifteen lines on Scotch Modern type] | The book was designed by W. A. Dwiggins and | manufactured by The Plimpton Press, Norwood, | Massachusetts.'

8⅝" × 5¾": [A–B i–iv] v–xi [xii–xvi 1–2] 3–313 [314–18] = 336 pp.

[1–21]⁸ = 168 leaves. A nonconjugate leaf is inserted after p. [ii], with a photograph of Mencken on the verso dated 'MAY 20 1904'.

Contents: p. A: blank; p. B: '*Mr. Mencken has also written* | [fifteen titles]'; p. i: half title; p. ii: blank; p. iii: title; p. iv: copyright; pp. v–xi: 'PREFACE'; p. xii: blank; p. xiii: 'NOTE' [four-line acknowledgment to the *New Yorker*]; p. xiv: blank; p. xv: 'TABLE OF | CONTENTS'; p. xvi: blank; p. 1: half title; p. 2: blank; pp. 3–313: text; p. 314: blank; p. 315: colophon; pp. 316–18: blank.

Text: "Allegro Con Brio,"# "Drill For a Rookie,"# "Sergeant's Stripes,"# "Approach to Lovely Letters,"# "Fruits of Diligence,"# "The Gospel of Service,"° "Scent of the Theatre,"# "Command,"# "Three Managing Editors,"# "Slaves of Beauty,"° "The Days of the Giants,"° "The Judicial Arm,"° "Recollections of Notable Cops,"° "A Genial Restauranteur,"# "A Girl From Red Lion, P.A.,"° "Scions of the Bogus Nobility,"° "Aliens, but Not Yet Enemies,"# "The Synthesis of News,"° "Fire Alarm,"° "Sold Down the River."#

Typography and paper: 6⁷⁄₁₆" (6¹⁄₁₆") × 3¼"; 30 lines per page. Running heads: recto and verso, 'PREFACE' (pp. vi–xi), chapter titles (pp. 4–313). Wove paper.

Binding: Oatmeal coarse grain linen cloth. Front, stamped in red, as on first trade binding of *Treatise on the Gods* (A 40): 'HLM'. Spine: '[stamped in blue, appearing as oatmeal showing through blue background] [rule] | [sun ornament] | [rule] | [stamped in red] NEWS= | PAPER | DAYS | 1899•1906 | [same blue stamping as before] | [red script] *H. L.* | *Mencken* | [red roman] ALFRED A [sic] | KNOPF'. Back: Borzoi device stamped in blue. Top edge trimmed, stained blue or purple, fore edge rough trimmed, bottom edge unevenly trimmed. White end papers.

Dust jacket: Red, blue, and black on white paper. Front: [all as white showing through in framed compartments amongst four vignettes] '[script] *Newspaper* | [roman] DAYS | 1899–1906 | H.L.Mencken [periods raised] | Here is the volume of journalistic memories that | you would expect from H. L. Mencken—shrewd, | good-natured, and completely free from portentous | whim-wham and other forms of bunk.' Spine: '[script] *News-* | *paper* | [roman] DAYS | [short rule] | H. L. | Mencken | [vignette and frame lines continuing from front] | [Borzoi Books logo] | [script] *Alfred A.* | *Knopf* | [vignette continuing from front]'. Back: blurbs for the fourth edition of *The American*

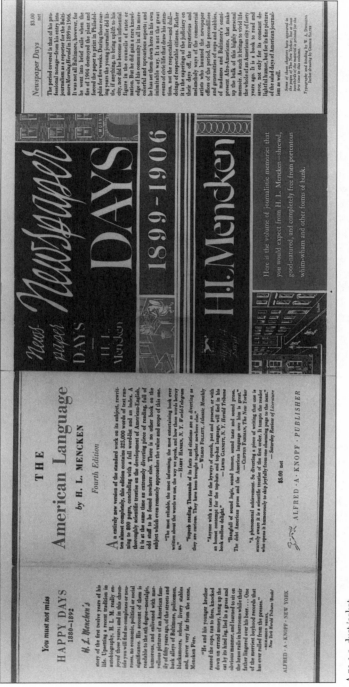

A 51.1.a, dust jacket

Language. Front flap: blurb; price $3.00; credit to George Salter for jacket drawing. Back: ad for *Happy Days.*

Publication: Published 20 October 1941. $3.00. Copyright #A158247. 17,400 copies of Knopf printings sold.

Printing: See colophon.

Locations: InU-Li (dj), LC (20 August 1941, cloth has turned brownish), MBU, MCR, RJS (dj).

Notes: Thickness 1⅟₁₆″. According to a publicity pamphlet ("Shrewd, good-natured . . ."), it was to be published 6 October (GHT). A copy reported with "Knopf rubber stamp on title—a publisher's presentation?" (D). For publication in box, see under *Happy Days* (A 49.1.c). "Some of these chapters have appeared, either wholly or in part, in the *New Yorker*" (p. [xiii]). No copies with a Canadian imprint were found. Adler 17, 18, 156–57; S2.13, 21; Bulsterbaum 8, 9.

Review copy: Same as above except bound in the dust jacket as wrappers, attached at spine, flaps folding over "pastedowns"; 8½″ × 5⁹⁄₁₆″; trimmed, unstained, stamped 'SAMPLE COPY' on top edge. 500 copies (Blanche Knopf to Mencken 10 November 1941 [EPL]). *Locations:* GHT, InU-Li, RJS. Copy reported stamped on bottom edge (D).

Salesman's dummy: Contents: pp. [i–ii] tipped in to free front end paper; p. [iii]: as above; p. [iv]: blank; pp. v–viii: 'PREFACE' (different setting of type); pp. [ix–x]: 'TABLE OF | CONTENTS' (different setting of type); pp. 3–10: 'I | ALLEGRO | CON BRIO' (different setting of type); the rest blank. Trade binding, top edge stained blue; 8⁹⁄₁₆″ × 5¾″. *Location:* EPL.

A 51.1.b
Only edition, second printing (first English printing) (1942)

Copyright page: 'First published in England 1942 | NOTE | [four-line acknowledgment to the *New Yorker*] | PRINTED IN GREAT BRITAIN BY LOWE AND BRYDONE PRINTERS LIMITED, LONDON, N.W.10'

8⁹⁄₁₆″ × 5⁷⁄₁₆″: [i–iv] vi–xi [xii–xiv 1–2] 3–313 [314] = 328 pp.

[A]⁴ B–I¹⁶ K–L¹⁶ = 164 leaves.

Contents: p. i: half title; p. ii: 'Mr. *Mencken has also written* | [fifteen titles]'; p. iii: title; p. iv: copyright; pp. v–xi: 'PREFACE'; p. xii: blank; p. xiii: 'TABLE OF | CONTENTS'; p. xiv: blank; p. 1: half title; p. 2: blank; pp. 3–313: text, same as in first printing; p. 314: blank. Photo of Mencken on glossy paper tipped in to p. ii.

Typography and paper: Typography same as in first printing. Wove paper.

NEWSPAPER

DAYS

1899 - 1906

H. L. MENCKEN

LONDON
KEGAN PAUL, TRENCH, TRUBNER & CO., LTD.
BROADWAY HOUSE, 68-74 CARTER LANE, E.C.

A 51.1.b

Binding: Light red V cloth stamped in black on spine: 'NEWS- | PAPER | DAYS | [diamond] | MENCKEN | KEGAN PAUL'. Trimmed, unstained. White end papers.

Dust jacket: White paper. Front: '[maroon] Newspaper | DAYS | 1899–1906 | [maroon bar over rule] | 'an impious history . . . . pure 100-proof | 220-volt Mencken' | [maroon rule over bar] | [maroon] by | H. L. MENCKEN | [maroon] author of "Happy Days," "The American | [maroon] Language," etc.' Spine: 'News- | paper | DAYS | [maroon] 1899– | [maroon] 1906 | by | H. L. | MENCKEN | KEGAN | PAUL'. Back: list of 'NEW AND RECENT BOOKS'. Front flap: blurb; price 16s.6d. Rear flap: blurbs for *Happy Days*.

Publication: Published May 1942 (ECB 15.396). 16s.6d.

Locations: BL (8 MAY 42, rebound), Bod (SEP | 9 | 1942), Camb (3 SP | 1942), GHT (dj), KU-S, RJS (dj).

Notes: Adler 17.

A 51.1.c
Third printing: New York: Knopf, 1943.

On copyright page: 'SECOND PRINTING, SEPTEMBER 1943'.

Location: EPL.

A 51.1.d
Fourth printing: New York: Knopf, 1945.

On copyright page: 'THIRD PRINTING, MARCH 1945'. Contains notice 'TO THE *Purchaser*' regarding wartime paper restrictions (p. [C]), thinner paper (8⅜″ × 5½″ ×⅝″), smooth binding.

Locations: EPL, JRS.

A 51.1.e
Fifth printing: New York: Knopf, 1947.

Reprinted in *The Days of H. L. Mencken*. See under *Happy Days* (A 49.1.f).

A 51.1.f
Sixth printing: New York: Knopf, 1955.

On copyright page: 'FOURTH PRINTING, JANUARY 1955'. Freak copy: bound upside-down (GHT).

Locations: D, EPL, GHT.

A 51.1.g
Seventh printing: New York: Knopf, 1963.

On copyright page: 'FIFTH PRINTING, AUGUST, 1963'.

Location: MBU.

A 51.1.h
Eighth printing: New York: Knopf, 1968.

On copyright page: '*Sixth Printing, December 1968*'.

Locations: D, Harv.

A 51.1.i
Ninth printing: New York: Knopf, 1975.

On copyright page: '*Seventh Printing, March 1975.*'

Location: D.

LATER REPRINTINGS WITHIN THE ONLY EDITION

A 51.1.j
New York: AMS, [n.d.].

Added title page (New York: Knopf, 1975, retained on original). On copyright page:
'. . . from the | edition of 1975'. Dated 1986 by OCLC.

Location: Harv.

A 51.1.k
New York: Dorset, 1989.

Second printing of *The Days of H. L. Mencken.* See under *Happy Days* (A 49.1.l).

A 51.1.l
Baltimore and London: Johns Hopkins University Press, [1996].

On copyright page: 'Maryland Paperback Bookshelf edition, 1996 | 05 04 03 02 01 00
99 98 97 96   5 4 3 2 1'. $8^{7}/_{16}'' \times 5^{7}/_{16}''$. White wrappers printed in green, black, and
beige.

Location: GHT.

A 52 A NEW DICTIONARY OF QUOTATIONS ADVERTISEMENT
[1942?]

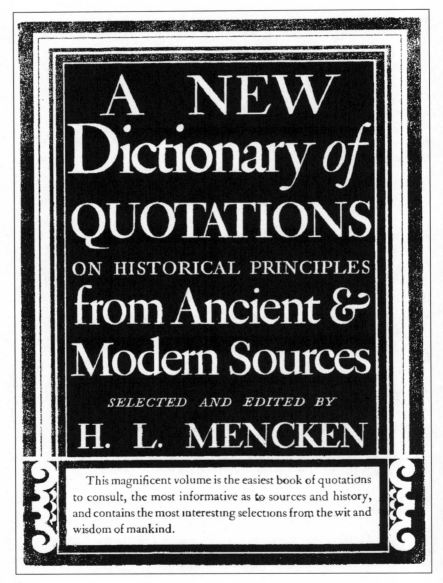

A 52

Title page: All within brown and white borders resembling the dust jacket of A 53. White letters show through blue field, remaining letters blue on white.

18½″ × 13¾″ sheet folded twice to make four uncut leaves.

Contents: blurbs, excerpts, and sample pages.

Typography and paper: No proper pages. Amount and size of type vary. No heads. Wove paper.

Binding: None.

Locations: GHT, Yale.

Notes: 'LIFT HERE . . . FOR A PREVIEW OF MR. MENCKEN'S REMARKABLE BOOK'. Order form on business reply card inserted in GHT copy. See salesman's dummy of *A New Dictionary of Quotations* (A 53.1.a). Not in Adler.

A 53.1.a
Only edition, first printing (1942)

A New

DICTIONARY OF

QUOTATIONS

ON *HISTORICAL* PRINCIPLES

FROM

ANCIENT AND MODERN SOURCES

Selected and Edited by

H. L. MENCKEN

NEW YORK : ALFRED A. KNOPF : 1942

A 53.1.a

Copyright page: 'Copyright 1942 by Alfred A. Knopf, Inc. All rights reserved. No part | [two lines reserving rights] | passages in a review to be printed in a magazine or newspaper. Manu- | factured in the United States of America. | FIRST EDITION'

Colophon: 'A NOTE ON THE TYPE | [six lines on Caledonia type, designed by W. A. Dwiggins] | *Mr. Dwiggins contrived the typographic scheme and designed the | binding and jacket. The book was composed, printed, and bound by | The Plimpton Press, Norwood, Massachusetts.* | [Borzoi device]'

9¼" × 6½": [A–B i–v] vi–x [xi] xii–xiii [xiv 1–3] 4–1347 [1348–52] = 1368 pp.

[1–3]⁸ [4–43]¹⁶ [44]⁴ [45–46]⁸ = 684 leaves.

Contents: p. A: blank; p. B: '*Mr. Mencken has also written* | [sixteen titles]'; p. i: half title; p. ii: blank; p. iii: title; p. iv: copyright; pp. v–x: 'Preface'; pp. xi–xiii: 'Acknowledgments'; p. xiv: blank; p. 1: half title; p. 2: blank; pp. 3–1347: text; p. 1348: blank; p. 1349: colophon; pp. 1350–52: blank.

Typography and paper: 7⅞" (7⅝") × 4¹⁵⁄₁₆"; 59 lines in left column, 54 in right (lines vary with number of entries). Columns divided by vertical rule. Headed above horizontal rule by first topic (flush left) and last topic (flush right) on page (pp. 4–1347). Wove paper.

Binding: Blue V cloth, stamped in gilt. Front: shield from the Mencken arms. Spine: '[rows of diamonds with circle in center before and after bar] | A NEW | DICTION-ARY | OF | QUOTATIONS [first T tall] | [rows of diamonds etc.] | ON HISTORICAL | PRINCIPLES | FROM ANCIENT | AND MODERN | SOURCES | [rows of diamonds etc.] | SELECTED | AND EDITED BY | H. L. MENCKEN | [rows of diamonds etc.] | KNOPF | [rows of diamonds etc.]'. Back: Borzoi Books logo blind-stamped. Trimmed, edges speckled in red. Drab end papers.

Dust jacket: Blue and gold on white paper. Front: [all in multiple borders] 'A NEW | Dictionary *of* | QUOTATIONS | ON HISTORICAL PRINCIPLES | from Ancient & | Modern Sources | *SELECTED AND EDITED BY* | H. L. MENCKEN | [in box separate from that containing the above] This magnificent volume is the easiest book of quotations | to consult, the most informative as to sources and history, | and contains the most interesting selections from the wit and | wisdom of mankind.' Spine: '[five rules and bars of various thickness] | A NEW | Dictionary | OF | Quotations | [five rules etc.] | ON HISTORICAL | PRINCIPLES | FROM ANCIENT | AND MODERN | SOURCES | SELECTED & EDITED | BY | *H. L. Mencken* | [five rules etc.] | [bar] | BORZOI | [rule] | [Borzoi device] | [rule] | BOOKS | [bold rule] | KNOPF | [bar]'. Back: blurbs for the fourth edition of *The American Language*. Front flap: blurb; price $7.50. Back flap continues the blurb.

Publication: Published 20 April 1942. $7.50. Copyright #A163330. 36,800 copies of Knopf printings sold.

A 53.1.a, dust jacket

Printing: See colophon.

Locations: GHT, LC (28 January 1942, rebound review copy?; second copy deposited 6 March 1942), RJS (dj), Yale.

Notes: Mencken wrote in a copy presented to Rosalind C. Lohrfinck: 'This is no. 1 | copy, received January | 29, 1942' (Yale). An inscribed set of uncorrected galley proofs was auctioned by Sotheby in 1984 (Cat. 5184). A dealer in 1996 sold a copy in "publisher's box" covered with slate blue paper; a label on the front reproduces the central panel of the dust jacket, but with an additional border (JRS). Adler 33; Bulster-baum 8.

Review copy: As above, with blue slip (2⁹⁄₁₆″ × 4″): 'This book will be published: | DATE: [red stamp] APR 20 1942 | PRICE: [handwritten in red] 7⁵⁰ pre pub. 6⁷⁵ | Please do not release reviews until the | above date. We would appreciate two | copies of your review. | *Alfred A. Knopf, Inc.*' Slip tipped in to free front end paper of copy examined (Yale).

Salesman's dummies: (1) *Contents:* p. [i]: blurb; p. [ii]: blank; p. [1]: title; p. [2]: blank; pp. [3]–5, 78–79, 136–37, 248–49, 324–26; the rest blank. Trade binding; 9¼″ × 6⁷⁄₁₆″. *Location:* EPL. (2) No print (first gathering perhaps missing); different collation; trade binding; 9³⁄₁₆″ × 6½″; dust jacket. *Location:* GHT. In a letter to Dwiggins (18 September 1941), Sidney R. Jacobs of Knopf requested a dummy to be ready for "the hands of the booksellers early in October." He also wanted to be able to photograph the bound dummy with a dust jacket on it for the prospectus under preparation (see A 52) (Dwiggins Collection at MB).

A 53.1.b
Second printing: New York: Knopf, 1942.

On copyright page: '*Second Printing, April 1942.*'

Location: EPL.

A 53.1.c
Third printing: New York: Knopf, 1946.

On copyright page: '*Third Printing, June 1946.*'

Location: EPL.

A 53.1.d
Fourth printing: New York: Knopf, 1952.

Published May 1952. Data from OCLC and subsequent printings. Not seen.

A 53.1.e
Fifth printing: New York: Knopf, 1957.

On copyright page: '*Fifth Printing, September 1957.*' For this printing in a boxed set, see *The American Language* (A 19.4.p).

Location: GHT.

A 53.1.f
Sixth printing: New York: Knopf, 1960.

On copyright page: '*Sixth Printing, September 1960.*' For this printing in a boxed set, see *The American Language* (A 19.4.p).

Location: GHT.

A 53.1.g
Seventh printing: Pirated sixth printing, probably done in Taiwan.

Title page blank between 'MENCKEN' and date ('1960'). Copyright page blank except for publishing history: '*Published April 20, 1942* | [four lines] | *Sixth Printing, September 1960.*' 8″ × 5⅜″; green cloth with silver lettering, no publisher shown; dust jacket.

Location: GHT (dj).

A 53.1.h
Eighth printing: New York: Knopf, 1962.

On copyright page: '*Seventh printing, August 1962.*' For this printing in a boxed set, see *The American Language* (A 19.4.p).

Location: RJS.

A 53.1.i
Ninth printing: New York: Knopf, 1966.

Data from OCLC. Not seen.

A 53.1.j

Tenth printing: Not seen.

A 53.1.k
Eleventh printing: New York: Knopf, 1977.

On copyright page: '*Tenth printing, June 1977.*'

Location: JRS.

A 53.1.l

Twelfth printing: Not seen.

A 53.1.m.i

Thirteenth printing, American issue: New York: Knopf, 1982.

On copyright page: '*Twelfth printing, June 1982.*' Data from next entry.

A 53.1.m.ii

Thirteenth printing, English issue: [London and Glasgow: Collins, n.d.].

White label (1¼" × 3⁹⁄₁₆") pasted above Borzoi device on copyright page: '*First published in the British Commonwealth 1982 | as* H. L. Mencken's Dictionary of Quotations *by | William Collins Sons and Company Limited* | ISBN 0 00 434569 10.' P. A: blank; p. B: '*Books by H. L. Mencken* | [sixteen titles]'; . . . . [1–31]¹⁶ [32–33]⁸ [34–41]¹⁶ [42]¹² [43–44]¹⁶.

Locations: BL reading room (30 MAR 84), MBAt (2, 18 April '84).

A 53.1.n

Only edition, fourteenth printing (first English printing) (1982)

Copyright page: 'First published 1942 | First published in this edition 1982 | Published by William Collins, Sons and Company Limited | Copyright 1942 by Alfred A. Knopf Inc. | [four lines reserving rights] | Printed and bound in the United States of America | ISBN 0 00 434569 10'

Colophon: 'A NOTE ON THE TYPE | [six lines on Caledonia type, designed by W. A. Dwiggins] | *Mr. Dwiggins contrived the typographic scheme and designed the | binding and jacket. The book was composed by The Plimpton Press, | Norwood, Massachusetts.* | [Borzoi device]'

9³⁄₁₆" × 6½": [A–B i–v] vi–x [xi] xii–xiii [xiv 1–3] 4–1347 [1348–52] = 1368 pp.

[1–40]¹⁶ [41]¹² [42–43]¹⁶ = 684 leaves.

Contents: pp. A–B: blank; p. i: half title; p. ii: blank; p. iii: title; p. iv: copyright; pp. v–x: 'Preface'; pp. xi–xiii: 'Acknowledgments'; p. xiv: blank; p. 1: half title; p. 2: blank; pp. 3–1347: text; p. 1348: blank; p. 1349: colophon; pp. 1350–52: blank.

Typography and paper: Typography same as in first printing. Wove paper.

Binding A: Black V cloth stamped in gilt. Front: shield of Mencken arms. Spine: 'H.L. MENCKEN'S | DICTIONARY OF | QUOTATIONS | [bar] | ON HISTORICAL PRINCIPLES | FROM ANCIENT & | MODERN SOURCES | [reading down] DICTIONARY OF [over] QUOTATIONS | [horizontal] COLLINS'. Trimmed, edges speckled in red. White end papers.

H.L.MENCKEN'S DICTIONARY OF QUOTATIONS

ON HISTORICAL PRINCIPLES FROM ANCIENT AND MODERN SOURCES

Selected and Edited by H.L.Mencken

Collins
London & Glasgow

A 53.1.n

Binding B: Like binding A except front unstamped, bar over rule on spine.

Publication: See dates of accession under *Locations*. Price unknown.

Dust jacket: White paper, lettering on front, spine, and back as white showing through light green field above continuous tan bar, showing through dark green below bar; flaps printed in green. Front: 'H.L.MENCKEN'S | [tan bar] | DICTIONARY OF | QUOTATIONS | ON HISTORICAL PRINCIPLES FROM | ANCIENT AND MODERN SOURCES | H. L. Mencken's classic selection | of the wit and wisdom of mankind. | Full information on sources and history. | Arranged thematically | for quick and easy reference.' Spine: 'H.L.MENCKEN'S | DICTIONARY OF | QUOTA-TIONS | [tan bar] | ON HISTORICAL PRINCIPLES | FROM ANCIENT & | MODERN SOURCES | [reading down] DICTIONARY OF [over] QUOTATIONS | [horizontal] COLLINS'. Back repeats front. Front flap: lengthy description. Rear flap: biography of Mencken, ISBN, 'Printed in the United States of America'.

Locations: BL (5 AUG 82, binding A), BL Lending Division (21 FEB 1983, binding B), Bod (12 AUG 1982, binding A), Camb (5 AUG 1982, binding A), GHT (dj, binding B).

A 53.1.o
Fifteenth printing: Not seen.

A 53.1.p
Sixteenth printing: New York: Knopf, 1985.

Data from OCLC. Not seen.

A 53.1.q
Seventeenth printing: New York: Knopf, 1987.

Data from OCLC. Not seen.

A 53.1.r
Eighteenth printing: New York: Knopf, 1989.

Data from OCLC. Not seen.

A 53.1.s
Nineteenth printing: New York: Knopf, 1991.

Stated seventeenth printing published May 1991. Data from OCLC and D. Not seen.

A 54.1.a
First edition, first printing (1943)

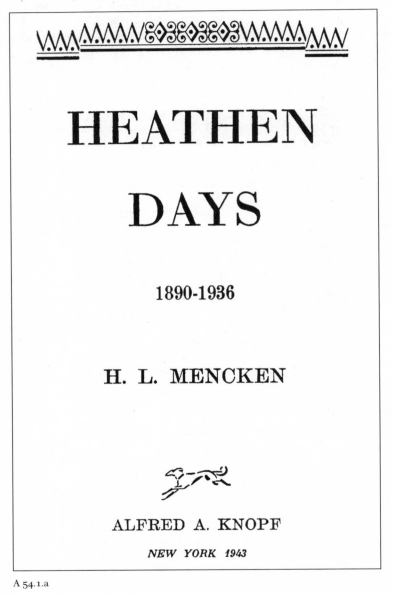

HEATHEN

DAYS

1890-1936

H. L. MENCKEN

ALFRED A. KNOPF

NEW YORK 1943

A 54.1.a

Copyright page: 'Copyright *1941, 1942, 1943 by Alfred A. Knopf, Inc. All* | [four lines reserving rights] | *or newspaper. Manufactured in the United States of* | *America. Published simultaneously in Canada by The* | *Ryerson Press.* | FIRST EDITION'

Colophon: 'THE TYPE | [fifteen lines on Scotch Modern type] | The book was designed by W. A. Dwiggins and | manufactured by The Plimpton Press, Norwood, | Massachusetts.'

8⅝″ × 5¾″: [A–B i–iv] v–x [xi–xiv 1–2] 3–299 [300–04] = 320 pp.

[1–20]⁸ = 160 leaves. A nonconjugate leaf is inserted after p. [ii], with a photograph of Mencken on the verso dated 'MARCH 30 1942'.

Contents: p. A: blank; p. B: '*Mr. Mencken has also written* | [seventeen Borzoi titles]'; p. i: half title; p. ii: blank; p. iii: title; p. iv: copyright; pp. v–x: 'PREFACE'; p. xi: 'NOTE | [six lines of acknowledgments to the *New Yorker* and *Esquire*]'; p. xii: blank; p. xiii: 'TABLE OF | CONTENTS'; p. xiv: blank; p. 1: half title; p. 2: blank; pp. 3–299: text; p. 300: blank; p. 301: colophon; pp. 302–04: blank.

Text: "Downfall of a Revolutionary,"° "Memoirs of the Stable,"° "Adventures of a Y.M.C.A. Lad,"# "The Educational Process,"# "Finale to the Rogue's March,"# "Notes on Palaeozoic Publicists,"° "The Tone Art,"# "A Master of Gladiators,"° "A Dip into Statecraft,"° "Court of Honor,"# "A Roman Holiday,"# "Winter Voyage,"# "Gore in the Caribbees,"° "Romantic Intermezzo,"° "Old Home Day,"° "The Noble Experiment,"# "Inquisition,"# "Vanishing Act,"# "Pilgrimage,"# "Beaters of Breasts."#

Typography and paper: 6⁷⁄₁₆″ (6¹⁄₁₆″) × 3⁵⁄₁₆″; 30 lines per page. Running heads: recto and verso, 'PREFACE' (pp. vi–x), chapter titles (pp. 4–299). Wove paper.

Binding: Oatmeal coarse grain linen cloth. Front, stamped in red, as on first trade binding of *Treatise on the Gods*: 'HLM'. Spine: '[stamped in blue, appearing as oatmeal showing through blue background] [rule] | [hollow diamond with two triangles on both right and left] | [rule] | [red] HEA= | THEN | DAYS | 1890 [small diamond]1936 | [same blue ornament as before] | [red script] *H. L.* | *Mencken* | [roman] ALFRED A *[sic]* | KNOPF'. Back: Borzoi device stamped in blue. Top edge trimmed, stained blue, fore and bottom edges roughly and unevenly trimmed. White end papers.

Dust jacket: Orange, black, and green on white paper. Front: [all within ornate borders, two lines above, four below] 'Heathen | [vignette signed 'Salter'] Days | [with ribbons above and below] 1890•1936 | H.L.Mencken | Further informal memoirs of H. L. M., who has been observing | the American scene for half a century with a shrewd eye, and | writes about it with brilliant wit and no illusions whatever [no period]'. Spine: '[top and bottom the lines continue from the front] Heathen | Days | [bracket pointing down] | H•L• | MENCKEN | [bracket pointing up] | ALFRED•A | [Borzoi Books logo] | KNOPF'. Back: ad for *Happy Days* and *Newspaper Days*. Front flap: blurb; price $3.00; credit for jacket design to George Salter. Rear flap: appeal to buy war bonds and stamps and to donate the book to the U.S.O.

A 54.1.a, dust jacket

Publication: Published 1 March 1943. $3.00. Copyright #A171801 (first copy received 22 December 1942). 16,400 copies of Knopf printings sold.

Printing: See colophon.

Locations: Harv, InU-Li (dj), LC (26 March 1943, rebound), MBU, RJS (dj).

Notes: Thickness 1″. "Some of these chapters have appeared, either wholly or in part, in the *New Yorker,* and one, 'Downfall of a Revolutionary,' was first published in *Esquire*" (p. [xi]). No copies with a Canadian imprint were found. Adler 17, 18, 156, 156–58; S1.9; S2.13, 19; Bulsterbaum 8, 9.

Salesman's dummy: Portrait (tipped in) and title page but no copyright page (pp. [i–iv]), pp. v–x, 3–10, the rest blank; 8⅝″ × 5¾″; trade binding, top edge may not be stained, drab end papers (Dwiggins Collection at MB).

A 54.1.b
First edition, second printing: New York: Knopf, 1943.

On copyright page: '*Second Printing, April 1943.*'

Location: EPL.

A 54.1.c
First edition, third printing: New York: Knopf, 1943.

Published June 1943. Data from D. Not seen.

A 54.1.d
First edition, fourth printing: New York: Knopf, 1945.

On copyright page: '*Fourth Printing, March 1945*'. Contains a notice 'To THE Pur-*chaser*' regarding wartime paper restrictions (p. [C]), thinner paper (8⅜″ × 5⅝″ ×⅝″), smooth binding.

Locations: EPL, GHT, JRS.

A 54.1.e
First edition, fifth printing: New York: Knopf, 1946.

On copyright page: '*Fifth Printing, May 1946.*'

Locations: EPL, GHT.

A 54.1.f
First edition, sixth printing: New York: Knopf, 1947.

Reprinted in *The Days of H. L. Mencken.* See under *Happy Days* (A 49.1.f).

A 54.1.g
First edition, seventh printing: New York: Knopf, 1955.

On copyright page: '*Sixth printing, January 1955.*'

Locations: EPL, MCR.

A 54.1.h
First edition, eighth printing: New York: Knopf, 1963.

On copyright page: '*Seventh printing, August 1963.*'

Location: MBU.

A 54.1.i
First edition, ninth printing: New York: Knopf, 1968.

On copyright page: '*Eighth printing, December 1968.*'

Locations: EPL, Harv.

A 54.1.j
First edition, tenth printing: New York: Knopf, 1975.

On copyright page: '*Ninth printing, January 1975.*'

Location: D.

LATER REPRINTINGS WITHIN THE FIRST EDITION

A 54.1.k
New York: AMS, [n.d.].

Added title page (New York: Knopf, 1975, retained on original). On copyright page: '. . . from the edition | of 1973 *[sic]*'. Dated 1986 by OCLC.

Locations: GHT, Harv.

A 54.1.l
New York: Dorset, 1989.

Second printing of *The Days of H. L. Mencken*. See under *Happy Days* (A 49.1.l).

A 54.1.m
Baltimore and London: Johns Hopkins University Press, [1996].

On copyright page: 'Maryland Paperback Bookshelf edition, 1996 | 05 04 03 02 01 00 99 98 97 96   5 4 3 2 1'. 8⁷⁄₁₆″ × 5⁷⁄₁₆″. White wrappers printed in purple, black, and beige.

Location: GHT.

A 54.2.a
Second edition, only printing (1943?)

Title page: '[all within double-rule box] [to left of vertical rule] PUBLISHED BY ARRANGEMENT WITH | ALFRED A. KNOPF, NEW YORK | *Copyright 1941, 1942, 1943 by Alfred A. Knopf,* | [five more lines reserving rights] || [to right of rule] HEATHEN | DAYS | 1890–1936 | *By* H. L. MENCKEN | *Armed Services Editions* | COUNCIL ON BOOKS IN WARTIME, INC. | NEW YORK'

Copyright page blank.

3¹⁵⁄₁₆″ × 5⁷⁄₁₆″: [1–4] 5–9 [10] 11–254 [255–56] = 256 pp.

Apparently [1–8]¹⁶ = 128 leaves, glued not sewed.

Contents: p. 1: title; p. 2: blank; p. 3: '*TABLE OF CONTENTS*'; p. 4: blank; pp. 5–9: '*PREFACE*'; p. 10: blank; pp. 11–254: text, same as in first edition, first printing; p. 255: 'NOTE' [same as above]; p. 256: blank.

Binding: Stapled front to back and glued beneath red, white, light and dark blue, and black stiff paper wrappers (series no. A–13).

Locations: EPL, GHT, RJS (2).

Notes: EPL copy signed and dated 1943 by Mencken; also the date assigned by OCLC. Adler 17.

A 55 SUNPAPERS STYLEBOOK
1944

STYLEBOOK

THE SUNPAPERS OF BALTIMORE

A 55

Copyright page: 'PRINTED OCTOBER, 1944'

$8^{13}/_{16}'' \times 5^{5}/_{16}''$: [1–3] 4–60 [61] 62–95 [96] = 96 pp.

$[1]^{48}$ = 48 leaves.

Contents: p. 1: title; p. 2: copyright; p. 3: 'PREFACE'; pp. 4–60: text; p. 61: blank; pp. 62–65: 'SPELLING'; pp. 66–71: 'APPENDIX'; pp. 72–95: ruled pages, headed A–Z; p. 96: 'Note On Typography'.

Typography and paper: $7^{1}/_{2}''$ ($7^{3}/_{16}''$) $\times$ 4''; 43 lines per page (number of lines varies with number of entries). Running heads, all over rules: recto, 'OF BALTIMORE [last entry on page]' (pp. 5–59), 'OF BALTIMORE' (p. 61), 'OF BALTIMORE [page number]' (pp. 63–95); verso, '[first entry on page] THE SUNPAPERS' (pp. 4–60), '[page number] THE SUNPAPERS' (pp. 62–94). Page numbers at bottom of pp. 4–60. Wove paper.

Binding: Dull orange paper wrappers. Front duplicates title page. All edges trimmed. Two staples.

Locations: EPL (2), GHT.

Notes: An EPL copy is inscribed by Mencken to Knopf: "I wrote the preface, but had only a fatherly hand in the rest." According to Adler, "This project was inspired by HLM, who wrote and revised most of the book. It has been subsequently used as a model by many U. S. newspapers." The GHT copy contains an errata sheet ($8^{3}/_{4}'' \times 5^{1}/_{8}''$). Adler 33; Busterbaum 69.

A 56 SUPPLEMENT I: THE AMERICAN LANGUAGE

A 56.1.a
Only edition, first printing (1945)

SUPPLEMENT I

T H E

American Language

AN INQUIRY

INTO THE DEVELOPMENT OF ENGLISH

IN THE UNITED STATES

BY

H. L. Mencken

1945
ALFRED A. KNOPF
NEW YORK

A 56.1.a

Copyright page: 'COPYRIGHT 1945 *by Alfred A. Knopf, Inc. All rights reserved. No part* | [three lines reserving rights] | *factured in the United States of America. Published simultaneously in* | *Canada by The Ryerson Press.* | FIRST EDITION'

Colophon: 'A NOTE ON THE TYPE | [fifteen lines on Janson type] | *The book was composed, printed, and bound by The Plimp-* | *ton Press, Norwood, Massachusetts. Typography and binding* | *designs by W. A. Dwiggins.* | [five lines on compliance with government regulations]'

9⁵⁄₁₆″ × 6³⁄₁₆″: [A–D i–iv] v–xv [xvi–xviii] 1–683 [684] 685–739 [740] i–xxxv [xxxvi–xxxviii] = 800 pp.

$[1-25]^{16}$ = 400 leaves.

Contents: pp. A–C: blank; p. D: eighteen Borzoi Books titles by Mencken; p. i: half title; p. ii: blank; p. iii: title; p. iv: copyright; pp. v–x: 'PREFACE'; pp. xi–xii: 'Table of Contents'; pp. xiii–xv: 'ABBREVIATIONS'; p. xvi: blank; p. xvii: half title; p. xviii: blank; pp. 1–683: text; p. 684: blank; pp. 685–739: 'LIST OF WORDS AND | PHRASES'; p. 740: blank; pp. i–xxxv: 'INDEX'; p. xxxvi: colophon; pp. xxxvii–xxxviii: blank.

Typography and paper: 7⅜″ (7⅛″) × 4⅛″; 48 lines per page (lines vary with amount of reduced type and number of footnotes, which are in double columns). Running heads: recto, '*Preface*' (pp. vii–ix), '*Abbreviations*' (p. xv), section titles (pp. 3–683), '*List of Words of Phrases*' (pp. 687–739), '*Index*' (pp. iii–xxxv); verso, '*Preface*' (pp. vi–x), '*Table of Contents*' (p. xii), '*Abbreviations*' (p. xiv), '*The American Language: Supplement I*' (pp. 2–682), '*List of Words of Phrases*' (pp. 686–738), '*Index*' (pp. ii–xxxiv). Laid paper.

Binding: Black S cloth. Front: blindstamped shield from Mencken arms. Spine, stamped in gilt: '[ornament with spread eagle, thick bar above it, three rules below] | THE | AMERICAN | LANGUAGE | *Supplement One* | [double rule] | [script] *H. L. Mencken* | [double rule, bar, rule, bar, rule] | K N O P F | [double rule, bar, double rule, ornament, bar]'. Back: Borzoi Books logo blindstamped. Top edge trimmed and stained black, fore and bottom edges rough trimmed. White end papers.

Dust jacket: Red and black printing on white paper. Front: [all between ornate red and black border at top, ornate black borders left and right] '*Supplement One* | T H E | American | Language | [red] H. L. MENCKEN | [eight-line blurb inside ornate black borders top, right, and left, red bar at bottom]'. Spine: '[red ornament] | *Supplement One* | The | American | Language | H. L. | MENCKEN | [red ornament] | [Borzoi device] | ALFRED • A • KNOPF | [red ornament]'. Back: 'THE | American Language | *FOURTH EDITION* | By H. L. M E N C K E N | [blurb, quotations from reviews, Knopf imprint]'. Front flap: blurb, price $5.00. Rear flap: ad for the *Days* books; '.82 TP 7–45' at bottom.

A 56.1.a, dust jacket

Publication: Published 20 August 1945. $5.00. Copyright #A189436 (two copies received 29 July 1945). 31,100 copies of Knopf printings sold (8,500 copies of the three-volume set).

Printing: See colophon.

Locations: Harv (2), InU-Li (dj), MChB, MCR, RJS (dj).

Notes: Reported separately boxed (D). No copies with a Canadian imprint were found. Adler 10; S2.6; Bulsterbaum 5.

A 56.1.b
Second printing: New York: Knopf, 1945.

On copyright page: 'SECOND PRINTING, SEPTEMBER 1945'.

Locations: EPL, MBU.

A 56.1.c
Third printing: New York: Knopf, 1945.

On copyright page: 'THIRD PRINTING, OCTOBER 1945'.

Locations: EPL, MBU.

A 56.1.d.i
Fourth printing, American issue: New York: Knopf, 1948.

On copyright page: 'FOURTH PRINTING, JUNE 1948'.

Location: EPL.

A 56.1.d.ii
Fourth printing, English issue (1948)

Title page: A label (1⁵⁄₁₆" × 4¼") with the RKP imprint covers 'ALFRED A. KNOPF | NEW YORK | [Borzoi device]'. See A 59.1.a.ii.

Copyright page: '[in a box formed by thick-thin rule at top, thin-thick rule at bottom, two sprigs on each side] THIS IS A BORZOI BOOK, | PUBLISHED BY ALFRED A. KNOPF, INC. | [below box] COPYRIGHT 1945 *by Alfred A. Knopf, Inc. All rights reserved. No part* | [three lines reserving rights] | *Manufactured in the United States of America. Published simultane-* | *ously in Canada by The Ryerson Press.* | PUBLISHED AUGUST 20, 1945 | SECOND PRINTING, SEPTEMBER 1945 | THIRD PRINTING, OCTOBER 1945 | FOURTH PRINTING, JUNE 1948'

Colophon: 'A NOTE ON THE TYPE | [fifteen lines on Janson type] | *The book was composed, printed, and bound by The Plimp-* | *ton Press, Norwood, Massachusetts. Typography and binding* | *designs by W. A. Dwiggins.*'

SUPPLEMENT I

T H E

American Language

AN INQUIRY

INTO THE DEVELOPMENT OF ENGLISH

IN THE UNITED STATES

BY

H. L. Mencken

9⅜″ × 6⅛″: [A–D i–iv] v–xv [xvi–xviii] 1–683 [684] 685–739 [740] i–xxxv [xxxvi–xxxviii] = 800 pp.

[1–25]¹⁶ = 400 leaves.

Contents: pp. A–C: blank; p. D: '*Also by H. L. Mencken* | [eight titles] | [double rule] | *These are Borzoi Books* | *published by* **ALFRED A. KNOPF** '; p. i: half title; p. ii: blank; p. iii: title; p. iv: copyright; pp. v–x: 'PREFACE'; pp. xi–xii: 'Table of Contents'; pp. xiii–xv: 'ABBREVIATIONS'; p. xvi: blank; p. xvii: half title; p. xviii: blank; pp. 1–683: text; p. 684: blank; pp. 685–739: 'LIST OF WORDS AND | PHRASES'; p. 740: blank; pp. i–xxxv: 'INDEX'; p. xxxvi: colophon; pp. xxxvii–viii: blank.

Typography and paper: Typography same as in first printing. Laid paper.

Binding: Black V cloth. Front: blindstamped shield from Mencken arms. Spine, stamped in gilt: '[ornament with spread eagle, thick bar above it, three rules below] | THE | AMERICAN | LANGUAGE | *Supplement One* | [double rule] | [script] *H. L. Mencken* | [double rule, bar, rule, bar, rule] | K N O P F | [double rule, bar, double rule, ornament, bar]'. Back: Borzoi Books logo blindstamped. Trimmed, unstained. White end papers.

Dust jacket: Not seen.

Publication: Published September 1948 (ECB 16.522). 30s.

Locations: BL (12 NOV 48), Bod (19 | NOV | 1948), Camb (19 NO | 1948).

Notes: The two supplements were issued simultaneously with *The American Language* (A 19.4.m.ii, A 59.1.a.ii). No copies with a Canadian imprint were found.

A 56.1.e
Fifth printing: New York: Knopf, 1952.

On copyright page: 'FIFTH PRINTING, MARCH 1952'.

Locations: EPL, OCanS.

A 56.1.f
Sixth printing: New York: Knopf, 1956.

On copyright page: 'SIXTH PRINTING, OCTOBER 1956'. Data from Senjo printings below. Not seen.

A 56.1.g
Seventh printing: New York: Knopf, 1960.

On copyright page: '*seventh printing, June* | *1960.*' For this printing in a boxed set, see *The American Language* (A 19.4.p).

Location: GHT.

A 56.1.h
Eighth printing: New York: Knopf, 1961.

On copyright page: '*eighth printing, October 1961.*' For this printing in a boxed set, see *The American Language* (A 19.4.p).

Locations: D, GHT.

A 56.1.i
Ninth printing: Same title page as sixth printing, for Senjo (Tokyo).

Wove paper. In a set with *The American Language* and the second supplement (A 19, A 59; on copyright page: August 1957 [*AL*], October 1956 [I], March 1956 [II]). Black cloth stamped in gilt, with 'KNOPF | SENJO' at the base of the spine of the cover. Senjo (of Tokyo) imprint and that of Knopf also on the front and spine of dust jacket, with table of contents in Japanese on the front flap, a Mencken chronology in Japanese on the back flap. A pale yellow-orange strip (white on the verso) wraps around the dust jacket, identifying the book in Japanese. Published 20 January 1962, and "500 (?)" printed, according to a distributor's label pasted onto the free front end paper of the EPL copy of *The American Language* (cf. S1.4).

Location: EPL (dj).

A 56.1.j
Tenth printing: New York: Knopf, 1962.

On copyright page: '*ninth printing, August 1962*'. Laid paper.

Location: MChB.

A 56.1.k
Eleventh printing: Same title page as tenth printing, for Book-of-the-Month Club.

The Book-of-the-Month Club dividend for May 1962 included the book in a set with *The American Language* and the second supplement. Wove paper; blindstamped dot on back cover; 'W' on copyright page; '4322' on spine of dust jacket.

Locations: GHT (dj), Harv, MB, RJS (dj).

A 56.1.l
Twelfth printing: New York: Knopf, 1966.

On copyright page: '*tenth printing, December 1966.*'

Locations: D, GHT, MB.

A 56.1.m
Thirteenth printing: Same title page as sixth printing, for Senjo (Tokyo).

Wove paper. In a set with *The American Language* and the second supplement (A 19, A 59; on copyright page: August 1957 [*AL*], October 1956 [I], March 1956 [II]). Taupe cloth stamped in gilt. Printed and published in July 1968, according to slip (printed in Japanese) tipped in to recto of rear end paper.

Location: GHT.

A 56.1.n
Fourteenth printing: New York: Knopf, 1975.

Data from OCLC. Not seen.

A 56.1.o
Fifteenth printing: New York: Knopf, 1977.

On copyright page: 'Twelfth Printing, August 1977'. Data from next entry. Not seen.

A 56.1.p
Sixteenth printing: Same title page as fifteenth printing, for Book-of-the-Month Club.

Book-of-the-Month Club premium for September 1979, with *The American Language* and second supplement. Wove paper; blindstamped square on back cover.

Locations: D, GHT.

A 56.1.q
Seventeenth printing: New York: Knopf, 1984.

On copyright page: 'Thirteenth Printing, January 1984'.

Location: D.

A 57 CHRISTMAS STORY

A 57.1.a
Only edition, first printing (1946)

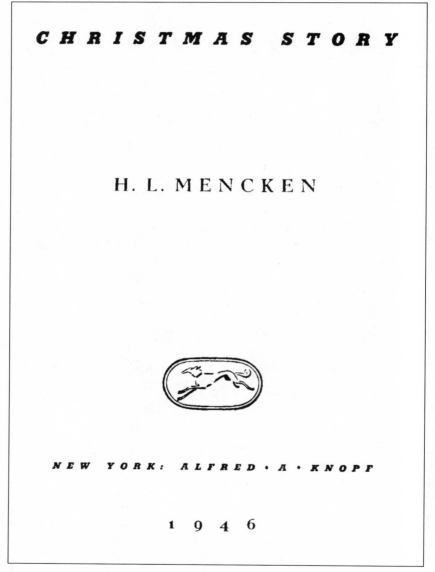

Copyright page: 'THIS STORY | was first printed in the *New Yorker*, to whose | editors I am indebted for permission to republish | it. In writing it I had valuable suggestions from | my brother, August Mencken. | [flush right] H.L.M. | *Copyright 1944, 1946 by H. L. Mencken. All rights reserved. No* | [four lines reserving rights] | *tured in the United States of America. Published simultaneously* | *in Canada by The Ryerson Press.* FIRST EDITION | *This is a Borzoi Book, published by Alfred A. Knopf, Inc.'*

Colophon: 'NOTE | [five lines on Caledonia type] | *The book was set by* THE COMPOSING ROOM, INC. *New York;* | *printed by* COLORGRAPHIC OFFSET COMPANY, *New York; and* | *bound by* H. WOLFF, *New York. Typography by* SIDNEY R. JACOBS.'

$6\frac{5}{8}'' \times 5\frac{7}{16}''$: [1–5] 6–31 [32] (unpaginated on pages of all but the last illustration) = 32 pp.

$[1–2]^8$ = 16 leaves.

Contents: p. 1: half title; p. 2: '*ILLUSTRATIONS BY* | *BILL CRAWFORD*'; p. 3: title; p. 4: copyright; pp. 5–31: text; p. 32: colophon. Illustrations on pp. 5, 9, 11, 13, 15, 16–17, 19, 21, 24, 29, 31.

Typography and paper: $5\frac{3}{16}''$ ($4\frac{3}{4}''$) $\times$ 4''; 25 lines per page. Running heads: recto, '*CHRISTMAS STORY*' (pp. 7–31); verso, '*H. L. MENCKEN*' (pp. 6–30). Wove paper.

Binding A: Light blue V cloth. Front: in blue, black, and orange on a white paper label, a bum picking up a cigar. Spine, stamped in gilt: '[ornament] | [reading down, off line] CHRISTMAS STORY H. L. MENCKEN [same ornament upside-down] KNOPF'. Back: Borzoi Books logo blindstamped. Edges trimmed, unstained. Front end papers white with multicolored illustration of feasting bums at a burlesque show. Back end papers colored the same, illustration of a bum at a feast with his hand raised.

Binding B: Same but darker blue cloth and a different texture, vertical grain slants left to right, stamping on spine is straight, and the end papers are as above or reversed.

Dust jacket A: Front: [all over a multicolored illustration of a bum ascending above his fellows through light from a cloud] '[white] CHRISTMAS STORY | [black, at bottom] H. L. MENCKEN | ILLUSTRATED BY BILL CRAWFORD'. Spine as on spine of cover, except ornaments black, lettering white. Back: a bum panhandling Mencken, inscribed in script: 'Mr. Mencken | and friend'. Flaps have continuous blurb; price $1.00. Parts of design missing, including the right lens of Mencken's glasses on the back.

Dust jacket B: Same but design complete.

Publication: Published 18 October 1946. $1.00. Copyright #A6800. 26,000 copies of Knopf printings sold.

Printing: See colophon.

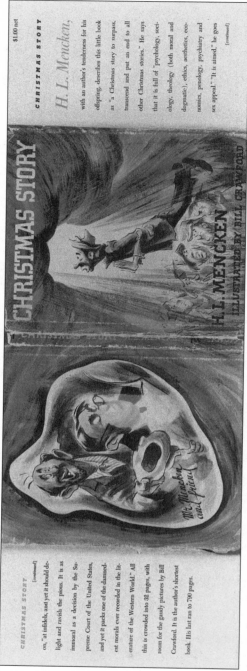

A 57.1.a, dust jacket A

A 57.1.a, dust jacket B

Locations: GHT (3, bindings A and B [2] in dj), Harv (binding B), InU-Li (2, bindings A [dj] and B), LC (28 August 1946, two copies in binding A, one of them in dj B), RJS (2, bindings A and B in dj).

Notes: Notwithstanding the prior offprint of "Stare Decisis" from *New Yorker*, 30 December 1944 (E 48), *Christmas Story* is the first separately published appearance. No copies with a Canadian imprint were found. Adler 17, 158; Bulsterbaum 12.

Review copy: Laid-in drab slip (6⅝″ × 4¹³⁄₁₆″): [all in a red box] '[red ornamental Borzoi device] | *This advance copy* | *is sent to you with the compliments* | [six more lines] | PUBLICATION DATE | [handstamped in red] NOV 14 1946'. *Location:* RJS (original copy in which it was placed unknown).

A 57.1.b
Second printing: New York: Knopf, [n.d.].

The presumed second printing (unstated) is in tan or dark blue cloth, no date on title page, copyright notice revised (distributed by Random House), the Mencken arms blindstamped on front cover, bum with raised hand on front end paper, complete design on dust jacket.

Locations: GHT (2, dj), JRS.

A 57.1.c
Third printing: New York: Knopf, [1969].

On copyright page: '*Published November 14, 1946* | *Third Printing, June 1969.*' Brown cloth, the Mencken arms stamped in gilt on the front.

Location: MBU.

A 58 VACHEL LINDSAY
1947

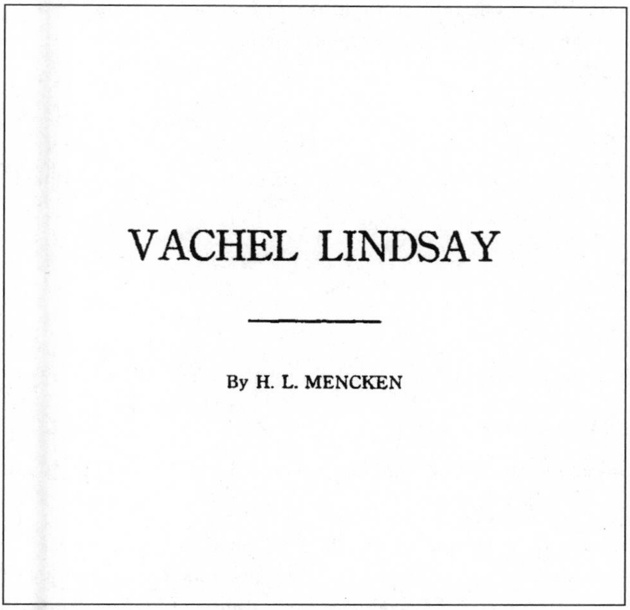

VACHEL LINDSAY

———

By H. L. MENCKEN

A 58, cover title

Copyright page: 'Copyright 1947 | By John S. Mayfield | Printed for John S. Mayfield by Keystone Press, | Washington, D. C.'

Statement of limitation: 'This tribute to the poet—written | shortly after his death—is printed | here for the first time. The edition | consists of one hundred numbered | copies of which this is | Copy Number | [number penned in]'

$7\frac{5}{16}'' \times 5\frac{1}{4}''$: [1–8] = 8 leaves.

[1]⁴ = 4 leaves.

Contents: p. 1: cover title; p. 2: copyright; pp. 3–5: text; p. 6: limitation; p. 7: blank; p. 8: union label.

Typography and paper: $4\frac{3}{4}'' \times 4''$; 24 lines (p. 4; each page of text has a different number of lines). No heads. Wove paper (see Notes).

Binding: Self wrappers. All edges trimmed. Two staples.

Publication: Published 11 April 1947. $5.00. Copyright #AA49903.

Printing: Manufactured by Keystone Press, Washington, D.C.

Locations: BL (30 AUG 60, no. 19, rebound), EPL, GHT, InU-Li, JRS, LC (17 April 1947, no. 13).

Notes: Originally composed 1931. "Mencken checked the proof, and the eight-page small octavo, with self-printed wrappers, stapled, all edges trimmed, was completed on 11 April 1947. . . . When I numbered the copies in ink, I noticed that two kinds of paper had been used: Gilbert Bond and Hamilton Bond" (John S. Mayfield, "Vachel Lindsay: The True Voice of Middle America By H. L. Mencken," *The Courier* [Syracuse Univ.] 2.4 [December 1962]: 13–16, which reprints Mencken's essay). All observed copies were watermarked 'GILBERT BOND | 25% COTTON FIBRE | U S A'; the other paper would indicate a second printing. Adler 18; S1.4; Bulsterbaum 12.

A 59 SUPPLEMENT II: THE AMERICAN LANGUAGE

A 59.1.a.i
Only edition, first printing, first issue (1948)

SUPPLEMENT II

THE

American Language

AN INQUIRY
INTO THE DEVELOPMENT OF ENGLISH
IN THE UNITED STATES

BY

H. L. Mencken

1948
ALFRED A. KNOPF
NEW YORK

A 59.1.a.i

Copyright page: [in a box formed by thick-thin rule at top, thin-thick rule at bottom, two sprigs on each side] 'THIS IS A BORZOI BOOK, | PUBLISHED BY ALFRED A. KNOPF, INC.' | 'COPYRIGHT *1948 by Alfred A. Knopf, Inc. All rights reserved. No part* | [three lines reserving rights] | *factured in the United States of America. Published simultaneously in* | *Canada by The Ryerson Press.* | FIRST EDITION'

Colophon: Same as in *Supplement I* (A 56.1.a) but without the five lines on government regulations.

9⅜″ × 6³⁄₁₆″: [A–B i–iv] v–vii [viii–x] xi–xiii [xiv 1–2] 3–890 i–xliii [xliv–xlvi] = 952 pp.

[1–28]¹⁶ [29]⁴ [30]¹⁶ [31]⁸ = 476 leaves.

Contents: p. A: blank; p. B: 'Also by H. L. Mencken | [ten titles]'; p. i: half title; p. ii: blank; p. iii: title; p. iv: copyright; pp. v–vii: 'PREFACE'; p. viii: blank; p. ix: 'Table of Contents'; p. x: blank; pp. xi–xiii: 'ABBREVIATIONS'; p. xiv: blank; p. 1: half title; p. 2: blank; pp. 3–786: text; pp. 787–890: 'LIST OF WORDS AND | PHRASES'; pp. i–xliii: 'INDEX'; p. xliv: blank; p. xlv: colophon; p. xlvi: blank.

Typography and paper: 7⅜″ (7⅛″) × 4³⁄₁₆″; 45 lines per page (lines vary with amount of reduced type and number of footnotes, which are in double columns). Running heads: recto, 'Preface' (p. vii), 'Abbreviations' (p. xiii), section titles (pp. 5–785), 'List of Words and Phrases' (pp. 789–889), 'Index' (pp. iii–xliii); verso, 'Preface' (p. vi), 'Abbreviations' (p. xii), 'The American Language: Supplement II' (pp. 4–786), 'List of Words and Phrases' (pp. 788–890), 'Index' (pp. ii–xlii). Laid paper.

Binding: Same as in *Supplement I,* except, on spine: '. . . | *Supplement Two* | . . .'. V cloth.

Dust jacket: Blue and black printing on white paper. Front: [all between ornate blue and black border at top, ornate black borders left and right] 'Supplement Two | T H E | American | Language | [blue] H. L. MENCKEN | [eight-line blurb inside ornate black borders top, right, and left, blue bar at bottom]'. Spine: '[blue ornament] | *Supplement Two* | The | American | Language | H. L. | MENCKEN | [blue ornament] | [Borzoi device] | ALFRED • A • KNOPF | [blue ornament]'. Back: '[blue] The American Language | *By* H. L. MENCKEN | [quotations from reviews, Knopf imprint]'. Front flap: blurb, price $7.50. Rear flap: reviews for *Supplement One.*

Publication: Published 12 March 1948. $7.50. Copyright #A16408 (two copies received 18 March 1948). 15,500 copies of Knopf printings sold (8,500 copies of the three-volume set).

Printing: See colophon.

Locations: InU-Li (dj), MChB, MCR, RJS (dj), Yale.

Notes: Errata sheet (9⅛″ × 6″) printed on both sides, laid in. Adler 10, 160; S2.6; Bulsterbaum 5.

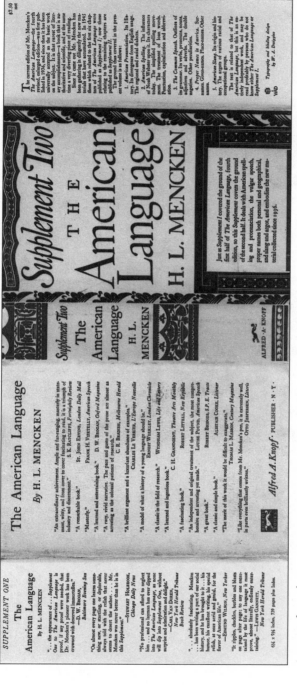

A 59.1.a.i, dust jacket

Review copy: Same as above, with blue slip (2½″ × 4″): 'This book will be published: | DATE: [red stamp] APR 5 | PRICE: [red stamp] $7.50 | Please do not release reviews until the | above date. We would appreciate two | copies of your review. | *Alfred A. Knopf, Inc.*' *Location:* Yale.

Salesman's dummy: Title and copyright pages, preface, table of contents, pp. 3–10; the rest blank; 9¼″ × 6¼″ × 1⅜″, regular binding, top edge stained purple. EPL copy signed and dated 1947 by Mencken.

A 59.1.a.ii
First printing, English issue (1948)

Same as A 59.1.a.i except:

Title page: As with A 56.1.d.ii, a label (1⁵⁄₁₆″ × 4¼″) covers everything beneath the date: 'LONDON | ROUTLEDGE AND KEGAN PAUL LTD. | BROADWAY HOUSE, 68–74 CARTER LANE, E.C. 4'.

Dust jacket: Not seen.

Publication: Published September 1948 (ECB 16.522). 37s.6d.

Locations: BL (12 NOV 48), Bod (19 | NOV | 1948), Camb (19 NO | 1948).

Notes: The two supplements were issued simultaneously with *The American Language* (A 19.4.m.ii, A 56.1.d.ii).

A 59.1.b
Second printing: New York: Knopf, 1952.

On copyright page: 'SECOND PRINTING, MARCH 1952'. Contains the corrections on the errata sheet.

Location: EPL.

A 59.1.c
Third printing: New York: Knopf, 1956.

On copyright page: 'THIRD PRINTING, MARCH 1956'. Wove paper, thickness 1¾″.

Location: OCanS.

A 59.1.d
Fourth printing: New York: Knopf, 1960.

On copyright page: '*fourth printing, May 1960*'. For this printing in a boxed set, see *The American Language* (A 19.4.p).

Location: GHT.

A 59.1.e
Fifth printing: New York: Knopf, 1961.

On copyright page: '*fifth printing, October 1961*'. For this printing in a boxed set, see *The American Language* (A 19.4.p).

Location: GHT.

A 59.1.f
Sixth printing: Same title page as third printing, for Senjo (Tokyo).

Wove paper, thickness 2⅛16″. In a set with *The American Language* and the first supplement (A 19, A 56; on copyright page: August 1957 [*AL*], October 1956 [I], March 1956 [II]). Black cloth stamped in gilt, with 'KNOPF | SENJO' at the base of the spine of the cover. Senjo (of Tokyo) imprint and that of Knopf also on the front and spine of dust jacket, with table of contents in Japanese on the front flap, a Mencken chronology in Japanese on the back flap. A pale yellow-orange strip (white on the verso) wraps around the dust jacket, identifying the book in Japanese. Published 20 January 1962, and "500 (?)" printed, according to a distributor's label pasted onto the free front end paper of the EPL copy of *The American Language* (cf. S1.4).

Location: EPL (dj).

A 59.1.g
Seventh printing: New York: Knopf, 1962.

On copyright page: '*sixth printing, August 1962.*' Laid paper. For this printing in a boxed set, see *The American Language* (A 19.4.p).

Location: MChB.

A 59.1.h
Eighth printing: Same title page as seventh printing, for Book-of-the-Month Club.

The Book-of-the-Month Club dividend for May 1962 included the book in a set with *The American Language* and the first supplement. Wove paper; blindstamped dot on back cover; 'W' on copyright page; '4322' on spine of dust jacket.

Locations: GHT (dj), Harv, MB.

A 59.1.i
Ninth printing: New York: Knopf, 1967.

Data from OCLC. Not seen.

A 59.1.j
Tenth printing: Same title page as third printing, for Senjo (Tokyo).

Wove paper, thickness 2¼″. In a set with *The American Language* and the first supplement (A 19, A 56; on copyright page: August 1957 [*AL*], October 1956 [I], March 1956 [II]). Taupe cloth stamped in gilt. Printed and published in July 1968, according to slip (printed in Japanese) tipped in to recto of rear end paper.

Location: GHT.

A 59.1.k
Eleventh printing: New York: Knopf, 1975.

Data from OCLC. Not seen.

A 59.1.l
Twelfth printing: New York: Knopf, 1978.

On copyright page: '*Ninth Printing, January 1978*'. Wove paper.

Location: MBU.

A 59.1.m
Thirteenth printing: Same title page as twelfth printing, for Book-of-the-Month Club.

Book-of-the-Month Club premium for September 1979, with *The American Language* and first supplement. Wove paper; blindstamped square on back cover.

Location: GHT.

A 60 MENCKENIANA: A SELECTION FROM A
MENCKEN CHRESTOMATHY
1949

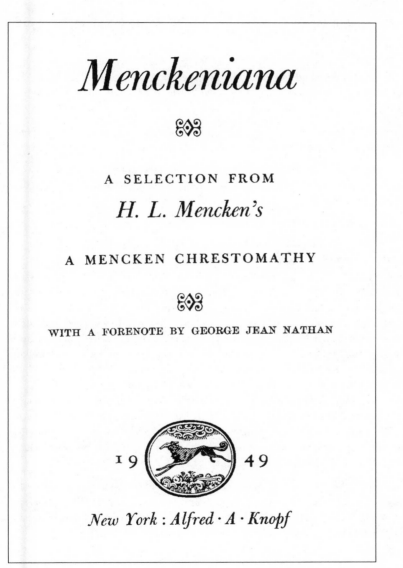

Menckeniana

᭓

A SELECTION FROM

H. L. Mencken's

A MENCKEN CHRESTOMATHY

᭓

WITH A FORENOTE BY GEORGE JEAN NATHAN

1 9 **49**

New York : Alfred · A · Knopf

Copyright notice: 'Copyright 1949 by Alfred A. Knopf, Inc.'

9¼″ × 6⅛″: [1–16] = 16 pp.

[1]⁸ = 8 leaves.

Contents: p. 1: title; p. 2: 'Forenote by | GEORGE JEAN NATHAN', copyright notice; pp. 3–16: text.

Text: "*From* the Preface," "The Good Man," "*From* War," "Art and Sex," "The Altruist," "*From* The Poet and His Art," "*From* Meditation on Meditation," "*From* The Critical Process," "*From* Portrait of an Ideal World," "*From* Immune," "In Memoriam: W. J. B.," "To Him That Hath," "Sententiæ," "Pater Patriæ." See Notes.

Typography and paper: 6¹¹⁄₁₆″ × 3¹³⁄₁₆″; 34 lines per page (lines vary with number of items on page). No heads. Laid paper, watermarked 'WARREN'S | OLDE STYLE'.

Binding: Light blue-green wrappers of stiff paper folded double (10″ × 6½″). Gold foil label on front, printed in red: [within ornate border] 'Menckeniana'. All edges trimmed. Three staples.

Locations: EPL, InU-Li, JRS, RJS, Yale.

Inserts: (1) On thick yellow paper (9½″ × 2¾″): 'These excerpts from | A MENCKEN | CHRESTOMATHY | were specially | prepared for distribution | at the annual convention | of the American | Booksellers Association | Washington, D. C. | May 1949. | [stylized Borzoi device]' (Yale). (2) On Knopf letterhead, blue paper (8½″ × 5½″): 'We prepared a limited number of | these Mencken brochures as souvenirs | of the 1949 ABA convention. Just in | case you didn't get a copy, here you | are. It contains selections from A | MENCKEN CHRESTOMATHY, to be published | on June 10th, at $5.00.' (RJS). (3) On same: 'As an antidote for spring fever, we have | prepared the enclosed MENCKENIANA brochure. | This is a chrestomathy chosen from the book | A MENCKEN CHRESTOMATHY, which we are publishing | June 13. | . . . | [signed] William Cole | Publicity Director' [another version concludes: 'Mrs. Stagg is no longer with Alfred A. Knopf, Inc. William Cole is now the Publicity Director.'] (JRS, EPL). (4) On same: 'To Friends of H. L. Mencken | The enclosed brochure was prepared in | conjunction with our recent publication of | Mr. Mencken's CHRESTOMATHY | . . . | [signed] Richard C. Ernst' (Yale).

Notes: Preceded *A Mencken Chrestomathy* (A 61). First appearance of "*From* the Preface"; the others previously appeared in books, except "*From* War" (*American Mercury*, September 1929), "*From* Immune" (*American Mercury*, March 1930), and "To Him That Hath" (*Smart Set*, May 1920). Adler 18.

A 61 A MENCKEN CHRESTOMATHY

A 61.1.a
Only edition, first printing (1949)

H. L. MENCKEN

A MENCKEN CHRESTOMATHY

EDITED AND ANNOTATED
BY THE AUTHOR

1949

ALFRED A KNOPF
NEW YORK

Copyright page: '[in a box formed by thick-thin rule at top, thin-thick rule at bottom, two sprigs on each side] THIS IS A BORZOI BOOK, | PUBLISHED BY ALFRED A. KNOPF, INC. | [below box] *Copyright 1916, 1918, 1919, 1920, 1921, 1922, 1924, 1926, 1927, 1932, 1934,* | [four lines reserving rights] | *United States of America. Published simultaneously in Canada by McClel-* | *land & Stewart Limited.* | FIRST EDITION'

Colophon: 'PRINTER'S NOTE | [six lines on Electra type, designed by W. A. Dwiggins] | *This book was composed, printed, and bound by* THE PLIMPTON | PRESS, *Norwood, Massachusetts. The typography and binding* | *are designed by* W. A. DWIGGINS. | [ornament with linked 'WAD']'

$8^{5}\!/_{16}'' \times 5^{9}\!/_{16}''$: [A–B i–iv] v–xvi [1–2] 3–627 [628–30] = 648 pp.

[1–18]^{16} [19]^4 [20–21]^{16} = 324 leaves.

Contents: p. A: blank; p. B: 'BOOKS BY | *H. L. Mencken* | [eight titles]'; p. i: half title; p. ii: blank; p. iii: title; p. iv: copyright; pp. v–viii: 'PREFACE'; pp. ix–xvi: 'TABLE OF CONTENTS'; p. 1: half title; p. 2: blank; pp. 3–627: text; p. 628: blank; p. 629: colophon; p. 630: blank.

Typography and paper: $6^{3}\!/_{4}''$ ($6^{9}\!/_{16}''$) $\times 3^{13}\!/_{16}''$; 39 lines per page. Running heads: recto, *'Preface'* (p. vii), *'Contents'* (pp. xi–xv), section titles (pp. 5–625); verso, *'Preface'* (pp. vi–viii), *'Contents'* (pp. x–xvi), *'A Mencken* CHRESTOMATHY' (pp. 4–626). Wove paper, watermarked with interlinked 'AAK' and the Borzoi device.

Binding: Blue V cloth. Front: shield of Mencken arms blindstamped. Spine, stamped in gilt: '[floral ornament over rule] | *H•L•Mencken* | [rule] | [bar] | A | MENCKEN | CHRES= | TOMATHY | [flower] | [double rule] | [bar] | [script] Knopf'. Back: Borzoi Books logo blindstamped. Top edge trimmed, stained blue, fore and bottom edges rough trimmed. White end papers.

Dust jacket: White paper. Front: [all on a blue field] '[gold] A | MENCKEN | CHRES-TOMATHY | [white] A selection from H.L.M.'s out-of-print writings. | [six more lines of blurb] | [black and white photo of Mencken beside flowers under glass]'. Spine: [all on a continuation of blue field, in three columns, each reading down] '[top, white] *A SELECTION FROM H.L.M.'S OUT OF PRINT WRITINGS* ‖ [middle, gold] A MENCKEN CHRESTOMATHY ‖ [bottom, white] ALFRED•A•KNOPF ‖ [top and middle columns above horizontal Borzoi Books logo in black]'. Back: seven quotations from the book. Flaps are a continuous blurb; on front typography and binding design credit to Dwiggins, jacket photograph by A. Aubrey Bodine; price clipped on examples seen.

Publication: Published 1 June 1949. $5 (insert 2 of A 60). Copyright #A33402. 27,000 hardback copies and 15,428 paperback copies of Knopf printings sold.

Printing: See colophon.

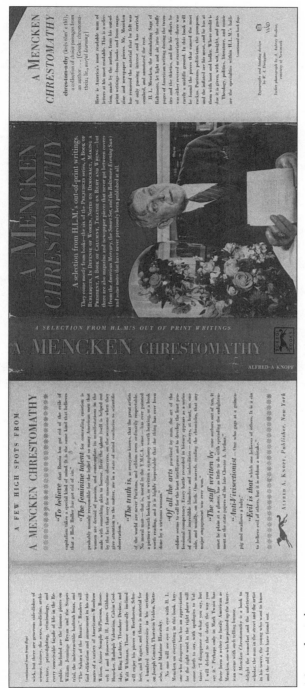

A SELECTION FROM H.L.M'S OUT OF PRINT WRITINGS

A MENCKEN CHRESTOMATHY

ALFRED·A·KNOPF

A MENCKEN CHRESTOMATHY

chres·tom·a·thy (krĕs-tŏm´ə-thĭ), a collection of choice passages from an author ... [Greek: *chrestomatheia*, lit., *useful learning*]

Here is America's most readable man of letters at his most readable. This is a selection, made by the author, from his out-of-print writings—from books and from magazine and newspaper pieces. Mr. Mencken has removed the material that he felt was of only passing interest and has carried, combed, and annotated the rest.

H. L. Mencken, the stimulating Sage of Baltimore, let light and air into the stuffy pages of American writing during the twenties and the thirties, and for his efforts he was either revered or excoriated—there was rarely a middle ground. In this book will be found the pieces that caused the most ruckus. Puritans, politicians, the pompous, and the inflated are his meat, and he has at them with taunt and holler. Where credit is due it is given, with wit, insight, and gusto. Theology, politics, literature, and music are the specialties within H. L. M.'s bailiwick

continued on back flap

A selection from H.L.M.'s out-of-print writings. They come mostly from books—the six of the *Prejudices* series, *A Book of Burlesques*, *In Defense of Women*, *Notes on Democracy*, *Making a President*, *A Book of Calumny*, *Treatise on Right and Wrong*—but there are also magazine and newspaper pieces that never got between covers (from the *American Mercury*, the *Smart Set*, and the *Baltimore Evening Sun*) and some notes that have never previously been published at all.

Typography and binding design by W. A. Dwiggins

Jacket photograph by A. Aubrey Bodine, courtesy of Newsweek

A FEW HIGH SPOTS FROM

A MENCKEN CHRESTOMATHY

¶*To believe* that Russia has got rid of the evils of capitalism takes a special kind of mind. It is the same kind that believes that a Holy Roller has got rid of sin."

¶*The feminine talent* for concealing emotion is probably mainly responsible for the belief of so many American men that women are devoid of passion, and contemplate its manifestations in the male with something akin to horror. Here the talent itself is helped out by the fact that very few masculine observers, on the occasions when they give attention to the matter, are in a state of mind conducive to scientific observation."

¶*The truth is*, as everyone knows, that the great artists of the world are never Puritans, and seldom even ordinarily respectable. No moral man—that is, moral in the Y.M.C.A. sense—has ever painted a picture worth looking at, or written a symphony worth hearing, or a book worth reading, and it is highly improbable that the thing has ever been done by a virtuous woman."

¶*Of all the arts* practiced by man, the art of the soldier seems to call for the least intelligence and to develop the least professional competence. Every battle recorded in history appears as a series of almost incredible blunders and imbecilities—always, at least, on one side, and usually, on both. One marvels, reading the chronicles, that any major engagement was ever won."

¶*The stuff written by* nine authors out of ten, it must be plain at a glance, has as little to do with spreading the enlightenment as the state papers of the late Chester A. Arthur."

¶*Anti-Vivisectionist*—One who ages at a guinea-pig and swallows a baby."

¶*Evil is that* which one believes of others. It is a sin to believe evil of others, but it is seldom a mistake."

ALFRED A. KNOPF, *Publisher, New York*

---

continued from front flap

wick, but there are generous side-dishes of science, history, the news, medicine, architecture, prize-fighting, criminology, and every conceivable facade of life in the Republic. Included are the famous pieces on William Jennings Bryan and the Scopes trial, the indestructible bathtub hoax, and "The Sahara of the Bozart." Readers will find edification and amusement in his estimates of a variety of Americans—Woodrow Wilson, Aimee Semple McPherson, Roosevelt I and Roosevelt II, James Gibbons Huneker, Rudolph Valentino, Calvin Coolidge, Ring Lardner, Theodore Dreiser, and Walt Whitman. Those musically inclined will enjoy his pieces on Beethoven, Schubert, and Wagner, and there is material for a hundred controversies in his sections on Joseph Conrad, Thorstein Veblen, Nietzsche, and Madame Blavatsky.

No one will see eye to eye with H. L. Mencken on everything in this book. Anyone who disagrees but has an appreciation for the right word in the right place will come forth to say, with apologies to Voltaire: "I disapprove of what you say, but I will defend to the death the way you say it." Perhaps only in Mark Twain has there been a writer so lucidly American as Mencken, one who has pointed up the American scene with each telling humor.

A Mencken Chrestomathy is a book to delight the iconoclast and the unfettered scholar, the man in the street and the artist in his tower, the young who want to know and the old who have found out.

A 61.1.a, dust jacket

Locations: GHT (dj), LC (9 June 1949, rebound), MBU, RJS (dj).

Notes: The numerous entries, with a few deliberate changes, "come mostly from books, but others are magazine or newspaper pieces that never got between covers, and a few of them are notes never previously published at all" (p. vi). The preface and annotation are also original. No copies with a Canadian imprint were found. Adler 18, 57, 161; S1.8, 9, 10, 15; S2.8, 14, 21; Bulsterbaum 13–23, 76.

Review copy: Unbound galleys of above, prelims a different setting of type, no table of contents, held with pin, 10¹³⁄₁₆″ × 6⁹⁄₁₆″, cheap paper covers, green Knopf mailing label pasted on front; publication date 20 June 1949. *Location:* GHT.

Salesman's dummies: (1) Different title and copyright pages, end papers, spine, prelims, and collation of printed pages; blank after p. 20; 8⅜″ × 5⅝″; trade binding but darker blue cloth. *Location:* GHT. (2) Blank after title page and copyright page, which are pasted to free front end paper; a gap follows as if a gathering were removed; 8¼″ × 5⅝″. *Location:* Dwiggins Collection at MB.

A 61.1.b
Second printing: New York: Knopf, 1949.

On copyright page: 'SECOND PRINTING, AUGUST 1949'.

Location: EPL.

A 61.1.c
Third printing: New York: Knopf, 1949.

On copyright page: 'THIRD PRINTING, SEPTEMBER 1949'.

Locations: EPL, MCR.

A 61.1.d
Fourth printing: New York: Knopf, 1953.

On copyright page: 'FOURTH PRINTING, JANUARY 1953'.

Location: EPL.

A 61.1.e
Fifth printing: New York: Knopf, 1956.

On copyright page: 'FIFTH PRINTING, JUNE 1956'.

Location: D.

A 61.1.f
Sixth printing: New York: Knopf, 1962.

On copyright page: 'SIXTH PRINTING, NOVEMBER 1962'.

Locations: Harv (2), MB.

A 61.1.g
Seventh printing: New York: Knopf, 1967.

On copyright page: 'SEVENTH PRINTING, DECEMBER 1967'.

Location: D.

A 61.1.h
Eighth printing: New York: Knopf, 1974.

On copyright page: 'EIGHTH PRINTING, JANUARY 1974'.

Location: JRS.

A 61.1.i
Ninth printing: New York: Knopf, 1976.

Published January 1976. Data from D. Not seen.

A 61.1.j
Tenth printing: New York: Knopf, 1978.

On copyright page: 'TENTH PRINTING, AUGUST 1978'.

Location: MC.

A 61.1.k
Eleventh printing: Franklin Center, Pa.: Franklin Library, 1980.

P. [v]: 'THE 100 GREATEST MASTERPIECES | OF AMERICAN LITERATURE | a limited edition collection | is published under the auspices of | The American Revolution | Bicentennial Administration | [logo]'. Portrait by Al Hirschfeld. Bound in leather stamped in gilt, all edges gilt, ribbon bookmark bound in, watered silk end papers. Twenty-two-page insert: 'NOTES FROM THE EDITORS'.

Locations: GHT, JRS, RJS.

A 61.1.l
Twelfth printing: New York: Knopf, 1981.

Published January 1981. Data from D. Not seen.

LATER REPRINTINGS WITHIN THE ONLY EDITION

A 61.1.m
New York: Vintage Books, [1982].

On copyright page: '*First Vintage Books Edition, May 1982*'. 8″ × 5⅛″. White wrappers printed in brown, tan, black, red, and blue.

Locations: GHT, RJS.

A 61.1.n–t

Later Vintage Books printings through eighth (May 1996). Indicated by lowest number in a line of type added to copyright page. Seventh printing ('798') seen (D).

A 62 MINORITY REPORT

A 62.1.a *Only edition, first printing (1956)*

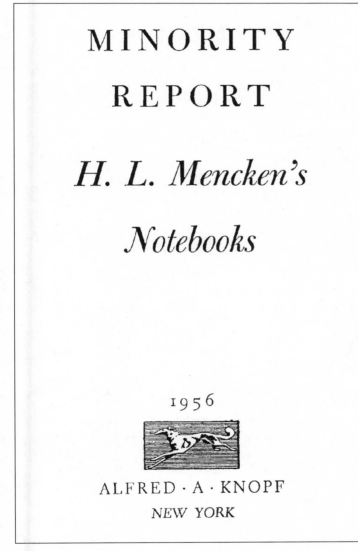

MINORITY

REPORT

H. L. Mencken's

Notebooks

1956

ALFRED · A · KNOPF

NEW YORK

Copyright page: 'L. C. *catalog card number: 56–7717* | © *Alfred A. Knopf, Inc., 1956* | [in a box formed by thick-thin rule at top, thin-thick rule at bottom, two sprigs on each side] THIS IS A BORZOI BOOK, | PUBLISHED BY ALFRED A. KNOPF, INC. | [below box] COPYRIGHT 1956 *by* ALFRED A. KNOPF, *Inc. All rights reserved. No* | [three lines reserving rights] | *Manufactured in the United States of America. Published simultane-* | *ously in Canada by McClelland and Stewart Limited.* | FIRST EDITION'

Colophon: 'PRINTER'S NOTE | [six lines on Electra type, designed by W. A. Dwiggins] | *The book was composed, printed, and bound by* THE PLIMPTON | PRESS, *Norwood, Massachusetts. The paper was made by* S. D. | WARREN COMPANY, *Boston. The typography and binding are* | *based on original designs by* W. A. DWIGGINS.'

$8\frac{5}{16}'' \times 5\frac{9}{16}''$: [A–B i–v] vi [1–2] 3–293 [294–96] = 304 pp.

$[1–9]^{16} [10]^8$ = 152 leaves.

Contents: p. A: blank; p. B: 'BOOKS BY | *H. L. Mencken* | [eleven titles]'; p. i: half title; p. ii: blank; p. iii: title; p. iv: copyright; pp. v–vi: 'PREFACE'; p. 1: half title; p. 2: blank; pp. 3–293: text; p. 294: colophon; pp. 295–96: blank.

Typography and paper: $6\frac{9}{16}''$ $(6\frac{1}{4}'') \times 3\frac{13}{16}''$; 29 lines per page (lines vary with number of items on the page). Running heads: recto, '*H. L. Mencken's Notebooks*' (pp. 5–293); verso, '*Preface*' (p. vi), 'MINORITY REPORT' (pp. 4–292). Wove paper.

Binding: Blue V cloth. Front: shield from Mencken arms blindstamped. Spine, stamped in gilt: '[floral ornament over rule] | [mirroring ornament over rule] | [bar] | MINOR= [lines slanting up] | ITY | REPORT | [double rule over bar] | *H•L•* | *Mencken's* | *Notebooks* | [flower] | [script] *Knopf*'. Back: Borzoi Books logo blindstamped. Top edge trimmed, various degrees of blue stain, fore and bottom edges rough and unevenly trimmed. White end papers.

Dust jacket A: Black field on white paper. Front: '[white] Minority Report | [orange] H. L. MENCKEN[S] | NOTEBOOKS | [four circles: white within orange within black within green] | [orange] Alfred A. Knopf : *Publisher, New York*'. Spine: '[orange] MENCKEN | [white, reading down] Minority Report | [orange] [Borzoi device] | Alfred A. Knopf'. Back: '[in green square] Mencken at the top of his form in a | manuscript completed prior to the fall of 1948 | (before the onset of his illness). | [black and white photo of Mencken credited to Knopf]'. Flaps are a continous blurb; price $3.95; jacket design credit to Herbert Bayer.

Dust jacket B: Same except circles on front replaced with nine squares (two white, one orange, six in shades of gray) and publisher's imprint omitted. Title on spine reduced in size and followed by orange rectangle. Square on back is orange.

Publication: Published 18 April 1956. $3.95. Copyright #A236675. 22,500 copies of Knopf printings sold.

A 62.1.a, dust jacket A

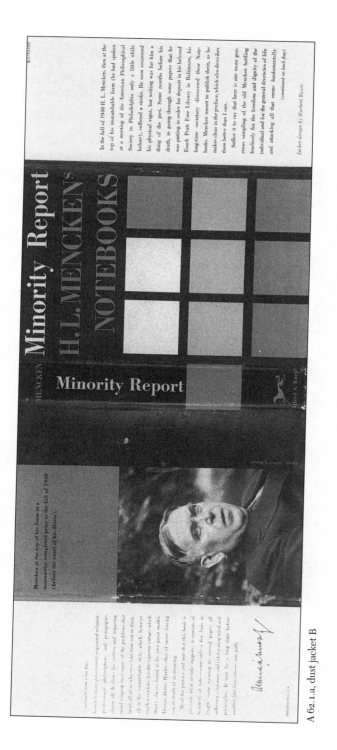

A 62.1.a, dust jacket B

Printing: See colophon.

Locations: Harv, MBU (2), InU-Li (2 in dj A and B), LC (23 April 1956, dj A), RJS (2 in dj A and B).

Notes: Stain not visible or missing on some copies. The two styles of dust jacket appeared simultaneously, each on half of the copies published (*Menckeniana* 22.13). "This is not a book, but a notebook. It is made up of selections chosen more or less at random from the memoranda of long years devoted to the pursuit, anatomizing and embalming of ideas" (p. [v]). Some of the material not selected was published in *Menckeniana* 31–33, 38, 42, 44. No copy with a Canadian imprint was found. The second review copy, below, would indicate that there was no separate printing or issue. Adler 19; S1.15; S2.11, 14, 17; Bulsterbaum 43, 80.

Review copies: (1) Same as above (top edge blue, dust jacket with squares on front), white slip laid in (6″ × 3¾″), all but date blue: '*This book | is sent to you with our compliments. | We would appreciate receiving | two copies of any mention of it | which you may publish. | But no review should appear | before publication date which is |* [black] May 21, 1956 | [Borzoi Books logo and Knopf address]'. *Location:* GHT (dj). (2) Same as above (dust jacket with squares), white slip pasted on free front end paper (6″ × 4″): '*This is a review copy of* | MINORITY REPORT: THE NOTEBOOK *[sic]* | OF H.L. MENCKEN | *by* H.L. Mencken | *price* $4.50 | *It is sent to you with* | *the compliments of* | McCLELLAND & STEWART LIMITED | 25 Hollinger Road— Toronto 16, Canada | [device and request for copies of reviews]'. *Location:* GHT (dj).

A 62.1.b
Second printing: New York: Knopf, 1956.

On copyright page: 'PUBLISHED MAY 21, 1956 | SECOND PRINTING, JUNE 1956'.

Location: MBU.

A 62.1.c
Third printing: New York: Knopf, 1956.

On copyright page: 'THIRD PRINTING, AUGUST 1956'.

Location: D.

A 62.1.d
Fourth printing: New York: Knopf, 1967.

On copyright page: 'FOURTH PRINTING, JANUARY 1967'.

Location: D.

A 63 A CARNIVAL OF BUNCOMBE

A 63.1.a
First edition, first printing (1956)

A 63.1.a

Copyright page: '© 1956, The Johns Hopkins Press, Baltimore 18, Md. | Distributed in Great Britain by | Geoffrey Cumberlege, Oxford University Press, London | Printed in U.S.A. by the William Byrd Press, Richmond | Library of Congress Catalog Card No. 56–11658'

8³⁄₁₆″ × 5⅜″: [i–iv] v–xix [xx–xxii] 1–289 [290] 291–336 [337–38] 339–61 [362] 363–70 = 392 pp.

[1–10]¹⁶ [11]⁴ [12–13]¹⁶ = 196 leaves.

Contents: p. i: half title; pp. ii–iii: title; p. iv copyright; pp. v–viii: 'Contents'; pp. ix–xviii: 'Introduction'; p. xix: 'ACKNOWLEDGMENTS'; p. xx: blank; p. xxi: half title; p. xxii: blank; pp. 1–336: text; p. 337: divisional half titles; p. 338: blank; pp. 339–61: 'Glossary'; p. 362: blank; pp. 363–70: 'Index'. Blank page of text: p. 290.

Text: "A Carnival of Buncombe," "The Clowns in the Ring," "Bayard vs. Lionheart," "Campaign Notes," "The Last Round," "In Praise of Gamaliel," "The Last Gasp," "Optimistic Note," "Gamalielese," "Gamalielese Again," "Who's Loony Now?," "Making Ready for 1924," "Next Year's Stuggle," "Calvinism (Secular)," "The Impending Plebiscite," "The Clowns March In," "Post-Mortem," "Breathing Space," "Labor in Politics," "The New Woodrow," "Meditations on the Campaign," "Notes on the Struggle," "The Coolidge Buncombe," "Mr. Davis' Campaign," "The Voter's Dilemma," "Autopsy," "Twilight," "Cal as Literatus," "The Coolidge Mystery," "Al Smith and His Chances," "The Struggle Ahead," "Al," "The Impending Combat," "Real Issues at Last," "Civil War in the Confederacy," "Al and the Pastors," "The Hoover Manifesto," "Onward, Christian Soldiers!," "The Campaign Opens," "The Show Begins," "Der Wille zur Macht," "Prophetical Musings," "Al in the Free State," "The Eve of Armageddon," "Autopsy," "The Men Who Rule Us," "Looking Ahead," "Little Red Ridinghood *[sic]*," "The Hoover Bust," "Hoover in 1932," "Imperial Purple," "The Men Who Rule Us," "The Impending Carnage," "Where Are We At?," "The Hoover Bust," "Pre-Mortem," "A Time to be Wary," "The Tune Changes," "Vive le Roi!," "Roosevelt," "1936," "The Show Begins," "The More Abundant Dialectic," "The Combat Joins," "Burying the Dead Horse," "After the New Deal," "Sham Battle," "The Choice Tomorrow," "Coroner's Inquest." See Notes.

Typography and paper: 6½″ (6⅛″) × 4″; 34 lines per page. Running heads: recto, 'CONTENTS' (p. vii), 'INTRODUCTION' (pp. xi–xvii), section titles (pp. 3–335), 'GLOSSARY' (pp. 341–61), 'INDEX' (pp. 365–69); verso, 'CONTENTS' (p. vi–viii), 'INTRODUCTION' (pp. x–xviii), 'A CARNIVAL OF BUNCOMBE' (pp. 2–336), 'GLOSSARY' (pp. 340–60), 'INDEX' (pp. 364–70). Wove paper.

Binding: Blue V cloth covering two-thirds of boards; red V cloth spine stamped in white, reading down: 'A CARNIVAL OF BUNCOMBE [over] H. L. Mencken / Edited by Malcolm Moos / JOHNS HOPKINS'. Trimmed, unstained. White end papers.

A 63.1.a, dust jacket

Dust jacket: White paper. Front: '[red] a CARNIVAL | of BUNCOMBE | [to right of photo of Mencken, black with red underline] H. L. Mencken | at his best . . . *[sic]* | on politics | [beneath photo, red] Edited by Malcolm Moos'. Spine, reading down: '[red] H. L. Mencken [black] JOHNS HOPKINS [over] a Carnival of Buncombe'. Back: quotations from the book. Front flap: blurb, jacket photo credit to Robert F. Kniesche, price $4.50. Back flap: continuation of blurb.

Publication: Published 10 October 1956. $4.50. Copyright #A256649 (two copies received 25 October 1956).

Printing: Printed by William Byrd Press, Richmond, Va.; bound by Haddon Bindery, Camden, N.J.

Locations: BL (2 MAY 57), Camb (9 MY | 1957), GHT (dj), MChB, MCR, RJS (dj).

Notes: Monday articles from the Baltimore *Evening Sun*, 1920–36, most of them previously uncollected. Published in England by Oxford University Press, 2 May 1957; 36s (ECB 1957: 209). Adler 19; S1.7; Bulsterbaum 78.

Review copy: Same as above with pale blue slip (8⅜″ × 3½″) printed in red laid in: '[ornate rule] | *your* | *Review Copy* | of [handwritten on line] A Carnival of Buncombe | [line] | by [handwritten on line] H. L. Mencken | [two lines] | Publication date: [handwritten on line] Oct. 10, 1956 | . . . | Its price is: [handwritten on line] $4.50 | . . . | [ornate rule]'. *Location:* GHT (dj).

A 63.1.b
First edition, second printing: A Carnival of Buncombe. Westport, Conn.: Greenwood, [1983].

On copyright page: 'Reprinted in 1983'.

Location: GHT.

A 63.2.a
Second edition, first printing (1960)

Title page: 'H. L. MENCKEN | ON POLITICS | A CARNIVAL OF | BUNCOMBE | [star] | EDITED, WITH AN INTRODUCTION | AND GLOSSARY, BY | MAL-COLM MOOS | [device: sun with face] | [French rule] | VINTAGE BOOKS | NEW YORK | *1960*'

Copyright page: '© THE JOHNS HOPKINS PRESS, 1956. | PUBLISHED BY VINTAGE BOOKS, INC. | Reprinted by arrangement with The JOHNS HOPKINS PRESS. | [four lines reserving rights] | magazine or newspaper. Manufactured in the United States of | America. Published simultaneously in Canada by McClelland & | Stewart, Ltd. | FIRST VINTAGE EDITION'

Colophon: '[five lines on Granjon type] | This book was composed, printed, and bound by THE COLONIAL | PRESS, INC., Clinton, Massachusetts. Paper manufactured by S. D. | WARREN COMPANY, Boston. Cover design by PAUL RAND.'

7¼" × 4¹⁵⁄₁₆": [A–D i–v] vi–xvi [xvii] xviii [xix] xx–xxi [xxii 1–3] 4–63 [64] 65–140 [141] 142–223 [224] 225–96 [297] 298–342 [342A–B 343] 344–65 [366 i] ii–xi [xii– xxii] = 416 pp.

Perfect bound.

Contents: pp. A–D: blank; p. i: half title; p. ii: blank; p. iii: title; p. iv: copyright; pp. v– xvi: 'INTRODUCTION'; pp. xvii–xviii: 'ACKNOWLEDGMENTS'; pp. xix–xxi: 'CONTENTS'; p. xxii: blank; p. 1: half title; p. 2: blank; pp. 3–342: text; p. 342A: half title; p. 342B: blank; pp. 343–65: 'GLOSSARY'; p. 366: blank; pp. i–xi: 'INDEX'; p. xii: blank; p. xiii: biographies of Mencken and Moos, colophon; p. xiv: blank; pp. xv– xix: catalogs; pp. xx–xxii: blank. Text same as in first edition.

Binding: White wrappers printed in red, black, and blue (series no. K-101; price $1.45).

Locations: GHT, InU-Li, RJS.

Notes: No copies with a Canadian imprint were found.

A 63.2.b
Second edition, second printing: Baltimore and London: Johns Hopkins University Press, [1996].

On copyright page: 'Maryland Paperback Bookshelf edition, 1996 | 05 04 03 02 01 00 99 98 97 96   5 4 3 2 1'. 8⁷⁄₁₆" × 5⁷⁄₁₆". White wrappers printed in black, white, pink, and tan.

Location: GHT.

A 63.3.a
Third edition, only printing (1984)

Title page: 'A Carnival of | Buncombe | Writings on Politics | H. L. Mencken | Edited by Malcolm Moos | With a New Foreword by | Joseph Epstein | THE UNIVERSITY OF CHICAGO PRESS | CHICAGO AND LONDON'

Copyright page: 'The University of Chicago Press, Chicago 60637 | The University of Chicago Press, Ltd., London | Reprinted by arrangement with The Johns Hopkins University Press. | © 1980, 1984 by Joseph Epstein | © 1956 by The Johns Hopkins University Press | All rights reserved. Published 1956 | University of Chicago Press edition 1984 | 93 92 91 90 89 88 87 86 85 84   1 2 3 4 5 | [twelve lines of Library of Congress Cataloging in Publication Data]'

8½″ × 5⅜″: [i–iv] v–xxvii [xxviii] xxix–xxxix [xl–xlii] 1–289 [290] 291–336 [337–38] 339–61 [362] 363–70 [371–74] = 416 pp.

Perfect bound.

Contents: p. i: half title; p. ii: blank; p. iii: title; p. iv: copyright; pp. v–viii: 'Contents'; pp. ix–xxvii: 'Foreword | Joseph Epstein'; p. xxviii: blank; pp. xxix–xxxviii: 'Introduction'; p. xxxix: 'ACKNOWLEDGMENTS'; p. xl: blank; p. xli: half title; p. xlii: blank; pp. 1–336: text; p. 337: divisional half titles; p. 338: blank; pp. 339–61: 'Glossary'; p. 362: blank; pp. 363–70: 'Index'; pp. 371–74: blank. Blank page of text: p. 290. Text same as in first edition.

Binding: White wrappers printed in black, gray, and yellow-orange (ISBN 0–226–51977–5).

Locations: GHT, RJS.

A 64 THE BATHTUB HOAX

A 64.1.a
Only edition, first printing (1958)

THE

BATHTUB HOAX

AND OTHER

BLASTS & BRAVOS

FROM THE *CHICAGO TRIBUNE*

BY

H. L. Mencken

EDITED,
WITH AN INTRODUCTION AND NOTES,
BY ROBERT McHUGH

ALFRED · A · KNOPF

NEW YORK · 1958

A 64.1.a

Copyright page: '[Borzoi device with intertwined 'AKB'] | *L. C. Catalog card number: 58–12629* | © *Alfred A. Knopf, Inc., 1958* | [in a box formed by thick-thin rule at top, thin-thick rule at bottom, two sprigs on each side] THIS IS A BORZOI BOOK, | PUBLISHED BY ALFRED A. KNOPF, INC. | [below box] *Copyright 1958 by Alfred A. Knopf, Inc. All rights reserved. No* | [three more lines reserving rights] | *or newspaper. Manufactured in the United States of America.* | *Published simultaneously in Canada by McClelland & Stewart* | *Ltd.* | FIRST EDITION'

Colophon: 'PRINTER'S NOTE | [six lines on Electra type, designed by W. A. Dwiggins] | *The book was composed, printed, and bound by* The PLIMPTON | PRESS, *Norwood, Massachusetts. The paper was made by* S. D. | WARREN COMPANY, *Boston. The typography and binding are* | *based on original designs by* W. A. DWIGGINS.'

$8\frac{5}{16}'' \times 5\frac{9}{16}''$: [A–D i–vi] vii–xiii [xiv] xv–xvi [1–2] 3–19 [20] 21–45 [46] 47–50 [51] 52–66 [67] 68–85 [86] 87–90 [91] 92–95 [96] 97–114 [115] 116–19 [120] 121 [122] 123–40 [141] 142–69 [170] 171–76 [177] 178–81 [182] 183–201 [202] 203–08 [209] 210–13 [214] 215–18 [219] 220–28 [229] 230–58 [259] 260–63 [264] 265–68 [269] 270–73 [274] 275–86 [287–92] = 312 pp.

[1–7]^{16} [8]^{12} [9–10]^{16} = 156 leaves.

Contents: pp. A–C: blank; p. D: 'BOOKS BY | *H. L. Mencken* | [thirteen titles and imprint]'; p. i: half title; p. ii: blank; p. iii: title; p. iv: copyright; p. v: quotations from *Minority Report* in eight lines; p. vi: blank; pp. vii–xiii: 'ABOUT H. L. MENCKEN' [by Robert McHugh]; p. xiv: blank; pp. xv–xvi: 'CONTENTS'; p. 1: half title; p. 2: blank; pp. 3–278: text; pp. 279–86: 'GLOSSARY'; p. 287: 'H. L. MENCKEN' [biography]; p. 288: blank; p. 289: colophon; pp. 290–92: blank. Blank pages of text: pp. 120, 170, 202.

Text: "A Neglected Anniversary (The Bathtub Hoax)," "Melancholy Reflections," "Hymn to the Truth," "The Believing Mind," "The Bill of Rights," "The Comstockian Imbecility," "The Anatomy of Wowserism," "Padlocks," "The Battle of Ideas," "The Birth Control Hullabaloo," "Equality Before the Law," "Essay on Constructive Criticism," "Hints for Novelists," "Yet More Hints for Novelists," "Poe's Start in Life," "The Case of Dreiser," "H. L. Mencken on Mark Twain," "Robert Louis Stevenson," "Beethoven, Obit. March 26, 1827," "The Music of the American Negro," "On Realism," "View of Literary Gents," "The Avalanche of Books," "Fundamentalism: Divine and Secular," "The Rev. Clergy," "Cousin Jocko," "Jacquerie," "Man as a Mammal," "Havelock Ellis," "On Eugenics," "Human Monogamy," "Another Long-Awaited Book," "Holy Writ," "The United States Senate," "The National Conventions," "Notes on Government," "Blackmail Made Easy," "A Long-Felt Want," "Vive le Roi!," "The Pedagogue's Utopia," "On Going to College," "The Language We Speak," "Babel," "The Emperor of Dictionaries," "The American Scene," "On Connubial Bliss," "Dreams of Peace," "On Human Progress," "The South Rebels Again," "The

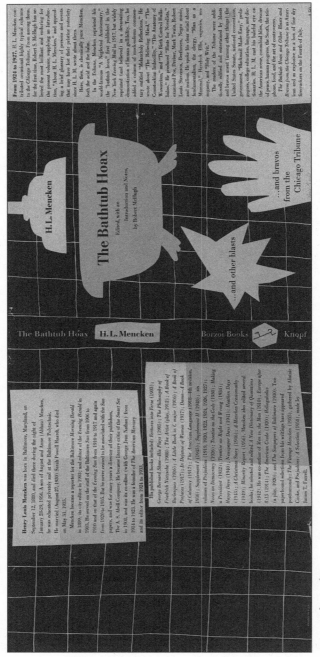

A 64.1.a, dust jacket

Sad Case of Tennessee," "The Movies," "The Telephone Nuisance," "Victualry as a Fine Art," "On Controversy." See Notes.

Typography and paper: 6½″ (6¼″) × 3¹³⁄₁₆″; 32 lines per page. Running heads: recto, 'About H. L. Mencken' (pp. ix–xiii), essay titles (pp. 5–277), 'Glossary' (pp. 281–85); verso, 'ROBERT McHUGH' (pp. viii–xii), 'CONTENTS' (p. xvi), section titles (pp. 4–278), 'Glossary' (pp. 280–86). Wove paper.

Binding: Bright blue V cloth. Front: blindstamped shield of Mencken arms. Spine, stamped in gilt: '[ornaments over rule over bar] | THE | BATHTUB | HOAX | AND | OTHER | BLASTS | AND | BRAVOS | [double rule over bar] | *H•L•* | *Mencken* | [flower] | [script] *Knopf'*. Back: Borzoi Books logo blindstamped. Top edge trimmed and stained yellow, fore and bottom edges rough and unevenly trimmed. White end papers.

Dust jacket: White paper, the designs against a black and white background resembling bathroom tile. Front: '[within white plunger] H. L. Mencken | [next four lines within pink bathtub] The Bathtub Hoax | Edited, with an | Introduction and Notes, | by Robert McHugh | [within yellow starburst] . . . and other blasts | [next four lines within white hand] . . . and bravos | from the | Chicago Tribune | [pink script] Paul Rand'. Spine, reading down: '[pink] The Bathtub Hoax [black in yellow rectangle] H. L. Mencken [white] Borzoi Books [stylized Borzoi device in pink hexagon] [white] Knopf'. Back: biography of Mencken. Front flap: blurb, jacket design credit to Paul Rand, price $4.50. Rear flap: '[white over tile design] PRINTED IN U.S.A.'

Publication: Published 19 August 1958. $4.50. Copyright #A350693. 8,200 copies sold.

Printing: See colophon.

Locations: InU-Li (dj), LC (25 August 1958), MB (dj), MBU, RJS (dj).

Notes: Articles from the Chicago *Tribune*, 1924–27, most of them previously uncollected. No copies with a Canadian imprint were found. Adler 19, 113; S2.8; Bulsterbaum 80.

Review copy: Reported with slip laid in (D).

A 64.1.b
Second printing: New York: Octagon, 1977.

Locations: EPL, GHT, MChB.

A 64.1.c
Third printing: New York: Octagon, 1977 *[sic]*.

On copyright page: '*Second Octagon printing 1981*'.

Location: EPL.

A 65 LETTERS OF H. L. MENCKEN

A 65.1.a
Only edition, first printing (1961)

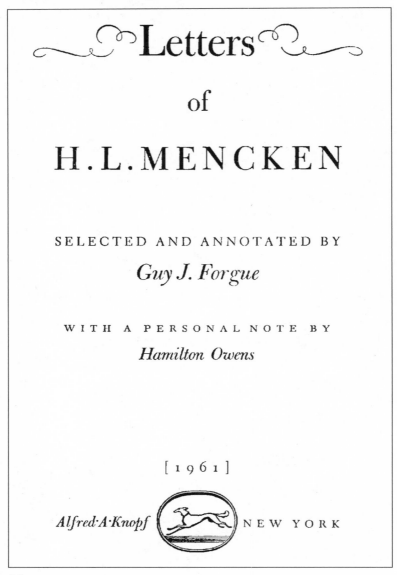

SELECTED AND ANNOTATED BY
Guy J. Forgue

WITH A PERSONAL NOTE BY
Hamilton Owens

[1 9 6 1]

Alfred·A·Knopf   NEW YORK

A 65.1.a

Copyright page: '[Borzoi device beneath intertwined 'AKB'] | L. C. catalog card number: 61–12312 | [French rule] | THIS IS A BORZOI BOOK, | PUBLISHED BY ALFRED A. KNOPF, INC. | [French rule] | Copyright © 1961 by Alfred A. Knopf, Inc. | [five lines reserving rights] | paper. Manufactured in the United States of America. | Published simultaneously in Canada by | McClelland & Stewart, Ltd. | FIRST EDITION'

Colophon: 'A *Note on the Type* | [ten lines on Caledonia type, designed by W. A. Dwiggins] | Composed, printed, and bound by | KINGSPORT PRESS, INC., Kingsport, Tennessee. | Paper manufactured by | S. D. WARREN COMPÀNY, Boston. | Typography and binding based on designs by | W. A. DWIGGINS | [Borzoi device]'

9⁵⁄₁₆″ × 6³⁄₁₆″: [A–B i–iv] v–xiv [xv–xvi] xvii–xix [xx] xxi [xxii] xxiii–xxxviii [xxxix–xl 1–2] 3–506 i–xxii [xxiii–xxviii] = 576 pp.

[1–18]¹⁶ = 288 leaves.

Contents: p. A: blank; p. B: 'BOOKS BY | *H. L. MENCKEN* | [fifteen titles]'; p. i: half title; p. ii: blank; p. iii: title; p. iv: copyright; pp. v–xv: 'H. L. MENCKEN | *A Personal Note*' [by Hamilton Owens]; p. xvi: blank; pp. xvii–xx: 'A NOTE FROM THE EDITOR' [by Guy Jean Forgue]; pp. xxi–xxii: 'ACKNOWLEDGMENTS'; pp. xxiii–xxxix: 'CONTENTS'; p. xl: blank; p. 1: half title; p. 2: blank; pp. 3–506: text: letters 1900–56; pp. i–xxiii: 'INDEX'; p. xxiv: '*A Note About the Author*'; p. xxv: blank; p. xxvi: colophon; pp. xxvii–xxviii: blank. Photo of Mencken (credit to 'ALFRED A. KNOPF') tipped in to p. ii.

Typography and paper: 7⅞″ (7⁹⁄₁₆″) × 4⁵⁄₁₆″; 40 lines per page (size and number of lines depend on whether a letter starts or ends on the page). Running heads: recto and verso, 'A PERSONAL NOTE' (pp. vi–xv), 'A NOTE FROM THE EDITOR' (p. xviii–xx), 'ACKNOWLEDGMENTS' (p. xxii), 'CONTENTS' (pp. xxiv–xxxix), year of the letters in parentheses (pp. 3–506), 'INDEX' (pp. ii–xxiii). Laid paper.

Binding: Medium blue V cloth. Front: blindstamped shield of Mencken arms. Spine, stamped in gilt: '[bar, double rule, row of dots, rule] | [script] *Letters* [ornate L] *of* | H•L• | Mencken | [reverse of bar, etc.] | [script] *Selected by* | GUY • J • FORGUE | [bar, double rule] | [script] Knopf'. Back: Borzoi Books logo blindstamped. Top edge trimmed and stained purple, fore edge rough cut, bottom edge trimmed. White end papers.

Dust jacket: White paper. Front, over photo of Mencken: '[blue] LETTERS *of* | [white] H•L•Mencken | [blue] Selected and annotated by GUY•J•FORGUE | [blue] WITH A PERSONAL NOTE BY HAMILTON OWENS'. Spine: '[white ornament] | LETTERS | *of* | H•L• | Mencken | [white ornament] | Selected and | Annotated | by | GUY•J• | FORGUE | [triple white ornament] | [Borzoi Books logo] | ALFRED•A• | KNOPF'. Back: '[blue] *by H. L. Mencken* | [ornament] | [fifteen titles]'. Front flap: '[price ($7.95) over blurb] | [blue] PHOTOGRAPH OF H. L. MENCKEN | BY

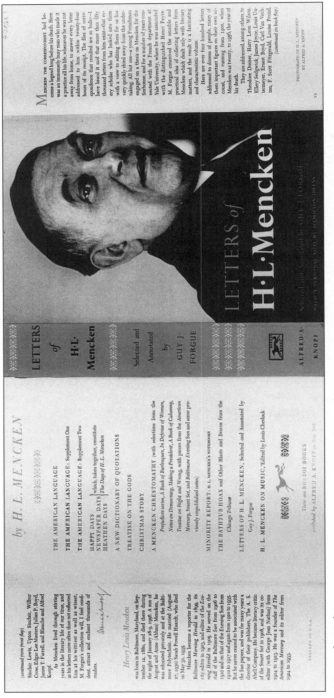

(continued from front flap)

Sinclair Lewis, Upton Sinclair, Wilbur Cross, Edgar Lee Masters, Julian P. Boyd, James T. Farell, and Blanche and Alfred Knopf.

As Mencken lived through stirring years in the literary life of our time, and as his letters more often than not reflected him at his wittiest as well as wisest, Mr. Forgue's collection will, I feel confident, attract and enchant thousands of readers.

Hamilton Owens

Henry Louis Mencken

was born in Baltimore, Maryland, on September 12, 1880, and died there during the night of January 28-9, 1956. A son of August and Anna (Abhau) Mencken, he was educated privately and at the Baltimore Polytechnic. He married (August 27, 1930) Sarah Powell Haardt, who died on May 31, 1935.

Mencken became a reporter for the Baltimore *Morning Herald* in 1899, its city editor in 1903, and editor of the *Evening Herald* in 1905. He served on the staff of the Baltimore *Sun* from 1906 to 1910 and on that of the *Evening Sun* from 1910 to 1917 and again from 1920 to 1935. But he never ceased to be associated with the *Sun* papers, and was for many years a director of their publishers, The A. S. Abell Company. He became literary critic of the *Smart Set* in 1908, and was its co-editor (with George Jean Nathan) from 1914 to 1923. He was a founder of *The American Mercury* and its editor from 1924 to 1933.

by H. L. MENCKEN

THE AMERICAN LANGUAGE

THE AMERICAN LANGUAGE: Supplement One

THE AMERICAN LANGUAGE: Supplement Two

HAPPY DAYS ⎱
NEWSPAPER DAYS ⎰ which, taken together, constitute
HEATHEN DAYS   *The Days of H. L. Mencken*

A NEW DICTIONARY OF QUOTATIONS

TREATISE ON THE GODS

CHRISTMAS STORY

A MENCKEN CHRESTOMATHY (with selections from the *Prejudices* series, *A Book of Burlesques, In Defense of Women, Notes on Democracy, Making a President, A Book of Calamny, Treatise on Right and Wrong*, with pieces from the *American Mercury, Smart Set,* and *Baltimore Evening Sun* and some previously unpublished notes)

MINORITY REPORT: H. L. MENCKEN'S NOTEBOOKS

THE BATHTUB HOAX and Other Blasts and Bravos from the *Chicago Tribune*

LETTERS OF H. L. MENCKEN, Selected and Annotated by Guy J. Forgue

H. L. MENCKEN ON MUSIC, Edited by Louis Cheslock

These are BORZOI BOOKS
published by ALFRED A. KNOPF in New York

LETTERS
of
H·L·
Mencken

Selected and
Annotated
by
GUY·J·
FORGUE

ALFRED·A·
KNOPF

LETTERS *of* H·L·Mencken

Selected and Annotated by GUY J· FORGUE
WITH A PERSONAL NOTE BY HAMILTON OWENS

ALFRED·A· KNOPF

MENCKEN THE CORRESPONDENT had become a legend long before his death. Here was an immensely busy man who made it a practice all his life, whenever he was not away from home, to answer every letter addressed to him within twenty-four hours of its receipt. The files of correspondence that resulted are so bulky—I have heard it said that more than fifty thousand letters from him exist—that every scholar who has looked into them with a view to editing them for us has very quickly shied away from the undertaking. All but one—a young Frenchman engaged on a thesis on Mencken for the Sorbonne, and for a number of years connected with the French department at Yale University, where he was associated with the distinguished Henri Peyre. M. Forgue conceived the sensible and practical idea of collecting letters from Mencken which dealt only with literary matters, and the result is a fascinating and characteristic volume.

Here are over four hundred letters addressed to dozens of people, many of them important figures on their own account, and running from 1900, when Mencken was twenty, to 1936, the year of his death.

They are addressed, among others, to Theodore Dreiser, Harry Leon Wilson, Ellery Sedgwick, James Joyce, Louis Untermeyer, Ernest Boyd, Carl Van Vechten, F. Scott Fitzgerald, Louise Pound,

(continued on back flap)

PHOTOGRAPH OF H. L. MENCKEN
BY ALFRED A. KNOPF

YA

A 65.1.a, dust jacket

ALFRED A. KNOPF | YA 0961'. Rear flap: continuation of blurb with signature of Knopf, biography of Mencken, 'PRINTED IN U.S.A.'

Publication: Published 22 August 1961. $7.95. Copyright #A519055 (two copies received 29 August 1961). 5,700 copies of Knopf printings sold.

Printing: See colophon.

Locations: Harv, InU-Li (dj), MBU, MCR, RJS (dj).

Notes: Recommended by Book-of-the-Month Club, September 1961. No copies with a Canadian imprint were found. Adler 273; S2.28–29; Bulsterbaum 94.

Review copies: (1) Spiral bound; light blue paper covers, yellow label on front: '[all within box] ADVANCE PROOFS | [UNCORRECTED] | TITLE: [typed] LETTERS OF H. L. MENCKEN, | Selected and Annotated by Guy J. Forgue, | with a Personal Note by Hamilton Owens | AUTHOR: [typed] H. L. Mencken | PRICE: [typed] $6.50 | PUBLICATION DATE: [typed] Sept. 12, 1961 | *All information is tentative. Please check for | final details.* | [imprint and device]'. $11^{7}\!/_{16}'' \times 5^{15}\!/_{16}''$. Printed on recto only. Prelims and text have typographical differences from trade printing. *Location:* GHT. (2) Trade printing with slip laid in reported (D).

A 65.1.b
Second printing: New York: Knopf, 1973.

On copyright page: 'Published September 12, 1961 | Second Printing, March 1973'.

Location: MBU.

A 65.1.c
Third printing: Boston: Northeastern University Press, 1981.

On copyright page: 'First Northeastern Edition, 1981'. Foreword by Daniel Aaron. Published as paperback and clothbound.

Locations: GHT (2), Harv, MBU.

A 66.1.a
Only edition, first printing (1961)

H·L·Mencken
ON MUSIC

A Selection of

HIS WRITINGS ON MUSIC

together with an Account of

H·L·MENCKEN'S MUSICAL LIFE

and a History of

THE SATURDAY NIGHT CLUB

B Y

Louis Cheslock

1 9   6 1

ALFRED·A·KNOPF   NEW YORK

A 66.1.a

Copyright page: '[Borzoi device beneath intertwined ⁖AKB'] | L. C. catalog card number: 61–13949 | [French rule] | THIS IS A BORZOI BOOK, | PUBLISHED BY ALFRED A. KNOPF, INC. | [French rule] | Copyright 1916, 1918, 1919, 1920, 1922, 1924, 1926, | 1927, 1940, 1949, © 1961 by Alfred A. Knopf, Inc. Re- | [six more lines reserving rights] | zine or newspaper. Manufactured in the United States | of America. Published simultaneously in Canada | by McClelland & Stewart, Ltd. | FIRST EDITION'

Colophon: 'A NOTE ON THE TYPE | [eight lines on Electra type, designed by W. A. Dwiggins] | *Composed, printed, and bound by* | *Kingsport Press, Inc., Kingsport, Tenn.* | *Paper manufactured by* | *S. D. Warren Co., Boston.* | *Typography and binding design* | *based on originals by* | W. A. DWIGGINS | [ornament]'

8⅜″ × 5⁹⁄₁₆″: [A–D i–ix] x [xi] xii–xiii [xiv–xv] xvi [1–3] 4–16 [17–19] 20–50 [51] 52–100 [101] 102–16 [117] 118–25 [126] 127 [128] 129–31 [132] 133–34 [135] 136–41 [142] 143–54 [155] 156–62 [163] 164–72 [173] 174–75 [176] 177–81 [182] 183–85 [186] 187–90 [191] 192–94 [195] 196 [197] 198–204 [205–07] 208–15 [216] 217–22 [223–24] i–iv [v–xii] = 256 pp.

[1–8]¹⁶ = 128 leaves.

Contents: pp. A–C: blank; p. D: 'BOOKS BY | *H. L. MENCKEN* | [fifteen titles]'; p. i: half title; p. ii: blank; p. iii: title; p. iv: copyright; p. v: 'HENRY LOUIS MENCKEN | BALTIMORE | *September 12, 1880—January 29, 1956*'; p. vi: blank; p. vii: " 'A–440' " [excerpt from letter to Fanny Butcher of 20 February 1921]; p. viii: blank; pp. ix–x: 'ACKNOWLEDGMENTS'; pp. xi–xiii: 'CONTENTS'; p. xiv: blank; pp. xv–xvi: 'IL-LUSTRATIONS'; p. 1: divisional half title; p. 2: blank; pp. 3–16: 'PRELUDE | [ornament] | LOUIS CHESLOCK'; p. 17: half title; p. 18: blank; pp. 19–204, 216–22: text; p. 205: divisional half title; p. 206: blank; pp. 207–15: 'POSTLUDE | [ornament] | LOUIS CHESLOCK | (The Saturday Night Club)'; p. 223: divisional half title; p. 224: blank; pp. i–iv: 'INDEX OF COMPOSERS | AND PERFORMERS'; p. v: blank; p. vi: 'H. L. MENCKEN' [biography]; p. vii: blank; p. viii: colophon; pp. ix–xii: blank. Illustrations inserted after pp. ii, 44, 76, 108, 140, 172.

Text: "Bach at Bethlehem (May, 1923)," "Bach at Bethlehem (May, 1928),"° "Bach at Bethlehem (May, 1929),"° "Two Days of Bach,"° "Beethoven," "Old Ludwig and his Ways,"° "Beethoveniana,"° "Brahms," "Schubert,"° "Schubert," "Wagner (Symbiosis and the Artist)," "Wagner (The Eternal Farce)," "Franz Joseph Haydn,"° "Johann Strauss," "Schumann (*O Fruehling, Wie Bist Du So Schoen!*),"° "Mendelssohn,"° "Dvořák (An American Symphony),"° "Opera," "Grand Opera in English,"° "The Tower Duet in *Il Trovatore*,"° "*The Mikado*,"° "The Passing of Gilbert,"° "*Pinafore* at 33,"° "Italian Bands,"° "Wind Music,"° "Tempo di Valse," "New Wedding March Needed,"° "Enter the Church Organist," "Catholic Church Music,"° "English Songs,"° "Russian Music,"° "A Plea for the Old Songs,"° "The Folk-Song,"° "American Folk-Song,"° "The Music of the American Negro,"° "Virtuous Vandalism,"° "Music After the War,"° "Ernest Newman and Others,"° "The Poet and the Scientist,"° "Music as a Trade," "The Reward of the Artist," "Little Concert-Halls,"° "On Tenors,"° "Mysteries of the Tone-Art,"° "Masters of Tone," "Music and Sin," "The Music-Lover," "Potpourri" (excerpts from *A Mencken Chrestomathy*), "Musical Allusions to Authors" (ibid.), "From a Letter to Isaac Goldberg" (6 May 1925), "The End of a Happy Life."°

Typography and paper: 6⁹⁄₁₆″ (6³⁄₁₆″) × 3¾″; 29 lines per page. Running heads: recto, 'Contents' (p. xiii), 'Prelude' (pp. 5–15), section titles (pp. 21–203), 'The Saturday Night Club' (pp. 209–15), 'The End of a Happy Life' (pp. 217–21), 'Index' (pp. i–iii); verso, 'Acknowledgments' (p. x), 'Contents' (p. xii), 'Illustrations' (p. xvi), 'Prelude' (pp. 4–16), 'H. L. Mencken ON MUSIC' (pp. 20–204), 'Postlude' (pp. 208–14), 'Vale' (pp. 218–22), 'Index' (pp. ii–iv). Wove paper.

Binding: Blue V cloth. Front: shield of Mencken arms blindstamped. Spine, stamped in gilt: '[ornament over rule and bar] | [script] H.L. | Mencken | ON | MUSIC | [parallel rules over bar] | *Selected by* | LOUIS | CHESLOCK | [ornament] | [script] Knopf'. Back: Borzoi Books logo blindstamped. Top edge trimmed and stained violet, fore edge rough trimmed, bottom edge trimmed. White end papers.

Dust jacket: White paper with black field on front and spine. Front: '[white] H•L• MENCKEN | [blue] on Music | [blue] A SELECTION BY Louis Cheslock | [nine squares in white, blue, and shades of gray]'. Spine: '[reading down] [pale yellow-orange] H•L•MENCKEN [blue] on Music | [horizontal, blue] [Borzoi Books logo] | Alfred•A• | Knopf'. Back: photo of Mencken under brief description. Front flap: price $4.50, blurb and beginning of biography, jacket design credit to Herbert Bayer, at bottom 'YA 0961'. Rear flap: continuation of Mencken biography, brief biography of Cheslock.

Publication: Published 22 August 1961. $4.50. Copyright #A519056 (two copies received 29 August 1961). 3,100 copies sold.

Printing: See colophon.

Locations: Harv, MBU, RJS (dj).

Notes: No copies with a Canadian imprint were found. Adler 19; S2.9; Bulsterbaum 82.

Review copy: Spiral bound; light blue paper cover, yellow label on front: '[all within box] ADVANCE PROOFS | [UNCORRECTED] | TITLE: [typed] H. L. MENCKEN ON MUSIC | [typed] EDITOR: Louis Cheslock | [line X'd out] | PRICE: [typed] $4.50 | PUBLICATION DATE: [typed] 12 September 1961 | *All information is tentative. Please check for | final details.* | [imprint and device]'. 11¾″ × 5¹³⁄₁₆″. Printed recto only; no copyright page. *Location:* GHT.

A 66.1.a, dust jacket

A 66.1.b

Second printing: New York: Schirmer Books, [1975].

On copyright page: 'First Paperback Printing 1975' | . . . | 1 2 3 4 5 6 7 8 9 10'.

Location: RJS.

A 67.1.a
Only edition, first printing (1968)

H. L. MENCKEN'S

Smart Set Criticism

Selected and Edited by
WILLIAM H. NOLTE

Cornell University Press

ITHACA, NEW YORK

A 67.1.a

Copyright page: 'Copyright © 1968 by Cornell University | [five lines reserving rights] | *First published 1968* | Library of Congress Catalog Card Number: 68–16387 | PRINTED IN THE UNITED STATES OF AMERICA | BY VAIL-BALLOU PRESS, INC.'

$8^{15}\!/_{16}'' \times 5^{15}\!/_{16}''$: [i–vi] vii–xxxvii [xxxviii–xl] 1–8 [9] 10–14 [15] 16–30 [31] 32–37 [38] 39–53 [54] 55–59 [60] 61–63 [64] 65–72 [73] 74–78 [79] 80–102 [103] 104–10 [111] 112–14 [115] 116–118 [119] 120–31 [132] 133–46 [147] 148–58 [159] 160 [161] 162–81 [182] 183–203 [204] 205–07 [208] 209–36 [237] 238–75 [276] 277–86 [287] 288–319 [320] 321–49 [350–52] = 392 pp.

[1–9]^{16} [10]^{20} [11–12]^{16} = 196 leaves.

Contents: p. i: half title; p. ii: blank; p. iii: title; p. iv: copyright; p. v: '*For Alice and Ann*'; p. vi: blank; pp. vii–x: '*Contents*'; pp. xi–xxxvii: '*Editor's Introduction*'; p. xxxviii: blank; p. xxxix: half title; p. xl: blank; pp. 1–334: text; pp. 335–49: '*Index*'; pp. 350–52: blank. Photograph of Mencken tipped in to p. iii.

Text: "Diagnosis of Our Cultural Malaise," "Our Literary Centers," "William Lyon Phelps and Others" ("The Plague of Books"), "The Professor Doctors," "Paul Elmer More" ("Books About Books—II—III"), "Private Reflections," "Professor Pattee and Professor Sherman" ("Adventures Among Books—II"), "The Novelist as Messiah" ("The Good, the Bad, and the Best Sellers"), "A Definition" ("A Road Map of the New Books"), "O. Henry" ("The Best Novels of the Year"), "The Raw Material of Fiction," "Point of View" ("Novels for Indian Summer"), "On Playgoers—And on Hauptmann, Synge, and Shaw" ("The New Dramatic Literature"), "Getting Rid of an Actor," "Chesterton's Picture of Shaw" ("George Bernard Shaw as a Hero"), "Shaw as Plati-tudinarian" ("The Ulster Polonius"), "Strindberg—A Final Estimate" ("A Counter-blast to Buncombe"), "The Greatest Stylist of Modern Times" ("Synge and Others"), "Lizette Woodworth Reese" ("In Praise of a Poet"), "Ezra Pound" ("The Meredith of Tomorrow"), "The Troubadours A-Twitter," "Holy Writ," "Huneker in Motley" ("Galsworthy and Others"), "An Apostle of Rhythm" ("The Tone Art"), "A First-Rate Music Critic" ("Shocking Stuff"), "Hall Caine and John D. Rockefeller" ("The Books of the Dog Days"), "George Moore" ("A Review of Reviewers"), "Henry Ford" ("Confidences"), "In the Altogether" ("Notices of Books—III—In the Altogether"), "The Style of Woodrow" ("Consolation—III—The Late Master-Mind"), "*Vox Populi*" ("Demagoguery as Art and Science"), "The Taste for Romance" ("Novels—The Spring Crop"), "The New Thought, Dreams, and Christian Science" ("A 1911 Model Dream Book"), "*Zuleika Dobson*" ("A Dip Into the Novels"), "Havelock Ellis" ("A Visit to a Short Story Factory"), "Osculation Anatomized" ("The Ulster Polonius—III—The Labial Infamy"), "The Advent of Psychoanalysis" ("Rattling the Subcon-scious"), "The Anatomy of Ochlocracy," "The Way to Happiness" ("The Novels That Bloom in the Spring, Tra-La!"), "To Drink or Not to Drink" ("The Books of the Dog Days"), "A Novel Thus Begins," "The Story of a Resourceful Wife" ("A Hot Weather Novelist"), "A Non-Cure for the World's Ills" ("The Leading American Novelist"), "A

Faded Charmer" ("Novels—The Spring Crop"), "Earnest Messages" ("A Counter-blast to Buncombe"), "Brief Dismissals" ("A Review of Reviewers"), "Mush for the Multitude," "Lachrymose Love," "Popularity Index" ("The Greatest of American Writers"), "Twain and Howells" ("The Leading American Novelist"), "Our One Authentic Giant" ("The Burden of Humor"), "Final Estimate" ("Discussion of Twain"), "The Prophet of the Superman," "Transvaluation of Values" ("The Bugaboo of the Sunday Schools"), "Importer of Foreign Flavors" ("The Prometheus of the Western World"), "Huneker's Confessions" ("Chiefly Americans—II—Huneker's Confessions"), "A Note on Oscar Wilde" ("George Bernard Shaw as a Hero"), "The Accounting of a Tartuffe" ("Critics of More or Less Badness"), "Portrait of a Tragic Comedian," "H. G. Wells *Redivivus*" ("A Soul's Adventures"), "Probing the Russian Psyche" ("Conrad, Bennett, James Et Al."), "Conrad's Self-Portrait" ("Synge and Others"), "*Victory*" ("The Grandstand Flirts with the Bleachers"), "A Good Book on Conrad" ("Partly About Books—3—Conrad Again"), "Conrad Revisited" ("The Monthly Feuilleton—IV"), "A Modern Tragedy" ("A Novel of the First Rank"), "The Creed of a Novelist," "*De Profundis*" ("More Notes From a Diary"), "A Gamey Old Gaul," "Her First Novel" ("A Visit to a Short Story Factory"), "Willa Cather vs. William Allen White" ("Sunrise on the Prairie"), "*Youth and the Bright Medusa*" ("Chiefly Americans"), "A Refined Scoffer" ("The Flood of Fiction"), "Something New Under the Sun" ("Novels, Chiefly Bad—II"), "The Two Andersons" ("Chiefly Americans"), "Muddleheaded Art" ("Some New Books"), "The Story of an American Family" ("Consolation—I—An American Novel"), "Portrait of an American Citizen," "Two Years Too Late" ("Chiefly Americans"), "A Step Forward" ("The Niagara of Novels—II"), "A Book for the Gourmet" ("A Guide to Intelligent Eating"), "The Nature of Vice," "Novels to Reread" ("Various Bad Novels"), "A Review of Reviewers," "An Autobiographical Note," "The Incomparable Billy" ("Savanarolas A-Sweat"), "The Irish Renaissance" ("The Books of the Irish"), "Taking Stock," "The Negro as Author" ("Groping in Literary Darkness"), "Scherzo for the Bassoon" ("Reflections on Prose Fiction—II—Scherzo for the Bassoon"), "Fifteen Years." See Notes.

Typography and paper: 7⁵⁄₁₆″ (7¹⁄₁₆″) × 4⁵⁄₁₆″; 39 lines per page. Running heads: recto, 'CONTENTS' (p. ix), 'EDITOR'S INTRODUCTION' (pp. xiii–xxxvii), '*SMART SET CRITICISM*' (pp. 3–333), 'INDEX' (pp. 337–49); verso, 'CONTENTS' (pp. viii–x), 'EDITOR'S INTRODUCTION' (pp. xii–xxxvi), 'H. L. MENCKEN' (pp. 2–334), 'INDEX' (pp. 336–48). Wove paper.

Binding: Brown V cloth stamped in gilt on spine: 'NOLTE | *Editor* | [reading down] H. L. MENCKEN'S *Smart Set* Criticism | [horizontal] CORNELL | UNIVERSITY | PRESS'. Trimmed, unstained. White end papers.

Dust jacket: Tan paper with brown field on front and spine. Front: [all within ornate frame] '[tan] H. L. MENCKEN'S | SMART SET [tall S's in logo form] | [tan] CRITICISM | [masked devil holding two bat-winged hearts on strings] | [tan] Edited by | [tan] WILLIAM H. NOLTE'. Spine: '[tan] NOLTE | EDITOR | [reading down] [tan]

A 67.1.a, dust jacket

H. L. MENCKEN'S [black, tall S's] SMART SET [tan] CRITICISM | [horizontal] CORNELL | UNIVERSITY | PRESS'. Back: blurb for *Willa Cather and Her Critics,* ed. James Schroeter. Front flap: blurb, price $10.00. Rear flap: biography of Nolte, cover design credit to Norm Forgit.

Publication: Published 6 June 1968. $10.00. Copyright #A6908 (two copies received 5 July 1968).

Printing: Manufactured by Vail-Ballou Press, Binghamton, N.Y.

Locations: Harv, InU-Li (dj), MBU, RJS (dj).

Notes: From the *Smart Set* 1908–23. "The vast majority of the contents, well over 90 per cent, appears here for the first time in book form" (p. xxxvi). S1.5; Bulsterbaum 85.

A 67.1.b
Second printing: Washington, D.C.: Gateway Editions, [1987].

On copyright page: '© 1987'. Paperback.

Locations: GHT, MB.

A 68 THE YOUNG MENCKEN: THE BEST OF HIS WORK

A 68.1.a
Only edition, only printing (1973)

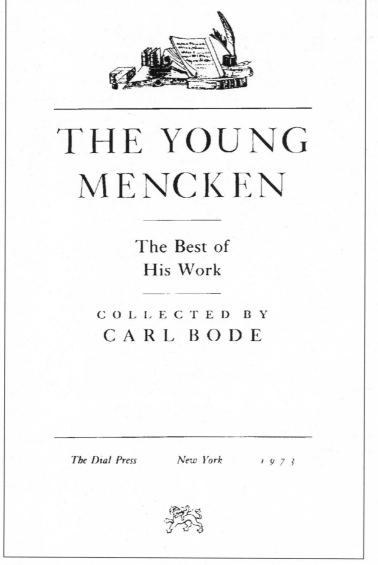

THE YOUNG
MENCKEN

The Best of
His Work

COLLECTED BY
CARL BODE

The Dial Press   *New York*   1 9 7 3

A 68

Copyright page: 'Copyright © 1973 by Carl Bode | [five lines reserving rights] | *Printed in the United States of America* | *First Printing 1973* | *Designed by Margaret McCutcheon Wagner* | [Library of Congress Cataloging in Publication Data in five lines]'

9⅛" × 6": [i–vi] vii–xi [xii–xiv] xv–xxxii [1–2] 3–4 [5–6] 7–8 [9–10] 11–21 [22–24] 25–29 [30–32] 33–46 [47–48] 49–56 [57–58] 59–77 [78–80] 81–83 [84–86] 87–109 [110–12] 113–14 [115–16] 117–45 [146–48] 149–216 [217–18] 219–38 [239–40] 241–365 [366–68] 369–443 [444–46] 447–80 [481–82] 483–547 [548–50] 551–73 [574–75] 576 = 608 pp.

[1–19]^{16} = 304 leaves.

Contents: p. i: half title; p. ii: McKee Barclay caricature of Mencken; p. iii: title; p. iv: copyright; p. v: '[ornament] *To Richard Hart*'; p. vi: blank; pp. vii–xi: 'CONTENTS'; p. xii: blank; p. xiii: divisional title; p. xiv: blank; pp. xv–xxxii: '[rule] | MENCKEN | ON HIS WAY'; pp. 1–573: text; p. 574: blank; pp. 575–76: '[ornament beside rule] | Acknowledgments'. Blank pages of text (° after chapter title): pp. 2,° 6,° 10,° 22, 24,° 30, 32,° 48,° 58,° 78, 80,° 84, 86,° 110, 112,° 116,° 146, 148,° 218,° 240,° 366, 368,° 444, 446,° 482,° 548, 550.°

Text: "Ode to the Pennant on the Centerfield Pole," "Y.M.C.A. Star Course," "Academy of Sciences," "Sewer Sleuths Rescued Her Boa," "The Flight of the Victor," "How J. Atticus Pluto Became an Expert Handholder and Subsequently Hit the Cobbles," "The Tin-Clads," "A Rondeau of Statesmanship," "The Song of the Slapstick," "The Ballad of Ships in Harbor," "Charles J. Bonaparte, a Useful Citizen," "Senator Fairbanks Will Accept the Second Place on the Ticket," "A Jewish African State," "By Way of Introduction" (from *George Bernard Shaw: His Plays*), "Grossvater Wilhelm," "Education" (from *The Philosophy of Friedrich Nietzsche*), "Sauerkraut Redivivus," "The Good, the Bad and the Best Sellers," "Afterwards," "Mencken's Reply to La Monte's Sixth Letter" (from *Men Versus the Man*), "The Common Negro," "The Two Englishes," "The Expurgators," "The Dramatic Critic," "'Der Rosenkavalier'," "Round One!," "The Varieties," "The Meredith of Tomorrow," "Up the Valley," "On Dreams," "A Symphony," "On Bartenders," "On Alcohol," "The Free Lance" (9 and 13 May 1911; 5 March 1912), "The Bards in Battle Royal," "The Free Lance" (15 March 1913), "Pertinent and Impertinent," "The Beeriad," "Good Old Baltimore," "The American," "The American: His Morals," "The American: His Language," "The American: His Ideas of Beauty," "The American: His Freedom," "The American: His New Puritanism," "The Free Lance" (8 July 1914), "Song," "The Barbarous Bradley," "The Mailed Fist and Its Prophet," "The Old Trails," "Litany for Magazine Editors," "The Flapper," "The Wedding: A Stage Direction," "Invocation," "The Free Lance" (9 June, 16 July, 23 October 1915), "Mobilizing the Mountebanks," "Eine Kleine Sinfonie in F Dur," "Doctor Seraphicus et Ecstaticus," "James Huneker," "Answers to Correspondents," "Joseph Conrad," "Epigrams" (from *A Little Book in C Major*), "For Americanos" (from "Litanies for the Overlooked" in *A Book of*

Burlesques), "If You Have Tears to Shed—!," "The Dreiser Bugaboo," "Mark Twain's Americanism," "The Sahara of the Bozart." See Notes.

Typography and paper: 6¹¹⁄₁₆″ (6¼″) × 4¹⁄₁₆″; 35 lines per page. Running heads: recto, 'Contents' (pp. ix–xi), 'Mencken on His Way' (pp. xvii–xxxi), chapter titles (pp. 15–573); verso, 'Contents' (pp. viii–x), 'The Young Mencken' (pp. xvi–576). Wove paper.

Binding: Dark green paper-covered boards, texture of LG cloth. Front, stamped in copper: title page illustration. Spine, stamped in gilt: 'BODE | [rule] | [reading down] THE YOUNG [over] MENCKEN | [horizontal] [rule] | *The Dial Press* | [device]'. Trimmed, top edge stained orange. Green end papers, texture similar to paper over boards.

Dust jacket: Brown paper. Front: ' The Young | [word curved, open capitals filled with yellow] MENCKEN | [title page illustration] | [the rest bordered right and left with vertical rules] [double rule] | THE BEST OF HIS WORK • COLLECTED BY CARL BODE | [double rule over excerpts from essays in three columns]'. Spine: 'BODE | [reading down, title and illustration as on front] | [horizontal] [device] | THE | DIAL | PRESS'. Back: title and illustration as on front, photograph of Bode. Front flap: '$15.00 | 9816 | [illustration and blurb]'. Rear flap: continuation of blurb, biography of Bode, design credit to Sandy Bernstein, '0473'.

Publication: Published 27 April 1973. $15.00. Copyright #A434464 (officially received 15 May 1973).

Printing: Manufactured by The Haddon Craftsmen, Scranton, Pa.

Locations: GHT, LC (10 April 1973), MBU, RJS (dj).

Notes: From various books and periodicals; most of the items were previously uncollected. Reader's Subscription main selection May 1973. S2.8; Bulsterbaum 87.

Review copy: Light blue wrappers printed in black: 'UNCORRECTED | GALLEYS | Publication Date: [stamped] APR 27 1973 | Price: [written] $15.00 | [rule] | The Young | Mencken | THE BEST OF | HIS WORK | Collected by | Carl Bode | *The Dial Press   New York*   1973 | [device]'. 8⅝″ × 5¾″. First page a blurb. Different prelims; other typographical differences from trade printing. In trade dust jacket (9½″ tall) with unprinted flaps and no photo on back. *Location:* GHT.

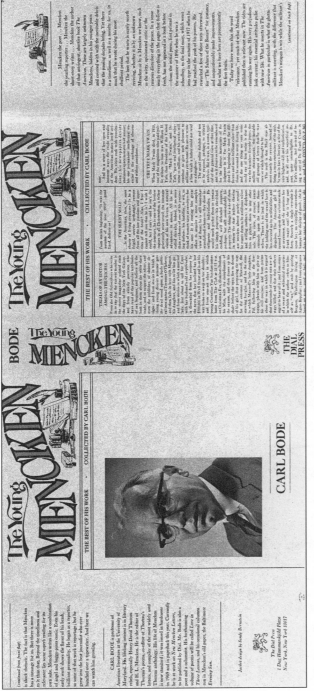

A 68, dust jacket

A 69 MENCKEN'S BALTIMORE

1974

A 69, cover title

Cover title: The illustrations are multicolored.

Copyright page: None.

10¼″ × 8″: [1] 2–6 [7] 8–13 [14] 15–39 [40] = 40 pp.

[1]²⁰ = 20 leaves.

Contents: p. 1: cover title; p. 2: 'Mencken's Baltimore', '*CONTENTS*', 'CREDITS'; pp. 3–4: 'H. L. Mencken, Sage of Baltimore | [rule] | By JOHN DORSEY'; pp. 5–39: text: numerous excerpts concerning Baltimore; p. 40: color photograph of Mencken.

Typography and paper: 9¾″ (9³⁄₁₆″) × 7⅜″; 60 lines per page (text in three columns; lines in each vary with number of entries and illustrations). Footers: recto, 'SEPTEM-BER 8, 1974' (pp. 3–39); verso, 'THE SUNDAY SUN' (pp. 2–38). Newsprint.

Binding: Self wrappers. All edges trimmed. Glued.

Locations: EPL, RJS (2).

Notes: A supplement with numerous illustrations. Selected by John Dorsey. Credits include design by Lois Moriconi, drawings by Charles R. Hazard, photograph by A. Aubrey Bodine. All but a piece on Cardinal Gibbons (pp. 17–18) were previously published in various books and periodicals, primarily the Baltimore *Sun*. Most were previously uncollected. S2.9, 20.

A 70 QUOTATIONS FROM CHAIRMAN MENCKEN
1974

QUOTATIONS FROM CHAIRMAN MENCKEN

or

POOR HENRY'S ALMANACK

Edited by Fenwick Anderson

Institute of Communications Research

University of Illinois

A 70

Copyright page: None.

10^{13}⁄₁₆″ × 8¼″: [i–v 1] 2–57 = 124 pp., mimeographed and paginated on recto only.

Perfect bound.

Contents: p. i: title; pp. ii–iii: 'INTRODUCTION'; pp. iv–v: 'TABLE OF CON-TENTS'; pp. 1–57: text.

Typography and paper: 9³⁄₁₆″ × 6⁷⁄₁₆″ (right margin not justified); 42 lines per page (lines vary with number of entries on the page). No heads. Wove paper.

Binding: Heavy light green paper wrappers, black tape spine. Front, slanting green line connecting first line to last: '[green] INSTITUTE OF COMMUNICATIONS RESEARCH | [on white paper label, typed in black] QUOTATIONS FROM CHAIR-MAN MENCKEN | OR | POOR HENRY'S ALMANACK | [below label, typed in black] EDITED BY FENWICK ANDERSON | [green] THE UNIVERSITY OF ILLINOIS, URBANA'. All edges trimmed.

Locations: CW, GHT, I.

Notes: Evidently prepared in 1974 at the Urbana campus (p. [iii]). Quotations of Mencken from the *American Mercury* during his editorship (1924–33), with a few items from 1934–39; most were previously uncollected. S2.9.

A 71 A GANG OF PECKSNIFFS

A 71.1.a
Only edition, first printing (1975)

A 71.1.a

Copyright page: 'Copyright © 1975 Theo Lippman, Jr., for Introduction. | "Journalism in America" copyright © 1927 by Alfred A. Knopf, Inc. and renewed 1955 by | H. L. Mencken. Reprinted from *Prejudices: A Selection*, by H. L. Mencken, edited by James | T. Farrell, by permission of the publisher. | [three lines reserving rights] | Manufactured in the United States of America | [Library of Congress Cataloging in Publication Data in six lines]'

$8^{15}/_{16}'' \times 5^{7}/_{8}''$: [1–12] 13–41 [42] 43–206 [207–08] = 208 pp.

$[1–4]^{16} [5]^{8} [6–7]^{16}$ = 104 leaves.

Contents: p. 1: half title; p. 2: 'Books by Theo Lippman, Jr. | [three titles]'; p. 3: title; p. 4: copyright; p. 5: 'This book is for Madeline'; p. 6: blank; pp. 7–8: 'Contents'; p. 9: half title; p. 10: blank; pp. 11–12: 'Acknowledgments'; pp. 13–41: 'Introduction: "The Life of Kings"'; p. 42: blank; pp. 43–206: text; pp. 207–08: blank.

Text: "Newspaper Morals," "The Public Prints," "On Journalism," "A Gang of Pecksniffs," "Max Ways as H. L. Mencken Knew Him," "Watterson's Editorials Reveal 'Vacuity of Journalism'," "The Newspaper Man," "The Reporter at Work," "Memoirs of an Editor," "A Wholesaler in Journalism," "Joseph Pulitzer," "Reflections on Journalism," "Learning How to Blush," "More Tips for Novelists," "Notes on Journalism," "Adams as an Editor," "Journalism in America," "The Case of Hearst," "Georgia Twilight," "Twenty Years," "Journalism in the United States," "Tainted News," "Twenty-Five Years," "Speech to the Associated Press" (20 April 1936), "The Public Prints," "Speech to the American Society of Newspaper Editors" (6 April 1937), "A Note on News," "The Newspaper Guild," "Memo to Paul Patterson," "On False News," "Speech to the National Conference of Editorial Writers" (14 [16] October 1947), "Interview with Donald H. Kirkley." See Notes.

Typography and paper: $7^{5}/_{16}'' \times 4^{1}/_{2}''$; 39 lines per page. No heads. Wove paper.

Binding A: Brown paper-covered boards, texture of LG cloth, stamped in copper. Front: [in double-rule box] 'A'. Spine: '[reading down] H. L. MENCKEN A Gang of Pecksniffs | [horizontal] ['A' in double-rule box] | ARLINGTON | HOUSE'. Trimmed, unstained. White end papers.

Binding B: Like binding A but brown V cloth.

Dust jacket: White paper. Front, over sepia photograph of Mencken: '[orange] A Gang | of | Pecksniffs | [black or dark brown] AND OTHER | COMMENTS ON | NEWS- PAPER | PUBLISHERS, | EDITORS AND | REPORTERS | BY H. L. | MENCKEN | [white] SELECTED, EDITED AND INTRODUCED | WITH A PROFILE OF MENCKEN AS NEWSMAN | BY THEO LIPPMAN, JR.' Spine: '[reading down] H. L. MENCKEN [orange] A Gang of Pecksniffs | [horizontal] ['A' in double-rule box] | ARLINGTON | HOUSE'. Back: quotations from the essays. Front flap: blurb, price $8.95. Rear flap: blurb continues, jacket photograph credit to Philip Wagner, jacket design by Marge Terracciano.

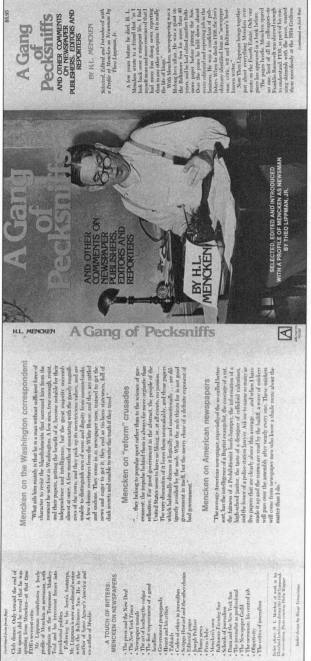

A 71.1.a, dust jacket

Publication: Published 12 September 1975. $8.95. Copyright #A680706 (officially received 23 October 1975).

Printing: Manufactured by the Haddon Craftsmen, Scranton, Pa.

Locations: GHT (binding B, dj), LC (15 August 1975, binding A), MBU (binding A), RJS (binding A, dj).

Notes: All the items were previously published in periodicals or *Prejudices: Sixth Series* (A 36) except the three speeches, "The Newspaper Guild," "Memo," and "Interview." Most were previously uncollected. S2.9, 22; Bulsterbaum 89.

A 71.1.b
Second printing: New Rochelle, N.Y.: Arlington House, [1977].

On copyright page: 'Second Printing, May 1977'.

Location: RJS.

A 72 MENCKEN'S LAST CAMPAIGN

A 72.1.a
Only edition, only printing (1976)

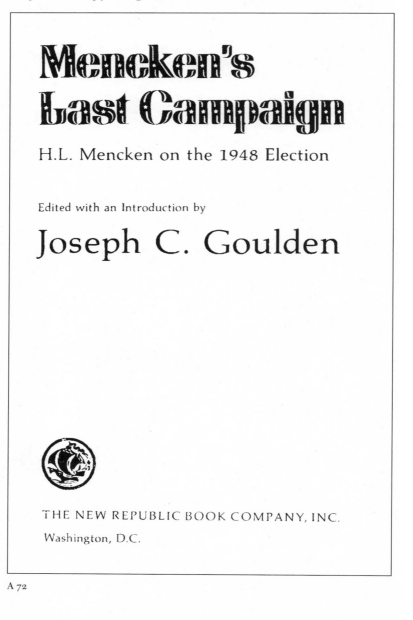

Mencken's Last Campaign

H.L. Mencken on the 1948 Election

Edited with an Introduction by

Joseph C. Goulden

THE NEW REPUBLIC BOOK COMPANY, INC.

Washington, D.C.

Copyright page: 'Published in the United States of America in 1976 | by The New Republic Book Company, Inc. | 1220 Nineteenth St., N.W., Washington, D.C. 20036 | © 1976 by Joseph C. Goulden | *All rights reserved* | [eight lines of acknowledgements] | [seven lines of Library of Congress Cataloging in Publication Data] | Printed in the United States of America'

Colophon: '[device with ship] | Composed in Palatino by the New Republic Book | Company, Inc. | Printed and bound by The Maple Press Company, | York, Pennsylvania. | Designed by Gerard Valerio.'

8^{15}⁄$_{16}$″ × 5^{15}⁄$_{16}$″: [i–vii] viii [ix–x] 1–22 [23–24] 25–38 [39–40] 41–70 [71–72] 73–90 [91–92] 93–135 [136–42] = 152 pp.

[1–2]^{16} [3]^{12} [4–5]^{16} = 76 leaves.

Contents: p. i: half title; p. ii: 'Books by Joseph C. Goulden | [eight titles]'; p. iii: title; p. iv: copyright; p. v: 'For Trey and Jimmy Goulden | Two good guys I'm proud to have as sons'; p. vi: blank; pp. vii–viii: 'Sources and | Acknowledgments'; p. ix: 'Contents'; p. x: blank; pp. 1–22: " 'All Bla-a-ah.' " [introduction]; pp. 23–135: text; p. 136: colophon; pp. 137–42: blank. Blank pages of text, all following divisional half titles: pp. 24, 40, 72, 92.

Text: Baltimore *Sun* articles of 18, 19, 20, 21 June, 9, 10, 11, 12 (2), 13, 15, 22, 24 (3), 25 July, 1, 4, 8, 22 August, 13, 15, 22 September, 2, 3, 5, 18, 23, 26 October, 7 November 1948 ("Mencken Tunes In," "Mencken Listens," "Mencken's Bottlescope," "Mencken Counts 'Em," "Mencken at Gettysburg," "Mencken Hears the Drums," "Mencken is Let Down," "Mencken Wipes Brow," "Mencken Lifts an Eyebrow," "Mencken Gets His Battle," "Doves for the Victors," "Mencken and the Swami," "Mencken and the Votaries," "Mencken at Hall and Park . . . Day . . . and Night," "Mencken Tastes the Cake," "Home to Roost," "Mencken Probes Mystery," "Truman and Herring," "Mencken on the Red Blight," "Mencken Hears Wallace," "Wallace's Motives," "Mencken in Gloomy Mood," "Mencken on Thurmond, Suh," "Mencken and GOP Decorum," "War Scare in Campaign," "Mencken Thanks Thomas," "Mencken on Barkley," "Two Truman Mistakes," "Truman's Election"). See Notes.

Typography and paper: 7^{9}⁄$_{16}$″ (7^{3}⁄$_{16}$″) × 4^{5}⁄$_{16}$″; 38 lines per page. Running heads: recto, divisional titles (pp. 3–135); verso, '*Sources and Acknowledgments*' (p. viii), '*Mencken's Last Campaign*' (pp. 2–134). Wove paper.

Binding: Blue V cloth. Spine: '[reading down] [silver] Goulden [red] Mencken's Last Campaign | [horizontal, silver] [device] | New | Republic'. Trimmed, unstained. White end papers.

Dust jacket: White paper, red field front to back. Front, over black and white photograph of Mencken: '[white and red] Mencken's | Last Campaign | [black] H. L. Mencken | on the | 1948 | Election | Edited with | an Introduction by | [red] Joseph C. |

$8.95

H.L. Mencken and American politics. He professed one but practiced the other, and the two were not reconciled without even a passing nod at objectivity, yet for more than forty years Mencken lived a literary journalistic double life. Whatever his business elsewhere, as reporter, editor and man of letters, each four years Mencken roared away to a "spectacle as fascinating as a hanging, and often as grisly."
—Joseph C. Goulden

Mencken covered eleven presidential conventions, beginning in 1904, finding in them sufficient material for his curmudgeonly wit. "Because they perform in public, their every utterance and gesture seen by a thousand onlookers," Goulden writes, "politicians were a species peculiarly vulnerable to Mencken."

In his introduction Goulden brings Mencken to life, filling in his professional background, his writing for the *Baltimore Herald* and *Sun* and the *American Mercury*, and setting the stage for the 1948 election.

The 1948 presidential campaign—Mencken's last—marked his return to politics after occupying a shadowy place in the public consciousness since just before World War II. And what subjects for the great iconoclast of American journalism: panting Republicans, certain they would return to power after sixteen years; unhappy Democrats, stuck with the hapless and seemingly unpopular Truman; a Gideon's Army of Progressives led by Henry Wallace and including an inimitable conglomeration of crackpots, communists, and idealists; and the protesting Dixiecrats, steadfastly pushing their state's rights platform.

The Sage of Baltimore made an art form of political reporting: he had no peers then and, regrettably, has none today.

Cover photo of H.L. Mencken taken by Kuhn of *The Wilmington Star*, Philadelphia, 1948.

Menckenisms
by the Greatest Iconoclast of American journalism

Mencken on American politics:
"A carnival of buncombe"

Mencken on political conventions:
"These conventions are all the same. They don't vary by one per cent. All bla-a-ah."

Mencken on political candidates:
"I am completely neutral. I'm against them all."

Mencken on Henry Ballan
"He can't win himself, but he can at least, he figures, drive a few nails into Truman's political coffin. This he is now trying to do. Like Li'l Eustis, his hammer has a greased handle and may slip and mash his thumb."

Mencken on Henry Truman
"If he did not come out for spiritualism, chiropractic, psychochutney, and extra sensory perception it was only because no one demanded that he do so. If there had been any formidable body of cannibals in the country he would have promised to provide them with free missionaries fattened at the taxpayers' expense."

Mencken on Thomas Dewey
"He is by nature cute but cautious. He is a good trial lawyer, but an incompetent rabble-rouser. He addressed great multitudes, as if they were ninnies—drooling judges, all of them austere in their hangman's gowns, but consumed inwardly by an expectant thirst. Truman made no such mistake..."

Mencken on the Presidency
"It is my firm conviction, reached after long experience, profound pondering and incessant prayer, that no man who is worth a host will ever be president of the United States hereafter. We are bound to suffer an endless procession of quacks—until, that is, the republic itself blows up."

THE NEW REPUBLIC BOOK COMPANY, INC.
Washington, D.C.

0-915220-38-0

JOSEPH GOULDEN, best-selling writer and reporter, is a longtime Mencken buff whose interest in HLM and the 1948 election was rekindled during his research for his most recent book, THE BEST YEARS.

Goulden was born in Marshall, Texas, in 1934 and worked for the *Dallas Morning News* and then the *Philadelphia Inquirer*, first as investigative reporter, later as Washington bureau chief. Since 1968 he has been a free-lance writer, contributing frequently to *The Nation* and *The Washington*. His fascination with power has resulted in THE BENCHWARMERS, a study of the federal judiciary; THE SUPER LAWYERS, about Washington lawyers; THE CURTIS CAPER; MONOPOLY: TRUTH IS THE FIRST CASUALTY; THE MONEY GIVERS; and MEANY.

THE NEW REPUBLIC
BOOK COMPANY, INC.
Washington, D.C.

THE NEW REPUBLIC BOOK COMPANY, INC.
Washington, D.C.

Spine: Goulden · Mencken's Last Campaign · New Republic

Front cover: Mencken's Last Campaign — H.L. Mencken on the 1948 Election — Edited with an Introduction by Joseph C. Goulden

A 72, dust jacket

Goulden'. Spine: '[reading down] Goulden [white and red] Mencken's Last Campaign | [horizontal, black] [device] | New | Republic'. Back: quotations. Front flap: blurb, jacket photograph credit to Kuhn, price $8.95. Rear flap: biography of Goulden.

Publication: Published 15 June 1976. $8.95. Copyright #A756075.

Printing: See colophon.

Locations: EPL (dj), Harv, LC (28 June 1976), RJS (dj).

Notes: All but the article of 25 July ("Mencken Tastes the Cake," which appears in *The Vintage Mencken* [AA 5]) were previously uncollected. S2.9; Bulsterbaum 90.

A 73.1.a
Only edition, first printing (1977)

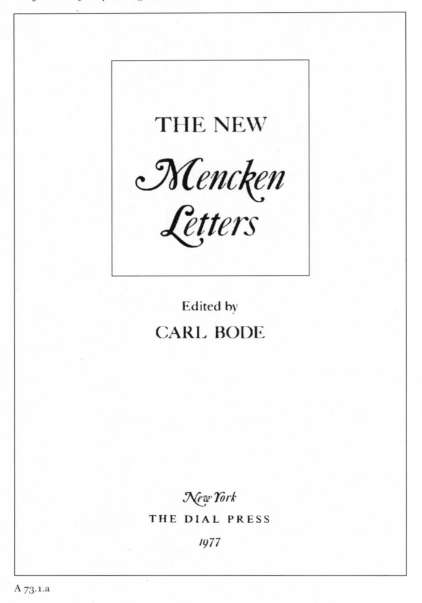

THE NEW

Mencken

Letters

Edited by

CARL BODE

New York

THE DIAL PRESS

1977

A 73.1.a

Copyright page: 'Copyright © 1976, 1977 by Carl Bode and The Mercantile-Safe Deposit and | Trust Co., as Trustees for the Estate of H.L. Mencken | [four lines reserving rights] | Manufactured in the United States of America | First printing 1977 | [eight lines of Library of Congress Cataloging in Publication Data]'

$8^{15}\!/_{16}'' \times 5^{15}\!/_{16}''$: [i–xvi 1–2] 3–606 [607] 608–35 [636–40] = 656 pp.

$[1–18]^{16} [19]^8 [20–21]^{16}$ = 328 leaves.

Contents: p. i: half title; p. ii: blank; pp. iii–iv: credit and drawing of Mencken at the piano; p. v: title; p. vi: copyright; p. vii: '*To Charlotte*'; p. viii: 'A Micro-Chrestomathy | [quotations from letters]'; pp. ix–xvi: '[in box] *Contents*'; p. 1: half title; p. 2: blank; pp. 3–16: "'Sincerely, H.L.M.'" [introduction]; p. 17: 'Abbreviations for Sources'; p. 18: 'Abbreviations for Modes of Text'; pp. 19–606: text: letters 1905–55; pp. 607–10: 'ACKNOWLEDGMENTS'; pp. 611–35: '[in box] *Index*'; pp. 636–40: blank.

Typography and paper: $7^5\!/_{16}'' \times 4^5\!/_{16}''$; 42 lines per page (lines vary with number of letters on the page). No heads. Wove paper.

Binding: Beige paper-covered boards. Red V cloth spine stamped in gilt: '[reading down] The New Mencken Letters Bode, ed. | [horizontal] [device] | THE DIAL | PRESS'. Trimmed, unstained. Beige end papers.

Dust jacket: White paper, beige field front and back. Front, over ornate black, gray, and dull gold background, letters outlined in dull gold: 'The | New | [red] Mencken | Letters | Edited by | Carl Bode'. Spine: '[reading down] [red] The New Mencken Letters [black] Bode, ed. | [horizontal] [red device] | THE DIAL | PRESS'. Back: letter to Dreiser of 26 May 1936. Front flap: '$19.95 | 1379 | [blurb]'. Rear flap: biography of Bode, jacket design credit to Holly McNeely, '1076'.

Publication: Published 7 January 1977. $19.95. Copyright #A827268 (officially received 1 February 1977).

Printing: Manufactured by the Haddon Craftsmen, Scranton, Pa.

Locations: GHT (dj), Harv, InU-Li (dj), LC (17 December 1976), MChB, RJS (dj).

Notes: S2.29; Bulsterbaum 95.

Review copies: (1) Olive-green wrappers printed in black on front: 'UNCORRECTED | GALLEYS | Publication Date: [written] OCT. 29, 1976 | Price: [written] $19.95 | [in box] THE NEW | *Menckin [sic]* | *Letters* | [outside box] Edited by CARL BODE | *New York* | THE DIAL PRESS | • 1976 •'. $9\frac{1}{2}'' \times 5^9\!/_{16}''$. Different setting of type; same error in Mencken's name on title page. *Location:* GHT. (2) Trade printing with laid-in slip ($8\frac{1}{8}'' \times 3''$): '[all within red frame] [device, address, and phone number of The Dial Press in red] | [black] THE NEW MENCKEN LETTERS | Edited by Carl Bode | $19.95 | November 30, 1976 | [red] This book is sent to you with our | compliments. Should you publish any mention of it, we would be | grateful for two clippings of your |

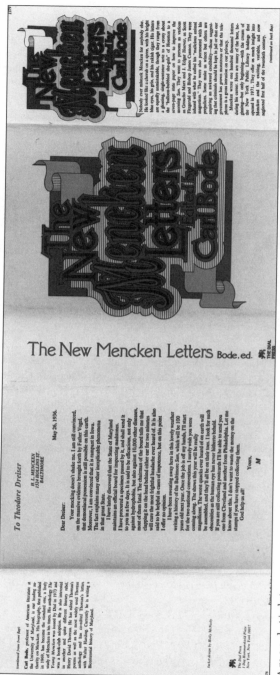

A 73.1.a, dust jacket

article. Please do not review the book before its publication date.' *Location:* GHT.

A 73.1.b
Second printing: Same title page as A 73.1.a, for Book-of-the-Month Club.

"A few months later [than the initial publication] the Book-of-the-Month Club picked it up for its Quality Paper Back subsidiary" (Bode in *Menckeniana* 62.1). No change in title page and copyright page. 8⅞″ × 5⅞″. Gatherings glued, not sewed. Stiff paper wrappers which are a replica of the above dust jacket, without indication of price.

Location: GHT.

A 74 LETTERS FROM BALTIMORE

A 74.1.a
Only edition, only printing (1982)

Letters from Baltimore

The Mencken-Cleator Correspondence

Edited by P. E. Cleator

Rutherford ● *Madison* ● *Teaneck*
Fairleigh Dickinson University Press
London and Toronto: Associated University Presses

A 74

Copyright page: 'Also by P. E. Cleator: | [sixteen titles in two columns] | © 1982 by Associated University Presses, Inc. | [American, English, and Canadian addresses of AUP in eight lines] | [Library of Congress Cataloging in Publication Data in twelve lines] | Printed in the United States of America'

$9\frac{3}{16}'' \times 6\frac{1}{16}''$: [1–10] 11–15 [16] 17–18 [19–20] 21–23 [24] 25–31 [32–36] 37–40 [41] 42–52 [53] 54–70 [71–72] 73–94 [95–96] 97–109 [110] 111–33 [134] 135–52 [153] 154–78 [179–80] 181–84 [185–86] 187–89 [190] 191–98 [199] 200–07 [208] 209–17 [218] 219–27 [228] 229–38 [239–40] 241–80 = 280 pp.

$[1–6]^{16} [7]^{12} [8–9]^{16}$ = 140 leaves.

Contents: p. 1: half title; p. 2: photograph of Mencken; p. 3: title; p. 4: copyright; p. 5: 'To the memory of Rosalind C. Lohrfinck, | "Mr. Mencken's secretary for twenty-seven years"'; p. 6: blank; p. 7: 'CONTENTS'; p. 8: blank; p. 9: 'LIST OF ILLUSTRA-TIONS'; p. 10: blank; pp. 11–15: 'FOREWORD | *By Carl Bode*'; p. 16 blank; pp. 17–18: 'ACKNOWLEDGMENTS'; p. 19: 'ABBREVIATIONS FOR | SOURCES'; p. 20: blank; pp. 21–23: 'EDITORIAL NOTE'; p. 24: blank; pp. 25–31: 'PERSONAL PRE-AMBLE'; p. 32: mock imprimatur; p. 33: half title; p. 34: blank; pp. 35–255: text: letters 1936–55; pp. 256–65: 'AFTERMATH'; p. 266: 'REFERENCES'; pp. 267–80: 'INDEX'. Blank pages of text, all after divisional titles: pp. 36, 96, 179, 240.

Typography and paper: $7\frac{1}{16}'' \times 4\frac{5}{16}''$; 40 lines per page (lines vary with number of letters on the page and amount of reduced type). No heads. Wove paper.

Binding: Blue V cloth stamped in silver on spine: 'Cleator | [reading down] Letters from Baltimore | [horizontal, FD device]'. Trimmed, unstained. White end papers.

Dust jacket: White paper. Front: '[white showing through blue field] Letters from | Baltimore | [black on white field] *The Mencken-Cleator Correspondence* | [on light blue field, to left of caricature of a clergyman] Edited by P. E. Cleator'. Spine, on light blue field: 'Cleator | [reading down] Letters from Baltimore | [horizontal, FD device]'. Back: 'About the Editor'. Flaps: continuous blurb.

Publication: Published 2 October 1982. $32.50. Copyright #TX-1-014-923.

Printing: Manufactured by the Haddon Craftsmen, Scranton, Pa.

Locations: Harv, LC (17 November 1982), MBU, RJS (dj).

Notes: Bulsterbaum 96.

Review copy: Trade printing with laid-in slip ($4'' \times 4''$): '[FD device to left of next three lines] *A Review Copy* | *with our* | *compliments* | PUBLICATION DATE [stamped over dotted line] OCT 2 1982 | PRICE [stamped over dotted line] $32.50 | We shall appreciate receiving two copies of any notice | or review of this book. | [address]'. *Location:* SL.

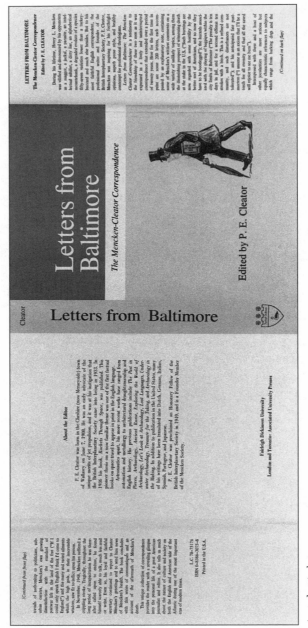

LETTERS FROM BALTIMORE
The Mencken-Cleator Correspondence
Edited by P. E. CLEATOR

During his lifetime, Henry L. Mencken was vilified and denounced by his opponents as a mugwort, a pickal, a cynnotic, an iconoclast—and, a thirty far, an indefensible mountebank, a degraded evolute of a species which, far fifty-seven varieties lower than a turkeybuzzard and much else beside. But to his post-natal circle of fond correspondents, of the British Interplanetary Society, P. E. Cleator, Mencken was inspiring for his forthright opinions, superb prose style, and healthy contempt for professional damfoolgery.

Letters from Baltimore: The Mencken-Cleator Correspondence is a testimony to the friendship of these two men as it was unfolded in a lively and uninterrupted correspondence that extended over a period of twenty years. Here for the first time in print are some 300 letters, each accompanied by an explanatory note, containing some of Mencken's wittiest comments on a wide variety of unlikely topics, among them the diminishing prospect of witnessing death at the stake in the U.S. ("Such diversions are now unhappily forbidden in the better sort of Americans, and no more they have to be hoodlegged"), the hazards associated with the playing of bagpipes within the city limits, the problem of why the monkey is ten days in jail, and for a second offense ten strokes with a birch. This is a refined community, and such disturbances are not tolerated"), and his anticipated four interments ("I mourn at an axiom that I'll be a touch for all eternity, and that all the saved will rejoice to see me burn").

(Continued on back flap)

Cleator
Letters from Baltimore

Letters from Baltimore

The Mencken-Cleator Correspondence

Edited by P. E. Cleator

Fairleigh Dickinson University

London and Toronto: Associated University Presses

About the Editor

P. E. Cleator was born in the Cheshire (now Merseyside) town of Wallasey on June 7, 1908. He was an early advocate of the unique merits of jet propulsion, and it was at his instigation that the British Interplanetary Society came into being in 1933. In 1936 his book, *Rockets Through Space*, was published. This pioneer thesis on a now familiar theme was one of the first factual books on space travel to appear in print in the English language.

Astronautics apart, his more recent works have ranged from automation and metallurgy to architectural draughtsmanship and English history. His previous publications include *The Past in Pieces, Archaeology, Ancient Rome, Exploring the World of Archaeology, Let's Look at Archaeology, Lost Languages, Underwater Archaeology, Treasure for the Taking*, and *Archaeology in the Making*. In addition to publication in the United States, many of his writings have been translated into Dutch, German, Italian, Spanish, Portuguese, and Japanese.

P. E. Cleator was proclaimed an Honorary Fellow of the British Interplanetary Society in 1949, and is a Founder Member of the Mencken Society.

(Continued from front flap)

travails of authorship to politicians, suburban centers, Mencken's own growing dissatisfaction with the standard of postwar life in the land of the free ("If I could only speak English I think I'd come to England") and the many and varied ailments which, near the high peak, in their inexorable window, saw fit to inflict upon his person.

In November, 1948, Mencken suffered a crippling stroke. Typically, throughout the long period of incapacitation he was then after called upon to endure, he found himself scarcely able to talk, much less read or write. Even so, his loyal and faithful secretary continued to report to Cleator Mencken's greetings and to send him news of Mencken's health. The book concludes with this series of communiqués and an account of the aftermath of Mencken's death.

This unique collection of correspondence provides the reader with a revealing glimpse into the personal life of a great American journalist and editor. It also tells us much about the nature of culture and society on both the European and American side of the Atlantic during one of the most important eras of modern times.

L.C. 78-75176
ISBN 0-8386-3073-4
Printed in the U.S.A.

A 75 ICH KUSS DIE HAND

A 75.1.a
Only edition, only printing (1986)

Edited by

Peter W. Dowell

"Ich Kuss die Hand"

The Letters of

H. L. Mencken

to Gretchen Hood

The University of

Alabama Press

A 75

Copyright page: 'Copyright © 1986 by | The University of Alabama Press | University, Alabama 35486 | All rights reserved | Manufactured in the | United States of America | [Library of Congress Cataloging-in-Publication Data in eleven lines]'

8⅜″ × 5⅜″: [i–iv] v [vi] vii–viii [ix–x] 1–30 [31–32] 33–150 [151–58] = 168 pp.

[1–4]¹⁶ [5]⁴ [6]¹⁶ = 84 leaves.

Contents: p. i: half title; p. ii: blank; p. iii: title; p. iv: copyright; p. v: '[rule] | *Contents*'; p. vi: blank; pp. vii–viii: '[rule] | *Acknowledgments*'; p. ix: half title; p. x: blank; pp. 1–24: '[rule] | *Introduction*'; pp. 25–27: '[rule] | *Notes to | Introduction*'; pp. 28–30: '[rule] | *Editorial Note*'; pp. 31–145: text: letters 1926–37; pp. 146–50: '[rule] | *Index*'; p. 151: 'About the Editor | [four lines]'; pp. 152–58: blank. Blank page of text: p. 32.

Typography and paper: 6⅞″ (6⁷⁄₁₆″) × 4″ (right margin not justified for text of letters); 31 lines per page (lines vary with number of letters on the page and amount of reduced type). Running heads, all above rule and preceded by page number and slash: recto, '*Introduction*' (pp. 3–23), '*Notes to Introduction*' (p. 27), '*Editorial Note*' (p. 29), '*The Letters*' (pp. 35–145), '*Index*' (pp. 147–49); verso, '*Acknowledgments*' (p. viii), '*Introduction*' (pp. 2–24), '*Notes to Introduction*' (p. 26), '*Editorial Note*' (p. 30), '*The Letters*' (pp. 34–144), '*Index*' (pp. 148–50). Wove paper.

Binding: Gray V cloth stamped in gilt on spine, reading down: 'DOWELL *"Ich Kuss die Hand"* ALABAMA [over] The Letters of H. L. Mencken to Gretchen Hood'. Trimmed, unstained. Lavender end papers.

Dust jacket: White paper. Front: 'Edited by Peter W. Dowell | [lavender bar] | "ICH KUSS DIE HAND" [first and last letters extend to bottom of next two lines, which are in lavender, as are the quotation marks] | The Letters of H. L. Mencken | to Gretchen Hood | [framed black and white photograph of Hood against lavender background]'. Spine, reading down: 'Dowell [on lavender background] [white] "ICH KUSS DIE HAND" [black] The Letters of H. L. Mencken [over] to Gretchen Hood [on white] Alabama'. Back: blurb. Flaps: continuous blurb, jacket design credit to Cameron Poulter.

Publication: Published 20 November 1986. $19.95. Copyright #TX-1-953-269.

Printing: Manufactured by the Composing Room, Grand Rapids, Mich.; Cushing-Malloy, Ann Arbor, Mich.; John H. Dekker, Grand Rapids.

Locations: Harv, LC (8 December 1986), MBU, RJS (dj).

Notes: Bulsterbaum 96.

"Ich Kuss Die Hand"
The Letters of H. L. Mencken to Gretchen Hood
Edited by Peter W. Dowell

H. L. Mencken's letters to Gretchen Hood recount a little-known chapter in the life of "the sage of Baltimore." His acquaintance with Hood, initiated by her suggestion to the New York World that Mencken run for President, ripened into a proud friendship that led to several meetings, including notable episodes with the Speaker of the House, Nicholas Longworth, and with a prominent Fiorello La Guardia, and produced a frequent exchange of letters, highlighted by the fiction that when Mencken entered the White House, Hood would become the First Lady.

Hood was a free-spirited woman from Washington, D.C., who had a short career as an opera singer and had been a part of the artistic community in Greenwich Village for a few years before returning to Washington to live. Her familiarity with the journalistic and political life of the nation's capital, her musical interests, and her keen interest in the contemporary cultural scene all made her a receptive audience for Mencken. He found her a witty and charming respondent to his characteristic traits of personality and style, one who challenged him to display his celebrated manner at its best. Their relationship and correspondence flourished for four years between 1926 and 1930, when Mencken's marriage brought the correspondence to an abrupt end.

(continue on back flap)

Edited by Peter W. Dowell

"ICH KUSS DIE HAND"
The Letters of H. L. Mencken
to Gretchen Hood

Dowell   **"ICH KUSS DIE HAND"** The Letters of H. L. Mencken to Gretchen Hood   **Alabama**

"Ich Kuss Die Hand"
The Letters of H. L. Mencken to Gretchen Hood
Edited by Peter W. Dowell

H. L. Mencken's letters to Gretchen Hood between 1926 and 1930 recount a little-known chapter in his life. His friendship with Hood, a free-spirited Washingtonian keenly interested in the contemporary cultural scene, produced a body of letters that display Mencken's celebrated manner at its best. This ample selection of the letters, many of them annotated with Hood's later observations about the relationship, presents a close-up look at the most well-known and controversial American man of letters in the 1920s at the height of his popular acclaim. His ever-present wit and verve make them lively and entertaining reading.

"This is a fascinating portrait of the private Mencken, all the more helpful because his relationships with women have never been explored as other aspects of his life"

Fred Hobson
The University of Alabama

The University of Alabama Press
University, Alabama 35486-2877

ISBN 0-8173-0296-4

(continued from front flap)

The letters Mencken wrote Hood vividly portray the most well-known and controversial American man of letters in the 1920s at the height of his popular acclaim. Here one sees with particular immediacy and fullness Mencken in the period following the Scopes trial and Hatrack case, when he was continually in the public eye, his opinions were widely circulated and argued about, and the press regularly carried stories about his activities, both as a social critic — here depicting his two worlds as a journalist and loyal son of Baltimore and as the editor of American Mercury and a national celebrity in New York. Mencken, the satiric commentator on the American scene, speaks out in these letters with his distinctive pungency and humor, whether airing his cordial representations of public personalities, discoursing on current ideas like companionate marriage, or observing such public events as the 1928 Presidential campaign or the Ruth Snyder-Judd Gray murder case. They express as well, however, several more personal sides of the man — his day-to-day comings and goings, his unpretentious tastes, his simple joys for family and friends, his idiosyncrasies and crotchets. In particular, his epistolary affair with Hood casts intriguing light on his relationships with women. This couple selection of the letters, many of them annotated with Hood's later observations about the friendship, presents a close-up look at the man of many parts, and his ever-present wit and verve make them lively and entertaining reading.

Peter W. Dowell is Associate Professor of English, Emory University, Atlanta, Georgia.

Jacket design: Cameron Poulter

A 75. dust jacket

A 76 DREISER-MENCKEN LETTERS

A 76.1.a
Only edition, only printing (1986)

Dreiser-Mencken
LETTERS

The Correspondence of
Theodore Dreiser & H. L. Mencken
1907–1945

VOLUME ONE

Edited by Thomas P. Riggio

University of Pennsylvania Press · Philadelphia

A 76, vol. 1

Title pages: Those of the second volume replace 'O N E' with 'T W O'.

Copyright page of both volumes: '*The Theodore Dreiser letters to Henry L. Mencken are copyright © 1986 | by the Trustees of the University of Pennsylvania | The Henry L. Mencken letters to Theodore Dreiser are copyright © 1986 | by the Trustees of the Enoch Pratt Free Library | Prefatory matter, introductions, and notes by Thomas P. Riggio | are copyright © 1986 by the University of Pennsylvania Press | All rights reserved | [Library of Congress Cataloging-in-Publication Data in eleven lines] | Printed in the United States of America | Designed by Adrianne Onderdonk Dudden*'

Volume 1: 8¹⁵⁄₁₆″ × 5¹³⁄₁₆″: [i–vii] viii [ix] x [xi] xii–xiii [xiv–xv] xvi–xix [xx–xxi] xxii–xxiii [xxiv 1] 2–7 [8–9] 10–14 [15] 16–29 [30] 31–48 [49] 50–53 [54–55] 56–60 [61] 62 [63] 64–120 [121] 122–66 [167] 168–73 [174–75] 176–86 [187] 188 [189] 190–214 [215] 216–48 [249] 250–91 [292] 293 [294] 295–320 = 344 pp. Volume 2: 8¹⁵⁄₁₆″ × 5⅞″: [i–vii] viii [ix] x [321] 322–28 [329] 330–60 [361] 362–460 [461] 462–503 [504–05] 506–10 [511] 512–52 [553] 554 [555] 556–62 [563] 564–66 [567] 568–87 [588] 589–98 [599] 600–46 [647–48] 649–60 [661] 662 [663] 664–71 [672] 673–710 [711] 712–20 [721–24] 725–35 [736–37] 738–812 [813] 814–23 [824–25] 826–37 [838–39] 840–43 [844–46] = 536 pp.

Volume 1: [1–2]¹⁶ [3]⁴ [4]⁸ [5–12]¹⁶ = 172 leaves. Volume 2: [1–2]¹⁶ [3]⁴ [4]⁸ [5–18]¹⁶ = 268 leaves.

Contents: Volume 1: p. i: half title; pp. ii–iii: title; p. iv: copyright; p. v: '*For Milla*'; p. vi: blank; p. vii–viii: '*Contents*'; pp. ix–x: '*Illustrations*'; pp. xi–xiii: '*Preface*'; p. xiv: blank; pp. xv–xix: '*Editorial Note*'; p. xx: blank; pp. xxi–xxiii: '*Acknowledgments*'; p. xxiv: blank; pp. 1–320: text. Blank pages of text: pp. 8, 54, 174. Volume 2: pp. i–x same as in Volume 1; pp. 321–812: text, including two appendices; pp. 813–23: 'Appendix 3 | [thick-thin rule] | *Annotated List of Omitted Letters* | (*1907–1945*)'; p. 824: blank; pp. 825–37: '*Index of Names and Subjects*'; p. 838: blank; pp. 839–43: '*Index of Works by Dreiser | and Mencken*'; pp. 844–46: blank. Blank pages of text: pp. 504, 722, 736.

Text: Volume 1: letters 1907–18. Volume 2: letters 1919–45; letters to Helen Dreiser 1945–49; "A Novel of the First Rank" (rev. of *Jennie Gerhardt*), "Dreiser's Novel the Story of a Financier Who Loved Beauty" (rev. of *The Financier*), "Adventures Among the New Novels" (rev. of *The Titan*), "A Literary Behemoth" (rev. of *The "Genius"*), "A Soul's Adventures" (rev. of *Plays of the Natural and the Supernatural*), "The Creed of a Novelist" (rev. of *A Hoosier Holiday*), "Dithyrambs Against Learning" (rev. of *Free and Other Stories*), "The Dreiser Bugaboo," "Theodore Dreiser" (from *A Book of Prefaces*), "H. L. Mencken Tells of Dreiser's New Book" (rev. of *Twelve Men*), "More Notes from a Diary" (rev. of *Hey Rub-a-Dub-Dub*), "Adventures Among Books" (rev. of *A Book About Myself*), "Dreiser in 840 Pages" (rev. of *An American Tragedy*), "Ladies, Mainly Sad" (rev. of *A Gallery of Women*), "Footprints on the Sands of Time" (rev. of *Dawn*), "A Protest Against the Suppression of Theodore Dreiser's "The 'Genius'"," "The Orf'cer Boy" (from *Ventures into Verse*), "A Eulogy for Dreiser," "The Life of an Artist." See Notes.

Typography and paper: Volume 1: 7½" (6¹⁵⁄₁₆") × 4⁵⁄₁₆" (heights vary); 38 lines per page (lines vary with number of letters and notes on the page). Running heads, all over rules: recto, 'Preface' (p. xiii), 'Editorial Note' (pp. xvii–xix), 'Acknowledgments' (p. xxiii), years covered in the sections (pp. 3–319); verso, 'Contents' (p. viii), 'Illustrations' (p. x), 'Preface' (p.xii), 'Editorial Note' (pp. xvi–xviii), 'Acknowledgments' (p. xxii), years covered in the sections (pp. 2–320). Wove paper. Volume 2: 7⁷⁄₁₆" (6⅞") × 4⁵⁄₁₆" (heights vary); 37 lines per page (lines vary with number of letters and notes on the page). Running heads, all over rules: recto, years covered in the sections (pp. 323–719), 'Appendix 1' (pp. 725–35), 'Appendix 2' (pp. 739–811), 'Appendix 3' (pp. 815–23), 'Index of Names and Subjects' (pp. 827–37), 'Index of Works by Dreiser and Mencken' (pp. 841–43); verso, 'Contents' (p. viii), 'Illustrations' (p. x), years covered in the sections (pp. 322–720), 'Appendix 1' (pp. 726–34), 'Appendix 2' (pp. 738–812), 'Appendix 3' (pp. 814–22), 'Index of Names and Subjects' (pp. 826–36), 'Index of Works by Dreiser and Mencken' (pp. 840–42). Wove paper.

Binding: Yellowish brown V cloth stamped in red on spine: '[reading down] *Riggio* DREISER-MENCKEN LETTERS *Volume One [Two]* | [horizontal] upp'. Trimmed, unstained. Red end papers.

Dust jacket: Brown paper. Front: '[David Levine caricature of Dreiser and Mencken] | Dreiser-Mencken Letters | [red rule] | *The Correspondence of* | Theodore Dreiser & H. L. Mencken | 1907–1945 | *edited by Thomas P. Riggio* | [red rule] | [red] VOLUME ONE [TWO] | [short black rule]'. Spine: [reading down] [red] *Riggio* [black] Dreiser-Mencken Letters [red] *Volume One [Two]* | [horizontal] upp'. Back: ad for four books. Front flap: blurb. Rear flap: three lines on Riggio, jacket illustration credit to David Levine, design credit to Adrianne Onderdonk Dudden.

Publication: Published 20 December 1986. $69.95 the set. Copyright #TX-2-025-263 (two copies received 9 March 1987).

Printing: Type set by G & S Typesetters, Austin, Tex.; printed and bound by Edwards Brothers, Ann Arbor, Mich.

Locations: Harv, MChB, RJS (dj).

Notes: Except for the "Eulogy," Mencken's reviews and reminiscences of Dreiser were previously published in numerous books and periodicals. Most of the letters were previously uncollected. Bulsterbaum 96.

Review copy: Laid-in slip (5½" × 4¼"): 'upp [to left of American address, which is over English address, in eight lines] | It is a pleasure to send on one of our recent books | for your consideration and review. Please send | two tearsheets of the published review. | *Title* Dreiser-Mencken Letters | *Author* Thomas P. Riggio, editor | Volume 1, $34.95 £29.70 | *Price* Volume 2, $39.95 £33.95 | Two volume set, $69.95 £59.45 | *Publication Date* January 1987 | We appreciate your interest in our books.' *Location:* D.

Dreiser-Mencken Letters
The Correspondence of Theodore Dreiser
and H. L. Mencken, 1907–1945
Volume One
Edited by Thomas P. Riggio

The Dreiser-Mencken correspondence began in 1907, when Mencken first wrote for Dreiser's *Delineator*. The two men first met, however, in 1908, to discuss a series of articles that Mencken had agreed to ghost-write. This meeting began the long collaboration between the two men, who at the time had little in common beyond their large literary ambitions and a marked disdain for the intellectual timidity of American writing.

Their friendship lasted four decades, their letters among the main literary exchanges in American literature. Their correspondence covered philosophical topics such as religion and politics, historical events including the two world wars, prohibition, the struggle against censorship and persecution, and the turmoil of the Great Depression, as well as the practical trivia of the magazine work that brought them together.

In addition to their straightforward content, the letters show how Mencken provided Dreiser with a context and a vocabulary to define his persona, and how Dreiser helped to place Mencken in print that would win him a wide audience. In 1916 F. Scott Fitzgerald called these two men "the greatest living writers in America." Dreiser was the uncontested novelist and Mencken its critic and their indelible imprint linked in the public's mind.

Appendices include key documents, such as reviews and reminiscences, that are essential to understanding the interaction between the two men.

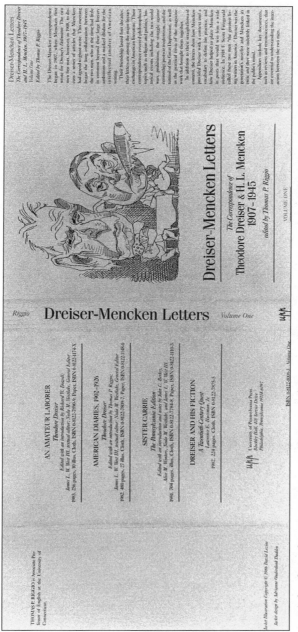

Dreiser-Mencken Letters

The Correspondence of
Theodore Dreiser & H. L. Mencken
1907–1945

edited by *Thomas P. Riggio*

VOLUME ONE

Riggio   **Dreiser-Mencken Letters**   *Volume One*

AN AMATEUR LABORER
Theodore Dreiser
Edited with an introduction by Richard W. Dowell;
James L. W. West III, textual editor; Neda M. Westlake, General Editor.
1983. 256 pages. 10 illus. Cloth. ISBN 0-8122-7896-9. Paper. ISBN 0-8122-3174-X

AMERICAN DIARIES, 1902–1926
Theodore Dreiser
Edited with an introduction by Thomas P. Riggio.
James L. W. West III, textual editor; Neda M. Westlake, General Editor.
1982. 480 pages. 27 illus. Cloth. ISBN 0-8122-7869-7. Paper. ISBN 0-8122-1486-7

SISTER CARRIE
The Pennsylvania Edition
Edited with an introduction and notes by John C. Berkey,
Alice M. Winters, Neda M. Westlake, and James L. W. West III.
1981. 704 pages. illus. Cloth. ISBN 0-8122-7784-8. Paper. ISBN 0-8122-1119-3

DREISER AND HIS FICTION
A Twentieth-Century Quest
Lawrence E. Hussman Jr.
1982. 224 pages. Cloth. ISBN 0-8122-7875-5

University of Pennsylvania Press
Blockley Hall, 418 Service Drive
Philadelphia, Pennsylvania 19104-6097

ISBN 0-8122-8039-3 Volume One

THOMAS P. RIGGIO is Associate Professor of English at the University of Connecticut.

A 76, vol. 1, dust jacket

A 77 MENCKEN AND SARA

A 77.1.a
Only edition, first printing (1987)

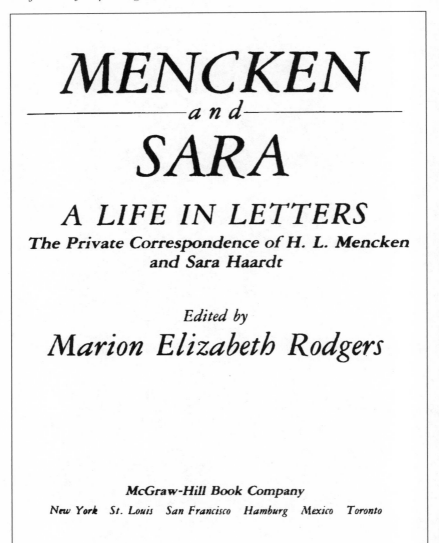

MENCKEN
———————*a n d*———————
SARA

A LIFE IN LETTERS
The Private Correspondence of H. L. Mencken
and Sara Haardt

Edited by

Marion Elizabeth Rodgers

McGraw-Hill Book Company
New York   St. Louis   San Francisco   Hamburg   Mexico   Toronto

A 77.1.a

Copyright page: 'Copyright © 1987 by Marion E. Rodgers and The Enoch Pratt Free Library | as Trustees for the Estate of H. L. Mencken | [five lines reserving rights] | 1 2 3 4 5 6 7 8 9 D O H D O H 8 7 6 | ISBN 0–07–041505–6 | [eleven lines of Library of Congress Cataloging-in-Publication Data] | *Book design by Mary A. Wirth*'

8^{15}⁄₁₆″ × 6″: [i–vi] vii–ix [x] 1–69 [70] 71–73 [74–76] 77–236 [236A–L] 237–417 [418–20] 421–515 [516] 517–31 [532] 533–35 [536] 537–51 [552–54] = 576 pp.

Perfect bound.

Contents: p. i: half title; p. ii: blank; p. iii: title; p. iv: copyright; p. v: '*To my father and mother* | [rule]'; p. vi: blank; pp. vii–viii: permissions; p. ix: '*CONTENTS*'; p. x: blank; pp. 1–69: '*INTRODUCTION*'; p. 70: blank; pp. 71–73: '*EDITORIAL NOTE*'; p. 74: photograph of letter of 10 November 1924; pp. 75–515: text: letters 1923–35; p. 516: blank; pp. 517–31: '*NOTES*'; p. 532: blank; pp. 533–35: '*APPENDIX*' [on Sara Haardt and Sara Mayfield]; p. 536: blank; pp. 537–40: '*ACKNOWLEDGMENTS*'; pp. 541–51: '*INDEX*'; pp. 552–54: blank. Blank pages of text, following divisional titles: pp. 76, 420. Pp. 236A–L contain illustrations.

Typography and paper: 7^{11}⁄₁₆″ (7¼″) × 4^5⁄₁₆″; 33 lines per page (lines vary with number of letters and amount of reduced type on the page). Running heads, all over rules: recto, '*Introduction*' (pp. 3–69), '*Mencken and Sara*' (p. 73), '*The Courtship Years*' (pp. 79–417), '*The Marriage Years*' (pp. 423–515), '*Notes*' (pp. 519–31), '*Appendix*' (p. 535), '*Acknowledgments*' (p. 539), '*Index*' (pp. 543–51); verso, '*Permissions*' (p. viii), '*Mencken and Sara*' (pp. 2–514), '*Notes*' (pp. 518–30), '*Appendix*' (p. 534), '*Acknowledgments*' (p. 538–40), '*Index*' (pp. 542–50). Wove paper.

Binding: Light blue paper-covered boards, blue V cloth spine. Front: blindstamped border. Spine, stamped in silver: '[reading down] MENCKEN & SARA | [horizontal] Rodgers, ed. | [device]'. Back: ISBN stamped in silver. Unstained, top and bottom edges trimmed, fore edge unevenly cut. White end papers.

Dust jacket: White paper. Front: '[black and light blue] MENCKEN | [photograph of Mencken framed in violet] | [violet] *A Life in Letters* | H. L. Mencken and Sara Haardt Mencken | edited by Marion Elizabeth Rodgers | [photograph of Sara framed in violet] | [black and light blue] & SARA'. Spine: '[reading down] [black and light blue] MENCKEN & SARA [violet vertical bar and rule] [black] edited by [over] Marion [over] Elizabeth [over] Rodgers | [horizontal device]'. Back: '*Advance praise for* | MENCKEN & SARA', ISBN. Front flap: price $22.95, blurb. Rear flap: continuation of blurb, jacket credits.

Publication: Published 11 March 1987. $22.95. Copyright #TX-2-027-016 (officially received 11 March 1987).

Printing: Manufactured by R. R. Donnelley & Sons, Chicago.

Locations: Harv, LC (5 January 1987), MBU, RJS (dj).

A 77.1.a, dust jacket

Notes: Bulsterbaum 96.

Review copy: Light blue wrappers printed in black on front: 'UNCORRECTED PAGE PROOF | *MENCKEN* | [rule] *and* [rule] | *SARA* | *The Letters of H. L. Mencken and Sara Haardt* | *Edited by* | *MARION E. RODGERS* | Trim size—6 × 9 | # Pages—576 (includes 12 page photo section) | Prob. Pub. Date—12/86 | Prob. Price — $19.95 | *McGraw-Hill Book Company* [wavy line] *New York*'. 8⅝6″ × 5⅜″. Typographical differences in the prelims. *Location:* GHT.

A 77.1.b
Second printing: New York etc.: Anchor Books / Doubleday, [1992].

On copyright page: 'FIRST ANCHOR BOOKS EDITION: FEBRUARY 1992 | 1 3 5 7 9 10 8 6 4 2'. Paperback.

Location: GHT.

A 78 THE EDITOR, THE BLUENOSE, AND THE PROSTITUTE

A 78.1.a.i
Only edition, only printing, limited issue (1988)

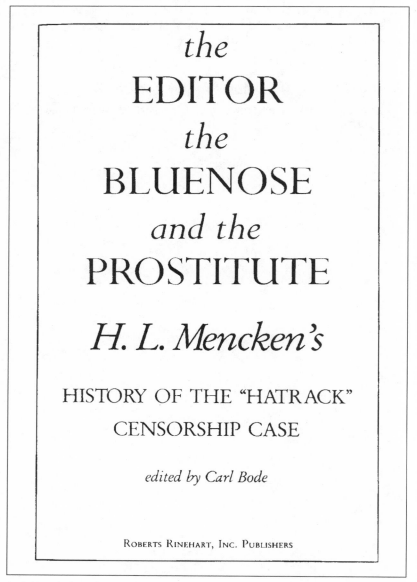

the
EDITOR
the
BLUENOSE
and the
PROSTITUTE

H. L. Mencken's

HISTORY OF THE "HATRACK"
CENSORSHIP CASE

edited by Carl Bode

ROBERTS RINEHART, INC. PUBLISHERS

A 78

Copyright page: 'to Barbara with love | H. L. Mencken text copyright ©1988 by the Enoch Pratt Free | Library, as trustee for the Mencken estate; "Hatrack" text copyright | ©1988 by Edith Evans Asbury; Introductory text copyright ©1988 | by Carl Bode. | Published by Roberts Rinehart, Inc. Publishers, Post Office Box | 3161, Boulder, Colorado 80303 | International Standard Book Numbers 0–911797–40–8 (trade edition) | and 0–911797–48–3 (limited edition) | Library of Congress Catalog Card Number 87–92066 | Printed in the United States of America | Typography, jacket, and binding design by Frederick R. Rinehart | First Printing March 1988'

Statement of limitation: 'OF THE FIRST PRINTING OF | THE EDITOR, THE BLUENOSE, AND THE PROSTITUTE | 250 COPIES HAVE BEEN SPECIALLY BOUND AND SLIP-CASED | AND NUMBERED 1 TO 250 | EACH COPY IS SIGNED BY THE EDITOR, CARL BODE | THIS IS NUMBER [number written in black ink] | [signature]'

$8^{5/16}'' \times 5^{7/16}''$: [i–x] 1–24 [25–26] 27–36 [37–38] 39–48 [49] 50–55 [56] 57–61 [62] 63–74 [75] 76–92 [93] 94–118 [119] 120–49 [150] 151–72 [173] 174 [175–78] = 188 pp.

$[1–2]^{16}$ $[3]^2$ $[4]^{16}$ $[5]^4$ $[6]^{16}$ $[7]^8$ $[8]^{16}$ = 94 leaves.

Contents: p. i: limitation notice; p. ii: blank; p. iii: half title; p. iv: cartoon; p. v: title; p. vi: copyright; p. vii: '*Contents*'; p. viii: blank; p. ix: divisional title; p. x: cartoon; pp. 1–24: 'THE CONTEXT | BY CARL BODE'; p. 25: divisional title; p. 26: blank; pp. 27–36: 'HATRACK | BY HERBERT ASBURY'; p. 37: divisional title; p. 38: blank; pp. 39–174: 'THE "HATRACK" CASE | THE AMERICAN MERCURY | VS. | THE NEW ENGLAND | WATCH AND WARD SOCIETY, | THE POSTMASTER-GENERAL | OF THE UNITED STATES, | ET AL. | BY H. L. MENCKEN | 1937'; p. 175: '*Acknowledgments*'; pp. 176–78: blank. Illustrations on pp. 49, 56, 62, 75, 93, 119, 150, 173.

Typography and paper: $6^{3/4}''$ ($6^{9/16}''$) × $3^{5/8}''$; 35 lines per page (lines vary with amount of reduced type). Running heads: recto, 'THE CONTEXT' (pp. 3–23), 'HATRACK' (pp. 29–35), 'THE "HATRACK" CASE' (pp. 41–171); verso, 'THE EDITOR, THE BLUENOSE, AND THE PROSTITUTE' (pp. 2–174). Wove paper (see Notes).

Binding: White V cloth. Spine, stamped in red: 'MENCKEN | [reading down] THE EDITOR, THE BLUENOSE, AND THE PROSTITUTE *edited by Carl Bode* ROBERTS [over] RINEHART'. Trimmed, unstained. Gray-green end papers. In box covered by the binding cloth; shrink-wrapped.

Dust jacket: None.

Publication: Published 25 March 1988. $50.00. No record of copyright could be found.

Printing: Type set by Lyn Chaffee, Longmont, Colo.

Location: GHT.

Notes: Laid in, on thick, pale gray paper: [all within double-rule border broken by a rhinoceros at top] 'A NOTE FROM THE PUBLISHER | [twenty-three lines on design, type, paper, and limitation]'. Type set directly from Mencken's "Fair Copy . . . with Corrections, 1937" in "a modern version of the Garamond face used in the *Mercury*"; 60# Warren's Old Style paper; endsheets Lindenmeyr Multicolor Ash Gray; boards and slipcase covered in Joanna Kennett 36121.

A 78.1.a.ii
Only edition, only printing, trade issue

Same as A 78.1.a.i except:

Statement of limitation: None.

Contents: pp. i–ii: blank;. . . .

Binding: No box.

Dust jacket: Light green paper (white on the inside). Front: [all within ornate *American Mercury* borders] '*the* | [maroon] EDITOR | *the* | [maroon] BLUENOSE | *and the* | [maroon] PROSTITUTE | [ornate rule] | [maroon] *H. L. Mencken's* | HISTORY OF THE "HATRACK" | CENSORSHIP CASE | [maroon] *edited by Carl Bode*'. Spine, reading down: '[maroon] THE EDITOR, THE BLUENOSE, AND THE PROSTITUTE [black] ROBERTS | *edited by Carl Bode*   RINEHART'. Back: photo of Mencken at typewriter. Flaps: a continuous blurb followed by biographies of Mencken and Bode.

Publication: $19.50.

Locations: Harv, LC (28 August 1989), MChB, RJS (dj).

THE EDITOR, THE BLUENOSE, AND THE
PROSTITUTE
H.L. Mencken's History of the "Hatrack"
Censorship Case
edited by Carl Bode

the
EDITOR
the
BLUENOSE
and the
PROSTITUTE

H. L. Mencken's

HISTORY OF THE "HATRACK"
CENSORSHIP CASE

edited by Carl Bode

THE EDITOR, THE BLUENOSE, AND THE PROSTITUTE
edited by Carl Bode

ROBERTS
RINEHART

H. L. MENCKEN

ROBERTS RINEHART, INC. PUBLISHERS

ISBN 0-911797-40-8

A 78.1.a.ii, dust jacket

A 79 FANTE / MENCKEN

A 79.1.a.i
Only edition, only printing, trade issue (1989)

FANTE/MENCKEN

JOHN FANTE & H.L. MENCKEN A PERSONAL CORRESPONDENCE 1930–1952

▲ ▲

Edited by Michael Moreau
Consulting Editor Joyce Fante

▼ ▼

BLACK SPARROW PRESS ▲ SANTA ROSA ▲ 1989

A 79

Title page: The triangles are red.

Copyright page: 'JOHN FANTE & H. L. MENCKEN: A PERSONAL CORRE-SPONDENCE. Copyright | © 1989 by Joyce Fante for the Estate of John Fante. | Copyright © 1989 by The Enoch Pratt Free Library for the Estate of H. L. | Mencken. | INTRODUCTION and NOTES. Copyright © 1989 by Michael Moreau. | [five lines reserving rights] | [Library of Congress Cataloging-in-Publication Data in seventeen lines]'

Colophon and statement of limitation: '[Black Sparrow device] | Printed June 1989 in Santa Barbara & Ann | Arbor for the Black Sparrow Press by Graham | Mackintosh & Edwards Brothers, Inc. Design by | Barbara Martin. This edition is published in | paper wrappers; there are 750 hardcover trade | copies; & 176 numbered deluxe copies have | been handbound in boards by Earle Gray.'

9″ × 5¹³⁄₁₆″ (binding A), 9″ × 5¹⁵⁄₁₆″ (bindings B–F): [1–6] 7–11 [12–14] 15 [16] 17–80 [80A–V] 81–141 [142] 143–59 [160] 161–72 [173–78] = 200 pp.

Perfect bound (binding A); [1]² [2–3]¹⁶ [4]² [5–8]¹⁶ = 100 leaves (bindings B–F).

Contents: p. 1: 'By John Fante | [eleven titles]'; p. 2: blank; p. 3: title; p. 4: copyright; p. 5: 'TABLE OF CONTENTS'; p. 6: blank; pp. 7–11: 'INTRODUCTION | by | Michael Moreau'; p. 12: blank; p. 13: half title; p. 14: blank; p. 15: note; p. 16: blank; pp. 17–141: text: letters 1930–52; p. 142: blank; p. 143–59: 'ENDNOTES'; p. 160: blank; pp. 161–68: 'FANTE AND MENCKEN: | A SELECTED BIBLIOGRAPHY'; pp. 169–72: 'INDEX'; p. 173: colophon; p. 174: blank; pp. 175–77: biographies of Fante and Mencken; p. 178: blank. Pp. 80A–V contain photographs.

Typography and paper: 7¼″ × 4″; 36 lines per page (number of lines varies). No heads. Wove paper.

Binding A: White stiff paper wrappers. Front: '[white showing through black] FANTE / MENCKEN | [the rest on a yellow-orange field] [three inverted red triangles] | [to left of photograph of Fante framed in red] JOHN FANTE & | H. L. MENCKEN | [two inverted red triangles] | A PERSONAL | CORRESPONDENCE | 1930–1952 | [to right of photograph of Mencken framed in red] Edited by | MICHAEL MOREAU | [red triangle] | Consulting Editor | JOYCE FANTE | [small red triangle over large one]'. Spine, reading down: '[continuation of black field] [on continuation of yellow-orange field] [red] FANTE/MENCKEN [black] BLACK SPARROW PRESS'. Back: continuation of the two fields with red triangle on the black. Inside of wrappers unprinted. Trimmed, unstained. Red "end papers" inserted.

Binding B: Paper corresponding in design to above wrappers covering boards; red V cloth spine with paper label (½″ × 5⅝″) corresponding to printed part of spine of wrappers. Trimmed, unstained. Red end papers.

Binding C: Like binding B but light gray V cloth spine.

Binding D: Like binding C but spine label (¾″ × 2¼″) contains only 'FANTE/ MENCKEN'.

Dust jacket: Unprinted acetate (bindings B–F).

Publication: Published 25 August 1989. $10.00 (binding A); $20.00 (B–D); $30.00 (E–F). Copyright #TX-2-739-128, 129, 130.

Printing: See colophon; Mackintosh of Santa Barbara, Edwards of Ann Arbor, and Gray of Gardena, Calif.

Locations: GHT (3, binding A, bindings B and D in dj), Harv (binding B), InU-Li (binding B), LC (16 October 1989, binding B), MBU (binding D), MChB (binding B), NjP (binding B), RJS (2, binding A, binding C in dj).

Review copy: Spiral-bound, clear acetate in front, dark red plastic-coated paper in back, 11″ × 8½″, different title page and copyright page, added page-length blurb; with slip (5″ × 3¼″), all particular information typed in: '[device] | We take pleasure in sending you this book | for review. | JOHN FANTE & H. L. | Title: MENCKEN: A PERSONAL | CORRESPONDENCE 1930–1952 | Author: Ed. by Michael Moreau | Publication Date: August 11, 1989 | Price: $10.00 (paper) | $20.00 (cloth) | Please send us two copies of the published review. . . . | . . . | [address]'. *Location:* SL.

A 79.1.a.ii
Only printing, limited binding issue

Same as A 79.1.a.i except:

Colophon and statement of limitation: '. . . Earle Gray. | [letter or number written in red]'

Binding E: Like binding B but gray and white V cloth spine (twenty-six lettered copies).

Binding F: Like binding B but gray V cloth spine (150 numbered copies).

Locations: GHT (2, bindings E and F in dj), RJS (binding F, dj).

A 80.1.a
Only edition, first printing (1989)

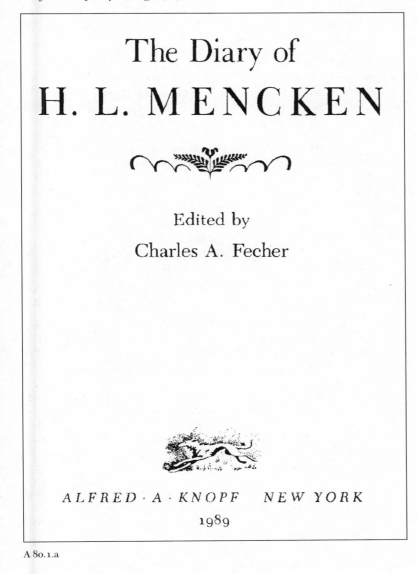

The Diary of
H. L. MENCKEN

Edited by

Charles A. Fecher

ALFRED · A · KNOPF   NEW YORK

1989

Copyright page: 'THIS IS A BORZOI BOOK | PUBLISHED BY ALFRED A. KNOPF, INC. | Copyright © 1989 by Enoch Pratt Free Library | All rights reserved under International and Pan- | American Copyright Conventions. Published in the | United States by Alfred A. Knopf, Inc., New York, and | simultaneously in Canada by Random House of Canada | Limited, Toronto. Distributed by Random House, Inc., | New York | [fifteen lines on acknowledgments to follow index, Library of Congress cataloging data] | Manufactured in the United States of America | First Edition'

Colophon: 'A NOTE ON THE TYPE | [fourteen lines on Caledonia type, designed by W. A. Dwiggins, whose services to Knopf and Mencken are surveyed] | This book was composed by Creative Graphics, Inc., | Allentown, Pennsylvania, and was printed and bound | by Fairfield Graphics, Fairfield, Pennsylvania. The de- | sign and ornamentation were appropriated from W. A. | Dwiggins by Peter A. Andersen.'

9³⁄₁₆″ × 6⁵⁄₁₆″: [A–B i–vii] viii–xxvii [xxviii–xxix] xxx [1–3] 4–463 (first page for each year 1930–1948 unpaginated) [464–65] 466–76 [477–80] = 512 pp.

[1–16]¹⁶ = 256 leaves.

Contents: p. A: Knopf 75th anniversary device; p. B: 'ALSO BY CHARLES A. FECHER | *Mencken: A Study of His Thought*'; p. i: half title; p. ii: blank; p. iii: title; p. iv: copyright; p. v: 'List of Illustrations'; p. vi: blank; pp. vii–xxvii: 'Introduction'; p. xxviii: blank; pp. xxix–xxx: 'Notes on the Text'; p. 1: half title; p. 2: blank; pp. 3–463: text; p. 464: blank; pp. 465–76: 'Index'; p. 477: acknowledgments (28 lines); p. 478: blank; p. 479: 'A NOTE ABOUT THE EDITOR | [9 lines]'; p. 480: colophon. Eight pages of illustrations follow p. 224.

Typography and paper: 7⁹⁄₁₆″ (7¼″) × 4⁹⁄₁₆″; 38 lines per page (lines vary with number of footnotes and breaks between entries). Running heads: recto, '*INTRODUCTION*' (pp. ix–xxvii), dates of entries (pp. 5–463), '*INDEX*' (pp. 467–75); verso, '*INTRODUCTION*' (pp. viii–xxvi), '*NOTES ON THE TEXT*' (p. xxx), dates of entries (pp. 4–462), '*INDEX*' (pp. 466–76). Wove paper.

Binding: Beige V cloth. Front, stamped in gilt: 'HLM'. Spine: '[gilt ornament] | [on a green field, in gilt] [bar over rule] *The Diary of* | H. L. | MENCKEN | [rule] | *KNOPF* | [rule over bar] | [gilt on beige, a long ornament]'. Back: Borzoi Books logo blind-stamped. Top and bottom edges trimmed, unstained, fore edge unevenly trimmed. White end papers.

Dust jacket: White paper. Front: 'EDITED BY CHARLES A. FECHER | [three small squares, red and yellow to left, black to right] | [on a light green field with black borders and a mauve frame, partly superimposed over a sepia photo of Mencken with corncob pipe above white border] THE DIARY OF | H.L. *[sic]* | MENCKEN'. Spine: '[black square over red and yellow squares] | [smaller version of framed title on front, partly superimposed on overlapping sepia field] | [reading down, in white] E D I T E D   B Y [over] CHARLES A. FECHER | [white Borzoi device in mauve

A 80.1.a, dust jacket

rectangle] | [white] K N O P F | [white border continuing from front]'. Back: 'About *H. L. Mencken*'. Front flap: blurb; price $30.00. Back flap: biographies of Mencken and Fecher; photo credit to Knopf; jacket design credit to Archie Ferguson.

Publication: Published 29 November 1989. $30.00. Copyright #TX-2-786-784 (officially received 13 April 1990).

Printing: See colophon.

Locations: Harv, InU-Li (dj), LC (5 December 1989), MBU, RJS (dj).

Notes: No copies with a Canadian imprint were found.

Review copies: (1) Like above except different prelims, 'Introduction', 'Notes on the Text', and footnotes; uncorrected proof in stiff gray wrappers, 8⅜″ × 5¼″, tentative publication date January 1989. *Locations:* GHT, RJS. (2) Trade printing, with white slip laid in (4″ × 5½″), printed in blue and black: 'A REVIEW COPY FROM | Alfred • A • Knopf | [Borzoi device] | [request for two copies of review, price $30.00, publication date 15 January 1990, plea not to run review before publication date]'. Also laid in is a promotional announcement: 'Coming from Knopf on January 15, 1990'; address of Knopf Publicity Department on verso. *Location:* GHT (dj).

A 80.1.b
Second printing: New York: Knopf, 1990.

On copyright page: 'Second Printing, February 1990'.

Location: MCR.

A 80.1.c
Third printing: New York: Vintage Books, [1991].

On copyright page: 'FIRST VINTAGE BOOKS EDITION, JANUARY 1991 | . . . | 10 9 8 7 6 5 4 3 2 1'. 8″ × 5³⁄₁₆″. White wrappers printed in black, rust, maroon, and green.

Locations: GHT, MB, RJS.

A 81.1.a
Only edition, only printing (1990)

Tall Tales and Hoaxes
of H.L. Mencken

Mencken's Baltimore Sunday Sun Hoaxes, 1908-1910
Edited with an Introduction by John W. Baer

Copyright page: '© 1990 John W. Baer. All rights Reserved. | Franklin Printing, Annapolis, Maryland'

8⁷⁄₁₆″ × 5⁵⁄₁₆″: [A–F] i–vii [viii] 1–62 = 76 pp.

[1]³⁸ = 38 leaves.

Contents: p. A: title; p. B: copyright; p. C: 'Sources and Acknowledgments' (dated July 1989); p. D: blank; p. E: 'Contents'; p. F: blank; pp. i–vii: 'INTRODUCTION TO H. L. MENCKEN | AND HIS HUMOR'; p. viii: blank; pp. 1–62: text. Illustrations on pp. 9, 42, 54, 58.

Text: "Baltimore Poet Demonstrates Poetic Skills At Amusement Park,"° "Pennsylvania Dutch Poet Translates Shakespeare,"° "A Science of Alcohol Needed In USA,"° "The Role of Alcohol in Psychological Therapy,"° "The Mint Julep Club in Annapolis,"° "European and Swedish Capacity for Alcohol,"° "The Invention of the Cocktail in Maryland,"° "Maryland Mountaineers See Their First Automobile,"° "Prohibition Arrives in Hell,"° "Former President Teddy Roosevelt Hunts Exotic Game in Africa."°

Typography and paper: 7¾″ × 4½″; 40 lines per page. No heads. Wove paper.

Binding: Off-white thick paper wrappers, title page duplicated on front. All edges trimmed. Two staples.

Publication: Published 19 January 1990. $11.00. Copyright #TX-2-833-313 (two copies received 25 May 1990).

Printing: See copyright page.

Locations: GHT, JRS, RJS.

A 82 THE GIST OF MENCKEN

A 82.1.a.i
Only edition, only printing, first issue (1990)

**THE
GIST
OF
MENCKEN:**

Quotations
from
America's
Critic

*Gleaned from Newspapers, Magazines,
Books, Letters, and Manuscripts by*
Mayo DuBasky

**The Scarecrow Press, Inc.
Metuchen, N.J., & London
1990**

A 82

Copyright page: '[credit for drawings and photographs in thirteen lines] | British Library Cataloguing-in-Publication data available | [Library of Congress Cataloging-in-Publication Data in thirteen lines] | Copyright © 1990 by Enoch Pratt Free Library | Manufactured in the United States of America | Printed on acid-free paper'

8$\frac{7}{16}$" × 5$\frac{3}{8}$": [A–D i–iv] v–vii [viii] ix–xi [xii] xiii [xiv] xv–xvii [xviii 1–2] 3–344 [345–46] 347–537 [538–40] 541–862 [863–66] = 888 pp.

[1–2]^{16} [3]^4 [4]^8 [5–29]^{16} = 444 leaves.

Contents: pp. A–C: blank; p. D: photograph of Mencken; p. i: title; p. ii: copyright; p. iii: Mencken arms; p. iv: blank; pp. v–vii: '[between rules] CONTENTS'; p. viii: blank; pp. ix–xi: '[between rules] ACKNOWLEDGMENTS'; p. xii: blank; p. xiii: '[between rules] EXPLANATION OF ARRANGEMENT'; p. xiv: blank; pp. xv–xvii: '[between rules] PREFACE'; p. xviii: blank; pp. 1–786: text; pp. 787–94: '[between rules] BIBLIOGRAPHY'; pp. 795–862: '[between rules] INDEX'; pp. 863–66: blank. Blank pages of text (°following divisional titles with illustrations): pp. 2,° 346,° 538, 540.°

Typography and paper: 7$\frac{3}{16}$" (6$\frac{7}{8}$") × 4$\frac{1}{16}$" (right margin not justified); 49 lines per page (lines vary with number of entries on the page). Running heads: recto, titles of sections (pp. 5–785), 'Bibliography' (pp. 789–93), 'Index' (pp. 797–861); verso, titles of parts (pp. 4–786), 'Bibliography' (pp. 788–94), 'Index' (pp. 796–862). Wove paper.

Binding: Blue-gray V cloth. Front: '[in gilt on black within gilt frame, to left of caricature of Mencken] THE | GIST | OF | MENCKEN: | Quotations | from | America's | Critic | [below frame, in gilt] *Mayo DuBasky*'. Spine, stamped in gilt: '*DuBasky* | [reading down] THE GIST OF MENCKEN: [over] Quotations from America's Critic | [horizontal device]'. Trimmed, unstained. White end papers.

Dust jacket: None.

Publication: Published 5 April 1990. $80.00. Copyright #TX-2-818-070 (two copies received 9 May 1990).

Printing: Printed and bound by Edwards Brothers, Ann Arbor, Mich.

Locations: GHT, Harv, MChB.

Notes: Most of the numerous paragraph-sized excerpts were previously published in various periodicals and books.

A 82.1.a.ii
Second issue (1993)

Same as A 82.1.a.i, except on p. [C]: [all in double-rule box] 'Special Edition | for | Laissez Faire Books'. Printed at the same time as the first issue. On sale from March 1993 by Cato Institute Books, San Francisco; price $49.95. *Locations:* GHT, RJS.

A 83.1.a
Only edition, presumed first printing (1991)

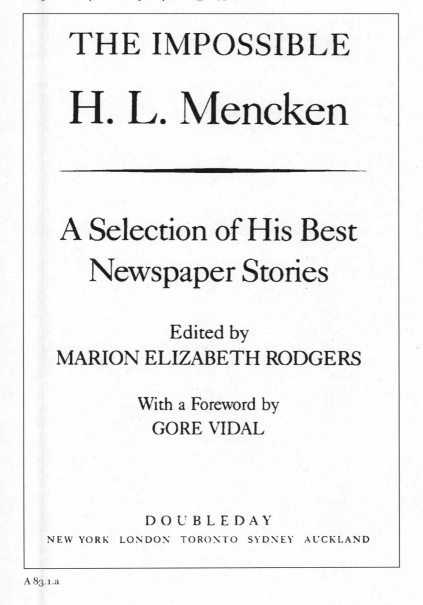

THE IMPOSSIBLE

H. L. Mencken

A Selection of His Best
Newspaper Stories

Edited by
MARION ELIZABETH RODGERS

With a Foreword by
GORE VIDAL

DOUBLEDAY
NEW YORK LONDON TORONTO SYDNEY AUCKLAND

A 83.1.a

Copyright page: '[device: anchor with dolphin] | PUBLISHED BY DOUBLEDAY | a division of Bantam Doubleday Dell Publishing Group, Inc. | 666 Fifth Avenue, New York, New York 10103 | Doubleday and the portrayal of an anchor with a dolphin are trademarks | of Doubleday, a division of Bantam Doubleday Dell Publishing Group, Inc. | *The Impossible H. L. Mencken* is published simultaneously in a paperback edition | by Anchor Books, a division of Bantam Doubleday Dell Publishing Group, Inc. | [Library of Congress Cataloging-in-Publication Data in nine lines] | ISBN 0–385–26207–8 | Copyright © 1991 by Marion Elizabeth Rodgers and the Enoch Pratt Free Library as | Trustees for the Estate of H. L. Mencken | Foreword © 1991 by Gore Vidal | Frontispiece photograph of H. L. Mencken by Robert Kniesche. Courtesy | Enoch Pratt Library. | All Rights Reserved | Printed in the United States of America | August 1991 | First Edition | 1 3 5 7 9 10 8 6 4 2'

9³⁄₁₆″ × 6¹⁄₁₆″: [i–viii] ix–xxxv [xxxvi] xxxvii–lx 1–707 [708] = 768 pp.

Perfect bound.

Contents: p. i: half title; p. ii: 'BOOKS BY MARION ELIZABETH RODGERS | [two titles]'; p. iii: quotation from Walter Lippmann in four lines; p. iv: photograph of Mencken; p. v: title; p. vi: copyright; p. vii: '*Dedicated to the working journalist*'; p. viii: blank; pp. ix–xvi: 'Contents'; pp. xvii–xxxv: 'Foreword'; p. xxxvi: blank; pp. xxxvii–lviii: 'Introduction'; pp. lix–lx: 'Editorial Notes'; pp. 1–683: text; pp. 684–85: 'Acknowledgments'; pp. 686–90: 'Notes to the | Introduction'; pp. 691–707: 'Index'; p. 708: blank.

Text: "Reminiscence," "Twenty-five Years," "Notes on Journalism," "Journalism in the Republic," "A Gang of Pecksniffs," "The American," "On Being an American," "More Notes for a Work upon the Origin and Nature of Puritanism," "The Psychic Follies," "The Gospel of Service," "A Boon to Bores," "Radio Programs," "The Movies," "Traffic," "Parade Unlike Anything Since Days of Roosevelt," "Outside, Looking In," "The Constitution," "The Bill of Rights," "On Liberty," "The Land of the Free," "Communism," "Morals and the Moron," "Object Lesson," "The State of the Nation," "Crime as a Trade," "On Controversy," "The American Scene," "New York," "San Francisco: A Memory," "How to Improve Arkansas," "The Age of Horses," "On Living in Baltimore," "Notes of a Baltimorean," "Aesthetic Diatribe," "Spring in These Parts," "Valentino," "Sister Aimée," "Thomas Henry Huxley 1825–1925," "The Case of Edward W. Bok," "On Bald Heads," "Two Wasted Lives," "The Exile of Enzesfeld," "Meditations on the Fair," "Answers to Correspondents," "The Holy Estate," "How Much Should a Woman Eat?," "The Woman of Tomorrow," "Negro Spokesman Arises to Voice His Race's Wrongs," "The Murray Case," "Sound and Fury," "The Lynching Psychosis," "Mencken Calls Tennis Order Silly, Nefarious," "On Banks," "Hard Times," "On Babbitts," "Empty Pessimism," "The Choice of a Career," "Theodore Roosevelt Named for President; Charles W. Fairbanks for Vice-President," "Hon. Henry G. Davis for Vice-President . . . ," "A Carnival of Buncombe," "It's All in Wilson's Hands . . . ," "Mencken Says All's Set to Put 'Young William' Over If Wilson

Gives the Word," "Battle at San Francisco Absolutely Free and Open . . . ," "Bayard vs. Lionheart," "The Clowns March In," "Mencken Forced to Flee Before Burton's Oratory . . . ," "Vice-Presidential Battle Thrills Mencken . . . ," "Mencken Decides Klan's Enemies Have Hurt Their Cause . . . ," "Conventions Have Become Ill Managed and Inefficient Carnivals . . . ," "Post-Mortem," "Breathing Space," "Strife Rends Democrats . . . ," "Episode," "Analysis Fails Mencken . . . ," "Al in the Free State," "The Eve of Armageddon," "Drys Are Done For . . . ," "Allies Block Stampede . . . ," "Mencken Finds Both Sides Sour . . . ," "Mencken Tells How Magic Word 'Beer' Brought the Cheers," " 'Three Long Years' Usurps Honor . . . ," "Roosevelt and Garner Told of Nomination . . . ," "Coroner's Inquest," "Hon. Herbert Hoover Brings Down House at Convention," "Wonder Man," "Roosevelt Statement Flabbergasts Delegates," "Triumph of Democracy," "There He Is!," "Music and Spellbinders Entertain Willkie Crowd," "Coroner's Inquest," "Television Lamps Stir Up 2-Way Use for Beer" ("Mencken's Bottlescope"), "Anti-Rights Rebs Due . . ." ("Mencken Hears the Drums"), "Mencken Finds Several Raisins in Paranoic Confection" ("Mencken Tastes the Cake"), "Truman's Election: Mencken Says Country Jolly Well Deserves It," "Lame Ducks," "Imperial Purple," "Harding Faces Task with Air of Confidence," "Gamalielese," "The Coolidge Buncombe," "The Coolidge Mystery," "Little Red Ridinghood *[sic]*," "The Men Who Rule Us," "Roosevelt," "Brief Battle Was Hopeless for Carpentier from First," "How Legends Are Made," "Notes on Victuals," "Victualry as a Fine Art," "Callinectes Hastatus," "Meditations on a Day in June," "Hot Dogs," "Beethoven," "Bach at Bethlehem," "Brahms," "Night Club," "Spoken American," "Essay in American," "Making New Words," "Hopeful Purists," "Why Are We Yankees?," "The American Novel," "The Sahara of the Bozart," "A Chance for Novelists," "On Literary Gents," "Mark Twain's Americanism," "Ambrose Bierce," "Poe's Start in Life," "James Huneker," "Joseph Conrad," "Peasant and Cockney," "Sherwood Anderson," "Two Dreiser Novels," "Short Story Courses," "The Trade of Letters," "Advice to Young Authors," "The Avalanche of Books," "The Critic and His Job," "The Golden Age of Pedagogy," "Homo Neanderthalensis," "Mencken Finds Daytonians Full of Sickening Doubts About Value of Publicity," "Impossiblity of Obtaining Fair Jury . . . ," "Mencken Likens Trial to a Religious Orgy . . . ," "Yearning Mountaineers' Souls Need Reconversion Nightly . . . ," "Darrow's Eloquent Appeal Wasted . . . ," "Law and Freedom . . . Yield Place to Holy Writ in Rhea County," "Mencken Declares Strictly Fair Trial Is Beyond Ken of Tennessee Fundamentalists," "Malone the Victor . . . ," "Battle Now Over . . . ," "Ready for New Jousts," "Tennessee in the Frying Pan," "Bryan," "Aftermath," "A Neglected Anniversary," "Hymn to the Truth," "Reflections on War," "Reminiscence," "Conference Notes," "Etiquette Makes Rapid Progress Impossible at London . . . ," "Help for the Jews," "A Word for the Japs," "England Revisited," "Erez Israel," "The Sixth Pan American Conference," "The Goosegreasers at Work," "Mr. Hughes Runs Things, Though Not a Spaniard," "Gin Guzzling American Tourists Crowd Havana," "Mencken Misses Pupils at University of Havana," "The Spanish Main," "Manifest Destiny," "Below the Rio Grande," "Off the Grand Banks." See Notes.

Typography and paper: 7⅝″ (7⁵⁄₁₆″) × 4⁵⁄₁₆″; 41 lines per page (number of lines varies). Running heads, all over rules: recto, 'CONTENTS' (pp. xi–xv), 'FORE-WORD' (pp. xix–xxxv), 'INTRODUCTION' (pp. xxxix–lvii), essay titles (pp. 3–683), 'ACKNOWLEDGMENTS' (p. 685), 'NOTES TO THE INTRODUCTION' (pp. 687–89), 'INDEX' (pp. 693–707); verso, 'THE IMPOSSIBLE H. L. MENCKEN' (pp. x–lx, 688–706), section titles (pp. 2–682). Wove paper.

Binding: Gray paper-covered boards. Black V cloth spine stamped in silver: 'THE | IMPOSSIBLE | H. L. | MENCKEN | Edited by | Marion | Elizabeth | Rodgers | [device] | DOUBLEDAY'. Trimmed, unstained. Red end papers.

Dust jacket: White paper. Front, all over gray background and two white vertical lines: '[as white through red field with white borders top and bottom] The Impossible | H. L. MENCKEN | [caricature of Mencken by David Levine] | A SELECTION OF HIS BEST | NEWSPAPER STORIES | [as white through red field with white borders top and bottom] EDITED BY | MARION ELIZABETH RODGERS | WITH A FORE-WORD BY GORE VIDAL'. Spine: [reading down, as white through red field with white borders top and bottom] The Impossible [over] H. L. MENCKEN | [horizon-tal] A SELECTION | OF HIS BEST | NEWSPAPER | STORIES | [caricature] | [reading down, white] EDITED BY [over] MARION ELIZABETH RODGERS | [horizontal, as white through red field with white borders top and bottom] [device] | DOUBLEDAY'. Back: blurb and quotations, bar code. Front flap: blurb, price U.S. $27.50, Canada $35. Rear flap: continuation of blurb, jacket credits, '1191 | [white through black bar] AG'.

Publication: Published 1 November 1991. $27.50. Copyright #TX-3-181-674.

Printing: No indication in copyright records.

Locations: Harv (2), MChB (2 in dj), LC (12 November 1991).

Notes: The order of the first two printings could not be determined. "I have concen-trated on the major signed contributions to the Baltimore *Herald,* the Baltimore *Sunpapers* . . . , the New York *Evening Mail,* the Chicago *Sunday Tribune,* and the New York *American.* . . . At least two thirds of the essays have not been seen since their first appearance in the newspapers where they were praised or damned over sixty years ago" (pp. lix–lx).

Review copy: Blue wrappers printed in black on front: 'THE IMPOSSIBLE | H. L. Mencken | [French rule] | A Selection of His Best | Newspaper Stories | Edited by | MARION ELIZABETH RODGERS | With a Foreword by | GORE VIDAL | TEN-TATIVE PUBLICATION: SEPTEMBER 1991 | TENTATIVE HARDCOVER PRICE: U.S.$27.50 *[sic]* / CANADA $35.00 | TENTATIVE PAPERBACK PRICE: U.S. $15.00 / CANADA $19.00 | [rule] | PUBLISHED SIMULTANEOUSLY AS A DOUBLEDAY HARDCOVER | AND AS AN ANCHOR PAPERBACK | [rule] | THIS IS AN UNCORRECTED PROOF. | PLEASE NOTE THAT ANY QUOTES

A 83.1.a, dust jacket

FOR REVIEWS | MUST BE CHECKED AGAINST THE FINISHED BOOK. | [device] | ANCHOR BOOKS'. 9¹⁄₁₆″ × 5¹⁵⁄₁₆″. *Location:* GHT.

A 83.1.b
Presumed second printing

Same as A 83.1.a except:

Copyright page: 'AN ANCHOR BOOK | PUBLISHED BY DOUBLEDAY | a division of Bantam Doubleday Dell Publishing Group, Inc. | 666 Fifth Avenue, New York, New York 10103 | ANCHOR BOOKS, DOUBLEDAY and the portrayal of an anchor | are trademarks of Doubleday, a division of Bantam Doubleday Dell | Publishing Group, Inc. | *The Impossible H. L. Mencken* is published simultaneously in a hardcover edition by | Doubleday, a division of Bantam Doubleday Dell Publishing Group, Inc. | [Library of Congress Cataloging-in-Publication Data in nine lines] | ISBN 0–385–26208–6 | Copyright © 1991 by Marion Elizabeth Rodgers and the Enoch Pratt Free Library as | Trustees for the Estate of H. L. Mencken | Foreword © 1991 by Gore Vidal | All Rights Reserved | Printed in the United States of America | August 1991 | 1 3 5 7 9 10 8 6 4 2'

9¹⁄₈″ × 6⁷⁄₈″.

Perfect bound.

Binding: Stiff paper wrappers like dust jacket above; different bar code on back; on spine: '. . . [device in oval] | Anchor Books'.

Publication: $15.00.

Location: GHT.

A 83.1.c–d
Third and fourth printings: New York etc.: Doubleday, [n.d.].

Second and third hardcover printings indicated by lowest numbers on copyright page.

Locations: MB (third), MBU (fourth), RJS (third).

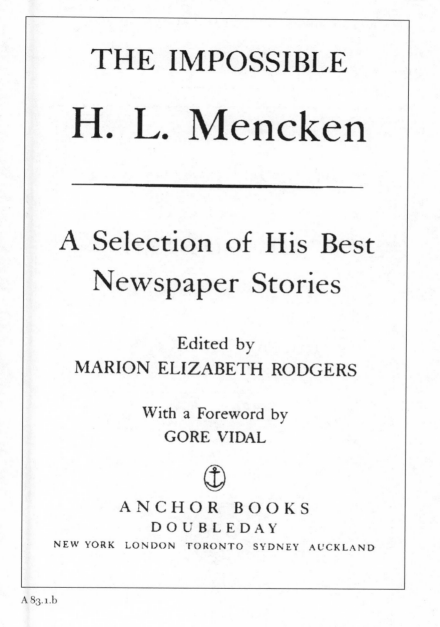

THE IMPOSSIBLE

H. L. Mencken

A Selection of His Best Newspaper Stories

Edited by
MARION ELIZABETH RODGERS

With a Foreword by
GORE VIDAL

ANCHOR BOOKS
DOUBLEDAY
NEW YORK LONDON TORONTO SYDNEY AUCKLAND

A 83.1.b

A 84 MY LIFE AS AUTHOR AND EDITOR

A 84.1.a
Only edition, first printing (1993)

MY LIFE AS
AUTHOR
AND EDITOR

H. L. MENCKEN

*Edited and
with an Introduction by
Jonathan Yardley*

ALFRED A. KNOPF   NEW YORK
1993

A 84.1.a

Copyright page: 'THIS IS A BORZOI BOOK | PUBLISHED BY ALFRED A. KNOPF, INC. | Copyright © 1992 by Enoch Pratt Free Library | Introduction, annotations and editing | copyright © 1992 by Alfred A. Knopf, Inc. | All rights reserved under International and Pan-American | Copyright Conventions. Published in the United States by | Alfred A. Knopf, Inc., New York, and simultaneously in | Canada by Random House of Canada Limited, Toronto. | Distributed by Random House, Inc., New York. | [nineteen lines on acknowledgments to follow index, Library of Congress Cataloging-in-Publication Data] | Manufactured in the United States of America | First Edition'.

Colophon: 'A NOTE ON THE TYPE | [fifteen lines on Caledonia type, designed by W. A. Dwiggins, whose services to Mencken and Knopf are surveyed] | *My Life As Author and Editor* was composed by Cre- | ative Graphics, Inc., Allentown, Pennsylvania, printed | and bound by R. R. Donnelly & Sons, Harrisonburg, | Virginia, and designed by Peter A. Andersen.'

9¼" × 6¼": [A–B i–vi] vii–xvi (versos unpaginated) [xvii–xviii] xix [xx] xxi [xxii 1–4] 5–450 (versos and 69, 81, 205, 217, 241, 249, 267, 283, 323, 379, 395, 411, 415, 423, 425 unpaginated) [451–56] = 480 pp.

[1–15]¹⁶ = 240 leaves.

Contents: p. A: blank; p. B: 'ALSO BY H. L. MENCKEN | [twenty-one titles]'; p. i: half title; p. ii: blank; p. iii: title; p. iv: copyright; pp. v–xvi: '*EDITOR'S INTRODUC-TION*'; pp. xvii–xxi: '*PREFACE*'; p. xxii: blank; p. 1: half title; p. 2: blank; pp. 3–409: text; p. 410: blank; pp. 411–14: '*APPENDIX I* [in box like that on title page] | *A NOTE TO AUTHORS*'; pp. 415–22: '*APPENDIX II* [in same box] | *A PERSONAL WORD BY* | *H. L. MENCKEN*'; pp. 423–24: '*APPENDIX III* [in same box] | *SUGGESTIONS TO OUR VISITORS*'; pp. 425–50: '*INDEX*'; pp. 451–52: blank; p. 453: acknowledgments (twenty-six lines); p. 454: blank; p. 455: colophon; p. 456: blank.

Typography and paper: 7⅝" (7¼") × 4⁷⁄₁₆"; 39 lines per page. Running heads on versos only, all unpaginated (rectos have page numbers at same height as heads): '*EDITOR'S INTRODUCTION*' (pp. vi–xvi), '*PREFACE*' (pp. xviii–xx), '*MY LIFE AS AUTHOR AND EDITOR*' (pp. 4–408), '*APPENDIX I*' (pp. 412–14), '*APPENDIX II*' (pp. 416–22), '*APPENDIX III*' (p. 424), '*INDEX*' (pp. 426–50). Wove paper.

Binding: Cream paper-covered boards, beige V cloth spine. Front: gilt silhouette of Mencken. Spine: [all within gilt frame as on title page] '[gilt on dark gray field] [bar over rule] | *My* | *Life* | *As* | *Author* | *and* | *Editor* | [rule] | H. L. | MENCKEN | [rule over bar] | [gilt on separate dark gray field] [rule] | [Borzoi device in oval] | KNOPF'. Top and bottom edges trimmed, unstained, fore edge unevenly trimmed. White end papers.

Dust jacket: White paper. Front: [all on dark gray field wrapping around through the back, in gold frame like that on title page] '[gold on deep blue field] H. L. MENCKEN

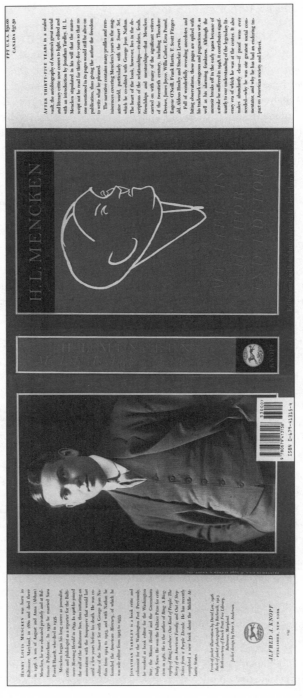

FPT U.S.A. $30.00
CANADA $37.50

AFTER THIRTY-FIVE YEARS in a sealed vault, the autobiography of America's great social and literary critic now comes to light, edited and with an introduction by Jonathan Yardley. H. L. Mencken stipulated in his will that the manuscript not be read for thirty-five years so that no one mentioned in its pages would still be alive on publication, thus giving the author the freedom to write what he pleased.

The narrative contains many profiles and reminiscences covering Mencken's years in the magazine world, particularly with the Smart Set, which he co-edited with George Jean Nathan. The heart of the book, however, lies in the descriptions of the relationships—rivalries, feuds, friendships and mentorships—that Mencken carried on with many of the significant writers of the twentieth century, including Theodore Dreiser, James Joyce, Willa Cather, Ezra Pound, Eugene O'Neill, Frank Harris, F. Scott Fitzgerald, Aldous Huxley and Sinclair Lewis.

Full of wonderfully revealing anecdotes and biting observations, these pages are spiked with his trademark outrageous and pugnacious wit, as well as his alarming frankness. Although the memoir breaks off in the early 1940s because of a stroke he suffered in 1948, it contributes significantly to our understanding of the legendary literary era of which he was at the center. It also makes abundantly clear—if proof were ever needed—why he was our greatest social commentator, and why he had had an enduring impact on American society and letters.

H. L. MENCKEN

HENRY LOUIS MENCKEN was born in Baltimore, Maryland, in 1880 and died there in 1956. A son of August and Anna (Abhau) Mencken, he was educated privately and at Baltimore Polytechnic. In 1930 he married Sara Powell Haardt, who died in 1935.

Mencken began his long career as a journalist, critic, and philologist as a reporter for the Baltimore Morning Herald in 1899. In 1906 he joined the staff of the Baltimore Sun, thus initiating an association with the newspaper that would last until a few years before his death. He was co-editor of the Smart Set with George Jean Nathan from 1914 to 1923, and with Nathan he founded the American Mercury, of which he was sole editor from 1925 to 1933.

JONATHAN YARDLEY is a book critic and columnist for the Washington Post. Previously he worked at book culture for the Washington Star, the Miami Herald and the Greensboro Daily News. He won the Pulitzer Prize for criticism in 1981. He is the author of Ring: A Biography of Ring Lardner; Our Kind of People: The Story of an American Family; and Out of Step: Notes from a Purple Decade. He has recently completed a new book about the Middle Atlantic States.

Front-of-jacket illustration by David Levi, 1998. Back-of-jacket photograph by Rasband, 1913. Both courtesy of Enoch Pratt Free Library, Baltimore, Maryland.

Jacket design by Peter A. Anderson

ALFRED A KNOPF
PUBLISHERS, NEW YORK

A 84.1.a, dust jacket

| [rule touching frame] | | [white sketch of Mencken on maroon field] | | [on same, in gold] *MY LIFE AS | AUTHOR | AND EDITOR* | [below frame, in gold] Edited and with an Introduction by Jonathan Yardley'. Spine: [all within same style of gold frame] '[on maroon field, reading down] H. L. MENCKEN [over] *My Life As Author and Editor* | [gold rule] | [remainder horizontal on deep blue field] [maroon and white Borzoi device] | [gold] KNOPF'. Back: photo of Mencken and bar code. Front flap: blurb on tan field; price $30.00 USA, $37.50 Canada. Back flap: biographies of Mencken and Yardley on tan field; jacket sketch credit to David Low, photograph credit to Bachrach; jacket design by Peter A. Andersen; '1/93' at bottom.

Publication: Published 4 January 1993. $30.00. Copyright #TX-3-607-091 (officially received 29 June 1993).

Printing: See colophon.

Locations: Harv, LC (19 January 1993), MBU, MCR (dj), RJS (dj).

Notes: No copies with a Canadian imprint were found.

Review copies: (1) Resembling above but text differently set (uncorrected proof), [A–B i–vi] . . . [432], index omitted, perfect bound in olive wrappers (white inside), 9″ × 6″, tentative publication date January 1993. *Location:* GHT. (2) Trade printing, with white slip laid in (4″ × 5½″), printed in blue and black: 'A REVIEW COPY FROM | Alfred • A • Knopf | [Borzoi device] | [request for two copies of review, price $30, publication date 29 January 1993, plea not to run review before publication date]'. *Location:* GHT (dj).

A 84.1.b
Second printing: New York: Knopf, 1993.

On copyright page: 'Published January 29, 1993 | Second Printing'.

Locations: D, Harv.

A 84.1.c
Third printing: New York: Vintage Books, [1995].

On copyright page: 'FIRST VINTAGE BOOKS EDITION, JANUARY 1995'. 8″ × 5⅛″. Black wrappers printed in yellow, lavender, and gold.

Location: GHT.

A 85.1.a
Only edition, first printing (1994)

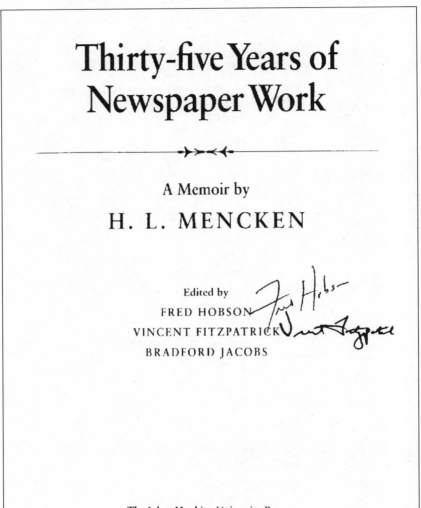

Thirty-five Years of Newspaper Work

➔➤⬥⬥⬅

A Memoir by

H. L. MENCKEN

Edited by
FRED HOBSON
VINCENT FITZPATRICK
BRADFORD JACOBS

The Johns Hopkins University Press
Baltimore and London

A 85.1.a

Copyright page: 'Frontispiece: H. L. Mencken at forty-two. 1922. E. O. Hoppé. | ©
1994 The Johns Hopkins University Press | All rights reserved | Printed in the United
States of America on acid-free paper | 03 02 01 00 99 98 97 96 95 94   5 4 3 2 1 | The
Johns Hopkins University Press | 2715 North Charles Street | Baltimore, Maryland
21218–4319 | The Johns Hopkins Press Ltd., London | ISBN 0–8018–4791–5 |
Library of Congress Cataloging-in-Publication Data | will be found at the end of this
book. | A catalog record of this book is available from the British Library.'

$8^{15}/_{16}'' \times 5^{15}/_{16}''$: [i–vi] vii–xxi [xxii] xxiii–v [xxvi] xxvii–xxxvi [xxxvii–viii] 1 [2] 3–42 [43]
44–55 [56] 57–177 [178] 179–204 [205] 206–23 [224] 225–84 [285] 286–345 [346]
347–71 [372] 373–75 [376] 377–90 [391–94] = 432 pp.

$[1–3]^{16} [4]^8 [5–14]^{16}$ = 216 leaves.

Contents: p. i: half title; p. ii: photo of Mencken; p. iii: title; p. iv: copyright; p. v: '*In
Memoriam* | Carl Bode, 1911–1993'; p. vi: blank; pp. vii–viii: 'CONTENTS'; pp. ix–
xxi: 'INTRODUCTION'; p. xxii: blank; pp. xxiii–xxv: 'NOTE ON THE MANU-
SCRIPT | AND EDITORIAL METHOD'; p. xxvi: blank; pp. xxvii–xxxii: 'CHRO-
NOLOGY'; pp. xxxiii–xxxvi: 'DRAMATIS PERSONAE'; p. xxxvii: half title; p. xxxviii:
blank; pp. 1–6: 'Preface' [by Mencken]; pp. 7–354: text; pp. 355–67: 'APPENDIX A |
An Editorial Memorandum | 1919'; pp. 368–71: 'APPENDIX B | Gridiron Club
Speech | (December 8, 1934)'; p. 372: blank; pp. 373–75: 'EPILOGUE'; p. 376: blank;
pp. 377–78: 'ACKNOWLEDGMENTS'; pp. 379–90: 'INDEX'; pp. 391–93: blank; p.
394: Library of Congress Cataloging-in-Publication Data. Illustrations on pp. 2, 31,
43, 56, 68, 107, 157, 169, 178, 195, 205, 224, 285, 334, 346.

Typography and paper: $7^{11}/_{16}''$ ($7^5/_{16}''$) $\times$ $4^5/_{16}''$; 40 lines per page. Running heads, all
preceded and followed by a rule: recto, 'Introduction' (pp. xi–xxi), 'Note on Manu-
script' (p. xxv), 'Chronology' (pp. xxix–xxxi), 'Dramatis Personae' (p. xxxv), 'Preface'
(pp. 3–5), chapter titles (pp. 9–353), 'Appendix A' (pp. 357–67), 'Appendix B' (pp.
369–71), 'Epilogue' (p. 375), 'Index' (pp. 381–89); verso, 'Contents' (p. viii), 'Introduction' (pp. x–xx), 'Note on Manuscript' (p. xxiv), 'Chronology' (pp. xxviii–xxxii),
'Dramatis Personae' (p. xxxiv–vi), 'Thirty-five Years of Newspaper Work' (pp. 4–370),
'Epilogue' (p. 374), 'Acknowledgments' (p. 378), 'Index' (pp. 380–90). Wove paper.

Binding: Blue V cloth front and back. Black V cloth spine stamped in silver: '[reading
down] MENCKEN [heavy dot] Thirty-five Years of Newspaper Work | [horizontal]
Johns | Hopkins | [silver shield with black 'jh']. Top and bottom edges trimmed,
unstained, fore edge rough trimmed. White end papers.

Dust jacket: White paper. Front, all superimposed on black and white photo: '[within
box in blue frame] [on black field] [blue] Thirty-five Years of | Newspaper Work |
[white] [rule] A MEMOIR BY [rule] | [blue] H. L. MENCKEN | [colorized photo of
Mencken at work] | [below box, in black] *Edited by* | FRED HOBSON | VINCENT
FITZPATRICK | BRADFORD JACOBS'. Spine duplicates that of cover except au-
thor and title in blue, press in white, black letters on gray shield, all on black field.

In January 1991 the Enoch Pratt Free Library opened the sealed manuscript of H. L. Mencken's "Thirty-five Years of Newspaper Work." Written in 1941–42 and bequeathed to the library under time-lock upon Mencken's death in 1956, it is among the very last of his papers opened to the public. *Thirty-five Years of Newspaper Work*, a one-volume abridgment of Mencken's much longer memoir, vividly pictures the excitement of newspaper life in the heyday of print journalism.

Here Mencken colorfully recalls his years —mostly with the Baltimore *Evening Sun*—as a reporter and a writer of editorials that always caused a stir among the public and sponsors of indignation among his enemies. The volume includes important new material on his coverage of presidential candidacies from 1912 to 1940 (Mencken on Harding's inaugural address: "a string of wet sponges") and the 1925 trial of the man he called the "infidel Scopes." Mencken also describes his brief stint as a war correspondent on Germany's subzero Eastern Front in 1917 and the perilous voyage back, which took him through Havana just as a revolution was breaking out. (He stayed to cover it.) He writes, with curious detachment, about the "suicidal" war and likely fate of Germany's Jews during a final visit to his ancestral homeland in summer 1938. And he describes colorful Baltimore personalities, shares local gossip, and offers candid—usually unflattering— portraits of the politicians and clerics he mostly despised.

Thirty-five Years of Newspaper Work

A MEMOIR BY
H. L. MENCKEN

Edited by
FRED HOBSON
VINCENT FITZPATRICK
BRADFORD JACOBS

MENCKEN · Thirty-five Years of Newspaper Work

Johns Hopkins

"The thing to do, I argued, was to use the case to make Tennessee forever infamous, and to that end the sacrifice of Scopes would be a small matter. Above all, the thing to do was to lay all stress, not on Scopes, who was a nobody, but on Bryan, who was an international figure — to lure him on the stand if possible, to make him taste his barbaric credo in plain English, and to make a monkey of him before the world. Getting Scopes acquitted would be worth a day's headlines in the newspapers, and then no more, but smearing Bryan would be good for a long while."

— H. L. Mencken, on his discussions of the upcoming Scopes trial with lawyers for the defense; 1925

The Johns Hopkins University Press
Baltimore and London

Fred Hobson is professor of American literature at the University of North Carolina, Chapel Hill. He is the author of *Mencken: A Life* and *Serpent in Eden: H. L. Mencken and the South*.

Vincent Fitzpatrick is assistant curator of the Mencken Collection at the Enoch Pratt Free Library in Baltimore and the author of *H. L. Mencken*.

Bradford Jacobs is former editorial page editor of the Baltimore *Evening Sun* and the author of *Thimbleriggers: The Law vs. Governor Marvin Mandel*.

Jacket design by Ann Walston
Jacket illustration from a photograph of Mencken at the Republican convention in Cleveland, Ohio, that nominated Governor Alf Landon for President in June, 1936. The Enoch Pratt Free Library, H. L. Mencken Collection

A 85.1.a, dust jacket

Back: excerpt and bar code. Front flap: blurb; price $34.95. Rear flap: biographies of the three editors; jacket design credit to Ann Walston; credit for jacket photo.

Publication: Published 22 August 1994. $34.95. Copyright #TX-3-873-667.

Printing: Type set by G & S Typesetters, Austin, Tex. Printed and bound by Maple Press, Manchester, Pa.

Locations: LC (1 September 1994), MBU, MChB, RJS (dj).

Review copy: Same as above except uncorrected proof in glossy wrappers printed in tan, black, and blue, 9″ × 6″; on copyright page: 'MANUFACTURED BY | THE COUNTRY PRESS INC. | MIDDLEBOROUGH MA'; publication date 20 September 1994; with promotional letter dated 23 June 1994, and announcing publication date of August. Some differences from above in introductory sections and appendices. *Location:* GHT.

A 85.1.b
Second printing: Baltimore and London: Johns Hopkins University Press, [1996].

Data from next item. Not seen.

A 85.1.c
Third printing: Baltimore and London: Johns Hopkins University Press, [1996].

On copyright page: 'Johns Hopkins Paperbacks edition, 1996 | 96 97 98 99 00 01 02 03 04 05   5 4 3 2'. It is presumed that this indicates the second paperback printing and not the second overall printing. In none of the several copies examined did the line of numbers end with '1'.

Locations: D, GHT.

A 86 A SECOND MENCKEN CHRESTOMATHY

A 86.1.a
Only edition, first printing (1995)

H. L. Mencken

A SECOND MENCKEN CHRESTOMATHY

Selected, Revised, and Annotated by the Author
Edited and with an Introduction by Terry Teachout

¹995

ALFRED A. KNOPF
New York

A 86.1.a

Copyright page: 'THIS IS A BORZOI BOOK | PUBLISHED BY ALFRED A. KNOPF, INC. | Copyright © 1994 by Enoch Pratt Free Library | Editing and annotations copyright © 1994 by Alfred A. Knopf, Inc. | Introduction copyright © 1994 by Terry Teachout | All rights reserved under International and Pan-American Copyright | Conventions. Published in the United States by Alfred A. Knopf, Inc., | New York, and simultaneously in Canada by Random House of Can- | ada Limited, Toronto. Distributed by Random House, Inc., New York. | [eleven lines of Library of Congress Cataloging-in-Publication Data] | Manufactured in the United States of America | First Edition'

Colophon: 'A NOTE ON THE TYPE | [fourteen lines on Electra type and its designer, W. A. Dwiggins] | Composed by Creative Graphics, Allentown, Pennsylvania | Printed and bound by R. R. Donnelley & Sons, Harrisonburg, Virginia'

$8\frac{5}{16}'' \times 5\frac{5}{8}''$: [A–D i–iv] v–xxvi [1–2] 3–491 [492–98] = 528 pp.

Perfect bound.

Contents: pp. A–C: blank; p. D: 'ALSO BY H. L. MENCKEN | [twenty-two titles]'; p. i: half title; p. ii: blank; p. iii: title; p. iv: copyright; pp. v–xii: 'Contents'; pp. xiii–xxvi: 'EDITOR'S INTRODUCTION'; p. 1: half title; p. 2: blank; pp. 3–491: text; p. 492: blank; p. 493: 'A NOTE ABOUT THE AUTHOR | [eleven lines]'; p. 494: blank; p. 495: 'A NOTE ABOUT THE EDITOR | [eleven lines]'; p. 496: blank; p. 497: colophon; p. 498: blank.

Typography and paper: $7\frac{1}{8}''$ ($6\frac{13}{16}''$) $\times$ 4''; 38 lines per page. Running heads: recto, 'Contents' (pp. vii–xi), 'Editor's Introduction' (pp. xv–xxv), section titles (pp. 5–491); verso, 'Contents' (pp. vi–xii), 'Editor's Introduction' (pp. xiv–xxvi), 'A SECOND MENCKEN CHRESTOMATHY' (pp. 4–490). Wove paper.

Binding: White paper-covered boards stamped in gilt on front; white V cloth spine stamped in gilt. Front: 'H. L. Mencken | [ornament]'. Spine: 'H. L. | Mencken | [reading down] A SECOND [over] MENCKEN [over] CHRESTOMATHY | [horizontal] [Borzoi device] | ALFRED A. | KNOPF'. Top and bottom edges trimmed, fore edge unevenly trimmed. White end papers.

Dust jacket: White paper. Front: [simulating a light brown and pale yellow label taped to a light brown background, the lines flush right] 'A SECOND MENCKEN | CHRESTOMATHY | A New Selection from the Writings | of America's Legendary | EDITOR, CRITIC, and WIT | [maroon rule] | [maroon] SELECTED, REVISED, AND ANNOTATED BY THE AUTHOR | [maroon rule] | [black] EDITED AND WITH AN INTRODUCTION | BY TERRY TEACHOUT | H.L.MENCKEN'. Spine: '[on same background, another taped label, the lines flush right, reading down] [maroon] A SECOND MENCKEN [over] CHRESTOMATHY [over] [black] H.L. MENCKEN | [horizontal, as light brown showing through blue, a round Borzoi device] | [blue] KNOPF'. Back: on same backround a photo of Mencken in shades of

FPT U.S.A. $30.00
CANADA $42.00

THIS WONDERFUL SEQUEL to the best-selling *A Mencken Chrestomathy* of nearly half a century ago is full of the iconoclastic common sense that marked H. L. Mencken's astonishing career as the premier American social critic of the twentieth century. Gathered by Mencken himself before he died in 1956, this second chrestomathy ("a collection of selected literary passages" — with the accent on the *fun*) contains writings about a variety of subjects — politics, war, music, literature, men and women, lawyers, bumfrom of the South. Some of his essays have beguiling titles — "Notes for an Honest Autobiography," "The Commonwealth of Morons," "Le vrai Anglais," "Acres of Babah," "Hooch for the Artist." All of them are a pleasure to read, and we are reminded that what Mencken wrote in the early years of this century remains applicable to a very different America.

TERRY TEACHOUT, who discovered the manuscript of this volume among Mencken's private papers and edited it for publication, writes in his introduction, "Mencken's own character got into every word he wrote, and it is writ large on every page of this book: witty and abrasive, self-confident and self-contradictory, sometimes maddening, often exasperating, always inimitable." Just so.

A SECOND MENCKEN
CHRESTOMATHY

A *New Selection from the Writings*
of America's Legendary
EDITOR, CRITIC, and WIT

SELECTED, REVISED, AND ANNOTATED BY THE AUTHOR

EDITED AND WITH AN INTRODUCTION
BY TERRY TEACHOUT

H.L. MENCKEN

A SECOND MENCKEN
CHRESTOMATHY
H.L. MENCKEN

VINTAGE / KNOPF

HENRY LOUIS MENCKEN was born in Baltimore in 1880 and died there in 1956. His long career as journalist, critic, and philologist began at the Baltimore *Morning Herald* in 1899. In 1906 he joined the staff of the Baltimore *Sun*, thus initiating an association with the *Sunpapers* that would last until a few years before his death. He was coeditor of the *Smart Set* with George Jean Nathan from 1914 to 1923, and with Nathan he founded the *American Mercury*, of which he was sole editor from 1925 to 1933.

TERRY TEACHOUT is arts columnist for the *New York Daily News* and associate editor of the *New Dance Review*. He also writes for *The American Scholar, Commentary, Mirabella, National Review, The New Criterion, The New York Times Book Review, The Wall Street Journal,* and the *Washington Post Book World.* His biography of H. L. Mencken is due out in 1996.

"What impresses most about this collection is Mencken's breadth. Few contemporary writers would assume such a broad brief, writing not only about politics, law and the clergy but also about biography, literature, music and drink. To apply a Mencken sobriquet, he was no lesser eminence."
— *Publishers Weekly*

AUTHOR PHOTOGRAPH BY ROBERT F. KNIESCHE, COURTESY OF
ENOCH PRATT FREE LIBRARY, BALTIMORE, MARYLAND

JACKET DESIGN BY
BARBARA DE WILDE / CHIP KIDD

ALFRED A. KNOPF, PUBLISHER, NEW YORK

Printed in U.S.A. © 1995 ALFRED A. KNOPF, INC.

ISBN 0-679-42624-3

A 86.1.a, dust jacket

brown and, on a pale yellow simulated piece of paper held by staples, the bar code. The flaps: blurbs and biographies of author and editor; price $30, in Canada $42; photo credit to Robert F. Kniesche; jacket design by Drenttel Doyle Partners; dated '1/95'.

Publication: Published 30 January 1995. $30.00. Copyright #TX-4-140-014, 015, 016.

Printing: See colophon.

Locations: GHT (dj), MChB, RJS (dj).

Notes: The book is based on numerous typescripts that Mencken edited for use in a planned second *Chrestomathy*. They are mostly excerpts "from his uncollected newspaper and magazine articles and from ten of his books" (p. xxiii). Most of the introductory notes and footnotes are by Mencken. The editor claims, "The arrangement of this book, though modeled on the original *Chrestomathy*, is entirely my own doing" (p. xxiv). No copies with a Canadian imprint were found.

Review copy: Like above except uncorrected proof in gray wrappers, 8⅜″ × 5⅝″; on front: 'PUBLICATION DATE: 30 JANUARY 1995'. *Location:* RJS.

A 86.1.b
Second printing: New York: Vintage Books, [1995].

On copyright page: 'FIRST VINTAGE BOOKS EDITION, OCTOBER 1995'. 8″ × 5³⁄₁₆″. Multicolored pictorial wrappers.

Location: GHT.

A 86.1.c
Third printing: New York: Vintage Books, [1996].

Second Vintage Books printing May 1996. Not seen.

A 87 DO YOU REMEMBER?

A 87.1.a.i
Only edition, only printing, limited issue (1996)

A 87

Copyright page: 'Maryland Historical Society | 201 West Monument Street | Baltimore, Maryland 21201 | *Founded 1844* | Copyright © 1996 by Maryland Historical Society. | All rights reserved. | First Edition | Manufactured in the United States of America | The letters on pages 25–182 are published by arrangement with the pro- | prietors, the Enoch Pratt Free Library and Ruth Goodman Goetz, whose per- | mission the editor and the publisher gratefully acknowledge. | BOOK DESIGN BY MARTHA FARLOW | [Library of Congress Cataloging-in-Publication Data in fifteen lines] | The paper used in this publication meets the minimum requirements | of the American National Standard for Permanence of Paper | for Printed Library Materials Z39.48–1984'

Statement of limitation: 'THIS EDITION OF | Do You Remember? | HAS BEEN LIMITED | TO ONE HUNDRED COPIES | AND SIGNED BY THE EDITOR | [signature in black] | THIS COPY IS NUMBER | [number written in black]'

8″ × 5^{15}⁄$_{16}$″: [A-B i–viii] ix–xv [xvi–xviii] 1–189 [190] = 210 pp.

[1]^{16} (1 + 1₁) [2]^{16} [3]^{8} [4–7]^{16} = 105 leaves. The limitation leaf is tipped in between the free front end paper and the first integral leaf.

Contents: p. A: limitation; p. B: reproduction of Mencken Christmas card on tan paper tipped in above four lines of description; p. i: half title; pp. ii–iii: title; p. iv: copyright; p. v: '*For Lily and Sara.* | *All men have better wives than they deserve.*'; p. vi: credit for title photos; p. vii: 'CONTENTS'; p. viii: blank; pp. ix–xv: 'PREFACE'; p. xvi: blank; p. xvii: half title; p. xviii: blank; pp. 1–24: 'INTRODUCTION'; pp. 25–182: text; pp. 183–84: 'AFTERWORD'; pp. 185–88: 'ACKNOWLEDGMENTS'; p. 189: 'ABOUT THE AUTHOR'; p. 190: blank.

Typography and paper: 6⅞″ × 4″; 30 lines per page (number of lines varies). No heads. Wove paper.

Binding: Gray V cloth. Front: '[stamped in gilt on black field, within double-rule box, outer rule thicker] The | Whimsical | Letters of | H. L. | Mencken | AND | Philip | Goodman | [below box, in gilt] Do You | Remember?'. Spine, stamped in gilt: '[reading down] SANDERS [on black field within double-rule box, outer rule thicker] Do You Remember? | [horizontal] MARYLAND | HISTORICAL | SOCIETY'. Trimmed, unstained. White end papers flecked with gray. In box covered in gray "elephant hide" paper, unprinted.

Dust jacket: None.

Publication: Published 21 September 1996. $75.00.

Printing: Set by Blue Heron Typesetters; printed and bound by Edwards Brothers.

Location: RJS.

$24.95

IN 1918, HENRY LOUIS MENCKEN WAS EDITING *The Smart Set* in New York, to which he traveled weekly, and working on *The American Language* in his native Baltimore. Philip Goodman, a New York advertising man, bon vivant, and fledgling publisher, later to be a Broadway impresario, was Mencken's closest friend. Knowing that Mencken was depressed about the state of the German-American community during World War I, Goodman offered cheer in a letter "reminiscing" about their old German-American neighborhood in the 1880s and 1890s. (Goodman actually had grown up in Philadelphia.) He invented characters and events and wrote with irony and affection for those better times. Mencken rose instantly to the challenge and wrote a letter in similar vein. For three years these correspondents—both superb storytellers—tried to outdo each other in tall tales that catch the vivacity and boisterousness of German and Jewish immigrants on the eastern seaboard in the late nineteenth century. Since Mencken's death in 1956 fragments and copies of the letters have reposed in the Enoch Pratt Free Library in Baltimore. Jack Sanders has devoted three years to reconstructing and annotating this correspondence, the most playful writing of Mencken's life.

The Whimsical Letters of

H. L. Mencken AND Philip Goodman

Do You Remember?

EDITED BY JACK SANDERS

SANDERS   Do You Remember?   MARYLAND HISTORICAL SOCIETY

"*Superb, just right.... a pleasure to read.*"
FRED HOBSON, author of *Mencken: A Life*

Dear Mencken:

Why have we not mentioned Charlie Grushek's barber shop? I was reminded of it today, when apropos me in the subway I beheld the living image of old Gus Schmidlapp, who used to have the second chair. Did you know that Gus had more private mugs on his shelf than even Charlie himself had? I have seen of a Sunday morning during those memorable waits as many as six men pass up their turn so that Gus could tend them. Also did you know that the *Tonsorial Review*, issue of May 8th, 1894, gave him a writeup and among other things said that he was the first barber ever to use hot towels after shaving? I used to play checkers with him on summer evenings. My God, what combinations he knew!

Goodman

Dear Goodman:

Charlie Grushek! I know quite well. Upon the death of Jacob Wichman, the bay and fied king, Charlie was summoned to the house of grief to deplume the corpse. He was so overcome by his sorrow that he allowed his razor to slip, and nearly cut off the defunct Jacob's nose. The slash, observed by the pallbearers of Schaimsheet Lodge, No. 74, A. F. & A. M., caused them to suspect that Jacob had met with foul play, and for a while there was a violent (though whispered) scandal, and talk of a coroner's inquest. It was hushed up by Dr Buddenbohn, who had attended Jacob in his last moments. He actually died, as everyone knows, of *Leberfrankheit*.

Mencken

JACK SANDERS lives and works in San Diego, California. By training he is a lawyer, by occupation a manager of real estate, by inclination a scholar. He describes himself as a humanist, libertarian, skeptic, and curmudgeon. The scion of a family of robust German peasants, he nevertheless acquired, he says, the trappings of a pedant. He claims that he could be dropped into any Heidelberg café and find perfect camouflage among the assembled anarchists.

Sanders is an avid collector of Menckeniana and a devoted member of the Mencken Society. He began work on *Do You Remember?* after reading Philip Goodman's story of a Philadelphia childhood, *Franklin Street*, and seeking the remaining work of this great observer of human character. In this volume he presents what is, in effect, Goodman's second book and Mencken's most outrageous book of letters.

MARYLAND HISTORICAL SOCIETY
201 West Monument Street
Baltimore, Maryland 21201

ISBN 0-938420-54-2

A 87.1.a.ii, dust jacket

Notes: "The 'Do You Remember?' letters were intended as the starting point for what would have been a wonderfully witty book about the German and Jewish immigrants in America, but the book was never completed. As a first step toward the book, the correspondence that had kept Goodman and Mencken entertained for three years had been snipped into fragments. It was the wreck of a magnificent exchange, but I thought I had the foundation for repairing the stories and restoring to readability a touching part of American literary history" (p. x).

A 87.1.a.ii
Only printing, trade issue

Same as A 87.1.a.i except:

Statement of limitation: None.

[i–viii] . . . = 208 pp.

[1–2]^{16} [3]^8 [4–7]^{16} = 104 leaves.

Contents: p. i: half title;. . . .

Binding: No box.

Dust jacket: White paper. Front, on black field: '[black, in red box] The | Whimsical | Letters of | [below box] [white] H. L. Mencken | [gray] AND | [white] Philip Goodman | [red] Do You | Remember? | [gray] EDITED BY JACK SANDERS'. Spine, on black field: '[reading down] [gray] SANDERS [red] Do You Remember? | [horizontal, white] MARYLAND | HISTORICAL | SOCIETY'. Back: blurb, two excerpts, ISBN, bar code. Front flap: '$24.95 | [red] 0996 | [blurb]'. Rear flap: photograph and biography of Sanders, address of Society.

Publication: $24.95. 1,900 copies of this issue.

Locations: MChB, RJS (2 in dj).

AA. Collections

AA 1 PREJUDICES
1925

Title page: 'PREJUDICES | *By* | H. L. MENCKEN | [JC device] | JONATHAN
CAPE LIMITED | THIRTY BEDFORD SQUARE LONDON'

On copyright page: 'FIRST PUBLISHED IN MCMXXV'.

Contents: "Note" (by Mencken, dated 12 September 1925), "The Poet and His Art,"
"Footnote on Criticism," "Reflections on the Drama," "Toward a Realistic Æsthetic,"
"The Divine Afflatus," "Ad Imaginem Dei Creavit Illum" 1–5, "High and Ghostly
Matters" 1–6, "On a Tender Theme" 1–13, "Types of Men" 1–14, "The Genealogy of
Etiquette," "Scientific Examination of a Popular Virtue," "Exeunt Omnes," "Educa-
tion," "Das Kapital," "On Government," "Roosevelt," "Portrait of an Immortal Soul,"
"James Huneker: A Memory."

[1–4] 5–7 [8–10] 11–77 [78–80] 81–165 [166–68] 169–201 [202–04] 205–56. 7³⁄₁₆″
× 5¹³⁄₁₆″. In wrappers (not seen).

Publication: Date of publication and price unknown. 3,317 copies of this printing sold.

Location: EPL (recased).

Notes: Mencken's "Note" indicates that the essays are drawn from the first four series
of *Prejudices,* selected jointly by Cape and Mencken; some minor changes were made
to the text for the benefit of English readers. Adler 12, 13bot.

Other editions and printings: Second printing in hard cover in 1926 as *Selected
Prejudices.* On copyright page: 'FIRST PUBLISHED IN VARIOUS | VOLUMES
1922–1925 | REPRINTED IN THE TRAVELLERS' LIBRARY 1926'. Published
April 1926 (ECB 12.1037). Second printing as such 1926; third in 1927; fourth in
1928; fifth in 1930 as *Selected Prejudices: First Series*; another in 1937 (NUC). 5,101
copies of these printings sold.

AA 2 SELECTED PREJUDICES: SECOND SERIES
1927

Title page: 'SELECTED PREJUDICES | SECOND SERIES | by | H. L. MENCKEN | [device with satyr] | LONDON | JONATHAN CAPE 30 BEDFORD SQUARE'

On copyright page: 'FIRST PUBLISHED IN VARIOUS | VOLUMES 1922–1927 | REPRINTED IN THE TRAVELLERS' LIBRARY 1927'.

Contents: "Note" (by Mencken, dated 1927), "On Being an American," "Notes on the Human Species" 1–15 (from "On the Nature of Man," "Advice to Young Men," "From a Critic's Notebook," and "Miscellaneous Notes"), "The Hills of Zion," "The Old Subject" 1–6 (from "Rondo on an Ancient Theme," "The Blushful Mystery," and "Reflections on Human Monogamy"), "Women as Novelists" (from "The Novel"), "Observations on Government" 1–3 (from "Matters of State," "Four Moral Causes," and "Miscellaneous Notes"), "The Art Eternal" (from "Contributions to the Study of Vulgar Psychology"), "Four Men at Random" 1–4 (from "Four Makers of Tales," "Beethoven," "An Unheeded Law-Giver," and "Five Men at Random"), "Five Americans" 1–5 (from "Four Makers of Tales," "Five Men at Random," and "Jack London"), "Literary Notes" 1–2 (from "The Fringes of Lovely Letters"), "The American Novel," "The Critic as Artist" (from "From a Critic's Notebook"), "Painting and its Critics" (from "The Fringes of Lovely Letters"), "On Living in the Provinces" ("On Living in Baltimore"), "Zoos" (from *Damn*), "Three American Immortals" 1–3, "Portrait of an Ideal World," "Funeral March" ("Memorial Service"), "Suite Américane [sic]" 1–3. Catalogue with fifty-three titles.

[1–4] 5–7 [8–10] 11–223 [224–36]. 6¾" × 4⅝". Blue cloth stamped in gilt; dust jacket.

Publication: Published October 1927 (ECB 12.1037). 3s.6d. 5,528 copies of Cape printings sold.

Locations: EPL, GHT (2, dj), RJS.

Notes: Mencken's "Note" indicates that the essays were drawn from the first five series of *Prejudices,* with some changes in the text for the benefit of English readers. ("Zoos," as stated above, is from *Damn* [A 17].) Two inserted catalogues at end noted: six-leaf (46 titles published, 7 projected) and eight-leaf (53 titles). Adler 12, 13bot.

Other editions and printings: Later printings in 1932 (D), 1937 (NUC).

AA 3 SELECTED PREJUDICES
1927

Title page: [all within ornate borders inside green double rule box] 'SELECTED |
[green] PREJUDICES | BY | H. L. MENCKEN | [green Borzoi device in oval] |
MCMXXVII | *NEW YORK*•ALFRED•A•KNOPF'

On copyright page: 'COPYRIGHT 1927'.

Contents: "Note" (signed 'H. L. M.'), "High and Ghostly Matters" 1–7, "Bryan,"
"Conrad" (from "Four Makers of Tales"), "Beethoven," "Three American Immortals"
1–3, "The Husbandman," "The Politician," "Totentanz," "Birth Control" (from "Four
Moral Causes"), "Lovely Letters" 1–3 (from "The Fringes of Lovely Letters"), "Por-
trait of an Immortal Soul," "Types of Men" 1–15, "Memorial Service," "On Living in
Baltimore," "Catechism."

[i–x] 1–166. 7″ × 5″. Blue or green cloth stamped in gilt and black, front also blindstamped; dust jacket.

Publication: Published 2 September 1927. $2.50. Copyright #A999738. 2,400 copies
sold.

Locations: D (2), EPL, GHT (dj), InU-Li, LC (6 September 1927, rebound), RJS (dj).

Notes: Mencken's "Note" indicates that these were drawn from the first five series of
Prejudices, with some unimportant changes; and that the English collections with the
same title are not identical with this one. Adler 13; Andes 129.

Other editions and printings: Advance review copy in wrappers (dust jacket) reported
(D), also "advance copy for review with tag on endpaper" (Sotheby cat. 5184, item 485).
Reprinted from Knopf plates, New York: Modern Library, [1930]; on copyright page:
'*First Modern Library Edition* | 1930'; dust jacket. In print 1930–1935; later copy noted
without the indication on copyright page. Four varieties of binding observed on stated
first ML edition: blue, maroon, red, green (corresponding end papers green, brown,
orange, green). These were published simultaneously, according to Gordon B. Neavill.

AA 4 H. L. MENCKEN'S ESSAYS
1928

Title page: 'H. L. MENCKEN'S ESSAYS | SELECTED WITH NOTES | BY | Gen
Sakuma | Keibundo | Tokyo'

Copyright page: Blank.

Contents: "National Characters" (from "On the Nature of Man"), "Portrait of an Ideal
World," "Types of Men," "The American Literature" ("The American Novel"), "Re-

flections on Human Monogamy," "On Music-Lovers" (from "The Allied Arts"), "The Nature of Love" (from "Appendix on a Tender Theme"), "The Blushful Mystery," "English or American?" (from *The American Language*), "Footnote on Criticism," "Three American Immortals," "Education." See Notes.

[i–iv 1–3] 4–7 [8–9] 10 [11] 12–13 [14] 15–20 [21] 22–28 [29] 30–36 [37] 38–46 [47] 48–49 [50] 51–56 [57] 58–60 [61] 62–69 [70] 71–92 [93] 94–98 [99] 100–27 [128–30]. 7⅝₁₆″ × 4⅞″.

Publication: Published 25 March 1928 (p. [129], in Japanese). 1 yen.

Location: GHT (damaged and rebound).

Notes: Previously published (first four series of *Prejudices* [A 20, A 24, A 26, A 29]; third edition of *American Language* [A 19.3]); Adler 14.

Other editions and printings: Revised printing 5 April 1929; adds "The Nature of Art" (from "Toward a Realistic Aesthetic") and "On Living in Baltimore" (EPL). This was probably the copy examined by Adler, accounting for her date of 1929.

AA 5 THE VINTAGE MENCKEN
1955

Title page: 'THE VINTAGE | MENCKEN | [star] | GATHERED BY | ALISTAIR COOKE | [French rule] | VINTAGE BOOKS | NEW YORK | *1955*'

On copyright page: 'FIRST VINTAGE EDITION'.

Contents: "Introduction to the Universe," "The Baltimore of the Eighties," "Adventures of a Y.M.C.A. Lad," "Text for Newspaper Days" (from the preface to the book), "First Appearance in Print," "Recollections of Notable Cops," "Theodore Dreiser," "Gore in the Caribbees," "Pater Patriae," "Quid est Veritas" (from *Damn*), "The Art Eternal" (from "Contributions to the Study of Vulgar Psychology"), "The Skeptic" (from "Types of Men"), "The Incomparable Buzz-Saw" (from "Appendix on a Tender Theme"), "A Blind Spot," "Abraham Lincoln" (from "Five Men at Random"), "Lodge," "Cavia Cobaya" (from "Reflections on Human Monogamy"), "The National Letters," "Star-Spangled Men," "The Archangel Woodrow" (from "From the Memoirs of a Subject of the United States"), "The Libertine" (from *In Defense of Women*), "The Lure of Beauty" (from *In Defense of Women*), "The Good Man," "The Anglo-Saxon" (from "The American Tradition"), "Holy Writ," "Masters of Tone," "The Noble Experiment," "The Artist," "Chiropractic" (from "Dives into Quackery"), "The Hills of Zion," "In Memoriam: W. J. B.," "The Author at Work" (from "The Fringes of Lovely Letters"), "Valentino," "A Glance Ahead" (from *Notes on Democracy*), "The Libido for the Ugly" (from "Five Little Excursions"), "Travail," "A Good Man Gone Wrong," "The Comedian," "Mr. Justice Holmes," "The Calamity of Appomattox,"

"The New Architecture," "The Nomination of F. D. R." ("Allies Block Stampede"), "A Good Man in a Bad Trade," "Coolidge," "The Wallace Paranoia" ("Mencken Tastes the Cake"), "Mencken's Last Stand" ("Mencken Calls Tennis Order . . . "), "Sententiae," "Exeunt Omnes," "Epitaph." See Notes.

[i–iv] v–xiv [1–2] 3–240 [241–42]. 7¼" × 4¼". Red, black, white, and yellow wrappers.

Publication: Published 29 August 1955 (on copyright page of second printing: 'VINTAGE EDITION PUBLISHED SEPTEMBER 12, 1955'). 95¢. Copyright #A204293. 128,436 copies of Knopf printings sold.

Locations: GHT, InU-Li, LC (12 September 1955), RJS.

Notes: Vintage Book K-25. All but "The Nomination of F.D.R." (Baltimore *Evening Sun*, 1–2 July 1932), "The Wallace Paranoia" (ibid., 6 July 1948), and "Mencken's Last Stand" (ibid., 9 November 1948) appeared in Mencken's own books, including the *Chrestomathy* (A 61). Adler 18; Bulsterbaum 77.

Other editions and printings: Second printing October 1955; third in March 1956; fourth in July 1956; fifth in January 1958; sixth in August 1958; seventh in August 1959 (line repeated in printing history on copyright page); eighth in February 1961. At some point after the eighth, the printings are no longer stated. A later one has the indication 'D987654321' after the copyright notices. One later printing is bound in brown cloth stamped in gilt and black ('BUCKRAM | REINFORCED | V-25' on spine) (GHT, MB). Reprinted New York: Vintage Books, [1990], in larger format (8" × 5⅛") with different wrappers; on copyright page: 'Vintage Books Edition, March 1990 | . . . | . . . Originally published, | in hardcover, by Alfred A. Knopf, Inc., in 1955.' Later Vintage Books printings indicated by lowest of a row of numbers on copyright page. Latest noted is fourth printing; fifth due July 1996.

AA 6 PREJUDICES: A SELECTION
1958

Title page: 'H. L. MENCKEN | PREJUDICES | A SELECTION | [star] | MADE BY | JAMES T. FARRELL | AND WITH AN INTRODUCTION BY HIM | [French rule] | VINTAGE BOOKS | NEW YORK | 1958'

On copyright page: 'FIRST VINTAGE EDITION'.

Contents: (*First Series*) "Criticism of Criticism of Criticism," "George Ade," "The Genealogy of Etiquette," "The Ulster Polonius," "George Jean Nathan," "Three American Immortals," (*Second Series*) "Roosevelt: An Autopsy," "The Sahara of the Bozart," "The Cerebral Mime" (from "The Allied Arts"), "The Cult of Hope," (*Third Series*) "On Being an American," "Huneker: A Memory," "The Nature of Liberty,"

"Memorial Service," "The King" (from "Types of Men"), "The Dismal Science," "Patriotism" (from "Advice to Young Men"), "Virtue" (from "Suite Américaine"), (*Fourth Series*) "The Husbandman," "The Politician," "On Government," "The Capital of a Great Republic" (from "People and Things"), "Bilder aus Schöner Zeit" (from "People and Things"), (*Fifth Series*) "Conrad" (from "Four Makers of Tales"), "Lardner" (from "Four Makers of Tales"), "Heretics" (from "From the Files of a Book Reviewer"), "On Living in Baltimore," "The Champion" (from "Miscellaneous Notes"), "Definition" (from "Miscellaneous Notes"), (*Sixth Series*) "Journalism in America," "On Controversy" (from "The Human Mind"), "The Emperor of Wowsers" (from "Souvenirs of a Book Reviewer"), "Hymn to the Truth," "Chiropractic" (from "Dives into Quackery"), "The Executive Secretary."

[A–B i–iv] v–xx [1–2] 3–258 [259–66]. 7¼″ × 4¼″. Red, black, blue, and white wrappers. Copy noted in blue cloth stamped in gilt and green (D).

Publication: Published 17 January 1958. $1.25. Copyright #A324248. 70,622 copies of Knopf printings sold.

Locations: GHT, Harv, InU-Li, LC (24 January 1958), RJS.

Notes: Vintage Books K 58. Adler 19; Bulsterbaum 81.

Other editions and printings: Second printing June 1958. Later undated printings include Random House in the imprint. Reprinted Baltimore and London: Johns Hopkins University Press, [1996]; paperback.

AA 7 THE AMERICAN LANGUAGE ABRIDGED
1963

AA 7.1
American printings

Title page: 'ONE-VOLUME ABRIDGED EDITION | [French rule] | T H E | *American Language* | AN INQUIRY | INTO THE DEVELOPMENT OF ENGLISH | IN THE UNITED STATES | BY | H. L. Mencken | *The Fourth Edition and the Two Supplements, abridged, with | annotations and new material, by* | RAVEN I. McDAVID, JR. | *With the assistance of David W. Maurer* | [Borzoi device against barred background in rectangle within ornate frame] | NEW YORK • ALFRED•A•KNOPF | 1963'

On copyright page: 'FIRST ABRIDGED EDITION'.

[A–B i–v] vi–xvi [xvii] xviii–xix [xx–xxi] xxii–xxv [xxvi 1–3] 4–97 [98] 99–109 [110] 111–42 [143] 144–97 [198] 199–266 [267] 268–400 [401] 402–78 [479] 480–508 [509] 510–571 [572] 573–701 [702] 703–61 [762] 763–77 [778 i] ii–xcv [xcvi–vii] xcviii–cxxiv [cxxv–cxxx]. 9⅝₁₆″ × 6¼″. Green or maroon cloth stamped in gilt on front and spine, blindstamped on rear. Dust jacket blue or red with black and gold (both found on maroon binding); red, black, and gold one also on green binding. All dust jackets inspected have '11/63' on front flap.

Publication: Published 23 October 1963. $12.95. Copyright #A655858 (two copies received 4 November 1963). 22,600 hardback copies and 28,900 paperback copies of Knopf printings sold.

Locations: GHT (2 in dj), Harv, RJS (2 in dj).

Notes: Publication date of 11 November 1963 found on later printings. S1.4, 44; S2.6; Bulsterbaum 5.

Other editions and printings: Advance proofs, uncorrected, in two spiral bound volumes, no publication date. Copy reported with presentation card from editor taped in (D). Second printing January 1967; . . . ; fifth in December 1974; sixth in 1977; seventh in October 1979; eighth in 1985. Reprinted as paperback 25 March 1977. Second printing thus in June 1977; . . . ; sixth in July 1985; seventh in 1986 (OCLC); eighth in March 1989; ninth in August 1992; tenth in August 1995. Reader's Subscription main selection 1964 (in the red, black, and gold dust jacket, which lacks price?).

AA 7.2
English issue

Title page: 'ONE-VOLUME ABRIDGED EDITION | [French rule] | T H E | *American Language* | AN INQUIRY | INTO THE DEVELOPMENT OF ENGLISH | IN THE UNITED STATES | BY | H. L. Mencken | *The Fourth Edition and the Two Supplements, abridged, with | annotations and new material, by* | RAVEN I. McDAVID, Jr. | *With the assistance of David W. Maurer* | [RKP device] | LONDON | ROUTLEDGE & KEGAN PAUL | 1963'

On copyright page: 'Manufactured in the United States of | America. | FIRST ABRIDGED EDITION'.

[A–B i–v] vi–xvi [xvii] xviii–xix [xx–xxi] xxii–xxv [xxvi 1–3] 4–97 [98] 99–109 [110] 111–42 [143] 144–97 [198] 199–266 [267] 268–400 [401] 402–78 [479] 480–508 [509] 510–571 [572] 573–701 [702] 703–61 [762] 763–77 [778 i] ii–xcv [xcvi–vii] xcviii–cxxiv [cxxv–cxxx]. 9⅝₁₆″ × 6¼″. Red cloth stamped in gilt on front and spine; back clear. Dust jacket blue with black and gold, no date, price 90s.

Publication: Published 6 December 1963 (ECB 1963: 161). 90s.

Locations: BL (22 NOV 63), Bod (3 JAN 1964), Camb (3 JA | 1964), GHT (dj), NhD.

AA 8 THE AMERICAN SCENE
1965

Title page: 'H•L•MENCKEN | *The American Scene* | A READER | [rule] | SE-
LECTED AND EDITED, AND | WITH AN INTRODUCTION AND COMMEN-
TARY, BY | HUNTINGTON CAIRNS | [Borzoi device in rectangle] | *New York* :
Alfred•A•Knopf | 1965'

On copyright page: 'FIRST EDITION'.

Contents: "On Being an American," "The Husbandman," "The National Letters,"
"Theodore Dreiser," "The Sahara of the Bozart," "Criticism of Criticism of Crit-
icism," "Footnote on Criticism," "The Poet and His Art," "Professor Veblen," "The
Politician," "Imperial Purple," "In Memoriam: W.J.B.," "Last Words" (from *Notes on
Democracy*), "Journalism in America," "The Hills of Zion," "The Spell of Journalism"
(preface to *Newspaper Days*), "The American Language" (from *The American Lan-
guage,* fourth edition), "Hell and Its Outskirts," "The Vocabulary of the Drinking
Chamber," "The Nature and Origin of Religion" (from *Treatise on the Gods*), "The
Nature and Origin of Morality" (from *Treatise on Right and Wrong*), "James Feni-
more Cooper" (intro. to *The American Democrat*), "Mark Twain" ("The Burden of
Humor"), "James Gibbons Huneker" (intro. to *Essays by James Huneker*), "Ambrose
Bierce," "Beethoven," "Recollections of Notable Cops," "A Girl from Red Lion, P.A.,"
"Beaters of Breasts," "Letters" (10), "Christmas Story," "The Divine Afflatus," "Star-
Spangled Men," "Death: A Philosophical Discussion," "The Libertine" (from *In De-
fense of Women*), "Random Notes" (from *Minority Report*), "Gnomes" (from *A Little
Book in C Major*), "The Shrine of Mnemosyne" (from "People and Things"), "Three
American Immortals." See Notes.

[A–B i–iv] v–vi [vii–viii] ix–xxvii [xxviii 1–2] 3–49 [50–52] 53–210 [211–12] 213–35
[236–38] 239–71 [272–74] 275–341 [342–44] 345–93 [394–96] 397–428 [429–30]
431–60 [461–62] 463–87 [488–90] 491–542 [543–46]. 9⅝6″ × 6¼″. Blue cloth blindstamped front and back, gilt on spine; dust jacket.

Publication: Published 9 March 1965. $8.95. Copyright #A755471 (two copies re-
ceived 15 March 1965). 10,200 hardback copies and 12,744 paperback copies of
Knopf printings sold.

Locations: GHT (dj), Harv, InU-Li, RJS (dj).

Notes: The essays appeared previously in Mencken's books, with the exception of
"Hell and Its Outskirts" (*New Yorker,* 23 October 1948) and "The Vocabulary of the
Drinking Chamber" (ibid., 6 November 1948). S1.5; Bulsterbaum 84.

Other editions and printings: Advance proofs, uncorrected and unbound, tied, publication date April 1965. Review copy of first printing has slip laid in. Second printing

1969; . . . ; fourth in May 1977; fifth in February 1982. Recommended by Book-of-the-Month Club July 1965. Reprinted New York: Vintage Books, [May 1982]; paperback.

AA 9 SALVOS FROM THE SAGE OF BALTIMORE
1973

Contents: '[white showing through black] AN H. L. MENCKEN MISCELLANY | [rule] | SALVOS | [script] from the | [script] Sage of | [script] Baltimore | [black, white, and tan illustrated poster with six quotations from Mencken and, at lower right, in white showing through black:] [EP monogram] | This broadside has been published | by the Enoch Pratt Free Library | to honor Betty Adler . . . | . . . | . . . Enoch Pratt Free Library, | Baltimore, Maryland 21201. September, 1973 | [at bottom, in white showing through black] Copyrighted quotations reproduced with permission. . . . Design and illustrations by Jerry Litofsky.'

22″ × 17″ broadside.

Locations: RJS (2), TxU.

Notes: From various of his books and *Smart Set,* October 1919.

AA 10 ON BEING AN AMERICAN AND OTHER ESSAYS
1973

Title page: 'Kenkyusha Modern English Readers 7 | ON BEING AN AMERICAN | and Other Essays | by | H. L. Mencken | *Edited and Annotated by* | Shigehisa Narita | *Selected and Introduced by* | Cinna | KENKYUSHA'

On copyright page: 'This edition is first published in 1973 by Kenkyusha | Limited . . . Tokyo . . . '.

Contents: "On Being an American," "Huneker: A Memory," "Christmas Story," "The Hills of Zion," "The Nature of Liberty," "The Noble Experiment (an excerpt)," "Holy Writ," "Pater Patriae," "Abraham Lincoln" (from "Five Men at Random"), "Valentino." See Notes.

[i–ii] iii–viii [ix–x] 1–130 [131] 132–217 [218–22]. 7⅛″ × 4⅞″. Buff wrappers printed in black, enclosed in pictorial dust jacket (black and yellow on white).

Locations: GHT (dj), RJS (dj).

Notes: Notes in Japanese. "American," "Huneker," and "Liberty" from *Prejudices: A Selection* (AA 6); "Christmas" (allegedly; see A 57) and "Zion" from *Prejudices: Third Series* (A 26); the rest from *The Vintage Mencken* (AA 5). S2.8.

AA 11 THE MATING GAME AND HOW TO PLAY IT
1974

Title page: '[purplish red outlined in black] The | Mating | Game | [black] And How to Play It | Tips and Pointers | From the Collected Wisdom | Of H. L. Mencken | (Over Fifty Years a Bachelor!) | Edited by C. Merton Babcock | Illustrated by Charles Saxon | [crown] HALLMARK EDITIONS'

On copyright page: 'Copyright © 1974 by Hallmark Cards, Inc., Kansas City, Missouri.'

Contents: "The Hazards of the Game" (from "Appendix on a Tender Theme"), "Suing for Peace," "Hits and Misses," "Women Always Want to Change the Rules," "Game Points," "Male Strategy" ("Clinical Notes"), "Why Blondes Have More Fun," "The Art of Camouflage," "How Not to Catch a Man," "Waterloo," "How Men 'Pick a Winner'," "Is Woman Intelligent?," "Psychological Warfare," "Grand Slams," "Women: A Scouting Report," "The Libertine," "And the Game Goes On," "In the Trenches," "Playing Dirty," "How to be a Good Loser," "The Thinking Man's Guide to Marriage," "Uneasy Truce," "Fire and Cross Fire." See Notes.

[i–ii 1–4] 5–7 [8] 9–15 [16] 17–20 [21] 22–27 [28] 29–32 [33] 34–35 [36] 37–45 [46]. 7½″ × 4⁷⁄₁₆″. Light reddish purple paper-covered boards with streaks of white, black printing on front (white field) and spine; dust jacket.

Publication: Published 1 August 1974. $3.50. Copyright #A596330 (two copies received 23 December 1974).

Locations: GHT (dj), RJS (dj).

Notes: "Male Strategy" credited to *American Mercury,* May 1924; the rest to *A Mencken Chrestomathy* (A 61), *Prejudices: Second Series* (A 24), and *Prejudices: Fourth Series* (A 29), without citation. Some of these retitled excerpts were traced to *In Defense of Women* (A 18). S2.8.

AA 12 H. L. MENCKEN'S UN-NEGLECTED ANNIVERSARY
1980

Title page: 'H. L. MENCKEN'S | UN-NEGLECTED | ANNIVERSARY | By P. J. Wingate | Frontispiece by Nancy Sawin'

On copyright page: 'Published by THE HOLLY PRESS | P.O. Box 306, Hockessin | Delaware 19707 | 1980'.

Contents: "A Neglected Anniversary," "Melancholy Reflections," "Hymn to the Truth." See Notes.

[i–iii] iv–vi 7–21 [22] 23–37 [38] 39–51 [52] 53–61 [62] 63–73 [74–80]. 7″ × 4¹⁵⁄₁₆″.
Tan cloth stamped in gilt on front, spine, and back; dust jacket.

Publication: Published 1 February 1980. $6.00. Copyright #TX-430-408.

Locations: GHT (dj), LC (10 March 1980), RJS (dj).

Notes: On the "Bathtub Hoax." Previously published (New York *Evening Mail,* 28 December 1917; Chicago *Tribune,* 23 May and 25 July 1926; all in A 64); S2.14.

AA 13 A CHOICE OF DAYS
1980

Title page: '[all framed by rules on four sides, diamond ornaments in corners] | H. L. Mencken | [rule swelling to diamond in center] | [rule] | A CHOICE | OF DAYS | [rule] | *Essays from* | HAPPY DAYS, | NEWSPAPER DAYS, | *and* HEATHEN DAYS | *selected and with* | *an introduction by* | EDWARD L. GALLIGAN | [rule swelling to diamond in center] | Alfred A. Knopf • New York | *19* [Borzoi device] *80*'

On copyright page: 'First Edition'.

Contents: (From *Happy Days*) "Introduction to the Universe," "The Caves of Learning," "The Baltimore of the Eighties," "The Head of the House," "The Training of a Gangster," "Larval Stage of a Bookworm," "Strange Scenes and Far Places," (from *Newspaper Days*) "Allegro Con Brio," "Drill for a Rookie," "The Days of the Giants," "Recollections of Notable Cops," "A Girl from Red Lion, P.A.," "The Synthesis of News," "Fire Alarm," (from *Heathen Days*) "Adventures of a Y.M.C.A. Lad," "The Tone Art," "Gore in the Caribbees," "Romantic Intermezzo," "The Noble Experiment," "Vanishing Act."

[A–B i–iv] v–xxiii [xxiv 1–2] 3–129 [130–32] 133–247 [248–50] 251–337 [338–42]. 8⁵⁄₁₆″ × 5⅝″. Light gray cloth stamped in blue on front and spine; dust jacket.

Publication: Published 29 August 1980. $12.95. Copyright #TX-594-386 (officially received 1 December 1980). 8,200 hardback copies and 12,782 paperback copies of Knopf printings sold.

Locations: GHT (dj), LC (8 September 1980), RJS (dj).

Notes: On copyright page of second printing: 'Published September 12, 1980'. S2.9; Bulsterbaum 90.

Other editions and printings: Uncorrected galleys, unbound, publication date 12 September 1980. Review copy of first printing has slip laid in. Second printing October 1980; third in November 1980. Reprinted New York: Vintage Books, [September 1981]; paperback.

B. First Appearances in Books and Pamphlets

Works edited and/or introduced by Mencken, or containing other material (including interviews and words for songs) appearing in a book or pamphlet for the first time.

B 1 MONOGRAPH OF THE NEW BALTIMORE COURT HOUSE
1899

A MONOGRAPH OF THE NEW | BALTIMORE COURT HOUSE. | [City of Baltimore seal] | One of the Greatest Examples of | American Architecture, and the Foremost Court House of | the United States, Including an Historical Sketch of the Early Courts of Maryland. | 500 ILLUSTRATIONS.

On copyright page: [all in middle column] 'COPYRIGHT, 1899, | BY FRANK D. THOMAS, | BALTIMORE, MD. | [all within ornament on device] PRESS of | A. HOEN & C° [dot beneath o] | Balto. Md.' Thomas signed the 'PUBLISHER'S NOTICE' on the following page. 10¾″ × 14″. Multicolored cardboard covers with black cloth spine; front: [beneath allegorical figures presenting the building, in brown] 'SOU-VENIR OF THE | NEW COURT HOUSE | BALTIMORE.' "Frank [Thomas] paid me $25 for the job" (Mencken quoted in Adler). *Locations:* GHT, KU-S. Adler 20.

'OLD COURT HOUSES OF MARYLAND' (unsigned), pp. [9–28].

B 2 OUR FLAG SONG BOOK
1900

[cover title] Our Flag Song Book. | [ornamental border] | [flag] | [double rule] COM-PILED BY [double rule] | CHARLES P. CLEAVELAND, | [credentials and poem in sixteen lines] | [rule] |–FOR SALE BY–| H. M. Biden Co., Printers and Publishers, 112 W. Fayette Street, Baltimore.

6⅞″ × 4⅞″. Self wrappers. "I wrote this dreadful drivel in September, 1900" (inscrip-tion on EPL copy). If Mencken's date is correct, the poem predates his contributions to "Rhyme and Reason" in the Baltimore *Herald* (see Adler 40). Reprinted from the *Herald* in this Republican pamphlet for the election of 1900, but not among his clippings in the scrapbook "Prose and Verse . . . Baltimore Morning Herald 1900–1902" (EPL). *Location:* EPL. Not in Adler.

'ONE MAN BAND.' (unsigned poem), p. [3].

B 3 THAT'S HIS BUSINESS
1900

[head title] [within scroll that passes through loop] THAT'S HIS BUSINESS [heavy dot] |
Words by HENRY L. MENCKEN.   Music by | JULIAN K. SCHAEFER. | [text
follows] | COPYRIGHT, 1900   GEO. WILLIG & CO.

12¼″ × 10⅛″ (bound in a collection and probably trimmed). Sheet music. Published
in Baltimore, according to Adler. *Location:* EPL. Adler 339 (title wrong).

Lyrics to song.

B 4 LOUDON PARK CEMETERY COMPANY
1902

[gothic, capitals centered with respect to lower-case letters] Loudon Park Cemetery
Company | 1853 = 1902

Unsigned. Recto of back cover: 'WILLIAMS & WILKINS COMPANY | ART PRESS
| BALTIMORE, MD.' 6″ × 7¹¹⁄₁₆″. Gray wrappers printed in white (possibly silver;
6⅛″ × 7¹⁵⁄₁₆″). "I wrote this in 1902" inscribed on EPL copy. "I also, at various times,
did jobs for advertisers. I remember very well composing a pamphlet for the Loudon
Park Cemetery Company of Baltimore, setting forth the comforts of eternal life in its
cemetery with great eloquence. I also did pamphlets for a piano manufacturer, Stieff,
for a wholesale milk dealer, and for the United Fruit Company" ("Autobiographical
Notes 1925" [TS A29 (EPL)], p. 100). *Location:* EPL. Adler 4.

Photographs on rectos, text on versos, pp. [2–15].

B 5 ECHOES FROM THE HUB
[1902?]

[cover title, printed ornately in gold] ECHOES | FROM THE HUB

Unsigned (his signature is on the EPL copy). Date from Adler. Verso of back cover:
'E. B. READ & SON CO., PRS. | BALTIMORE.' 6³⁄₁₆″ × 4⅛″. Stiff white paper
wrappers. Also referred to as *A Word at the Start.* The text is comprised of testimo-
nials for the Stieff Piano Co.; see Mencken's comment at B 4. *Location:* EPL. Adler 4.

'A WORD AT THE START.' (preface), pp. [1]–2.

B 6 SIXTIETH ANNIVERSARY CHARLES M. STIEFF
1902

1842   1902 | [next two lines against rectangular box containing ornaments] Sixtieth [breaking through left rule] | Anniversary [breaking through right rule] | CHARLES M. STIEFF, | DARLEY PARK, ° BALTIMORE. | JUNE 2, 1902.

Unsigned (his signature is on the EPL copy). On p. [24]: 'E.B. READ & SON, PRS., BALTO.' 6¹¹⁄₁₆″ × 5″. Light yellow stiff paper wrappers, printed in gold on front: [within ornamental design] 'A RECORD | OF | THREE SCORE | YEARS | [outside design] 1842   1902'. The pamphlet is also referred to by this title. An advertising brochure for Stieff Pianos; see Mencken's comment at B 4. *Location:* EPL. Adler 4.

'HISTORY OF THE FIRM.', pp. [6–7].

B 7 STIEFF PIANOS
[1902?]

[within harp held by female figure] STIEFF | PIANOS

Unsigned (his signature is on the EPL copy). Date from Adler. Verso of back cover, in green: 'E. B. READ & SON CO., PRINTERS, BALTIMORE.' 6¾″ × 5¹⁄₁₆″. Stiff paper wrappers, light green outside, white inside. See Mencken's comment at B 4. *Location:* EPL. Adler 4.

Advertising text, pp. [2–3, 11–14]; illustrations and descriptions of pianos, pp. [4–10].

B 8 THE VAGABONDS
1905

[all in a box] FIRST ANNUAL REUNION | [short rule] | [gothic] The Vagabonds | [roman] NEW YEAR'S EVE | 1905 | HOTEL CASWELL | BALTIMORE, MD.

9⁷⁄₁₆″ × 6¼″. Off-white thick paper wrappers folded double; cover title: '[all in double-rule box] AUTOBIOGRAPHIES | AND SKETCH OF | THE VAGABONDS | *Esto Perpetua*'. *Location:* EPL. Adler 20 (uses cover title).

'HENRY LOUIS MENCKEN.' (autobiography), p. 16.

B 9 BY RAIL OR WATER
1908

"BY RAIL OR WATER." | [short rule] | Copyright, 1906, | By ARTHUR W. ROB-SON. | [short rule] | [*All rights reserved.*]

Title on p. [1]. 9″ × 5¹⁵⁄₁₆″. Black cloth with large white label on front printed in black and orange; cover title over illustration: 'BY RAIL OR | WATER | FACTS of | INTER-EST | to TRAVELERS | and IMPORTERS | EDITION 1908 | ARTHUR W. ROB-SON BALTIMORE, MD.' *Location:* EPL. Adler 20; Frey 47; West 190.

'SUMMER IN JAMAICA', pp. 125–26.

B 10 WHO'S WHO IN AMERICA
1908

WHO'S WHO | IN AMERICA | A BIOGRAPHICAL DICTIONARY OF NOTA-BLE LIVING | MEN AND WOMEN OF THE UNITED STATES | 1908–1909 | FOUNDED, 1899. FOUNDED AND EDITED BY | ALBERT NELSON MAR-QUIS | REVISED AND REISSUED BIENNIALLY | CHICAGO: A. N. MARQUIS & COMPANY | LONDON: KEGAN PAUL, TRENCH, TRUBNER & CO., LTD.

On copyright page: 'Copyright, 1908'. 7⁹⁄₁₆″ × 5¼″. Red cloth stamped in gilt and blindstamped. Mencken's first appearance in the series. *Location:* Harv. Not in Adler.

Biographical information presumably supplied by Mencken, pp. 1281–82.

B 11 BY RAIL OR WATER
1911

By RAIL OR WATER | PUBLISHED ANNUALLY | IN THE INTERESTS OF THE TRAVELING PUBLIC | By ARTHUR W. ROBSON | GENERAL STEAMSHIP AND RAILROAD PASSENGER AGENT | AND CUSTOM HOUSE BROKER | [five lines of Baltimore addresses and phone number] | [between double rules in three columns] ALL RIGHTS RESERVED | COPYRIGHT || PHOTOS AND NOTES OF TRAVEL FOR INSERTION | IN NEXT ISSUE GRATEFULLY ACKNOWL-EDGED || VOL. NO. 10 | 1911 EDITION

Title on p. 7; text fills remainder of page. 9″ × 6″. Buff wrappers printed in blue and yellow ochre. *Location:* JRS. Not in Adler.

'SAN SALVADOR, OR WATLING'S ISLAND', pp. 41–42.

B 12 ANNOUNCEMENT OF AWARDS
[1911?]

[everything, including cover, printed with spine side as top and fore edge as bottom] [head title] ANNOUNCEMENT *of AWARDS* | [double rule] | IN THE PRIZE CONTEST FOR REVIEWS OF | The Prodigal Judge | [text follows]

On p. 3: 'THE BOBBS-MERRILL | COMPANY'. 8½″ × 7½″. White wrappers printed in brown. The book is by Vaughn Kester (Indianapolis: Bobbs-Merrill, 1911). *Location:* EPL. Previously published (Baltimore *Evening Sun*, 14 March 1911); Adler 23; Frey 58.

'IN JACKSON'S DAY', pp. [11, 13].

B 13 BLANCHETTE AND THE ESCAPE
1913

BLANCHETTE AND THE | ESCAPE • TWO PLAYS BY | BRIEUX • WITH PREFACE | BY H. L. MENCKEN • TRANS- | LATED FROM THE FRENCH | BY FREDERICK EISEMANN | JOHN W. LUCE & COMPANY | BOSTON MCMXIII

The author was Eugène Brieux. Copyright page: '*Copyright, 1913* | *By L. E. Bassett*'. 7⁷⁄₁₆″ × 5³⁄₁₆″. Green cloth with white paper label on spine printed in black and either orange or yellow (black and red according to Frey). Price $1.25 (*Books*). *Locations:* GHT, InU-Li, MCR, RJS (2). Adler 23; Frey 48; Bulsterbaum 65.

'PREFACE', pp. i–xxxvi. Listed among the works edited by Mencken in Fanfare 30.

B 14 WHY I AM OPPOSED TO SOCIALISM
1913

Why I Am | Opposed to Socialism | [ornament] | Original Papers by | Leading Men and Women | [ornament] | EDWARD SILVIN | [ornament] | SACRAMENTO, CAL- IFORNIA | U. S. A.

On copyright page: 'Copyright, 1913'. 9⅛″ × 6¹⁄₁₆″. Brown wrappers printed in black, or green cloth stamped in gilt. (Cloth bindings, stamped on either front or spine, may be recasings.) *Locations:* EPL (cloth), GHT (wrappers), Harv (no covers), NhD (cloth). Adler 23; Frey 47.

Statement opposing socialism, pp. 6–7.

B 15 BALTIMORE
[1914?]

[cover title] BALTIMORE [M overlaps O] | [ten-line puff] | [city seal on a ribbon]

On recto of back wrapper: 'Munder-Thomsen Press'. 8⅛" × 5⅜". Wrappers comprised of stiff paper sheet folded twice, printed in black and yellow-orange. An invitation to the 2–6 February 1914 Convention of the National Canners' Association in Baltimore. *Location:* Yale. Previously published (*Smart Set,* May 1913); Adler 131 (*The Souvenir Program of the Baltimore Canned Goods Exchange*); S2.14, 16; Frey 58.

'*Good Old Baltimore* | (Mencken in the "Smart Set" for April)', pp. [3–7].

B 16 BY RAIL OR WATER
1914

BY RAIL OR WATER | PUBLISHED ANNUALLY | IN THE INTERESTS OF THE TRAVELING PUBLIC | BY ARTHUR W. ROBSON | [nine lines of Baltimore address and phone numbers] | [double rule] | [the rest in three columns] ALL RIGHTS RESERVED | COPYRIGHT 1914 || PHOTOS AND NOTES OF TRAVEL FOR INSERTION | IN NEXT ISSUE GRATEFULLY ACKNOWLEDGED || VOL. NO. 13 | 1914 EDITION

Title on p. 5; 'INTRODUCTION' follows. 9" × 6". (1) White wrappers (three staples front to back) printed in orange and maroon with pictorial front. *Location:* Yale. (2) Black cloth with large label, like wrapper, on front. *Location:* EPL. Adler 24 (misdated 1916); Frey 48; West 190.

'STRANGE, FAR-OFF PLACES', pp. 25–28.

B 17 1001 PLACES TO SELL MANUSCRIPTS
1915

[all in a box] "1001 PLACES TO SELL | MANUSCRIPTS" | Compiled by   WILLIAM R. KANE | [device] | THE AMERICAN WRITER'S | YEAR BOOK AND DIRECTORY | TO MARKETS FOR MANU- | SCRIPTS | Ridgewood - - New Jersey | THE EDITOR COMPANY

On copyright page: 'Copyright, 1915'. 8⅝" × 5¹¹⁄₁₆". Blue cloth stamped in yellow. *Location:* Harv. Not in Adler.

Statement concerning editorial policy of the *Smart Set,* p. 299.

B 18 ONE MAN
1915

ONE MAN | A NOVEL | BY | ROBERT STEELE | [MK device] | NEW YORK | MITCHELL KENNERLEY | MCMXV

Steele was the pen name of R. A. Lindsey. 7⁵⁄₁₆″ × 5″. Orange brown cloth stamped in gilt on front and spine, 'MK' ligature blindstamped on back. Two states of dust jacket: cream with black lettering, Kennerly imprint, one-sentence Mencken quotation on front and long blurb by him on front flap, price $1.50 on spine; ecru with black lettering, Argus Books imprint, 'Revisions Suggested and Title Furnished by H. L. Mencken,' price $3.00 on spine. *Locations:* GHT (2, both states of dj), RJS (first state of dj). Adler 344 (misdated 1913).

Edited by Mencken; dust jacket blurbs as above. See MLAE 378 and "Portrait of an Immortal Soul" (*Prejudices: First Series* [A 20]).

B 19 A NEW NOVEL BY JOSEPH CONRAD
1915

[head title] A New Novel by | JOSEPH CONRAD | *Author of "Chance," "Youth," "Lord Jim"* | [statue of headless winged Victory] | *"VICTORY"* | [text follows]

On p. [1], following blurbs: 'JUST OUT'. 6⁵⁄₁₆″ × 3¼″. Folio. Advertising brochure with price and address of Doubleday/Page. The book was published in 1915 (London: Methuen; New York: Doubleday-Page). Not from Mencken's review in *Smart Set,* April 1915. *Locations:* InU-Li, Yale. Previously published?; not in Adler.

Four-line quotation, p. [1]. "A tale indeed! I think it will do a lot for Conrad. . . ."

B 20 THEODORE DREISER: AMERICA'S FOREMOST NOVELIST
[1917?]

THEODORE DREISER | *America's Foremost Novelist* | [illustration: Dreiser's book-plate?] | NEW YORK: JOHN LANE COMPANY | LONDON: JOHN LANE, THE BODLEY HEAD

On p. 32 is an ad for *The Bulwark,* 'To be Published in the Spring, 1917.' 6⅝″ × 3¾″. Brown wrappers printed in gilt, and with gray-brown bust on ivory. Reprinted n. p.: Folcroft Library Editions, 1973 (omits Mencken review). *Locations:* GHT, MBU. Previously published (*Smart Set,* October 1916); not in Adler.

Excerpt from review of *A Hoosier Holiday* ("The Creed of a Novelist"), p. 24.

B 21 THE BLESSING OF BUSINESS
1918

[all in a double-rule box, outer rule thicker] *The* | *Blessing of Business* | [short double rule] | By E. W. HOWE | Author of "The Story of a Country Town," | "A Moonlight Boy," etc. | [short double rule] | Crane & Company, Publishers | Topeka, Kansas | 1918

6″ × 4½″. Gray paper-covered boards stamped in black. *Location:* Harv. Previously published?; Adler 24.

Quotation from unknown source serving as preface (p. [3]) and on p. 73. "Astounding hypocrisy is the chief symbol of our American life. . . ."

B 22 THE PROFESSION OF JOURNALISM
1918

THE PROFESSION OF | JOURNALISM | A Collection of Articles on Newspaper Editing | and Publishing, Taken from the | Atlantic Monthly | EDITED WITH AN INTRODUCTION | AND NOTES BY | WILLARD GROSVENOR BLEYER, PH.D. | *Author of "Newspaper Writing and Editing" and "Types of News* | *Writing"; Professor of Journalism in the* | *University of Wisconsin* | [device] | [gothic] The Atlantic Monthly Press | BOSTON

On copyright page: '*Copyright, 1918*'. 7⁷⁄₁₆″ × 5″. Maroon cloth blindstamped on front, stamped in gilt on spine. *Location:* MChB. Previously published (*Atlantic Monthly,* March 1914); Adler 132; S2.13; Frey 49.

'NEWSPAPER MORALS', pp. 52–67.

B 23 THE MASTER BUILDER, PILLARS OF SOCIETY,
HEDDA GABLER
1918

B 23.1
First edition (1918)

[all in double-rule box] THE MASTER BUILDER | PILLARS OF SOCIETY | HEDDA GABLER | [rule extending the width of the inner box] | By HENRIK IBSEN | [rule extending the width of the inner box] | INTRODUCTION BY H. L. MENCKEN | [rule extending the width of the inner box] | [Modern Library/BL device] | [rule extending the width of the inner box] | BONI AND LIVERIGHT, INC. | [rule extending the width of the inner box] | PUBLISHERS [two pyramids of three dots each] NEW YORK

On verso of title page is a thirty-five-title catalogue (dated September 1917 by Andes) ending with *Evolution in Modern Thought,* no copyright information. 6⁷⁄₁₆″ × 4⅛″. Leatherette binding stamped in gilt on front and spine (single rule on spine), marbled end papers matching color of covers: tan, brown, blue-green, or green. Dated 1917 by Andes, NUC, and OCLC, 1918 by Adler and by Mencken in Fanfare, in MLAE, and in his 1918 *Books.* Published spring 1918; in print 1918–37 (Gordon B. Neavill). Title page reset 1919; see Andes for differences in later printings. *Locations:* EPL, GHT (2), LC (14 July 1919, brown covers), RJS (2). Introduction previously published ("Ibsen: Journeyman Dramatist," *Dial* 63 [11 October 1917]: 323–26); reprinted in 1935 ML Giant *Eleven Plays.* Adler 24, 136; S1.6; Frey 48; Bulsterbaum 26, 65, 68; Fanfare 30; MLAE 292; Andes 100 (photo of title page), 102–03.

Edited and 'INTRODUCTION' (dated September 1917), pp. v–xii.

B 23.2
Second edition (ca. 1940)

A Doll's House | Ghosts | An Enemy of the People | The Master Builder | *by* | HENRIK IBSEN | [figure running to left with torch] | [rule] | THE MODERN LIBRARY • NEW YORK | [rule]

Copyright page: Random House imprint. Found in gray buckram stamped in green and gilt, 7″ × 4⅝″; and green stamped in black and gilt, 7″ × 4¹¹⁄₁₆″. Blumenthal binding with Kent end papers. New plates; in print until 1950; reprints include altered title and contents pages. 1948 dust jacket on GHT copy. A further revision (1950–57) replaced Mencken's introduction with one by Eric Bentley. *Locations:* GHT (dj), MBU, RJS. Not in Adler; Andes 101–02 ("1940's").

'INTRODUCTION', pp. vii–xiv.

B 24 A HOUSE OF POMEGRANATES
1918

BEN KUTCHER'S | Illustrated Edition of | A | HOUSE *of* POMEGRANATES | and the story of | THE NIGHTINGALE *and* THE ROSE | *By* OSCAR WILDE | with an introduction by | H. L. MENCKEN | [device] | NEW YORK | MOFFAT, YARD AND COMPANY | 1918

8⅜″ × 5⅞″. Brown paper-covered boards, yellow cloth spine, paper labels on front and spine. Second printing as *A House of Pomegranates* (New York: Dodd, Mead, 1925); reprinted 1926, 1928. *Locations:* GHT, RJS. Adler 24; Frey 49.

'PREFACE', pp. i–viii. Listed among the works edited by Mencken in Fanfare 30.

B 25 VENTURES IN COMMON SENSE
1919

[all within double-rule borders on left, single on right, both the length of the page] THE FREE LANCE BOOKS. II | EDITED WITH INTRODUCTIONS BY H. L. MENCKEN | [double rule from left side of page to right border, interrupting left vertical rules] | VENTURES | IN COMMON SENSE | By E. W. HOWE | [Borzoi device over bold rule] | [rule] | NEW YORK ALFRED • A • KNOPF MCMXIX | [rule]

7¼″ × 5″. Blue "Toyogami" paper-covered boards, black cloth spine with blue paper label (dated 1919). Two titles in catalogue on p. [2]. Second printing as Borzoi Pocket Book January 1924; reprinted October 1927. 1500 copies of Knopf printings sold. *Locations:* Harv, RJS (2). Adler 24; Frey 55; Bulsterbaum 66.

Edited and 'INTRODUCTION', pp. 7–29.

B 26 TWELVE MEN, BY THEODORE DREISER
[1919?]

TWELVE MEN | BY | THEODORE DREISER | [BL device] | [thirteen-line blurb] | BONI & LIVERIGHT | :-: :-: PUBLISHERS :-: :-: | 105 W. 40th ST., NEW YORK

6¼″ × 3⁵⁄₁₆″. Self wrappers. *Location:* EPL. Previously published (New York *Sun*, 13 April 1919); Adler 24; Frey 59.

Review ("H. L. Mencken Tells of Dreiser's New Book"), pp. 4–8.

B 27 THE AMERICAN LITERARY YEARBOOK
1919

THE | AMERICAN LITERARY | YEARBOOK | [rule] | A BIOGRAPHICAL AND BIBLIOGRAPHICAL DICTIONARY OF | LIVING NORTH AMERICAN AU-THORS; A RECORD | OF CONTEMPORARY LITERARY ACTIV- | ITY; AN AUTHOR'S MANUAL AND | STUDENTS' TEXT BOOK. | VOL. 1 | 1919 | EDITED BY | HAMILTON TRAUB | FOUNDED, 1918 | REVISED AND REISSUED AN-NUALLY | PAUL TRAUB, Publisher | HENNING, MINNESOTA

On copyright page: 'FIRST EDITION | Copyright, 1919'. 7¹¹⁄₁₆″ × 5¼″. White cloth stamped in black. Reprinted Detroit: Gale Research, 1968 (OCLC). *Location:* NhU. Not in Adler.

Editorial requirements of *Smart Set*, p. 271. Such material was "compiled from information sent in by the publishers and editors" (p. 269).

B 28 JURGEN AND THE CENSOR
1920

[all in a box] [red] JURGEN | [red] AND THE CENSOR | REPORT OF THE EMERGENCY COMMITTEE | ORGANIZED TO PROTEST AGAINST THE | SUPPRESSION OF JAMES BRANCH CABELL'S | JURGEN | [row of small vertical lines] | PRIVATELY PRINTED FOR THE EMERGENCY COMMITTEE | EDWARD HALE BIERSTADT   BARRETT H. CLARK   SIDNEY HOWARD | [row of small vertical lines] | *ONE THOUSAND NINE HUNDRED AND TWENTY* | NEW YORK

On p. [2]: 'FOUR HUNDRED AND FIFTY-EIGHT COPIES | OF JURGEN AND THE CENSOR HAVE | BEEN PRINTED AND NUMBERED, OF | WHICH FOUR HUNDRED AND | FORTY ARE FOR SALE. THIS | IS COPY NUMBER | [number stamped on line in blue]'. 9⁵⁄₁₆″ × 6″. Brown paper covering tan cloth front and back (outer corners exposed), paper label on spine printed in red and black. *Locations:* Harv, InU-Li, RJS. Adler 25; Frey 50.

Undated letter, pp. 53–54.

B 29 H. L. MENCKEN
1920

[thick-thin rule] | H. L. MENCKEN | [rule] | FANFARE | By Burton Rascoe | THE AMERICAN CRITIC | By Vincent O'Sullivan | BIBLIOGRAPHY | By F. C. Henderson | [Borzoi device in oval] | NEW YORK ALFRED • A • KNOPF 1920 | [rule]

Also referred to as *Fanfare*. The bibliography, by Mencken as "F. C. Henderson" (MLAE 320), is his first. First book appearance of the other two. 7¼″ × 4¾″. Rose wrappers. Reprinted (with two title pages) Folcroft, Pa.: Folcroft Press and Darby, Pa.: Darby Books, [1969]; Folcroft, Pa.: Folcroft Library Editions, 1973. *Locations:* EPL, RJS. Adler 1, 274; Frey 69; Bulsterbaum 99.

'BIBLIOGRAPHY', pp. 21–32.

B 30 YOUTH AND EGOLATRY
1920

[all within double-rule borders on left, single on right, both the length of the page] THE FREE LANCE BOOKS. I | EDITED WITH INTRODUCTIONS BY H. L. MENCKEN | [double rule from left side of page to right border, interrupting left vertical rules] | YOUTH | AND EGOLATRY | By PÍO BAROJA | TRANSLATED

FROM THE SPANISH | By JACOB S. FASSETT, Jr. | and FRANCES L. PHILLIPS | [Borzoi device in oval] | [rule] | NEW YORK ALFRED • A • KNOPF MCMXX | [rule]

On copyright page: 'COPYRIGHT, 1920'. 7¾6″ × 4¹⁵⁄₁₆″. Red "Toyogami" paper-covered boards, black cloth spine with red paper label (dated 1919). Four titles in catalogue on p. [2]. Copy noted with extra dust jacket of Argus Books, Chicago. 800 copies sold. *Locations:* GHT (dj), Harv, InU-Li, RJS (dj). Adler 25; Frey 55; Bulster-baum 66.

Edited and 'INTRODUCTION', pp. 11–20.

B 31 WE MODERNS
1920

[all within double-rule borders on left, single on right, both the length of the page] THE FREE LANCE BOOKS. IV | EDITED WITH INTRODUCTIONS BY H. L. MENCKEN | [double rule from left side of page to right border, interrupting left vertical rules] WE MODERNS: | ENIGMAS AND GUESSES | By EDWIN MUIR | [Borzoi device in oval] | [rule] | NEW YORK ALFRED • A • KNOPF MCMXX | [rule]

On copyright page: 'COPYRIGHT, 1920'. 7¾6″ × 5″. Green "Toyogami" paper-covered boards, black cloth spine with green paper label (dated 1920). Four titles in catalogue on p. [2]. First American edition of Muir's first book. *Locations:* GHT, Harv, InU-Li, RJS. Adler 26; Frey 56; Bulsterbaum 66.

Edited and 'INTRODUCTION', pp. 7–21.

B 32 THE ST. FRANCIS LOBBYIST
1920

The St. Francis Lobbyist | Edition de Luxe | Published at the Hotel St. Francis during the National Democratic Convention, | San Francisco, June 23 to July 6, 1920. | THOS. J. COLEMAN, Publisher

Foreword by Coleman. 13⅛″ × 9¹¹⁄₁₆″. Plain boards stamped in black on front, black cloth spine and corners. Mencken's first piece prefaces twelve bound numbers, 23 June to 3 August (Vol. I, nos. 1–12), published during the Democratic Convention. *Location:* MChB. Preface previously published (Baltimore *Evening Sun,* 21 July 1920); neither the book nor Mencken's second entry in Adler.

'SAN FRANCISCO: A MEMORY', p. [iv]; 'AT LAST! A MAN | WITH GOOD EYES!', no. 6 (29 June): 1.

B 33 THE ART OF JAMES BRANCH CABELL
1920

[all within double-rule box] THE ART OF | JAMES BRANCH CABELL | *By* | HUGH WALPOLE | WITH AN APPENDIX OF INDIVIDUAL | COMMENT UPON THE CABELL BOOKS | [device with Liberty Bell] | NEW YORK | ROBERT M. McBRIDE & CO. | 1920

7$\frac{7}{16}$" × 4$\frac{15}{16}$". Tan wrappers printed in brown. Copies noted with and without 'Compliments of the Book Fair | Marshall Field & Company | 1920' printed on front wrapper. Reprinted 1924; Folcroft, Pa.: Folcroft Press, 1969; [Folcroft, Pa.:] Folcroft Library Editions, 1974; Norwood, Pa.: Norwood Editions, 1978. Walpole's essay is reprinted in *James Branch Cabell Three Essays* (see A 35.1.c). *Locations:* AAP, GHT, RJS, InU-Li. Previously published (*Smart Set,* March 1919); not in Adler.

Review of *Beyond Life* ("Mainly Fiction–II"), pp. 18–19.

B 34 ON AMERICAN BOOKS
1920

ON AMERICAN BOOKS | *Edited by* | FRANCIS HACKETT | A symposium by five American critics | as printed in the London *Nation* | [Huebsch device] | NEW YORK | B. W. HUEBSCH, INC. | MCMXX

On wrapper: 'THE FREEMAN PAMPHLETS'. 7$\frac{3}{8}$" × 4$\frac{7}{8}$". Gray wrappers printed in black. Reprinted Folcroft, Pa.: Folcroft Press, [1969]. *Locations:* GHT, InU-Li, RJS. Previously published (*Nation* [London], 17 April 1920); Adler 138; Frey 50; Bulsterbaum 27.

'The Literary Capital of the United States', pp. 31–38.

B 35 THE BORZOI 1920
1920

THE BORZOI 1920 | *Being a sort of record* | *of five years' publishing* | [Borzoi device in oval] | *New York* | ALFRED·A·KNOPF | 1920

Foreword by Knopf, introduction by Maxim Gorky. *Presumed first printing:* On p. [ii]: 'OF THIS EDITION ONE HUNDRED COPIES | HAVE BEEN PRINTED ON SAN MARCO HAND- | MADE PAPER BY ALFRED A. KNOPF FOR HIS | FRIENDS. | THIS, NUMBER [number written in], IS FOR | [recipient's name written in] | CHRISTMAS, 1920'. Frontispiece portrait signed by Knopf. 7$\frac{5}{8}$" × 5$\frac{1}{2}$". Violet paper-covered boards flecked in black and with sparkles, vellum spine stamped in gilt. Paper label with recipient's name on front cover ($^{11}/_{16}''$ × $2^3/_8''$). *Locations:* EPL, GHT, InU-Li. *Presumed second printing:* Laid paper. $7^1/_4''$ × $4^{15}/_{16}''$. Pictorial boards in purple, black, and yellow, top edge dark gray. *Locations:* Harv, InU-Li, RJS. Adler 27; Frey 51; Bulsterbaum 66.

'WILLA CATHER', pp. 28–31.

B 36 PAINTED VEILS
[1920?]

[head title] *Printed for Private Circulation and sold only to Subscribers* | [green] Painted Veils | By JAMES GIBBONS HUNEKER | [double green rule] | [text follows]

The advertised book was published in 1920 (New York: Boni and Liveright). $8^1/_4''$ × $5^1/_2''$. Two-leaf brochure on brown paper. Form with New York address of Christian Gerhardt on p. [3]. The same reader's report by Mencken is quoted on the dust jacket of the 1928 reprint of *Painted Veils* by Liveright. *Location:* NhD. Not in Adler.

Quotation of what Mencken wrote on first reading the MS, p. [2]. "'Ishtar' is a sort of scherzo . . . no other American writing."

B 37 THE LINE OF LOVE
1921

B 37.1
First American printing (1921)

The | *Line of Love* | *Dizain des Mariages* | *By* | JAMES BRANCH CABELL | WITH AN INTRODUCTION BY | H. L. MENCKEN | [ornament] | [four lines of Latin poetry] | [ornament] | ROBERT M. McBRIDE & COMPANY | NEW YORK ------ 1921

$7^1/_2''$ × $5^1/_8''$. Brown cloth stamped in gilt. Second printing September 1923; third in August 1926. Reprinted Freeport, N.Y.: Books for Libraries Press, 1969; New York: AMS, 1970. *Locations:* Harv, InU-Li, RJS. Adler 27; Frey 51; Bulsterbaum 66.

'*Introduction*' (dated 1 October 1921), pp. vii–xiii.

B 37.2
First English printing (1929)

THE LINE OF LOVE | *Dizain des Mariages* | BY | JAMES BRANCH CABELL | WITH AN INTRODUCTION BY | H. L. MENCKEN | [four lines of Latin poetry] | LONDON | JOHN LANE THE BODLEY HEAD LIMITED

On copyright page: '*First Published in* 1929 | PRINTED IN GREAT BRITAIN FROM ELECTRO-PLATES'. Published February 1929 (ECB 12.258). 7⁵⁄₁₆″ × 4¾″. Blue cloth stamped in black, or black cloth stamped in yellow. One GHT copy stamped 'COLONIAL EDITION' on copyright page. *Locations:* BL, GHT (2), InU-Li, MBU.

'*Introduction*' (dated 1 October 1921), pp. vii–xiii.

B 38 TALES OF MEAN STREETS
1921

[all in double-rule box] TALES OF MEAN | STREETS | [rule extending the width of the inner box] | By ARTHUR MORRISON | [rule extending the width of the inner box] | PREFACE | By H. L. MENCKEN | [rule extending the width of the inner box] | [Modern Library/BL device] | [rule extending the width of the inner box] | BONI AND LIVERIGHT | [rule extending the width of the inner box] | PUBLISHERS [two triangles of three dots each] NEW YORK

On copyright page: '*Copyright, 1921*'. Fanfare (1920) dates it "(1920)," and Frey follows suit. The EPL copy is signed and dated 1921 by Mencken. Published fall 1921 (Gordon B. Neavill). 6½″ × 4⅛″. Deep green (top edge blue), green (top edge green or blue), or brown (top edge brown) leatherette stamped in gilt, double rules at top and bottom of spine, Brodsky end papers. Catalogue begins "Four years ago . . ." (p. [252]) and ends with three titles on p. [260]; includes titles up to ML no. 104, though this volume is no. 100. In print 1921–30; later printings differ in covers, end papers, catalogue, etc. Originally "projected by Philip Goodman, probably in 1918" (MLAE 293). *Locations:* EPL, GHT, RJS (3). Adler 27; Frey 50; Fanfare 31; Andes 135 (claims wrongly that p. [260] is blank).

Edited and 'PREFACE' (dated 1918), pp. vii–xi.

B 39 THE NIETZSCHE-WAGNER CORRESPONDENCE
1921

B 39.1
First American printing (1921)

THE NIETZSCHE-WAGNER | CORRESPONDENCE | EDITED BY | ELIZ-ABETH FOERSTER-NIETZSCHE | TRANSLATED BY | CAROLINE V. KERR | INTRODUCTION BY | H. L. MENCKEN | BONI and LIVERIGHT | PUBLISH-ERS NEW YORK

On copyright page: 'COPYRIGHT, 1921'. On p. [iii]: '*This edition is limited to 1500 num-* | *bered copies of which this volume is* | *No.. . . . . .* [number written in blue ink]'.

8¹⁄₁₆″ × 5⅜″. Brown cloth, paper label on spine. Reprinted New York: Liveright, [1949] (cloth), [1985] (paperback). *Locations:* GHT, Harv, RJS. Adler 27; Bulsterbaum 66.

'INTRODUCTION', pp. xi–xvii.

B 39.2
First English printing (1922)

THE NIETZSCHE-WAGNER | CORRESPONDENCE | EDITED BY | ELIZ-ABETH FOERSTER-NIETZSCHE | TRANSLATED BY | CAROLINE V. KERR | WITH AN INTRODUCTION BY | H. L. MENCKEN | [device] | LONDON : DUCKWORTH & CO. | 3, HENRIETTA STREET, COVENT GARDEN

On copyright page: '*First published in 1922* | PRINTED IN GREAT BRITAIN'. Published October 1922 (ECB 11.1107). No limitation notice. 9⅜″ × 6″. Red cloth, yellow spine label printed in black; spare label tipped in to back end paper. *Locations:* BL, GHT.

'INTRODUCTION', pp. xi–xvii.

B 40 DEMOCRACY AND THE WILL TO POWER
1921

[all within double-rule borders on left, single on right, both the length of the page] THE FREE LANCE BOOKS. V | EDITED WITH INTRODUCTIONS BY H. L. MENCKEN | [double rule from left side of page to right border, interrupting left vertical rules] | DEMOCRACY AND | THE WILL TO POWER | By JAMES N. WOOD | [Borzoi device in oval] | [rule] | NEW YORK ALFRED • A • KNOPF MCMXXI | [rule]

7¼″ × 5″. Light green "Toyogami" paper-covered boards, black cloth spine with light green paper label (dated 1921). Six titles in catalogue on p. [2]. Variant binding: green cloth stamped in black, blank on front, lettering on spine, Borzoi Books logo on back. *Locations:* GHT, Harv, RJS (2). Adler 27; Frey 56; Bulsterbaum 67.

Edited and '*INTRODUCTION*', pp. 7–17.

B 41 THE REVIEWER
1921

[head title] THE REVIEWER | A Monthly Magazine | Richmond, Va. | [short rule] | EDITORS | EMILY CLARK   HUNTER STAGG | MARY STREET   MARGA-RET FREEMAN | [text follows]

5‷₁₆″ × 6¼″. Folio. Announcement of continuation of the magazine as a monthly beginning 1 October 1921. *Location:* JRS. Previously published (*Smart Set,* August 1921); not in Adler.

Quotation from "The South Begins to Matter," p. [3]. Cf. Fred C. Hobson, Jr., *Serpent in Eden: H. L. Mencken and the South* (Chapel Hill: Univ. of North Carolina, [1974]), p. 39.

B 42 TWENTY-ONE LETTERS OF AMBROSE BIERCE
1922

B 42.1
First edition (1922)

Twenty-one Letters | of Ambrose Bierce | *Edited* | with a Note | *by* | SAMUEL LOVEMAN | GEORGE KIRK | Cleveland | 1922

Presumed first printing: On p. [iii]: 'This edition is limited to 50 copies on | Japan Vellum and 950 copies on An- | tique Paper. Of the edition on Japan | Vellum this is No. [number written in] | [signature of Samuel Loveman]'. 7″ × 5″. Light green paper-covered boards with white paper label on front printed in black. *Location:* Harv. *Presumed second printing:* On p. [iii]: 'This edition is limited to 50 copies on | Japan Vellum and 950 copies on An- | tique Paper. Of the edition on Antique | Paper this is No. [number written in]'. 7″ × 5″. Grayish-blue paper-covered boards with white paper label on front printed in black. *Locations:* GHT, RJS. Vincent Starrett, *Ambrose Bierce: A Bibliography* (Philadelphia: Centaur Book Shop, 1929), p. 81. Not in Adler.

Quotation from a 1913 Mencken letter, p. 30.

B 42.2
Second edition (1991)

[bar] | [number 21 in gray, extending to bottom of third line, behind first two letters of second line] letters of | Ambrose | Bierce | Edited by Samuel Loveman | Introduction by Donald R. Burleson | [device: cat over book] | Necronomicon Press | [bar]

On copyright page: 'First edition | July 1991'. 8½″ × 6⅞″. Yellow wrappers printed in black and gray. *Location:* GHT.

Quotation from a 1913 Mencken letter, p. 19.

B 43 CIVILIZATION IN THE UNITED STATES
1922

B 43.1
First American printing (1922)

CIVILIZATION IN THE | UNITED STATES | *AN INQUIRY BY THIRTY AMERI-CANS* | EDITED BY HAROLD E. STEARNS | [square HB device] | NEW YORK | HARCOURT, BRACE AND COMPANY | 1922

On copyright page: 'COPYRIGHT, 1922'. Later (?) published without date on title page (the date appears in Frey's transcription). 8⅝″ × 5¾″. Light blue cloth stamped in gilt and blindstamped. Reprinted St. Clair Shores, Mich.: Scholarly Press, 1970; Westport, Conn.: Greenwood, [1971]. *Locations:* EPL, GHT (no date on title page), Harv (2, rebound), Yale. Adler 27; Frey 51; Bulsterbaum 67.

'POLITICS', pp. 21–34, and bibliographical note, p. 532.

B 43.2
First English issue (1922)

CIVILIZATION | IN THE UNITED STATES | AN ENQUIRY BY THIRTY AMER-ICANS | EDITED BY HAROLD E. STEARNS | [JC device in circle] | JONATHAN CAPE | ELEVEN GOWER STREET, LONDON

The title leaf is a cancel. On copyright page: '*First published* 1922'. Published March 1922 (ECB 11.1447). 8¾″ × 5⅝″. Deep blue cloth stamped in gilt. *Locations:* BL (rebound), EPL.

'POLITICS', pp. 21–34, and bibliographical note, p. 532.

B 44 A BOOK ABOUT MYSELF
1922

[all within double-rule box] A BOOK ABOUT | MYSELF | THEODORE DREISER | BONI AND LIVERIGHT | PUBLISHERS   NEW YORK

On copyright page: 'COPYRIGHT, 1922'. 8⁷⁄₁₆″ × 5⅝″. Red vertically ribbed cloth stamped in gilt. For subsequent publishing history see Donald Pizer et al., *Theodore Dreiser: A Primary Bibliography and Reference Guide,* 2nd edn. (Boston: Hall, 1991), pp. 9–10. *Locations:* GHT, Harv, InU-Li, RJS. Not in Adler.

Edited by Mencken without acknowledgment. See MLAE 354–55.

B 45 POE'S GESAMMELTE WERKE
1922

EDGAR ALLAN POE | GESAMMELTE WERKE | HERAUSGEGEBEN VON | FRANZ BLEI

Last of six volumes. On p. [2]: 'SECHSTER BAND | [French rule] | MÜNCHEN / RÖSL & CIE. VERLAG | MDCCCCXXII'. On p. [3]: 'DIE GEDICHTE | UND AUFSÄTZE'. (1a) 8⅟₁₆″ × 5¼″. Glossy paper-covered boards, design in shades of purple, grayish green, black, and white; leather spine stamped in gilt and black. *Location:* NjMD. (1b) 8⅟₁₆″ × 5⁵⁄₁₆″. Black cloth stamped in gilt. *Location:* GHT. (2) Limited printing: fifty numbered copies of the six volumes on special paper and leather-bound (D); not seen. S1.6.

'DER KRITIKER POE' ('H. L. Mencken' at conclusion), pp. [5]–12.

B 46 THESE UNITED STATES
1923

[all within double-rule box, outer rule thicker] THESE | UNITED STATES | *A SYMPOSIUM* | Edited by | ERNEST GRUENING | *FIRST SERIES* | [B&L device] | BONI and LIVERIGHT | Publishers :: New York

On copyright page: '*Copyright, 1923*'. First printing dated April in subsequent printings. 8⅟₁₆″ × 5½″. Blue cloth blindstamped front and back, stamped in gilt on spine. Second printing January 1925; third March 1925; fourth June 1925. Reprinted Freeport, N.Y.: Books for Libraries, 1971. *Location:* Harv. Previously published (*Nation*, 3 May 1922); Adler 141; Frey 51; Bulsterbaum 28.

'MARYLAND | APEX OF NORMALCY', pp. 13–24.

B 47 THE BOOKMAN ANTHOLOGY
1923

THE | BOOKMAN ANTHOLOGY | OF ESSAYS | [*1923*] | EDITED BY | JOHN FARRAR | NEW [Doran device with rising sun] YORK | GEORGE H. DORAN COMPANY

On copyright page: 'COPYRIGHT, 1923'. 7½″ × 5⅟₁₆″. Red cloth blindstamped on front, stamped in gilt on spine. A reply to Hugh Walpole. *Locations:* GHT, Harv, RJS. Previously published (*The Bookman*, June 1922); Adler 141; Frey 52.

'MR. MENCKEN REPLIES', pp. 66–68.

B 48 UPTON SINCLAIR
1923

[cover title] [all within box] [first three lines within another box whose bottom line is broken in the middle; the rest in another box whose top line is the same] UPTON SINCLAIR | *Biographical and Critical* | *Opinions* | *From:* | [six lines of countries] | *Including :* | [thirteen lines of names]

The latest book advertised is from 1923. Gray-green wrappers. (1) $7\frac{1}{4}'' \times 4\frac{1}{2}''$. Recto of back wrapper blank. (2) $6\frac{7}{8}'' \times 4\frac{3}{16}''$. On recto of back wrapper: 'Proposition to Reprint | The Early Books of Upton Sinclair'. (He proposes to reprint them himself in the summer of 1923 if there is enough demand.) Reprinted 1931 ($6\frac{7}{8}'' \times 4\frac{1}{4}''$, gray-green wrappers); on top of p. 1: '[This pamphlet, first printed in 1923, is reprinted in | 1931 in response to continual demands from readers.]'. *Locations:* GHT, InU-Li (2), RJS (2), Yale (3). Not in Adler.

Four sentences from a letter of 14 October 1917, p. 11. Cf. Bode, *Letters* 76.

B 49 AMERICAN MERCURY AD
1924

[head title] THE | AMERICAN MERCURY | *A new monthly Review* | [text follows]

Text: 'EUGENE [E occupies two lines] O'NEILL's play, *All God's Chillun Got Wings*, appeared | [further on contents of 1924 issues, prices, address]'. $7'' \times 4\frac{7}{8}''$ sheet on *Mercury* green paper. *Locations:* D, GHT, RJS. Previously published (*The Nation*, 5 December 1923); not in Adler.

Quotation on verso from "H. L. Mencken, by Himself."

B 50 AMERICAN MERCURY, VOL. I, NO. 1
January 1924

No separate title page. On p. [ii]: 'TWO HUNDRED LARGE-PAPER COPIES | OF THIS FIRST ISSUE OF | THE AMERICAN MERCURY | HAVE BEEN SPE-CIALLY PRINTED AND BOUND | FOR FRIENDS OF | THE EDITORS AND PUBLISHERS | THIS IS NUMBER | [number penned in]'. $13'' \times 10''$. Red and black (Frey), orange and blue (GHT, RJS), deep blue and brown (JRS) Borzoi boards #21, vellum spine and corners, stamped in gilt, uncut. Laid in the JRS copy is a founder subscriber's certificate ($8\frac{7}{16}'' \times 10\frac{7}{8}''$), blue on pale blue paper, subscriber's name and number (no. 901 in this case) penned in, signed and dated by Alfred A. Knopf.

Locations: GHT, JRS, RJS. (Note: the regular printing of this first number, in wrappers, is found with spine lettering reading either up or down.) Frey 56; not in Adler.

Edited by Mencken and George Jean Nathan, with other contributions.

B 51 BEN SILBERT CATALOGUE
1924

[on wrapper] BEN SILBERT | "DE CHICAGO" | EXHIBITION OF | PAINTINGS AND | AQUARELLES | [ornament] | FEBRUARY THIRTEEN | TO MARCH NINE, 1924 | THE BALTIMORE | MUSEUM OF ART | MOUNT VERNON PLACE–101 W. MONUMENT ST. | 17–24–2 | CATALOGUE TEN CENTS

$7\frac{5}{8}'' \times 5\frac{1}{8}''$. Shiny coffee-colored wrappers ($8'' \times 5\frac{1}{4}''$). *Location:* AJG. Not in Adler.

Two-sentence forenote, p. [1].

B 52 A ROUND-TABLE IN POICTESME
1924

[orange] A Round—Table in | Poictesme | [black] A Symposium | Edited by | DON BREGENZER | and | SAMUEL LOVEMAN | [eight-line quotation credited to Anatole France] | Privately Printed | by Members of | [orange] THE COLOPHON CLUB | [black] CLEVELAND | 1924

On copyright page: 'Published March, 1924'. P. [v]: *'This Edition of A ROUND-TABLE IN POICTESME | consists of 774 numbered copies as follows: two hundred | and forty-eight copies on American Vellum, bound in | cloth, and five hundred and twenty-six copies on Rox- | burghe book paper and bound in cloth. This is | COPY NO.* _____ [number penned in red]'. *Presumed first printing:* $9'' \times 5\frac{7}{8}''$ (Vellum). The first 248. Brown cloth stamped in gilt. *Locations:* GHT, InU-Li, RJS. *Presumed second printing:* $8\frac{3}{16}'' \times 5\frac{3}{16}''$ (Roxburghe). Same binding as previous. Review copy, stamped in blue on title page between quotation and imprint: 'ADVANCE | [bar] | REVIEW | COPY'; also on limitation notice, where the bar covers '*COPY NO.* _____' (Harv). *Locations:* GHT, Harv, InU-Li, RJS. Adler 27; Frey 53.

'*The Style of Cabell*', pp. [113]–17.

B 53 A BIBLIOGRAPHY OF THE WRITINGS OF H. L. MENCKEN
1924

A Bibliography | of the Writings of | H. L. Mencken | By | Carroll Frey | With a Foreword by H. L. Mencken | [device: centaur] | PHILADELPHIA | THE CENTAUR BOOK SHOP | 1924

Presumed first printing: P. [1]: 'THIS IS NUMBER [ten small dashes forming a line, number written in red] OF THE LARGE | PAPER EDITION LIMITED TO EIGHTY-FIVE | COPIES SEVENTY-FIVE OF WHICH ARE FOR | SALE. | [signatures of Mencken and Frey]'. 9⁵⁄₁₆″ × 6¹⁄₁₆″. Laid paper. Black paper-covered boards, gilt paper label on front; black cloth spine with gilt paper label. Transparent spiderweb paper dust jacket. Uncorrected and unbound first state in three reported copies (D). A GHT copy is blank on p. 69 after Van Doren entry; p. 70 begins with description of Fanfare ("[a *double rule*] . . ."), down to "exhausted"; unsigned and unnumbered; see next printing. *Locations:* GHT (2, dj), RJS.

Presumed second printing: On p. [71]: 'THIS IS NUMBER [eight small dashes forming a line, number written in red] OF THREE HUN- | DRED NUMBERED COPIES | THE FOURTH OF THE CENTAUR BIBLIOG- | RAPHIES DONE BY THE BOOKFELLOWS AT | THE TORCH PRESS, CEDAR RAPIDS, IOWA, | PUBLISHED BY THE CENTAUR BOOKSHOP, | PHILADELPHIA'. 7⁹⁄₁₆″ × 4⅝″. Wove paper. Bound as above. Copy numbered R, with 'PRESENTATION COPY' embossed above it on the limitation page and on p. [73] (GHT). Copy blank on p. 69 after Van Doren entry; p. 70 begins with description of Fanfare ("[a *double rule*] . . ."), down to "exhausted"; unnumbered (GHT). Centaur Book Shop announcement (9 August 1924): ". . . owing to a major error in the text, discovered after binding, the publication of the bibliography . . . has been postponed until corrections can be made" (EPL). The error was corrected by a cancel for pp. 69–70, where the description of Fanfare begins on p. 69. *Locations:* GHT (3), InU-Li, MB, RJS.

Reprinted Folcroft, Pa.: Folcroft Press, 1969; Folcroft, Pa.: Folcroft Library Editions, 1976; Norwood, Pa.: Norwood Editions, 1977; Philadelphia: R. West, 1978 (all via OCLC and S2). Adler 1; S2.1; Bulsterbaum 99.

'FOREWORD' (dated 20 May 1924), pp. [3]–6.

B 54 H. L. MENCKEN
1924

LITTLE BLUE BOOK NO. 611 [the number extends from top of this line to bottom of next, which ends under 'NO.'] | Edited by E. Haldeman-Julius | H. L. Mencken | Isaac Goldberg | HALDEMAN-JULIUS COMPANY | GIRARD, KANSAS

On copyright page: 'Copyright, 1924'. Published 15 November 1924 (Johnson and Tanselle). 5″ × 3⅜″. Blue-gray wrappers printed in black. The work was previously published in *Life and Letters* 2.12 (August 1924, "H. L. Mencken Number"), ed. E. Haldeman-Julius (RJS; not in Adler). *Locations:* EPL, InU-Li, RJS (2). Adler 274; Frey 65, 68; Bulsterbaum 105; Richard C. Johnson and G. Thomas Tanselle in *PBSA* 64 (1970): 67; MLAE 408.

Introductory letter, p. [2].

B 55 THREE IMPORTANT OPINIONS
1925

[head title] *THREE IMPORTANT OPINIONS | ABOUT NEWSPAPERS AND | NEWSPAPER MEN |* [rule] | Published by the Department of Journalism of the University of Colo- | rado for the benefit of journalism students and Colorado newspaper men. | [rule] | JUNE, 1925 | [rule] | [text follows]

9″ × 6⅛″. Self wrappers. *Location:* Yale. Previously published (Chicago *Tribune*, 19 April 1925; here credited to the New York *World*, undated); Adler 28.

'*Mr. Mencken Reflects on Journalism*' ("Reflections on Journalism"), pp. [1]–3.

B 56 A BOOK ABOUT THEODORE DREISER
[1925?]

[all within rectangular box] A BOOK ABOUT | THEODORE | DREISER | AND HIS WORK

On wrapper: 'THEODORE | DREISER | [four dots] | [nine titles] | BONI & LIVERIGHT'. Last title in biographical note on p. [24] is *An American Tragedy* (1925). 6″ × 3³⁄₁₆″. Heavy brown paper wrappers printed in maroon and green. Reprinted [Folcroft, Pa.: Folcroft, 1973], without new title page. *Locations:* InU-Li, MBU. Previously published (Chicago *Sunday Tribune*, 15 March 1925); not in Adler.

'The Case of Dreiser', pp. [8–15].

B 57 THE MAN MENCKEN BROCHURE
1925

[on white field, within three ornamental borders, the middle one red] THE MAN | MENCKEN [rest of the page red]

9½″ × 6½″. Folio. Simon and Schuster brochure advertising Isaac Goldberg's book of that title (B 58). *Location:* EPL (2). Not in Adler.

Letter to Goldberg dated 28 July 1925, p. [4]. Cf. Forgue 280.

B 58 THE MAN MENCKEN
1925

[all within a triple-rule box, the middle rule blue] THE | MAN MENCKEN | [rule touching sides of inner box] | *A Biographical and Critical Survey* | [rule touching sides of inner box] | BY ISAAC GOLDBERG | [rule touching sides of inner box] | [the Mencken arms in a gothic arch contained within another, a blue strip between them except at bottom] | [rule touching sides of inner box] | ILLUSTRATED *and* DOCU-MENTED | [rule touching sides of inner box] | SIMON AND SCHUSTER | NEW YORK • 1925

On copyright page: 'PUBLISHED IN OCTOBER, 1925'. 8¹⁄₁₆″ × 5⁷⁄₁₆″. Blue cloth blindstamped on front and stamped in gilt on front and spine. Second printing November 1925. Reprinted New York: AMS, [1968]. *Locations:* GHT, MBU, RJS. Previously published (*Red Book,* February 1905; *Short Stories,* August 1900; Baltimore *Sunday Herald,* 1901); Adler 40, 128, 129, 274; C1.

'THE BEND IN THE TUBE', 'THE COOK'S VICTORY', 'Specimens of the | *Untold Tales* | Baltimore *Herald,* 1901', and poems from *Ventures into Verse* (A 1) and elsewhere (uncredited), pp. 85–86, 134–46, 303–10, 313–24, 325–39, 343–70.

B 59 AMERICAN SPEECH
1925

PM-ASp-95 | [the rest in a box] AMERICAN SPEECH | *A Journal Devoted to New-World English* | EDITED BY | LOUISE POUND, *University of Nebraska* | KEMP MALONE, *Johns Hopkins University* | ARTHUR G. KENNEDY, *Stanford University* | [typical contributors and contents in sixteen lines] | *ISSUED MONTHLY* | *FIRST ISSUE–OCTOBER, 1925* | [prices in four lines] | The Williams & Wilkins Company | Baltimore, Maryland

5½″ × 3½″. Folio. *Location:* EPL. Previously published (*American Mercury,* September 1925); not in Adler.

On news of this forthcoming journal, p. [3].

B 60 A PORTRAIT GALLERY OF AMERICAN EDITORS
1925

A | Portrait Gallery | OF AMERICAN EDITORS | BEING | A GROUP OF XLIII LIKENESSES | BY | DORIS ULMANN | WITH CRITICAL ESSAYS BY THE EDITORS | AND AN INTRODUCTION | BY | LOUIS EVAN SHIPMAN | [ornament] | NEW YORK | WILLIAM EDWIN RUDGE | 1925

P. [iii]: 'William Edwin Rudge *certifies that this copy of* | A PORTRAIT GALLERY OF AMERICAN EDITORS *by* Doris Ulmann | *is one of an edition of 375 copies, of which 350 only are for sale. The types, designed* | *and arranged by Frederic W. Goudy, have been set by Bertha M. Goudy at the Village* | *Press, Marlborough-on-Hudson, New York.* | *Presswork by William Edwin Rudge, Mt. Vernon, New York.* | [ornament] | *This is No.* _____ [number written in red]'. 15¾" × 11⁵⁄₁₆". Blue paper-covered boards stamped in gilt on front, tan cloth spine. Translucent paper dust jacket. In light blue paper-covered cardboard box with lift-off front with paper label on it. *Locations:* GHT, Harv. Adler 28.

Statement on magazines, pp. 108, 111; photo with blank verso, pp. 109–10.

B 61 GULLIVER'S TRAVELS
1925

[row of ten deep red ornaments] | [black] GULLIVER'S TRAVELS | [three dark red diamond-shaped ornaments] | [black] JONATHAN SWIFT | [three dark red diamond-shaped ornaments] | [black] *With an introduction* | *by* H. L. MENCKEN | [two diamond-shaped ornaments] | [dark red Borzoi device in oval] | [two black diamond-shaped ornaments] | ALFRED • A • KNOPF | *New York* • 1925 | [row of ten deep red ornaments]

P. [B]: 'THE FIRST EDITION OF THIS | BOOK CONSISTS OF THREE | THOUSAND NUMBERED COPIES | THIS IS NUMBER | [number penned in]'. (1) 8¼" × 5½". Red cloth stamped in gilt and blindstamped, top edge unstained and uncut. Signed by Mencken under limitation notice. Noted on free front end paper of Harv copy: "One of a few large paper copies signed by Mencken." *Location:* Harv (no. 2008). (2) 8⅛" × 5½". Bound as previous but top edge trimmed and gilt. *Locations:* EPL (no. 1259), GHT (no. 383), PB (no. 41), RJS (no. 667), TxU (Knopf's copy, not numbered). (3) 8" × 5⁷⁄₁₆". Green cloth stamped in yellow, all edges trimmed, top edge stained orange. *Location:* GHT (not numbered). Adler 28.

'INTRODUCTION', pp. v–vii.

B 62 THE BORZOI 1925
1925

[all within double-rule box framed by ornate border featuring Borzoi devices and two linked AK's at top, bottom, and sides] T H E | B O R Z O I | 1 9 2 5 | [Borzoi device in oval] | *Being a sort of record* | *of ten years of* | *publishing* | ALFRED • A • KNOPF | NEW YORK

On copyright page: '*Copyright,* 1925'. *Presumed first printing:* On p. [353]: '*Of the* B O R Z O I   1 9 2 5 | *there were printed in the month of December* | *five hundred copies on Borzoi all rag paper* | . . . | *The book was designed by Elmer Adler*'. Laid paper watermarked with Borzoi Books logo. Willa Cather's birth year hand-corrected from 1867 to 1876 on p. 246. 9⅛" × 5¹³⁄₁₆". (a) Borzoi boards design #7 (green and white), white cloth spine stamped in green. (b) Same binding but boards blue and white, spine stamped in blue. Some copies signed by Alfred, Blanche, and Samuel Knopf. Reported in slipcase (D). *Locations:* D (blue), GHT (blue), InU-Li (2 in blue), RJS (green), TxU (blue).

Presumed second printing: On p. [353]: '*Of the* B O R Z O I   1 9 2 5 | *there were printed in the month of December* | *five thousand copies on laid India tint paper* | . . . | *The book was designed by Elmer Adler*'. Laid paper without logo watermark. 7⁹⁄₁₆" × 5⅛". Borzoi boards design ##5 (violet or rose and tan) and 6 (purple and beige), black cloth spine stamped in gilt. *Two states:* Cather's birth year on p. 246 uncorrected, corrected by hand. *Locations:* GHT (2, #5 corr., #6 uncorr.), Harv (2 in #6 uncorr.), InU-Li (#5 uncorr.), RJS (3, #5 in both states, #6 uncorr.), TxU (#6 uncorr.).

Third printing: Same as second but Cather's birth year printed correctly. Borzoi boards design ##5, 6, and 22 (brown and light brown). *Locations:* GHT (#6), JRS (#5), RJS (#22).

Adler 28; S1.10; Bulsterbaum 67; Joan Crane, *Willa Cather: A Bibliography* (Lincoln and London: Univ. of Nebraska, [1982]), p. 312 (does not note uncorrected state and refers to the third printing as second state).

'MEMORANDUM', pp. 138–41.

B 63 A TRIBUTE TO A GREAT SEAFARER
[1925?]

[below portrait of Joseph Conrad and credit] A Tribute | to | A Great Seafarer

On p. [2] is a letter from Mrs. Conrad dated 25 May 1925. 8" × 5⁵⁄₁₆". Self wrappers; printed in brown. *Location:* EPL. Not in Adler.

Quotation from an undated letter supporting a memorial reading room at the Seamen's Church Institute of New York, p. [6].

B 64 HAROLD W. GAMMANS
[ca. 1925?]

Lectures & Lecture | Recitals | [photo] | HAROLD W. GAMMANS | Author of | "Common Men and Women", | "The Corner Store", Etc. | Recently Manager of | Community Theatre | of New London

6⅜″ × 3½″. Folio. The two books were published in 1917 and 1922; his next appeared in 1927. *Location:* Yale. Previously published (*Smart Set,* June 1918); not in Adler.

Quotation from "Hark, Hark, the Lark!," p. [2].

B 65 THE ENCYCLOPÆDIA BRITANNICA
1926

THE | ENCYCLOPÆDIA BRITANNICA | A DICTIONARY OF ARTS, | SCIENCES, LITERATURE | & GENERAL INFORMATION | [rule] | *The Three New Supplementary Volumes | constituting with the Volumes of the | Latest Standard Edition* | THE THIRTEENTH EDITION | [rule] | VOLUME I | AALAND ISLANDS *to* EYE | [rule] | *LONDON* | The Encyclopædia Britannica Company, Ltd. | *NEW YORK* | The Encyclopædia Britannica, Inc.

On copyright page: 'Copyright, in the United States of America, 1922, 1926'. The eleventh edition (1911) had twenty-nine volumes; the next had three "new volumes" (1922) which, with the eleventh, constituted the twelfth. 11½″ × 8⅝″. Dark brown leatherette stamped in gilt. Revised for the fourteenth (1929); reprinted through the 1957 edition. *Locations:* GHT, Harv (rebound). Adler 28 ("29:104–05"); Bulsterbaum 67.

'AMERICANISM', pp. 104–05.

B 66 MENCKEN IN BRONZE
1926

[head title] MENCKEN IN BRONZE | [rule] | [text follows]

Ad for the 1926 Annette Rosenshine bust of Mencken; at bottom: 'E. WEYHE • *Art Books in All Languages* • 794 LEXINGTON AVE., N. Y.' 12″ × 9¼″ glossy sheet printed on one side. *Locations:* NhD, Yale. Not in Adler.

Quotation of his congratulations from a letter. Cf. *Menckeniana* 37.8–10.

B 67 THE THEATRE OF GEORGE JEAN NATHAN
1926

[all within triple-rule box, outer rule bold] THE THEATRE OF | GEORGE JEAN NATHAN | [red rule] | CHAPTERS AND DOCUMENTS TOWARD A | HISTORY OF THE NEW AMERICAN DRAMA | [red rule] | *by Isaac Goldberg* | [red rule] | [red S&S device] | [red rule] | *New York* SIMON AND SCHUSTER *Mcmxxvi*

8″ × 5½″. Black vertically ribbed cloth stamped in gilt and blindstamped. Noted on free front end paper of a Harv copy: "One of ten copies signed by Goldberg and Nathan"; signatures on title page. *Locations:* GHT, Harv (2), JRS. *Suggestions* previously published (A 27); Adler 6 (s.v. *Suggestions*).

'SUGGESTIONS TO OUR VISITORS', letter, and scenario, pp. 71–73, 214–16.

B 68 STERLING
1926

[all framed ornately, mourning figures on left and right, row of books at bottom, portrait of Sterling at top above and overlapping an oblong box containing a double-rule box; within it:] STERLING | [Mencken's essay within double-rule box overlapped at top by previous box and at bottom by:] [within oblong box containing a double-rule box] SAN FRANCISCO: PRINTED BY | JOHN HENRY NASH FOR HIS FRIENDS | MDCCCCXXVI [all in brown except quoted printing, which is in black]

On p. [3] is a statement by Nash indicating that 300 copies were printed, three of them bound (for the club The Family, for Mencken, and for William Andrews Clark Jr.). (1) Six leaves (four outer leaves blank). 18¹⁵⁄₁₆″ × 12⁹⁄₁₆″. Marbled paper-covered boards, brown morocco spine and corners (19½″ × 13″); cover title in gilt within blindstamped box: 'TO | REMEMBER | GEORGE | STERLING'. *Location:* EPL. (2) Folio, unbound. 19¼″ × 12⅝″. *Locations:* EPL (2), Yale. Adler 14 (wrongly dated 1927); S2.40.

Essay by Mencken, p. [1].

B 69 MAJOR CONFLICTS
1926

[all in ornate purple frame] THE WORK *[sic]* OF | STEPHEN CRANE | *Edited by Wilson Follett* | •X• | MAJOR CONFLICTS | • GEORGE'S MOTHER • | • THE

BLUE HOTEL • MAGGIE • | *Introduction by* | H. L. MENCKEN | *New York* | ALFRED • A • KNOPF

Tenth of twelve volumes (1925–27). On copyright page: '*Copyright* 1896, 1899, 1926'. On p. [220]: '*designed and printed under supervision of Elmer Adler,* | *seven hundred and fifty numbered copies have been made* | . . . *Number* [number written in]'. 7½″ × 5¼″. White cloth-covered boards, black and gold cloth label on front, black cloth spine stamped in gilt. Individual volumes boxed, uncut. *Locations:* GHT, Harv (2), InU-Li. Ames W. Williams and Vincent Starrett, *Stephen Crane: A Bibliography* (1948; New York: Burt Franklin, [1970]), p. 63; Adler 29.

'Introduction' (dated September 1926), pp. ix–xiii.

B 70 THE BEST HUMOR OF 1925
1926

[all within double-rule box, outer rule thicker] The | Best Humor | *of* 1925 | *Edited* | *by* | Nathan Haskell Dole | *and* Harold S. Dole | [Stratford device] | 1926 | THE STRATFORD COMPANY, *Publishers* | BOSTON, MASSACHUSETTS

7³⁄₁₆″ × 4⅞″. Yellow-orange cloth stamped in black. Reprints some items not in *Americana 1925* or *1926* (A 30, A 32). *Location:* RJS. Previously published (*American Mercury,* 1925); not in Adler.

'Americana° | *By* H. L. MENCKEN *and* G. J. NATHAN | *From the American Mercury*', pp. 71–78. The asterisk points to copyright credit in a note.

B 71 READINGS FROM THE AMERICAN MERCURY
1926

[rule] | READINGS FROM | THE AMERICAN MERCURY | [rule] | *Edited by* | GRANT C. KNIGHT | *Associate Professor of English, University of Kentucky* | [Borzoi device in oval] | NEW YORK ALFRED•A•KNOPF MCMXXVI

7⁵⁄₁₆″ × 5″. Blue cloth blindstamped and stamped in gilt. Ad for the *AM* laid in (D); ad for the book laid in (RJS). *Locations:* GHT, JRS, RJS. Previously published (*American Mercury,* October 1924, March 1925, April 1925, July 1924); not in Adler.

'EDITORIAL', 'WHAT IS STYLE?' (review of W. C. Brownell, *The Genius of Style*), 'ARROWSMITH' (review), and 'HOW TO WRITE SHORT STORIES' ("Ring W. Lardner"), pp. 19–29, 127–38.

B 72 CURRENT REVIEWS
1926

CURRENT REVIEWS | *EDITED BY* | LEWIS WORTHINGTON SMITH | PRO-
FESSOR OF ENGLISH AND COMPARATIVE LITERATURE, | DRAKE UNI-
VERSITY | Author of "The Sky Line in English Literature," etc. | [Holt device with
owl] | NEW YORK | HENRY HOLT AND COMPANY

On copyright page: 'COPYRIGHT, 1926'. 7⅜" × 4⅞". Blue-gray cloth, blue-green
paper label printed in black on spine. *Locations:* GHT, Harv, RJS. Previously published (*Smart Set*, December 1922; *Atlantic*, November 1925); Adler 184, 204.

Reviews of *The Bright Shawl*, by Joseph Hergesheimer ("The Monthly Feuilleton–I–
Cuba in Stained Glass"), and *Indians of the Enchanted Desert*, by Leo Crane, pp.
189–91, 358–59.

B 73 THREE YEARS
1927

THREE YEARS | 1924 to 1927 | *The Story of a New Idea* | *And Its Succesful Adapta-
tion* | With a Postscript by | H. L. MENCKEN | [AM device] | NEW YORK | THE
AMERICAN MERCURY | MCMXXVII

On p. [ii]: '*Six hundred Copies of Three Years have been printed* | *by The Plimpton
Press from Poliphilus type on Utopian* | *Laid paper in January, 1927, and each copy
signed by the* | *Editor and publisher of the American Mercury.* | *This is Number*_____
[number penned in purple, signatures of Mencken and Alfred A. Knopf below]'. 9⅞"
× 6¹⁵⁄₁₆". Borzoi boards designs ##9 (green on beige) or 10 (shades of green), green
cloth spine stamped in gilt. *Locations:* GHT, RJS. Adler 29.

'*POSTSCRIPT BY H. L. MENCKEN*', pp. 33–36.

B 74 MIND YOUR P'S AND Q'S
1927

MIND YOUR | *p's* and *q's* [p and q large] | A useful and entertaining book | which puts
graphology entirely | in the hands of the layman and | enables him to analyze any |
handwriting whatsoever without | study or knowledge of the subject | BY | JEROME
S. MEYER | [S&S device] | SIMON AND SCHUSTER

On copyright page: 'Copyright, 1927'. Published September 1927. 10¼" × 7¾". Blue
cloth, white paper labels printed in black on front and spine. Later printings: September 1927, October 1927, January 1928, March 1928. Seventh (revised) printing: *How*

to Read Character From Handwriting (Mind Your P's and Q's) (New York: Blue Ribbon Books, 1931). *Locations:* NjHM, Yale. Adler 347.

Handwritten passage (4 Kings 2:23–24), p. 116. Analysis on pp. 117–18.

B 75 MORROW'S ALMANACK FOR 1928
1927

[all in antique typography, all rules irregular, within a box inside a double-rule box bordered by diamond-shaped ornaments] MORROW'S | ALMANACK | for the Year of Our Lord | 1928 | [three lines on the year] | [rule] | [seven lines on the contents] | [rule] | BURTON RASCOE, *Philom.* | [rule] | NEW [Morrow device] YORK | *Published by* WILLIAM MORROW & COMPANY | [three lines on the publisher]

On copyright page: '*Copyright,* 1927'. *Presumed first issue:* P. [A]: '[Rascoe's signature above wavy line] | *This edition of* Morrow's ALMANACK *for* 1928 | *is limited to 500 autographed copies,* | *Numbers 1 to 365 being for* | *sale. This copy is* | *Number* [number penned in]'. 8″ × 5″. Light violet paper-covered boards printed in black, tan cloth spine stamped in gilt. Boxed. *Location:* GHT. *Presumed second issue:* 8⅛″ × 5⅛″. White paper-covered boards printed in black and orange on front, white cloth spine stamped in gilt. *Locations:* GHT, Harv, RJS (2). Adler 29.

'FROM THE JOURNAL OF A VOY- | AGE TO HOBOKEN, N. J.', p. 89.

B 76 ANTHONY COMSTOCK
1927

No title page. On p. [1]: '[in simulated handwriting] Finish this story | for yourself | [beginning of first chapter, in type]'. 8⁷⁄₁₆″ × 5½″. Folio. Advertises *Anthony Comstock: Roundsman of the Lord,* by Margaret Leech and Heywood Broun (New York: Boni, 1927). On p. [4]: 'Out March 3rd.' *Location:* TxU (2). Previously published (New York *Herald Tribune Books,* 6 March 1927); not in Adler.

'THE EMPEROR OF WOWSERS | Extracts from an article in the Herald-Tribune', p. [4].

B 77 DREISER ACCORDING TO
1927

[all within triple-rule box] DREISER | *according to* | [vertical rule] | THOMAS BURKE | ARNOLD BENNETT | T. P. O'CONNOR | SARAH GERTRUDE MIL-

LIN | CARL VAN DOREN | EDWIN MUIR | H. L. MENCKEN | AND | GERALD
GOULD | [outside box] *No. 5 of "Critics and Constable Books"*

Among the titles listed is *The Financier,* "just published" by Constable (1927). Evidently a 5½" × 16½" sheet folded three times to make eight "pages." *Location:* EPL
(bound in a book). Previously published?; not in Adler.

'THEODORE DREISER | according to | H. L. MENCKEN', p. [8]. "Dreiser's defect
as a novelist lies in his lack of superficial charm. . . ."

B 78 OLD SOX ON TRUMPETING
[1927?]

Untitled two-leaf pamphlet on green paper advertising *Old Sox on Trumpeting,* by
E. T. Gundlach [Chicago: Consolidated Book Publishers, 1927; second and third
"editions" in 1928]. First page has photographs and quotations from Roger W. Babson, Mencken, and William Wrigley. 6¼" × 3⅛". *Location:* EPL. Previously published (*American Mercury*); not in Adler.

Quotation on Gundlach from a review, p. [1].

B 79 ERNEST BOYD
1927

[all within double-rule box] ERNEST BOYD | *CRITIC—ESSAYIST - SCHOLAR* |
[photo of Boyd and credit] | *LECTURE SUBJECTS:* | [four subjects on five lines] |
[outside box] Exclusive Management–EMMERICH LECTURE BUREAU, 1480
Broadway, New York City

The last work of Boyd's noted is *Literary Blasphemies* (New York and London: Harper, 1927), and two paragraphs from Mencken's essay are used as a blurb on the rear
of the dust jacket of that book. 11" × 8" brochure, glossy paper. *Locations:* EPL, RJS.
Mencken's essay not from any of his six *Smart Set* or *American Mercury* reviews of
Boyd. Not in Adler.

'ERNEST BOYD', p. [2].

B 79A BALLYHOO
1927

[all within quadruple-rule box] BALLYHOO | THE VOICE OF THE PRESS | BY |
SILAS BENT | [ornament] | ILLUSTRATED | [B&L device] | NEW YORK | BONI
AND LIVERIGHT | 1927

8″ × 5½″. Black cloth stamped in red. *Locations*: GHT, Harv. Previously published (*Smart Set,* April 1920); not in Adler.

Quotation on the average American newspaper (from "On Journalism"), p. 321.

B 80 VANDOVER AND THE BRUTE
1928

[orange] VANDOVER | AND THE BRUTE | [black] BY | [orange] FRANK NORRIS | [black] WITH AN INTRODUCTION BY | H. L. MENCKEN | VOLUME V | [nautical device with letters DD] | 1928 | [orange] DOUBLEDAY, DORAN & COM-PANY, INC. | [black] GARDEN CITY, NEW YORK

Fifth of ten volumes. 'FOREWORD' by Charles G. Norris. 8⁹⁄₁₆″ × 5¾″. Parchment over orange paper over parchment-covered boards, the orange showing as a thin strip near the spine on front and back covers and at corners; stamped in gilt. On p. [i]: 'THE ARGONAUT MANUSCRIPT LIMITED | EDITION OF FRANK NORRIS'S | WORKS'. Statement of limitation (245 sets) in first volume only. Reprinted 1929 from same plates, 1928 remaining on title page; 8⁹⁄₁₆″ × 5¹¹⁄₁₆″; black cloth stamped in gilt; on spine of dust jacket: 'THE COMPLETE | EDITION OF | FRANK NORRIS' (GHT [dj], Harv). Third printing Port Washington, N.Y.: Kennikat, 1967. *Location:* MWelC. Joseph R. McElrath, Jr., *Frank Norris: A Descriptive Bibliography* (Pittsburgh: University of Pittsburgh Press, 1992), pp. 190–92. Not in Adler.

'INTRODUCTION', pp. ix–x.

B 81 A NÖK VÉDELMÉBEN!
1928

[all within green double-rule box set in foliage design of white showing through green] MENCKEN | A NÖK | VÉDEL- | MÉBEN! | FORDITOTTA | Dʳ FEKETE | OSZKÁR | BEVEZETTE | Dʳ JUHÁSZ | ANDOR | RÉVAI KIADÁS

Translation of *In Defense of Women* (A 18). Juhász's preface dated 31 January 1928; Mencken's Hungarian foreword ends 'Baltimore, 1928. tavaszán [Spring]. | [facsimile signature]'. Series: Kötet Világ Könyv Tár 49. (1) 6½″ × 4⅜″. Wrappers printed in black. (2) 6⅛″ × 4⅛″. Gray cloth stamped in green. *Location:* EPL (2, both signed and dated 1928 by Mencken). Adler 9.

'H. L. MENCKEN | elöszava | a magyar kiadáshoz.' (foreword to the Hungarian edition), pp. 1–2.

B 82 MY VIEW OF COMPANIONATE MARRIAGE
[1928?]

[head title, all within box] "MY VIEW OF | COMPANIONATE MARRIAGE" | Pro and Con Discussion of the Biggest | Social Problem Now Before the Public | By 12 FAMOUS THINKERS | [text follows]

17¼" × 22¼" sheet, printed on both sides. Published by the Philadelphia *Public Ledger,* probably to promote advertising, in advance of the series' appearance in the paper. Mencken's contribution was separately published at that time (see E 28). *Location:* D. Not in Adler.

'*My View of* | *COMPANIONATE MARRIAGE* | [rule] | *As Told to Hannah Stein* | *By H. L. MENCKEN*', on first two columns of verso.

B 83 THE ENCYCLOPEDIA AMERICANA
1929

[all within box inside ornate frame] THE | ENCYCLOPEDIA | AMERICANA | [next five lines within oval frame entwined with three leaves] *A* | *LIBRARY* | *of* | *UNIVERSAL* | *KNOWLEDGE* | *IN THIRTY VOLUMES* | 1929 | AMERICANA CORPORATION | NEW YORK CHICAGO

Volume 1. 9¹⁵⁄₁₆" × 6⅞". Dark blue cloth blindstamped front and back, gilt on spine, edges marbled. The article was supposedly in subsequent editions to at least 1961. *Location:* MB. Adler 29 (wrong pagination).

'Americanisms', pp. 522–25. Unsigned and uncredited; attribution from Adler. The bibliography for the article cites among its authorities the 1921 (2nd) and not the 1923 (3rd) edition of Mencken's *The American Language.*

B 84 ON PARADE
1929

[resembling block printing] ON PARADE | CARICATURES by | EVA HERRMANN | [five marching figures] | EDITED BY ERICH POSSELT | CONTRIBUTIONS | BY PROMINENT AUTHORS | 1929 | COWARD-McCANN NEW YORK

9⁹⁄₁₆" × 7". Green paper-covered boards printed in black and blue, black cloth spine stamped in gilt. *Locations:* GHT, Harv, RJS. Adler 29.

Contribution, p. 106; her caricature, p. 107; bibliography, p. 109.

B 85 FRANCES NEWMAN'S LETTERS
1929

FRANCES NEWMAN'S | LETTERS | *Edited by* | HANSELL BAUGH | *With a* | *Prefatory Note* | *by James Branch Cabell* | NEW YORK | HORACE LIVERIGHT : 1929

8⅛" × 5½". Purple cloth front and back, dark red cloth spine stamped in gilt. *Locations:* GHT (dj), MB, RJS. Blurb previously published (F 14); Adler 273; Bulsterbaum 93.

Blurb on back of dust jacket and five letters, pp. 64, 65, 82, 84.

B 86 ESSAYS BY JAMES HUNEKER
1929

B 86.1
First American printing (1929)

ESSAYS BY | JAMES HUNEKER | SELECTED WITH AN INTRODUCTION | BY | H. L. MENCKEN | [circular ornament: man on steeple with telescope, letters JGH] | NEW YORK | CHARLES SCRIBNER'S SONS | 1929

8¾" × 6". Green cloth stamped in gilt. Reprinted [New York: AMS, 1976]. *Locations:* GHT, InU-Li, MCR, RJS (2). Adler 29; S2.12; Bulsterbaum 68.

Edited and 'INTRODUCTION', pp. ix–xxiii.

B 86.2
First English issue (1930)

ESSAYS BY | JAMES HUNEKER | SELECTED WITH AN INTRODUCTION | BY | H. L. MENCKEN | [circular ornament: man on steeple with telescope, letters JGH] | LONDON | T. WERNER LAURIE | 1930

The title leaf is a cancel. On copyright page: 'Printed by The Scribner Press | New York, U.S.A.' Published August 1930 (ECB 12.780). 8¹¹⁄₁₆" × 5⅞". Same binding as American printing ('SCRIBNERS' on spine) but different dust jacket. *Locations:* BL, GHT (dj), Harv. Adler 29.

Edited and 'INTRODUCTION', pp. ix–xxiii.

B 87 LIFE AND LETTERS OF HENRY WILLIAM THOMAS
1929

Life and Letters | of | Henry William Thomas | Mixologist | *(Privately Printed)* | SECOND EDITION | Revised from the First Edition of MCMXXVI, 1000 copies printed on the | Planograph at Washington, D. C., C. V. Wheeler, Editor. (Mem. Ancient | Order of Froth Blowers, Carleton Bar Vat, London, and Hon. Mem. Inde- | pendent Order of Bar Flies, Harry McElhone's New York Bar Trap, Paris.) | [illus. of bartender] | "Ye happy mixtures of more happy days." | *Byron.*

On copyright page: 'Second Printing [i.e., edition], Copyrighted 1929. | Charles V. Wheeler'. 9⅛" × 6¹⁄₁₆". Mottled brown and gray wrappers. *Locations:* GHT, LC. Previously published (*American Mercury,* February 1927); Adler 254.

'In Honor of an Artist' (review of first edition), pp. 12–14.

B 88 HAVELOCK ELLIS: IN APPRECIATION
1929

[all within quadruple-rule six-sided frame printed over blue rectangles, the outer rule spaced wider] HAVELOCK ELLIS [orange] | *IN APPRECIATION* | BY | ELIE FAURIE, BERTRAND RUSSELL, H. L. MENCKEN, | [three lines of contributors] | *and thirty-four other important contributors* | WITH AN UNPUBLISHED LET-TER BY THOMAS HARDY | TO HAVELOCK ELLIS, AND A FOREWORD BY ISAAC | GOLDBERG & EMBELLISHMENTS BY LOUIS MOREAU | *compiled, edited and printed by* | JOSEPH ISHILL | [device: compositor and hand press] | PUBLISHED PRIVATELY BY THE ORIOLE PRESS | BERKELEY HEIGHTS, NEW JERSEY | 1929

On copyright page: '*The edition is limited to 450 copies printed* | *on American Egg Shell paper and 50 copies* | *on Alexandra Japan vellum. This is No.* | [number written]'. On p. [300]: 'FINISHED IN JULY, 1929'. *Presumed first printing* (vellum): 7¹³⁄₁₆" × 6". Golden brown paper-covered boards with blue sprigs, white parchment spine with brown label printed in black. *Location:* Harv. *Presumed second printing* (eggshell): 7¹⁵⁄₁₆" × 5⅞". Gray-green paper-covered boards and spine label (printed in black), cream cloth spine. Harv copy (donated by Ishill) has '(personal)' instead of a limitation number. *Locations:* GHT, RJS. Previously published (based on two articles: New York *Evening Post,* 24 September 1921; *The Birth Control Review,* February 1926); Adler 144; Bulsterbaum 68. The advertising pamphlet of the same title is at B 89.

'HAVELOCK ELLIS: | THE MOST ADMIRABLE ENGLISHMAN OF HIS TIME', pp. 55–60.

B 89 AD FOR HAVELOCK ELLIS: IN APPRECIATION
1930

[all in a box surrounded by an ornate orange frame] HAVELOCK ELLIS | *IN APPRE-CIATION* | BY | ELIE FAURE, BERTRAND RUSSELL, H. L. MENCKEN, | [three lines of contributors] | *and thirty-four other important contributors* | WITH AN UNPUBLISHED LETTER BY THOMAS HARDY | TO HAVELOCK ELLIS, AND A FOREWORD BY ISAAC | GOLDBERG & EMBELLISHMENTS BY LOUIS MOREAU | *compiled, edited and printed by* | JOSEPH ISHILL | [device: compositor and hand press] | PUBLISHED PRIVATELY BY THE ORIOLE PRESS | BERKELEY HEIGHTS, NEW JERSEY

Date from *American Book Collector* 25.1 (1974): 19. 7⁹⁄₁₆″ × 5½″. Blue-gray wrappers printed in red (8⅜″ × 5¾″), tied with blue thread. Publicity pamphlet for 1929 book of same title (B 88). *Locations:* GHT, Harv, Yale. Not in Adler.

Excerpt from letter upon receiving the 1929 book, p. 6.

B 90 GREATEST THOUGHTS ON IMMORTALITY
1930

GREATEST THOUGHTS | ON IMMORTALITY | COMPILED FROM | PER-SONAL LETTERS TO THE AUTHOR | AND FROM VARIOUS OTHER SOURCES | BY | JACOB HELDER, A.M., Ph.D. | FORMERLY PROFESSOR OF PHILOSOPHY AND THE GERMAN LANGUAGE | AND LITERATURE IN MOUNT UNION-SCIO COLLEGE. | EX-VICE-PRESIDENT MODERN LAN-GUAGE ASSOCIATION OF OHIO. | APPOINTED FELLOW IN PSYCHOLOGY AND PHILOSOPHY | AT CLARK UNIVERSITY | [device] | RICHARD R. SMITH, INC. | NEW YORK | 1930

7⅜″ × 4¹⁵⁄₁₆″. Blue cloth stamped in gilt (?) on spine. *Location:* MB. Adler 30.

Contribution, pp. 112–14.

B 91 THE WRITER'S MARKET
1930

The Writer's Market | *Edited by* ARON M. MATHIEU | COPYRIGHT | 1930 | WRIT-ER'S DIGEST | PUBLISHERS

Published in Cincinnati (OCLC). 8″ × 5⁷⁄₁₆″. Pale blue-green cloth stamped in black on front: '[ornately framed left and bottom] WRITER'S | MARKET | [slanting down] 1931 | [WD device]'. *Locations:* FMU, KU-S. Not in Adler.

Statement of *American Mercury* editorial requirements submitted by Mencken, p. 13. "Its theory is that quacks give good shows . . . ."

B 92 MODERN WRITERS AT WORK
1930

MODERN WRITERS | AT WORK | *Edited* | BY | JOSEPHINE K. PIERCY | IN-STRUCTOR IN ENGLISH, | INDIANA UNIVERSITY | [gothic] New York | THE MACMILLAN COMPANY | 1930

On copyright page: 'Published September, 1930'. $7^{11}/_{16}'' \times 5^{1}/_{8}''$. Purple cloth stamped in silver. Later printings: February 1931, January 1932, May 1933, September 1933, April 1939, June 1941. *Location:* MWelC. Essay previously published (*Prejudices: Sixth Series* [A 36]); Adler 30.

Letter and 'Back to Bach' ("From the Memoirs of a Subject of the United States"), pp. 84–91.

B 93 NOBLE EXPERIMENTS
1930

Noble | Experiments | [orange] *The* THIRD *Volume in the Famous* | HERE'S HOW *Series* | [black] *By* Judge Jr. | [man with cocktail shaker] | [red rule] | THE JOHN DAY COMPANY | *New York*

The compiler was Norman Anthony (OCLC). On copyright page: '*This volume published for Judge Pub-* | *lishing Company by the John Day Com-* | *pany, Inc.* | COPY-RIGHT, 1930'. $4^{13}/_{16}'' \times 3''$. Orange cloth stamped in gilt. *Locations:* GHT, RJS. Not in Adler.

'THE FAVORITE CONCOCTION OF | [orange] H. L. Mencken', p. 19.

B 94 A BOOK OF DAYS
1930

[red] A Book *of* Days | [black French rule] | *Being a Briefcase packed for his* | *own Pleasure by* CHRISTOPHER | MORLEY & *made into a Calendar* | *for sundry Paramours of Print* | [red decoration with hourglass, sun, moon, stars, and, on a scroll in black, 1931] | [black French rule] | *PUBLISHED* (appropriately enough) | *by* THE JOHN DAY COMPANY

On copyright page: 'COPYRIGHT, 1930'. 6¹⁄₁₆″ × 4¼″. Binding varieties: light green cloth printed in dark green, light violet printed in green, straw printed in dark green. *Locations:* GHT, Harv, RJS. Previously published (*Nation,* 7 December 1921; A 27); not in Adler.

'*On Living in the | United States*' and '*Suggestions to Our Visitors*', s.v. 3 February, 11 March.

B 95 THEODORE DREISER AND HIS BOOKS
[1930?]

[cover title] [photograph of Dreiser] | THEODORE | DREISER | and his books

5⅝″ × 3½″. Self wrappers. Advertising brochure of Constable (London), with listings for Spring and Autumn 1930 and probables for Spring and Summer 1931. *Location:* GHT. Previously published?; not in Adler.

Quotation, p. 6. "I know of no other novelist who has stuck to his ideas more resolutely. . . ."

B 96 LIVING PHILOSOPHIES
1931

[all in double-rule box, the inner rule thicker, surrounded by ornate borders] Living | Philosophies | BY | [twenty-two authors in double columns] | 19 [device: rising sun behind sower] 31 | SIMON AND SCHUSTER • NEW YORK

9⅜″ × 6¼″. Black cloth stamped in gilt and with ornate blindstamping. Reprinted as Tower Book (Cleveland and New York: World, [June 1941]). For second edition (*I Believe* [1939]) see B 142. *Locations:* GHT, Harv (2), RJS. Previously published ("What I Believe," *Forum,* September 1930). An excerpt from the essay appeared in the same year in *Problems and Opinions: A Book of Discussions of Persistent Questions for Classes in Speaking and Writing,* ed. Alexander M. Drummond and Russell H. Wagner (New York and London: Century, [1931]), p. 373. Adler 30, 147; Bulsterbaum 36, 68.

Statement, pp. 179–93. Photo between pp. 180 and 181.

B 97 HIGHLIGHTS
1931

[all within box] HIGHLIGHTS | A CARTOON HISTORY | OF THE NINETEEN TWENTIES | BY | *Rollin Kirby* | A SELECTION OF HIS CARTOONS IN | [gothic] The [*World* vignette] [gothic] World | WITH A FOREWORD BY | WALTER LIPP-MANN | *Frontispiece Portrait by Albert Sterner* | Edited, with Illuminating Excerpts | from Contemporary Sources, by | HENRY B. HOFFMAN | *NEW YORK* | WILLIAM FARQUHAR PAYSON | *1931*

11″ × 8⅝″. Light brown cloth printed in dark brown. *Locations:* GHT, Harv. Previously published (New York *Times,* 19 October 1927: 4e–f); neither book nor original interview in Adler.

Interview quoted, p. 82.

B 98 MODELS FOR WRITING PROSE
1931

[all within ornate green frame] MODELS FOR | WRITING PROSE | *EDITED BY* | ROGER SHERMAN LOOMIS | COLUMBIA UNIVERSITY | [green device] | RICHARD R. SMITH, INC. | NEW YORK | 1931

7¾″ × 5¼″. Green cloth stamped in silver. Second printing 1931. *Location:* MChB. Previously published (*American Mercury,* June 1930; *Prejudices: Fourth Series* [A 29]); not in Adler.

'THE EMBATTLED LITERATI' and 'THE AMERICAN NOVEL', pp. 182–84, 204–07.

B 99 THE AMERICAN DEMOCRAT
1931

B 99.1
First edition (1931)

[various bracketing with orange rules] *THE* | *AMERICAN* | *DEMOCRAT* | *BY* | *JAMES* | *FENIMORE* | *COOPER* | [orange Borzoi device] | *With an Introduction by* | *H. L. MENCKEN* | *NEW YORK*   ALFRED•A•KNOPF   *MCMXXXI*

On p. [D]: '*AMERICANA DESERTA* | [four titles] | *EDITED BY BERNARD DE VOTO*'. 8⅛″ × 5⅜″. Orange cloth stamped in gilt. Reprinted with additional introduction by J. Perry Leavell, Jr.: New York: Funk & Wagnalls, [1969]. *Locations:* GHT, Harv, MCR, RJS. Adler 30; Bulsterbaum 68.

'INTRODUCTION' (dated May 1931), pp. xi–xx.

B 99.2
Second edition (1956)

THE | AMERICAN DEMOCRAT | *O R* | *HINTS ON THE SOCIAL AND CIVIC RELATIONS* | *OF THE UNITED STATES OF AMERICA* | [ornate rule] | *B Y* | JAMES FENIMORE COOPER | [ornate rule] | *WITH AN INTRODUCTION BY H. L. MENCKEN* | *AND AN* | *INTRODUCTORY NOTE BY ROBERT E. SPILLER* | *NEW YORK VINTAGE BOOKS* | *1956*

On copyright page: 'FIRST VINTAGE EDITION'. $7^{3}/_{16}'' \times 4^{5}/_{16}''$. Red, white, blue, and black wrappers; series no. K 26. *Locations:* MBU, RJS. Adler 30.

'*INTRODUCTION TO THE SECOND* | *(1931) EDITION*', pp. v–xiv.

B 99.3
Third edition (1981)

[curved] [brown star] The American Democrat [brown star] | [in brown, eagle with scroll in its mouth, olive branch and arrows in claws, standing on shield] | [brown] James Fenimore Cooper | [black] With an Introduction by | H. L. Mencken | Liberty-Classics *[sic]*.

Among data on copyright page is Indianapolis: Liberty Fund, 1981. (1) $8^{15}/_{16}'' \times 5^{7}/_{8}''$. Dark brown paper-covered boards with white label on front printed in gilt, black, and tan, medium brown cloth spine stamped in gilt. *Location:* GHT. (2) $8^{7}/_{8}'' \times 5^{13}/_{16}''$. Dark brown wrappers printed in tan, black, white, and gold. *Location:* GHT. S2.14.

'Introduction', pp. ix–xxi.

B 100 ELMER GANTRY
1932

B 100.1
First edition (1932)

SINCLAIR LEWIS | *Elmer Gantry* | Roman traduit de l'anglais | par | RÉGIS MICHAUD | "*UNIVERS*" | A. FAYARD ET Cie, ÉDITEURS | 18 et 20, rue du Saint-Gothard | PARIS

On copyright page: 'IL A ÉTÉ TIRÉ DE CET OUVRAGE : | Soixante-quinze exemplaires | sur papier pur fil des Papeteries Lafuma, | numérotés de 1 à 75. | Copyright by A. Fayard et Cie 1932.' On p. [595]: 'ACHEVÉ D'IMPRIMER | LE 30 JANVIER MCMXXXII | PAR FIRMIN-DIDOT AU | MESNIL-SUR-L'ESTRÉE (FRANCE).' Series: Collection *"Univers,"* Série rouge. 8^{11}⁄$_{16}$" × 5^3⁄$_8$". Heavy white paper wrappers printed in black and maroon. Michaud notes (p. [7]) that Mencken wrote the preface specifically for this translation. *Locations:* IU (rebound), LC (original wrappers recased). Adler 31.

'*PRÉFACE*' (signed 'H. L. MENCKEN'), pp. [7]–12.

B 100.2
Second edition (1960–1961)

SINCLAIR LEWIS | (Prix Nobel) | ELMER GANTRY | Le charlatan | Roman | ÉDITIONS SEGHERS | 228, Boulevard Raspail—PARIS XIV[raised heavy dot]

On copyright page: '© . . . | . . . | 1961, by Éditions SEGHERS'. On p. [407]: 'ACHEVÉ D'IMPRIMER LE | 24 DÉCEMBRE 1960'. 8^3⁄$_{16}$" × 5^1⁄$_4$". Red wrappers with black and white lettering. *Location:* GHT. Not in Adler.

'*PRÉFACE*' (signed 'H. L. MENCKEN.'), pp. [7]–12.

B 101 EDITORIAL THINKING AND WRITING
1932

EDITORIAL THINKING | AND WRITING | A TEXTBOOK WITH EXERCISES | BY | CHILTON R. BUSH | ASSOCIATE PROFESSOR OF JOURNALISM, UNIVERSITY OF WISCONSIN | AUTHOR OF "NEWSPAPER REPORTING OF PUBLIC AFFAIRS" | [device] | D. APPLETON AND COMPANY | NEW YORK LONDON | 1932

8" × 5^1⁄$_4$". Red cloth blindstamped and stamped in black. *Location:* MWalB. Previously published (?; *American Mercury,* February 1925; Baltimore *Evening Sun,* 7 September 1925); not in Adler.

From an editorial, 'Joseph Pulitzer', and a *Sun* article, pp. 164, 306n, 358.

B 102 CANCER: WHAT EVERYONE SHOULD KNOW ABOUT IT
1932

[fourteen diamond-shaped ornaments with floral designs within] | CANCER | WHAT EVERYONE | SHOULD KNOW ABOUT IT | [French rule] | *By* JAMES A. TOBEY, Dr. P. H. | *Fellow, American Public Health Association* | *Associate Fellow, American*

Medical Association | *Member, American Society for the Control of Cancer* | With Introductions by | JOSEPH COLT BLOODGOOD, M. D. | *and* H. L. MENCKEN | [French rule] | *New York* [Borzoi device] *Mcmxxxii* | ALFRED • A • KNOPF | [fourteen diamond-shaped ornaments with floral designs within]

On copyright page: '*First Edition*'. 8⅛" × 5½". Pale green cloth stamped in maroon and gilt. *Locations:* GHT, MWelC. Adler 31.

'Introduction', pp. xix–xx.

B 103 AMERICANA
1932

[head title] E.C.S. Choral Songs, № 1634 | *To The A Capella Singers of New York* | AMERICANA | *A Sequence of Five Choruses* | *for Mixed Voices* | [title of first part in four lines] | Texts from *The American Mercury*° Randall Thompson | [musical text follows] | °*Used by permission of the Publishers.* | E.C.S. № 753 [ASCAP seal] Copyright, 1932, by E. C. Schirmer Music Co. [over] For all countries Orchestra Score and parts may be [over] obtained from the publishers on a [over] rental basis.

Not seen in original wrappers; later printings in stiff green paper wrappers printed in black; most recently self wrappers. Sheet music. *Locations:* MBMU, MBU, RJS. Previously published; Adler 339.

'May Every Tongue', 'The Staff Necromancer', 'God's Bottles', 'The Sublime Process of Law Enforcement', and 'Loveli-lines' (edited texts from the "Americana" series in the *Mercury*). Lyrics for the choruses, also printed on verso of front wrapper.

B 104 ON THE MEANING OF LIFE
1932

[all in blue double-rule box] ON | THE MEANING | OF LIFE | WILL DURANT | [device: initials above hammer and anvil in blue] | Ray Long & Richard R. Smith, Inc. | New York • • • • 1932

On copyright page: 'Copyright, September 1932'. 7¾" × 5⅛". Blue cloth stamped in gilt. *Locations:* Harv (partially rebound), Yale. Later printings: October 1932, December 1932. Adler 30.

Letter quoted, pp. 30–35.

B 105 THE INTIMATE NOTEBOOKS OF
GEORGE JEAN NATHAN
1932

THE INTIMATE NOTEBOOKS | *of* | *GEORGE JEAN NATHAN* | [six rules in descending degree of thickness] | 19 [Borzoi device in oval] 32 | ALFRED • A • KNOPF • NEW YORK | [six rules in descending degree of thickness]

On copyright page: 'FIRST EDITION'. 7⅜″ × 5″. Black cloth stamped in gilt and blindstamped, or stamped in red and gilt and blindstamped. *Locations:* GHT (2), Harv, InU-Li, RJS. Adler 286.

Letters quoted, pp. 94–121 *passim.*

B 106 MONETA'S
[1932?]

B 106.1
Presumed first edition (1932?)

[man raising glass] | [reading at angle up from left to right, red letters outlined in black, script] Moneta's | C. A. MONETA, Prop.

5¾″ × 3¾″. Four leaves; self wrappers. *Location:* EPL. Cf. Hobson 330–31 and n. Not in Adler.

Quotation, perhaps from letter, p. [1].

B 106.2
Presumed second edition (1936?)

Same title as B 106.1.

5¹¹⁄₁₆″ × 3⅞″. Eight leaves; self wrappers. Contains quotations from newspapers of April 1936. *Location:* EPL.

Quotation, perhaps from letter, p. [9].

B 107 1933 ESSAY ANNUAL
1933

[all bordered left and bottom with triple-rule frame] 1933 | Essay | Annual | *A Yearly Collection of Signif-* | *icant Essays, Personal, Critical,* | *Controversial, and Humorous* |

ERICH A. WALTER | *Department of English, University of Michigan* | SCOTT, FORESMAN AND COMPANY | CHICAGO–ATLANTA–DALLAS–NEW YORK

On copyright page: 'COPYRIGHT, 1933'. 7¼" × 4¹⁵⁄₁₆". Green cloth stamped in yellow. *Locations:* GHT, MChB. Previously published (Baltimore *Evening Sun,* 18 July 1932); not in Adler.

'Paying the Bill', pp. 335–39.

B 108 BALTIMORE IN THE EIGHTIES AND NINETIES
[1933?]

Baltimore in the | Eighties and Nineties | [beside red and black illustration of the fire] *often* | *referred to* | by the old timers | as | "Before | The | Fire" | [on illustration] by *Meredith Janvier*

8⅜" × 12½" heavy paper sheet with top folded over, then folded to make four pages. The book it advertises was published in 1933. *Location:* Yale. Previously published?; not in Adler.

Quotation, p. [4]. ". . . He has done a capital job."

B 109 PRESS SERVICE OF THE NAACP
1934

[head title] [printed] Press Service of the National Association | FOR THE | Advancement of Colored People | [address, officers, directors] | [double rule] | [hectographed] LYNCH EVIL MORE DANGEROUS | THAN COMMUNISM, CONGRESSWOMAN | TELLS SENATE COMMITTEE | [text follows]

For date cf. Bode, *Letters* 305–07. 13¹⁵⁄₁₆" × 8⁷⁄₁₆". Four stapled pages. *Location:* GHT. Not in Adler.

Mencken's testimony of February 14 in favor of the Costigan-Wagner anti-lynching bill excerpted on p. [1].

B 110 MODERN ENGLISH COMPOSITION
1934

[all within double-rule box] MODERN ENGLISH | COMPOSITION | BY | JOHN C. McCLOSKEY, M.A. | *University of Oregon* | [ornament] | FARRAR & RINEHART | ON MURRAY HILL   NEW YORK

On copyright page: 'COPYRIGHT 1934'. 8″ × 5⅜″. Red cloth stamped in gilt on spine. *Locations:* MU, MWelC. Previously published (*American Credo* [A 22]; *American Mercury,* June 1932); Adler 191.

'*Advertising in America*' and '*Mediums and Nonsense*' ("The Believing Mind"), pp. 7–8, 140–41.

B 111 THE RIGHTS AND PRIVILEGES OF THE PRESS
1934

THE | RIGHTS AND PRIVILEGES | OF THE PRESS | BY | FREDRICK [sic] SEATON SIEBERT, J. D. | *Assistant Professor of Journalism, University of Illinois* | *Member of the Illinois Bar* | [A-C device] | D. APPLETON-CENTURY COMPANY | INCORPORATED | NEW YORK LONDON

On copyright page: 'COPYRIGHT, 1934'. 8″ × 5³⁄₁₆″. Red cloth stamped in gilt on spine. Reprinted Westport, Conn.: Greenwood, 1970. *Location:* GHT. Previously published (source: 13 *Virginia Law Register* n.s. 121, quoting from a syndicated article); not in Adler.

Quotation, pp. 53–54n.

B 112 SURVEY OF CONTEMPORARY ECONOMICS
1934

[decorative border] | *SURVEY* | *of* | *CONTEMPORARY* | *ECONOMICS* | *Edited by* | NORMAN S. BUCK | *Yale University* | [device: house] | THOMAS NELSON AND SONS | New York 1934 | [decorative border]

8½″ × 5⅝″. Maroon cloth blindstamped on front, stamped in gilt on spine. *Locations:* Harv, MWC. Previously published (*Current History,* August 1934); Adler 151 (error in title).

'NOTES ON THE NEW DEAL', pp. 819–26.

B 113 NOT AN IDEA MISSING / MINIATURE ESSAYS
[1934?]

B 113.1
Presumed first edition

No title page on this advertising brochure. Facsimile signatures of notables on p. [1] show through open space in front wrapper. On p. [15] is the address of The Readers

Digest Association, Pleasantville, N. Y. 7⅝″ × 5½″. Plain white wrappers. *Locations:* EPL, GHT, Yale. Previously published (*Reader's Digest,* September 1934, back cover); Adler 151?; West 194. Priority of these two editions uncertain.

'Not An Idea | Missing', p. [7].

B 113.2
Presumed second edition

[cover title] [words of title slanting up] [blue] *Miniature* | [blue] *Essays* | [contents (seven titles) in column to right of blue oil lamp with black smoke rising]

The magazine was founded in 1922, "twelve years ago" (p. [1]). Same address as previous on recto of back wrapper. 8⁷⁄₁₆″ × 5½″. White wrappers printed in black. *Location:* GHT. Previously published; Adler 151?

'I Was Astonished', p. [3]. Same essay as above.

B 113A MORE FUN IN BED
1934

MORE FUN | IN BED | THE CONVALESCENT'S | HANDBOOK | Edited by *FRANK SCULLY* | *and an* | *ALL-STAR CAST* | *including* | [eight lines of names] | *and many others far too* | *humorous to mention.* | *SIMON AND SCHUSTER, INC.* | *386 Fourth Avenue   New York*

First printing not seen (1934); title page from third printing. *Location:* NNF. Previously published (*American Mercury,* March 1930); not in Adler.

'Comfort for the Ailing', pp. 167–68.

B 114 IDEAS AND MODELS
1935

IDEAS AND MODELS | BY || [left column] LOUISE POUND | UNIVERSITY OF NEBRASKA | THEODORE STENBERG | UNIVERSITY OF TEXAS | JAMES P. CALLAHAN | KANSAS STATE COLLEGE || [right column] ROBERT ADGER LAW | UNIVERSITY OF TEXAS | LOWRY C. WIMBERLY | UNIVERSITY OF NEBRASKA | NORMAN ELIASON | INDIANA UNIVERSITY || [Holt device] | NEW YORK | HENRY HOLT AND COMPANY

On copyright page: 'COPYRIGHT, 1935'. 8½″ × 5½″. Blue cloth stamped in white. *Location:* MBNU. Previously published (*Liberty,* 3 March 1934); not in Adler.

'THE BRAIN TRUST', pp. 157–63.

B 115 OF H. L. DAVIS
1935

[head title] [beneath ornamental border and to right of photograph of Mencken in a circle, which has an arrow connecting it to a photograph of Davis] *Says [sic]* H. L. | MENCKEN | of H. L. DAVIS | [text follows]

8⅜″ × 6″ green sheet. Contains other blurbs for the book. *Location:* EPL. Previously published (New York *Herald Tribune*, 25 August 1935); not in Adler.

Quotation from review of *Honey in the Horn* ("History and Fable and Very Good Stuff").

B 116 IN BEHALF OF SIDNEY LANIER
1935

[all within quadruple-rule box, outer rule bold] A BRIEF | Addressed to | *The Electors of the Hall of Fame* | *New York University, N. Y.* | In Behalf of | *Sidney Lanier, Poet and Musician* | By | The United Daughters of the Confederacy | of Thirty-Eight States | [ornament] | Edited by | MRS. WALTER D. LAMAR, Chairman of Committee | To Advance the Name of Sidney Lanier | For the Hall of Fame | Macon, Ga., April 1935

8″ × 4¹⁵⁄₁₆″. Self wrappers. *Location:* EPL. Adler 31.

Letter or statement (dated 30 September 1932) in support of Lanier's candidacy, p. 26.

B 117 YOU KNOW THESE LINES
1935

You Know These Lines! | *A Bibliography of the Most* | *Quoted Verses in American* | *Poetry* | *By* | *Merle Johnson* | [five lines of his works, three-line quotation from Burton E. Stevenson] | *Foreword by* | *H. L. Mencken* | [ornament] | *New York* | G. A. BAKER & COMPANY | 1935

On copyright page: '. . . A LIMITED EDITION OF 1000 COPIES | SIGNED BY THE AUTHOR | [signature of Johnson]'. 9″ × 5¹⁵⁄₁₆″. Brown cloth stamped in gilt on spine. Some copies unsigned (GHT, InU-Li). *Locations:* GHT, Harv, InU-Li (2), RJS. Adler 31; S1.7.

'Foreword', pp. ix–xi.

B 118 PORTRAITS AND SELF-PORTRAITS
1936

PORTRAITS AND | SELF-PORTRAITS | COLLECTED AND ILLUSTRATED BY | GEORGES SCHREIBER | 1936 | HOUGHTON MIFFLIN COMPANY   BOSTON | [gothic] The Riverside Press Cambridge

$9^{13}\!/_{16}''\times6^{15}\!/_{16}''$. Light tan cloth stamped in red and black. *Locations:* GHT, Harv, RJS. Adler 31.

Autobiographical essay, pp. 105–07. Sketch of Mencken, p. 104.

B 119 FAMOUS RECIPES BY FAMOUS PEOPLE
1936

B 119.1
First edition (1936)

[on wrapper, multicolored as below] FAMOUS [OU linked] | RECIPES | [man eating from pot] | BY | FAMOUS [OU linked] PEOPLE | HOTEL [square dot] DEL [square dot] MONTE. [on title page] [within an arc of seven orange stars] THE AMERICAN | ASSOCIATION | OF GOURMETS | . . . | Recipes Compiled and | Commented Upon by | HERBERT CERWIN | [heavy dot] | Illustrations by | PAUL WHITMAN | HOTEL DEL MONTE | DEL MONTE [heavy dot] CALIFORNIA | [orange star]

On copyright page: 'FIRST EDITION | [heavy dot] | Issued March 15, 1936'. Second printing 2 April 1936. $7\!^{1}\!/_{4}''\times5\!^{7}\!/_{8}''$. White wrappers printed in copper, black, gray, and shades of purple and orange-yellow. *Location:* TxU. Not in Adler.

One-sentence comment, p. 13.

B 119.2
Second edition (1940)

[in horseshoe shape above illustration of chef with huge fork over wreath, in yellow] FAMOUS RECIPES BY FAMOUS PEOPLE | COMPILED AND EDITED BY | HERBERT CERWIN | ILLUSTRATED BY SINCLAIR ROSS | COPYRIGHT 1940 BY LANE PUBLISHING CO., SAN FRANCISCO, CALIFORNIA | PUBLISHED BY SUNSET MAGAZINE IN COOPERATION WITH HOTEL DEL MONTE | PRINTED IN U. S. A.

$9\!^{1}\!/_{16}''\times6\!^{11}\!/_{16}''$. Ivory fabricoid stamped in gilt. *Locations:* GHT, MCR, RJS. *Menckeniana* 39.15.

One-sentence comment, p. 13.

B 120 SOUTHERN ALBUM
1936

[all within a double-rule box surrounded by stylized floral borders inside another box] *Sara Haardt* | SOUTHERN | ALBUM | Edited, with a Preface, by | H. L. MENCKEN | 1936 | DOUBLEDAY, DORAN & CO., INC. | *Garden City, New York*

On copyright page: 'FIRST EDITION'. 7⅞" × 5½". Blue-violet cloth stamped in gilt on spine. *Locations:* GHT, Harv, RJS. Adler 31; Bulsterbaum 68.

Edited and 'Preface', pp. vii–xxiii.

B 121 ADVENTURES IN ERROR
1936

B 121.1

[three rules in descending order of length] | A D V E N T U R E S | *in* | E R R O R | *By* | VILHJALMUR STEFANSSON | [device with Liberty Bell] | *New York* | R O B E R T M. M c B R I D E & C O M P A N Y | [three rules in reverse order of previous rules]

On copyright page: 'COPYRIGHT 1936 | . . . | FIRST EDITION'. 8⁹⁄₁₆" × 5¹¹⁄₁₆". Red cloth stamped in gilt. *Location:* Harv. Previously published (New York *Evening Mail*, 28 December 1917); Adler 288.

'A NEGLECTED ANNIVERSARY', pp. 280–86.

B 121.2
Offprint

[cover title] [within rules on four sides, diamonds in corners] [script] *History of the Bathtub in America* | [diamond] | A CHAPTER FROM | ADVENTURES IN ER-ROR | By VILHJALMUR STEFANSSON | [script] *Presented with the Compliments of* | ROBERT M. McBRIDE & COMPANY | [script] *publishers of "Adventures in Error"* | *by Vilhjalmur Stefansson*

8⁵⁄₁₆" × 5⁹⁄₁₆". Yellow paper wrappers printed in red. Form letter from Stanley Walker of McBride pasted on inside of wrapper, dated 6 November 1936, the day of publica-tion. *Location:* Yale. Not in Adler.

'A NEGLECTED ANNIVERSARY', pp. 280–86 (within reprinted chapter with head title '[three rules in descending order of length] | CHAPTER VIII. | HISTORY OF THE BATHTUB IN AMERICA').

B 122 THE MODERN WRITER'S ART
1936

[bordered at right by a pair of vertical double rules, the right ones thicker, ending above publisher's name] THE | MODERN | WRITER'S | ART | [the rest bordered at left by a pair of vertical double rules, the left ones thicker] *Edited by* | Theodore J. Gates | *and* | Robert E. Galbraith | *The Pennsylvania State College* | THOMAS NELSON AND SONS | New York 1936

8″ × 5⁵⁄₁₆″. Brown paper-covered boards, yellow-green cloth spine stamped in black. *Location:* MCR. Previously published (*American Mercury*, October 1931); not in Adler.

'POETRY (EDITORIAL)', pp. 107–09.

B 123 OUR LAND AND ITS LITERATURE
1936

OUR LAND | AND ITS | LITERATURE | [rule with star in center] | BY | ORTON LOWE | [five lines of credentials] | ILLUSTRATIONS BY PAUL WENCK | [Harper device] | [rule] | HARPER & BROTHERS PUBLISHERS | *NEW YORK AND LONDON* | 1936

9³⁄₁₆″ × 6″. Gray-green cloth stamped in black. *Locations:* CtNbT, Nc. Previously published (*American Mercury*, December 1930); Adler 191.

'*The American Cuisine*' (review of Fannie Farmer, *The Boston Cooking-School Cook-Book*), pp. 559–61.

B 124 THE NEW REPUBLIC ANTHOLOGY 1915–1935
1936

[all within double-rule box, the outer rule thicker] *The* | NEW REPUBLIC | *Anthology* | 1915 : 1935 | [heavy dot] | Edited by | GROFF CONKLIN | Introduction by | BRUCE BLIVEN | [Dodge device] | DODGE PUBLISHING COMPANY | New York

On copyright page: 'COPYRIGHT, 1936 | . . . | FIRST EDITION'. (1) 8⁵⁄₁₆″ × 5½″. Black and red lettering on gray cloth, top edge red. (2) 8⁵⁄₁₆″ × 5½″. Brown lettering on orange, top unstained; dust jacket has quotation about the book from H. W. Van Loon. (3) 8⅜″ × 5⅝″. Gray-brown stamped in black, top unstained. (4) 8⁵⁄₁₆″ × 5½″. Black lettering on light green cloth. *Locations:* GHT (3, dj), Harv (2), RJS. Previously published (*New Republic*, 8 September 1920); Adler 138.

'MEDITATION IN E MINOR', pp. 125–29.

B 125 AN ENTIRELY NEW VERSION
[1936?]

An entirely new version of a standard work | [rule] | *The* AMERICAN | LANGUAGE | *By* H. L. MENCKEN | [rule] | *Fourth Edition, Corrected, Enlarged and Rewritten. 800 pages,* | *with a full word-list and an index. 325,000 words of text.* | [rule] | [nineteen-line blurb and illustration of book] | [rule] | ALFRED•A• KNOPF•*Publisher*•730 Fifth Avenue•New York

9¹⁄₁₆″ × 24″ sheet folded three times to make 8 "pages." Contains specimen page and table of contents. *Location:* GHT. Not in Adler.

'Mr. Mencken *Says:*', pp. 2–3.

B 126 PROCEEDINGS, AMERICAN SOCIETY OF NEWSPAPER
EDITORS
1937

PROCEEDINGS | FIFTEENTH ANNUAL CONVENTION | AMERICAN SOCIETY OF | NEWSPAPER EDITORS | April 15 [dash slanted up] 16 [dash slanted up] 17, 1937 | National Press Club | Washington, D. C.

8¹¹⁄₁₆″ × 5⅞″. Green cloth stamped in gilt. *Locations:* MBU, NBu. Adler 270.

Mencken's speech during 16 April session, part of the discussion called 'Are Editorials Effective?' in table of contents, pp. 45–49.

B 127 FREE VISTAS, VOLUME II
1937

[orange] FREE VISTAS | [orange French rule] | A LIBERTARIAN OUTLOOK ON | LIFE & LETTERS • EDITED AND | PUBLISHED BY JOSEPH ISHILL | [woodcut of seated, partially nude woman] | PRINTED AT THE ORIOLE PRESS | BERKELEY HEIGHTS, N.J., 1937 | [French rule] | [orange] • VOLUME II •

7¹⁵⁄₁₆″ × 5″. Plain light gray-green wrappers thicker than the pages (8¼″ × 5³⁄₁₆″). Prospectus for B 128, in which the full context of the Mencken quotation appears (p. 302). *Location:* JRS. Not in Adler.

Letter quoted, p. xi.

B 128 FREE VISTAS, VOL. II
1937

FREE VISTAS–VOL. II | [sepia French rule] | A LIBERTARIAN OUTLOOK ON LIFE & | LETTERS • EDITED BY JOSEPH ISHILL | [sepia woodcut of nude man and woman] | PUBLISHED BY THE ORIOLE PRESS AT | BERKELEY HEIGHTS, N. J. | [French rule] | [sepia] • MCMXXXVII •

On copyright page: 'EDITION LIMITED TO TWO HUNDRED AND FIVE COPIES, | PRINTED ON ARAK ASH WHITE PAPER'. On p. [399]: 'APRIL : MCMXXXVII'. 8½" × 6¹⁄₁₆". Coarse bluish cloth without design or red cloth with black design, black cloth spine with light blue paper label printed in black and gold. *Locations:* Harv, JRS. Not in Adler.

'TWO LETTERS BY H. L. MENCKEN' (dated 31 January and 18 May 1935), pp. 301–02.

B 129 BREAKING INTO PRINT
1937

[all within sepia border containing authors' names showing through in white and separated by stars] Breaking into print | BEING A COMPILATION OF PAPERS | *WHEREIN* | EACH OF A SELECT GROUP OF AUTHORS | *TELLS* | OF THE DIFFICULTIES OF AUTHORSHIP | & | HOW SUCH TRIALS ARE MET | *TO-GETHER WITH* | Biographical Notes and Comment | BY AN EDITOR OF THE COLOPHON | *ELMER ADLER* | *NOW* | PUT IN A BOOK BY SIMON AND SCHUSTER | PUBLISHERS OF NEW YORK IN MCMXXXVII

9³⁄₁₆" × 6¹⁄₁₆". Black cloth blindstamped and stamped in gilt on front and spine. Reply card laid into RJS copy. Reprinted Freeport, N.Y.: Books for Libraries Press, 1968. At Yale and EPL is a gathering from *The Colophon, Part One* (February 1930), a hard-bound periodical issued to 2,000 subscribers: [head title] 'H • L • MENCKEN | [next three lines slanted down] ON | BREAKING | IN | TO TYPE | [alphabet divided by red diamonds]'; 10½" × 8½"; four unpaginated leaves tied; marked "Printers Copy"; [New York?: Pynson Printers, 1929?]. Articles therein were separate gatherings by various presses; Mencken's was "written" (and printed?) in August 1929. *Locations:* GHT, Harv (2), RJS. Essay previously published (*Colophon, Part One* [February 1930]); Adler 147; S1.14; Bulsterbaum 35.

Letter to Adler (dated 21 December 1936) and 'On Breaking into Type' (with illus. of typescript), pp. 139–46.

B 130 BALTIMORE YESTERDAYS
1937

Baltimore Yesterdays | BY | Meredith Janvier | ILLUSTRATED | [ornament] | BAL-
TIMORE | H. G. ROEBUCK & SON | 1937

7⅞″ × 5⅞16″. Black cloth stamped in gilt. *Locations:* GHT, RJS. Adler 31.

'*Preface*', pp. vii–xiv.

B 131 THE CHARLATANRY OF THE LEARNED
1937

B 131.1
Only printing, American issue (1937)

T H E | CHARLATANRY of the | L E A R N E D | (*De Charlataneria Eruditorum,
1715*) | B Y | Johann Burkhard Mencken | (1674–1732) | TRANSLATED FROM THE
GERMAN BY | FRANCIS E. LITZ | WITH NOTES AND AN INTRODUCTION
BY | *H. L. MENCKEN* | [ornament featuring owl in dunce cap] | [rule] | *NEW YORK :
: LONDON* | Alfred A. Knopf | 1937

On copyright page: 'FIRST EDITION'. On p. [xii] after index: '. . . *limited to 1475
copies*. . . .| . . . | . . . *Designed* | *by W. A. Dwiggins*.' 7¹³⁄₁₆″ × 5⅜″. Orange cloth with
white paper label on spine. *Second state:* handstamped correction on title page barr-
ing out 'GERMAN' and putting 'LATIN' above it. Letter from Mencken of 21 December 1938, formerly tipped in to MBU copy donated by him: ". . . It was designed
by Mr. Dwiggins, for whose talents I have the very highest respect. Rather curiously,
he made an error in his copy for the title page. As you will note, it has been corrected
with a rubber stamp." Mencken himself also corrected it by hand (JRS, SL). 1,400
copies sold. *Locations:* BL (17 SEP 37, first state), D (2 in second state), GHT (second
state), Harv (2 in first state), InU-Li (second state), MBU (second state), RJS (first
state). Adler 31; Bulsterbaum 69.

Edited and 'PREFACE BY THE EDITOR', pp. [3]–45.

B 131.2
Only printing, English issue (1938)

As above, but pasted on title page below '1937' (¹⁵⁄₁₆″ × 4⅝″): 'LONDON | KEGAN
PAUL, TRENCH, TRUBNER & Co., LTD. | BROADWAY HOUSE, 68–74 CAR-
TER LANE, E.C.' Published January 1938 (ECB 14.1124). *Locations:* Bod (AUG | 16
| 1938), GHT. Not in Adler.

B 132 1937 ESSAY ANNUAL
1937

1937 | [forming arc] Essay Annual | *A Yearly Collection of Significant Essays* | *Personal, Critical, Controversial, and Humorous* | Erich A. Walter | *Department of English, University of Michigan* | [ornament] | SCOTT, FORESMAN AND COMPANY | CHICAGO • ATLANTA • DALLAS • NEW YORK

On copyright page: 'COPYRIGHT, 1937'. 7³⁄₁₆″ × 4⅞″. Blue cloth stamped in yellow. *Locations:* Harv, JRS. Previously published (*Yale Review,* March 1936); Adler 152.

'The American Language', pp. 1–15.

B 133 BEFORE I FORGET
1937

Burton Rascoe | BEFORE I FORGET | [decoration: quill over book over tree] | MCMXXXVII | [French rule] | DOUBLEDAY, DORAN & COMPANY, INC. | *Garden City New York*

8⅜″ × 5⅝″. Green cloth blindstamped on front, stamped in gilt and black on spine. Reprinted New York: Literary Guild, 1937. *Location:* Harv. Adler 289.

Three sentences of February 1918 letter, p. 354n.

B 134 10,000 SNACKS
1937

[pp. [iv–v]] 10,000 | SNACKS | [rule] | a cookbook | [rule] | [decorations] | [rule] | of canapés, savories, relishes, hors | d'oeuvres, sandwiches, and appe- | tizers for before, after, and be- | tween meals || BY Cora, Rose | and Bob Brown | [rule] | [next three lines to left of decorations] | Pictures by | Julian | Brazelton | [rule] | Farrar & Rinehart Incorporated | Publishers . New York | [decorations]

On copyright page: 'COPYRIGHT, 1937, BY CORA, ROSE, AND ROBERT CARLTON BROWN'. 7¹⁵⁄₁₆″ × 5¼″. Light green cloth stamped in red. Reprinted Garden City, N.Y.: Halcyon House, [1949]. *Location:* MCR. Not in Adler.

Quotation from "a recent letter," p. 371; "My favorite snack is a sandwich made of sliced turkey . . .," p. 492.

B 135 THE STAG AT EASE
1938

[all within a frame of adjacent triangles surrounded by a box] A COOKBOOK | THE STAG AT EASE | Compiled by | MARIAN SQUIRE | Being the Culinary Pref-erences | of a Number of Distinguished | Male Citizens of the World | [rule] | [row of adjacent triangles pointing down] | [Caxton device] | The CAXTON PRINTERS, Ltd. | Caldwell, Idaho | 1938

On copyright page: '48508'. 8¼″ × 5⁷⁄₁₆″. Blue cloth stamped in gilt. *Locations:* InU-Li, MCR, RJS. Adler 32.

On Chesapeake crabs, p. 98.

B 136 GUIDE TO KULCHUR
1938

B 136.1
First English printing (1938)

EZRA POUND | GUIDE | *TO* | KULCHUR | [four heavy dots] | FABER & FABER LIMITED | *24 RUSSELL SQUARE* | *LONDON*

On copyright page: '*First published in June Mcmxxxviii*'. 8″ × 5⅛″. Green cloth stamped in gilt on spine. Proof copy at InU-Li has material deleted from published version; on copyright page: '*First published in May Mcmxxxviii*'. *Locations:* BL (re-bound), Camb, GHT, Harv (rebound), InU-Li, NBronSL (rebound), RJS. See Donald Gallup, *Ezra Pound: A Bibliography* (Charlottesville: University Press of Virginia, [1983]), pp. 61–64, for subsequent printings. Not in Adler.

Quotation from a "letter dated March 1st [1938]," p. 182. Cf. Bode, *Letters* 404.

B 136.2
First printing, American issue (1938)

EZRA POUND | CULTURE | NEW DIRECTIONS | *NORFOLK–CONNECTI-CUT* | *1938*

On copyright page: '*Printed in England | Published in London under the title | "Guide to Kulchur"*'. 7⅞″ × 5³⁄₁₆″. Blue cloth stamped in gilt on spine. Review copy with slip inviting comments ('With the compliments of the editor | James Laughlin IV'). *Locations:* GHT, InU-Li, MChB. Not in Adler.

Quotation from a "letter dated March 1st [1938]," p. 182.

B 137 TALES OF A WAYWARD INN
1938

TALES OF A | WAYWARD INN | By FRANK CASE | [within the first of four purple arches, in black, letters resembling those on a marquee] ALGONQUIN | [figure in tuxedo beneath arches] | Illustrated | FREDERICK A. STOKES COMPANY | NEW YORK   MCMXXXVIII

8⁹⁄₁₆″ × 5¾″. Black cloth stamped in gilt. Sixth printing Philadelphia and New York: Lippincott, [1938]. Reprinted New York: Garden City Pub. Co., [1940]. *Locations:* GHT, Harv, RJS. Adler 273.

Letter to Case (dated 24 October), pp. 348–52.

B 138 TONICS AND SEDATIVES
1938

TONICS and SEDATIVES | 1938 | *Incorporating also the* | *DIARY OF DR. PEPYS.* | Published by | Dr. and Mrs. Morris Fishbein | for their friends.

11⅜″ × 8½″. Pictorial wrappers printed in black and red on white. *Locations:* EPL, NhD. Previously published (*JAMA*, 26 March 1938); West 198; not in Adler.

'MAX BRÖDEL AS A | PIANIST', p. 17.

B 139 FUN IN BED
1938

Fun in Bed—Series Four | Rx Just What the | Doctor Ordered | *Edited by* FRANK SCULLY | *and an* | ALL-STAR CAST | *including* | [eight lines of names] | *SIMON AND SCHUSTER, INC.* | New York 1938

10″ × 6¾″. Orange cloth stamped in black, with loop for pencil. Latest noted printing is the seventh (1943). *Locations:* CtH (rebound), EPL, GHT. Previously published (*American Mercury*, November 1930); not in Adler.

'*Medicine and Morals*', pp. 129–30.

B 140 IN AMERICAN
1939

IN | AMERICAN | *THE COLLECTED POEMS OF* | JOHN V. A. WEAVER | *With a Foreword by* | H. L. M E N C K E N | [row of diamonds with dots in center] | [rule] |

NEW YORK [Borzoi device above six lines within a circle surrounded by a wreath] *LONDON* | ALFRED • A • KNOPF • 1939

On copyright page: 'FIRST EDITION'. Binding designed by W. A. Dwiggins (p. [318]). (1) 8¹¹⁄₁₆″ × 5⁹⁄₁₆″. Black cloth with embossed horizontal design, stamped in gilt on spine, bottom and fore edges rough trimmed, top edge trimmed and stained gray. (2) 8⁹⁄₁₆″ × 5⁷⁄₁₆″. Green cloth with orange on spine and back, all edges trimmed, top edge stained orange. (3) 8¹¹⁄₁₆″ × 5¾″. Black with embossed vertical design, spine stamped in gilt, top edge stained gray, fore and bottom edges unevenly and rough trimmed. (4) 8¾″ × 5¾″. Plain black cloth, stamped in gilt on spine, top edge trimmed and stained gray, fore and bottom edges rough and unevenly trimmed. (5) 8⅝″ × 5½″. Blue cloth stamped in orange on spine and back, top edge stained orange, all edges trimmed. Knopf published Weaver's *In American—Poems* (1921). *Locations:* GHT (4), Harv, RJS. Adler 32.

'*Foreword*' (dated January 1939), pp. v–xi.

B 141 FROM ANOTHER WORLD
1939

From Another World | THE AUTOBIOGRAPHY OF | LOUIS UNTERMEYER | HARCOURT, BRACE AND COMPANY, NEW YORK

On copyright page: 'COPYRIGHT, 1939 . . . | . . . | *first edition*'. 8⁷⁄₁₆″ × 5⁹⁄₁₆″. Blue cloth stamped in gilt. Second printing November 1939. *Locations:* GHT, Harv, InU-Li. Adler 290.

Letters quoted, pp. 184–205 *passim*.

B 142 I BELIEVE
1939

[all within red double-rule box] I BELIEVE | *The Personal Philosophies | of Certain Eminent | Men and Women | of Our Time* | [red rule] | Edited, with an Introduction | and Biographical Notes, by | CLIFTON FADIMAN | 19 [red device] 39 | [red rule] | SIMON AND SCHUSTER • NEW YORK

9³⁄₁₆″ × 6⅛″. Blue cloth stamped in red and gilt on spine. At least five printings 1939. This is the second edition of *Living Philosophies* (1931; B 96) but with a new affirmation by Mencken. *I Believe* (London: Allen & Unwin, 1940, 1952) omits his contribution. *Location:* MBU. Adler 30; Bulsterbaum 68 (error).

Statement, pp. 389–91.

B 143 THE COLLEGE BOOK OF ESSAYS
1939

[all within box inside double-rule box] THE COLLEGE BOOK | OF ESSAYS | [ornamental line] | BY | JOHN ABBOT CLARK | MICHIGAN STATE COLLEGE | NEW YORK | HENRY HOLT AND COMPANY

On copyright page: 'COPYRIGHT, 1939, | . . . | December, 1939'. 8⅜″ × 5⅜″. Yellowish tan cloth stamped in brown. Review copy has blue slip (4¼″ × 2½″) printed in blue, pasted on free front end paper, containing a blurb, price $2. *Locations:* MWelC, Yale. Previously published (*American Mercury,* June 1931; January 1930; February 1931); not in Adler.

'The Striated Muscle Fetish' ("Editorial"), 'The American Language' ("Editorial"), and 'The New Architecture', pp. 172–76, 204–09, 321–23.

B 144 SARGENT BULLETIN #10
1939

[top right of recto, mimeographed] Sargent Bulletin #10 | [printed and mimeographed text follows]

Boston: Porter Sargent. 11″ × 8½″ sheet printed on both sides. Verso has an essay by J. R. Burrow. Mencken's essay reprinted by Porter E. Sargent, *Getting U S into War* (Boston: The Author, [1941]), pp. 137–40; second printing September 1941. *Locations:* EPL, Harv. Essay previously published (Baltimore *Sun,* 8 October 1939); Adler 16, 17, 105; West 198 (wrongly dated 1944).

'Notes On A Moral War' and quotation from a letter, recto.

B 145 CENTENNIAL SOUVENIR
1940

[cover title] [within box, in gold] [gothic] Centennial Souvenir | DU | [gothic] Restaurant Antoine | [left to right: 1840 reading down in box, illustration in box, 1940 reading down in box] | [roman] FONDÉ EN 1840 | ROY L. ALCIATORE, PROPRIETOR | 713–717 ST. LOUIS STREET NEW ORLEANS, LA.

6¾″ × 5⅛″. Black wrappers printed in gold. *Locations:* GHT, RJS. Not in Adler.

One-sentence remark to Mr. Alciatore, p. 19.

B 146 ALFRED A. KNOPF QUARTER CENTURY
1940

19 [crown] 40 | ALFRED A. | KNOPF | *Quarter Century* | [ornament]

Copyright page: 'COPYRIGHT BY ELMER ADLER, 1940'. On p. [53]: 'DESIGNED BY W. A. DWIGGINS, | PRINTED BY THE PLIMPTON PRESS . . . | . . . COMPLETED IN THE | MONTH OF APRIL, MCMXL.' 7¾″ × 5⅜″. Green cloth, white paper labels on front and spine printed in blue. In box covered with brown and white decorated paper, glassine dust jacket. Copies reported with slip ('WITH MR. KNOPF'S | COMPLI-MENTS') (RAW, InU-Li). *Locations:* Harv (2), InU-Li (2), RJS (dj). Adler 32; S1.10; Bulsterbaum 69.

'COMPETENT MAN', pp. 17–21.

B 147 SUMNER TODAY
1940

SUMNER TODAY | *SELECTED ESSAYS OF* | WILLIAM GRAHAM SUMNER | *WITH COMMENTS BY* | *AMERICAN LEADERS* | *EDITED BY* | MAURICE R. DAVIE | *PROFESSOR OF SOCIOLOGY* | *IN YALE UNIVERSITY* | *NEW HAVEN* | YALE UNIVERSITY PRESS | LONDON • HUMPHREY MILFORD • OXFORD UNIVERSITY PRESS | 1940

8¹¹⁄₁₆″ × 5¹⁵⁄₁₆″. Gray cloth stamped in dark blue. Reprinted Westport, Conn.: Green-wood, [1971]. *Locations:* GHT, Harv (2), MWalB, RJS. Adler 32.

'COMMENT', pp. 13–14.

B 148 1941 ESSAY ANNUAL
1941

[shaky rule] | 1941 | Essay Annual | A YEARLY COLLECTION OF SIGNIFICANT ESSAYS | PERSONAL, CRITICAL, CONTROVERSIAL, AND | HUMOROUS | [shaky rule] | Erich A. Walter | DEPARTMENT OF ENGLISH | UNIVERSITY OF MICHIGAN | [shaky rule] | Scott, Foresman and Company | CHICAGO ATLANTA DALLAS NEW YORK

On copyright page: 'Copyright, 1941'. 8¹⁵⁄₁₆″ × 6″. Purple paper-covered boards, gray cloth spine stamped in purple. *Locations:* GHT, Harv. Previously published (*Yale Review*, March 1936; *Saturday Review*, 3 August 1940); Adler 153, 156.

'*The American Language*' and '*Vocabulary Glorification*', pp. 15–27.

B 149 BY THE NECK
1942

[all framed on left, right, and top, with a double rule on left and right] by [ascender of b rising to frame] | the | neck | *A Book of Hangings* | Selected from Contemporary Accounts | and Edited with an Introduction by | AUGUST MENCKEN | *Author of "First-Class Passenger," etc.* | *Foreword by* | *H. L. MENCKEN* | *Illustrated* | H A S T I N G S H O U S E | PUBLISHERS NEW YORK

On copyright page: 'Copyright, 1942'. 8⅛″ × 5½″. Seen in two shades of light brown cloth stamped in dark brown; cross-hatching more pronounced in darker cloth. *Locations:* GHT, Harv, InU-Li, RJS (2). Adler 32; Bulsterbaum 69.

'FOREWORD', pp. v–viii.

B 150 THE SCIENCE OF MATERIALISM
1942

THE SCIENCE OF MATERIALISM | By | CHARLES T. SPRADING | Author of | *Liberty and the Great Libertarians* | *Equal Freedom and Its Friends* | *Freedom and Its Fundamentals* | *War, Its Cause and Cure* | *Mutual Service and Cooperation* | *Science Versus Dogma* | THE TRUTH SEEKER COMPANY, INC. | 38 PARK ROW | NEW YORK

On copyright page: 'COPYRIGHT, 1942'. 7⅜″ × 5″. Orange wrappers printed in black. *Location:* IaAS. Previously published (New York *American*, 20 August 1934); not in Adler.

Quotation from "Philosophy: Organized Nonsense as a Form of Learning," pp. 14–16.

B 151 FEEDING THE LIONS
1942

Feeding | *the* | *Lions* | [two squiggles] | AN ALGONQUIN | COOKBOOK | [mirror image of previous squiggles] | *by* | *Frank Case* | [device] | THE GREYSTONE PRESS • NEW YORK

On copyright page: 'Copyright, 1942'. 9″ × 6″. Red cloth stamped in yellow orange. *Locations:* GHT, MCR, RJS. Not in Adler.

Nine-line quotation, probably from a letter, p. 21.

B 152 THIS IS MY BEST
1942

America's 93 Greatest Living Authors Present | [script] This Is My Best | [sprig]
OVER 150 SELF-CHOSEN AND | COMPLETE MASTERPIECES, TOGETHER
WITH | THEIR REASONS FOR THEIR SELECTIONS | [device: winged child
astride lion] *Edited by Whit Burnett* | Burton C. Hoffman THE DIAL PRESS New
York, 1942

8½″ × 5⅝″. Brownish gray cloth stamped in gilt on front, gilt and green on spine.
Book-of-the-Month Club selection. *Location:* Harv. Essay previously published
(*Newspaper Days* [A 51]); not in Adler.

'The Days of the Giants' with brief introduction (dated 26 June 1942), pp. 69–76.

B 153 THE NEW RIGHTS OF MAN
1942

The New Rights of Man | Text of Letter to Wells from Soviet Writer, Who Pictures the
Ordeal | and Rescue of Humanistic Civilization—H. G. Wells' | Reply and Program for
Liberated Humanity | H. G. WELLS | HALDEMAN-JULIUS PUBLICATIONS |
GIRARD, KANSAS

On copyright page: 'COPYRIGHT, 1942 | BY H. G. WELLS AND LEV USPENSKY'. Big
Blue Book no. 374 in the Haldeman-Julius catalogue. 8½″ × 5⁷⁄₁₆″. Dull blue-gray
wrappers. *Locations:* InU-Li, KPT, TxU. Not in Adler.

Remark by Mencken, p. 17. "I suspect that Wells's visions of the future will turn out to
be just as inaccurate this time. . . ."

B 154 LIFE IN A PUTTY KNIFE FACTORY
1943

H. Allen Smith [star] LIFE | IN A PUTTY KNIFE | FACTORY | *Doubleday, Doran* |
and Company, Inc., Garden City, New York   1943

On copyright page: 'FIRST EDITION'. 7¹³⁄₁₆″ × 5⅜″. Rust cloth stamped in black
and blue. *Locations:* GHT, KU-S, RJS. Adler 291.

Interview, pp. 170–77.

B 155 THE WRECKING OF THE EIGHTEENTH AMENDMENT
1943

The WRECKING *of the* | EIGHTEENTH AMENDMENT | *by* | ERNEST GOR-DON | THE ALCOHOL INFORMATION PRESS | FRANCESTOWN, NEW HAMPSHIRE

On copyright page: 'Copyright, 1943'. 8″ × 5⁵⁄₁₆″. Maroon cloth stamped in gilt. *Location:* RJS. Previously published (*American Mercury,* January 1931); not in Adler.

Quotation on prohibitionists as white trash (from "Editorial"), p. 273.

B 156 EDITING THE DAY'S NEWS
1943

AN INTRODUCTION TO NEWSPAPER | COPYREADING, HEADLINE WRIT-ING, | ILLUSTRATION, MAKEUP, AND | GENERAL NEWSPAPER METHODS | [in box shaded on right and bottom] *Editing the Day's News* | *BY* GEORGE C. BAS-TIAN | Late Copyreader on the *Chicago Daily Tribune* and Lecturer | in News Editing in the Medill School of Journalism of | Northwestern University | *AND* LELAND D. CASE | Formerly of the Staff of the Paris Edition of the *New York* | *Herald Tribune;* Formerly Assistant Professor, Medill School | of Journalism; Editor, *The Rotarian* Magazine | *Third Edition* | *NEW YORK* • *1943* | THE MACMILLAN COMPANY

On copyright page: 'PUBLISHED MARCH, 1943'. 9³⁄₁₆″ × 6¹⁄₁₆″. Grayish tan cloth stamped in red. Reprinted October 1944, April 1945, September 1946, February 1947; tenth printing 1950. *Location:* MB. Not in Adler.

Mencken credited (pp. v–vi) with assisting with chap. VIII, 'Streamlining Newspaper Copy'.

B 157 HARVEST OF MY YEARS
1943

HARVEST | OF MY YEARS | An Autobiography | [French rule] | By CHANNING POLLOCK | [French rule] | [three-line quotation from Ovid] | THE BOBBS-MER-RILL COMPANY | INDIANAPOLIS   NEW YORK

On copyright page: 'COPYRIGHT, 1943, BY CHANNING POLLOCK | *First Edition*'. 9⁵⁄₁₆″ × 6¼″. Maroon cloth stamped in gilt. *Locations:* GHT, InU-Li, NjP, RJS. Not in Adler.

Portion of letter to Pollock [13 July 1942], p. 81n. Cf. Forgue 466.

B 158 BOOKMEN'S HOLIDAY

1943

BOOKMEN'S HOLIDAY | *Notes and Studies* | *Written and Gathered in Tribute to* | HARRY MILLER LYDENBERG | *New York* | The New York Public Library | 1943

Copyright page: '1000 COPIES | PRINTED AT THE NEW YORK PUBLIC LIBRARY'. On p. [575]: 'Bound in Interlaken maroon vellum'. 9³⁄₁₆″ × 6″. Stamped in gilt on spine. For separate printing of Mencken's essay see E 44. *Locations:* Harv (2), RJS. Adler 33.

'Notes on American Given-names', pp. 70–80.

B 159 THE SHOCK OF RECOGNITION

1943

THE SHOCK | OF | RECOGNITION | [ornamental rule] | THE DEVELOPMENT OF LITERATURE | IN THE UNITED STATES | RECORDED BY THE MEN | WHO MADE IT | EDITED BY | EDMUND WILSON | [pictorial scene in oval] | DOUBLEDAY, DORAN AND COMPANY, INC. | GARDEN CITY   NEW YORK | 1943

On copyright page: 'FIRST EDITION'. 7⁷⁄₁₆″ × 4⁵⁄₁₆″. Blue cloth stamped in gilt and blindstamped. Second (?) printing 1947. Reprinted ("second edition") New York: Farrar, Straus, and Cudahy, [1955]. Reprinted New York: Grosset & Dunlap, paperback (Grosset's Universal Library UL17–18, 2 vols.), [1955], 2: 1160–1245; New York: Octagon, 1975, 2: 1160–1245. *Locations:* Harv (2), Yale. First book appearance of "Short View." Previously published (*Book of Prefaces* [A 16] [2], *Nation,* 27 August 1921, *Prejudices: Fifth Series* [A 34] [2]); Adler 140, 291.

'Theodore Dreiser', 'James Huneker', 'A Short View of Gamalielese', 'Want Ad' (from "The Fringes of Lovely Letters"), and 'Ring Lardner' (from "Four Makers of Tales"), pp. 1160–1245.

B 160 FOR LOVING A BOOK

1945

[rule] | With an Overture by H. L. MENCKEN | [rule] | [the rest between two vertical rules] [red] FOR LOVING A BOOK | [black] Further News Adventures | Among Bins and Bibliophiles | By CHARLES HONCE | [red eagle] | MOUNT VERNON | The Golden Eagle Press | 1945 | [rule extending to vertical rules] | Designed and Printed by S. A. JACOBS | [rule]

Printed at Mt. Vernon, N.Y. On p. [115]: *'Limited to one hundred and eleven copies on | Winterbourne mould-made paper . . . | . . . | . . . This copy is Number |* [number written in red]'. 9⅞″ × 6½″. Tan paper-covered boards stamped in gilt on spine. *Locations:* GHT, Harv, RJS. Adler 33.

'WHY I AM NOT A BOOK | COLLECTOR', pp. xvii–xx.

B 161 POPULATION ROADS TO PEACE OR WAR
1945

[head title] POPULATION ROADS | to | PEACE or WAR | By | GUY IRVING BURCH and ELMER PENDELL, Ph.D. | FOREWORD and POSTSCRIPT by WALTER B. PITKIN, Ph.D. | [text follows]

9″ × 6″. Folio. The book it advertises was published in 1945. *Location:* Yale. Not in Adler.

Quotation, presumably from a letter, p. [1].

B 162 ESQUIRE VS. POSTMASTER GENERAL
1945

B 162.1
Presumed first edition

[head title] [gothic] United States Court of Appeals | [roman] DISTRICT OF CO-LUMBIA | [rule] | No. 8899 | Esquire Incorporated, appellant, | V. | Frank C. Walker as Postmaster General of the United States, | APPELLEE. | Appeal from the District Court of the United States for the | District of Columbia | [rule] | [text follows]

Argued 20 April 1945, decided 4 June. 10⁷⁄₁₆″ × 8¹⁄₁₆″. Nine sheets printed and numbered on recto only, three or four staples front to back. The priority of the two editions is unknown. *Locations:* EPL, GHT, Yale. Not in Adler.

Testimony, pp. 8–9.

B 162.2
Presumed second edition

Title same except: ' . . . Appeal from the District Court of the United States for the | District of Columbia'. 9¼″ × 6¹⁄₁₆″. Six leaves; self wrappers. *Location:* Yale.

Testimony, pp. 8–9.

B 163 PROCEEDINGS AT TESTIMONIAL DINNER 1945

[head title] Proceedings At Testimonial Dinner On The | Retirement Of Hon. Eugene O'Dunne | As Member Of Supreme Bench | [rule] | Held At The Emerson Hotel On June 25, 1945 [. . . ; text follows]

9″ × 6″. Glossy wrappers, photo on front with names above and below, all print in box, beginning: 'Stenographic transcript of the proceedings. . . .' *Location:* EPL. Adler 270.

Transcript of speech, pp. 7–9.

B 164 AN AMERICAN TRAGEDY 1946

B 164.1
First edition (1946)

THEODORE DREISER | An American Tragedy | INTRODUCTION BY H. L. MENCKEN | Memorial Edition | TWO VOLUMES IN ONE | THE WORLD PUBLISHING COMPANY | CLEVELAND AND NEW YORK

On copyright page: 'MEMORIAL EDITION | *First printing March 1946* | HC'. 8$\frac{5}{16}$″ × 5$\frac{1}{2}$″. Black cloth stamped in red and gilt. The volumes are separately paginated (431, 409). A later printing coded HC2 (D). *Locations:* GHT, RJS. Adler 33; Bulsterbaum 69.

'INTRODUCTION', pp. ix–xvi.

B 164.2
Second edition (1948)

THEODORE DREISER | An American Tragedy | ILLUSTRATED BY GRANT REYNARD | INTRODUCTION BY H. L. MENCKEN | [illustration] | THE WORLD PUBLISHING COMPANY | CLEVELAND AND NEW YORK

On copyright page: 'ILLUSTRATED EDITION | FIRST PUBLISHED AUGUST 1948 | HC1'. 7$\frac{15}{16}$″ × 5$\frac{5}{16}$″. Blue cloth stamped in red and gilt. Later printings noted with codes 6WP153, 7HC455, 9HC958, 15HC767. Seventeenth printing in August 1971 (New York: World; styled 'Centennial Edition' on new dust jacket; no code on copyright page). Book-of-the-Month Club Special Members' Edition November 1948 with blindstamped dot on rear cover. Reprinted Cambridge, Mass.: Robert Bentley, Inc., [1978] ('by permission of T. Y. Crowell Co.'). *Locations:* GHT, RJS. Adler 33.

'INTRODUCTION', pp. 7–12.

B 165 ENCYCLOPÆDIA BRITANNICA
1946

[all within box, ornate borders at top and bottom] ENCYCLOPÆDIA BRITAN-
NICA | *A New Survey of Universal Knowledge* | Volume 20 | SARSAPARILLA to
SORCERY | [shield with book and phoenix] | THE UNIVERSITY OF CHICAGO |
ENCYCLOPÆDIA BRITANNICA, INC. | CHICAGO • LONDON • TORONTO

On copyright page: 'COPYRIGHT | . . . | 1929 . . . | . . . | 1946'. Fourteenth (1946)
printing of 1929 edition. 10⅞″ × 8¼″. Red cloth stamped in gilt. "HLM helped write
this article which appeared from 1946–1954 and entirely wrote the lists of American
slang included in this article. From 1955 *[sic]* to the present edition, he helped write
the section of American slang included in the article 'Slang' " (Adler). *Location:* NbU.
Adler 34.

'SLANG' (signed H[enry]. Br[adley]., G[eorge]. P. K[rapp]., H.L.M.), pp. 765–67,
followed by lists of American, British, and Australian slang, pp. 767–70.

B 166 CALIFORNIA FOLKLORE QUARTERLY
1946

[head title] *Reprinted from the* CALIFORNIA FOLKLORE QUARTERLY | VOLUME V •
NUMBER 3 • JULY, 1946 | Reviews of Books | [rule] | [text follows]

10″ × 6¾″ offprint paginated 317–28. No covers. *Location:* Yale (2). Not in Adler.

Review of *American Sayings,* by Henry F. Woods, pp. 319–20.

B 167 WRITERS AND WRITING
1946

[in box] WRITERS AND WRITING | by Robert van Gelder | [below box] Charles
Scribner's Sons New York 1946

On copyright page: 'A'. 7¹⁵⁄₁₆″ × 5⁷⁄₁₆″. Green cloth stamped in yellow, or blue cloth
stamped in gilt. *Locations:* GHT, Harv (rebound), InU-Li, NjP. Previously published
(*New York Times Book Review,* 11 February 1940); Adler 125.

'Mencken on Literature and Politics' (interview), pp. 20–22.

B 168 OF, BY, AND ABOUT HENRY MILLER
1947

OF–BY–AND ABOUT HENRY | MILLER a collection of pieces by Miller– | Herbert Read–Nicola Chiaromonte–Wallace | Fowlie–Paul Rosenfeld–H. L. Mencken– | [five more lines of names] | [ornament] | Printed by | Leo Porgie for the Alicat Bookshop Press | At 287 South Broadway, Yonkers, N. Y. | In June, 1947 | Of this edition of 1000 copies, | only 750 copies are for sale. | Copyright 1947 by Oscar Baradinsky, | Alicat Bookshop.

11″ × 8¼″. Beige wrappers (11⅞″ × 8¹⁵⁄₁₆″) printed in black and red. *Locations:* RJS, Yale. Not in Adler.

Quotation regarding *Black Spring* from letter, p. [3].

B 169 NATIONAL CONFERENCE OF EDITORIAL WRITERS
1947

[cover title] [all within double-rule box] STENOGRAPHIC TRANSCRIPT | FIRST ANNUAL MEETING | NATIONAL CONFERENCE | *of* | EDITORIAL WRITERS | STATLER HOTEL | WASHINGTON, D. C. | OCTOBER 16–18, 1947 | [heavy dot] | THURSDAY AFTERNOON | OCTOBER 16, 1947, | CONGRESSIONAL ROOM | [heavy dot] | GUILD REPORTING ASSOCIATES | 228 TUCKERMAN ST., N. W. | WASHINGTON 11, D. C. | [rule] | GEORGIA 6454

Text mimeographed. 10¾″ × 8⁵⁄₁₆″. Yellow-orange wrappers printed in black. *Location:* WMM. Adler 271.

Remarks, pp. 51–60.

B 170 THE LOST ART OF PROFANITY
1948

THE LOST ART | OF PROFANITY | [thick dot] | [script] *by* | BURGES JOHNSON | *Foreword by* H. L. MENCKEN | *Drawings by* | ORSON LOWELL | [thick dot] | THE BOBBS-MERRILL COMPANY • PUBLISHERS | INDIANAPOLIS NEW YORK

On copyright page: 'COPYRIGHT, 1948 . . . | . . . | *First Edition*'. 7⁷⁄₁₆″ × 5½″. Red cloth stamped in gilt. Dedicated to Mencken (p. [5]). *Locations:* GHT, Harv, RJS. Adler 34.

'FOREWORD', pp. [9–11].

B 171 STAR REPORTERS
1948

[all in double-rule box] STAR | REPORTERS | and 34 of their stories | [star] | Collected, with Notes and | an Introduction, by | WARD GREENE | [outside box] [Random House device] | RANDOM HOUSE • NEW YORK

On copyright page: 'FIRST PRINTING | Copyright, 1948'. 8³⁄₁₆″ × 5⁷⁄₁₆″. Gray cloth stamped in blue and gold on spine. Three printings 1948. *Locations:* GHT, INS (rebound), TxU (2). Previously published (Baltimore *Sun*, 9, 13, 14, 17, 18 July 1925; *Prejudices: Fifth Series* [A 34]); Adler 68, 99.

Scopes Trial dispatches ("Mencken Finds Daytonians . . . ," "Yearning Mountaineers' Souls . . . ," "Darrow's Eloquent Appeal . . . ," "Malone the Victor . . . ," "Battle Now Over . . . ") and 'Bryan', pp. 228–55.

B 172 LOOKING BACK
1948

[between ornate border at top and bottom] *Looking Back* | A Successful Author Reviews His Past | To Help Beginners On Their | Upward Climb | *By Harry Harrison Kroll* | (With Foreword by H. L. Mencken) | [ornament] | 35 c | COPYRIGHT, 1947 | THE AUTHOR & JOURNALIST | 1837 Champa Street | DENVER 2, COLORADO

Copyright page: 'This report is reprinted with | addition of Foreword by H. L. | Mencken, from the November 5, | 1947, issue of *The Author & Journalist*.' 8¹⁵⁄₁₆″ × 6⅛″. Self wrappers. *Location:* EPL (signed and dated 1948 by Mencken). Adler 34 (title wrong).

'Introduction', p. [3].

B 173 LITERARY HISTORY OF THE UNITED STATES
1948

LITERARY HISTORY | OF THE | UNITED STATES | *Editors* | ROBERT E. SPILLER • WILLARD THORP | THOMAS H. JOHNSON • HENRY SEIDEL CANBY | *Associates* | HOWARD MUMFORD JONES • DIXON WECTER | STANLEY T. WILLIAMS | *VOLUME II* | 1948 | THE MACMILLAN COMPANY • NEW YORK

On copyright page: '*First Printing*'. 9³⁄₁₆″ × 6¹⁄₁₆″. Dark blue cloth stamped in gilt. Three-volume set in dust jackets and maroon paper-covered box with pale blue label printed in dark blue and maroon. Reprinted in successive "editions" 1953, 1963, and 1974. *Locations:* GHT, Harv, InU-Li, RJS. Adler 34; Bulsterbaum 70.

'40. THE AMERICAN LANGUAGE' (credited to Mencken on p. 1394), pp. 663–75.

B 174 ALFRED A. KNOPF PRESENTS
1948

Alfred • A • Knopf presents | [within ornamental side borders] [blue] *Supplement Two* | T H E | American | Language | [blue] H. L. MENCKEN [borders end] | *Coming March 22nd • 864 pages • $7.50*

8¼″ × 16¹¹⁄₁₆″ sheet folded twice to make six "pages." Business reply card enclosed. *Location:* Yale. Not in Adler.

Sample pages.

B 175 ESSAYS IN CRITICISM AND GUIDANCE
1948

ESSAYS IN CRITICISM AND | GUIDANCE | STUDIES OF CURRENT LIFE, TRENDS OF THOUGHT, LINES OF | ACTION, CRITICISMS OF EVILS, AND GUIDANCE IN THE | DIRECTION OF REALISTIC THINKING | AND AC-TION | By E. HALDEMAN-JULIUS | HALDEMAN-JULIUS PUBLICATIONS | GIRARD, KANSAS

On copyright page: 'Copyright, 1948'. Big Blue Book B-695. 8⅜″ × 5¼″. Light yellowish-brown wrappers. *Locations:* InU-Li, KPT. Not in Adler.

Letter, p. 19. Cf. *Menckeniana* 80.11.

B 176 PHILOLOGICA
1949

PHILOLOGICA: | *THE MALONE ANNIVERSARY STUDIES* | Edited | *by* | THOMAS A. KIRBY | *and* | HENRY BOSLEY WOOLF | [ornament: shield] | *THE JOHNS HOPKINS PRESS : BALTIMORE* | *1949*

8¹⁵⁄₁₆″ × 5¹⁵⁄₁₆″. Brown cloth stamped in gilt. For offprint see E 53. *Location:* Harv. Adler 34; Bulsterbaum 70.

'THE BIRTH OF NEW VERBS', pp. 313–19.

B 177 NEWSMEN AT WORK
1949

[across pp. [ii–iii]] NEWSMEN AT WORK | [parallogram] REPORTING AND WRITING THE NEWS . . . *[sic]* | LAURENCE R. CAMPBELL and ROLAND E. WOLSELEY | [below respective names] *University of Oregon   Syracuse University* | HOUGHTON MIFFLIN COMPANY | BOSTON—NEW YORK—CHICAGO—DALLAS—ATLANTA—SAN FRANCISCO | THE RIVERSIDE PRESS, CAMBRIDGE

On copyright page: 'COPYRIGHT, 1949'. 9⁷⁄₁₆″ × 7″. Rust cloth stamped in black and gold and blindstamped. *Location:* GHT. Previously published (1947?; cf. *Fante/ Mencken* [A 79], p. 80S); not in Adler.

Excerpt from uncredited newspaper interview by Hal Boyle, p. 188.

B 178 A TREASURY OF GREAT REPORTING
1949

A TREASURY OF | [red] GREAT | [red] REPORTING | "Literature under Pressure" | from the Sixteenth Century | to Our Own Time | Edited by | [red] Louis L. Snyder | ASSOCIATE PROFESSOR OF HISTORY | THE COLLEGE OF THE CITY OF NEW YORK | AND | [red] Richard B. Morris | PROFESSOR OF HISTORY, COLUMBIA UNIVERSITY | [red] 1949 | SIMON AND SCHUSTER • NEW YORK

Preface by Herbert Bayard Swope. 9³⁄₁₆″ × 6″. Black cloth-covered boards stamped in gilt, white cloth spine stamped in gilt and red. Second "edition," revised and enlarged, 1962, cloth and paperback; Mencken on same pages. Cloth version reprinted three times 1962; third paperback printing 1967. *Locations:* Harv, MMeT. Previously published (Baltimore *Sun*, 13 July 1925; New York *Times*, 21 July 1925); not in Adler.

'Deep in "the Coca-Cola belt" ' ("Yearning Mountaineers' Souls . . . ") and 'Monkey business in Tennessee' ("Tennessee in the Frying Pan"), pp. 428–37.

B 179 PATTERNS IN WRITING
1950

B 179.1
First edition (1950)

[across pp. [ii–iii]] PATTERNS *in* WRITING | [French rule] | *A Book of Readings for College Students* || [on p. [ii]] [next three lines to left of WSA device] WILLIAM SLOANE | ASSOCIATES, INC: | *Publishers—New York* || [on p. [iii]] ROBERT B.

DOREMUS | • | EDGAR W. LACY | • | GEORGE BUSH RODMAN | *University of Wisconsin*

On copyright page: '*Copyright, 1950* . . . | . . . | *First Printing*'. 8³⁄₁₆″ × 5½″. Boards two-thirds covered by blue paper, remainder and spine gray cloth stamped in blue and gilt. Subsequent printings in March 1950, May 1951, January 1952, August 1952, March 1953, September 1953, June 1954. *Location:* MU. Previously published (*New Yorker,* 2 April 1949); not in Adler.

'*Scented Words*', pp. 572–78.

B 179.2
Second edition (1956)

[on p. [ii]] ROBERT B. DOREMUS | EDGAR W. LACY | GEORGE BUSH ROD-MAN | *University of Wisconsin* | THE DRYDEN PRESS | *Publishers* || [on p. [iii]] [script] Patterns | IN | [script] Writing | REVISED

On copyright page: '*Revised Edition* . . . | . . . | *First Printing, March 1956*'. 8¼″ × 5⁷⁄₁₆″. Blue-green cloth stamped in gilt and black. Reprinted July and November 1956. *Location:* MNoeS.

'*Scented Words*', pp. 582–88.

B 180 THE WORLD'S BEST
1950

105 GREATEST LIVING AUTHORS | *PRESENT* | *The World's Best* | STORIES • HUMOR • DRAMA • BIOGRAPHY | HISTORY • ESSAYS • POETRY | *Edited by* | WHIT BURNETT | *The Dial Press* [device] *New York* • *1950*

8³⁄₁₆″ × 5⁷⁄₁₆″. Gray cloth stamped in blue and gilt on spine. Book-of-the-Month Club selection. *Location:* MBU. Excerpt previously published; not in Adler.

Headnote and '*The Poetry of Christianity*' (end of *Treatise on the Gods* [A 40]), pp. 148–54.

B 181 F. SCOTT FITZGERALD: THE MAN AND HIS WORK
1951

B 181.1
First edition (1951)

F. Scott Fitzgerald: | [rule with bar superimposed at center] | THE MAN AND HIS

WORK | [rule] | *edited by* ALFRED KAZIN | [rule] | *Cleveland* [World device] *New York* | THE WORLD PUBLISHING COMPANY | [rule]

On copyright page: '*First Edition* | HC 351 | Copyright 1951'. 8⁵⁄₁₆″ × 5⅝″. Black cloth blindstamped and stamped in gilt. *Locations:* GHT, InU-Li. Previously published (Baltimore *Evening Sun*, 2 May 1925); not in Adler.

Review of *The Great Gatsby* ("As H. L. M. Sees It"), pp. 88–92.

B 181.2
Second edition (1962)

F. Scott Fitzgerald | THE MAN AND HIS WORK | Edited by ALFRED KAZIN | COLLIER BOOKS | *A Division of Macmillan Publishing Co., Inc.* | NEW YORK | COLLIER MACMILLAN PUBLISHERS | LONDON | [device]

On copyright page: '*First Collier Books Edition 1962*'. 7¹⁄₁₆″ × 4⅛″. White wrappers printed in green and black. Fifth printing 1974. *Locations:* EPL, MCL (rebound), MNoeS (rebound). S1.8.

Review of *The Great Gatsby* ("As H. L. M. Sees It"), pp. 89–92.

B 182 CHRONICLES OF BARABBAS
1952

Chronicles of | Barabbas | 1884–1934 | Further Chronicles and Comment | 1952 | BY GEORGE H. DORAN | *With candid portrait reviews by* | *Sinclair Lewis* | *W. Somerset Maugham* | *H. L. Mencken* | *Christopher Morley* | *"Now Barabbas was a publisher"* | *Twenty-first thousand* | RINEHART & COMPANY, INCORPORATED | *New York Toronto*

8⅜″ × 5½″. Blue paper-covered boards (front blindstamped), black cloth spine stamped in gilt. Copy with blank copyright page noted. Mencken's essay is his review of the 1935 edition, reprinted from the *Nation* (5 June 1935). *Locations:* GHT, RJS. Adler 188.

'A FRIEND OF LETTERS' and exchange of letters with Doran, pp. 422–26.

B 183 CHICAGO'S LEFT BANK
1953

CHICAGO'S | LEFT BANK | BY | ALSON J. SMITH | [device] | HENRY REGNERY COMPANY | CHICAGO 1953

8¼″ × 5⁷⁄₁₆″. Blue or maroon cloth stamped in gilt on spine. *Locations:* GHT (dj), MChB, RJS (dj). Previously published (*Smart Set,* August 1918); not in Adler.

Quotation on Chicago (from "A Sub-Potomac Phenomenon"), p. [3] and front flap of dust jacket.

B 184 THE STATURE OF THEODORE DREISER
1955

[across pp. [ii–iii]] THE STATURE OF THEODORE DREISER || [on p. [ii]] *a critical survey of the man and his work* | *edited by* ALFRED KAZIN *and* CHARLES SHAPIRO | *with an introduction by* ALFRED KAZIN | *Indiana University Press, Bloomington* || [on p. [iii]] [device]

On copyright page: '*Copyright* © *1955*'. 9″ × 6″. Dark gray cloth blindstamped and stamped in silver. Reprinted as a Midland Book Edition 1965. *Locations:* InU-Li, MChB. Previously published (*The Seven Arts,* August 1917); not in Adler.

'THE DREISER BUGABOO', pp. [84]-91.

B 185 THE PROVINCE OF PROSE
1956

The PROVINCE | *of PROSE* | Edited by | WILLIAM R. KEAST | Cornell University | and | ROBERT E. STREETER | University of Chicago | [Harper device] | *New York* | HARPER & BROTHERS, PUBLISHERS

On copyright page: '*Copyright* © *1956*'. 9¼″ × 6″. Light reddish-brown cloth stamped in black, white, and blue. *Location:* GHT. Previously published (*New Yorker,* 25 September 1948); not in Adler.

'*The Podunk Mystery*', pp. 296–302.

B 186 WHO: SIXTY YEARS OF AMERICAN EMINENCE
1958

[on p. [ii], in tall letters] WHO || [on p. [iii]] *Sixty Years of American Eminence* | *The Story of* WHO'S WHO IN AMERICA | *by Cedric A. Larson* | [device] MCDOWELL, OBOLENSKY, NEW YORK, N.Y.

On copyright page: 'COPYRIGHT © 1958 . . . | . . . | *First Printing*'. 8³⁄₁₆″ × 5½″. Red cloth-covered boards, black cloth spine stamped in gilt. *Locations:* GHT, Harv, RJS. Previously published (*Saturday Review*, 24 October 1936); S1.7.

'TAP-DAY IN AMERICA', pp. 337–43.

B 187 THE ARMCHAIR ESQUIRE
1958

B 187.1
First edition (1958)

THE ARMCHAIR | Esquire [in *Esquire* title font] | *Edited by* ARNOLD GIN-GRICH | *and* L. RUST HILLS | INTRODUCTION BY *Granville Hicks* | [Putnam's device] | G. P. PUTNAM'S SONS *New York*

On copyright page: '© 1958'. Published October 1958 (so the Popular Library edition). 8³⁄₈″ × 5½″. Black cloth stamped in red and silver. Second printing December 1958. *Locations:* GHT, InU-Li, MB, RJS. Previously published (*Esquire,* December 1943); Adler 158.

'AN EVENING ON THE HOUSE', pp. 172–80.

B 187.2
Second edition (1959)

The Armchair Esquire | [thick-thin rule, ornament superimposed at center] | Edited by ARNOLD GINGRICH | and L. RUST HILLS | [windmill device] | HEINEMANN | LONDON MELBOURNE TORONTO

On copyright page: 'First published in Great Britain 1959'. 8⁷⁄₁₆″ × 5½″. Blue cloth stamped in gilt on spine. *Locations:* BL, CtNbT, GHT. Not in Adler.

'An Evening on the House', pp. 165–73.

B 187.3
Third edition (1960)

Popular Library Edition | THE ARMCHAIR | Esquire [in *Esquire* title font] | ED-ITED BY | Arnold Gingrich | and L. Rust Hills | INTRODUCTION BY | Granville Hicks | POPULAR LIBRARY [heavy dot] NEW YORK

On copyright page: 'Published in October, 1960'. Popular Library Special W1100. 6⁷⁄₈″ × 4³⁄₁₆″. Red, white, black, green, blue-green, flesh, yellow, and gray wrappers. *Locations:* GHT, Harv, ViMvPHC. Adler 158.

'AN EVENING ON THE HOUSE', pp. 146–54.

B 188 THE HOME TEAM
1958

[across pp. [ii, 1]] [beneath photo] A PATRIOTIC STORY, TOLD BY JAMES H. BREADY |
WITH EMOTION, ARITHMETIC, GLASS PLATES & BAND MUSIC | Copyright, © 1958,
by James H. Bready || [on p. [1]] [within ornate frame] 1859 | A FULL CENTURY | OF
BASEBALL IN | BALTIMORE | 1959 | [below frame, to left of another photo] The |
Home | Team

Published "[Baltimore?]" (OCLC). 11^{15}⁄$_{16}$″ × 8^{15}⁄$_{16}$″. Orange cloth stamped in black.
According to a 1959 letter from a bookseller to Herbert F. West regarding this book, it
is the "only published appearance of any of Mencken's drawings" (NhD). Second
printing 1971. *Locations:* KU-S, MdBCC. Not in Adler.

1894 sketch of Oriole batterymates [George] Hemming and [Boileryard] Clarke,
p. [50B].

B 189 LETTERS OF THEODORE DREISER
1959

Letters of | THEODORE DREISER | A SELECTION | VOLUME ONE | *Edited
with Preface and Notes by* | Robert H. Elias | *Consulting Editors* | SCULLEY BRAD-
LEY *and* ROBERT E. SPILLER | [UPP device] | *Philadelphia* | University of Penn-
sylvania Press

On copyright page: '© 1959'. 8^{5}⁄$_{16}$″ × 5^{9}⁄$_{16}$″. Black cloth stamped in gilt on spine. One
of three volumes, boxed; letters *from* Mencken only in first volume. *Locations:* GHT,
Harv, InU-Li. Adler 273; Bulsterbaum 93.

Letters, pp. 114–16, 146–47, 179–80, 190–91, 229–30, 238–40, 242–43, 276–77,
288, 312, 319.

B 190 MY LIFETIME IN LETTERS
1960

MY LIFETIME | IN LETTERS | Upton Sinclair | UNIVERSITY OF MISSOURI
PRESS | COLUMBIA

On copyright page: 'Copyright 1960'. 9″ × 6″. Blue cloth stamped in gilt. *Locations:*
GHT, Harv, InU-Li, RJS. Adler 273; Bulsterbaum 93.

Letters, pp. 228–41, 249–53, 314–28.

B 191 VANITY FAIR
1960

B 191.1
First American printing (1960)

[peacock] | V A N I T Y   F A I R | SELECTIONS FROM AMERICA'S MOST MEMORABLE MAGAZINE | A CAVALCADE | *of the* | *1920s* AND *1930s* | [ornaments] | *Edited by* | CLEVELAND AMORY | *and* | FREDERIC BRADLEE | *Picture Editor:* KATHARINE TWEED | THE VIKING PRESS • PUBLISHERS • NEW YORK

On copyright page: 'Copyright © 1960'. 11⅞″ × 8¹⁵⁄₁₆″. Gray and white figured paper-covered boards, red cloth spine, stamped in gilt. Reprinted New York: Bonanza Books, n.d. Book-of-the-Month Club selection. *Location:* MBU. Previously published (*Vanity Fair*, August 1923); not in Adler.

Mencken's contribution to 'The Ten Dullest Authors: A Symposium', p. 76.

B 191.2
First English issue (1961)

CAVALCADE | of the 1920s and 1930s | *Selections from America's* | *most memorable* *magazine 'Vanity Fair'* | Edited by | CLEVELAND AMORY | and | FREDERIC BRADLEE | Picture Editor | KATHARINE TWEED | THE BODLEY HEAD | LONDON

The title page is a cancel. On copyright page: 'Printed in the U.S.A. . . . | . . . | *First published in Great Britain 1961'*. 11¹⁵⁄₁₆″ × 9″. Figured blue-gray and white paper-covered boards, blue cloth spine stamped in gilt. *Location:* MBU.

Mencken's contribution to 'The Ten Dullest Authors: A Symposium', p. 76.

B 192 JOSEPH HERGESHEIMER
1961

[cover title] [down left column, on gray] Joseph | Hergesheimer | [double rule] | *American* | *Man of Letters* | *1880–1954* | *An Exhibition* | *at the* | *Humanities Research* | *Center* | [rule] | THE | UNIVERSITY | OF TEXAS | [rule] | *January 1961* || [down right column, both in separate boxes] [signature of Hergesheimer to left of red ornament] | [illustration of Cytherea in gold, black, and gray]

On p. [32]: '[UT logo] | *One thousand copies* | *of this exhibition catalogue* | *have been* *made by The Printing Division for* | *The Humanities Research Center* | *The University of Texas* | *February 1961'*. 9¹¹⁄₁₆″ × 6¾″. Pictorial wrappers in black, gray, gold, and red. *Location:* GHT. Poem previously published (*Ventures into Verse* [A 1]); Adler 273; C1.11.

Quotations from letters, inscriptions, and 'An Ante-Christmas Rondeau', pp. 27–31.

B 193 BETWEEN FRIENDS
1962

BETWEEN FRIENDS | LETTERS OF | JAMES BRANCH CABELL | AND OTH-ERS | EDITED BY | PADRAIC COLUM | AND | MARGARET FREEMAN CA-BELL | WITH AN | INTRODUCTION | BY | CARL VAN VECHTEN | [HB device] | HARCOURT, BRACE & WORLD, INC. NEW YORK

On copyright page: '© 1962 . . . | . . . | *first edition*'. 9³⁄₁₆″ × 6¹⁄₁₆″. Grayish yellow cloth stamped in blue on spine. *Locations:* GHT, Harv, InU-Li, RJS. S1.17; Bulsterbaum 94.

Letters, *passim*.

B 194 THE ANXIOUS YEARS
1963

The Anxious Years | AMERICA IN THE NINETEEN THIRTIES | A COLLEC-TION | OF CONTEMPORARY WRITINGS | EDITED WITH AN INTRODUC-TION BY | *LOUIS FILLER* | [Putnam device] | *G. P. Putnam's Sons   New York*

On copyright page: '© 1963'. 7¹⁵⁄₁₆″ × 5¼″. Red cloth stamped in gilt on spine. Reprinted as *American Anxieties: A Collective Portrait of the 1930s* (New Brunswick, N.J.: Transaction, [1993]), paperback. *Locations:* Harv, MBMU, MWelC. Previously published (*American Mercury*, May 1936); S1.9.

'THE NEW DEAL MENTALITY', pp. 126–40.

B 195 ESQUIRE'S WORLD OF HUMOR
1964

B 195.1
First American printing (1964)

Esquire's [script] | World of Humor | By the editors of Esquire Magazine | Commentary by David Newman | Foreword by Malcolm Muggeridge | Published by Esquire, Inc., New York | in association with | Harper & Row, New York and Evanston, [1964] [*sic*]

10⅝″ × 8½″. Yellow cloth stamped in purple. *Locations:* GHT, MB. Previously published (*Esquire,* January 1944); S1.10.

'The Institution: Death | The Wrecker: H. L. Mencken' ("Obsequies in the Grand Manner"), pp. 191–94.

B 195.2
First English printing (1965)

Esquire's [script] | World of Humor | By the editors of Esquire Magazine | Commentary by David Newman | Foreword by Malcolm Muggeridge | ARTHUR BARKER LIMITED | 20 New Bond Street London W1

On copyright page: 'First published in Great Britain . . . 1965'. 10⁷⁄₁₆″ × 8⁵⁄₁₆″. Medium blue paper-covered boards printed in black. *Location*: GHT.

'The Institution: Death | The Wrecker: H. L. Mencken' ("Obsequies in the Grand Manner"), pp. 191–94.

B 196 BEHOLD THIS DREAMER
1964

Behold | This Dreamer! | *An Autobiography by* | FULTON OURSLER | *Edited and with Commentary by* | FULTON OURSLER, JR. | [LB device] | *Little, Brown and Company* • Boston • Toronto

On copyright page: 'COPYRIGHT © 1964 . . . | . . . | FIRST EDITION'. 8³⁄₁₆″ × 5¼″. Red cloth blindstamped and stamped in silver. *Location:* GHT.

Letter to Oursler quoted, p. 316.

B 197 LETTERS FROM BOHEMIA
1964

B 197.1
First American printing (1964)

Letters from Bohemia | *by* BEN HECHT | [two stars over one star] | 1964 | DOUBLEDAY & COMPANY, INC. | GARDEN CITY, NEW YORK

On copyright page: 'First Edition'. 8³⁄₁₆″ × 5⅜″. Green cloth-covered boards, gray cloth spine stamped in black. *Locations:* GHT (dj), Harv, InU-Li (dj), RJS (dj). S1.18, 27.

Letters, pp. 80–83, rear of dust jacket.

B 197.2
First English printing (1965)

Letters from Bohemia | *by* BEN HECHT | [two stars over one star] | LONDON | HAMMOND, HAMMOND & COMPANY

On copyright page: '*First published in Great Britain* 1965 | . . . | *Printed in Great Britain*'. 8½″ × 5½″. Black cloth stamped in silver on spine. *Locations:* BL, GHT, InU-Li.

Letters, pp. 81–84.

B 198 A CREATIVE CENTURY
1964

[across pp. [2–3]] AN EXHIBITION   SELECTIONS FROM THE TWENTIETH CENTURY | A [elaborate descender] | Creative Century [large capitals] | COLLECTIONS AT THE UNIVERSITY OF TEXAS | HELD IN NOVEMBER 1964 AT THE ACADEMIC CENTER & UNDERGRADUATE LIBRARY : THE UNIVERSITY OF TEXAS

On page 71: ' . . . *compiled by Andreas Brown* . . . | . . . | . . . *Three thousand copies* . . . | *were published by the Humanities Research Center and printed by* | *the Printing Division of The University of Texas in November 1964.*' (1) 9¹⁄₁₆″ × 5³⁄₁₆″. Gray paper-covered boards printed in black and white (500 copies). (2) 9¹⁄₁₆″ × 5¼″. Gray wrappers printed in black and white. Gray slip (2½″ × 5¹⁵⁄₁₆″) printed in red and black ('*With the compliments of* THE HUMANITIES RESEARCH CENTER') laid in one of the RJS copies in wrappers. *Locations:* Harv, RJS (2).

Photograph of presentation inscription in Shaw's copy of *George Bernard Shaw: His Plays* (A 2) and excerpt from letter to Shaw, pp. 42–43.

B 199 ONE HUNDRED YEARS OF THE NATION
1965

[four floral ornaments] | *One Hundred Years of* | *THE NATION* | A CENTENNIAL ANTHOLOGY | Edited by HENRY M. CHRISTMAN | ABRAHAM FELDMAN, Poetry Editor | Introduction by CAREY McWILLIAMS | THE MACMILLAN COMPANY, NEW YORK | COLLIER-MACMILLAN LIMITED, LONDON

On copyright page: 'Copyright © 1965'. 9¼″ × 6⅛″. Red cloth stamped in gilt. Reprinted New York: Capricorn Books, [1972], paperback (Capricorn Giant 368). *Locations:* GHT, MBU. Previously published (*Nation*, 5 December 1923).

'H. L. Mencken', pp. 136–39.

B 200 D-DAYS AT DAYTON
1965

[on p. ii] D-DAYS || [on p. iii] AT DAYTON | [rule] | *Reflections on the* | *Scopes Trial* | *Edited by* | *Jerry R. Tompkins* | LOUISIANA STATE UNIVERSITY PRESS Baton Rouge / 1965

8¹⁵⁄₁₆″ × 5⅞″. Goldenrod cloth stamped in black on spine. *Locations:* GHT, MBU. Previously published (Baltimore *Sun*, 9–11, 13–18 July 1925; some appeared in B 171 and B 178); S1.10.

Scopes Trial dispatches ("Mencken Finds Daytonians . . . ," "Impossibility of Obtaining . . . ," "Mencken Likens Trial . . . ," "Yearning Mountaineers' Souls . . . ," "Darrow's Eloquent Appeal," "Law and Freedom," "Mencken Declares Strictly Fair Trial . . . ," "Malone the Victor . . . ," "Battle Now Over . . . "), pp. 35–51.

B 201 THE SMART SET: A HISTORY AND ANTHOLOGY
1966

The SMART SET [in form of a typical *SS* cover, with large S's and masked devil holding two winged hearts on strings] | [in double-rule box, within the rules ornate brackets left and right] A HISTORY | AND ANTHOLOGY BY | Carl R. Dolmetsch | WITH AN INTRODUCTORY REMINISCENCE BY | S. N. Behrman | [below box] THE DIAL PRESS | [Dial device] | NEW YORK 1966

On copyright page: 'FIRST PRINTING, 1966'. 11⅞″ × 8¹³⁄₁₆″. White cloth stamped in gilt. The usual dust jacket is white paper printed in black, red, and blue. Another is printed in maroon and grayish green (probably on remainders or for a book club). Prepublication copy in spiral binding, unprinted yellow paper covers. *Locations:* GHT (2), RJS. Previously published (*Smart Set*, June 1923, September 1917); S1.22.

'*Répétition Générale* | SELECTIONS' (with George Jean Nathan) and '*Si Mutare Potest Aethiops Pellum Suam* | ABRIDGED', pp. 141–43, 243–48.

B 202 WINESBURG, OHIO: TEXT AND CRITICISM
1966

THE VIKING CRITICAL LIBRARY | [row of contiguous ornaments] | SHERWOOD ANDERSON | [script] *Winesburg, Ohio* | [rule] | *TEXT AND CRITICISM* | EDITED BY JOHN H. FERRES | MICHIGAN STATE UNIVERSITY | [Viking device] | NEW YORK: THE VIKING PRESS

On copyright page: '*First published in 1966*'. 7¾″ × 5⅛″. Gray cloth stamped in red and black. Reprinted 1968, 1969 (2), 1971, 1973 (2), 1974, 1975 (2), 1976. Reprinted [Harmondsworth and New York:] Penguin, [1977], 1977, 1980; paperback. *Location:* MChB. Previously published; *Menckeniana* 124.6.

'*Smart Set*, August 1919' ("Novels, Chiefly Bad—II"), pp. 257–58. Review of the novel.

B 203 A GIRL LIKE I
1966

[ornament] | A Girl Like I | ANITA LOOS | New York [leaf] THE VIKING PRESS

On copyright page: '*First published in 1966*'. 8⁵⁄₁₆″ × 5⁹⁄₁₆″. Red-orange paper-covered boards, black cloth spine stamped in gilt. *Locations:* GHT, InU-Li, MChB, RJS. S1.29.

Quotations from letters, pp. 218–19.

B 204 WILLA CATHER AND HER CRITICS
1967

Willa Cather | and Her Critics | *Edited by* | JAMES SCHROETER | CORNELL UNIVERSITY PRESS | ITHACA, NEW YORK

On copyright page: '*First published 1967*'. 9″ × 6″. Tan cloth stamped in silver on spine. *Location:* MB. Previously published (*Smart Set*, January 1916, February 1919, December 1920, October 1922); S1.12.

Reviews of *Song of the Lark* ("Partly About Books—4—Cinderella the Nth"), *My Ántonia* ("Sunrise on the Prairie"), *Youth and the Bright Medusa* ("Chiefly Americans"), and *One of Ours* ("Portrait of an American Citizen—II"), pp. 7–12.

B 205 WHAT HAPPENS WHEN YOU DIE?
1968

EDITED BY *August H. Wagner* | [rule] | WHAT | HAPPENS | WHEN | YOU DIE? | [rule] | *Twentieth Century Thought* | *on Survival After Death* | [A-S device] | ABELARD-SCHUMAN | LONDON NEW YORK TORONTO

On copyright page: '© Copyright 1968'. (1) 8¼″ × 5⅜″. Black cloth stamped on spine in metallic blue-green. (2) 8¼″ × 5⁷⁄₁₆″. Light gray cloth stamped in black on front and spine. *Locations:* MA, MGrefC. S1.12.

Letter to Wagner, p. 129.

B 206 THE LETTERS OF CARL SANDBURG
1968

THE LETTERS OF | *Carl Sandburg* | EDITED BY HERBERT MITGANG | *Harcourt, Brace & World, Inc. : New York*

On copyright page: 'Letters copyright © 1968 . . . | . . . | First edition'. 9³⁄₁₆″ × 6⅛″. Black cloth stamped in copper on spine. *Locations:* GHT, MChB.

Quotation from letter of 6 August 1927, p. 253.

B 206A THE LIBERTY YEARS
1969

THE Liberty | YEARS | 1924–1950 | *AN ANTHOLOGY* | Edited and with Commentary by | ALLEN CHURCHILL | *PRENTICE-HALL, INC. Englewood Cliffs, New Jersey*

On copyright page: '© 1969'. 10⅞″ × 8⅜″. Light blue cloth stamped in gilt on spine, blindstamped on front. *Location:* GHT. Previously published (*Liberty,* 26 December 1936).

'Why We Have | Wars' ("Peace on Earth–Why We Have Wars"), pp. 255–57.

B 207 KILLER
1970

[gray, in large letters] KILLER [black, smaller letters, superimposed against the LE] KILLER | A JOURNAL | OF MURDER | [gray] THOMAS E. | GADDIS & | JAMES O. | LONG | [black] THE MACMILLAN COMPANY

On copyright page: 'Copyright © 1970 . . . | . . . | FIRST PRINTING'. 8¼″ × 5½″. Brown cloth stamped in gilt. *Locations:* GHT, Harv. S1.18.

Letter to Henry Lesser (dated 25 May 1929), pp. 186–87.

B 208 WILLIAM MORTON WHEELER
1970

MARY ALICE EVANS and | HOWARD ENSIGN EVANS | William Morton Wheeler, Biologist | Harvard University Press | Cambridge, Massachusetts | 1970

9¼″ × 5⅞″. Light green cloth stamped in white on spine. *Location:* MWelC.

Letter to Wheeler of 3 April 1930, pp. 248–49.

B 209 THEODORE DREISER: THE CRITICAL RECEPTION
1972

Theodore Dreiser | [rule] | The Critical Reception | [rule] | Edited with an Introduction by | Jack Salzman | [device] | David Lewis New York 1972

On copyright page: 'First Edition'. 9⅛″ × 6⅛″. Blue cloth stamped in gilt on spine. *Locations:* GHT, MBU, MChB. Previously published (*Smart Set,* November 1911; *New York Times Book Review,* 10 November 1912; *Smart Set,* February 1914, August 1914, December 1915, June 1916, October 1916, November 1918; New York *Sun,* 13 April 1919; *Smart Set,* May 1920, March 1923; Baltimore *Evening Sun,* 12 January 1924; *American Mercury,* March 1926, February 1930, July 1931); S2.11.

"A Novel of the First Rank," "Dreiser's Novel the Story of a Financier Who Loved Beauty," "Anything But Novels," "Adventures Among the New Novels," "A Literary Behemoth," "A Soul's Adventures," "The Creed of a Novelist," "Dithyrambs Against Learning," "H. L. Mencken Tells of Dreiser's New Book," "More Notes from a Diary," "Adventures Among Books—III," "Mencken Becomes Reminiscent Over Dreiser's New York," "Dreiser in 840 Pages," "Ladies, Mainly Sad," "Footprints in the Sands of Time," pp. 61–64, 101–04, 159–60, 194–98, 237–42, 268, 275–81, 313–14, 319–21, 382–84, 414–15, 427–28, 476–79, 579–80, 612.

B 210 EZRA POUND: THE CRITICAL HERITAGE
1972

EZRA POUND | *THE CRITICAL HERITAGE* | *Edited by* | ERIC HOMBERGER | School of English and American Studies | University of East Anglia | [rule] | ROUT-LEDGE & KEGAN PAUL : LONDON AND BOSTON

On copyright page: '*First published 1972*'. 8⁷⁄₁₆″ × 5⁵⁄₁₆″. Light blue cloth stamped in gilt on spine. *Location:* MChB. Previously published (*Smart Set,* April 1911 [also A 67], August 1920).

Reviews of *Provença* ("The Meredith of Tomorrow") and *Instigations* ("Books More or Less Amusing—IV"), pp. 73–74, 190.

B 211 MANY LIVES—ONE LOVE
1972

Many Lives—One Love | [squiggle] | FANNY BUTCHER | HARPER & ROW, PUB-LISHERS | *New York, Evanston, San Francisco, London* | [device]

On copyright page: '© 1972 . . . | . . . | FIRST EDITION'. 8⅝₁₆″ × 5⁹⁄₁₆″. Orange cloth stamped in silver. *Locations:* GHT, MChB, RJS. S2.38.

Inscription and letters quoted, pp. 235–36, 403–10.

B 212 SOME VIEWS OF SANTA CLAUS
1973

SOME VIEWS | *of* | SANTA CLAUS | 50 YEARS AGO | [illustration of Santa] | *by* | JOSEPH CONRAD | H. L. MENCKEN | H. G. WELLS | & | G. BERNARD SHAW | [ornament] THE HART PRESS [ornament]

P. [10]: '[device] | Illustrated by Victor Anderson, & printed by Ruth | & James D. Hart, Berkeley, California, Mcmlxxiii.' 9⁹⁄₁₆″ × 6¼₁₆″. Deep red wrappers (9¹⁵⁄₁₆″ × 6⅜″) printed in black. Christmas greeting from the Harts on a printed slip laid in. *Locations:* Harv, InU-Li, KU-S, RJS. Previously published (*Colliers*, 15 December 1923).

Statement on whether modern children should believe in Santa Claus, p. [8].

B 213 THE BEST IN THE WORLD
1973

THE BEST IN | [gothic] The World | A Selection of News | and Feature Stories, | Editorials, Humor, | Poems, and Reviews | from 1921 to 1928 | [rule] | Edited, | with Introductions, by | John K. Hutchens and George Oppenheimer | THE VIKING PRESS NEW YORK

On copyright page: '© 1973'. 8⅝₁₆″ × 5⁷⁄₁₆″. Yellow cloth stamped in black and red on spine. *Locations:* GHT, MNodS, MWelC. Previously published (New York *World*, 19 July, 13 September 1925, 12 Sept, 7 November 1926); S2.12.

'*BALTIMORE SAGE VS.* | *ENGLISH LITERATURE*' ("The English Begin to Slip"), '*PITY THE* | *ARTIST'S WIFE*' ("Treason at the Domestic Hearth"), '*ADVICE TO THE YOUNG*' ("Another Long-Awaited Book"), and '*THE LAST REFUGE* | *OF A SCOUNDREL*' ("The Psychic Follies"), pp. 190–96, 291–98.

B 214 A CATALOGUE OF THE JOSEPH HERGESHEIMER
COLLECTION
1974

A CATALOGUE OF THE | *Joseph Hergesheimer Collection* | AT THE UNIVER-
SITY OF TEXAS | *Compiled by Herb Stappenbeck* | *Humanities Research Center* |
[rule] | THE UNIVERSITY OF TEXAS AT AUSTIN

On copyright page: '*Copyright © 1974*'. On p. [261]: '*900 copies of this catalogue have
been printed . . .*'. 9″ × 6″. Blue cloth stamped in gilt. *Locations:* InU-Li, RJS.

Photograph of letter to Hergesheimer (4 December 1924), p. [164].

B 215 CAST OF THOUSANDS
1977

ANITA | Cast of Thousands | LOOS | [olive green] Grosset & Dunlap | Publishers •
New York | A Filmways Company

On copyright page: 'Copyright © 1977 . . . | . . . | First printing'. (1) 10⁷⁄₁₆″ × 9⅛″. Gray
cloth-covered boards, black cloth spine stamped in silver. (2) 10½″ × 9⅛″. Boards and
spine covered in blue paper, stamped in silver on spine. *Locations:* GHT, Harv, InU-
Li, RJS. S2.45.

Letter of 29 December, p. 258.

B 216 F. SCOTT FITZGERALD: THE CRITICAL RECEPTION
1978

F. Scott Fitzgerald | [rule] | The Critical Reception | [rule] | Edited with an Introduc-
tion by | Jackson R. Bryer | Burt Franklin & Co., Inc.

On copyright page: '© 1978 . . . | . . . | . . . Series: The American | critical tradition (New
York, 1978–   )'. On p. [iii]: 'THE AMERICAN CRITICAL TRADITION 5'. 9¹⁄₁₆″ × 6¹⁄₁₆″.
Red cloth stamped in gilt on spine. *Location:* MChB. Previously published (*Smart Set,*
August, December 1920, April 1922, July 1923; Baltimore *Evening Sun,* 2 May 1925);
S2.13.

Reviews of *This Side of Paradise* ("Books More or Less Amusing—II") and *Flappers
and Philosophers* ("Chiefly Americans"), 'Fitzgerald and Others' ("The Niagara of
Novels—II"), review of *Tales of the Jazz Age* ("Some New Books—IV"), and 'As H. L.
M. Sees It', pp. 28, 48, 106–07, 163, 211–14.

B 217 LITERARY AMERICA 1903–1934
1979

Literary | America | 1903–1934 | THE | MARY AUSTIN | LETTERS | Selected and Edited by T. M. PEARCE | CONTRIBUTIONS IN WOMEN'S STUDIES, NUMBER 5 | [Greenwood device to left of next two lines] GREENWOOD, *[sic]* PRESS | WESTPORT, CONNECTICUT [heavy dot] LONDON, ENGLAND

On copyright page: 'First published in 1979 | . . . | 10 9 8 7 6 5 4 3 2 1'. 8¼″ × 5⅜″. Green cloth stamped in gilt. *Locations:* GHT, Harv.

Letter (dated 13 September [1925]), p. 197.

B 218 CORRESPONDENCE OF F. SCOTT FITZGERALD
1980

Correspondence of | F. SCOTT | FITZGERALD | [French rule] | Edited by | MATTHEW J. BRUCCOLI | and | MARGARET M. DUGGAN | with the assistance of | Susan Walker | [Random House device] | RANDOM HOUSE   NEW YORK

On copyright page: 'Copyright © 1980 . . . | . . . | 24689753 | First Edition'. 9³⁄₁₆″ × 6¹⁄₁₆″. Black cloth stamped in gilt on spine. *Locations:* GHT, Harv, InU-Li. S2.27; Bulsterbaum 96; Bruccoli 237.

Inscription and letters, pp. 74, 87, 158.

B 219 ON MENCKEN
1980

[all in a box] *On* MENCKEN | [ornament] | *Edited by JOHN DORSEY* | [Borzoi device] | ALFRED A. KNOPF | NEW YORK 1980

On copyright page: 'First Edition'. 8¼″ × 5⅝″. Brown cloth blindstamped front and back, stamped in gilt on spine. Review copy: uncorrected proof; different title, copyright, and contents pages; 10⅞″ × 5⅜″, heavy yellow paper wrappers with label announcing simultaneous publication with *A Choice of Days* (AA 13) on 12 September 1980 (GHT). Review copies of trade printing have Knopf newsletter and photo of Mencken laid in (GHT). Second printing October 1980; copyright page notes original publication date of 12 September. Contains eight essays on Mencken, with writings by Mencken interspersed. *Locations:* Harv, MBU, RJS. All of the Mencken essays appeared previously in books except "800,000" (Baltimore *Evening Sun,* 21 July 1930). S2.13.

Letters, pp. 251–82, and the following essays, *passim:* "In the Footsteps of Gutenberg," "Fire Alarm," "A Dip into Statecraft," "Good Old Baltimore," "800,000," "On
Metaphysicians" (from "The Human Mind"), "Sabbath Meditation" (from *A Mencken
Chrestomathy*), "The State of Religion Today" (from *Treatise on the Gods*), "The
Origin of Morality" (from *Treatise on Right and Wrong*), "The Essence of Democracy" (from *Minority Report*), "Last Words" (from *Notes on Democracy*), "The Iconoclast" (from "From a Critic's Notebook"), "The Politician," "The Last Gasp," "Gamalielese," "The Clowns March In," "Post-Mortem," "Onward, Christian Soldiers,"
"Imperial Purple," "The Choice Tomorrow," "Coroner's Inquest," "Criticism of Criticism of Criticism," "Portrait of an American Citizen," "Stephen Crane," "Joseph
Conrad" (from "Four Makers of Tales"), "Fifteen Years."

B 220 A BEGGAR IN PURPLE
1983

[all in a box] *A Beggar in Purple* | [rule] | A selection from | the commonplace book of |
RUPERT HART-DAVIS | 'He wrapped himself in quotations—as a beggar | would
enfold himself in the purple of Emperors.' | *Kipling* | [HH device] | HAMISH HAM-
ILTON | *London*

On copyright page: 'First published in Great Britain 1983'. 9³⁄₁₆″ × 5⅞″. Blue cloth
stamped in gilt on spine. *Locations:* BL (rebound), Harv, InU-Li, MB. *Menckeniana*
105.16.

Excerpt from letter to Hugh Walpole regarding Warren Harding (1921), p. 28.

B 221 THE AMERICAN MERCURY: FACSIMILE EDITION OF
VOLUME I
1984

THE | AMERICAN | MERCURY | Facsimile Edition of Volume I | The Issues of
January, February, March, April 1924 | A MONTHLY REVIEW | *Edited by* H. L.
MENCKEN | & GEORGE JEAN NATHAN | *Originally Published by* | ALFRED A.
KNOPF | Introduction to the Book Edition by | RICHARD K. RUSSELL | Freedeeds
Books | *(a division of Garber Communications, Inc.)* | Blauvelt, New York 10913 U.S.A.

On copyright page: 'FIRST EDITION | Published in Book Format | Copyright ©
1984'. 9¹⁵⁄₁₆″ × 6⅞″. Olive green cloth stamped in gold and black. Paperback review
copy has 'REVIEW COPY' printed on cover; facsimile covers of the four numbers
bound in; 9¹⁵⁄₁₆″ × 6⅞″, pale green wrappers printed in black. *Locations:* GHT, RJS.
Previously published; *Menckeniana* 92.16.

Edited by Mencken and Nathan, with other contributions.

B 222 INVENTED LIVES
1984

[contents of both pages all within box surrounding ornate frame, the printing beneath an illustration that is across the two pages] [on page [ii]] INVENTED | [ornament] LIVES | HOUGHTON MIFFLIN COMPANY BOSTON | *1984* || [on page [iii]] *F. Scott and Zelda | Fitzgerald* [mirror image of same ornament] | James R. Mellow

8⅞" × 6". Deep blue cloth stamped in red and silver on spine. *Locations:* GHT, InU-Li, MChB. First letter previously published (B 218, p. 158); *Menckeniana* 112.14.

Excerpts from letters (dated 16 April 1925 and 15 March 1927), pp. 232, 288.

B 223 MARYLAND WITS & BALTIMORE BARDS
1985

MARYLAND | WITS & [I above & in same space] | BALTIMORE | BARDS | A • LITERARY • HISTORY | WITH • NOTES • ON | WASHINGTON • WRITERS | [heavy mark] | BY•FRANK•R•SHIVERS•JR [dots to here represent marks] | MAC-LAY & ASSOCIATES [OC linked]•INC•BALTIMORE•1985

9" × 5¹⁵⁄₁₆". Blue cloth stamped in gilt on spine. Printed from untitled Mencken typescript at Yale (dated 1945). *Locations:* GHT, JRS, RJS.

Essay on the fireplace in the house on Hollins St. (excerpts), pp. 184–86.

B 224 F. SCOTT FITZGERALD: INSCRIPTIONS
1988

F. SCOTT FITZGERALD: | INSCRIPTIONS | [short rule] | Columbia, S.C.: Matthew J. Bruccoli, 1988.

On copyright page: 'Bruccoli Clark Layman | 2006 Sumter Street | Columbia, S.C. 29201'. On p. [88]: 'There are two hundred numbered copies of this book. | This is copy | [number penned in, followed by signature of MJB]'. 10¹³⁄₁₆" × 8⁷⁄₁₆". Gray cloth-covered boards and black cloth spine, stamped in gilt. *Locations:* InU-Li, RJS.

Photo of inscription in the copy of *Prejudices: Second Series* (A 24) presented to Fitzgerald (1920), p. [75].

B 225 MAX BRÖDEL

1991

Ranice W. Crosby | John Cody | Max Brödel | *The Man Who Put Art Into Medicine* | [Springer device] | Springer-Verlag | New York Berlin Heidelberg London | Paris Tokyo Hong Kong Barcelona

On copyright page: '© 1991 . . . | . . . | 9 8 7 6 5 4 3 2 1'. 9³⁄₁₆" × 8". Maroon paper-covered boards and spine, printed in white and dull yellow. Second printing noted. *Location:* Harv. Obituary previously published (Baltimore *Sun,* 28 October 1941).

Letters, pp. 167–68, 191–92, 220, 228; excerpt from editorial-obituary of Brödel, p. 272.

B 226 SPUD JOHNSON AND LAUGHING HORSE

1994

SHARYN UDALL | [script] Spud Johnson & | [letters of next two lines scattered] LAUGHING | HORSE | UNIVERSITY OF NEW MEXICO PRESS | ALBUQUERQUE

On copyright page: '*Copyright* © 1994 . . . | . . . | FIRST EDITION'. 8" × 5⅞". Violet cloth stamped in light violet on spine. *Locations:* GHT, MChB.

Letter to Johnson (16 April 1935), p. 68.

B 227 LETTERS OF AYN RAND

1995

[in a box] LETTERS | OF | AYN RAND | [below box] EDITED BY MICHAEL S. BERLINER | [rule] | INTRODUCTION BY LEONARD PEIKOFF | [device] | A DUTTON BOOK

Published New York. On copyright page: '*First Printing, June, 1995*'. 8¹⁵⁄₁₆" × 5⅞". Tan paper-covered boards, black cloth spine stamped in silver. *Locations:* GHT, MChB.

Quotations from letters to Gouverneur Morris (1934) and Rand (31 July 1934), pp. 10, 14.

B 228 JAMES THURBER: HIS LIFE AND TIMES
1995

[script] James Thurber | [rule] | HIS LIFE AND TIMES | [script] Harrison Kinney | HENRY HOLT AND COMPANY | NEW YORK

On copyright page: 'First Edition—1995 | . . . | 1 3 5 7 9 10 8 6 4 2'. 9⅛″ × 6¹⁄₁₆″. Mottled beige paper-covered boards blindstamped on rear, brown cloth spine stamped in gilt. *Locations:* GHT, InU-Li, MChB.

Letter of 29 November 1947 quoted on pp. 886 and 909.

B 229 WINESBURG, OHIO
1996

A NORTON CRITICAL EDITION | [rule] | Sherwood Anderson | WINESBURG, OHIO | [ornament resting on rule] | AUTHORITATIVE TEXT | BACKGROUNDS AND CONTEXTS | CRITICISM | *Edited by* | CHARLES E. MODLIN | VIRGINIA POLYTECHNIC INSTITUTE | AND STATE UNIVERSITY | and | RAY LEWIS WHITE | ILLINOIS STATE UNIVERSITY | [Norton device] | [rule] | W • W• NORTON & COMPANY • *New York* • *London*

On copyright page: 'Copyright © 1996 . . . | . . . | First Edition.' 8⁵⁄₁₆″ × 5¹⁄₁₆″. Multicolored wrappers. *Location:* RJS. Previously published (Chicago *American*, 28 June 1919; *Notes on Modern American Literature* 2.2 [spring 1978], p. 11; cf. *Menckeniana* 66.15).

'[A Book of Uncommon Merit]', pp. 162–63.

B 230 IN DEFENSE OF MARION
1996

[photograph of Marion Bloom] | IN DEFENSE OF | Marion | *The Love of Marion Bloom & H. L. Mencken* | [photograph of Mencken] | *Edited by Edward A. Martin* | THE UNIVERSITY OF GEORGIA PRESS | Athens & London

On copyright page: '© 1996 . . . | . . . | 00 99 98 97 96 C 5 4 3 2 1'. 9³⁄₁₆″ × 6¹⁄₁₆″. Green cloth stamped in gilt on spine. Review copy: spiral bound in stiff buff paper covers; on front: '*In Defense of Marion*'; two pages per sheet, recto only; 8½″ × 11″. Review copies of trade printing have laid-in letter from publisher. *Locations:* GHT, Harv, RJS.

Letters and excerpts from *Smart Set* and *In Defense of Women*, passim.

B 231 F. SCOTT FITZGERALD: CENTENARY EXHIBITION
1996

F *[sic]* Scott Fitzgerald [in facsimile handwriting] | CENTENARY EXHIBITION | September 24, 1896–September 24, 1996 | The Matthew J. and Arlyn Bruccoli Collection | The Thomas Cooper Library | [ornament] | University of South Carolina Press for | The Thomas Cooper Library

On copyright page: '©1996 . . . | . . . | 00 99 98 97 96   5 4 3 2 1'. $9^{15}/_{16}'' \times 7^{15}/_{16}''$. White wraps printed in blue, black, and gold. *Locations:* MChB, RJS. First item previously published (B 224).

Photo of inscription in the copy of *Prejudices: Second Series* (A 24) presented to Fitzgerald (1920), p. 38; letter of 17 June 1946 to a bookseller regarding *The Crack-Up*, p. 45.

C. Periodical Appearances

First appearances in magazines and newspapers, listing only those items lacking in Adler and its supplements.

C 1

"A Matter of Ethnology" (story), *The Sunday Magazine* 6.7 (3 June 1900): 3–5.

Location: EPL ("Miscellaneous Typescripts . . . 1900–37").

C 2

"A Footnote on Journalism," *The Optimist* (Boone, Iowa) 2.1 (March 1901): 39–44.

West 202. *Location:* KU-S.

C 3

"The Point of the Story" (a tale signed "H.L.M."), *Frank Leslie's Popular Magazine* 52.5 (September 1901): [512]–14.

The same issue contains Mencken's "The Flight of the Victor." Reprinted (still signed "H.L.M.") in the Brooklyn *Citizen* of 14 December 1904 and preserved thus as a clipping at EPL ("Miscellaneous Typescripts . . . 1900–37"). Cf. Adler 128. *Location:* RJS.

C 4

"Popular Medical Fallacies," *The American Magazine: For Thirty Years Leslie's Monthly* 62.6 (October 1906): 655–60.

Ghosted for and signed by Leonard Hirshberg, according to Markel and Oski (A 8.3.a), pp. 11, 185. *Location*: MB.

C 5

"Cancer, the Unconquered Plague," *The American Magazine: For Thirty Years Leslie's Monthly* 63.4 (February 1907): 374–78.

Ghosted for and signed by Leonard Hirshberg, according to Markel and Oski (A 8.3.a), pp. 11, 185. *Location*: MB.

C 6

"If Your Baby Had Pneumonia," *Delineator* 71.2 (February 1908): 233–34.

Ghosted for and signed by Leonard Hirshberg. Cf. Adler 130; *Menckeniana* 92.15. *Location:* MB.

C 7

"If My Baby Had Scarlet Fever," *Delineator* 72.2 (August 1908): 258–59, 293.

Ghosted for and signed by Leonard Hirshberg. Cf. Adler 130; *Menckeniana* 92.15. *Location:* MB.

C 8

"The Slaughter of the Innocents," *Delineator* 73.5 (May 1909): 681, 713–14.

Ghosted for and signed by Leonard Hirshberg. Cf. Adler 130; *Menckeniana* 92.15. *Location:* MB.

C 9

"How to Put on a Collar," *Delineator* 76.1 (July 1910): 80.

Reprinted in *Menckeniana* 90.3–4. *Location:* MB.

C 10

"The Legal Liabilities of the Best Man," *Delineator* 76.2 (August 1910): 152.

Reprinted in *Menckeniana* 90.4–5. *Location:* MB.

C 11

"At Last! A Man With Good Eyes!" *St. Francis Lobbyist* (San Francisco) 1.6 (29 June 1920): 1.

See B 32. *Location:* MChB.

C 12

Letter, *The Freeman* 3.59 (27 April 1921): 161.

Location: RJS.

C 13

"On Living in the United States," *The Nation* 113.2944 (7 December 1921), sec. II: 655–56.

Location: GHT.

C 14

Six-paragraph quotation on the New York businessman from a London newspaper, *The Bookman* 56.3 (November 1922): 376.

Location: GHT.

C 15

Contribution to "The Ten Dullest Authors: A Symposium," *Vanity Fair* 20.6 (August 1923): 58.

Reprinted in B 191. *Location:* Harv.

C 16

Untitled four-sentence contribution with facsimile signature in article "What I Think of Santa Clause: Signed Confessions Obtained by Perriton Maxwell from Eighteen Famous Writers," *Collier's: The National Weekly* 72.24 (15 December 1923): 10.

Reprinted in B 212. *Location:* MB.

C 17

Life and Letters 2.12 (August 1924, H. L. Mencken number).

First printing of Isaac Goldberg's *H. L. Mencken* (B 54) with Mencken's letter. *Location:* RJS.

C 18

"As H. L. M. Sees It" (review of *The Great Gatsby*), Baltimore *Evening Sun,* 2 May 1925: 9.

Reprinted in B 181 and B 216. Cf. Adler 109; S1.8 s.v. Kazin.

C 19

Interview, *New York Times,* 19 October 1927: 4e–f.

Reprinted in B 97.

C 20

"San Francisco," *The San Franciscan* 2.1 (January 1928): 9.

Reprinted from the San Francisco *Bulletin* (not "San Francisco: A Memory"). *Location:* GHT.

C 21

On responsibility for the World War, *The World Tomorrow* 13.10 (October 1930): 401.

Location: RJS.

C 22

Letter, *International Literature* 2–3 (1932): [8].

Location: GHT.

C 23

Contribution to "Mutation in Language: Inquiry on the Malady of Language," *Transition* 23 (July 1935): 150–51.

Locations: RJS, GHT.

C 24

Letter to Enrique Uribe White of 12 November 1935 (trans. into Spanish), *Pan* (Bogotá) 5 (December 1935): 79.

With "El sentido poético de la religión o la naturaleza de la fe" (from *Selected Prejudices*), trans. Uribe, pp. 79–82, 132–36. *Location:* TxU.

C 25

Letter, *Newsweek* 11.12 (21 March 1938): 2.

Location: GHT.

C 26

"Farmers—Real and Bogus," *Scribner's Commentator* 7.4 (February 1940): 51–57.

Location: Yale.

C 27

Comment on Knopf books, *The Dolphin* 4.1 (Fall 1940): 83.

Location: RJS.

C 28

"Letters to Jack Conroy" (24 October 1930; 17 March 1932; 25 July 1933), *New Letters: A Continuation of the University Review* 39.1 (October 1972): 16–17.

Bulsterbaum 95. *Location:* GHT.

D. Juvenilia, Jokes, Ephemera, and Other Private Printings by Mencken

This material was printed by Mencken himself or privately with his approval. Borderline items connected to *Smart Set* or *American Mercury* remain in Section A (11, 12, 25, 27, 28). Errata slips privately printed for Mencken are noted with the appropriate books.

D 1 AMERICAN INSTITUTE OF ARTS AND LETTERS

Elaborate letterhead on yellow stationery, 11⁵⁄₁₆″ x 8½″, headed (in various fonts): 'AMERICAN INSTITUTE OF ARTS AND LETTERS (*Colored*) | *Rev. Hannibal S. Jackson, A.B., A.M., Ph.D., LL.D., DD.* | Chancellor and Financial Secretary'. Matching envelope.

"This buffoonery [ca. 1925] was a double crack, first at the Southern Bourbons and then at the National Institute of Arts and Letters, always one of my favorite butts" (*Thirty-five Years* 152). *Location:* EPL.

D 2 KOSHER CHINESE RESTAURANT

3¹⁄₁₆″ x 5⅛″ card headed: 'Strictly Kosher Oriental and Yiddo-American Home Cooking | Chinese [Hebrew characters for kosher] Restaurant | Ming Aarons, *Prop.*'

Reproduced in *Menckeniana* 8.4. *Locations:* EPL, Yale.

D 3 W. EMIL HAMMERBACHER

3½″ x 5¼″ card headed: '[row of nine symbols of fraternal organizations] | W. EMIL HAMMERBACHER | ATTORNEY, SOLICITOR, & COUNSELLOR-AT-LAW | Practise limited to Real Estate, Testamentary and Building Association Business'.

Locations: EPL, Yale.

D 4 FORM OF BEQUEST

3⁷⁄₁₆″ x 5½″ card headed: 'FORM OF BEQUEST | [rule] | I give and bequeath unto Henry Louis Mencken, alias H. L. Mencken, a cit- | izen of Baltimore, in the Maryland Free State, the sum of [row of periods]'.

Reproduced in *Saturday Review of Literature* 9.29 (4 February 1933): 414. *Locations:* EPL, InU-Li, RJS, Yale.

D 5 FROM L'ACTION FRANÇAISE

3″ x 4¹⁵⁄₁₆″ card headed: 'From *L'Action Française*, September 14, 1933 | La revue de critique l'American Mercury, que dirige le Juif [last word bold] | Mencken, . . . '.

On this notice of Mencken in the reactionary periodical, see Forgue 366–67. *Locations:* EPL, Yale.

D 6 MADSTONE TAG

2⅞″ x 5¾″ card, left corners beveled, reinforced hole at left: 'Nᵒ [dot below the o] [serial number] [Maryland seal] | COMPLIMENTARY [handstamped at angle] | Maryland State Board of Madstone Examiners | State of Maryland, SS: | . . . | Annapolis, Md., ___ 193 ___ Inspector | . . . '.

Reproduced in *Letters from Baltimore* (A 74), p. [185] (no. 3244, signed and dated 8 June 1936 by Mencken). *Location:* EPL (2 signed with same date, nos. 3228 and 3241; other undistributed examples numbered in the 3200's).

D 7 CHANGE OF ADDRESS CARDS

D 7.1
1930

2¾″ x 4⅝″ card: 'PLEASE CHANGE YOUR MAILING LIST | H. L. MENCKEN HAS MOVED FROM | 1524 HOLLINS STREET, BALTIMORE, MD. | TO | 704 CATHEDRAL STREET, BALTIMORE, MD.'

Location: EPL.

D 7.2
1930

2⅝″ x 4⅝″ card: 'PLEASE NOTE CHANGE OF ADDRESS | H. L. MENCKEN HAS MOVED FROM 1524 | . . . '.

Location: EPL.

D 7.3
1936

3″ x 5⅛″ card with rounded corners: 'PLEASE CHANGE YOUR MAILING LIST | H. L. MENCKEN | HAS MOVED FROM | 704 CATHEDRAL STREET, BALTIMORE, MD. | TO | 1524 HOLLINS STREET, BALTIMORE, MD.'

Location: EPL (dated 1936 by Mencken).

D 7.4
1936

3″ x 5″ card: 'Please Change Your Mailing List | H. L. MENCKEN | *has moved to* | 1524 Hollins Street, Baltimore, Md. | Communications for him should NOT be addressed to | 704 Cathedral Street, Baltimore, or to The Sun Office, | Baltimore, or to The American Mercury.'

Location: EPL.

D 8 TOBACCO-CHEWERS' LEAGUE

6¼″ x 3⅜″ sheet headed: '[left column] SERIES B | No. 17 || [right column] July 1, 1927 | 250 M. | [the rest in one column] The Tobacco-Chewers' | Protective and Educational League | of America'.

Locations: EPL, Yale.

D 9 MANDOLOWITZ CARDS

D 9.1

2⅜″ x 3⅞″ card headed: '*Insurance and Real Estate   Notary Public* | *REV. M. MANDOLOWITZ* | *Sanitary Mohel*'.

Location: EPL.

D 9.2

3¼″ x 5⁹⁄₁₆″ card headed: 'INSURANCE IN ALL ITS BRANCHES   INVESTMENT SECURITIES | REV. I. MANDOLOWITZ | SANITARY MOHEL'.

Location: EPL.

D 10 HELL SALTS LABEL

1¾" x 4⁹⁄₁₆" buff label headed: '[all in ornate border] [skull and crossed bones beside next two lines] OLD DR. MENCKEN'S | HELL SALTS'.

Attached to a container, it was offered as a "souvenir" to *American Mercury* subscribers, according to an undated ad (JRS). An *AM* form letter dated 11 April 1929 offers Hell Salts to new subscribers (GHT). *Location:* EPL.

D 11 THE FRIENDS OF THE SALOON

8½" x 5½" folio, printing on first page only, headed: 'BULLETIN NO. 1 (Confidential) January, 1926 | PRELIMINARY ANNOUNCEMENT | THE FRIENDS OF THE SALOON'.

An EPL copy is inscribed "by Mencken" in his hand. Adler 12. *Locations:* EPL (2), InU-Li, Yale.

D 12 CALLING CARD

2⅛" x 3⅜" card: '[left column] HOTEL | ACCOMMODATIONS | NYLON HOSIERY | TIRES | GASOLINE COUPONS | SIRLOIN STEAKS | RACE TIPS | FINEST WHISKIES | TRAIN TICKETS | *Income Tax Expert* | [ornament] || [four vertical lines] || [right column] H. L. MENCKEN'.

Location: Yale (a typed note quotes a letter to Bradford Swan, 18 March 1948: the cards were made for Mencken by Wheeler Sammons, editor of *Who's Who,* perhaps three or four years earlier; "He lately sent me a new supply.").

D 13 CLUB DE FRANCE ET D'ANGLETERRE

12" x 9" sheet folded twice to make four leaves, top uncut. Contents: [p. 1] 'Club de France et d'Angleterre | *A SUPPER RENDEZVOUS* | MÄNNERCHOR HALL | *One Flight Up* | 56th Street, Just Off Third Avenue | Board of Governors | [thirty-two names in two columns, including Mencken and Nathan]'; pp. [2–3] blank; pp. [4–5] explanation and rules of membership: the club's only object is "to establish a supper place in New York where one may eat a Swiss cheese sandwich in peace and quiet"; pp. [6–8] blank.

Presumed that Mencken had a hand in it. *Location:* Yale (signed by Mencken).

D 14 BOOKPLATES

D 14.1–3

Printed in black or gray and in three sizes, which vary slightly. RJS examples: large (5″ x 3½″), medium (3½″ x 2½″), and small (1½″ x 1⅛″): '[all in a frame, a figure hunched over a table and writing with a quill; superimposed below him:] HENRY | LOUIS | MENCKEN | HIS BOOK | [script] JD'.

Bookplates designed by James Doyle Jr., of Baltimore (*The Courier* [Syracuse University] 35 [1970]: 6; *Menckeniana* 116.13). *Locations:* EPL, GHT, RJS, Yale (accompanying note: "The three states of my bookplate. The largest was the earliest. Only the smallest is now used. HLM").

D 15 I AM A 100 PERCENT AMERICAN

12″ x 9″ sheet printed on one side, headed: 'I Am a One Hundred Percent. American | By WILLIAM W. WOOLLCOTT, Op. 143'.

Music and lyrics, no credit to Mencken. "It was at one of these dinners in his own house that Woollcott wrote his song, 'I Am a 100 Percent. American, Goddamn!' He hummed the tune to me, and I took it down at the piano. Later it was harmonized by another member [of the Florestan Club], [Theodor] Hemberger. I printed it in the *American Mercury* and then circulated a reprint as a broadside" (*Thirty-five Years* 20). Cf. *Ich Kuss* (A 75), p. 41. *Location:* Yale.

D 16 CALLING CARD

Small card (1½″ x 2⅞″): 'MR. H. L. MENCKEN'.

Found with gift books: *Charlatanry of the Learned* (1937; B 131) (Harv, with bookplate indicating that he donated it); MBU copy of same (donated 1938); *Southern Album* (1936; B 120) (SL, donated 1937).

D 17 EARLY PRINTING EFFORTS

Pasted in the scrapbook "Souvenirs of Childhood and Schooldays 1880–1896." (1) Five 2″ x 3½″ cards: '[all to right of hand-drawn Masonic emblems] [gothic] Aug. Mencken. | [roman] BALTIMORE, MD.' (2) 2⅝″ x 2½″ brown slip: '[gothic] Tinted 6 colors. | [roman] ANY SIZE | 1 DOZ. 5CTS. | ¼ DOz. 2 CENTS'. (3) 2″ x 3⅛″ bluish card: 'CARDS PRINTED IN | [script] *Script or* [gothic] Old English | type.' (4) 2⅝″ x 2½″ brown slip: '[gothic] Advertisements. | [roman] SIZE 1   2 CTS. 100. | ' ' [= ditto]

1–2   3CTS. 100.' (5) 3″ x 3¾″ pink slip (a receipt): '[script] *Baltimore   1889* | *M* | [roman] *To* [gothic] H. L. Mencken & Co. [roman] *D* | JOB PRINTING | 1524 HOLLINS STREET, BALTO'. (6) 1¼″ x 2″ bluish card: '[gothic] H. L. Mencken | [roman script] *Card Printer* | 1524 HOLLINS ST. | BALTIMORE, MD.'

See "In the Footsteps of Gutenberg" in *Happy Days* (A 49), and Stephen O. Saxe et al., "H. L. Mencken: In the Steps of Gutenberg," *Printing History* 5.1 (1983): 29–32. *Location:* EPL.

D 18 AMERICAN CREDO ADDENDUM

7⁷⁄₁₆″ x 5¹⁄₁₆″ two-leaf addendum of bawdy credos with running head 'THE AMERI-CAN CREDO'; pp. 193–96; nos. 499–526.

Either 50 (Frey 46) or 100 copies (MLAE 324) were privately printed in December 1921. Watermarked 'WARREN'S OLDE STYLE'. See A 22; Bode, *Letters* 118 (contributions by Louis Untermeyer); Adler 25. *Locations:* GHT, NjP.

D 19 SOUVENIRS OF H. L. MENCKEN

7½″ x 4″ sheet printed on one side, beginning: 'SOUVENIRS OF H. L. MENCKEN | [double rule] | So many requests are received for souvenirs of | Mr. H. L. Menecken *[sic]*, that it has become necessary, | in order to save time, to have a printed answer to | hand to those making inquiries.'

Given the quality of the humor, it is presumed that Mencken had a hand in it. *Location:* Yale (photocopy at EPL).

D 20 A PETITION

11″ x 8¼″ sheet printed on one side, headed: '[gothic] A Petition | [roman] TO THE CONGRESS OF THE UNITED STATES'.

Ironic appeal to restore slavery. Reproduced in *Letters from Baltimore* (A 74), p. [185]. *Location:* EPL.

D 21 BOOKS BY H. L. MENCKEN

7¹¹⁄₁₆″ x 3⅛″ sheet printed on one side: '[all within box] BOOKS BY | H. L. MENCKEN | Ventures Into Verse. Baltimore: Marshall, | Beek and Gordon, 1903. 46 pp. $0.50. | Out of Print. | [seventeen more titles]'.

Latest titles 1918. "Some time toward the end of 1918 I got out a printed slip listing my books to date. . . . It showed eighteen volumes with my name attached . . ." (MLAE 233). *Locations:* EPL, Yale.

D 22 HATRACK CASE STATEMENT

13″ x 8½″ sheet mimeographed on one side: 'Private | This statement is not for publication, but is offered in the | thought that you are interested personally. | . . . | H. L. Mencken.'

Concerns the "Hatrack" case, in which the April 1926 issue of the *American Mercury* was suppressed in Boston on the grounds of obscenity. EPL copy signed and dated 1926 by Mencken. Adler 12. *Locations:* EPL, NhD, Yale.

D 23 A LITERARY CRITIC

Cover title: '[all within double rule box] [gothic] A | Literary | Critic | [cross] | [roman] FROM THE | CHRISTIAN REGISTER | OF JUNE 24, 1920'.

Four-leaf pamphlet on gray-green paper, uncut at top, 6⅜″ x 3½″, reprinting an unsigned article (see Adler 300). "I couldn't resist the temptation to have it reprinted in ecclesiastical form. A copy is going to every moralist and Methodist dervish in Baltimore. It should shake them up" (letter to August Mencken, 24 July [1920]). *Location:* EPL (2).

D 24 HIGHLAND LAKE GOLF CLUB

10¹⁵⁄₁₆″ x 8½″ form letter headed: 'HIGHLAND LAKE GOLF CLUB | ROCK POINT SUMMIT | ANNE ARUNDEL COUNTY, MD. | HOME OFFICE. | AFRO-PENN BUILDING | PITTSBURG *[sic]*, PA.' Matching envelope.

Invitation to help start a golf club for black people. *Location:* EPL.

E. Keepsakes, Offprints, Pamphlet Piracies, and Promotional Items

Works restricted to a small number of copies, whether privately or commercially printed. None was for sale. Borderline items such as *Erez Israel* (A 45) remain in Section A when their contents were specially revised by Mencken.

E 1 THE AMERICAN: HIS MORALS
1913

Title page: 'THE AMERICAN | HIS MORALS | By H. L. Mencken | [square orna-
ment: four daisies radiating from the center, each flower forming a corner of the
square] | 1913'

Copyright page: None.

9¾″ x 6⁵⁄₁₆″: [1–3] 4–12 = 12 pp.

[1]⁶ = 6 leaves.

Contents: p. 1: title; p. 2: blank; pp. 3–12: text in two columns. The ornament on the
title page is repeated on p. 12.

Typography and paper: 7¹¹⁄₁₆″ x 5⅛″; 50 lines per page. No heads. Wove paper.

Binding: Light brown wrappers. Front identical to title page. All edges trimmed. One
(KyLoU) or two (GHT) staples.

Locations: GHT, KyLoU.

Notes: A piracy (Robin Harris and R. H. Miller in *PBSA* 73 [1979]: 355–56). Previously published (*Smart Set*, July 1913); not in Adler.

E 2 THE OLD SUN AIN'T WHAT SHE USED TO BE
1914

Head title: '[double rule] | THE SUN, BALTIMORE, TUESDAY MORNING, OC-
TOBER 13. | [double rule] | [next three lines to right of a humorous portrait of
Mencken] The Old Sun Ain't What She Used | To Be. | By H. L. Mencken. | [twenty-
seven lines of text follow]'

Location: EPL.

Notes: Available only on microfilm of sealed first volume of Mencken's clippings; only
the first page is visible. Previously published (Baltimore *Sun*, 13 October 1914); Adler
6 ("[2] p.").

E 3 THE CREED OF A NOVELIST
1916

Head title: '°THE CREED OF A | NOVELIST | By H. L. MENCKEN | [text follows]'

$6\frac{1}{4}''$ x $3\frac{1}{2}''$: 1–16 = 16 pp.

$[1]^8$ = 8 leaves.

Contents: pp. 1–16: text.

Typography and paper: $5^{11}/_{16}''$ ($5^{7}/_{16}''$) x $2^{11}/_{16}''$; 32 lines per page. Running heads: recto, 'A HOOSIER HOLIDAY | [rule]' (pp. 3–15); verso, 'THE CREED OF A NOVEL-IST | [rule]' (pp. 2–16). Wove paper.

Binding: Pale yellow glossy wrappers printed in green. Front: 'A HOOSIER [OO linked] HOLIDAY | BY | THEODORE DREISER | WITH ILLUSTRATIONS | BY FRANKLIN BOOTH • | [illustration] | NEW YORK : JOHN LANE COMPANY | LONDON : JOHN LANE | THE BODLEY HEAD | MCMXVI'. Front verso: an illustration of Terre Haute. Back recto: list of Dreiser's books. Back verso: blurb for *A Hoosier Holiday.* All edges trimmed. Two staples.

Locations: EPL (2), Yale.

Notes: Asterisk in title refers to credit to *Smart Set,* October 1916, at bottom of page. Mencken penciled "1916" on an EPL copy. Adler 7; Frey 58; Bulsterbaum 11.

E 4 IRELAND: HER BOOKS
[1917?]

Head title: 'IRELAND | HER BOOKS | [rule] | *By* H. L. MENCKEN | [rule] | [text follows]'

$6\frac{1}{4}''$ x $3\frac{1}{2}''$: 1–7 [8] = 8 pp.

$[1]^4$ = 4 leaves.

Contents: pp. 1–7: text; p. 7: ad for *Ireland's Literary Renaissance,* published by John Lane; p. 8: blank.

Typography and paper: $5^{5}/_{16}''$ ($4^{15}/_{16}''$) x $2^{11}/_{16}''$; 32 lines per page. Running heads: recto, 'BY H. L. MENCKEN | [rule]' (pp. 3–7); verso, 'IRELAND: HER BOOKS | [rule]' (pp. 2–6). Wove paper.

Binding: Self wrappers. All edges trimmed. Two staples.

Locations: EPL (2), Yale.

Notes: Wrongly called *Ireland and Her Books* by Frey and West. It is a review of Ernest Boyd's *Ireland's Literary Renaissance* from the *Evening Sun,* 10 November 1916. Dated 1917 by Adler, Frey, and West. Dated 1922 by Mencken on an EPL copy, but this is a review of the 1916 Lane edition, not the revised edition of Knopf 1922. Adler 7, 52; Frey 59; West 195.

E 5 VIRTUOSI OF VIRTUE
1917

Head title: 'VIRTUOSI OF VIRTUE | [short rule] | [sixteen-line 'NOTE' on Mencken] | [double rule] | BY H. L. MENCKEN | [short rule] | [text follows]'

Location: EPL.

Notes: Available only on microfilm of sealed second volume of Mencken's clippings; only the first four pages are visible. Previously published (Chicago *Sunday Tribune,* 2 December 1917); Adler 7 ("[8] p.").

E 6 PROHIBITION AND THE MAILS
1918

Head title: 'Reprinted from the New York, N. Y. Mail, March 20, 1918 | [double rule] | [all within box above first two columns, to left of double vertical rules separating it from an introduction] Prohibition | and | the Mails | *By* | H. L. Mencken | [text follows]'

$13\frac{3}{4}$" x $7\frac{1}{2}$" sheet printed on one side.

Contents: Head title and introduction; text in three columns separated by vertical rules, horizontal rule at bottom.

Typography and paper: $12\frac{3}{4}$" x $6\frac{3}{4}$"; 17 lines in introduction; 104 lines in third column of text. Newsprint.

Location: D.

Notes: Not in Adler.

E 7 MR. CABELL OF VIRGINIA
1918

Title page: 'Mr. Cabell | of Virginia | *by* | H. L. Mencken | [device]'

Copyright page: None.

11¼″ x 7⅛″ sheet folded twice to make 8 unnumbered pp.

Contents: When fully open, recto reads from top to bottom in two columns of text; verso has four "pages": one for title, two of text, one a list of Cabell's books.

Typography and paper: 4¾″ x 2¹³⁄₁₆″; 32 lines per page. No heads. Wove paper.

Binding: None.

Locations: EPL (2), GHT.

Notes: Reprinted from the New York *Evening Mail,* 3 July 1918. Dated 1918 by Mencken in an EPL copy. Published in 1918 by McBride (New York), according to Frey. Adler 9, 58; Frey 59.

E 8 DITHYRAMBS ON ALCOHOL
1918

Cover title: [all within double rule box] 'DITHYRAMBS | ON ALCOHOL | BY | H. L. MENCKEN | *Envy of the other fellow lies at the root of all prohibition legis- | lation, insists H. L. Mencken, chanting the praise of potable alco- | hol for its contentment-bringing qualities. Even excessive drink- | ing has its high uses, the satirist argues, since a man who yields | to it is a man the world is well rid of.* | [all within circle] SAVE | [in box with torch symbol in upper left] W. S. S. | WAR SAVINGS STAMPS | ISSUED BY THE | UNITED STATES | GOVERNMENT | [outside box] SERVE'

Copyright page: None.

8¹⁵⁄₁₆″ x 5¾″: [1] 2–4 = 4 pp.

[1]² = 2 leaves.

Contents: p. 1: cover title; pp. 2–4: text; p. 4: union label.

Typography and paper: 6⅞″ x 4⅝″; 44 lines (p. 2; each page has a different number of lines). No heads. Wove paper.

Binding: None.

Location: Harv.

Notes: Four excerpts on alcohol, the last credited to the [New York] *Evening Mail* of 15 May [1918]. War Savings Stamps were issued 1917–20. The union label is of the Allied Printing Trades Council, New York City. Not in Adler.

E 9 REVIEW OF THE NEW INTERNATIONAL ENCYCLOPAEDIA
[ca. 1918]

Head title: '25M—9–22 | REVIEW OF | THE NEW INTERNATIONAL ENCY-
CLOPAEDIA | By H. L. MENCKEN | [text follows]'

9⅜" x 6": [1–4] = 4 pp.

[1]² = 2 leaves.

Contents: pp. 1–4: text; p. 4: ad for revised version and blurbs.

Typography and paper: 7¹⁵⁄₁₆" x 4⅛" (5⅛" with marginal rubrics); 46 lines per page.
No heads. Wove paper.

Binding: None.

Locations: GHT, LC, Yale.

Notes: The encyclopedia was published in New York by Dodd, Mead (1917). Mencken's review of the revised edition appeared in *Smart Set,* January 1918. West 199; not in Adler.

E 10 THE LITERARY CAPITAL OF THE UNITED STATES
1920

Title page: 'The | LITERARY CAPITAL | OF | THE UNITED STATES | By
HENRY L. MENCKEN'

Copyright page: 'This essay was first pub- | lished in the Nation of | London April 17,
1920, | and reprinted by permis- | sion on the Wednesday | Book Page of The Chicago |
Daily News May 12, 1920.'

7" x 5⅜": [1–12] = 12 pp.

[1]⁶ = 6 leaves.

Contents: p. 1: cover; p. 2: blank; p. 3: title; p. 4: credit; pp. 5–10: text; pp. 11–12:
blank.

Typography and paper: 5⁹⁄₁₆" x 4" (inside 6" x 4½" box); 37 lines per page. No heads.
Wove paper.

Binding: Self wrappers. Front: 'T H E | LITERARY CAPITAL | OF | THE UNITED
STATES | BY HENRY L. MENCKEN'. All edges trimmed. Two staples.

Locations: EPL (2), TxU.

Notes: Published by the *Daily News,* according to Frey. Adler 10, 138; Frey 59.

E 11 SPIRITUAL AUTOPSIES
1922

Title page: '[within ornate border] SPIRITUAL | AUTOPSIES | By H. L. MENCKEN | [device] | An Article on | GAMALIEL BRADFORD | Reprinted from the | Literary Review of the | *New York Evening Post*'

Copyright page: None.

6³⁄₁₆″ x 10½″ sheet folded twice into thirds to make six unnumbered "pages."

Contents: p. 1: title; pp. 2–5: text; p. 6: 'BOOKS BY GAMALIEL BRADFORD [with address of Houghton Mifflin]'.

Typography and paper: 5½″ x 2⁵⁄₁₆″; 36 lines per page. No heads. Wove paper.

Binding: None.

Locations: EPL (2), GHT, LC, RJS (2), Yale.

Notes: Dated 1921 by Adler and by Mencken on an EPL copy, 1922 (Boston and New York: Houghton, Mifflin) by Frey, which is when this review of *American Portraits 1875–1900* (1922) appeared. An undated reprint reported (S2.7). Previously published (New York *Evening Post*, 8 April 1922); Adler 11, 173; Frey 60.

E 12 SAVIORS OF CIVILIZATION
1923

Head title: 'Saviors of Civilization | By H. L. MENCKEN | A FAMOUS AMERICAN CRITIC ON FRANCE | [text follows]'

About 23½″ x 5½″ if a single sheet.

Contents: '[head title] | From the *Baltimore Evening Sun* | (Copyright, 1923) | Republication with credit permitted. | [rule] | *FOREWORD* | [nine lines] | [text in two columns]'.

Typography and paper: About 22¼″ x 5⅛″; 128 lines in right column. Wove paper?

Location: EPL.

Notes: The EPL copy was cut into sections and pasted into a scrapbook; measurements uncertain. Previously published (Baltimore *Evening Sun,* 9 April 1923); not in Adler.

E 13 THE NORDIC BLOND RENAISSANCE
[1923?]

Head title: 'The Nordic Blond Renaissance | [rule] | By H. L. MENCKEN | [text follows]'

24¹⁵⁄₁₆″ x 6¼″ sheet printed on one side.

Contents: '[head title] | [eleven-line note on Mencken] | (Copyright, 1923, by The Evening Sun, Baltimore, Maryland.) | [text in two columns]'.

Typography and paper: 23¼″ x 4¹³⁄₁₆″; 12 lines in single column of note and credit; 149 lines in second column of text. Wove paper.

Locations: EPL, NjP, Yale.

Notes: Previously published (Baltimore *Evening Sun*, 16 July 1923); Adler 65–66.

E 14 EDITORIAL JANUARY 1924
1924

Head title: 'EDITORIAL | by H. L. Mencken | from the first issue of THE | AMERI-CAN MERCURY—January 1924 | [text follows]'

14″ x 8½″: [1–6] = 6 pp. mimeographed on recto only. Second and third pages of text numbered 'Page Two' and 'Page Three' at top.

Three separate sheets.

Contents: pp. 1, 3, 5: text.

Typography and paper: p. [1]: 12½″ x 6½″ (right margin not justified); 71 lines (other pages vary in size and number of lines). No heads. Laid paper.

Binding: None. All edges trimmed. Stapled at top center.

Location: NjP.

Notes: The NjP copy is autographed by Mencken; provenance unknown. Not in Adler.

E 15 A REVIEW OF "AMERICANISM"
[1924?]

Cover title: '[all within ornamental border] A Review of | "Americanism" | by that Celebrated | American Critic | H. L. Mencken | Editor of that Leading Monthly Magazine | "The American Mercury"'

Copyright page: None.

6⅞" x 4⁷⁄₁₆": [1] 2–8 = 8 pp.

[1]⁴ = 4 leaves.

Contents: p. 1: cover title; pp. 2–8: text, head title: ' "AMERICANISM" | *Exterior View By H. L. Mencken*'.

Typography and paper: 5¾" x 3⅛"; 39 lines per page. No heads. Wove paper.

Covers: Self wrappers. All edges trimmed. Two staples.

Locations: EPL (4), GHT, Yale.

Notes: "This was privately printed by a Canadian lawyer" (Mencken's inscription in GHT copy). Mencken dated one EPL copy 1923, another 1924. It is a review of W. T. Colyer's *Americanism: A World Menace* from *Smart Set,* April 1923. Adler dates it 1924 but misdates the review as being from the same year. Adler 11, 181.

E 16 THE REWARDS OF VIRTUE
1925

Head title: 'The Rewards of Virtue | [rule] | By H. L. MENCKEN | (Copyright, 1925, by The Evening Sun, Balti- | more, Maryland. Reprinted by special | permission of the Editors.) | [rule] | [text follows]'

8½" x 12" sheet printed on both sides and folded in thirds to make columns numbered 5, 6, [1] on recto, 2–4 verso.

Contents: pp. 1–6: text.

Typography and paper: 7½" x 3"; 41 lines per page. No heads. Wove paper, water-marked 'INTERNATIONAL BROTHERHOOD OF PAPER MAKERS | REGIS-TERED | UNION MADE'.

Covers: None.

Locations: EPL (2), NjP, Yale.

Notes: The Yale copy was dated 1925 by Mencken. On the Burton Kendall Wheeler case. Previously published (Baltimore *Evening Sun,* 8 June 1925); Adler 12, 68.

E 17 H. L. MENCKEN ON THE NATION
1925

Head title: 'H. L. Mencken on The Nation | (Reprinted from the Baltimore *Evening Sun* for July | 6, 1925. Copyright the *Evening Sun*.) | [text follows]'

11$^{11}\!/_{16}''$ x 8$^{7}\!/_{8}''$ sheet printed on both sides, unpaginated.

Contents: Text in two columns; at end is a subscription form for *The Nation* (New York address) and for *The Nation* and *The American Mercury* in combination.

Typography and paper: Both pages framed by double rule box with ornaments inside the corners (9$^{15}\!/_{16}''$ x 7$^{9}\!/_{16}''$). 9'' x 6½''; 45 lines in second column of text, recto. Wove paper.

Locations: EPL, Yale.

Notes: Adler 11, 68, 144.

E 18 BRYAN
1925

Head title: 'BRYAN | By H. L. MENCKEN | (Reprinted from The Evening Sun of | July 27, 1925) | [text follows]'

12$^{3}\!/_{4}''$ x 5$^{1}\!/_{8}''$ sheet printed on one side.

Contents: Text in two columns.

Typography and paper: 11$^{15}\!/_{16}''$ x 5$^{1}\!/_{16}''$; 110 lines in right column. Wove paper or newsprint.

Location: EPL.

Notes: The EPL copy is pasted into a scrapbook. Not in Adler

E 19 AMERICAN MERCURY EDITORIAL OF DECEMBER 1925
1925

Head title: [all within ornate frame] '*Reprint* | *of* THE AMERICAN MERCURY *Editorial* | *of December,* 1925 | [text follows]'

10$^{15}\!/_{16}''$ x 4$^{1}\!/_{4}''$: [1–4] = 4 pp.

[1]^{2} = 2 leaves.

Contents: pp. 1–3: text: '[head title] | WITH this issue THE AMERICAN MERCURY | closes its sixth volume and second year. . . . '; p. 4: *American Mercury* logo.

Typography and paper: 6$^{3}\!/_{16}''$ (5$^{15}\!/_{16}''$) x 3½''; 27 lines per page. Running heads: recto and verso, '*Reprint of* THE AMERICAN MERCURY *Editorial*' (pp. 2–3). *Mercury* green wove paper, watermarked '[AM logo] | THE | AMERICAN | MERCURY'.

Binding: None.

Location: Yale.

Notes: Not in Adler.

E 20 MY DEAR WALPOLE
1925

Head title: 'MY DEAR WALPOLE° | An Open Letter from H. L. Mencken' | [text follows; at bottom of second column on p. 1: '°See Mr. Walpole's letter in November.']

9½" x 6⅝" sheet printed in two columns recto and verso, then folded twice into quarters to make 4¾" x 3⁵⁄₁₆"; paginated 1–2.

Contents: pp. 1–2: text.

Typography and paper: P. 1: 7¼" x 4¹³⁄₁₆"; 40 lines in right column. P. 2, with head 'THE BOOKMAN | [thick-thin rule]': 1½" (1³⁄₁₆") x 4¹³⁄₁₆"; 8 lines in both columns. Wove paper.

Binding: Thick paper wrappers, white inside. Front: [black on green, all within double rule box, then ornate frame including acorns and oak leaves] 'THE | BOOKMAN [OO linked] | [device] | MY DEAR WALPOLE | An Open Letter from | H. L. Mencken | (Reprinted from the December, | 1925, Issue of THE BOOKMAN) | GEORGE H. DORAN COMPANY | PUBLISHERS | 50 CENTS $4⁰⁰ Yearly'. Back: blurb for *The Bookman* on white, framed by black box surrounded by green. Folded sheet pasted in.

Locations: EPL (3), Yale.

Notes: One EPL copy signed and dated 1925 by Mencken. Adler 11, 144.

E 21 EYE EXERCISE FROM PREJUDICES: SECOND SERIES
[1925?]

Title page: None.

4⅛" x 2⅞" (outer corners rounded): [1–12] = 12 pp., printed on recto only.

[1]⁶ = 6 leaves.

Contents: p. 1: on Dr. W. H. Bates's discoveries regarding eyestrain, followed in EPL copy in binding B by 'E. F. DARLING, M.D. | 63 Park Avenue | New York City'; p. 3: introduction and permission; pp. 5, 7, 9, 11: text, headed: 'From | Prejudices, II. | By H. L. Mencken'.

Typography and paper: 2″ x 1¼″; 29 lines (p. 7 = full p. 15 of *Prejudices: Second Series;* number of lines varies). No heads apart from those reprinted from Mencken's book. Wove paper.

Binding A: Unprinted gray heavy-paper wrappers. All edges trimmed (outer corners rounded). Two staples. Dr. E. F. Darling's name and 41st St. address are handwritten on front verso of most copies.

Binding B: Same as binding A but buff wrappers without handwriting.

Locations: EPL (4, bindings A [3] and B), GHT (binding A), NhD (2 in binding A), TxU (binding A), Yale (binding A).

Notes: Signed and dated 1925 by Mencken in GHT copy. Pp. 5, 7, 9, and 11 reproduce pp. 14 (part), 15, 16, and again 16 of *Prejudices: Second Series* in progressively smaller type as an eye exercise, with the page numbers and heads of 15 and 16 as part of the text. The addition to p. 1 in binding B indicates a separate printing. The TxU copy has the 41st St. address written below the introduction on p. 3. Adler 10.

E 22 WHAT MENCKEN THINKS OF EL PASO AND JUAREZ
[1926?]

Cover title: '[woman in Spanish garb against oval with hanging foliage, red and black] | WHAT | *Mencken* | Thinks of | EL PASO AND | JUAREZ'

Copyright page: None.

6³⁄₁₆″ x 3½″: [1–4] = 4 pp.

[1]² = 2 leaves.

Contents: p. 1: cover title; p. 2: text; p. 3: on Mencken; p. 4: ad for Central Cafe, Juarez, Mexico.

Typography and paper: 5″ x 2½″; 22 lines on p. 3 (different number on each page). No heads. Wove paper.

Binding: None.

Locations: EPL, GHT, Yale.

Notes: Text is quotations from the El Paso *Times* of 27 October 1926 (wrongly given as 1928 in Adler). Cf. *Thirty-five Years* 160. Adler 14.

E 23 CHIROPRACTIC
1927

Cover title: [all within double rule box] 'CHIROPRACTIC | *By* H. L. MENCKEN | [ornament] | [Copyright : 1927 : By The Chicago Tribune.]'

Copyright page: None.

7½" x 4⅜" (?): [1–4] = 4 pp.

Probably [1]² = 2 leaves.

Contents: p. 1: cover title; pp. 2–4: text.

Typography and paper: 7¹⁄₁₆" x 3⁵⁄₁₆"; 49 lines per page. No heads. Wove paper.

Binding: None.

Location: EPL.

Notes: EPL copy bound in a book and probably trimmed; "1927" pencilled on it by Mencken. Previously published (Chicago *Tribune*, 13 February 1927); Adler 13, 111.

E 24 EDITORIAL, APRIL 1927
1927

Title page: [all within ornate frame] 'EDITORIAL | *From* | THE AMERICAN MER-CURY | April 1927 | [*American Mercury* logo] | *Copyright, 1927, by* | THE AMERI-CAN MERCURY, INC. | *730 Fifth Ave., New York*'

Copyright page: None.

10" x 6¹¹⁄₁₆": [1–8] = 8 pp.

[1]⁴ = 4 leaves.

Contents: p. 1: facsimile of cover of April 1927 issue; p. 2: blank; p. 3: title; pp. 4–6: text in two columns; p. 7: some contents of the forthcoming April 1927 issue; p. 8: *American Mercury* logo.

Typography and paper: 7¹⁵⁄₁₆" (7⁹⁄₁₆") x 5⅛"; 50 lines per page (size and number of lines vary). Running heads: 'THE AMERICAN MERCURY' (p. 5), 'EDITORIAL' (p. 6). *Mercury* green wove paper.

Binding: Self-wrappers; see pp. 1, 8, above. All edges trimmed. ? staples.

Location: EPL.

Notes: On peace and the likelihood of war. The EPL copy is bound in a book. Adler 13.

E 25 SATURNALIA
1927

Head title: 'THE EVENING SUN *Baltimore, July 18, 1927* | [thick-thin rule] | Saturnalia | [short rule] | By H. L. MENCKEN. | [Copyright, 1927, by The Evening Sun. Republication without permission prohibited.]' | [text follows]

17¼″ x 5¾″ sheet printed on one side, folded three times.

Contents: Text in two columns, with crude border at bottom.

Typography and paper: 16⅝″ x 4⅝″; 119 lines in right column below head title. Vertical rule between the columns. Newsprint.

Binding: None.

Locations: D, LC, NhD.

Notes: Facsimile of the article. Adler attributes it to William Feather of Cleveland, 1927. Adler 13.

E 26 A STATEMENT BY THE EDITOR
1927

Head title: [recto, right column] 'A STATEMENT BY THE EDITOR | [text follows]'

6″ x 4″ sheet printed on both sides.

Contents: Recto, left column: portrait of Mencken over AM logo; right column: '[head title] | THE | AMERICAN | MERCURY | is quite devoid of propagandist | purpose. It labors under no | [twenty-three more lines]'. Verso: ad and subscription form.

Typography and paper: Recto: 5⅜″ x 3¼″ (1¹¹⁄₁₆″, print only); 28 lines and head title. Verso: 5⅛″ x 3⁵⁄₁₆″; 24 lines and illustration, rules, and brackets. *Mercury* green wove paper.

Locations: GHT, JRS, RJS.

Notes: Drawn from first and last paragraphs of Mencken's "Postscript" in *Three Years* (1927; B 73), pp. 33, 35–36. JRS copy was found in George Jean Nathan's *The New American Credo* (1927; A 22.2 [Notes]). Not in Adler.

E 27 EDITORIAL, DEC. 1928
1928

Cover title: [all within red box and between brown vertical rules, in brown except where stated] '[rule with ornament] | [rule] | [red] EDITORIAL | [rule] | *by* H • L •

MENCKEN | [rule] | *which appeared in* | [rule] | *the* DECEMBER 1928 *number of* |
[rule] | [red] THE AMERICAN | MERCURY | [rule] | [rule with ornament]'

8" x 5¼": [1–8] = 8 pp.

[1]⁴ = 4 leaves.

Contents: pp. 1–8: text, beginning: '[red ornament] | WITH THIS ISSUE THE AMERI-
CAN MERCURY | COMPLETES ITS FIFTH YEAR. | . . .'.

Typography and paper: 6⅛" x 3¹³⁄₁₆"; 32 lines per page. No heads. Printed in brown
ink with red ornaments and section numbers. Wove paper, watermarked 'SUEDE |
[D within diamond] | FINISH'.

Binding: Green paper wrappers. Front: cover title. Back: [all within red box and
between brown vertical rules, in brown except where stated] '[rule with ornament] |
[rule] | THE AMERICAN MERCURY | [rule] | [red *American Mercury* logo] | [rule] |
ALFRED • A • KNOPF | *publisher* | NEW YORK CITY | *730 Fifth Avenue* | [rule] |
[rule with ornament]'. All edges trimmed. Red tie string.

Locations: EPL, NhD, Yale.

Notes: Adler 14.

E 28 MY VIEW OF COMPANIONATE MARRIAGE
[1928?]

Head title: 'NUMBER ONE | [in box] *My View of* | *COMPANIONATE MARRIAGE* |
[rule] | *As Told to Hannah Stein* | *By H. L.* MENCKEN | [text follows]'

11¼" x 6⅛" sheet printed on one side.

Contents: Head title; text in two columns separated by a vertical rule, with short
horizontal rule at bottom; at end of text: 'Tomorrow—Elinor Glyn | *Copyright by
Public Ledger*'. Also photo of Mencken in right column.

Typography and paper: 8⅞" x 4¼"; 64 lines in left column. Smooth wove paper.

Location: D.

Notes: Published by the Philadelphia *Public Ledger,* perhaps as an insert in connection with a feature on companionate marriage in the magazine section of the 6 May
1928 issue (cf. Adler 123 s.v. Stein). Mencken refers to Judge [Benjamin] Lindsey,
whose book on the subject he reviewed in the *American Mercury* of January 1928.
Previously published (B 82); not in Adler.

E 29 HOT DOGS
1929

Head title: 'THE EVENING SUN *November 4, 1929* | [thick-thin rule] | [the rest framed right, left, and bottom] Hot Dogs | [short rule] | By H. L. MENCKEN | [Copyright, 1929, by The Evening Sun. Republication without permission prohibited.]' | [text follows]

19¼″ x 7¾″ sheet printed on one side.

Contents: Text in two columns on reproduced page; beneath it: '*Reprinted by permission from* | *The Evening Sun, November 4, 1929.* | COMPLIMENTS OF OPPENHEIMER CASING CO.'

Typography and paper: 15⅞″ x 4⁷⁄₁₆″ (Mencken text only); 119 lines in right column below head title. Vertical rule between columns. Wove paper.

Location: NhD.

Notes: Reproduction of page as if torn from the *Sun,* with parts of adjacent articles visible and a shadow in the background. Not in Adler.

E 30 LO, THE POOR BOOKSELLER
[1930?]

Head title: '[to right of numerous parallel vertical rules forming a rectangle] LO, | THE POOR | BOOKSELLER | Copyright, 1930, The American Mercury, Inc. | *Reprinted by permission* | [text follows] | [at bottom right with four rules above and four below] B y   H . L . M e n c k e n'

Colophon: '[Stanley Rose logo] | Distributed by Stanley Rose ltd. | The Picador Press | AT 1625 NORTH VINE | HOLLYWOOD, CALIFORNIA | PRINTED AT THE LAKESIDE PRESS | R. R. DONNELLEY & SONS COMPANY, CHICAGO, ILL. | IN 10 PT. MONOTYPE BODONI NO. 175, | ON DRESDEN PAMPHLET BOOK PAPER, WITH A | COVER OF OCHRE GEORGIAN | TYPOGRAPHY AND FORMAT BY | LESLIE E. BAIRD, JR.'

7½″ x 5⅛″: 1–9 [10–12] = 12 pp.

[1]⁶ = 6 leaves.

Contents: pp. 1–9: text; p. 10: blank; p. 11: colophon; p. 12: blank.

Typography and paper: 5¹¹⁄₁₆″ x 3⅝″; 36 lines per page. No heads. Wove paper.

Binding: Drab stiff paper wrappers (7¾″ x 5¼″). Front: '[rectangle formed by vertical rules in top left corner] | Lo, | The Poor | Bookseller | By | H. L. Mencken | [rectangle formed by horizontal rules in bottom right corner]'. All edges trimmed. Three staples.

Locations: EPL (4), RJS.

Notes: Dated 1930 by Adler and OCLC. A GHT copy has Stanley Rose logo pasted on verso of rear wrapper. Previously published ("Editorial," *American Mercury,* October 1930); Adler 14; S2.12.

E 31 THE EDITOR REVIEWS HIS MAGAZINE
1930

Cover title: '[wavy line] | THE EDITOR | [wavy line] | REVIEWS | [wavy line] | HIS MAGAZINE | [wavy line] | [AM logo]'

Copyright page: None.

8½″ x 5½″: [1–4] = 4 pp.

[1]² = 2 leaves.

Contents: p. 1: cover title; pp. 2–3: text, ending with facsimile signature; p. 4: blurb from the Pittsfield *Eagle.* Text begins: 'Despite the effort of those who dislike it to credit | it with this or that sinister purpose, THE AMERICAN | MERCURY is, in reality, quite devoid of propagandistic | aim. . . .'

Typography and paper: 7″ x 4″; p. 2: 32 lines and head title between wavy lines; p. 3: 31 lines and facsimile signature. No heads. *Mercury* green wove paper, watermarked '[AM logo] | THE | AMERICAN | MERCURY'.

Binding: None.

Locations: EPL, SL.

Notes: With a few changes, the text, with the same title, is from *American Mercury,* September 1930: xxxiv–v. Not in Adler.

E 32 A SUGGESTION
[ca. 1930?]

Head title: 'A SUGGESTION | [text follows]'

4³⁄₁₆″ x 5¼″ card printed on one side.

Contents: [all within ornamental frame] '[head title] | *I have reason to believe that you are acquainted with* THE AMERICAN | MERCURY *and have found it not unin-*

teresting, but the Circulation | [ten lines of advertising] | [address of *AM* in left column; in right column: 'H. L. MENCKEN | *Editor*']'.

Typography and paper: 2⅞″ x 4″ within 3½″ x 4⅝″ frame; 17 lines. Wove paper.

Locations: EPL, RJS.

Notes: Not in Adler.

E 33 SO FAR AS I KNOW
[1930?]

8½″ x 5⁷⁄₁₆″ sheet printed on one side.

Contents: '[*American Mercury* logo] | THE AMERICAN MERCURY | 730 FIFTH AVE-NUE | NEW YORK | *OFFICE OF THE EDITOR   Telephone: CIRCLE 7670 • 7675* | So far as I know—and I'd certainly have got | [eleven lines] | the scenes. | [facsimile of Mencken's signature]'.

Typography and paper: 5¾″ (6½″ with facsimile signature; text beneath letterhead 2¹³⁄₁₆″) x 5″ (text 3⁵⁄₁₆″); 18 lines and facsimile (13 lines of text). *Mercury* green wove paper, watermarked '[AM logo] | THE | AMERICAN | MERCURY'.

Locations: EPL (2), NjP, TxU (2).

Notes: "The following, which bore no headline, was printed on an *American Mercury* letter-head, signed by me, and stuffed into the office mail. Its date I do not know, but it must have been 1930 or thereabout . . ." (*Second Chrestomathy* [A 86], p. 479). Not in Adler.

E 34 PROJECT FOR A LICENSING ACT
1933

Cover title: '[five parallel rules] | Project | For A | Licensing Act | For | Baltimore City | By | H. L. MENCKEN | From | The Evening Sun | [five parallel rules]'

Copyright page: 'COPYRIGHT, 1933 | BY | THE EVENING SUN | Reproduction in | whole or part not | permitted with- | out proper credit.'

9″ x 3¾″: [1–4] 5–22 [23–24] = 24 pp.

[1]¹² = 12 leaves.

Contents: p. 1: cover title; p. 2: copyright; p. 3: introduction signed 'THE EVENING SUN'; p. 4: blank; pp. 5–22: text; pp. 23–24: blank.

Typography and paper: 7⅝₁₆″ x 2¹³⁄₁₆″; 41 lines per page. No heads. Wove paper, watermarked 'Ticonderoga | Eggshell'.

Binding: Self wrappers. All edges trimmed. Two staples.

Locations: EPL, GHT, Yale.

Notes: The original articles were "soon afterward reprinted by the *Sunpapers* as a pamphlet for free distribution" (*Thirty-five Years* 228). Previously published (Baltimore *Evening Sun*, 23–25 January 1933); Adler 15, 77; S2.7.

E 35 THE SOUTH ASTIR
1935

Head title: 'Reprinted from The Virginia Quarterly Review, January 1935 | University, Virginia | THE SOUTH ASTIR | BY H.L. MENCKEN | [text follows]'

?: [47] 48–60 = 14 pp. Collation unknown.

Contents: pp. 47–60: text.

Typography and paper: 7⅐₁₆″ (7¹⁄₁₆″) x 4⅝₁₆″; 36 lines per page. Running heads: recto, 'THE SOUTH ASTIR' (pp. 49–59); verso, 'THE VIRGINIA QUARTERLY RE-VIEW' (pp. 48–60). Wove paper.

Binding: Unknown. All edges trimmed.

Location: ViU (2).

Notes: Both known copies are rebound. Not in Adler.

E 36 THE ANATOMY OF QUACKERY
1935

Head title: 'The Anatomy of Quackery | [short rule] | By H. L. MENCKEN | Copyright, 1935, by The Evening Sun of Baltimore. The reprinting of extracts is authorized, but the whole article may | not be reprinted without special permission.) *[sic]* | (*Italics not used in original.*) | [text follows]'

22″ x 6″ sheet printed on one side, folded five times.

Contents: text in two columns; beneath it: 'Printed by permission, and distributed by William Feather, | president, The William Feather Company, Printers and | Publishers, 812 Huron Road, Cleveland, Ohio | [union label] 10'.

Typography and paper: 20¾″ x 4¾″; 124 lines in right column between head title and Feather imprint. Vertical rule between the columns. Wove paper.

Binding: None.

Location: NhD.

Notes: A form cover note (7″ x 5″) dated 20 December 1935 states that the article is from the *Evening Sun* of 16 December. Adler 16 (misdates article); Bulsterbaum 11.

E 37 THE AVERAGE AMERICAN NEWSPAPER
[ca. 1935]

6¼″ x 5″ sheet printed on one side.

Contents: '[all within green vine as frame] THE [T descends to top of next line] average American | Newspaper, especially | of the so-called better sort, | has the intelligence of a | Baptist evangelist . . . | . . . | . . . and the | honor of a police station | lawyer.—*H. L. Mencken.*'

Typography and paper: 2¹³⁄₁₆″ x 2″ (frame 4½″ x 3″); 13 lines. Tan laid paper.

Location: RPB.

Notes: According to the dealer, it was printed in Greenfield, Mass., by the Hermitage Press between 1930 and 1939. Previously published (see B 79A); not in Adler.

E 38 THREE YEARS OF DR. ROOSEVELT
1936

Head title: 'Reprinted from THE AMERICAN MERCURY | *March, 1936* | THREE YEARS OF DR. ROOSEVELT | BY H. L. MENCKEN | [32 lines of text in two columns] | Copyright 1936, by The American Mercury, Inc.'

7⅝″ x 5⁷⁄₁₆″: 1–8 = 8 pp.

[1]⁴ = 4 leaves.

Contents: pp. 1–8: text in two columns.

Typography and paper: 6⁵⁄₁₆″ (6¹⁄₁₆″) x 5⁵⁄₁₆″; 40 lines per page. Running heads: recto, 'THREE YEARS OF DR. ROOSEVELT' (pp. 3–7); verso, 'THE AMERICAN MERCURY' (pp. 2–8). Wove paper.

Binding: Self wrappers. All edges trimmed. Two staples.

Location: NjP.

Notes: An excerpt from the essay appeared in the same year in *Surplus Prophets in Their Own Words* (New York: Viking, 1936), p. 61. Not in Adler.

E 39 THE INCOMPARABLE PHYSICIAN
1936

E 39.1
First edition (1936)

Title page: 'THE | INCOMPARABLE PHYSICIAN | *H. L. MENCKEN* | [three orange Chinese characters descending, one above the other] | 1936'

Copyright page: None.

Colophon: 'COPIES OF THIS REPRINT OF AN H. L. MENCKEN BURLESQUE | WERE MADE FOR MEMBERS OF THE SENIOR CLASS | OF THE SCHOOL OF MEDICINE OF THE | UNIVERSITY OF CALIFORNIA | SAN FRANCISCO | PRINTED BY T W MCDONALD'

6⅛" x 4": [i–iv 1–4] 5–14 [15–20] = 24 pp.

[1]^{12} = 12 leaves.

Contents: p. i: cover; pp. ii–iv: blank; p. 1: title; p. 2: blank; p. 3: motto; p. 4: blank; pp. 5–14: text; p. 15: blank; p. 16: colophon; pp. 17–20: blank.

Typography and paper: 4⅛" x 2½"; 15 lines per page. No heads. Chinese characters in orange on title page and p. 5. Laid paper, watermarked 'Made in U.S.A.'

Binding: Self wrappers. Front: '*The* | *Incomparable* [I extending into line above] | *Physician*'. All edges trimmed. Sewed with tied string.

Locations: EPL (3), GHT, Yale.

Notes: An EPL copy is inscribed by Mencken to Knopf: "This is a violation of the old Smart Set copyright—but I have forgiven him." "This piece has attracted the operators of private presses, and there have been half a dozen arty prints of it" (*A Mencken Chrestomathy* [A 61], p. 606). Previously published (from "Tales of the Moral and Pathological" in *Book of Burlesques* [A 14]); Adler 16, 134; Bulsterbaum 12.

E 39.2
Second edition (1940?)

Cover title: [written right to left around the edges, bottom of letters toward edges, no space between words] '[right edge] the incomparable [bottom] physician [left] a burlesque by h l [top] H mencken L [H and L right side up]'

Colophon: '529 | copies have been printed | with the permission of H L Mencken | by T W McD & Charles Gregory | for Dorothy McDonald, M D | The Gillick Press, Berkeley'

$4\frac{1}{2}''$ x $2\frac{1}{2}''$: [i–iv 1–2] 3–7 [8–12] = 16 pp.

$[1]^8$ = 8 leaves.

Contents: pp. i–iv: blank; p. 1: 'The eminent physician,'; pp. 2–7: text continues; p. 8: colophon; pp. 9–12: blank.

Binding: Yellow paper wrappers, folded around outer leaves. Front: cover title. Back, in same format as front: '[right edge] the good physician [bottom] bestows [left] what the gods merely [top] M promise D [M and D right side up]'. All edges trimmed. Sewed.

Locations: EPL, InU-Li, JRS, RJS.

Notes: Also referred to as *The Eminent Physician*. GHT copy signed and dated 27 January 1940 by Mencken. EPL copy signed and dated 1940 by him; also hand-stamped with design of his small bookplate (D 14.3).

E 40 THE JOHNS HOPKINS HOSPITAL
1937

Cover title: 'BALTIMORE SUN ARTICLES | ON | THE JOHNS HOPKINS HOS-PITAL | BY | H. L. MENCKEN | FROM | JULY, 6 TO 28, 1937 *[sic]*'

Copyright page: None.

$10\frac{3}{4}''$ x $8\frac{1}{4}''$: [1] 2–48 = 96 pp., mimeographed and paginated on rectos only.

Perfect bound.

Contents: pp. 1–48: text, headed 'THE JOHNS HOPKINS HOSPITAL', in twenty sections corresponding to the original articles.

Typography and paper: $9\frac{3}{16}''$ x $7\frac{1}{8}''$ (right margin not justified); 45 lines per page. No heads. Wove paper.

Binding: Stiff brown paper wrappers. Cover title typed or mimeographed on blue-gray sheet ($10\frac{11}{16}''$ x $6\frac{15}{16}''$) pasted to front.

Location: EPL.

Notes: Adler 16, 100.

E 41 TRIUMPH OF DEMOCRACY
1940

Head title: '[top right, mimeographed] Sargent Bulletin #70 | [above text, all within box] Triumph of Democracy | [rule] | By H. L. MENCKEN | [text follows]'

11″ x 8½″ sheet printed on one side.

Contents: Text within box in four columns (separated by vertical rules) in two parts (separated by double horizontal rule); beneath box, mimeographed credit, date 26 July 1940.

Typography and paper: 9″ (from head title of article to bottom of continuation) x 7⅞″ · within 9¼″ x 8⅟₁₆″ box; 60 lines in fourth column. Four unjustified mimeographed lines of credit below box (¾″ x 7″). Wove paper.

Locations: EPL, Harv, Yale.

Notes: Boston: Porter Sargent. For an earlier Mencken appearance in a "Sargent Bulletin" see B 144. From editorials in the Baltimore *Sun,* 7 and 21 July 1940. Adler 17, 106; West 198 (wrongly dated 1944).

E 42 QUICKSTEP TO WAR
1940

Head title: '[top right, mimeographed] Sargent Bulletin #74 | [above text, all within box] Quickstep to War | By H. L. MENCKEN | [text follows]'

11″ x 8½″ sheet printed on one side.

Contents: Text within box in four columns divided by vertical rules; beneath box, mimeographed credit, dated 7 August 1940.

Typography and paper: 9⅟₁₆″ x 8⅟₁₆″ within 10⅟₁₆″ x 8⅟₁₆″ box; 68 lines in fourth column. Two unjustified mimeographed lines of credit below box (⅜″ x 6⅞″). Wove paper.

Locations: EPL, Harv, Yale.

Notes: Boston: Porter Sargent. Editorials in the Baltimore *Sun,* 28 July and 4 August 1940. Reprinted in Porter E. Sargent, *Getting U S into War* (Boston: The Author, [1941]), pp. 405–10; second printing September 1941. Adler 17, 106; West 198 (wrongly dated 1944).

E 43 A GIRL FROM RED LION, P. A.
[ca. 1941]

Head title: 'A Girl from | Red Lion, P. A.° | BY H. L. MENCKEN | [twenty-five lines of text] | °Reprinted from NEWSPAPER DAYS by H. L. Mencken by permission of the publisher, | Alfred A. Knopf, Inc. Copyright 1941 by Alfred A. Knopf, Inc.'

6¾″ x 4⅜″: [1] 2–8 = 8 pp.

[1]⁴ = 4 leaves.

Contents: pp. 1–8: text.

Typography and paper: 5⁹⁄₁₆″ (5⁵⁄₁₆″) x 3⁷⁄₁₆″; 39 lines per page. Running heads: recto, 'A GIRL FROM RED LION, P.A.' (pp. 3–7); verso, 'H. L. MENCKEN' (pp. 2–8). Wove paper.

Binding: Thick pale green paper wrappers. Front: 'A Girl from | Red Lion, P. A. | BY H. L. MENCKEN'. All edges trimmed. Three staples.

Location: NNC.

Notes: Not an offprint from the book (1941). On bookplate: "Bequest of Frederic Bancroft 1860–1945." Not in Adler.

E 44 NOTES ON AMERICAN GIVEN-NAMES
1943

Head title: 'Notes on American Given-names | By Henry L. Mencken | [text follows]'

Copyright page: None.

Colophon: 'Reprinted from Bookmen's Holiday, Notes and Studies | Written in Tribute to Harry Miller Lydenberg. | Published by The New York Public Library, 1943'

9¼″ x 6⅛″: [1] 2–11 [12] = 12 pp.

[1]⁶ = 6 leaves.

Contents: pp. 1–11: text; p. 12: colophon.

Typography and paper: 6⅞″ (6⅝″) x 4⅛″; 33 lines per page. Running heads: recto, 'BOOKMEN'S HOLIDAY' (pp. 3–11); verso, 'HENRY L. MENCKEN' (pp. 2–10). Wove paper.

Binding: Self wrappers. All edges trimmed. Two staples.

Locations: EPL, Yale.

Notes: Separately published essay from *Bookmen's Holiday* (B 158), repaginated. Not in Adler.

E 45 WAR WORDS IN ENGLAND
1944

Head title: 'Reprinted from | AMERICAN SPEECH | February, 1944 | WAR WORDS IN ENGLAND | H. L. MENCKEN | *Baltimore, Maryland* | [text follows]'

$9\frac{1}{2}''$ x $6\frac{3}{4}''$: [3] 4–15 [16–18] = 16 pp.

$[1]^8$ = 8 leaves.

Contents: pp. 3–15: text; pp. 16–18: blank.

Typography and paper: $7\frac{3}{8}''$ ($7\frac{1}{8}''$) x $4\frac{1}{2}''$; 43 lines per page (varies with amount of reduced type). Running heads: recto, '*WAR WORDS IN ENGLAND*' (pp. 5–15); verso, '*AMERICAN SPEECH*' (pp. 4–14). Laid paper.

Binding: Self wrappers. All edges trimmed. One staple.

Locations: EPL (3), InU-Li, Yale.

Notes: Not in Adler.

E 46 DESIGNATIONS FOR COLORED FOLK
1944

Head title: 'Reprinted from | AMERICAN SPEECH | October, 1944 | DESIGNA-TIONS FOR COLORED FOLK | H. L. MENCKEN | *Baltimore, Maryland* | [text follows] | Copyright 1944 by Columbia University Press'

$9\frac{3}{4}''$ x $6\frac{11}{16}''$: [161] 162–74 [175–76] = 16 pp.

$[1]^8$ = 8 leaves.

Contents: pp. 161–74: text; pp. 175–76: blank.

Typography and paper: $7\frac{3}{4}''$ ($7\frac{1}{2}''$) x $4\frac{1}{2}''$; 45 lines per page (varies with amount of reduced type). Running heads: recto, '*DESIGNATIONS FOR COLORED FOLK*' (pp. 163–73); verso, '*AMERICAN SPEECH*' (pp. 162–74). Wove paper.

Binding: Self wrappers. All edges trimmed. One staple.

Locations: EPL (2), InU-Li, Yale.

Notes: Not in Adler.

E 47 AMERICAN PROFANITY
1944

Head title: 'Reprinted from | AMERICAN SPEECH | December, 1944 | AMERI-
CAN PROFANITY | H. L. MENCKEN | *Baltimore, Maryland* | [text follows] |
Copyright 1945 by Columbia University Press'

9¾" x 6¾": [241] 242–49 [250–52] = 12 pp.

[1]⁶ = 6 leaves.

Contents: pp. 241–49: text; pp. 250–52: blank.

Typography and paper: 7⅝" (7⅜") x 4½"; 49 lines per page (varies with amount of
reduced type). Running heads: recto, '*AMERICAN PROFANITY*' (pp. 243–49);
verso, '*AMERICAN SPEECH*' (pp. 242–48). Wove paper.

Binding: Self wrappers. All edges trimmed. One staple.

Locations: EPL (3), InU-Li, Yale.

Notes: Not in Adler.

E 48 STARE DECISIS
1944

Cover title: 'A *New Yorker Reprint* | STARE DECISIS | *By H. L. Mencken* | ISSUE
OF | DECEMBER 30, 1944'

Copyright page: None.

8⅜" x 6": [1–12] = 12 pp.

[1]⁶ = 6 leaves.

Contents: p. 1: cover title; p. 2: blank; pp. 3–10: text in two columns; pp. 11–12: blank.

Typography and paper: 6⁵⁄₁₆" x 4⅝"; 41 lines per page. No heads. Glossy wove paper.

Binding: Self wrappers. All edges trimmed. One staple.

Location: EPL (4).

Notes: Reprinted, presumably, for Mencken's private use. Cf. *Christmas Story* (A 57).
Not in Adler.

E 49 BULLETIN ON "HON."
1946

Head title: 'Reprinted from | AMERICAN SPEECH | April, 1946 | BULLETIN ON 'HON.' | H. L. MENCKEN | *Baltimore, Maryland* | [27 lines of text] | [rule] | [five-line footnote] | Copyright 1946 by Columbia University Press'

9¾" x 6¾": [81] 82–85 [86–88] = 8 pp.

[1]⁴ = 4 leaves.

Contents: pp. 81–85: text; pp. 86–88: blank.

Typography and paper: 9⅜" (9¹⁄₁₆") x 5½"; 50 lines per page (lines vary with amount of reduced type and number of footnotes). Running heads: recto, '*BULLETIN ON 'HON."* (pp. 83–85); verso, '*AMERICAN SPEECH*' (pp. 82–84). Wove paper.

Binding: Self wrappers. All edges trimmed. Two staples.

Locations: EPL (2), InU-Li, RJS.

Notes: Not in Adler.

E 50 NAMES FOR AMERICANS
1948

Head title: 'Reprinted from | AMERICAN SPEECH | December, 1947 | NAMES FOR AMERICANS | H. L. MENCKEN | *Baltimore, Maryland* | [text follows] | Copyright 1948 by Columbia University Press'

9¾" x 6¹¹⁄₁₆": [241] 242–56 = 16 pp.

[1]⁸ = 8 leaves.

Contents: pp. 241–56: text.

Typography and paper: 7¾" (7½") x 4½"; 46 lines per page (varies with amount of reduced type). Running heads: recto, '*NAMES FOR AMERICANS*' (pp. 243–55); verso, '*AMERICAN SPEECH*' (pp. 242–56). Wove paper, watermarked 'WARREN'S | OLDE STYLE'.

Binding: Self wrappers. All edges trimmed. Two staples.

Locations: EPL (2), Yale.

Notes: An EPL copy was signed and dated 1948 by Mencken. Not in Adler.

E 51 WHAT THE PEOPLE OF AMERICAN TOWNS CALL
THEMSELVES
1948

Head title: 'Reprinted from | AMERICAN SPEECH | October-December, 1948 | WHAT THE PEOPLE OF | AMERICAN TOWNS CALL THEMSELVES | H. L. MENCKEN | *Baltimore, Maryland* | [text follows]'

$9\frac{3}{4}''$ x $6\frac{3}{4}''$: [161] 162–84 = 24 pp.

$[1]^{12}$ = 12 leaves.

Contents: pp. 161–84: text.

Typography and paper: $7\frac{11}{16}''$ ($7\frac{7}{16}''$) x $4\frac{1}{2}''$; 41 lines per page (varies with amount of reduced type). Running heads: recto, '*WHAT AMERICAN TOWNSPEOPLE CALL THEMSELVES*' (pp. 163–83); verso, '*AMERICAN SPEECH*' (pp. 162–84). Wove paper.

Binding: Self wrappers. All edges trimmed. Two staples.

Locations: EPL, Yale.

Notes: Not in Adler.

E 52 SOME OPPROBRIOUS NICKNAMES
1949

Head title: 'Reprinted from | AMERICAN SPEECH | February, 1949 | SOME OP-PROBRIOUS NICKNAMES | H. L. MENCKEN | *Baltimore, Maryland* | [text follows]'

$9\frac{11}{16}''$ x $6\frac{3}{4}''$: [25] 26–30 [31–32] = 8 pp.

$[1]^{4}$ = 4 leaves.

Contents: pp. 25–30: text; pp. 31–32: blank.

Typography and paper: $7\frac{11}{16}''$ ($7\frac{7}{16}''$) x $4\frac{1}{2}''$; 46 lines per page (varies with amount of reduced type). Running heads: recto, '*SOME OPPROBRIOUS NICKNAMES*' (pp. 27–29); verso, '*AMERICAN SPEECH*' (pp. 26–30). Wove paper.

Binding: Self wrappers. All edges trimmed. Two staples.

Location: Yale.

Notes: Not in Adler.

E 53 THE BIRTH OF NEW VERBS
1949

Head title: 'THE BIRTH OF NEW VERBS | H. L. MENCKEN | [text follows]'

8¹⁵⁄₁₆″ x 5¹³⁄₁₆″: 313–19 [320] = 8 pp.

Pages separated.

Contents: pp. 313–19: text; p. 320: blank.

Typography and paper: 7″ (6¹¹⁄₁₆″) x 4³⁄₁₆″; 40 lines per page. Running heads: recto, 'The Birth of New Verbs' (pp. 315–19); verso, 'Philologica: The Malone Anniversary Studies' (pp. 314–18). Wove paper, watermarked 'WARREN'S | OLDE STYLE' (?).

Binding: None. All edges trimmed. Two staples, front to back.

Locations: EPL, GHT.

Notes: Separately published essay from *Philologica: The Malone Anniversary Studies* (B 176); verso of last leaf blank (unlike p. 320 in book). Not in Adler.

E 54 IN THE FOOTSTEPS OF GUTENBERG
1964

Title page: [in blue double rule box with blue ornaments on each side] 'IN THE | FOOTSTEPS OF | [gothic] GUTENBERG | BY | H. L. MENCKEN | CHRISTMAS, MCMLXIV | PRINCETON UNIVERSITY PRESS'

Copyright page: 'Copyright 1939, 1940 by Alfred A. Knopf, Inc. | "In the Footsteps of Gutenberg" | originally appeared in *The New Yorker* | This portion of the article is | here reprinted with the kind permission of | Alfred A. Knopf'

Colophon: '[star over ornament, in blue] | This portion of | "In the Footsteps of Gutenberg," by | H L M | was printed by | Princeton University Press | and is sent to you | with our best wishes for | The New Year | [ornament over star, in blue]'

7″ x 4½″: [1–16] = 16 pp.

[1]⁸ = 8 leaves.

Contents: pp. 1–4: blank; p. 5: title; p. 6: copyright; pp. 7–13: text; p. 14: colophon; pp. 15–16: blank.

Typography and paper: 5¼″ x 2¹³⁄₁₆″; 29 lines per page. No heads. Pagination within blue decorations in outer margins. Black and blue illustration at head of text. Wove paper.

Binding: Decorated paper wrappers folded over and pasted onto inside of outer leaves. Black and blue patterns on white, and on white rectangular label on front, within a double rule box (outer green, inner blue) which is flanked on left by green star and blue ornament and on right by blue ornament and green star: 'In the Footsteps of Gutenberg'. All edges trimmed. Two staples.

Locations: EPL, GHT.

Notes: Sent by P. J. Conkwright Jr., typographer of the press (S1.10), probably in an envelope like E 55. Previously published (*New Yorker,* 14 October 1939 and *Happy Days* [A 49]).

E 55 MEMORIALS OF GORMANDIZING
1965

Title page: '[green decoration] | MEMORIALS OF | GORMANDIZING | BY H. L. MENCKEN | ILLUSTRATIONS BY HENRY MARTIN | CHRISTMAS, MCMLXV | PRINCETON UNIVERSITY PRESS'

Copyright page: 'Copyright 1939, 1940 by Alfred A. Knopf, Inc. | "Memorials of Gormandizing" | originally appeared in *The New Yorker* | This portion of the article is | here reprinted with the kind permission of | Alfred A. Knopf'

Colophon: '[light green star] | This portion of | "Memorials of Gormandizing" | by H. L. Mencken | was printed by | Princeton University Press | and is sent to you | with best wishes for Christmas | and The New Year | [light green star]'

$7'' \times 4\frac{1}{2}''$: [1–16] = 16 pp.

[1]^8 = 8 leaves.

Contents: pp. 1–4: blank; p. 5: title; p. 6: copyright; pp. 7–13: text; p. 14: colophon; pp. 15–16: blank.

Typography and paper: $2\frac{1}{16}'' \times 2\frac{13}{16}''$; 11 lines per page. No heads. Green illustrations on each page of text. Wove paper, watermarked 'WARREN'S | OLDE STYLE'.

Binding: Decorated paper wrappers folded over and pasted onto inside of outer leaves. Black and white patterns on green, and in white on a purple rectangular label on front: 'MEMORIALS OF | GORMANDIZING'. All edges trimmed. Two staples.

Locations: EPL, GHT.

Notes: Enclosed in envelope. Previously published (*New Yorker,* 26 August 1939 and *Happy Days* [A 49]); S1.10.

E 56 H. L. MENCKEN REPLIES TO A LETTER
[ca. 1965]

Head title: '[brown] H. L. Mencken | replies to a letter which asks his opinions | [brown] On Book Reviews | [text follows]'

10⅞″ x 8⁷⁄₁₆″ broadside.

Contents: text: letter in twenty-three lines, beginning 'Dear Sir: | I have your note of April 6th, addressed to Mr. S. Mencken.'

Typography and paper: 9″ x 5¹⁵⁄₁₆″ (right margin not justified); 26 lines. Laid paper.

Location: TxU.

Notes: The letter is printed in *Menckeniana* 9.8 and is there dated 9 April and addressed to John William Rogers of Dallas. According to Betty Adler, *Man of Letters: A Census of the Correspondence of H. L. Mencken* (Baltimore: Enoch Pratt Free Library, 1969), p. 154, it is held by the Dallas Public Library; his dates are given as 1894–1965. The cataloguing data at TxU places the broadside in the 1960's. Not in Adler.

E 57 A LETTER FROM MENCKEN
1968

Cover title: 'A LETTER FROM MENCKEN | [ornament]'

Copyright page: None.

Colophon: '[device] | Printed at the Sign of the Rolling Stone | by members of English 450, Champaign, Illinois, | May 1968'

9″ x 5¾″: [1–4] = 4 pp.

[1]² = 2 leaves.

Contents: p. 1: cover title; p. 2: 'A note on Baskette:'; p. 3: text: letter to Ewing C. Baskette of 23 October 1929; p. 4: colophon.

Typography and paper: P. 2: 3⅝″ x 3¹³⁄₁₆″; 18 lines. P. 3: 5⅞″ x 3¹³⁄₁₆″; 18 lines. No heads. Wove paper, watermarked 'CURTIS RAG'.

Binding: Sewed into white paper wrappers with title page duplicated on front (Harv copy only).

Locations: GHT, Harv, RJS, RPB.

Notes: No device above colophon in RPB copy. Evidently printed two to the sheet: RJS a double copy, sheet folded twice to make four uncut leaves, 9¼″ x 5¾″.

E 58 WHAT'S AHEAD FOR BOOKS & AUTHORS?
1972

Title page: 'H. L. Mencken: | [green] WHAT'S AHEAD for BOOKS | [green] & AU-THORS? [purple and upside down] ?AUTHORS & | BOOKS for AHEAD WHAT'S | [black] Roxburghe / Zamorano / 1972'

Copyright page: None.

Colophon: 'This keepsake is presented to the Roxburghe and Zam- | orano Clubs at their joint meeting, September 10, 1972, by | David E. Belch, Carroll T. Harris, and Clifford Burke. | The type is Spectrum, designed by Jan Van Krimpen and | set by Mackenzie & Harris of San Francisco. The | printing was accomplished by Clifford Burke, under the | direct supervision of Mr. Belch.'

$8\frac{3}{4}''$ x $5\frac{13}{16}''$: [1–16] = 16 pp.

$[1]^8$ = 8 leaves.

Contents: pp. 1–2: blank; p. 3: 'Note:'; p. 4: caricature of Mencken; p. 5: title; p. 6: blank; pp. 7–12: text; p. 13: '2nd Note:'; p. 14: colophon; pp. 15–16: blank.

Typography and paper: $5\frac{15}{16}''$ x $3\frac{13}{16}''$; 27 lines per page. No heads. Laid paper.

Binding: Wrappers of same stock as pages, outsides with purple design. Front, in green: 'H. L. Mencken: What's Ahead for Books & Authors? | [same, upside down]'. Rough trimmed. Sewed.

Locations: EPL, GHT, LC, RJS.

Notes: A speech delivered to the American Booksellers Association on 13 May 1940. Previously published (*Menckeniana* 2.3–6); S1.16, S2.23.

E 59 H. L. MENCKEN ON PANTS-PRESSERS, PUBLISHERS, & EDITORS
1980

Title page: 'H. L. MENCKEN | on | Pants-Pressers, | Publishers, | & Editors | °'

Copyright page: None.

Colophon: 'The text of H. L. Mencken's remarks is taken | from a stenographic transcript of proceedings of | the first annual meeting of the National Conference | of Editorial Writers, at Washington, D.C., | October 16, 1947. The original work is in the | possession of the University of West Florida | Library. | Reprinted, October, 1980, by | Williamsburg Press, Inc. | Designed by S. F. Royall. | 200 copies.'

8½″ x 5⅜″: [1–12] = 12 pp.

[1]⁶ = 6 leaves.

Contents: p. 1: title; p. 2: 'UNIVERSITY OF WEST FLORIDA | JOHN C. PACE LIBRARY | [UWF monogram] | Library Publication | No. 11'; pp. 3–9: text; p. 10: colophon; pp. 11–12: blank.

Typography and paper: 6¼″ x 4″; 35 lines per page. No heads. Laid paper.

Binding: Heavy brown paper wrappers. Front: 'H. L. MENCKEN | *on* | *Pants-Pressers* | *Publishers* | *& Editors* | Remarks to the Annual Meeting of the | National Conference of Editorial Writers | October 16, 1947'. All edges trimmed. Three staples.

Locations: GHT, JRS.

Notes: A keepsake for the Library Associates. Previously published (*Stenographic Transcript* [B 169] and *Gang of Pecksniffs* [A 71]); cf. Adler 271, S2.22.

E 60 MENCKENIANA
1980

Title page: 'MENCKENIANA | [brown ornament] | The House of Type | Baltimore | 1980'

Copyright page: Blank.

Colophon: 'GUY BOTTERILL AT THE HOUSE OF TYPE | 5502 CRAIG AVE. BALTIMORE, MD. 21212 | 70 COPIES 5 X 8 BALTIMOREAN NO. 13 PRESS | PAPER: MOHAWK SUPERFINE SUB. 80'

5½″ x 4¼″: [i–ii] 1–28 [29–30] = 32 pp.

[1]¹⁶ = 16 leaves.

Contents: p. i: title; p. ii: blank; pp. 1–2: 'HENRY LOUIS MENCKEN' [biography]; pp. 3–28: text: quotations, one per page; pp. 29–30: '*Notes on the Type*'; p. 30: colophon.

Typography and paper: Various fonts and with entry titles in various colors. 3¾″ x 2⅜″ (height varies with font of entry title; right margin not justified); 4 lines per page (lines vary greatly with length of entry). No heads. Wove paper.

Binding: Heavy, grained, cream-colored paper wrappers. Front, in red: 'Menckeniana | [ornament: quill pen and sheet]'. All edges trimmed. Two staples.

Location: GHT.

Notes: Quotations uncredited.

E 61 THE SAGE OF BALTIMORE
1984

Title page: '[blue] THE SAGE | OF | BALTIMORE | [black] H. L. Mencken | [fuchsia ornament] | [black] The House of Type | Baltimore | 1984'

Copyright page: None.

Colophon: '*Sixty copies printed on a 5x8 Baltimorean No. 13 | hand press by Guy Botterill at the House of Type, | 5502 Craig Avenue, Baltimore, Maryland 21212*'

5½" x 4¼": [i–ii] 1–12 [13–14] = 16 pp.

[1]⁸ = 8 leaves.

Contents: p. i: title; p. ii: 'Henry Louis Mencken' [biography]; pp. 1–12: text: quotations, one per page; p. 13: 'Notes on the Type', colophon; p. 14: blank.

Typography and paper: Various fonts and with entry titles in various colors. 3½" x 3" (height varies with font of entry title; right margin not justified); 5 lines per page (lines vary greatly with length of entry). No heads. Wove paper, watermarked 'WARREN'S | OLDE STYLE'.

Binding: Heavy, grained, white paper wrappers. Front: 'THE SAGE | OF | BAL-TIMORE | [ornament: candle and books]'. All edges trimmed. Two staples.

Location: GHT.

Notes: Quotations uncredited.

E 62 A TEXAS SCHOOLMARM
1989

Head title: '[ornamental border] | A Texas Schoolmarm | *My First Thirty Years,* by Gertrude Beasley. | Paris: The Three Mountains Press. | [text follows]'

Colophon: 'This review first appeared in the January, 1926, issue | of *The American Mercury,* and has been reprinted as a keep- | sake for the second annual meeting of the Book Club of | Texas, November 4, 1989. The photograph of Edna | Gertrude Beasley comes from the 1914 year- | book of Simmons College. 750 copies of | this keepsake were printed at the | press of W. Thomas Taylor.'

9¼" x 6⅛": [1–8] = 8 pp.

[1]⁴ = 4 leaves.

Contents: pp. 1–2: blank; pp. 3–5: text, signed '—H.L. Mencken'; p. 6: blank; p. 7: colophon; p. 8: blank.

Typography and paper: 7⅛″ x 4¹¹⁄₁₆″; 35 lines per page (number of lines varies). No heads. Gray wove paper flecked with darker gray.

Binding: Heavy brown paper wrappers flecked with darker brown. Front: photograph of Beasley. All edges trimmed. Two staples.

Location: TxCM.

E 63 DEFINITIONS, SKEPTICISMS
1995

Title page: 'DEFINITIONS | [ornament] | SKEPTICISMS | [ornament] | IRREVER-ENCES | [ornament] | OBSERVATIONS | [ornament] | BARBS AND | [ornament] | OTHER ACERBITIES | *A Selection of Quotations from* | H. L. MENCKEN'

Copyright page: Blank.

Colophon: 'This keepsake was printed at the Arion Press | and presented by Andrew Hoyem and David | Belch on the occasion of an address by Mr. | Belch on the subject of H. L. Mencken at the | meeting of the Roxburghe Club of San Fran- | cisco on 21 February 1995.'

7⅛″ x 4¹¹⁄₁₆″: [i–ii 1–2] 3–12 [13–14] = 16 pp.

[1]^8 = 8 leaves.

Contents: pp. i–ii: blank; p. 1: title; p. 2: blank; pp. 3–11: text: quotations; p. 12: biography of Mencken (signed G. T.), colophon.

Typography and paper: 5¾″ x 3″; 28 lines per page (including ornaments dividing items). No heads. Laid paper.

Binding: Pale green wrappers. Front: [within ornate frame] 'MENCKEN'. All edges trimmed. Sewed with tied thread.

Locations: GHT, RJS.

Notes: G. T. is Glen Todd. Quotations uncredited.

F. Blurbs

Statements about other authors by Mencken printed on dust jackets and wrappers, or in prelims. These are either original contributions or appear in/on a book for the first time. Subsequent appearances of these blurbs are not listed.

F 1 JOSEPH CONRAD: A STUDY
1914

JOSEPH CONRAD | A STUDY | BY | RICHARD CURLE | AUTHOR OF | 'AS-PECTS OF GEORGE MEREDITH,' SHADOWS OUT OF THE CROWD | 'LIFE IS A DREAM' | WITH A FRONTISPIECE | [seven-line quotation from *The Mirror of the Sea*] | GARDEN CITY   NEW YORK | DOUBLEDAY, PAGE & COMPANY | 1914

$7^{15}/_{16}''$ × $5^{1}/_{4}''$. Blue cloth stamped in gilt. *Location:* GHT (dj). Previously published (*Smart Set,* July 1913); not in Adler.

Blurb about *Youth* (from "Various Bad Novels") on back of dust jacket.

F 2 AIRS AND BALLADS
1918

AIRS AND BALLADS | B y   J O H N   M c C L U R E | [Borzoi device over rule of same width] | New York ALFRED A. KNOPF Mcmxviii

$7^{3}/_{8}''$ × $5^{1}/_{16}''$. Light blue paper-covered boards stamped in dark blue. *Location:* KU-S (dj). Not in Adler.

Twenty-one-line blurb on front of dust jacket.

F 3 MY ÁNTONIA
1919

MY ÁNTONIA | BY | WILLA SIBERT CATHER | *Optima dies . . . prima fugit* | VIRGIL | WITH ILLUSTRATIONS BY | W. T. BENDA | [Riverside device] | BOS-TON AND NEW YORK | HOUGHTON MIFFLIN COMPANY | [gothic] The Riverside Press Cambridge | [roman] 1918

On copyright page: *'Published October 1918'*. $7^{1}/_{4}''$ × $4^{3}/_{4}''$. Brown cloth stamped in light yellow-orange. *Location:* MBU (dj from Joan Crane, *Willa Cather: A Bibliogra-*

phy [Lincoln: University of Nebraska Press, [1982]], p. 58). Previously published (*Smart Set*); not in Adler.

Blurb on 1919 dust jacket. Not on first printing of jacket.

F 4 MUSIC AND BAD MANNERS
1919

[all within double-rule box inside bold-rule box] Music | and Bad Manners | [rule] | *Carl Van Vechten* | [Borzoi device over rule] | New York Alfred A. Knopf | MCMXVI

7⁵⁄₁₆″ × 5″. Black paper-covered boards, yellow paper label on front and spine. Published in this (second) binding 16 June 1919 (Bruce Kellner, *A Bibliography of the Work of Carl Van Vechten* [Westport, Conn.: Greenwood, [1980]], pp. 6–7). *Location:* D (dj). Previously published (*Smart Set,* May 1917); not in Adler.

Blurb for the book on front of dust jacket (from "Shocking Stuff").

F 5 THE BLOOD OF THE CONQUERORS
1921

The Blood of the Conquerors | *by* | *Harvey Fergusson* | [Borzoi device in oval] | *New York* | *Alfred • A • Knopf* | *1921*

Published September 1921. 7³⁄₈″ × 4⅞″. Black ribbed cloth stamped in orange and blindstamped. See *Mencken and Sara* (A 77), p. 140, on his blurbs for Fergusson. *Location:* GHT (dj). Not in Adler.

Eight-line blurb on front of dust jacket.

F 6 ALEXANDER'S BRIDGE
1922

ALEXANDER'S BRIDGE | BY | WILLA SIBERT CATHER | NEW EDITION WITH A PREFACE | [Riverside device in oval] | BOSTON AND NEW YORK | HOUGHTON MIFFLIN COMPANY | [gothic] The Riverside Press   Cambridge | [roman] 1922

7⁵⁄₁₆″ × 4¹⁵⁄₁₆″. Blue cloth stamped in gilt. *Location:* MChB (dj from Crane, *Willa Cather: A Bibliography,* p. 24). Previously published (*Smart Set,* December 1912?); not in Adler.

Nine-line excerpt from review (probably from "A Visit to a Short Story Factory") on dust jacket.

F 7 THE VEGETABLE
1923

[all within double-rule box] THE VEGETABLE | or | from President to postman | [rule] | By | F. SCOTT FITZGERALD | [quotation in six lines *From a Current Magazine*] | [rule] | NEW YORK | CHARLES SCRIBNER'S SONS | 1923

Published 27 April 1923. $7\frac{7}{16}''$ × $5\frac{1}{16}''$. Green cloth stamped in gilt and blindstamped. *Location:* D (dj from Bruccoli 62). Previously published (*Smart Set*, August 1920); not in Adler.

Excerpt from review of *This Side of Paradise* ("Books More or Less Amusing—II") on rear flap of dust jacket.

F 8 THE CREATIVE LIFE
1924

[script] The | CREATIVE LIFE | LUDWIG LEWISOHN | [B&L device] | BONI AND LIVERIGHT | Publishers   New York | M C M X X I V

$8''$ × $5\frac{7}{16}''$. Gray paper-covered boards with gray design, gray buckram spine stamped in gilt. *Location:* GHT (dj). Previously published (*Nation,* 12 April 1922); not in Adler.

Blurb for *Up Stream* on front flap of dust jacket (from "Dream and Awakening").

F 9 THE GREAT GATSBY
1925

THE GREAT GATSBY | BY | F. SCOTT FITZGERALD | [poem attributed to Thomas Parke D'Invilliers in five lines] | NEW YORK | CHARLES SCRIBNER'S SONS | 1925

Published 10 April 1925. $7\frac{7}{16}''$ × $5''$. Dark bluish green cloth blindstamped and stamped in gilt. *Location:* GHT (dj from Bruccoli 66). Previously published (*American Mercury*, July 1924); not in Adler.

Blurb from review of Lardner's *How to Write Short Stories* ("Ring W. Lardner") on rear flap of dust jacket.

F 10 WHAT OF IT?

1925

WHAT OF IT | ? | BY | RING W. LARDNER | [rule] | [ship] | [rule] | NEW YORK • LONDON | CHARLES SCRIBNER'S SONS | MCMXXV

Published 10 April 1925. 7¼" × 5⅛". Dark grayish green cloth stamped in gilt. *Location:* Harv (dj from Matthew J. Bruccoli and Richard Layman, *Ring W. Lardner: A Descriptive Bibliography* [Pittsburgh: University of Pittsburgh Press, 1976], p. 66). Not in Adler.

On front flap of dust jacket is same blurb as on F 9, published on same day.

F 11 THE ODYSSEY OF A NICE GIRL

1925

[all within green frame] *The Odyssey of a | Nice Girl | Ruth Suckow* | [green Borzoi device in oval] | *New York | Alfred • A • Knopf* | 1925

7½" × 5¹⁄₁₆". Black cloth stamped in white and blue and blindstamped on front. *Locations:* D (dj), MWH. Not in Adler.

Blurb for *Country People* on rear flap of dust jacket. "I regard Ruth Suckow as the most promising. . . ."

F 12 AN AMERICAN TRAGEDY

1925

[all within double-rule box, outer rule thicker, inside ornate frame] AN AMERICAN | TRAGEDY | BY | THEODORE DREISER | VOLUME ONE [and TWO] | [BL device] | NEW YORK | BONI AND LIVERIGHT | MCMXXV

Trade printing, preceding limited. 7⅜" × 4⅞". Black cloth stamped in gilt. *Location:* GHT (dj). Donald Pizer et al., *Theodore Dreiser: A Primary Bibliography and Reference Guide,* 2nd ed. (Boston: Hall, 1991), pp. 10–12; not in Adler.

Blurb on back of dust jacket on both volumes. "He stands isolated today, a figure weatherbeaten and lonely. Yet I know no American novelist who seems so secure or likely to endure."

F 13 DOMNEI
1925

Domnei | *A Comedy of Woman-Worship* | *By* | JAMES BRANCH CABELL | *With an Introduction by* | JOSEPH HERGESHEIMER | [rule] | *"En cor gentil domnei per mort no passa."* | [rule] | NEW YORK | ROBERT M. McBRIDE & COMPANY | 1925

On copyright page: 'Revised Edition . . . | *Fourth Printing* | *December, 1925* | Published, October, 1920'. 7½″ × 5⅛″. Brown cloth stamped in gilt. First published as *The Soul of Melicent*. Earliest dust jacket located with the Mencken blurb is with a copy of the fourth printing of the revised edition. *Location:* GHT (dj). Previously published (*Smart Set*, August 1918); not in Adler.

Blurb on back of dust jacket (from "A Sub-Potomac Phenomenon").

F 14 THE HARD-BOILED VIRGIN
1926

[all within brown box formed by four lines crossing, with ornate borders on it, and contained within a black double-rule box, outer rule bold] THE | HARD-BOILED | VIRGIN | *by* | FRANCES NEWMAN | [brown B&L device] | BONI & LIVERIGHT | NEW YORK 1926

7⅜″ × 5⅛″. Orange and yellow paper-covered boards, black cloth spine stamped in gilt and blindstamped. *Locations:* GHT (dj), RJS (dj). Not in Adler.

Blurb from a letter on front of the dust jacket. Cf. *Mencken and Sara* (A 77), p. 268, n. 4; *Frances Newman's Letters* (B 85), pp. 227–28.

F 15 JARNEGAN
1926

[all within ornate frame] JARNEGAN | *By* | JIM TULLY | *Author of* | Beggars of Life | [star] | New York | Albert & Charles Boni | 1926

7⁵⁄₁₆″ × 5″. Green cloth-covered boards stamped in gilt, black cloth spine stamped in gilt. *Locations:* MWC, PB (dj). Previously published (*American Mercury*, December 1924); not in Adler.

Blurb for *Beggars of Life* ("Brief Notices") on rear flap of dust jacket.

F 16 GENTLEMEN PREFER BLONDES
1926

[all within double-rule box surrounded by ornate frame] *"Gentlemen Prefer Blondes"* | *The Illuminating Diary of a* | *Professional Lady* | *By* | Anita Loos | *Intimately Illustrated by* | RALPH BARTON | [B&L device in oval] | *NEW YORK* | BONI & LIVERIGHT | 1925

On copyright page: 'Thirteenth printing, May, 1926'. 7¼" × 4¹⁵⁄₁₆". Figured blue and white paper-covered boards with label on front, red cloth spine stamped in gilt. Earliest dust jacket located with the Mencken blurb is with copies of the thirteenth printing. *Locations:* GHT (dj), RJS (dj). Previously published (*American Mercury,* January 1926); not in Adler.

Blurb ("Brief Notices") on back of dust jacket.

F 17 THE STORY OF PHILOSOPHY
1926

F 17.1
First printing (1926)

The Story of | PHILOSOPHY | [green rule] | THE LIVES AND OPINIONS OF | THE GREATER PHILOSOPHERS | [green rule] | BY *Will Durant* PH.D. | [green squiggle] | [S&S device] | [green rule] | SIMON AND SCHUSTER | *NEW YORK* | 1926

Published May 1926. 9¼" × 6⅛". Black vertically ribbed cloth blindstamped on front and stamped in gilt on spine. *Location:* GHT (dj). Prviously published (*Smart Set,* April 1918); not in Adler.

Blurb for *Philosophy and the Social Problem* on front of dust jacket (from "Business– II").

F 17.2
Twenty-first printing (1927)

[all within box inside double-rule box] THE STORY | *of* | PHILOSOPHY | [green rule] | THE LIVES AND OPINIONS OF | THE GREATER PHILOSOPHERS | [green rule] | *BY* WILL DURANT, Ph. D. | [green squiggle] | [S&S device] | [green rule] | SIMON AND SCHUSTER | *NEW YORK   MCMXXVII*

On copyright page: 'Twenty-first printing, October, 1927'. 9⁵⁄₁₆" × 6¼". Black cloth blindstamped and stamped in gilt. Earliest dust jacket located with the Mencken blurb is with a copy of the twenty-first printing. *Location:* GHT (dj). Previously published (*American Mercury,* August 1926); not in Adler.

Blurb for the book on front of dust jacket.

F 18 EXCAVATIONS
1926

[all within ornate frame] [blue] EXCAVATIONS | [black] *a book of advocacies* | BY | CARL VAN VECHTEN | [blue Borzoi device in oval] | 1926 • ALFRED • A • KNOPF • *New York*

7⁷⁄₁₆″ × 5⅛″. Blue cloth blindstamped front and back and stamped in gilt on spine. The blurb may appear on the dust jacket of the third printing (May 1922) of *Peter Whiffle.* See Bruce Kellner, *A Bibliography of the Work of Carl Van Vechten* (Westport, Conn.: Greenwood Press, [1980]), p. 19. *Locations:* GHT (dj), MNS. Previously published (*Smart Set* [unlocated]); not in Adler.

Blurb on front flap of dust jacket regarding Van Vechten's *Peter Whiffle.* "A rambling puckish piece . . ."

F 19 THE OUTLOOK FOR AMERICAN PROSE
1927

THE OUTLOOK | FOR AMERICAN PROSE | *By* | JOSEPH WARREN BEACH | [device] | THE UNIVERSITY OF CHICAGO PRESS | CHICAGO • ILLINOIS

On copyright page: 'Second Impression April 1927'. 8½″ × 5¾″. Blue-green paper-covered boards printed in red, black cloth spine stamped in gilt. *Location:* GHT (dj). Previously published (*American Mercury,* October 1926); not in Adler.

Blurb for the book on front flap of dust jacket.

F 20 MEANWHILE
1927

MEANWHILE | (*The Picture of a Lady*) | BY H. G. WELLS | NEW YORK | GEORGE H. DORAN COMPANY

On copyright page: 'FIRST PRINTING IN AMERICA, AUGUST, 1927'. 7⅝″ × 5¼″. Blue cloth blindstamped and stamped in gilt. *Locations:* GHT (dj), RJS (dj). Previously published (*American Mercury,* December 1926); not in Adler.

Blurb from review of *The World of William Clissold* ("Wells Redivivus") on front flap of dust jacket.

F 21 ELMER GANTRY
1927

ELMER GANTRY | BY | SINCLAIR LEWIS | [device] | NEW YORK | HAR-COURT, BRACE AND COMPANY

On copyright page: 'COPYRIGHT, 1927'. 7½″ × 5⅛″. Blue cloth stamped in orange. Dedicated to Mencken. *Locations:* GHT (dj), RJS (dj). Cf. Adler 341.

Blurb for *Arrowsmith* on rear flap of dust jacket. "One of the best novels ever written in America."

F 22 CIRCUS PARADE
1927

Circus | *PARADE* | [rule] | By J I M   T U L L Y | [red] [circus tent] | Illustrated by WILLIAM GROPPER | [black] ALBERT & CHARLES BONI NEW YORK [red device] MCMXXVII

7¹⁵⁄₁₆″ × 5⁵⁄₁₆″. Red cloth-covered boards stamped in green and blindstamped, green cloth spine stamped in red. *Location:* PB (dj). Previously published (F 15; *American Mercury*, November 1926); not in Adler.

Blurbs for *Beggars of Life* and *Jarnegan* ("Certain Works of Fiction") on rear flap of dust jacket.

F 23 LATEST CONTEMPORARY PORTRAITS
1927

[row of squares] | LATEST | CONTEMPORARY | PORTRAITS | [row of squares] | BY | FRANK HARRIS | AUTHOR OF | "OSCAR WILDE: HIS LIFE AND CONFESSIONS" | NEW YORK | THE MACAULAY COMPANY

On copyright page: 'COPYRIGHT, 1927, BY NELLIE HARRIS'. 8½″ × 5¾″. Tan cloth stamped in black. *Location:* GHT (dj). Previously published (*Smart Set*, February 1922); not in Adler.

Blurb on front of dust jacket (from "Frank Harris and Others").

F 24 THE BONNEY FAMILY
1928

[olive ornamental border] | [olive rule] | T H E | *Bonney Family* | [olive rule] | *Ruth Suckow* | [olive Borzoi device] | [olive rule] | *New York* | ALFRED • A • KNOPF | 1928

7⁷⁄₁₆″ × 5⅛″. Olive cloth stamped in gilt and maroon. *Locations:* D (dj), ViU. Not in Adler.

Blurb for *Iowa Interiors* on rear flap of dust jacket. "Her short stories are wholly devoid. . . ."

F 25 SHANTY IRISH
1928

SHANTY IRISH | by *Jim Tully* | [device] | *Albert & Charles Boni* • *New York*

On copyright page: '*Copyright, 1928*'. 7⁵⁄₁₆″ × 4¹⁵⁄₁₆″. Pale green cloth stamped in black. *Location:* PB (dj). Second blurb previously published (F 22); not in Adler.

Blurb on p. [ii]: "If Tully were a Russian, read in translation, all the Professors would be hymning him. . . ." Blurb for *Beggars of Life* on rear flap of dust jacket.

F 26 POEMS IN PRAISE OF PRACTICALLY NOTHING
1928

[all in a box] POEMS IN | PRAISE OF | [concentric circles, outer one thicker] | [four ornaments over rule] | PRACTICALLY | NOTHING | [rule] | SAMUEL HOFFEN-STEIN | [rule] | BONI & LIVERIGHT • *NEW YORK*

On copyright page: '*Copyright, 1928*'. 7⁷⁄₁₆″ × 5³⁄₁₆″. Black, vertically ribbed cloth stamped in gilt and blindstamped. *Location:* GHT (dj). Previously published?; not in Adler.

Blurb on front of dust jacket. "'INCOMPARABLE,' says H. L. Mencken, whose authority on matters ironic is undisputed."

F 27 BALLYHOO
1928

[all within quadruple-rule box] BALLYHOO | THE VOICE OF THE PRESS | BY | SILAS BENT | [ornament] | ILLUSTRATED | [HL device] | NEW YORK | HORACE LIVERIGHT | 1927

On copyright page: 'Fourth Printing, November, 1928'. 8″ × 5½″. Black cloth stamped in red. Earliest dust jacket located with the Mencken blurb is with a copy of the fourth printing. *Location:* GHT (dj). Previously published (*American Mercury,* December 1927); not in Adler.

Blurb on rear flap of dust jacket.

F 28 WINGS ON MY FEET
1929

Wings on My Feet | [rule over rust twisted rule over rule] | BLACK ULYSSES | AT THE WARS | BY HOWARD W. ODUM | *Author of* Rainbow Round My Shoulder | [rule over rust twisted rule over rule] | THE BOBBS-MERRILL COMPANY | *Indianapolis   Publishers*

On copyright page: 'COPYRIGHT, 1929'. 7¹³⁄₁₆″ × 5¼″. Green cloth stamped in black. *Location:* GHT (dj). Previously published (*American Mercury,* September 1928); not in Adler.

Blurb for *Rainbow Round My Shoulder* ("Black Boy") on rear flap of dust jacket.

F 29 HELLO TOWNS!
1929

[red] HELLO TOWNS! | [black ornamental rule] | *by* | *SHERWOOD ANDERSON* | [red rule] | [black ornamental rule] | *19* [red HL device] *29* | [black ornamental rule] | *New York • Horace Liveright*

Published April 1929. 8⅛″ × 5½″. Light brown cloth blindstamped and stamped in gilt. *Locations*: GHT (dj), RJS (dj), MBU (rebound). Not in Adler.

Blurb for *Dark Laughter* on back of dust jacket. "One of the most profound American novels. . . ."

F 30 MENCKEN AND SHAW
1930

MENCKEN AND SHAW | THE ANATOMY OF | AMERICA'S VOLTAIRE | AND | ENGLAND'S OTHER JOHN *BULL* | BY | BENJAMIN DE CASSERES | [ornament: child's head with wings] | *NEW YORK* • SILAS NEWTON • *PUBLISHER*

On copyright page: 'COPYRIGHT 1930'. 8¹⁄₁₆″ × 5¹⁄₁₆″. Blue cloth stamped in silver. Dust jacket has wraparound band. *Locations:* GHT (dj), Harv, RJS (2, dj). Cf. Adler 275.

Letter quoted on front flap of dust jacket, two-word quotation on back.

F 31 NOTHING TO PAY
1930

CARADOC EVANS | [ornament] | NOTHING | TO PAY | [ornament] | NEW YORK | W. W. NORTON & COMPANY INC. | PUBLISHERS

On copyright page: 'Copyright, 1930 | . . . | FIRST EDITION'. 7⁷⁄₁₆″ × 5¹⁄₁₆″. Light brown cloth stamped in brown. *Location:* GHT (dj). Previously published (*Smart Set,* December 1918); not in Adler.

Four-line excerpt from review of *Capel Sion* ("The Late Mr. Wells—III") on front of dust jacket; one line of it on spine.

F 32 THE HUMAN BODY
[1930?]

[all within a box] A STAR BOOK | [rule] | THE | HUMAN BODY | BY | LOGAN CLENDENING, M.D. | Illustrations by | W. C. SHEPARD AND DALE BERONIUS | AND FROM PHOTOGRAPHS | [quotations from *Iolanthe* in five lines] | [Star Books device] | [rule] | GARDEN CITY PUBLISHING COMPANY, INC. | GARDEN CITY, NEW YORK

On copyright page: 'COPYRIGHT 1927, 1930, BY ALFRED A. KNOPF, INC.' 8¼″ × 5⁷⁄₁₆″. Light brown cloth stamped in brown. Blurb possibly on dust jacket of second revised Knopf edition (1930); not seen. *Location:* GHT (dj). Previously published (*Nation,* 19 October 1927); not in Adler.

Sentence (from "Man as Mechanism") quoted on front and spine of dust jacket.

F 33 CREATIVE CRITICISM
1931

Creative Criticism | AND OTHER ESSAYS | BY J. E. SPINGARN | A NEW AND ENLARGED EDITION | [leaf] | NEW YORK | HARCOURT, BRACE AND COMPANY | 1931

On copyright page: *first edition*. 7⅜″ × 5″. Blue cloth stamped in gilt. *Locations:* GHT (dj), NjP. Previously published?; not in Adler.

Quotation on back of dust jacket. "Mr. Spingarn is one of the most civilized men in America."

F 34 LET THERE BE BEER!
1932

LET THERE BE | BEER! | BY BOB BROWN | [woodcut] | NEW YORK • NINE-TEEN THIRTY-TWO | HARRISON SMITH & ROBERT HAAS

On copyright page: 'FIRST PUBLISHED | 1932'. 7¹⁵⁄₁₆″ × 5½″. Yellow cloth stamped in white and black. Dedicated to Mencken. *Location:* GHT (dj). Cf. Adler 340.

Blurb on back of dust jacket. "I hope every honest beer fanatic will buy two copies of 'Let There Be Beer!' one for himself and one for his pastor" *[sic]*.

F 35 PRISON DAYS AND NIGHTS
1933

[all between three vertical rules on left and right] PRISON | DAYS | and | NIGHTS | BY VICTOR F. NELSON | *With an Introduction by* | ABRAHAM MYERSON, M.D. | *Psychiatric Examiner of Prisoners* | *Commonwealth of Massachusetts* | BOSTON | LITTLE, BROWN, AND COMPANY | 1933

On copyright page: 'Published March, 1933'. 8¹⁄₁₆″ × 5⁷⁄₁₆″. Cloth that is part black (stamped in blue) and part blue (stamped in black). *Location:* GHT (dj). Not in Adler.

Letter to Nelson as blurb on front flap of dust jacket.

F 36 THE AMERICAN SPECTATOR YEAR BOOK
1934

The | AMERICAN SPECTATOR | YEAR BOOK | *Edited by* | GEORGE JEAN NATHAN SHERWOOD ANDERSON | ERNEST BOYD JAMES BRANCH CABELL | THEODORE DREISER EUGENE O'NEILL | [Stokes device: winged horse carrying torchbearer] | FREDERICK A. STOKES COMPANY | NEW YORK MCMXXXIV

8⅝″ × 5¾″. Black cloth stamped in red and gilt. *Locations:* GHT (dj), NjP. Previously published (*American Mercury,* October 1932); not in Adler.

Blurb for *Man's Rough Road,* by A. G. Keller (from "The Travail of Man"), on back of dust jacket.

F 37 TENDER IS THE NIGHT
1934

TENDER IS THE | NIGHT | A ROMANCE | By | F. Scott Fitzgerald | [decoration] | DECORATIONS BY | EDWARD SHENTON | NEW YORK | CHARLES SCRIBNER'S SONS | 1934

Published 12 April 1934. 7⁵⁄₁₆″ × 5¹⁄₁₆″. Green cloth stamped in gilt on spine and blindstamped. *Location:* GHT (dj). Previously published (*American Mercury,* July 1925); Bruccoli 91; not in Adler.

Excerpt from review of *The Great Gatsby* ("New Fiction") on front flap of dust jacket.

F 38 BRUISER
1936

THE BRUISER | [rule] | by | *JIM TULLY* | [device] | NEW YORK | GREENBERG : PUBLISHER | [rule]

On copyright page: 'COPYRIGHT, 1936'. 7½″ × 5″. Yellowish tan cloth stamped in black. *Location:* PB (dj). Not in Adler.

Blurb on back of dust jacket. "The Bruiser is capital stuff—one of the best books Jim Tully has ever written. . . ."

F 39 THE RAPE OF PALESTINE
1940

A DIGEST | *by* HARRY LOUIS SELDEN | *of* THE RAPE OF PALESTINE | *by* WILLIAM B. ZIFF | with an introduction | *by* FRANCES GUNTHER | Copyright, 1940 | THE AMERICAN FRIENDS OF A JEWISH PALESTINE | 285 Madison Avenue | New York City

7⅝″ × 5½″. White wrappers printed in red and blue with white showing through. *Location:* Harv. Previously published (unlocated reviews in New York *Herald Tribune* and Baltimore *Sun*); not in Adler.

Blurb from Mencken's reviews of first edition (1938) on back wrapper.

F 40 ELMER GANTRY
[1940?]

[all within box with double rule at top and bottom] [row of ornaments] | ELMER
GANTRY | [squiggle] | BY | SINCLAIR LEWIS | [script] *Avon Books* | NEW YORK |
JO. MEYERS E. B. WILLIAMS

First printing (1940?) not seen. Earliest copy located with the Mencken blurb is a
later printing. *Location:* GHT. Previously published (*American Mercury,* April 1927);
not in Adler.

Quotation from the review ("Man of God: American Style"), p. [i].

F 41 DODSWORTH
1941

[all in a box with ornate borders at top and bottom] Dodsworth | A NOVEL BY |
Sinclair Lewis | [double rule] | *Pocket* BOOKS, Inc. [device in circle superimposed
over double rule and bottom border] NEW YORK, N. Y.

On copyright page: '*Pocket* BOOKS *edition published September, 1941*'. 6½″ × 4¼″.
Multicolored wrappers. *Location:* GHT. Previously published (*American Mercury,*
April 1929); not in Adler.

Blurb (from "Escape and Return") on p. [iii] and on back wrapper.

F 42 THE REALNESS OF WITCHCRAFT IN AMERICA
1942

[cover title] [thick-thin rule] THE REALNESS OF | WITCHCRAFT | IN AMER-
ICA . . . *[sic]* | [next four lines divided by witch on broomstick in triangle] WITCH-
DOCTORS APPARITIONS | POW-WOWS HEXEREI | ANGELS DEVILS |
HEX   SEX | WITCHES OR NO WITCHES, YOU | SHOULD READ THIS AC-
COUNT! | [heavy dot] | By A. MONROE AURAND, Jr. | Author of | [three titles in
three lines] | [heavy dot] | Copyright by The Aurand Press.—*All rights reserved.* |
Privately Printed: THE AURAND PRESS, LANCASTER, PENNA. | [thin-thick
rule]

Published 1942 (OCLC). 8⁷⁄₁₆″ × 5¹¹⁄₁₆″. Pale yellow wrappers printed in black. *Location:* GHT. Not in Adler.

Blurb on back wrapper, probably from letter, concerning Aurand's series of books on
Pennsylvania Germans.

F 43 THE CASE OF MR. CRUMP
1947

The Case of | MR. CRUMP | BY | [script] *Ludwig Lewisohn* | FARRAR, STRAUS AND COMPANY | NEW YORK • 1947

Published March 1947; original printing 1926. 7^{15}⁄$_{16}$″ × 5^{5}⁄$_{16}$″. Maroon cloth blind-stamped on front, stamped in black and gilt on spine. *Locations:* GHT (dj), MChB. Previously published (*American Mercury*, March 1927); not in Adler.

Blurb (from "Portrait of a Lady") on back of dust jacket.

F 44 THE HISTRONIC MR. POE
1949

THE HISTRONIC | MR. POE | N. BRYLLION FAGIN | ASSOCIATE PROFESSOR OF ENGLISH AND DRAMA | THE JOHNS HOPKINS UNIVERSITY [shield] | BALTIMORE | THE JOHNS HOPKINS PRESS | 1949

8⅜″ × 5⅜″. Light orange cloth stamped in gilt. Mencken was among those who "have read my manuscript, in whole or in part," and offered advice (p. xi). *Locations*: MBU, NjP (rebound), Richard Copley (dj). Not in Adler.

Blurb on front of dust jacket. ". . . Of all the Poe books ever done in English . . . it seems to me the best, and by long odds."

F 45 DICTIONARY OF AMERICAN UNDERWORLD LINGO
1950

[within quadruple-rule box] DICTIONARY | OF AMERICAN | UNDERWORLD | LINGO | HYMAN E. GOLDIN | Editor in Chief | FRANK O'LEARY | General Editor | MORRIS LIPSIUS | Assistant Editor | TWAYNE PUBLISHERS, INC. | 42 Broadway, New York 4

On copyright page: 'Copyright 1950'. 9″ × 6″. Blue-gray buckram stamped in silver. This "prepublication comment" must have been written before his stroke in 1948. *Location:* PB (dj). Not in Adler.

Prepublication blurb on rear flap of dust jacket.

F 46 WORDS AND WAYS OF AMERICAN ENGLISH
1952

Words | and Ways | of | American | English | by Thomas Pyles

New York: Random House. On copyright page: '*First Printing | Copyright, 1952*'. 8¼″ × 5⁷⁄₁₆″. Black cloth stamped in red, white, blue, and gilt. *Locations:* GHT (dj), MNodS. Previously published (*Partisan Review,* March 1948); not in Adler.

Excerpt from review of the *American College Dictionary* ("Thousands of Words—All Good Ones") on back of dust jacket.

F 47 NIGHTS OF LOVE AND LAUGHTER
1955

Henry Miller | NIGHTS OF LOVE | AND | LAUGHTER | *With an Introduction by Kenneth Rexroth* | [device] | A SIGNET BOOK | Published by THE NEW AMERI-CAN LIBRARY

On copyright page: 'FIRST PRINTING, NOVEMBER, 1955'. 7¹⁄₁₆″ × 4¼″. White paper wrappers printed in black, blue, white, purple, and yellow. *Location:* D. Not in Adler.

Blurb on p. [1]. "His is one of the most beautiful styles today."

G. Ghosts and Unlocated Items

G 1

"Journalism as a Trade," in *How a Press Club Can Aid Its City; Issued by The Journalist Club of Baltimore for the Week of July 26, 1909*, pp. [5–6].

Entered in Adler 22. Not located.

G 2

Seeing the World [ca. 1916].

Entered in NUC 375.494. Chap. VI (pp. 103–32) of *A Book of Burlesques* (A 14); pages detached and rebound, not a separate publication. *Location:* ICU.

G 3

Baltimore Symphony programs 1916–18.

According to Adler (23–24), "Program annotations for the concerts of the Baltimore Symphony were written by HLM for the first concert, Friday Feb. 11, 1916, and for two years thereafter. These notes were reprinted on the editorial page of the [Baltimore] Evening Sun." Title page of only copy located (AJG): '[all within double rule box] [double rule] | BALTIMORE | SYMPHONY ORCHESTRA | Established and Maintained Exclusively by the City of Baltimore | FIRST SEASON, 1916 | GUSTAV STRUBE, Conductor | [double rule] | Programme of the | FIRST CONCERT | WITH DESCRIPTIVE NOTES BY | WILBERFOSS G. OWST | [ornament] | FRIDAY EVENING, FEBRUARY 11 | AT 8.30 | [rule] | PUBLISHED BY FREDERICK R. HUBER, MANAGER'. 9¼" x 5¹⁵⁄₁₆"; self wrappers. Owst is not a Mencken pseudonym. He had been music critic for the *Herald* and was Mencken's "old friend and music mentor" until they parted company with the outbreak of World War I (Hobson 183). Mencken's account: "When a Baltimore Symphony Orchestra was set up toward the end of 1915 I would sometimes give it a lift before a concert by printing an article on the symphony to be played. This I did mainly because the official program notes, written by a donkey named S. Broughton Tall, were stupid and inadequate" (*Thirty-five Years* 60).

G 4

Blurb, in *The Free Lance Books* (New York: Knopf, 1921).

Entered in Frey 59–60, West 196; not in Adler. Not located.

G 5
Books (New York: Knopf, [ca. 1922]).

Entered in West 199. No Mencken content (ad for fourth printing of *Book of Prefaces* [A 16], etc.). *Locations:* EPL, SL.

G 6
Review of Ernest Boyd's *Ireland's Literary Renaissance* (new ed.) "reprinted as a pamphlet" (1923?).

Entered in Adler 173. Probably refers to *Ireland: Her Books* (1917), the separately printed review of the first edition (E 4).

G 7
Foreword ("German Song Still Flourishes"), in *Program of the Diamant Jubiläum des Männer-Gesangsvereins Arion, Baltimore, Md., 26 Oktober, 1926.*

Entered in S1.6. Reprinted in *Menckeniana* 36.12–13. Not located.

G 8
A Comedy of Fig Leaves (New York: Knopf, 1927).

Entered in NUC 375.488 ("pamphlet" at Yale). Not at Yale; probably this review of James Branch Cabell's *Something About Eve* was detached from *American Mercury*, December 1927: 510.

G 9
Two Gay Rebels (New York: Knopf, [1928?]).

Entered in NUC 375.496 ("pamphlet" at Yale). Not at Yale; probably this review of the Storisende Edition of James Branch Cabell's works was detached from *American Mercury*, June 1928: 251–53.

G 10
Henry L. Mencken (New York: Knopf, n.d. [1928/9]).

Entered in West 199. No Mencken content (ad for forthcoming *Treatise on the Gods* [A 40; due "October 1929"] etc.). *Location:* EPL.

G 11
Fiction for Adept Hands [New York: Knopf, 1930].

Entered in NUC 375.489 ("pamphlet" at Yale). Not at Yale; probably this review of James Branch Cabell's *The Way of Ecben* was detached from *American Mercury*, January 1930: 126–27.

G 12

Mencken at Fifty (New York: The American Mercury, [1930]).

Entered in Adler 275, West 199. No Mencken content. *Locations:* EPL, Yale.

G 13

The Book Trade [1930?].

Entered in West 197 ("Reprint from the Baltimore *Evening Sun,* July 7, 1930"). Not located.

G 14

"Reflections on Homicide," *The Sandalwood Herald* [1934?].

Cited in *Behold This Dreamer!* (B 196), p. 310. Cf. "What to do With Criminals" (Adler 151). Not located: LC run (NUC 518.599) begins with vol. 2 (October 1935–September 1936).

G 15

Treatise on Right and Wrong (A 44.2), English edition "Subsequently issued by Routledge as no. 1 of their New World series."

Entered in Adler 15. In fact, the first three volumes in that series were published at the same time as Mencken's book. It is clear from the dust jacket and from the RKP catalogues examined (1934–36) that *Treatise* was not a part of the series. She also claims that there was a Canadian issue, but no evidence for it has been found.

G 16

A Proposed New Constitution for Maryland (1937).

Entered in Adler 96 (Baltimore *Sun* article of 12 April 1937 "Reprinted as a pamphlet"). Perhaps on the authority of the note, not by Mencken, with the typescript donated to EPL by Joseph Katz. Not located.

G 17

Read at a Luncheon Given by Fannie Hurst, Anne O'Hare McCormack, & H. L. Mencken to Blanche W. Knopf On December 18, 1940.

Entered in West 203. No Mencken content. *Location:* GHT.

G 18

Beethoven (1943).

Entered in Adler 17. Handcopied by a calligrapher, not a printed book. *Location:* EPL.

G 19

Treatise on the Gods (A 40.2), second edition "reprinted in London by G. Allen."

Entered in Adler 15. No record of publication.

G 20

Trattato Sugli Dei, trans. Aldo Devizzi (Milan: Il saggiatore, 1967).

Entered in *Index Translationum* 1967: 385. Not located.

G 21

R.I.P., trans. W. E. Richartz (Frankfurt a. M.: Patio-Verlag, 1968).

Entered in *Index Translationum* 1973: 106. Not located.

G 22

Musical settings of Mencken's works by Louis Cheslock, Emma Hemberger, and Howard R. Thatcher.

Entered in S1.71. Not printed for publication. *Location:* EPL.

G 23

Pamphlets ghosted for Dr. Joseph Bloodgood.

Claimed in MLAE 31. Not located.

G 24

The Battle of the Wilhelmstrasse.

Announced on the front dust jacket flap of the second printing of *A Book of Prefaces* (A 16; 1918) as "to be published after the war," and listed among his works in *Pistols for Two* (A 15; September 1917), p. 31. Never published; cf. Frey 42.

G 25

"Mencken has edited a collection of modern American short stories, in two volumes, to be translated into German by Franz Blei, and published in Munich by Georg Müller. The date is indefinite; German publishers are in a difficult position" (Frey 57). Never published.

G 26

"The 'brochure, privately printed, on the Battle of Tannenberg,' mentioned in *Pistols for Two* [A 15, p. 38], is imaginary" (Frey 60).

G 27

Note on *The American Songbag* (1927):

The | AMERICAN | SONGBAG | [row of asterisks and arrows] | CARL SANDBURG | [HB device] | *New York* | HARCOURT, BRACE & COMPANY

Copyright page: 'COPYRIGHT, 1927, BY | HARCOURT, BRACE AND COMPANY, INC. | PRINTED IN THE U. S. A.' Seven titles on p. ii, ending with 'ROOTABAGA PIGEONS'. 10¼" x 7⁷⁄₁₆". Black or very deep blue buckram stamped in orange; all edges stained orange. Four signed presentation copies at TxU had this binding and were not the printing with red cloth stamped in gilt on spine, top edge yellow, thicker and rougher paper (thickness 1½" as opposed to 1¼"), and different collation. *Locations:* RJS, TxU (6), Yale. Not in Adler.

Arrangement of 'THE DRUNKARD'S DOOM' credited to Mencken by Sandburg, pp. 104–05. Mencken denied the attribution in his *American Mercury* review of the book (March 1928: 383), and the MS of his contribution (dated 9 December 1926), in the RJS collection, bears him out. Sandburg probably had it rearranged by one of the professionals who handled the other entries in the book.

H. Translations and Braille Versions

Separate appearances and collections. Other contributions and periodical appearances excluded.

IN DEFENSE OF WOMEN (A 18)

H 1.1
German translation (1923)

[all within double-rule brown frame with ornate corners, gothic] Die Bücher der | Abtei Thelem | Begründet von | Otto Julius Bierbaum | [ornate rule] | H. L. Mencken | Verteidigung | der Frau | [star] | Übertragen | von | Franz Blei | [star] | 1923 | [ornate rule] | Georg Müller München

Three states of binding, all 5⅞″ × 3¾″: half bound leather with green and brown paper, spine stamped ornately in gilt and black, all edges stained maroon; green paper-covered boards and light green cloth spine, stamped in black, top edge stained yellow; green marbled boards with brown leather spine stamped in gilt, top edge possibly stained yellow. *Locations:* EPL (2), GHT (2). Adler 8; Frey 31.

H 1.2
Hungarian translation (1928). See B 81.

H 1.3
French translation (1934)

H. L. MENCKEN | *DÉFENSE DES* | FEMMES | *(In defence of women)* | PREFACE DE PAUL MORAND | *Traduit de l'anglais par Jean Jardin* | nrf [descender of f curves back under nr] | GALLIMARD | Paris — 43, rue de Beaune | *S.P.*

On p. [205]: 'ACHEVÉ D'IMPRIMER LE VINGT | FÉVRIER 1934'. 7⅜″ × 4¾″. Wrappers printed in black and red. Copy noted with tipped in card: 'Hommage du Traducteur'. *Locations:* EPL, GHT. Adler 9.

THE AMERICAN LANGUAGE (A 19)

H 2.1
German translation (1927)

DIE | AMERIKANISCHE SPRACHE | (DAS ENGLISCH DER VEREINIGTEN STAATEN) | VON | H. L. MENCKEN | DEUTSCHE BEARBEITUNG | VON | HEINRICH SPIES | [Teubner device] | 1927 | VERLAG UND DRUCK VON B. G. TEUBNER / [sic] LEIPZIG UND BERLIN

Translation of the third edition. On copyright page: '*Druck von B. G. Teubner in Dresden*'. Four pages of ads at the end (pp. [177–80]). Green cloth stamped in gilt on front and spine (9³⁄₁₆″ × 6¹⁄₁₆″), and gray paper wrappers (9¾″ × 6½″). A dealer reported blue cloth. *Locations:* EPL (2), NjP, RJS. Adler 9.

H 2.2
Braille version

A fourteen-volume Braille edition was prepared for the Library of Congress. Adler 9.

HELIOGABALUS (A 21)

H 3
German translation (1920)

[all gothic] Heliogabal | Schwank in drei Akten aus dem Amerikanischen | von | H. L. Mencken u. George Jean Nathan | Deutsch von | Peter Perpentikel | [ornament] | "Theatralia", Verlag und Vertrieb von Bühnenwerken | (Inh. Otto Rühlemann & A. H. Waechter)

On copyright page: 'Manuskript not for sale.— Copyright 1920 by "Theatralia".' 8⅝″ × 5½″. Stiff gray paper wrappers printed in black. Also unbound, 8⁷⁄₁₆″ × 5⅜″, stapled twice front to back and spine covered with brown tape; title page similar but headed 'Unverkäufliches Manuskript' and the English notice on the copyright page of the other transferred to the bottom of the title page. *Location:* EPL (2). Adler 26; Frey 44.

"SAVIORS OF CIVILIZATION" (E 12)

H 4
German translation (1923)

[head title, gothic] Retter der Civilization | [short rule] | Von H. L. Mencken. | Verlagsrecht, 1923, "The Evening Sun", Baltimore Md. Nachdruck mit | Unerkennung hiermit genehmigt.

After head title, announcement that the *American Mercury* will commence publication in January 1924. 14⅞″ × 11½″ sheet printed on one side in four columns, translating article of 9 April 1923. *Location:* D. Not in Adler.

NOTES ON DEMOCRACY (A 33)

H 5
German translation (1930)

[all in gothic] H. Mencken | [rule] | Demokratenspiegel | Übersetzung von | D. S. Kellner | Mit Lithographien | von | A. Paul Weber | 1930 | [rule] | Widerstands [lines slanting up:] = Verlag | Berlin

8¹⁵⁄₁₆″ × 6¹⁄₁₆″. Boards covered with orange and yellow paper. Yellow cloth spine stamped with black box containing gilt lettering. Top edge stained blue. Dust jacket has picture of Mencken on front. Actual translator may have been Leon and not Dora S. Kellner (*Ich Kuss* [A 75], p. 74). *Locations:* GHT (dj), RJS. Adler 12.

HAPPY DAYS (A 49)

H 6
Braille version

Embossed in three volumes for the Library of Congress: Mt. Healthy, O.: Clovernook Printing House for the Blind, 1941.

HEATHEN DAYS (A 54)

H 7
Braille version

Embossed in Press Braille grade 2, three volumes, for the Library of Congress: Los Angeles: Braille Instutute of America, 1943 (BRA 5784).

A MENCKEN CHRESTOMATHY (A 61)

H 8.1
Spanish translation (1971)

H. L. Mencken | [rule] | PRONTUARIO | DE LA ESTUPIDEZ | Y LOS PRE-JUICIOS | HUMANOS | [rule] | [device to left of next two lines] granica | editor.

On copyright page: '1ª [dot beneath the a] edición: 1971 | Traducción: Eduardo Goligorsky'. On p. [4]: 'Colección | Libertad y Cambio | [no. 12 on the list]'. On p. [231]: 'Este libro se terminó de imprimir . . . | . . . | Buenos Aires, el 24 setiembre de 1971.' 7¾″ × 5⅛″. Wrappers printed in red, black, and brown. Published October 1971; second printing January 1972. *Location:* TxU. *Menckeniana* 55.14.

Second edition: 'H. L. Mencken | Prontuario de la estupidez | humana | Prólogo de Fernando Savater | Traducción de Eduardo Goligorsky | ALCOR [stylized bird crossing the A]'

On p. [2]: 'Colección «Campo de Agramante»'. On copyright page: '© 1992, Ediciones Martínez Roca, S. A. | . . . Barcelona'. 8⁷⁄₁₆″ × 5¼″. Glossy thick paper wrappers in blue-green, mauve, and tan, printed in black. *Locations:* EPL, RJS.

H 8.2
Portuguese translation (1988)

O LIVRO | DOS INSULTOS DE | H. L. MENCKEN | Seleção, tradução e prefácio: | RUY CASTRO | 2ª [a over dot] *reimpressão* | [device] | COMPANHIA DAS LETRAS

Title from second printing, November 1988; on copyright page: '1988 | Editora Schwarcz Ltda. | Rua Barra Funda, 296 | 01152—São Paulo—SP'. First printing (1988) not seen. Selections. Fourth printing in April 1993. *Location:* NjN.

MINORITY REPORT (A 62)

H 9
Braille version

Embossed in handcopied Braille, in four volumes: New York: Jewish Guild for the Blind, 1958 (BRJ 2074).

GANG OF PECKSNIFFS (A 71)

H 10
Braille version

Embossed in handcopied Braille, in four volumes: New York: Jewish Guild for the Blind, 1977 (BRJ 1777).

THE EDITOR, THE BLUENOSE, AND THE PROSTITUTE (A 78)

H 11
Braille version

Embossed in Press Braille grade 2, in two volumes: Louisville, Ky.: American Printing House for the Blind, 1992 (BR 8834).

FANTE/MENCKEN (A 79)

H 12
French translation (1991)

JOHN FANTE / H.L. MENCKEN | CORRESPONDANCE | 1930 – 1952 | éditée par Michael Moreau | avec la collaboration de Joyce Fante | traduit de l'anglais | par Brice MATTHIEUSSENT | CHRISTIAN BOURGOIS ÉDITEUR

Published Paris (OCLC). On copyright page: '© Christian Bourgois Editeur *[sic]* 1991 pour la traduction française.' 7⅞" × 4⅝". Pictorial wrappers in blue-black, white, yellow, green, and orange. Reprinted 1993 in series 'Éditions 10/18'. *Locations:* GHT, RJS.

COLLECTIONS

H 13
Préjugés (1929)

ÉCRIVAINS ET PENSEURS AMÉRICAINS | *COLLECTION PUBLIÉE SOUS LA DIRECTION DE RÉGIS MICHAUD* | H. L. MENCKEN | [short rule] | PRÉJUGÉS | [short rule] | *Traduction et notes de RÉGIS MICHAUD* | [Bouvin device] | PARIS | ANCIENNE LIBRAIRIE FURNE | BOUVIN & Cⁱᵉ, ÉDITEURS | 3 ET 5, RUE PALATINE (VIᵉ)

On copyright page: '*Il a été tiré de cet ouvrage* | vingt-cinq exemplaires sur | vélin bibliophile numérotés | de 1 à 25'; added line on copyright page of limited printing: '*Exemplaire nº* [number written in]'. On p. 296: 'Poitiers.—Société française d'Imprimerie. 1929.' 7½" × 5½". Pictorial wrappers, black and bluish gray on tan (both limited and trade printings). *Locations:* EPL, GHT, NjP. Adler 14.

Contents: "Pourquoi je suis Américain" (III), "La Tradition américaine" (IV), "De la Démocratie" (ND), "Le politicien" (IV), "William Jennings Bryan" (V), "Théodore Roosevelt (Autopsie)" (III), "Le poète et son art" (III), "Beethoven" (V), "Puritanisme et Littérature" (BP), "Théodore Dreiser, ou le roman d'un romancier" (BP), "De l'Amour, des Femmes, du Mariage et du célibat" (IV), "Carnet d'un misogyne" (IDW), "Danse macabre" (IV). The series of *Prejudices* indicated above by roman numeral; else from *Notes on Democracy, Book of Prefaces,* or *In Defense of Women.*

H 14
Samlade fördomar artiklar och essayer (1931)

H. L. MENCKEN | SAMLADE FÖRDOMAR | ARTIKLAR OCH ESSAYER | URVAL OCH ÖVERSATTNINGAR | ANNA LENAH ELGSTRÖM | OCH | CID ERIK TALLQVIST | FÖRETAL AV | ANNA LENAH ELGSTRÖM | [device] | STOCKHOLM | ALBERT BONNIERS FÖRLAG

On copyright page: 'STOCKHOLM | ALB. BONNIERS BOKTRYCKERI | 1931'. 8¾" × 5¹⁵⁄₁₆". Gray wrappers printed in black; dust jacket. *Locations:* EPL, GHT (dj). Adler 14 (misdated).

Contents: "Att bo i Baltimore" (V), "Metropolis" (VI), "Den amerikaneka traditionen" (IV), "Zions berg" (V), "Söderns dekadans" (II), "Sex porträtt" 1–6 (VI, I, II, VI, I, VI), "Poesien i Amerika" (VI), "Dödsdansen" (IV), " 'Comstokeri' " (V), "Reflexioner kring det mänskliga engiftet" (IV), "Det outslitliga ämnet" (*Book of Burlesques*?), "Att vara amerikan" (III), "Den amerikanska litteraturen" (II). The series of *Prejudices* indicated above by roman numeral.

H 15
Fordomme (1943)

H. L. MENCKEN | F O R D O M M E | I UDVALG OG OVERSÆTTELSE | VED | HARTVIG ANDERSEN | [windmill device] | KØBENHAVN | STEEN HASSEL-BALCHS FORLAG | MCMXLIII

On copyright page: 'DYVA & JEPPESENS BOGTRYKKERI | AKTIESELSKAB KØBENHAVEN K'. On p. [1]: 'HASSELBALCHS KULTUR-BIBLIOTEK | RE-DAKTION: JACOB PALUDAN | BIND XXX | H. L. Mencken: Fordomme'. 7" × 4¾". Paper-covered boards printed in blue, white, and lavender. Laid into GHT copy is a two-leaf catalogue, dated February 1943, advertising the first twenty-one volumes in the series. Second printing 1951. *Location:* GHT. Not in Adler.

Contents: "Hymne til sandheden" (VI), "Valentino" (VI), "Om filosoffer" (VI), "Mennesketyper" (III), "Billede af en ideel verden" (IV), "Raad til unge mennesker" (III), "Slavesindet" (IV), "Forskellige notater" (V), "Til erindring om de døde" (III). The series of *Prejudices* indicated above by Roman numerals.

H 16
The Vintage Mencken (AA 5)
Braille versions

Embossed in three volumes: Louisville, Ky.: American Printing House for the Blind, 1956 (BRA 9758); in handcopied Braille, five volumes: New York: New York Association for the Blind, 1966 (BRA 9758 also).

H 17
Hombres y dioses en la picota (1972)

H. L. Mencken | [rule] | HOMBRES Y DIOSES | EN LA PICOTA | [rule] | [device beside next two lines] granica | editor

"Men and Gods at the Gibbet." Published Buenos Aires (OCLC). On copyright page: '1ª edición: julio 1972 | Traducción: Eduardo Goligorsky'. On p. [4]: 'Collección | LIBERTAD Y CAMBIO'. No. 23 in the series. 7¾" × 5¼". Stiff pictorial paper wrappers, printed in black, red, and green. *Location:* EPL. S2.11 *("Pilota")*; *Mencke-niana* 55.14.

Contents: (From *Treatise on the Gods*) "Magia y religión," "El sueño de la inmor-talidad," "Los vicios de los dioses," "Los castigos de ultratumba," "La educación religiosa," "Una religión, todas las religiones," "Cielos e infiernos," "Los Padres de la Iglesia," "Las enseñanzas éticas," "Un poco de historia," "La crisis de la teología," "Más sobre la crisis de la teología," "El ocaso de los dioses," (From *Minority Report*) "El altruismo," "Los argumentos teológicos," "El atraso intelectual," "La casuística," "Las certidumbres," "Ciencia y religión," "El clero," "La conducción del Universo," "El consuelo," "Los creyentes," "Los charlatanes," "La ética," "La eucaristía," "La expiación," "La fe," "El fin del mundo," "Guerra," "Los historiadores católicos," "El hombre perfecto," "La incompetencia divina," "La inmortalidad," "La justicia di-vina," "Los mártires," "El materialismo," "El miedo al cambio," "Los misioneros," "La moral," "Las panaceas universales," "Los profetas," "El progreso," "Las pruebas objetivas," "Las religiones orientales," "La salvación," "El sentido común," "El miedo al sexo," "El Talmud," "La tolerancia," "La voluntad suprema."

Index

Index

Mencken's essays and reviews are indexed by their original titles only; see the note under "Contents" in the introduction. Different essays with the same title are listed here separately and numbered chronologically, as are different versions of the same essay.